My Boyfriend is a VAMPIRE

Book 9 & 10

Yu-Rang Han

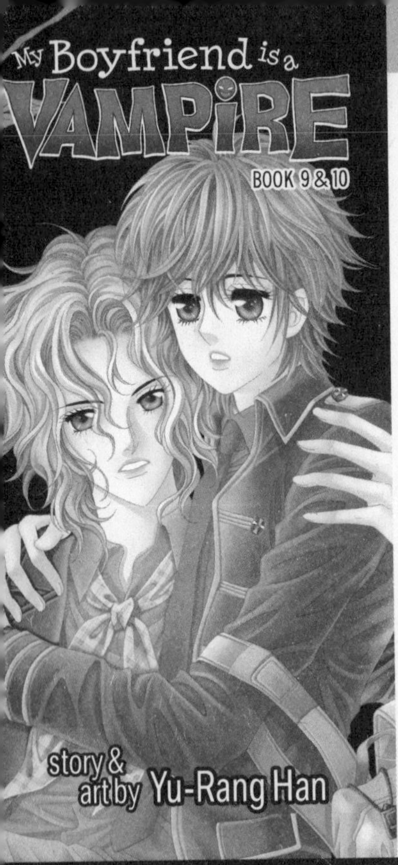
My Boyfriend is a
VAMPIRE
BOOK 9 & 10
story & art by Yu-Rang Han

STAFF CREDITS

translation ChanHee Grace Sung
adaptation Bambi Eloriaga-Amago
lettering Roland Amago
layout Mheeya Wok
cover design Nicky Lim
proofreader Danielle King
editor Adam Arnold

publisher Jason DeAngelis
Seven Seas Entertainment

MY BOYFRIEND IS A VAMPIRE BOOK 9 & 10

First published in Korea in 2010 by Samyang Publishing Co., Ltd.
English translation rights arranged by Samyang Publishing Co., Ltd. through TOPAZ Agency Inc.

ISBN: 978-1-937867-45-4

Printed in Canada

First Printing: September 2013

10 9 8 7 6 5 4 3 2 1

FOLLOW US ONLINE: www.gomanga.com

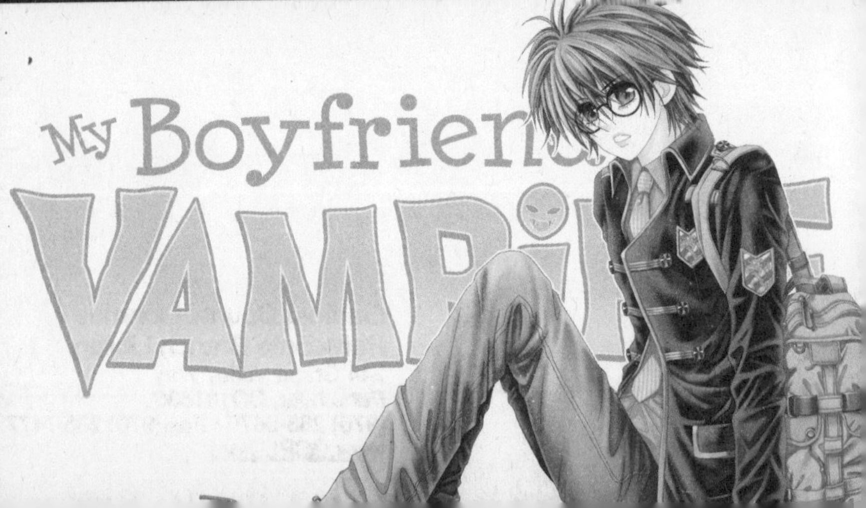

BOOK 9

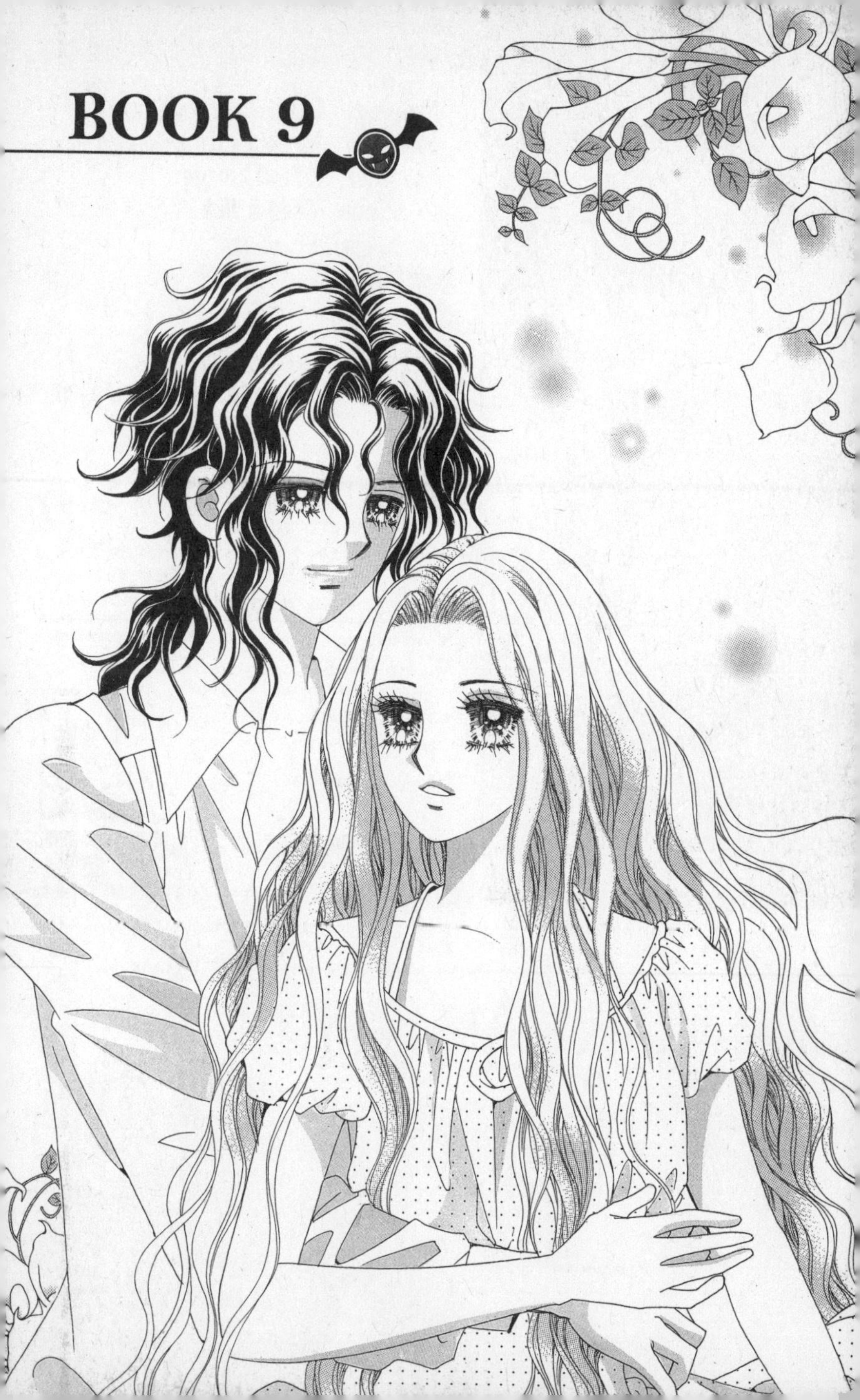

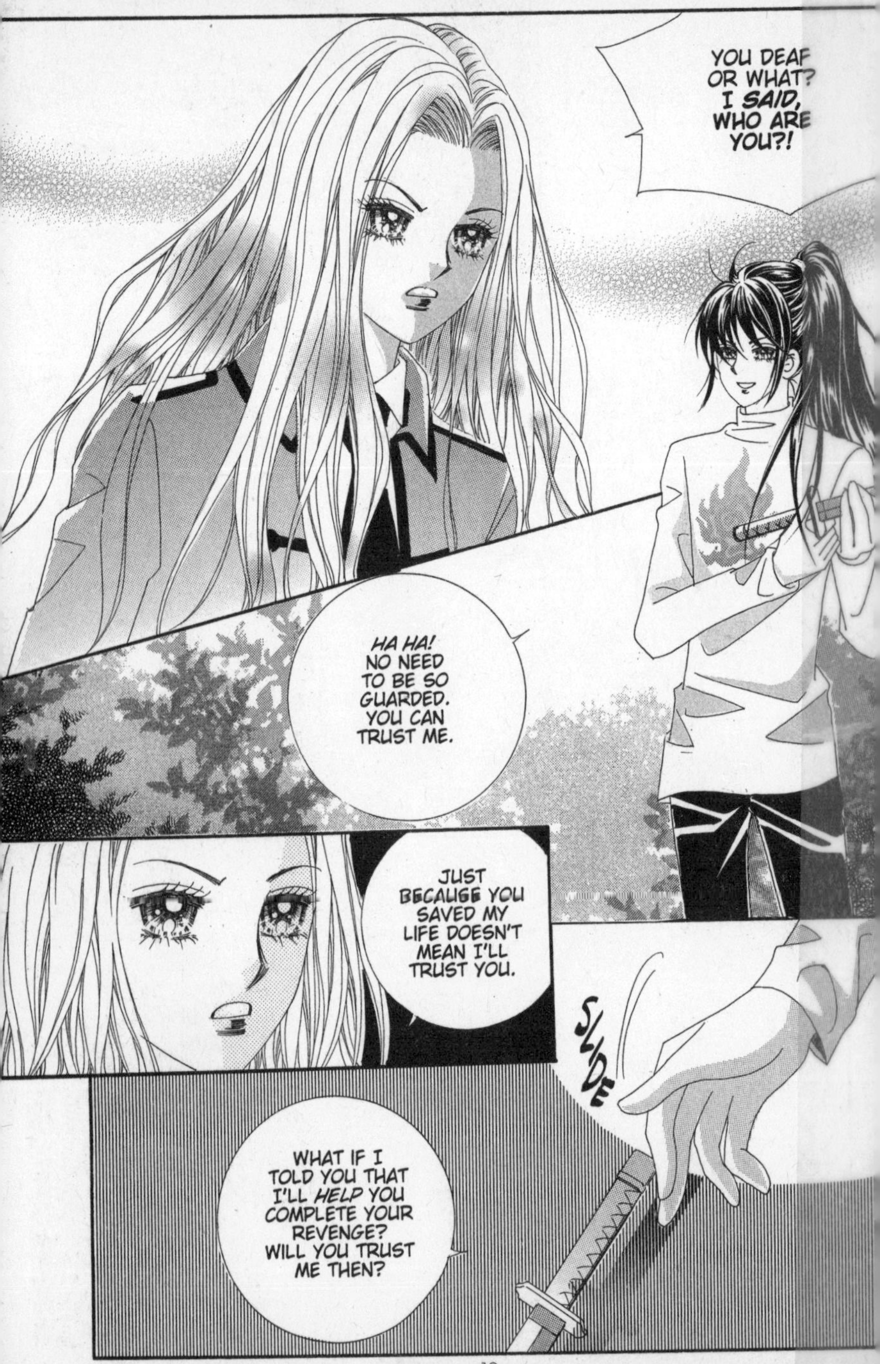
YOU DEAF OR WHAT? I *SAID*, WHO ARE YOU?!
HA HA! NO NEED TO BE SO GUARDED. YOU CAN TRUST ME.
JUST BECAUSE YOU SAVED MY LIFE DOESN'T MEAN I'LL TRUST YOU.
SLIDE
WHAT IF I TOLD YOU THAT I'LL *HELP* YOU COMPLETE YOUR REVENGE? WILL YOU TRUST ME THEN?

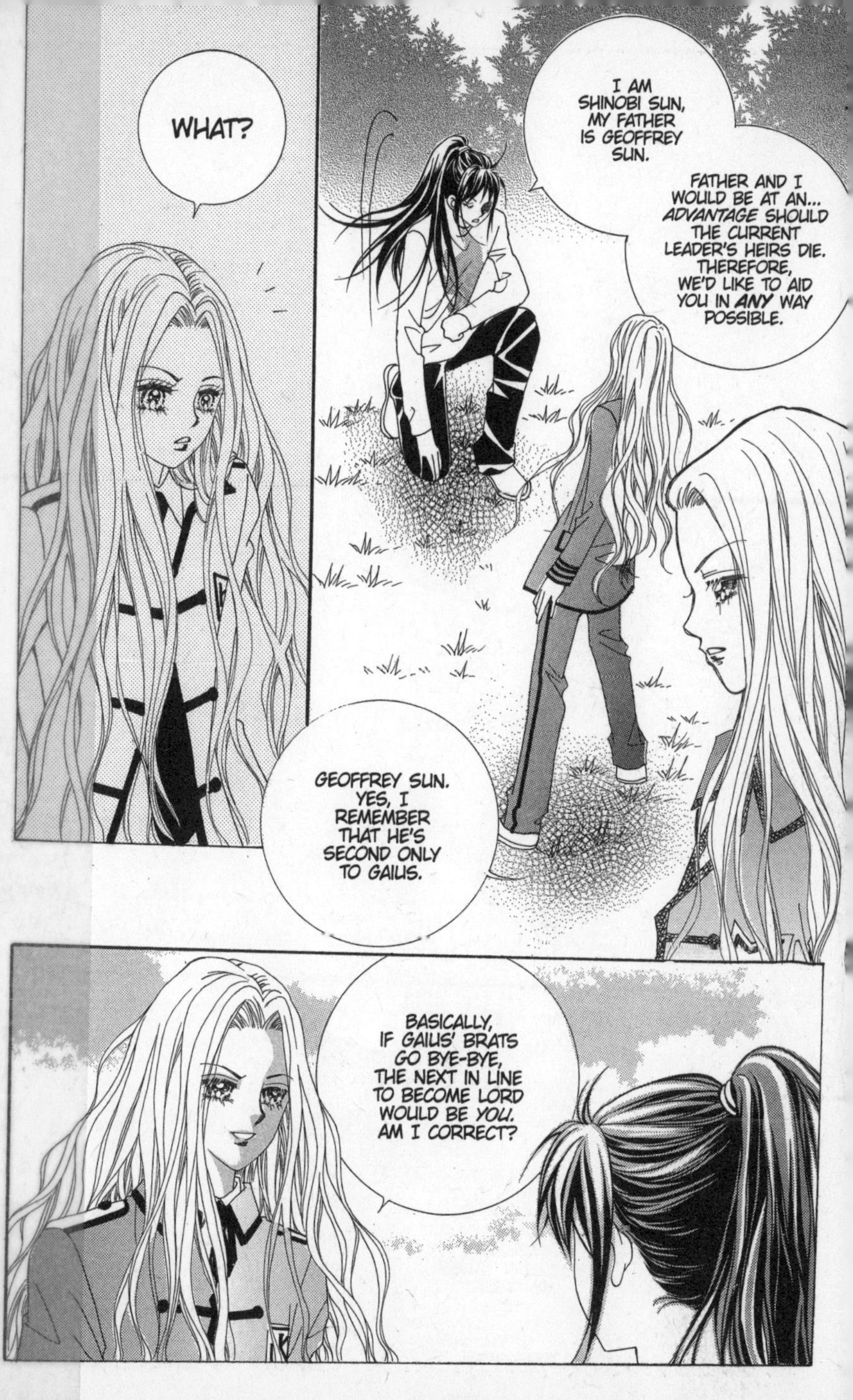
WHAT?
I AM SHINOBI SUN, MY FATHER IS GEOFFREY SUN.
FATHER AND I WOULD BE AT AN... *ADVANTAGE* SHOULD THE CURRENT LEADER'S HEIRS DIE. THEREFORE, WE'D LIKE TO AID YOU IN *ANY* WAY POSSIBLE.
GEOFFREY SUN. YES, I REMEMBER THAT HE'S SECOND ONLY TO GAIUS.
BASICALLY, IF GAIUS' BRATS GO BYE-BYE, THE NEXT IN LINE TO BECOME LORD WOULD BE *YOU*. AM I CORRECT?

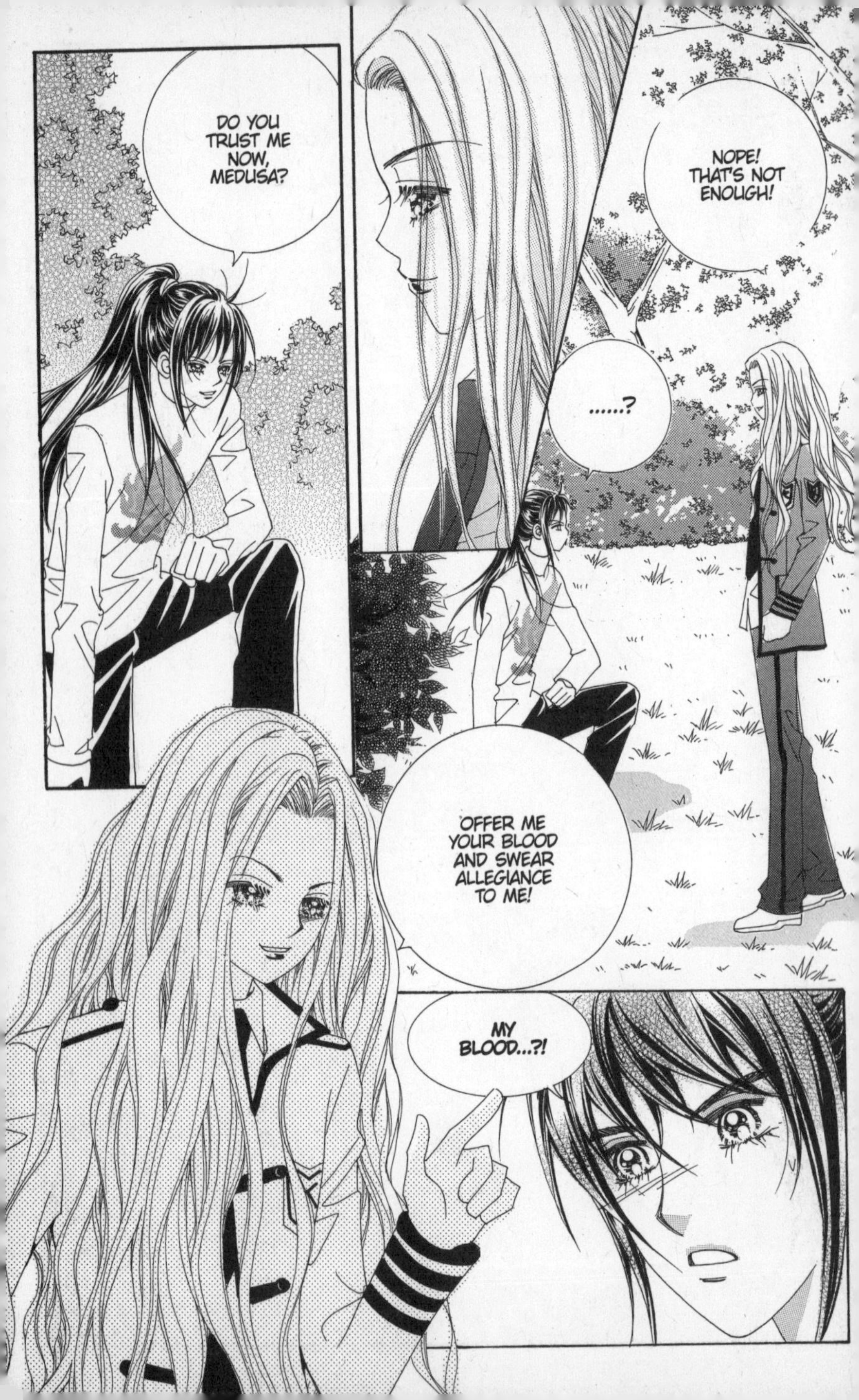
DO YOU TRUST ME NOW, MEDUSA?
NOPE! THAT'S NOT ENOUGH!
......?
OFFER ME YOUR BLOOD AND SWEAR ALLEGIANCE TO ME!
MY BLOOD...?!

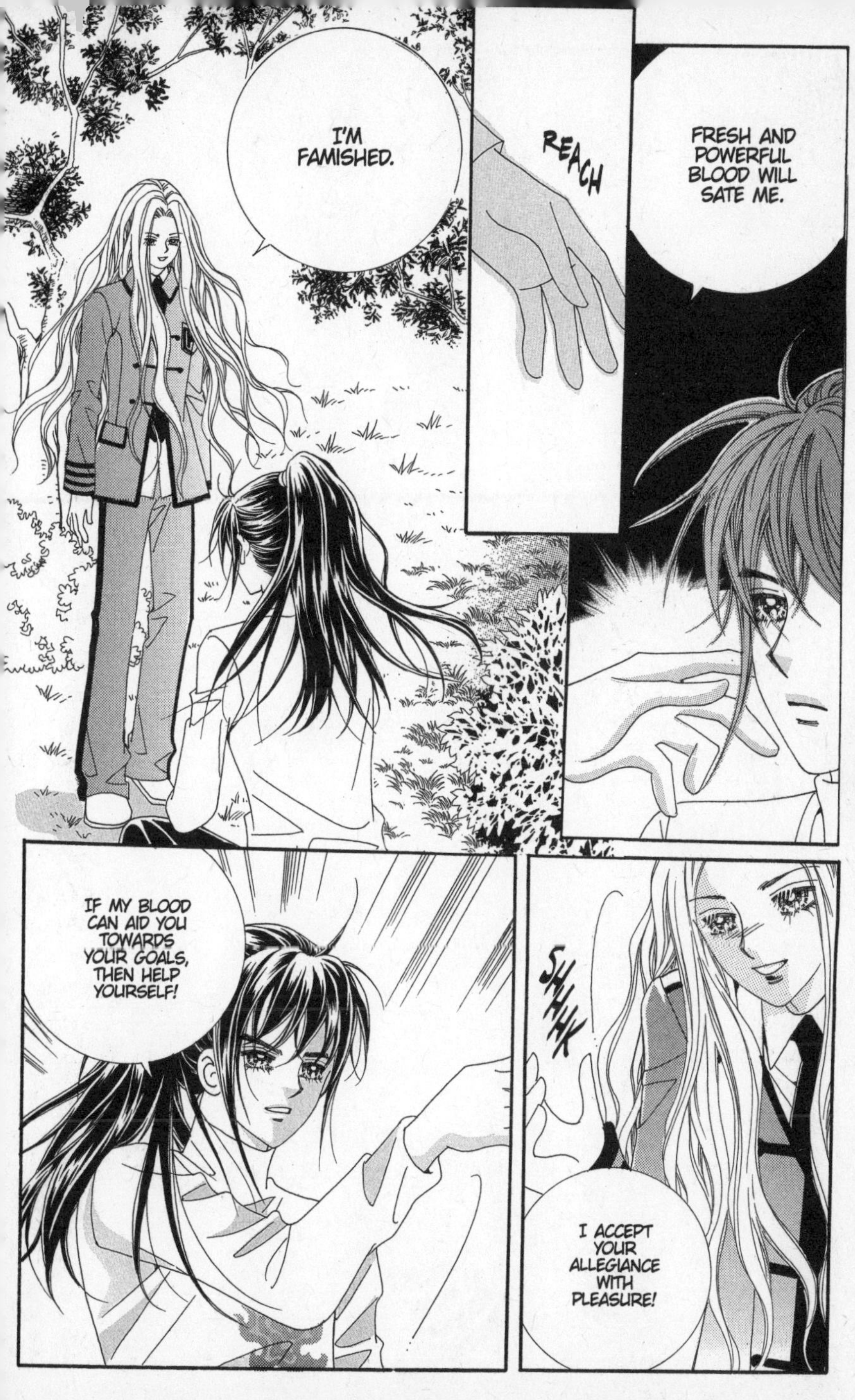
I'M FAMISHED.
REACH
FRESH AND POWERFUL BLOOD WILL SATE ME.
IF MY BLOOD CAN AID YOU TOWARDS YOUR GOALS, THEN HELP YOURSELF!
SHHHK
I ACCEPT YOUR ALLEGIANCE WITH PLEASURE!

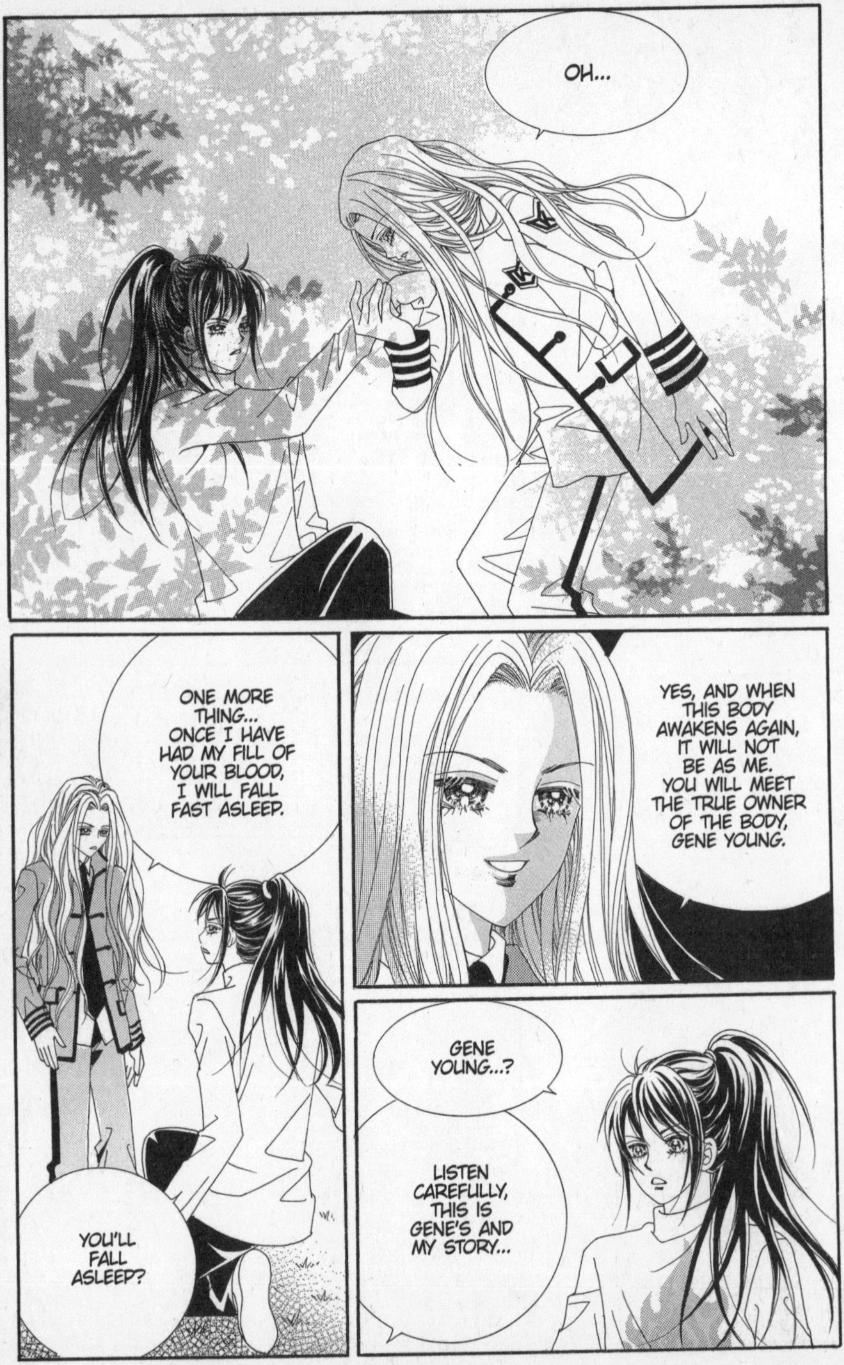
OH...
ONE MORE THING... ONCE I HAVE HAD MY FILL OF YOUR BLOOD, I WILL FALL FAST ASLEEP.
YOU'LL FALL ASLEEP?
YES, AND WHEN THIS BODY AWAKENS AGAIN, IT WILL NOT BE AS ME. YOU WILL MEET THE TRUE OWNER OF THE BODY, GENE YOUNG.
GENE YOUNG...?
LISTEN CAREFULLY, THIS IS GENE'S AND MY STORY...

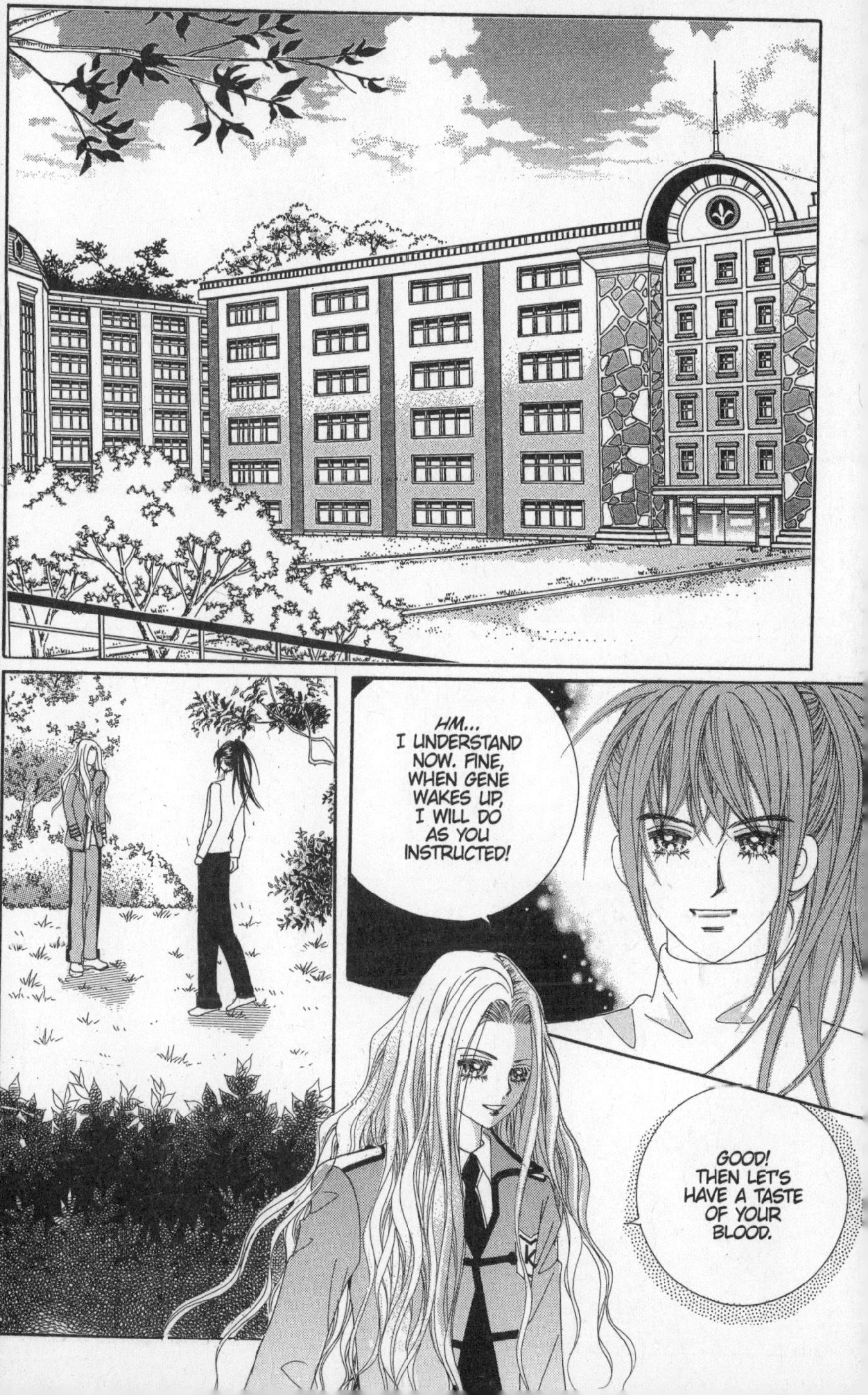
HM... I UNDERSTAND NOW. FINE, WHEN GENE WAKES UP, I WILL DO AS YOU INSTRUCTED!
GOOD! THEN LET'S HAVE A TASTE OF YOUR BLOOD.

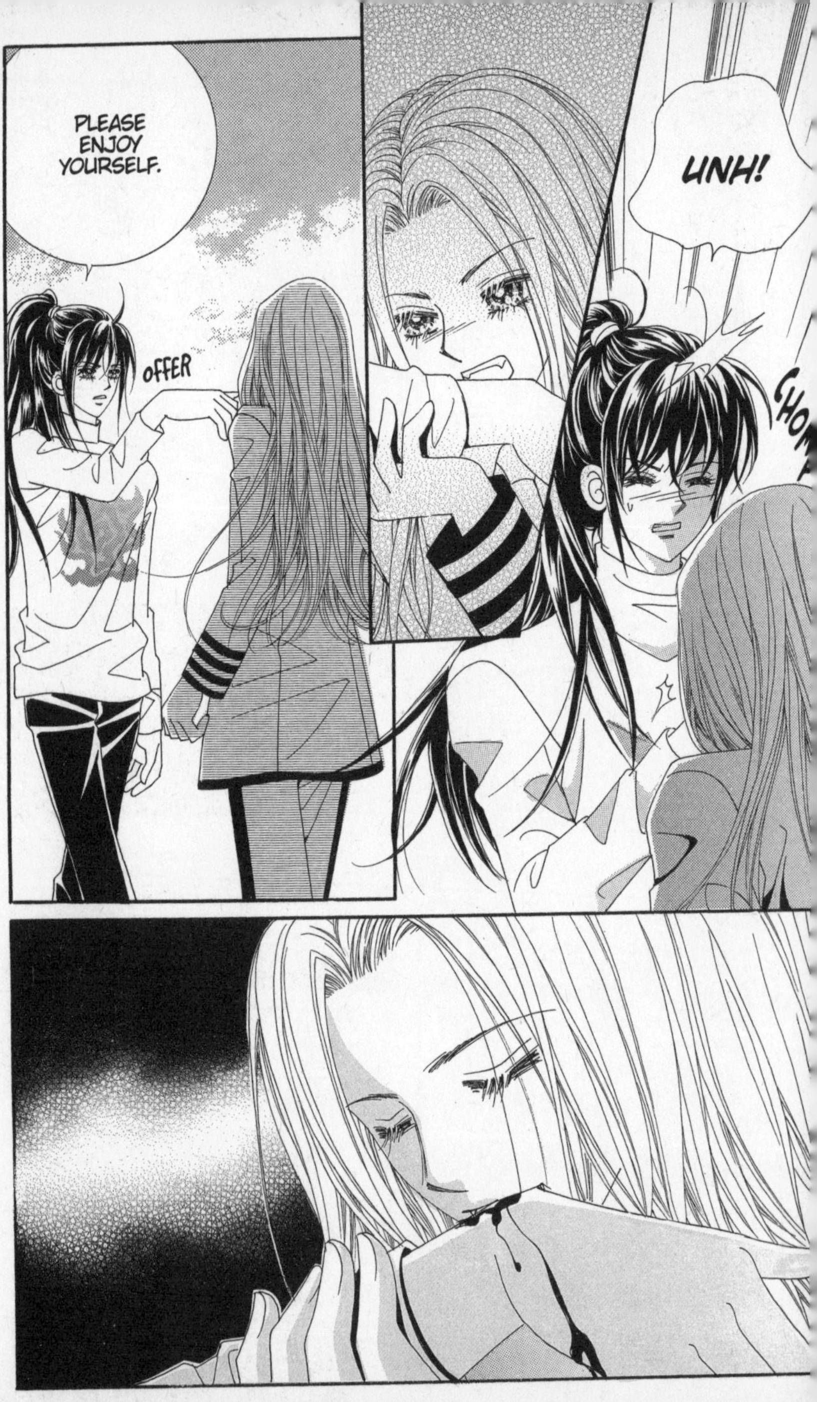
PLEASE ENJOY YOURSELF.
OFFER
UNH!

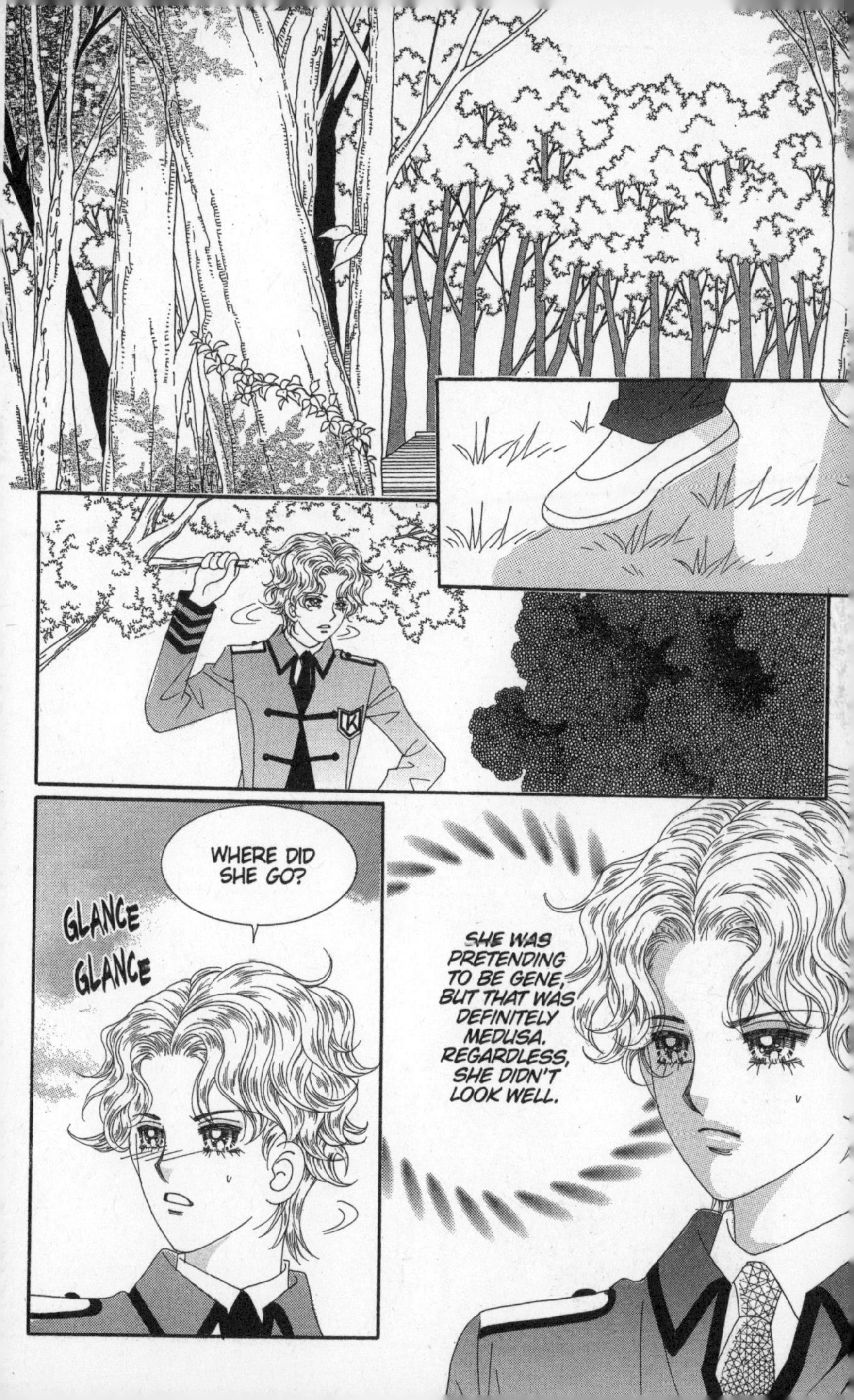
WHERE DID SHE GO?
GLANCE GLANCE
SHE WAS PRETENDING TO BE GENE, BUT THAT WAS DEFINITELY MEDUSA. REGARDLESS, SHE DIDN'T LOOK WELL.

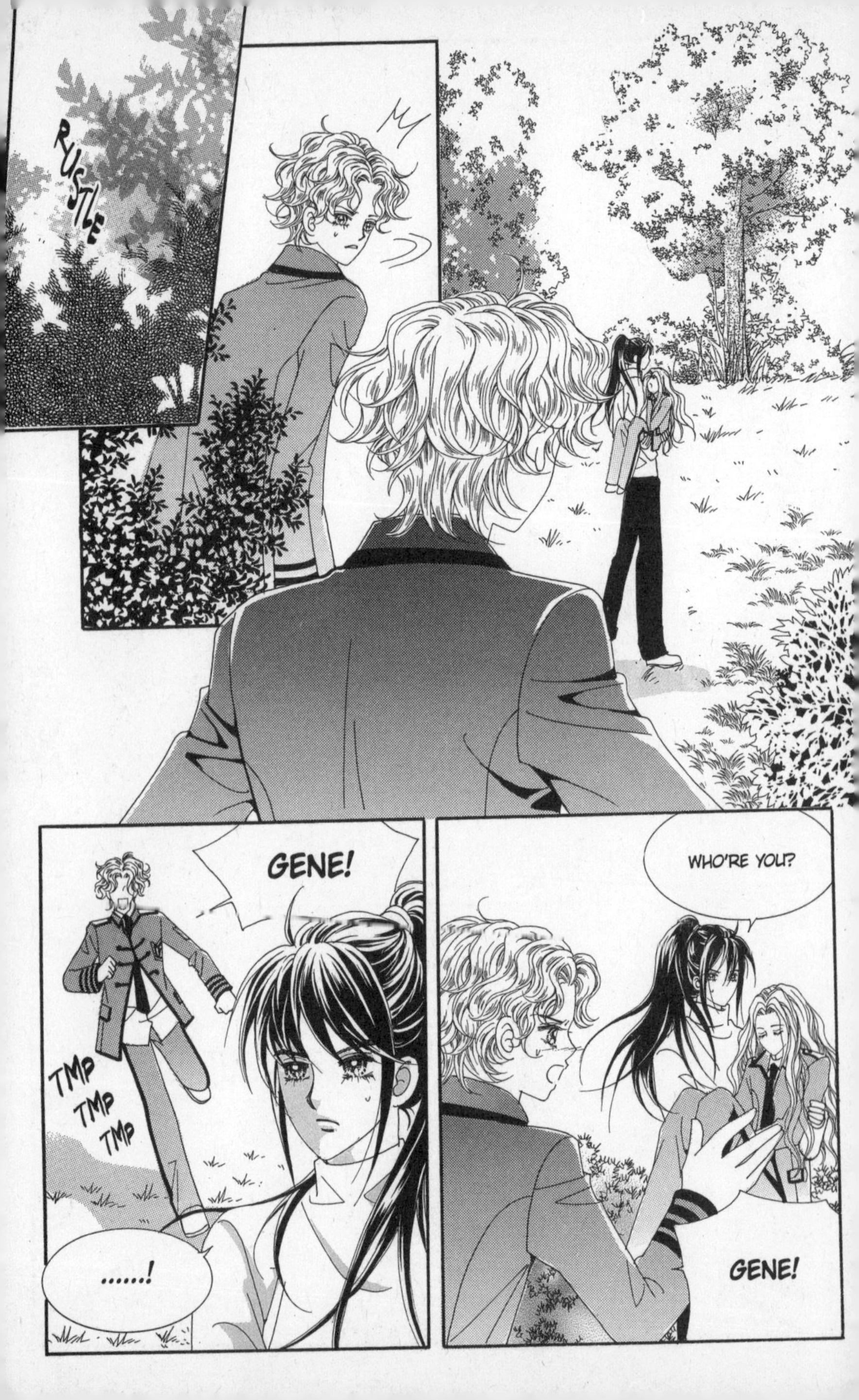
RUSTLE
GENE!
TMP TMP TMP
......!
WHO'RE YOU?
GENE!

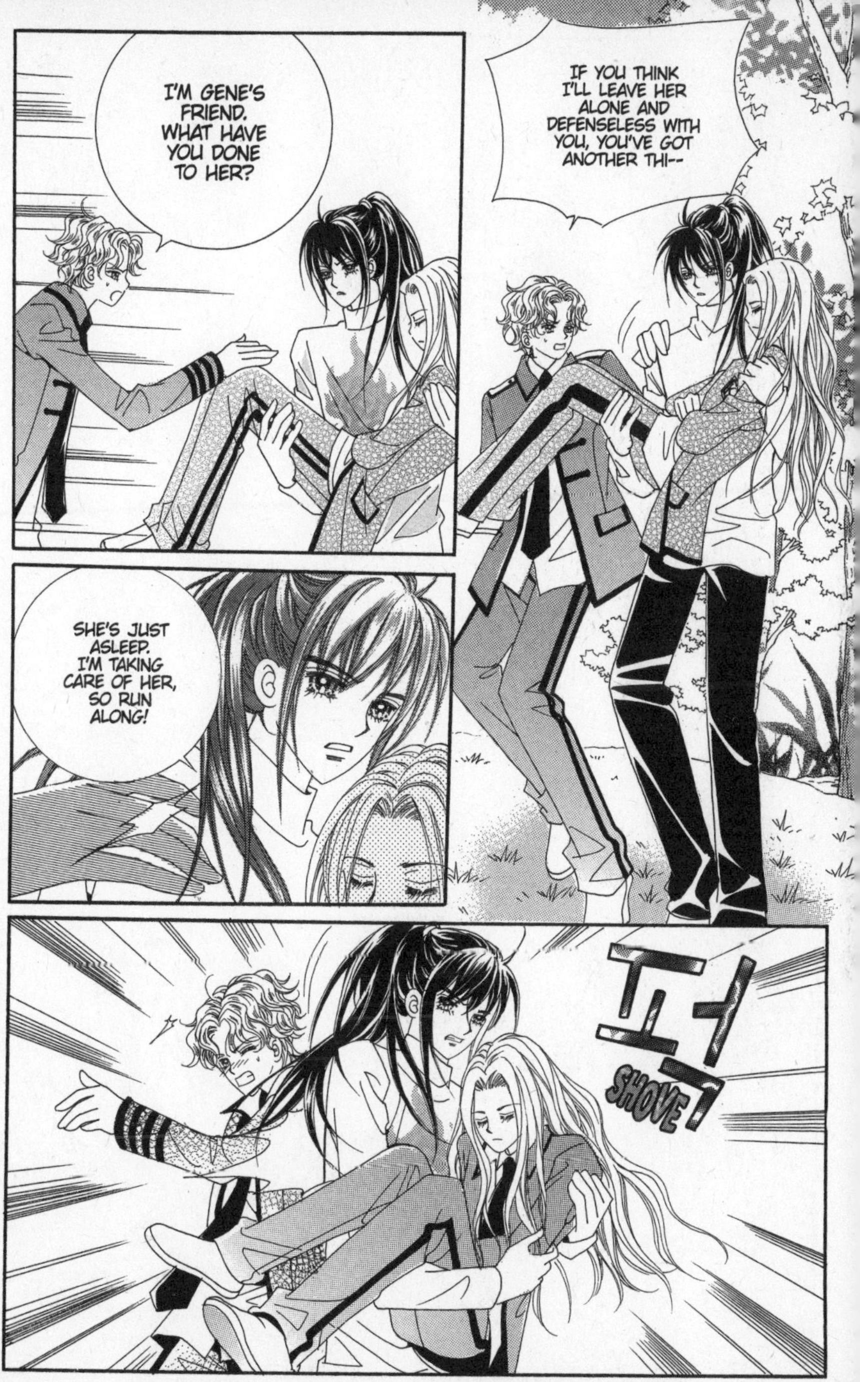
I'M GENE'S FRIEND. WHAT HAVE YOU DONE TO HER?
SHE'S JUST ASLEEP. I'M TAKING CARE OF HER, SO RUN ALONG!
IF YOU THINK I'LL LEAVE HER ALONE AND DEFENSELESS WITH YOU, YOU'VE GOT ANOTHER THI--
SHOVE

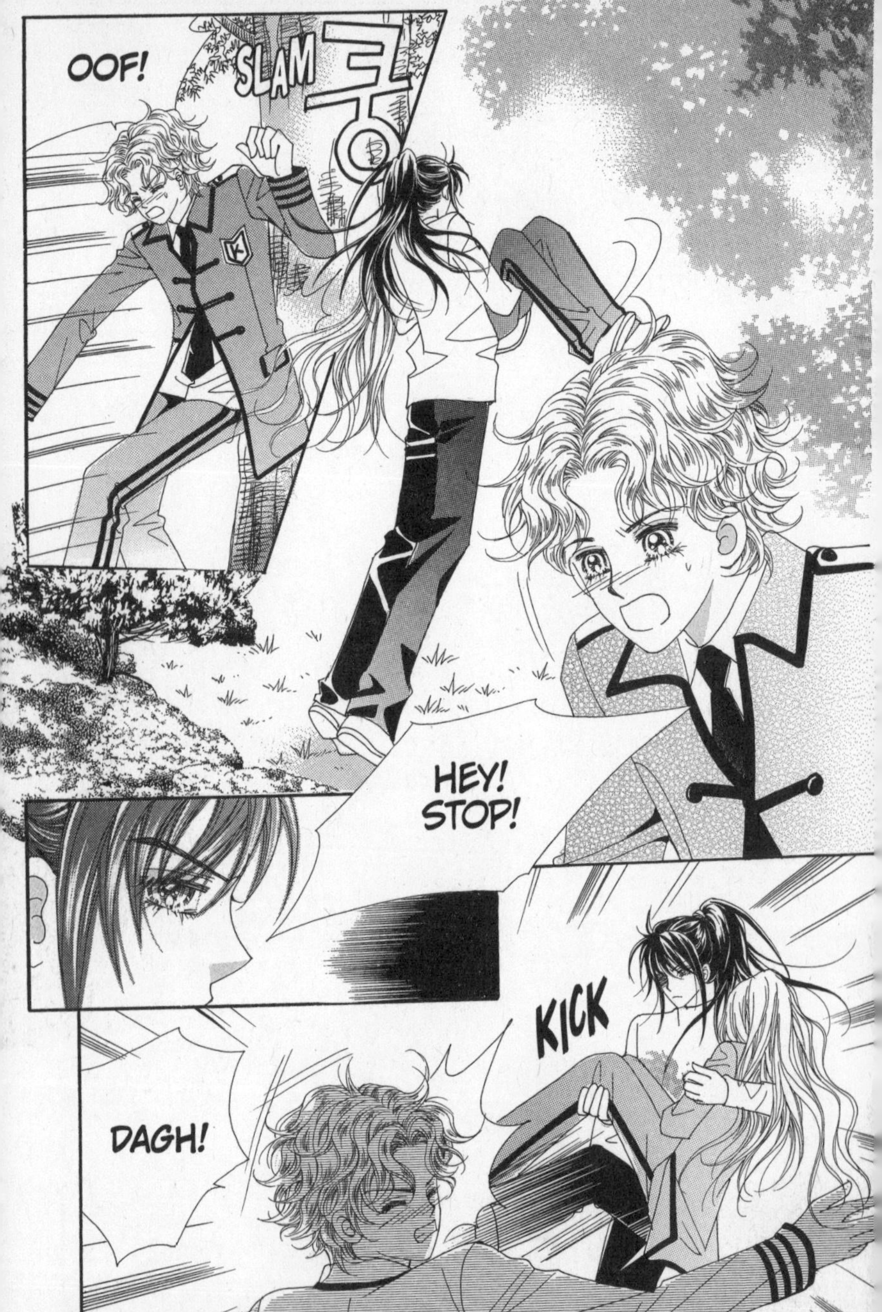
OOF!
SLAM
쿵
HEY! STOP!
KICK
DAGH!

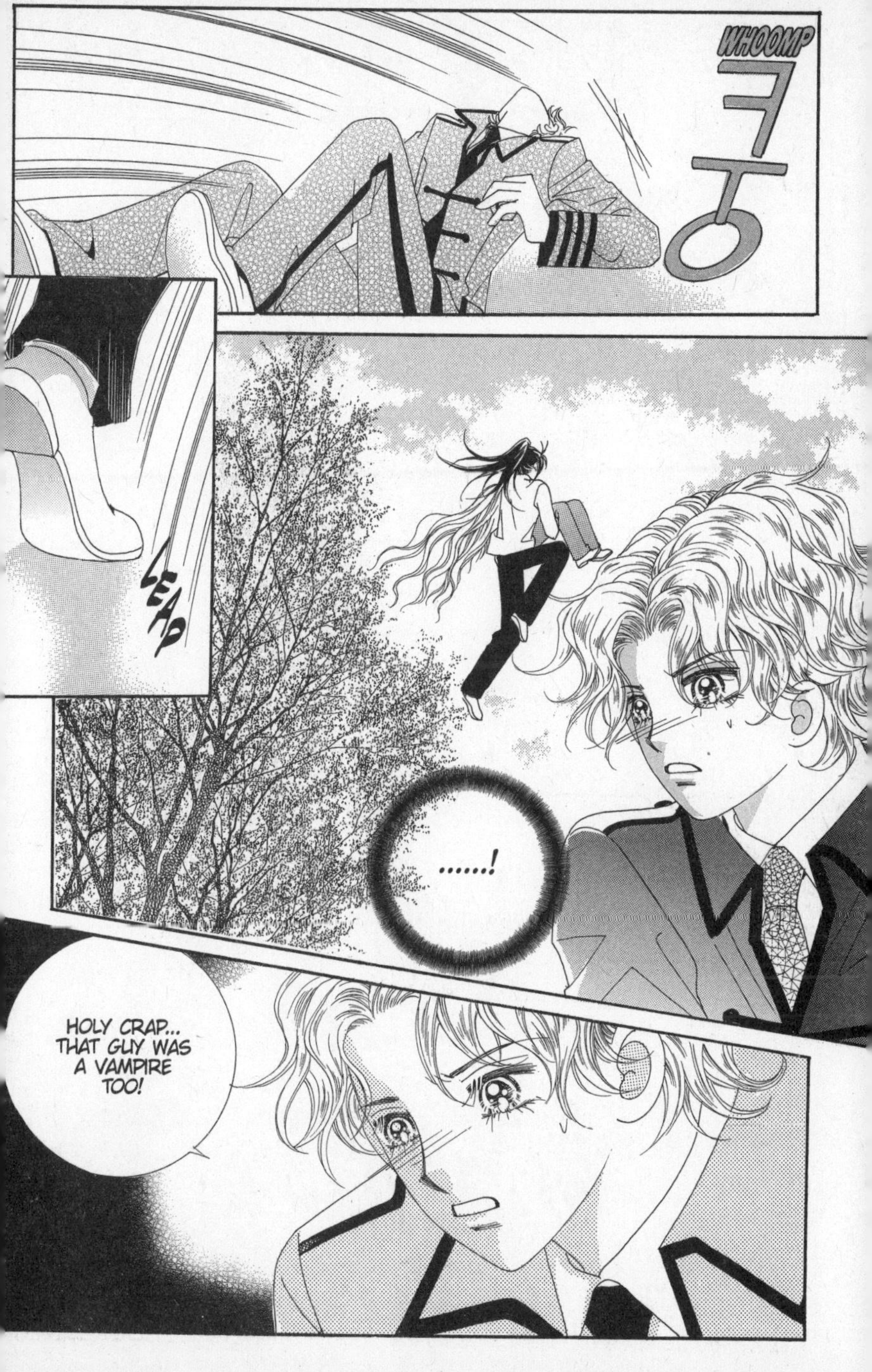
WHOOMP
LEAP
......!
HOLY CRAP... THAT GUY WAS A VAMPIRE TOO!

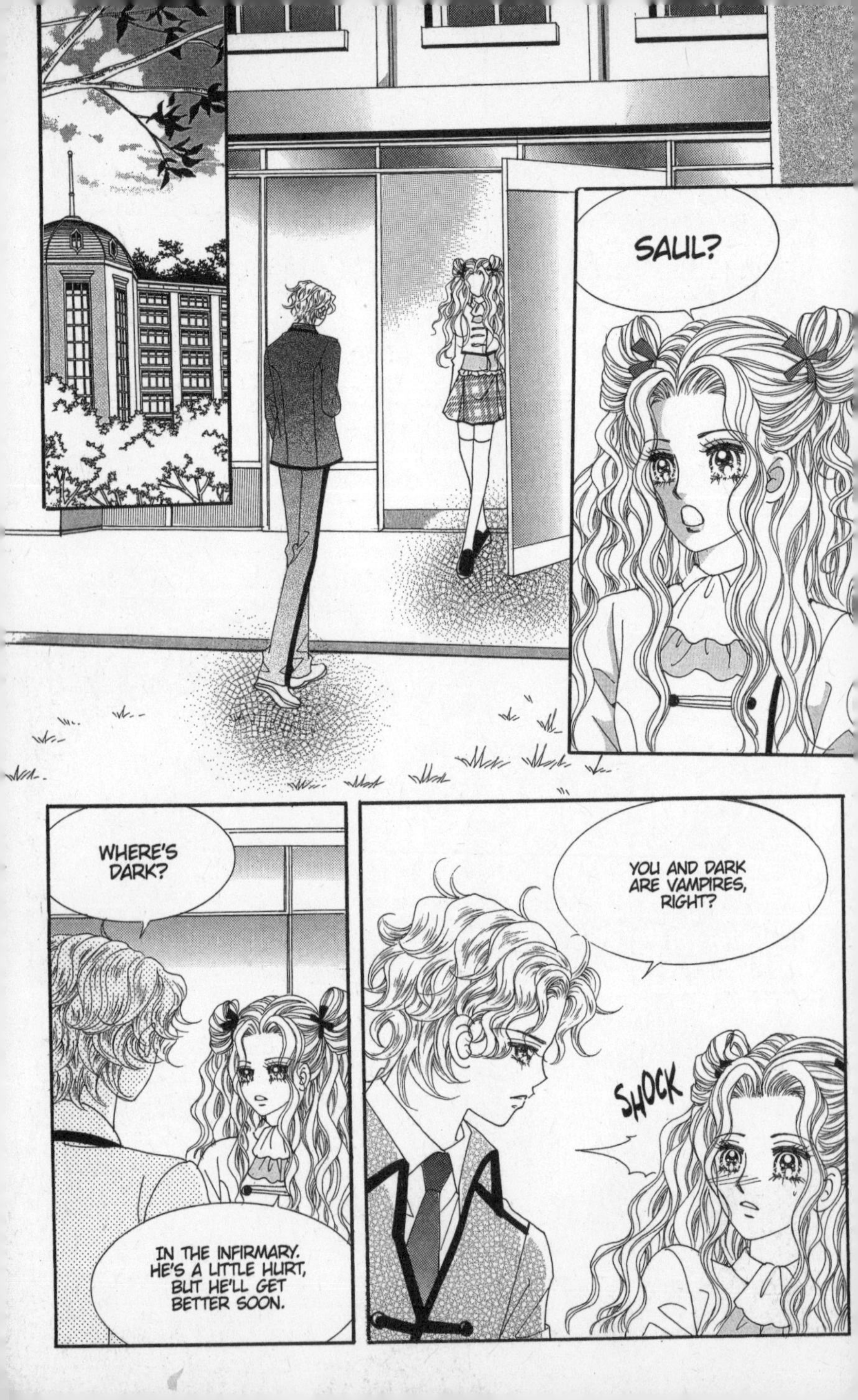
SAUL?
WHERE'S DARK?
IN THE INFIRMARY. HE'S A LITTLE HURT, BUT HE'LL GET BETTER SOON.
YOU AND DARK ARE VAMPIRES, RIGHT?
SHOCK

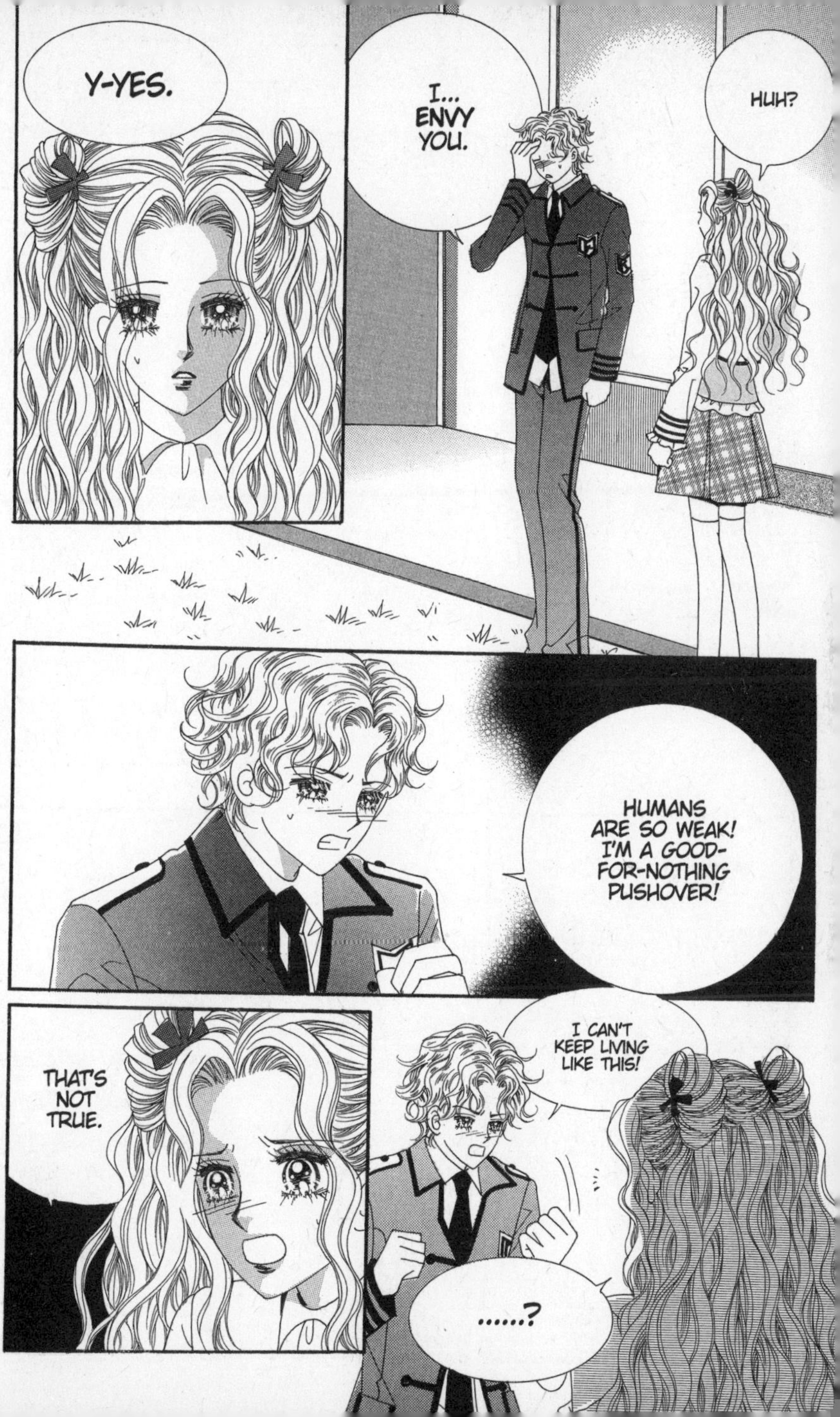
Y-YES.
I... ENVY YOU.
HUH?
HUMANS ARE SO WEAK! I'M A GOOD-FOR-NOTHING PUSHOVER!
THAT'S NOT TRUE.
I CAN'T KEEP LIVING LIKE THIS!
......?

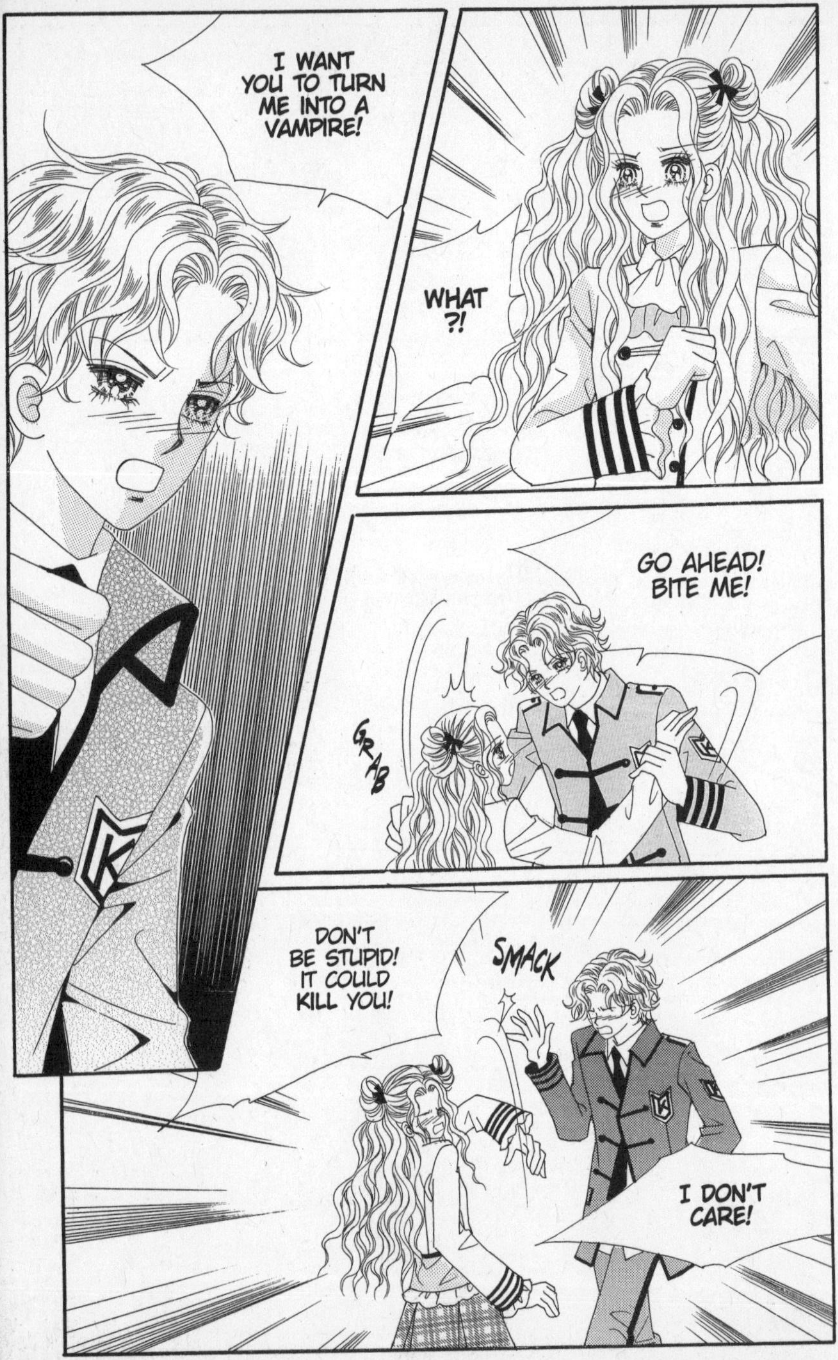
I WANT YOU TO TURN ME INTO A VAMPIRE!
WHAT ?!
GO AHEAD! BITE ME!
GRAB
DON'T BE STUPID! IT COULD KILL YOU!
SMACK
I DON'T CARE!

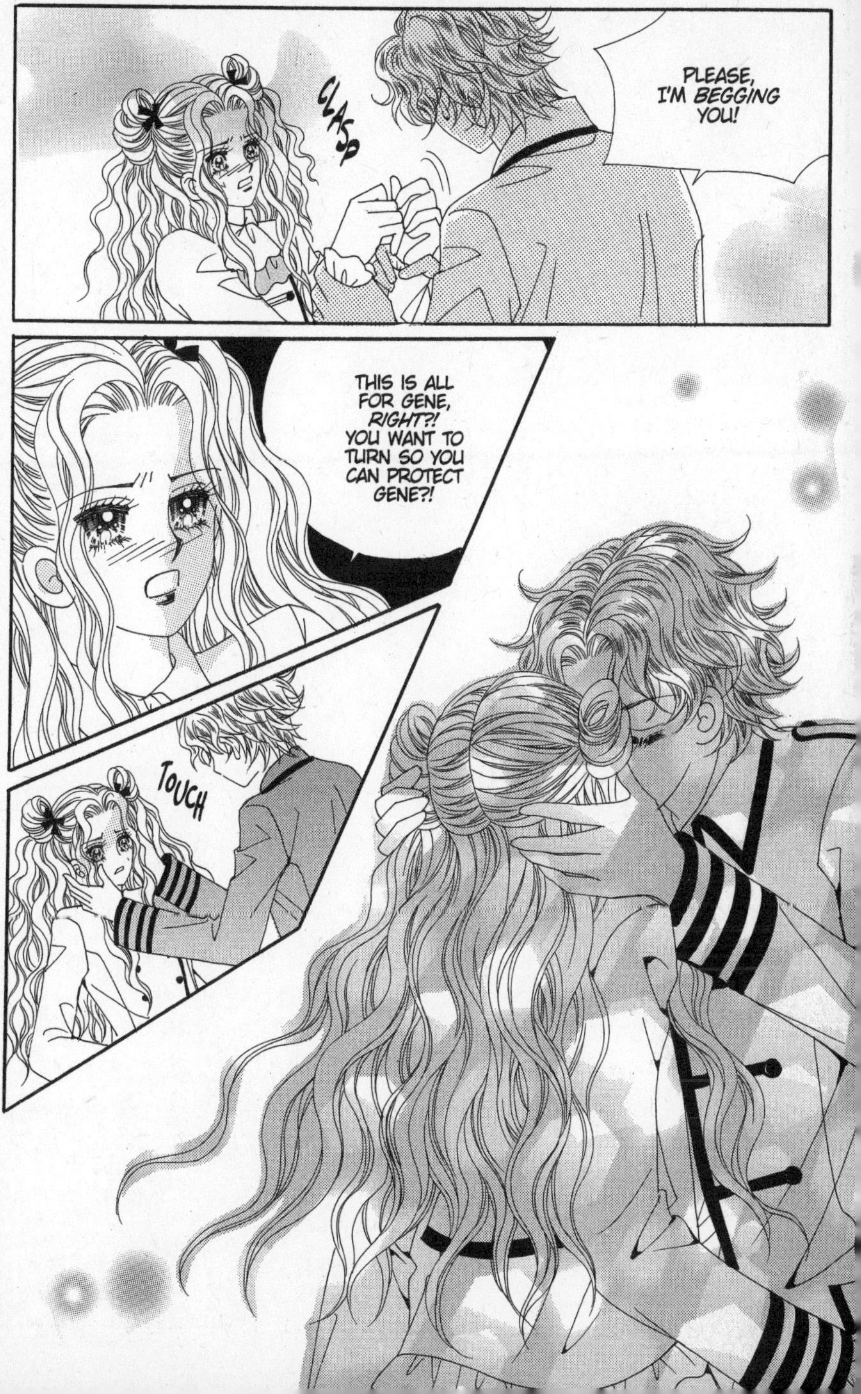
CLASP
PLEASE, I'M *BEGGING* YOU!
THIS IS ALL FOR GENE, *RIGHT?!* YOU WANT TO TURN SO YOU CAN PROTECT GENE?!
TOUCH

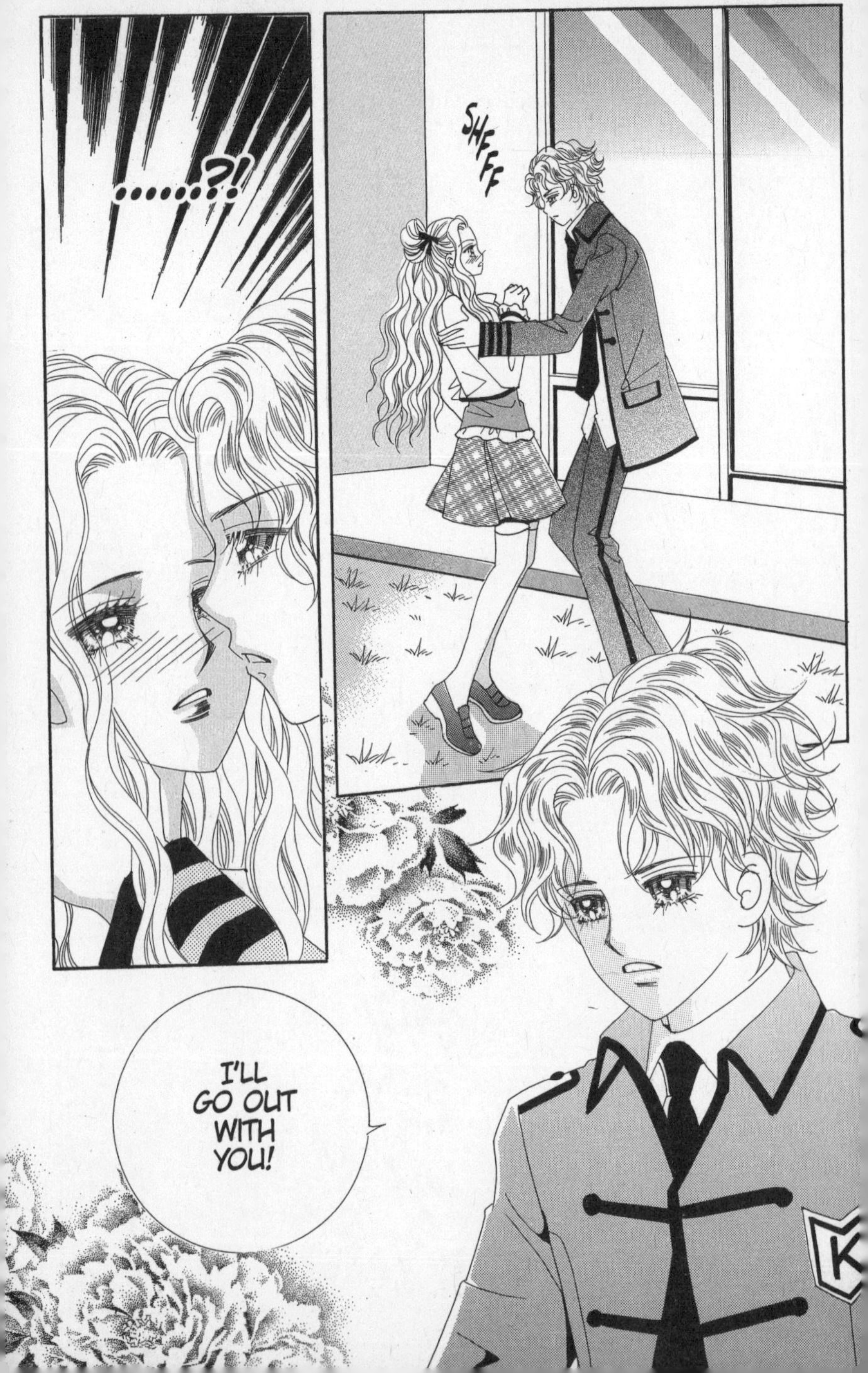
......?!
SHFFF
I'LL GO OUT WITH YOU!

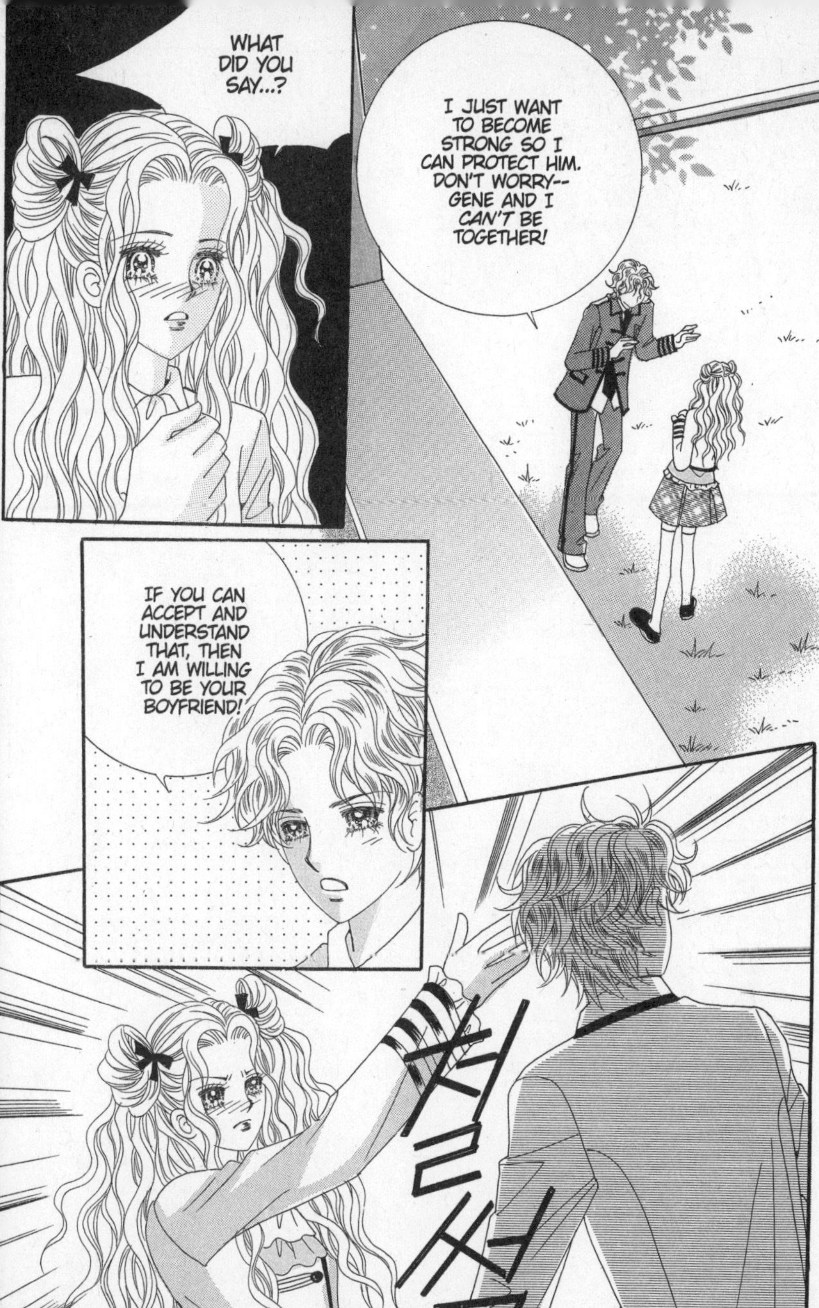
WHAT DID YOU SAY...?
I JUST WANT TO BECOME STRONG SO I CAN PROTECT HIM. DON'T WORRY-- GENE AND I *CAN'T* BE TOGETHER!
IF YOU CAN ACCEPT AND UNDERSTAND THAT, THEN I AM WILLING TO BE YOUR BOYFRIEND!
SLAP

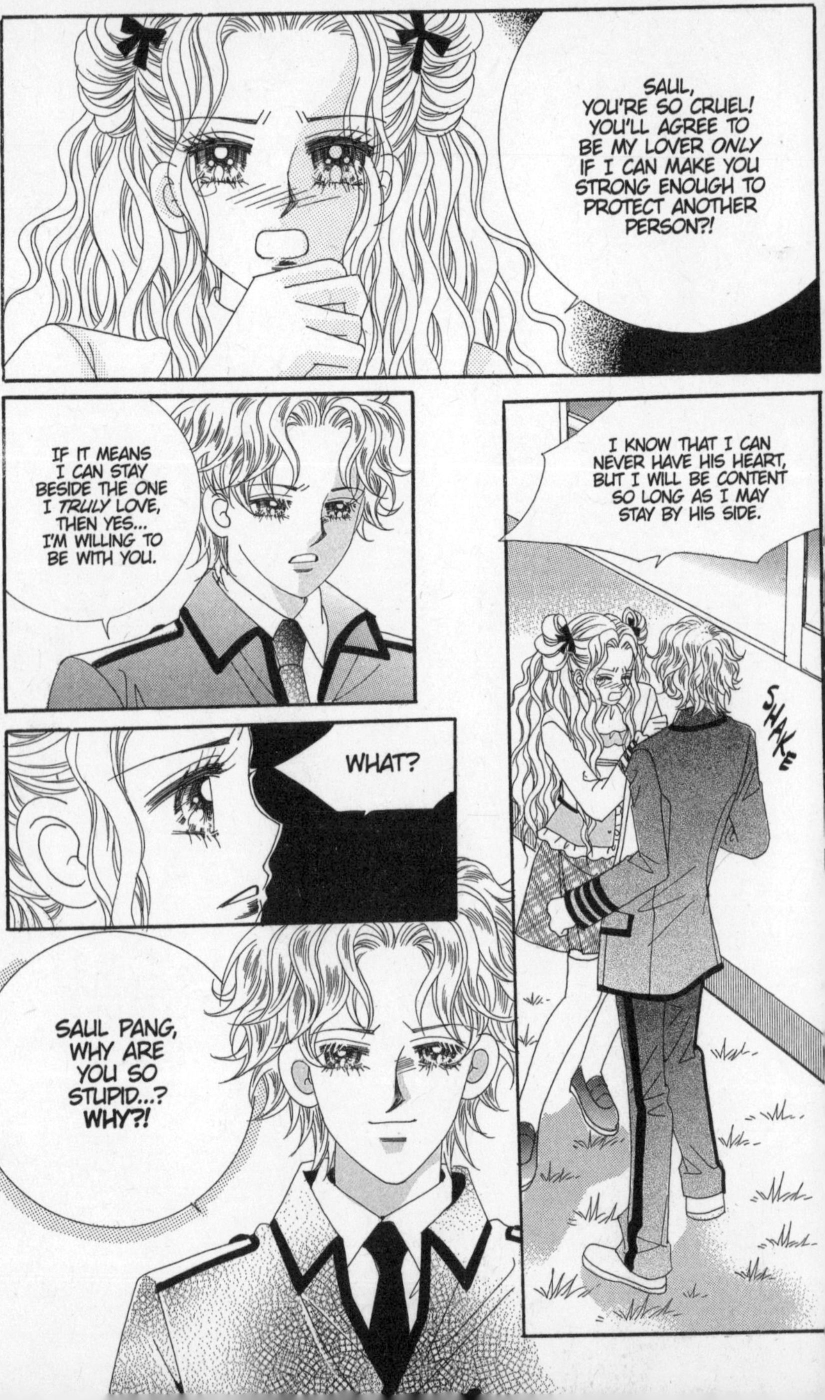
SAUL, YOU'RE SO CRUEL! YOU'LL AGREE TO BE MY LOVER *ONLY* IF I CAN MAKE YOU STRONG ENOUGH TO PROTECT ANOTHER PERSON?!
IF IT MEANS I CAN STAY BESIDE THE ONE I *TRULY* LOVE, THEN YES... I'M WILLING TO BE WITH YOU.
WHAT?
SAUL PANG, WHY ARE YOU SO STUPID...? WHY?!
I KNOW THAT I CAN NEVER HAVE HIS HEART, BUT I WILL BE CONTENT SO LONG AS I MAY STAY BY HIS SIDE.
SHAKE

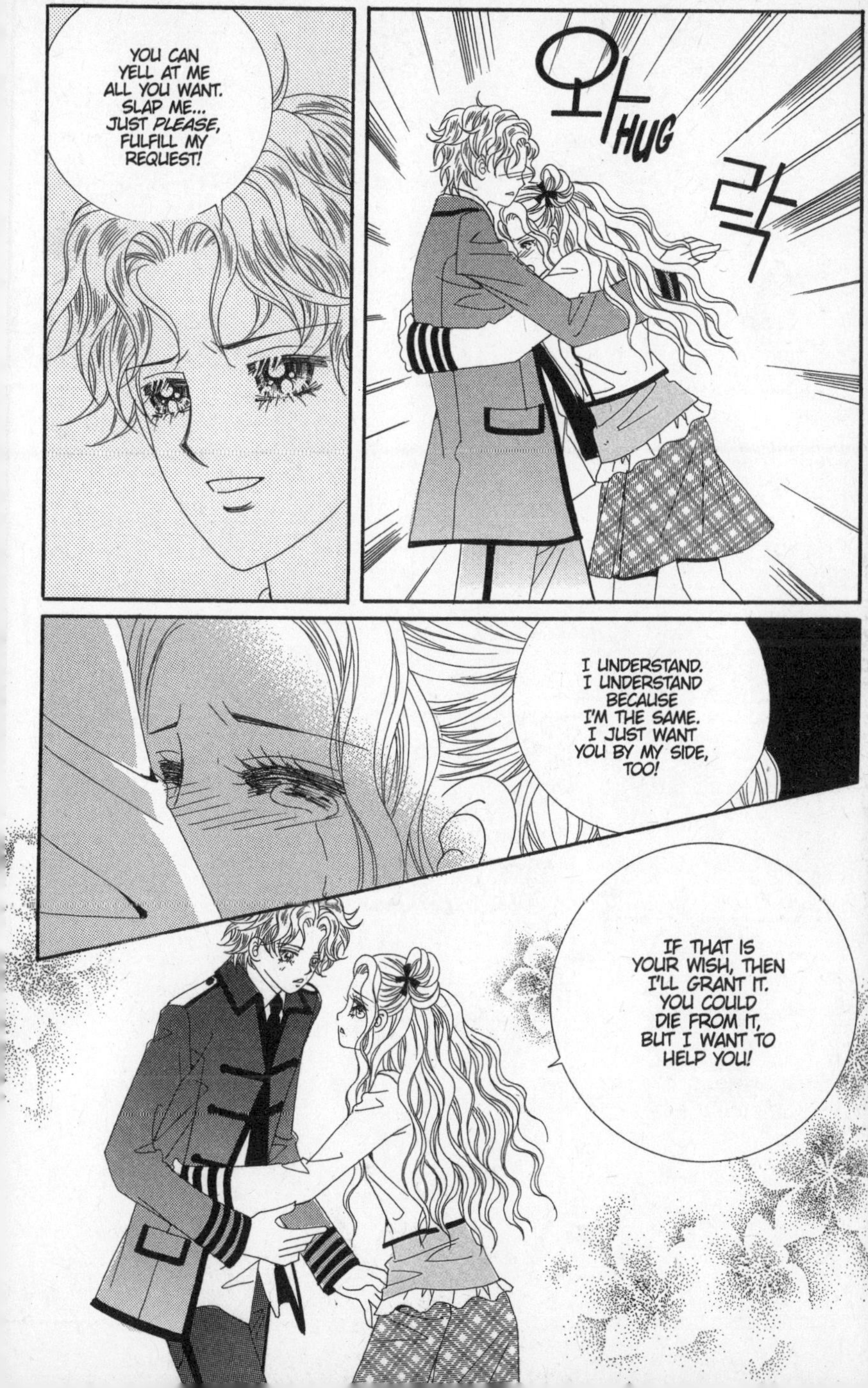
YOU CAN YELL AT ME ALL YOU WANT. SLAP ME... JUST *PLEASE*, FULFILL MY REQUEST!
와락
HUG
I UNDERSTAND. I UNDERSTAND BECAUSE I'M THE SAME. I JUST WANT YOU BY MY SIDE, TOO!
IF THAT IS YOUR WISH, THEN I'LL GRANT IT. YOU COULD DIE FROM IT, BUT I WANT TO HELP YOU!

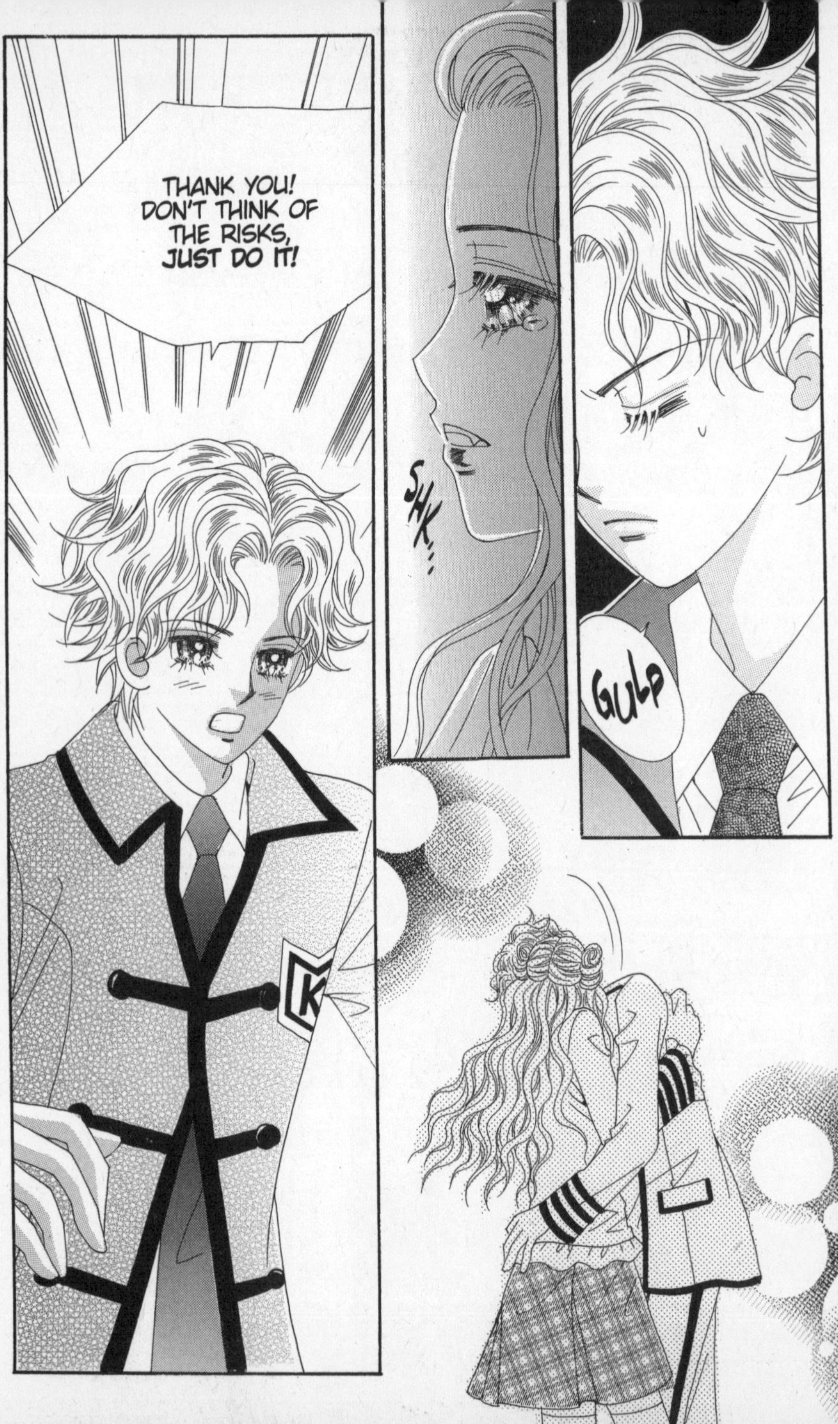
THANK YOU! DON'T THINK OF THE RISKS, JUST DO IT!
SHK..
GULP

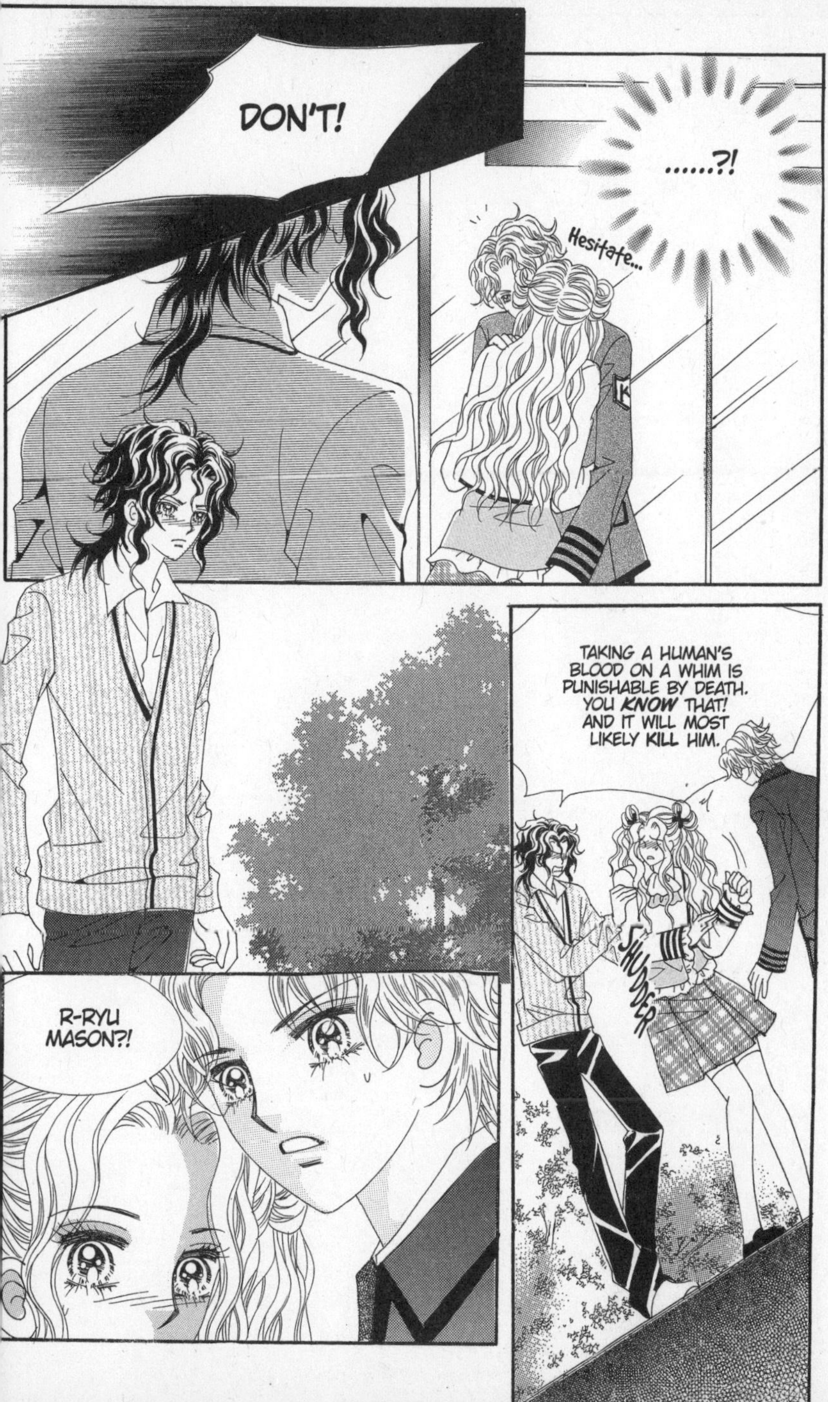
DON'T!
Hesitate...
......?!
TAKING A HUMAN'S BLOOD ON A WHIM IS PUNISHABLE BY DEATH. YOU KNOW THAT! AND IT WILL MOST LIKELY KILL HIM.
SHUDDER
R-RYU MASON?!

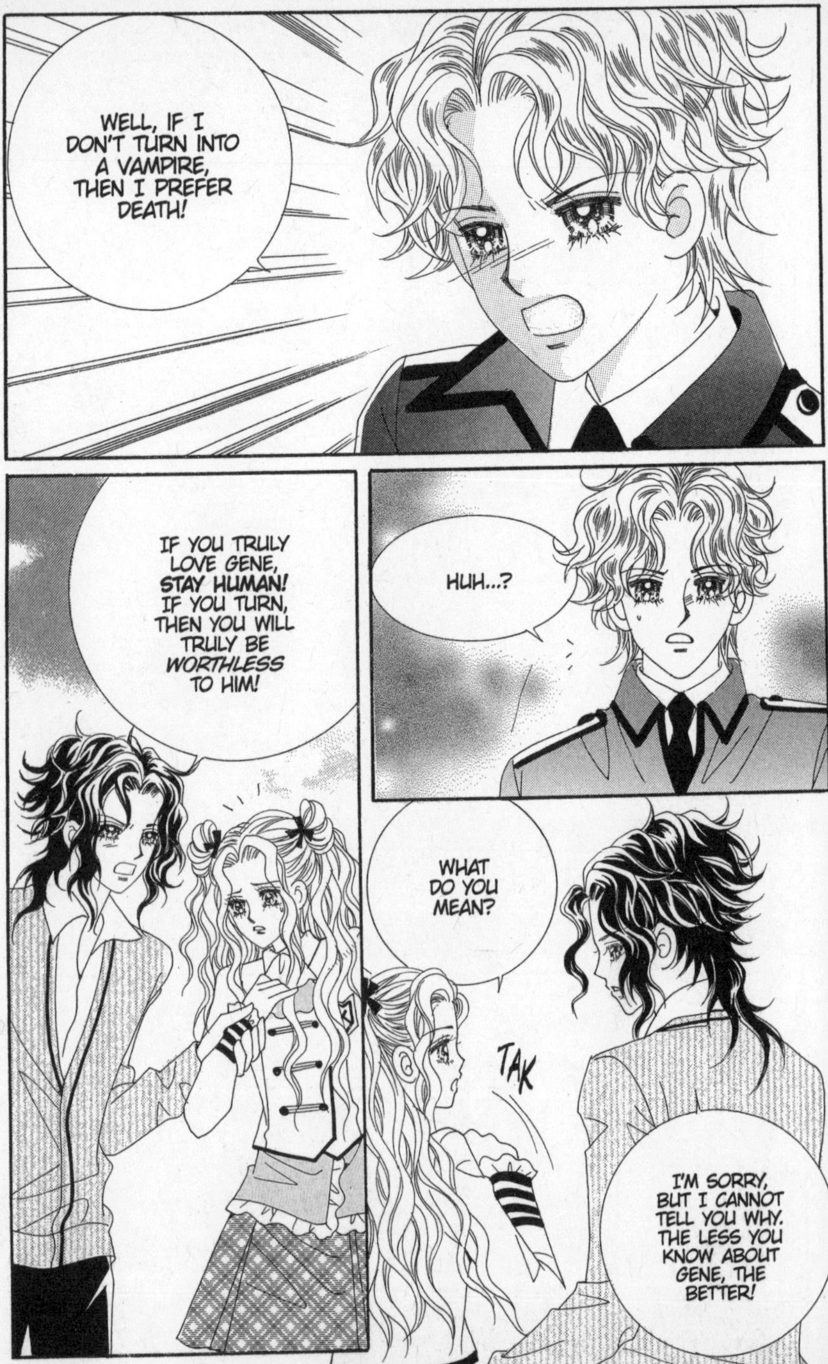
WELL, IF I DON'T TURN INTO A VAMPIRE, THEN I PREFER DEATH!
IF YOU TRULY LOVE GENE, STAY HUMAN! IF YOU TURN, THEN YOU WILL TRULY BE *WORTHLESS* TO HIM!
HUH...?
WHAT DO YOU MEAN?
TAK
I'M SORRY, BUT I CANNOT TELL YOU WHY. THE LESS YOU KNOW ABOUT GENE, THE BETTER!

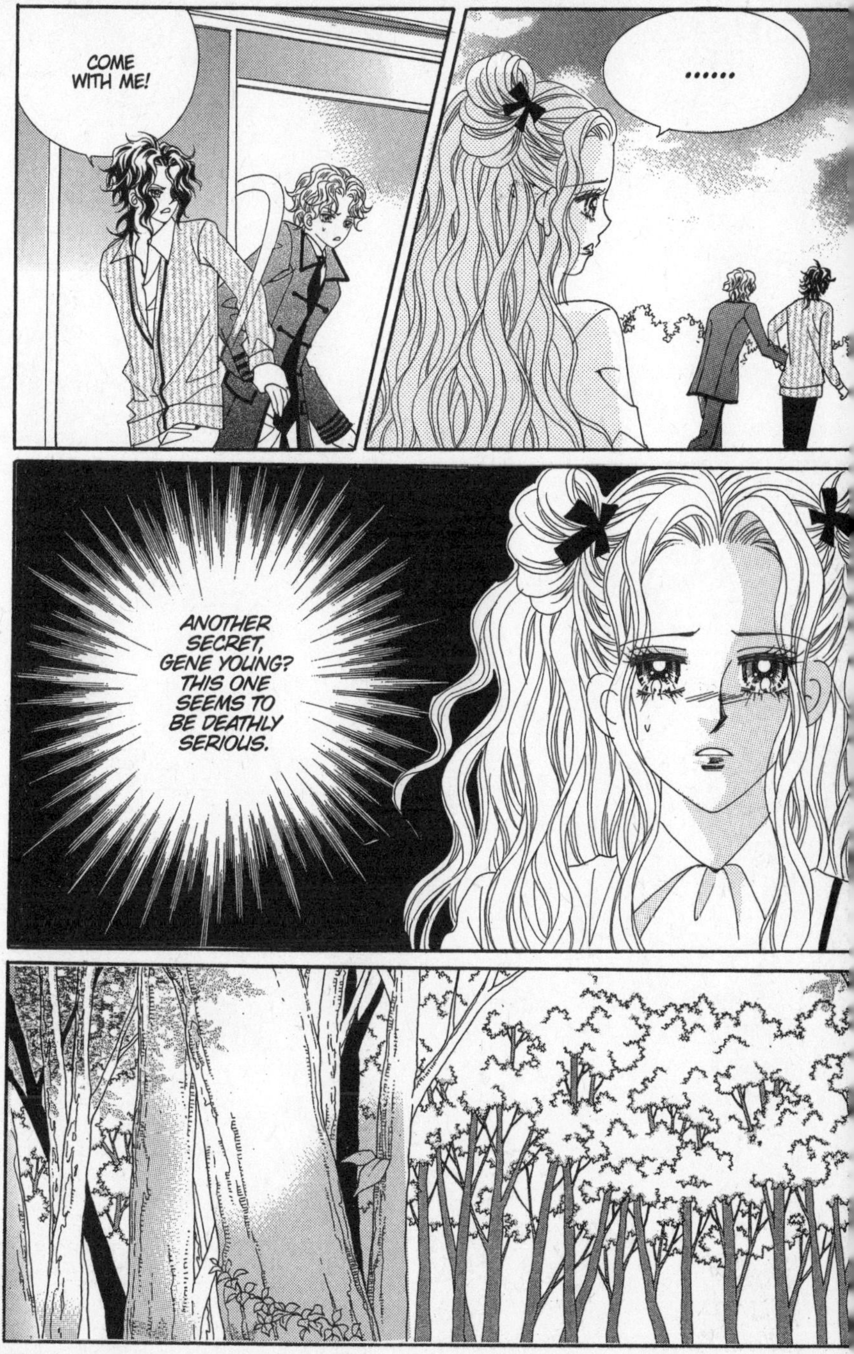
COME WITH ME!
......
ANOTHER SECRET, GENE YOUNG? THIS ONE SEEMS TO BE DEATHLY SERIOUS.

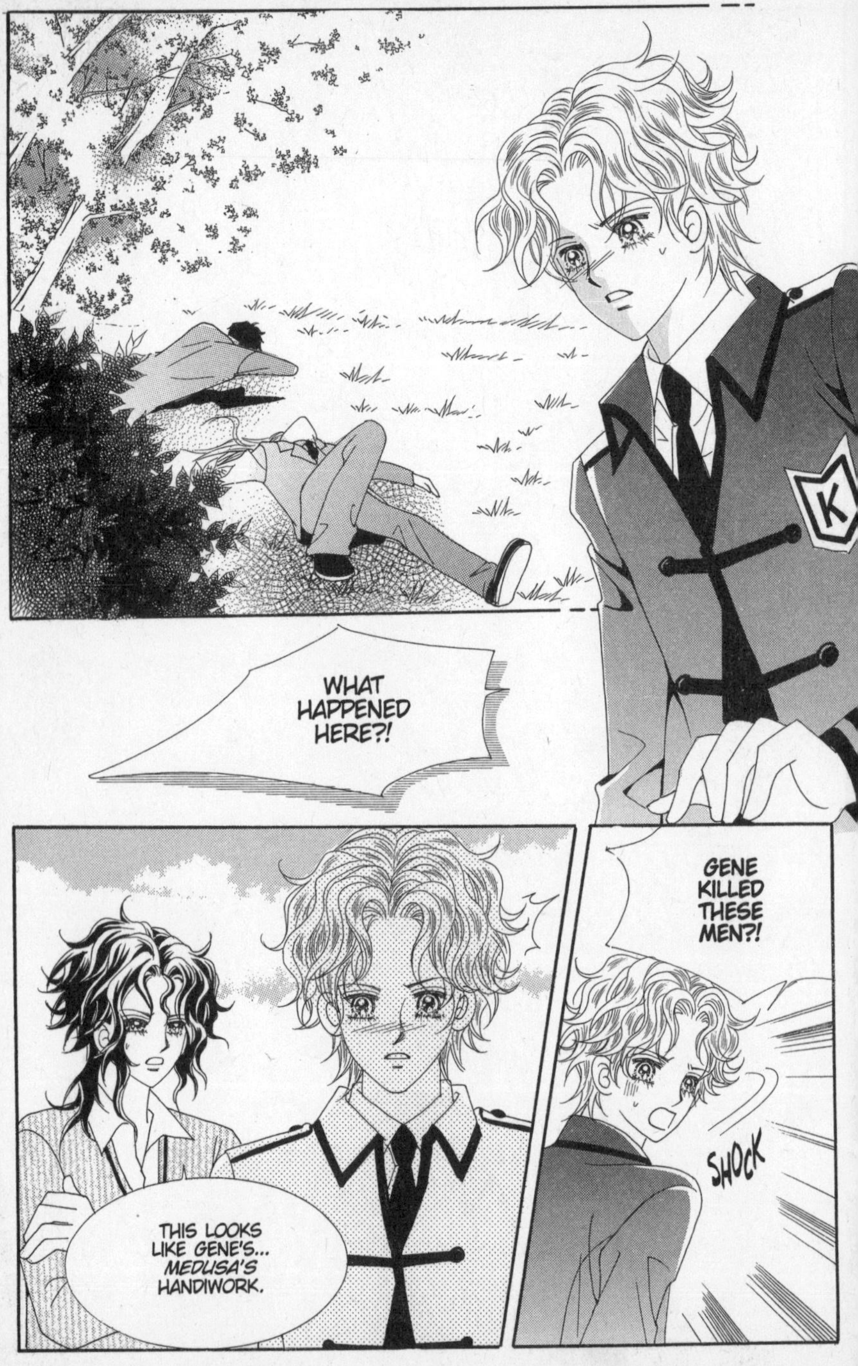
WHAT HAPPENED HERE?!
THIS LOOKS LIKE GENE'S... *MEDUSA'S* HANDIWORK.
GENE KILLED THESE MEN?!
SHOCK

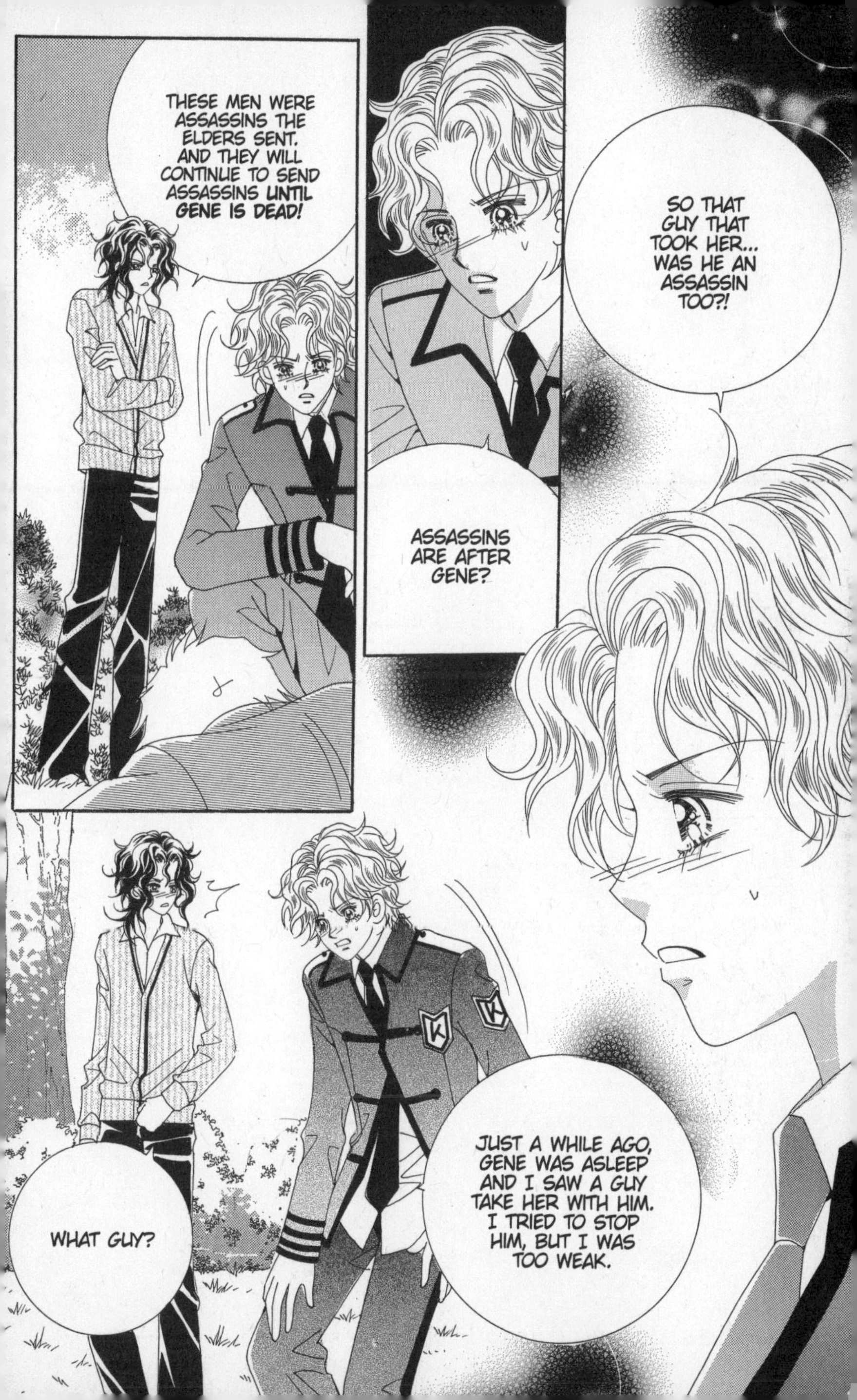
THESE MEN WERE ASSASSINS THE ELDERS SENT. AND THEY WILL CONTINUE TO SEND ASSASSINS UNTIL GENE IS DEAD!
ASSASSINS ARE AFTER GENE?
SO THAT GUY THAT TOOK HER... WAS HE AN ASSASSIN TOO?!
WHAT GUY?
JUST A WHILE AGO, GENE WAS ASLEEP AND I SAW A GUY TAKE HER WITH HIM. I TRIED TO STOP HIM, BUT I WAS TOO WEAK.

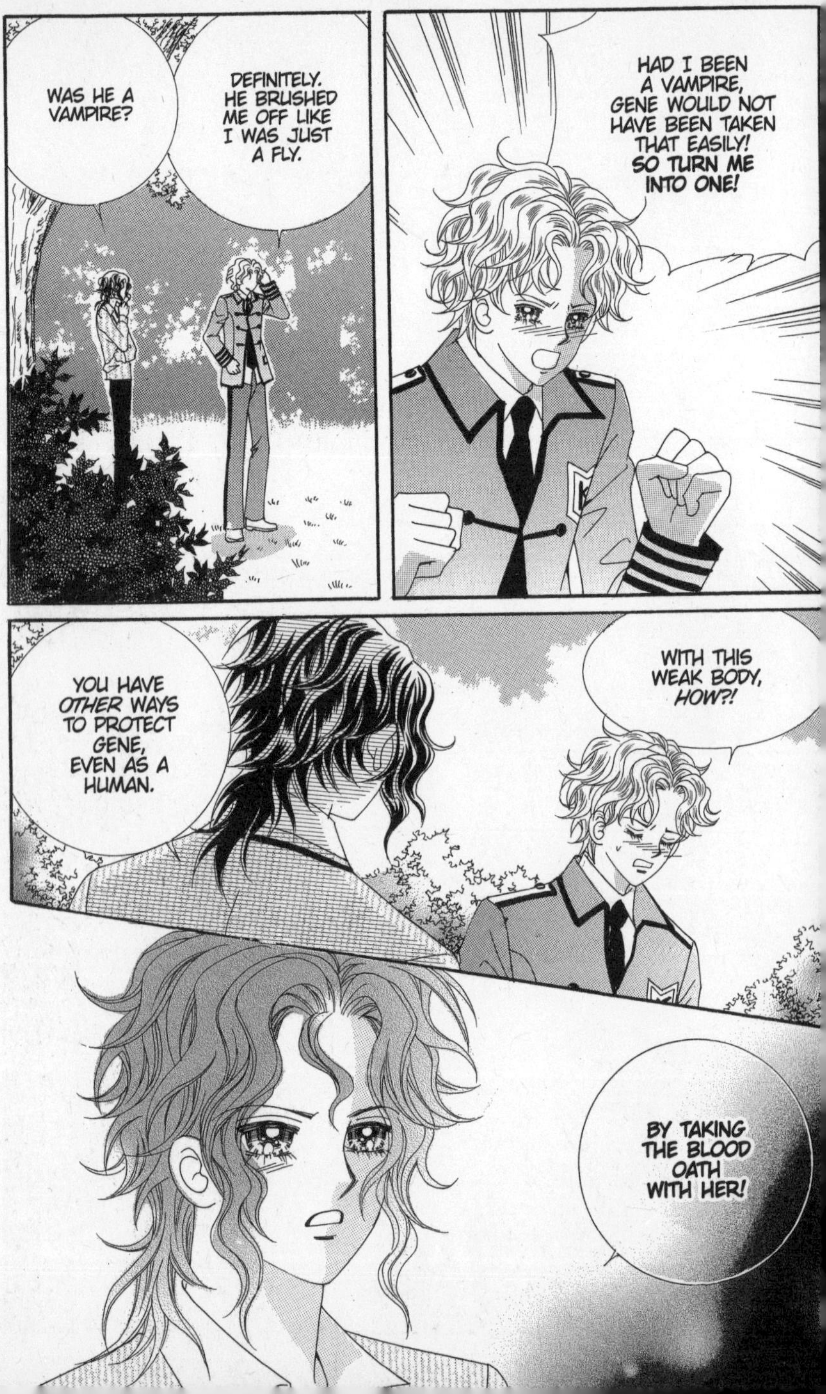
WAS HE A VAMPIRE?
DEFINITELY. HE BRUSHED ME OFF LIKE I WAS JUST A FLY.
HAD I BEEN A VAMPIRE, GENE WOULD NOT HAVE BEEN TAKEN THAT EASILY! SO TURN ME INTO ONE!
YOU HAVE *OTHER* WAYS TO PROTECT GENE, EVEN AS A HUMAN.
WITH THIS WEAK BODY, *HOW?!*
BY TAKING THE BLOOD OATH WITH HER!

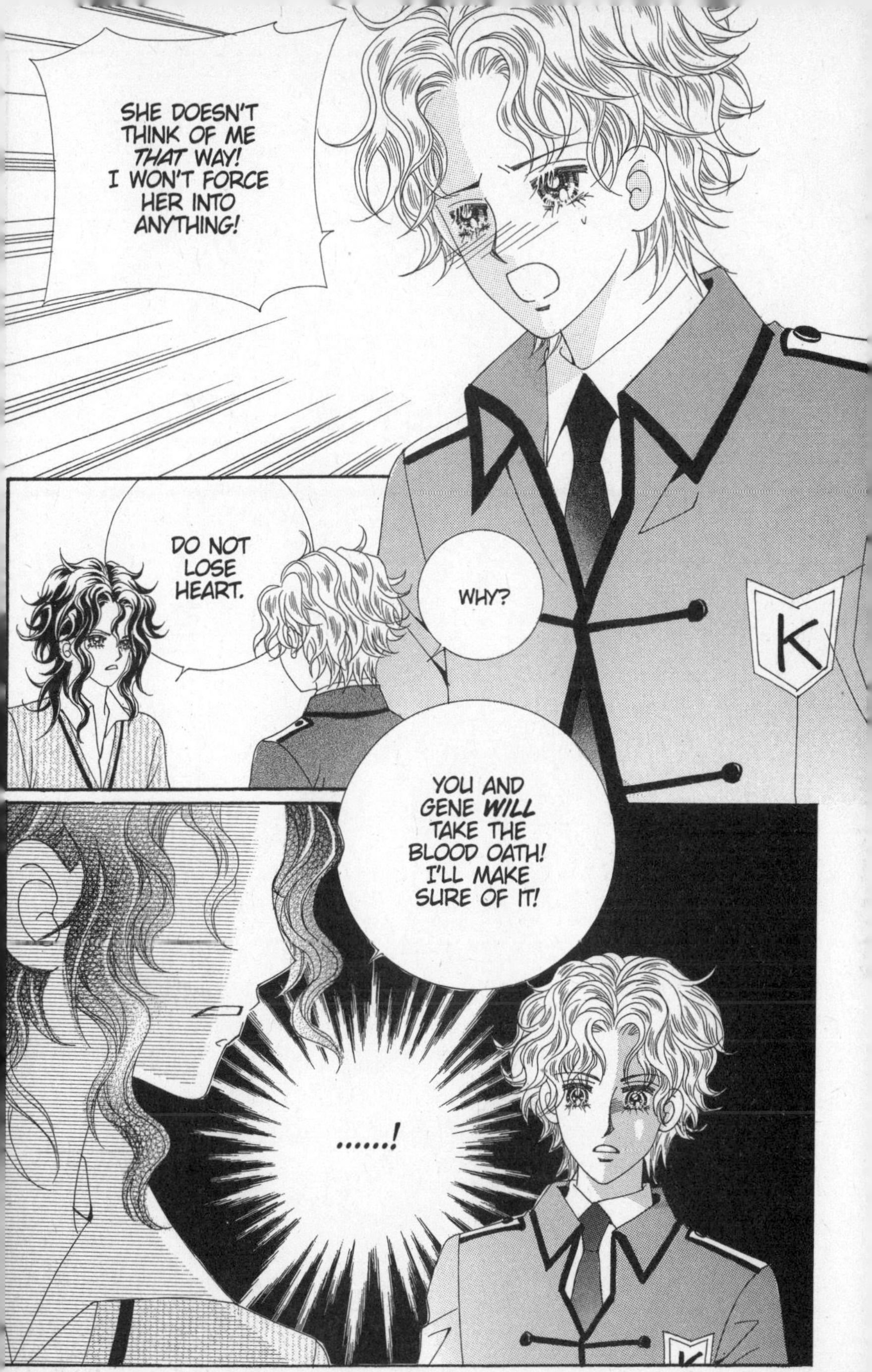
SHE DOESN'T THINK OF ME *THAT* WAY! I WON'T FORCE HER INTO ANYTHING!
DO NOT LOSE HEART.
WHY?
YOU AND GENE ***WILL*** TAKE THE BLOOD OATH! I'LL MAKE SURE OF IT!
......!

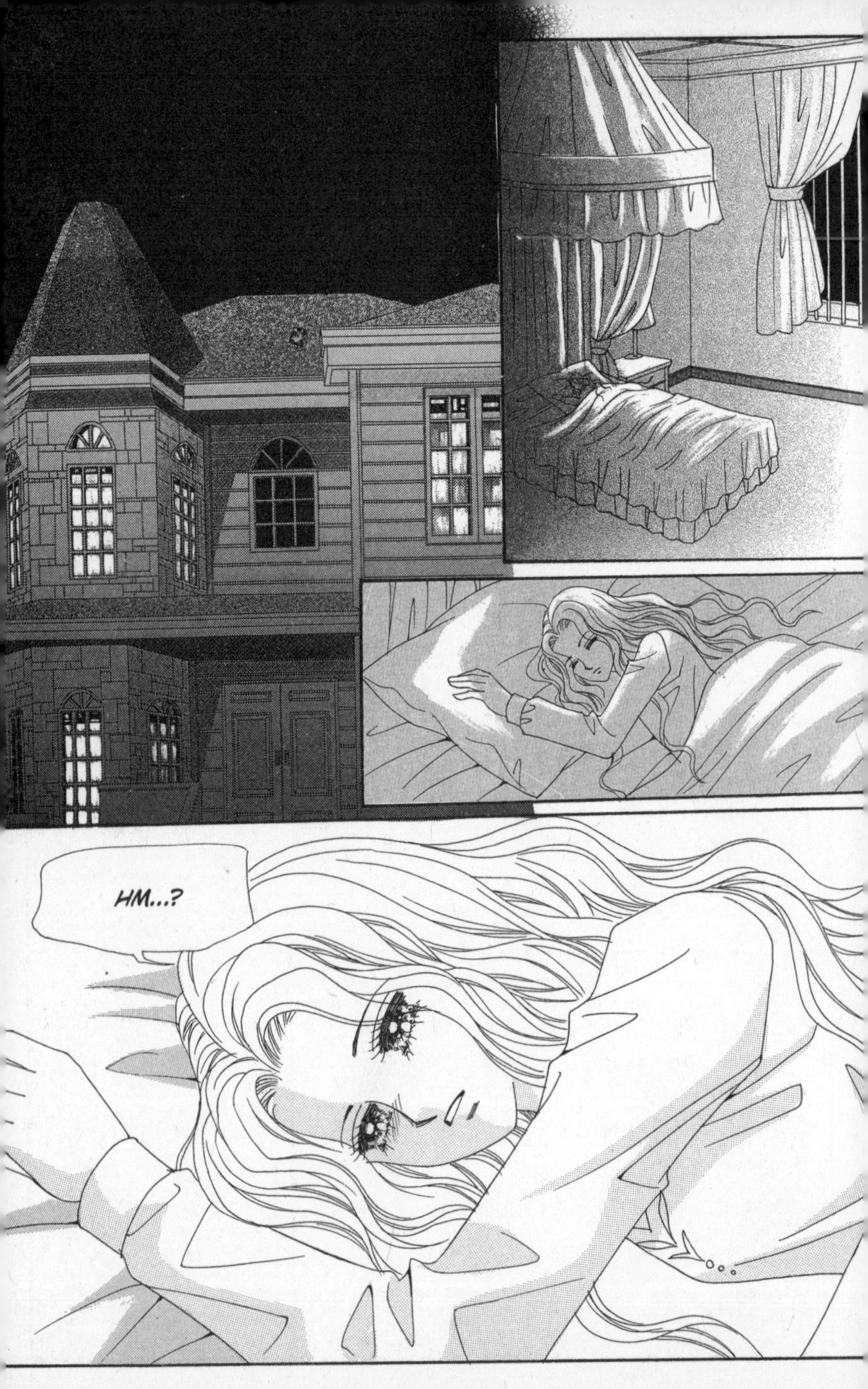
HM...?

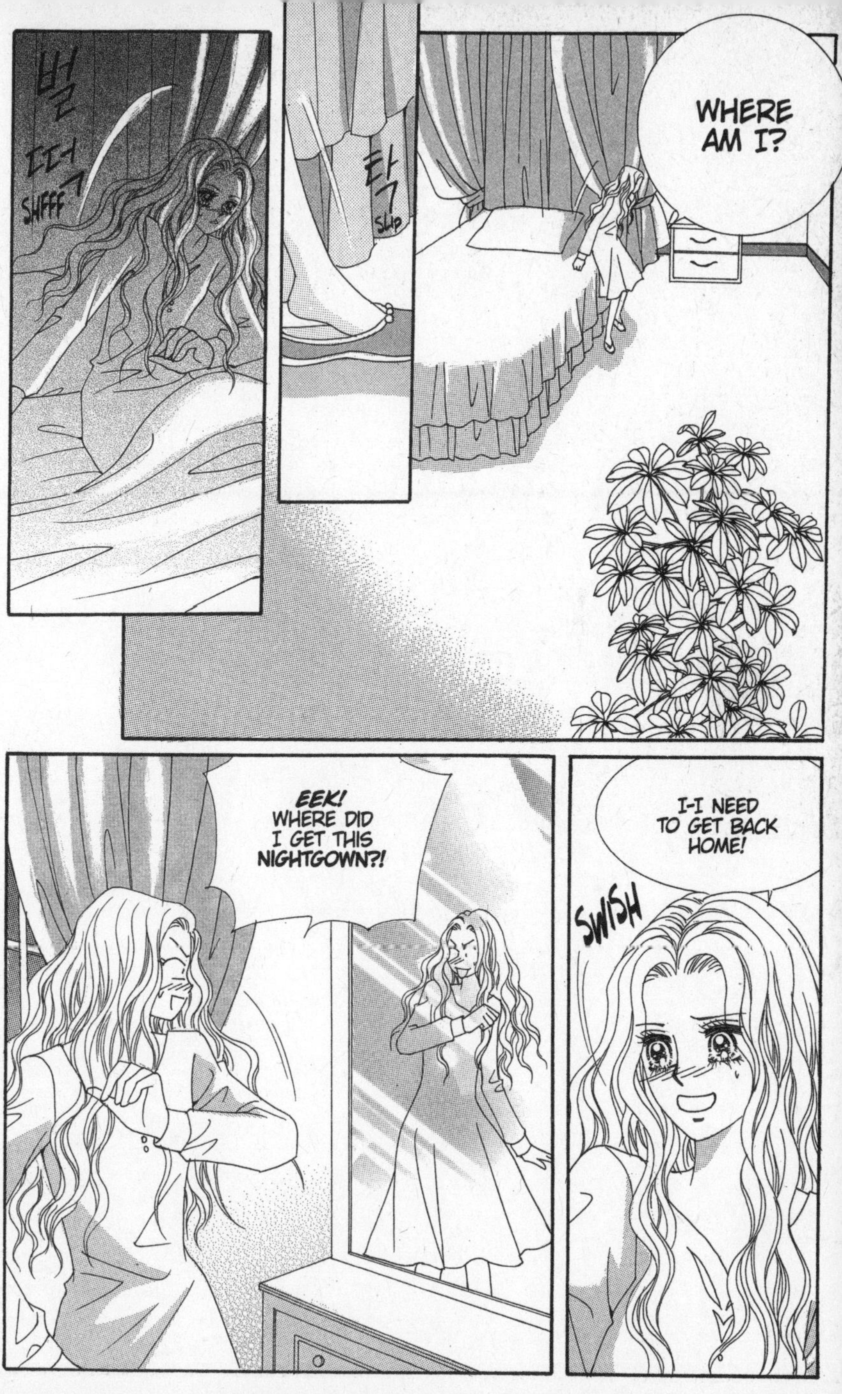
벌떡
SHFFF
탁
SLIP
WHERE AM I?
EEK! WHERE DID I GET THIS NIGHTGOWN?!
SWISH
I-I NEED TO GET BACK HOME!

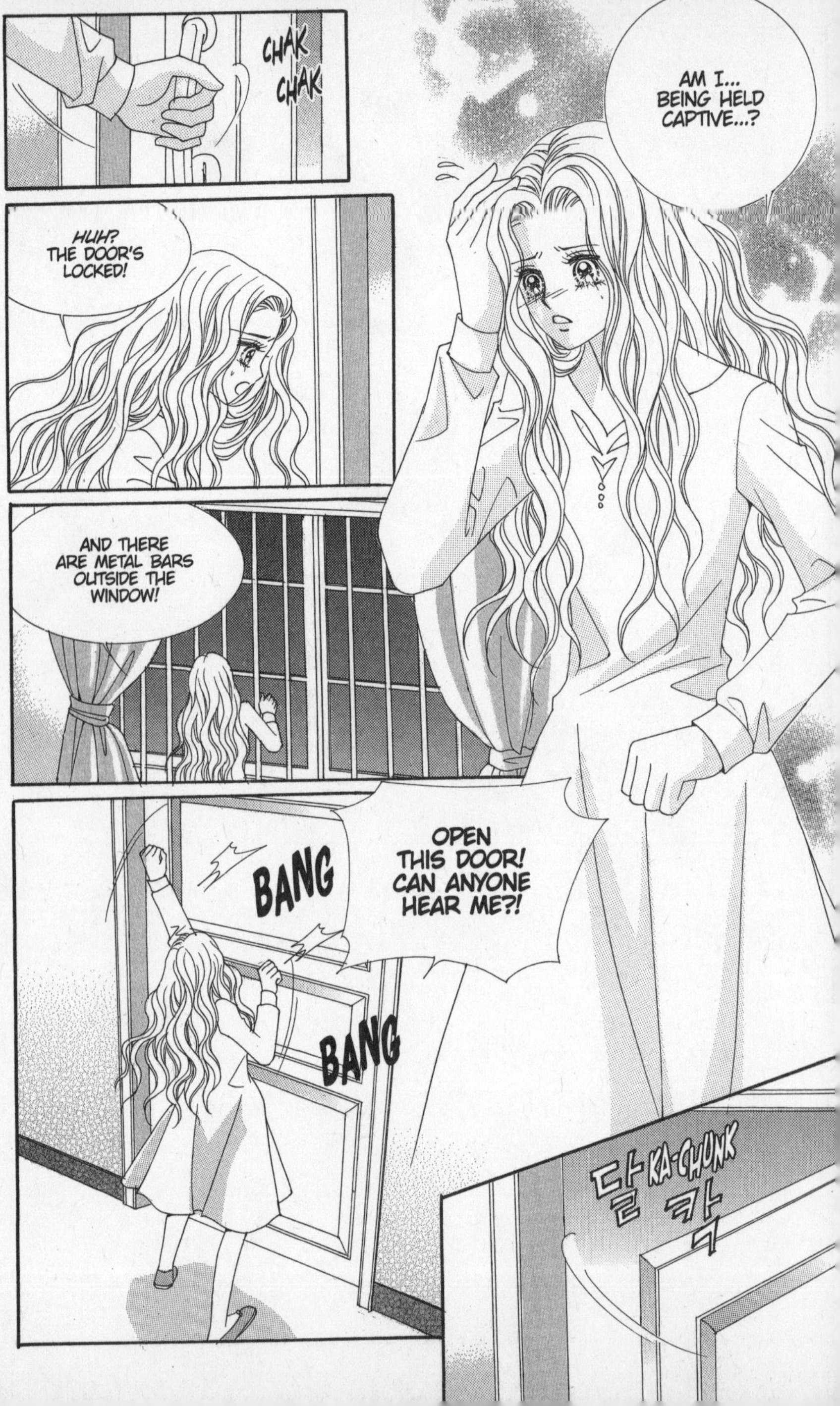
CHAK CHAK
HUH? THE DOOR'S LOCKED!
AND THERE ARE METAL BARS OUTSIDE THE WINDOW!
BANG
OPEN THIS DOOR! CAN ANYONE HEAR ME?!
BANG
AM I... BEING HELD CAPTIVE...?
달칵 KA-CHUNK

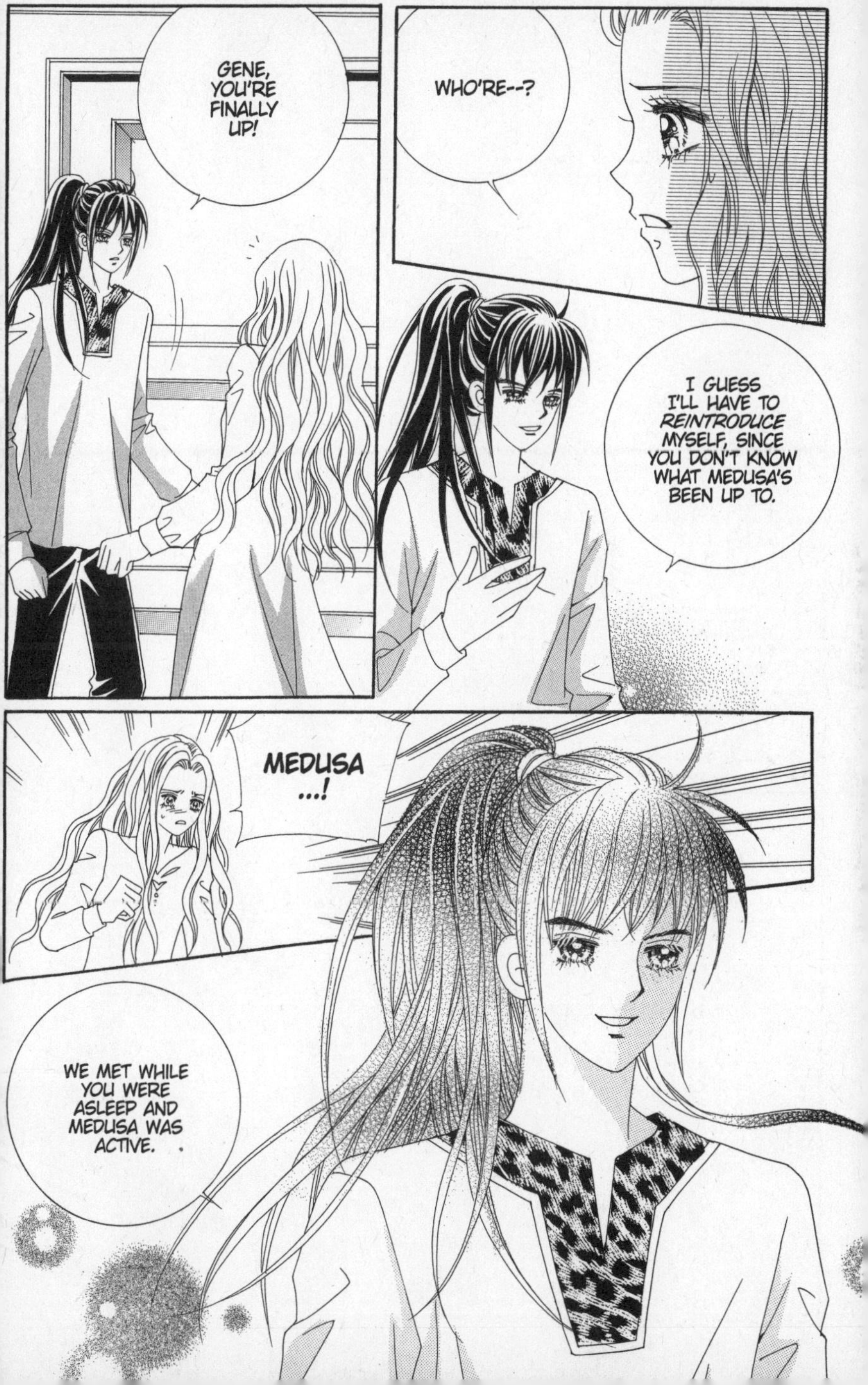
GENE, YOU'RE FINALLY UP!
WHO'RE--?
I GUESS I'LL HAVE TO *REINTRODUCE* MYSELF, SINCE YOU DON'T KNOW WHAT MEDUSA'S BEEN UP TO.
MEDUSA ...!
WE MET WHILE YOU WERE ASLEEP AND MEDUSA WAS ACTIVE.

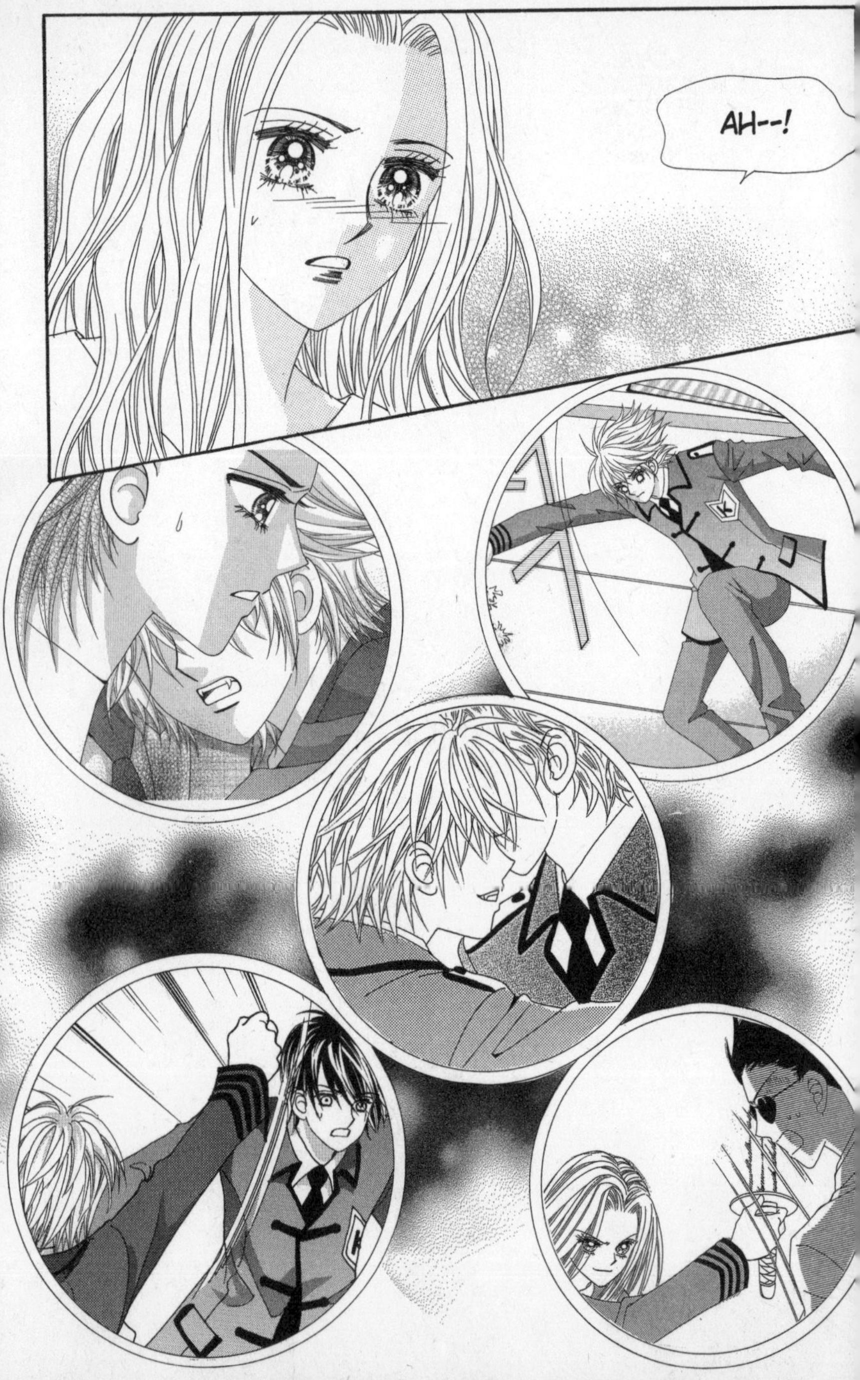
AH--!

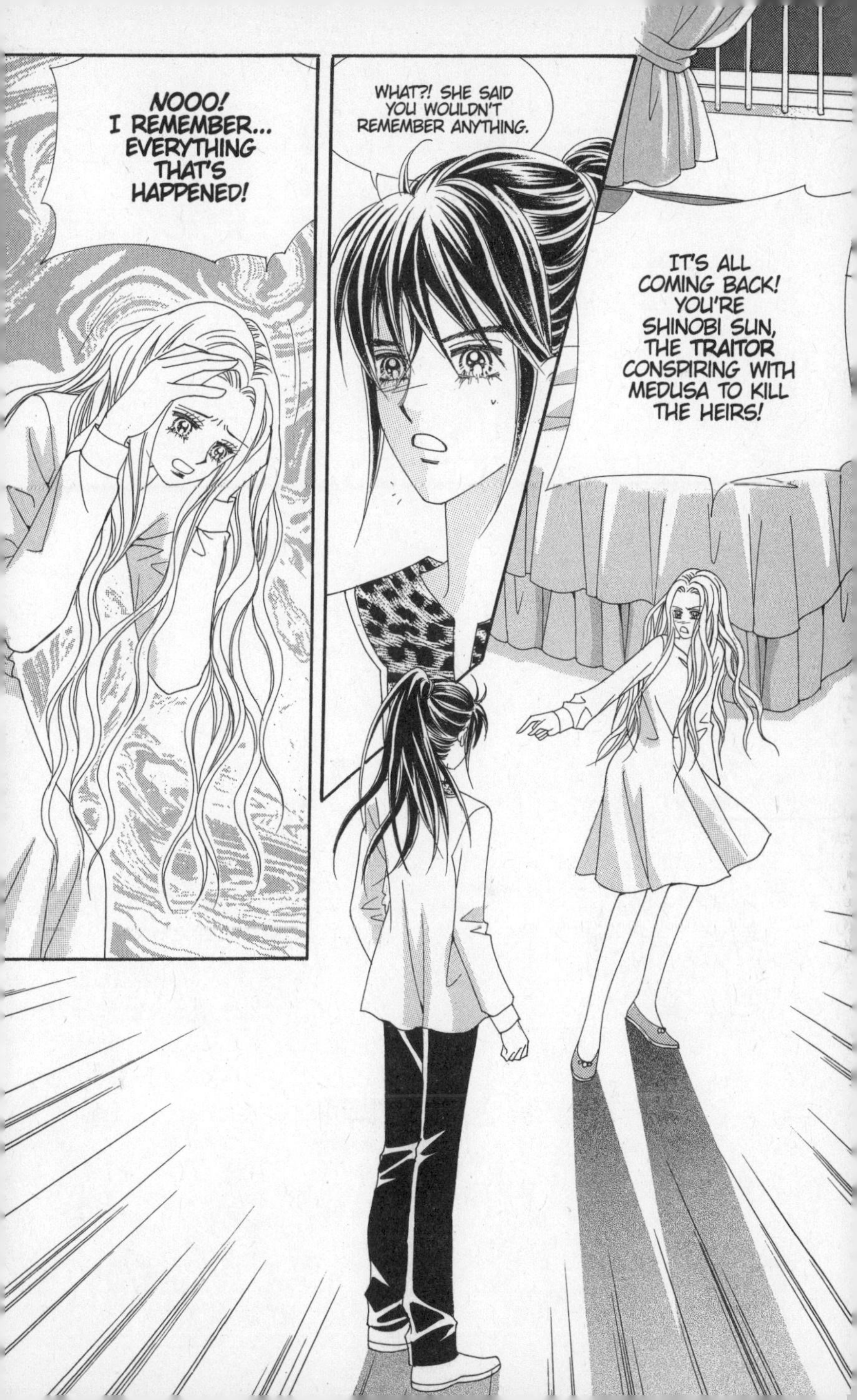
NOOO! I REMEMBER... EVERYTHING THAT'S HAPPENED!
WHAT?! SHE SAID YOU WOULDN'T REMEMBER ANYTHING.
IT'S ALL COMING BACK! YOU'RE SHINOBI SUN, THE TRAITOR CONSPIRING WITH MEDUSA TO KILL THE HEIRS!

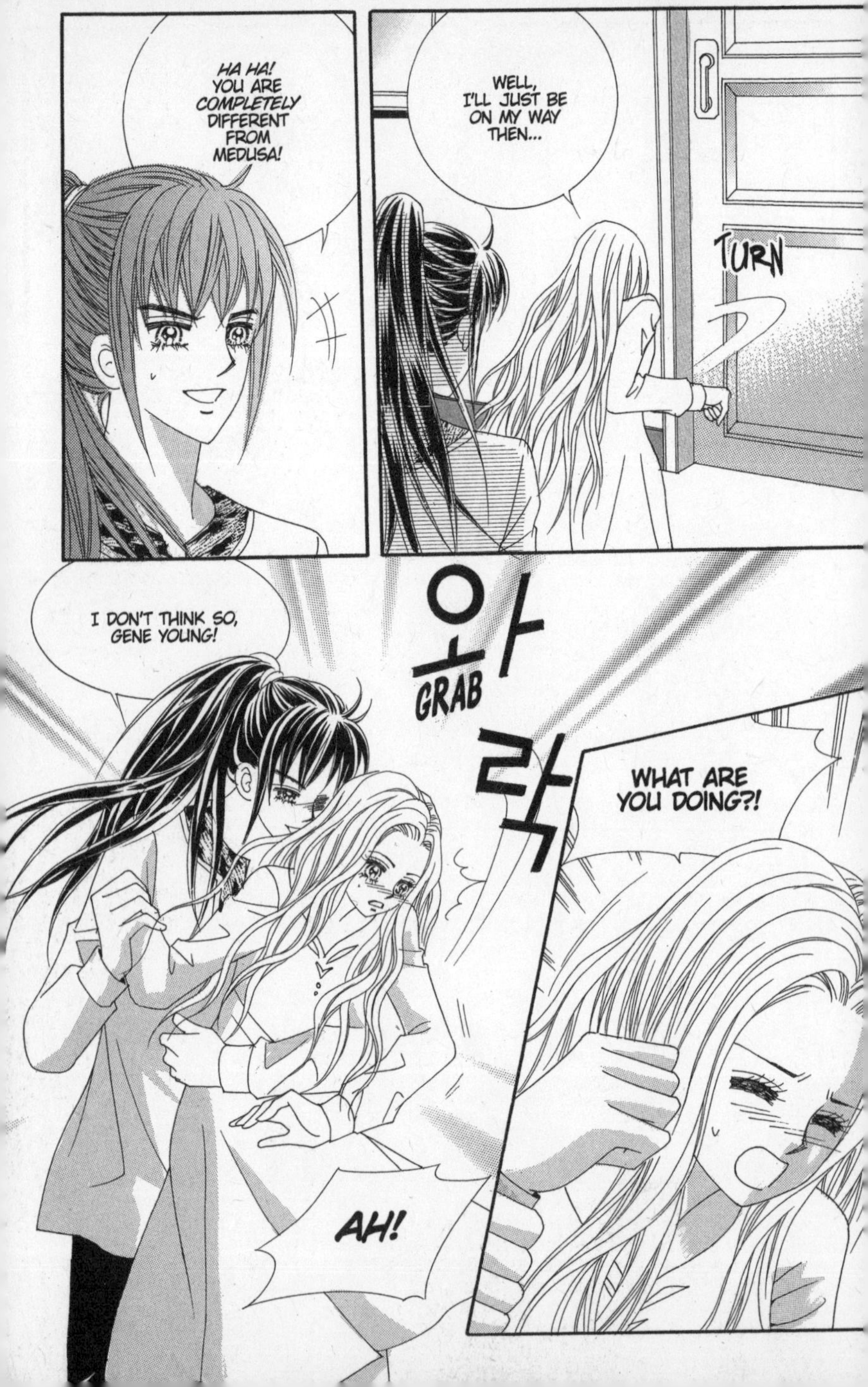
HA HA! YOU ARE COMPLETELY DIFFERENT FROM MEDUSA!
WELL, I'LL JUST BE ON MY WAY THEN...
TURN
I DON'T THINK SO, GENE YOUNG!
와락
GRAB
AH!
WHAT ARE YOU DOING?!

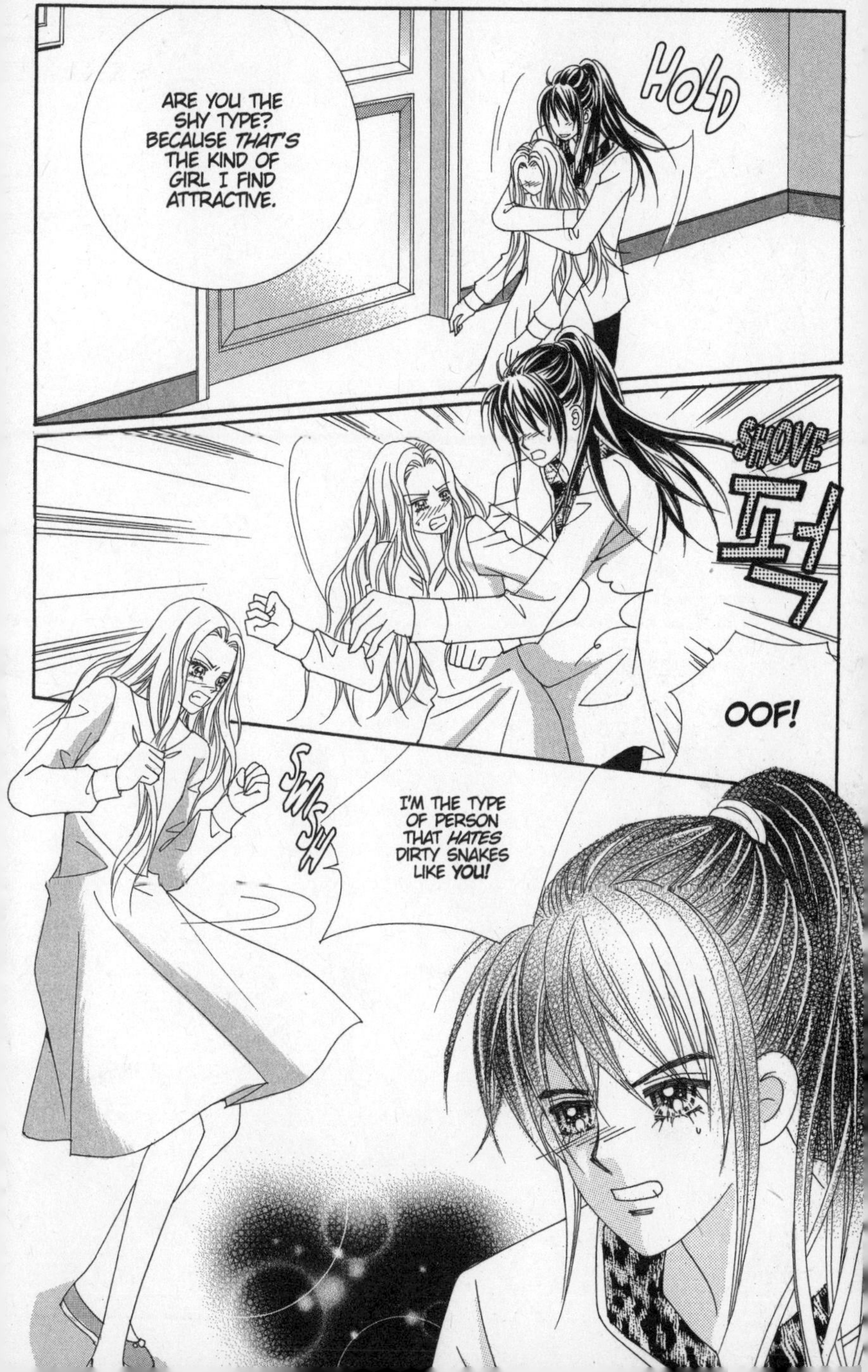
ARE YOU THE SHY TYPE? BECAUSE THAT'S THE KIND OF GIRL I FIND ATTRACTIVE.
HOLD
SHOVE
OOF!
SWISH
I'M THE TYPE OF PERSON THAT HATES DIRTY SNAKES LIKE YOU!

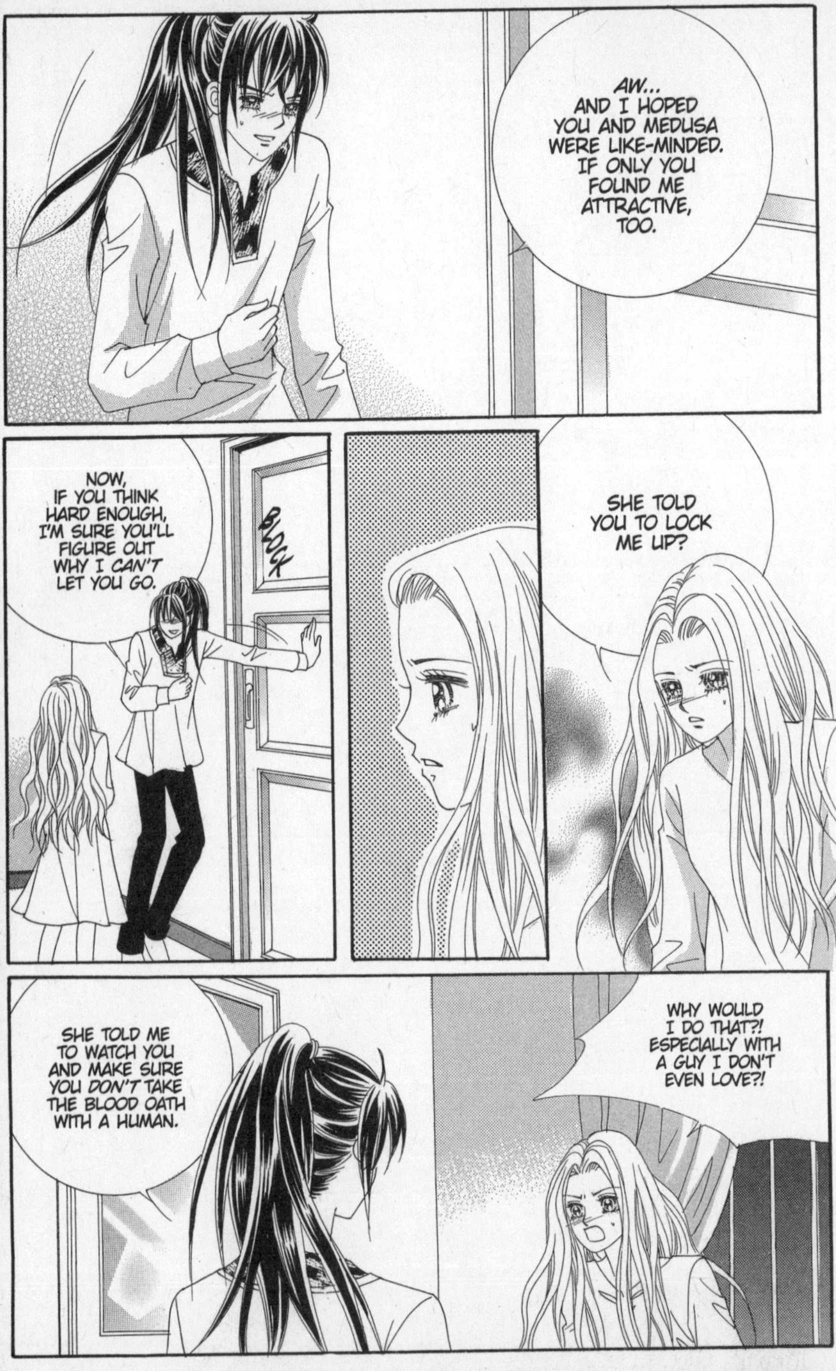
AW... AND I HOPED YOU AND MEDUSA WERE LIKE-MINDED. IF ONLY YOU FOUND ME ATTRACTIVE, TOO.
NOW, IF YOU THINK HARD ENOUGH, I'M SURE YOU'LL FIGURE OUT WHY I CAN'T LET YOU GO.
BLOCK
SHE TOLD YOU TO LOCK ME UP?
SHE TOLD ME TO WATCH YOU AND MAKE SURE YOU DON'T TAKE THE BLOOD OATH WITH A HUMAN.
WHY WOULD I DO THAT?! ESPECIALLY WITH A GUY I DON'T EVEN LOVE?!

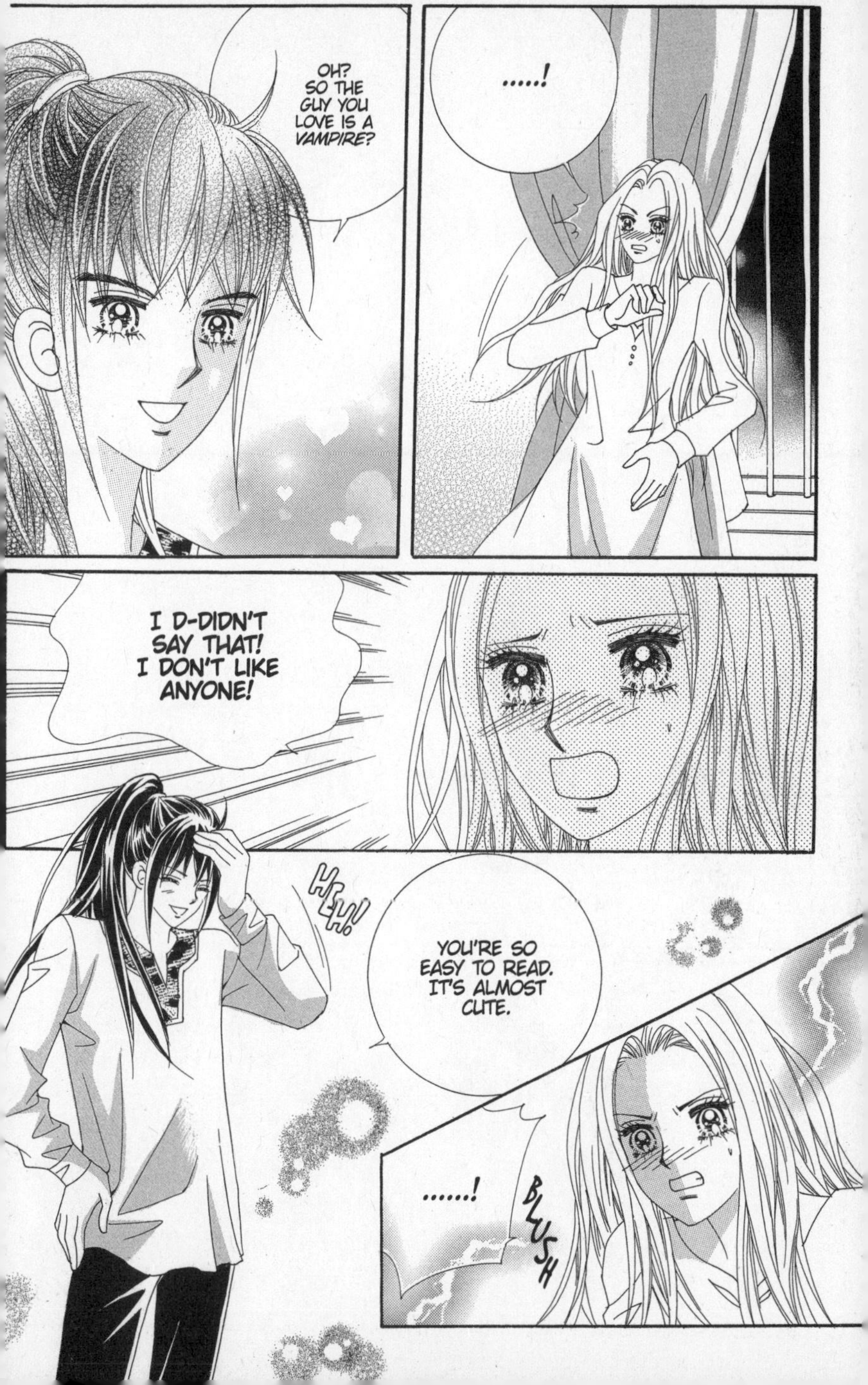
OH? SO THE GUY YOU LOVE IS A VAMPIRE?
......!
I D-DIDN'T SAY THAT! I DON'T LIKE ANYONE!
HEH!
YOU'RE SO EASY TO READ. IT'S ALMOST CUTE.
......!
BLUSH

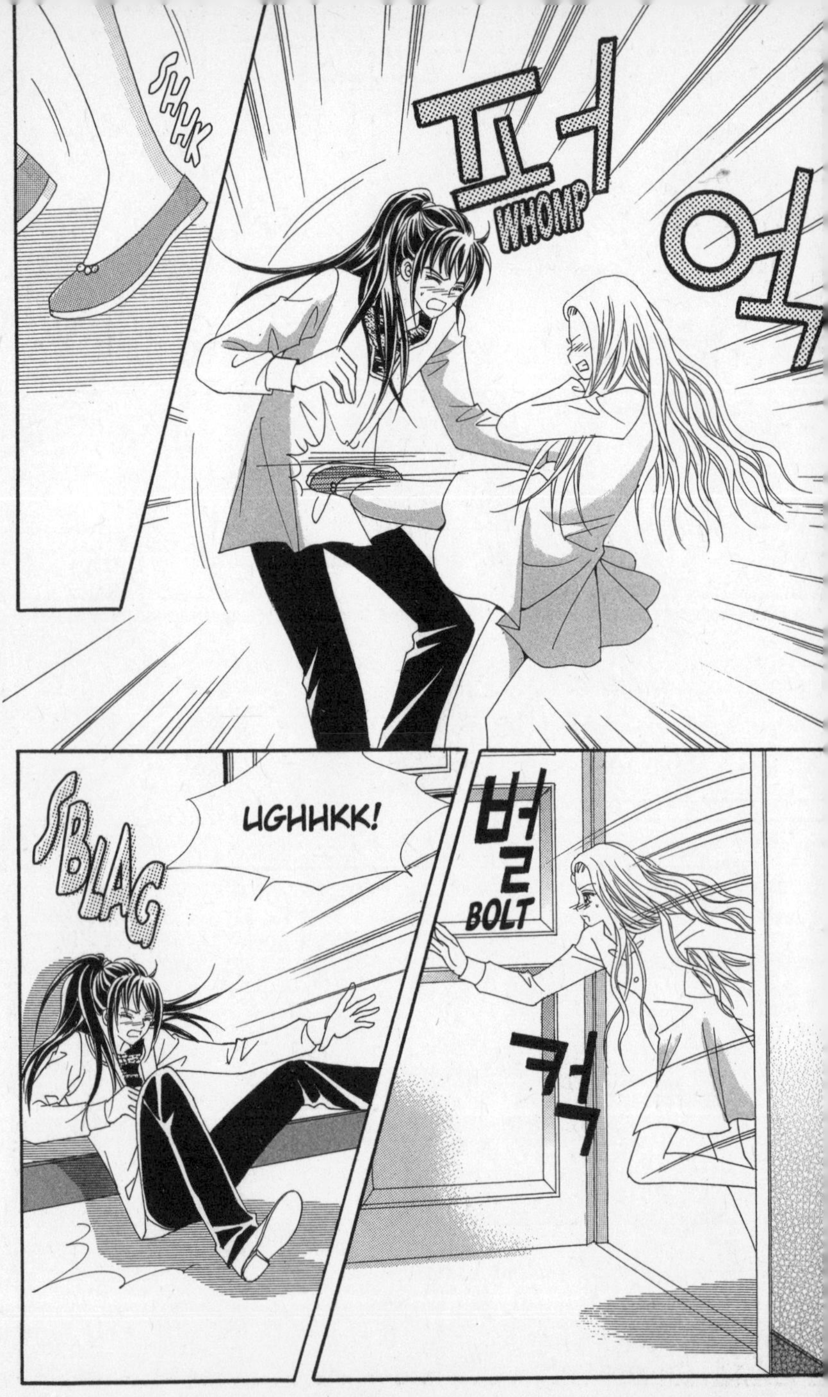
SHHK
퍼억
WHOMP
SBLAG
UGHHKK!
벌
BOLT
컥

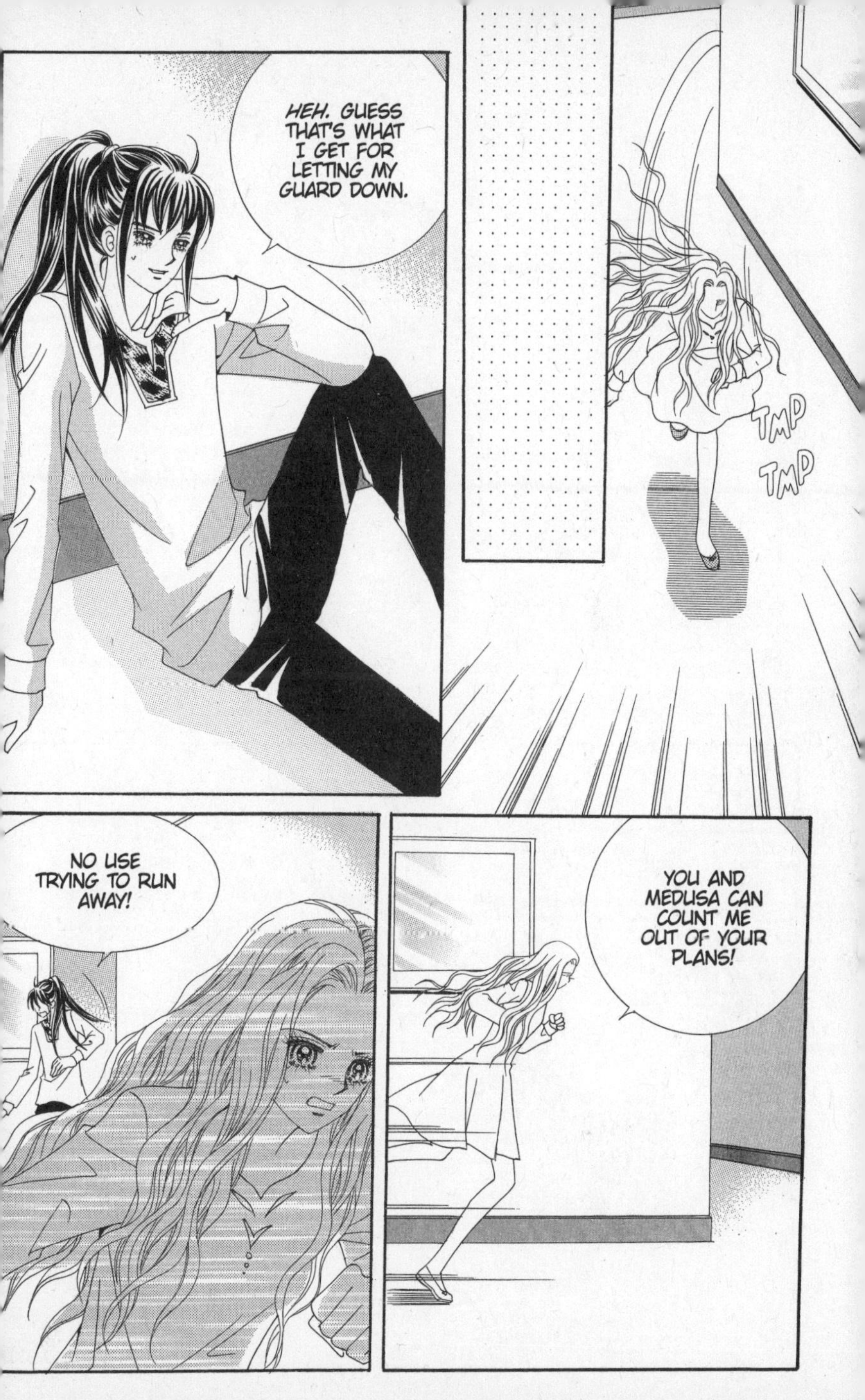
HEH. GUESS THAT'S WHAT I GET FOR LETTING MY GUARD DOWN.
TMP
TMP
NO USE TRYING TO RUN AWAY!
YOU AND MEDUSA CAN COUNT ME OUT OF YOUR PLANS!

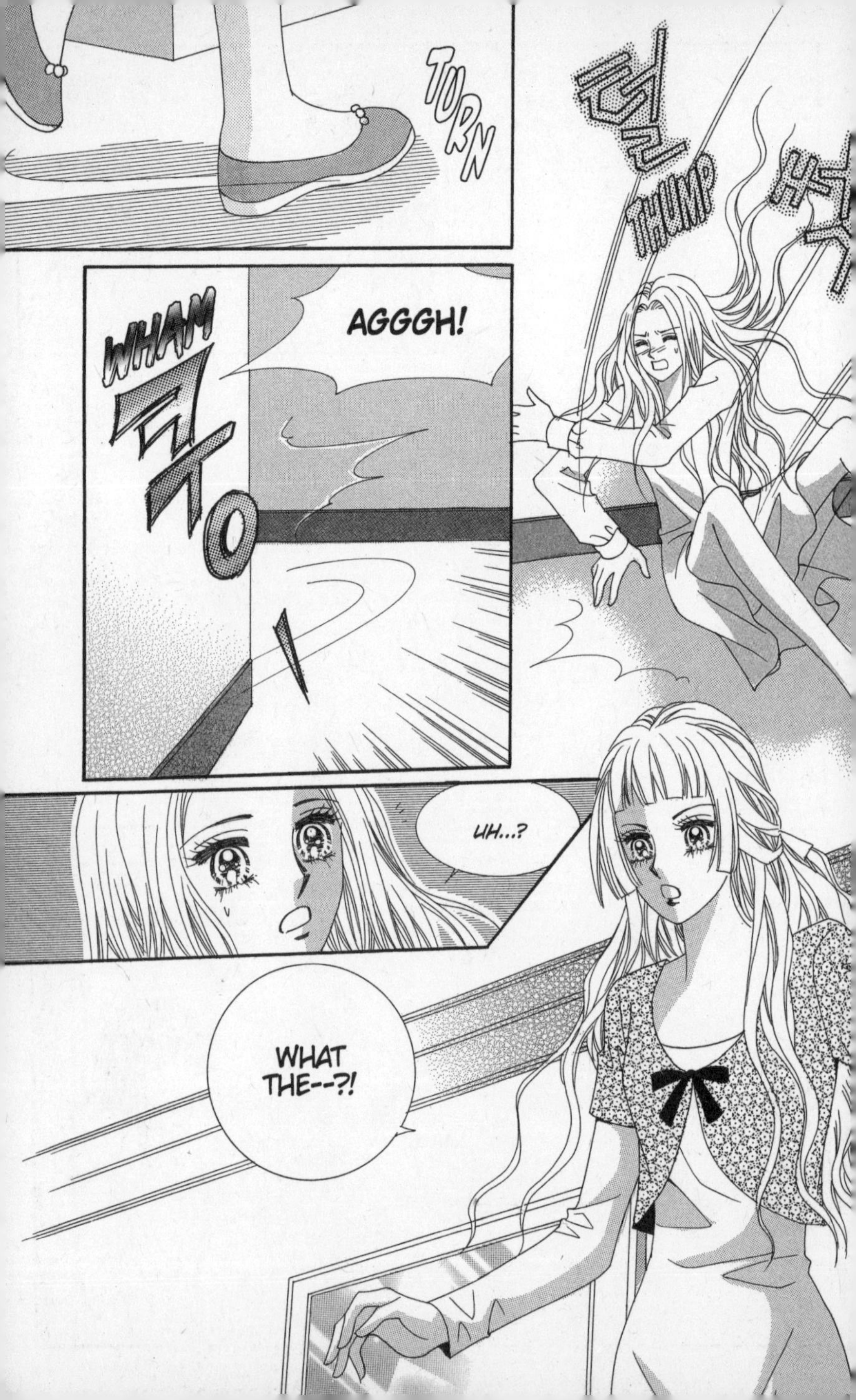
TURN
WHAM
AGGGH!
THUMP
UH...?
WHAT THE--?!

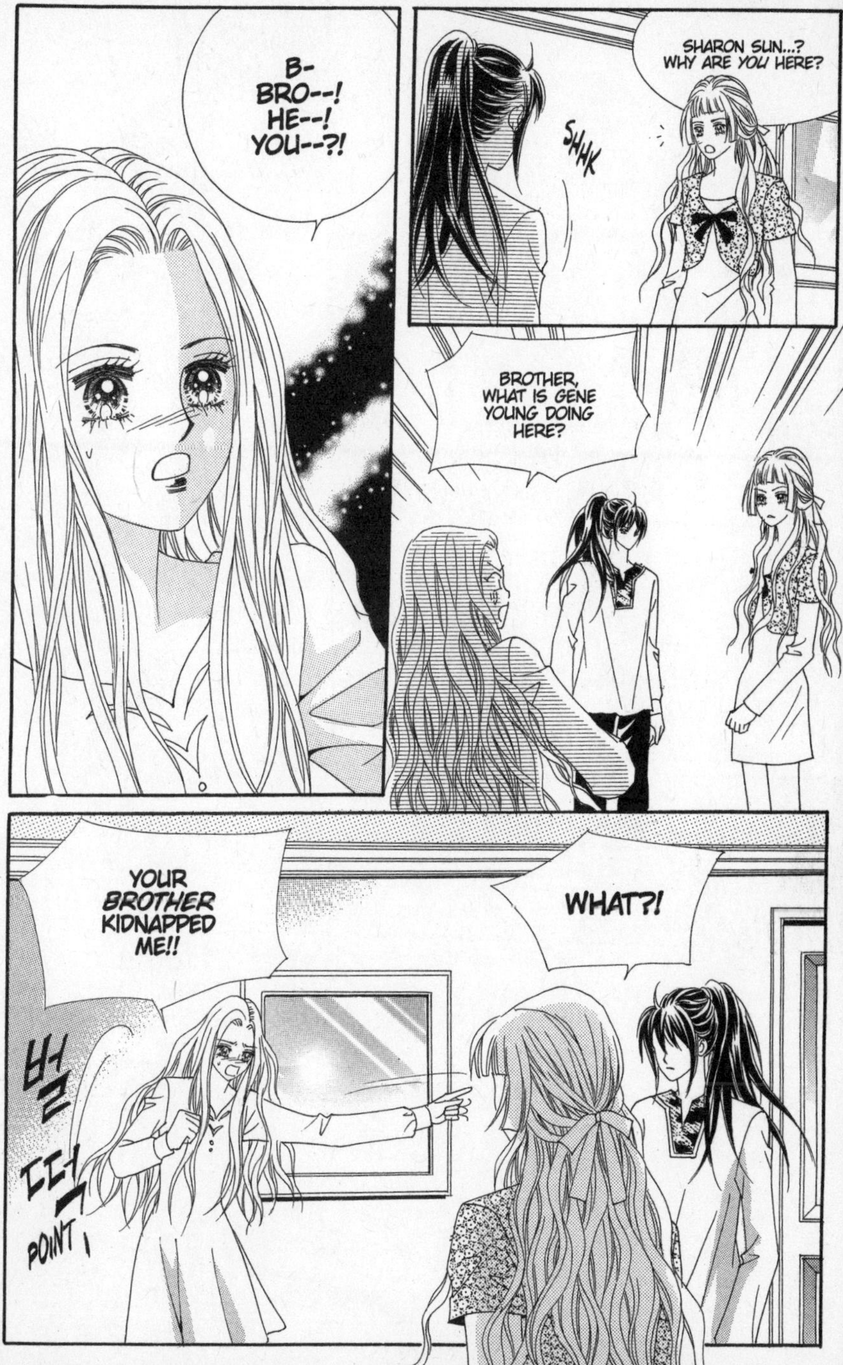
B-
BRO--! HE--! YOU--?!
SHARON SUN...? WHY ARE *YOU* HERE?
SHHK
BROTHER, WHAT IS GENE YOUNG DOING HERE?
YOUR *BROTHER* KIDNAPPED ME!!
WHAT?!
벌떡
POINT

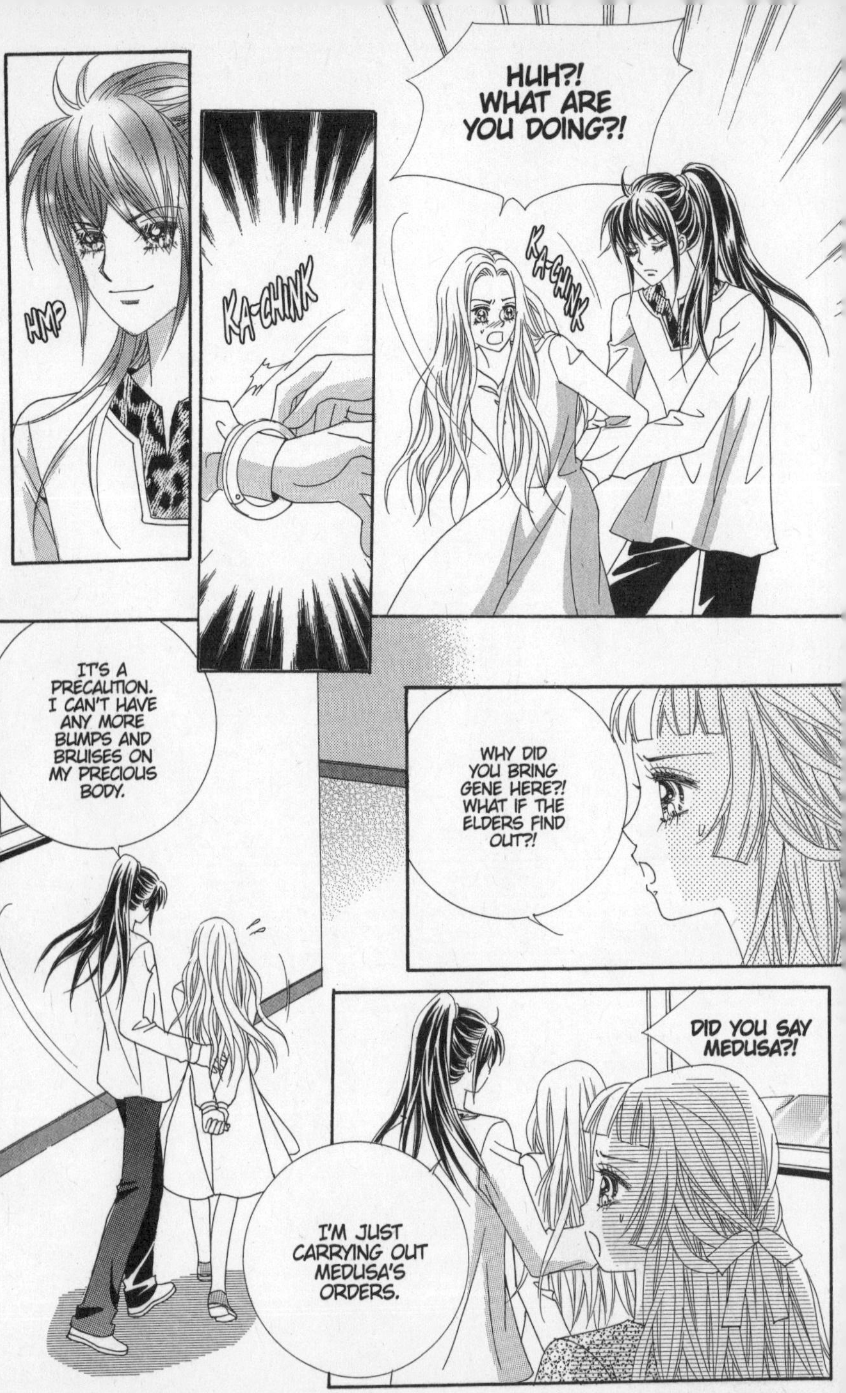
HMP
KA-CHINK
HUH?! WHAT ARE YOU DOING?!
KA-CHINK
IT'S A PRECAUTION. I CAN'T HAVE ANY MORE BUMPS AND BRUISES ON MY PRECIOUS BODY.
WHY DID YOU BRING GENE HERE?! WHAT IF THE ELDERS FIND OUT?!
I'M JUST CARRYING OUT MEDUSA'S ORDERS.
DID YOU SAY MEDUSA?!

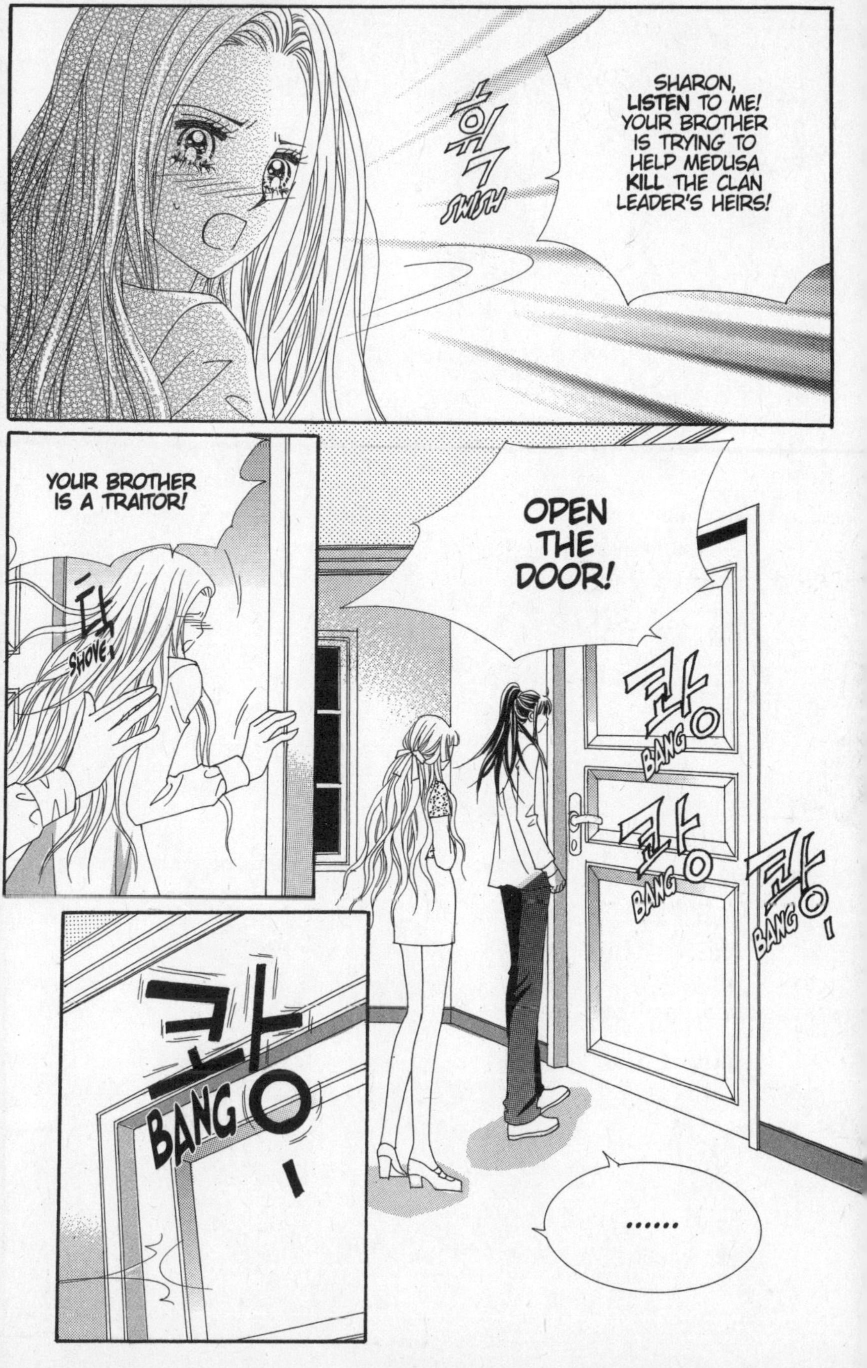
SHARON, LISTEN TO ME! YOUR BROTHER IS TRYING TO HELP MEDUSA KILL THE CLAN LEADER'S HEIRS!
SWISH
YOUR BROTHER IS A TRAITOR!
SHOVE
BANG
OPEN THE DOOR!
BANG
BANG
BANG
......

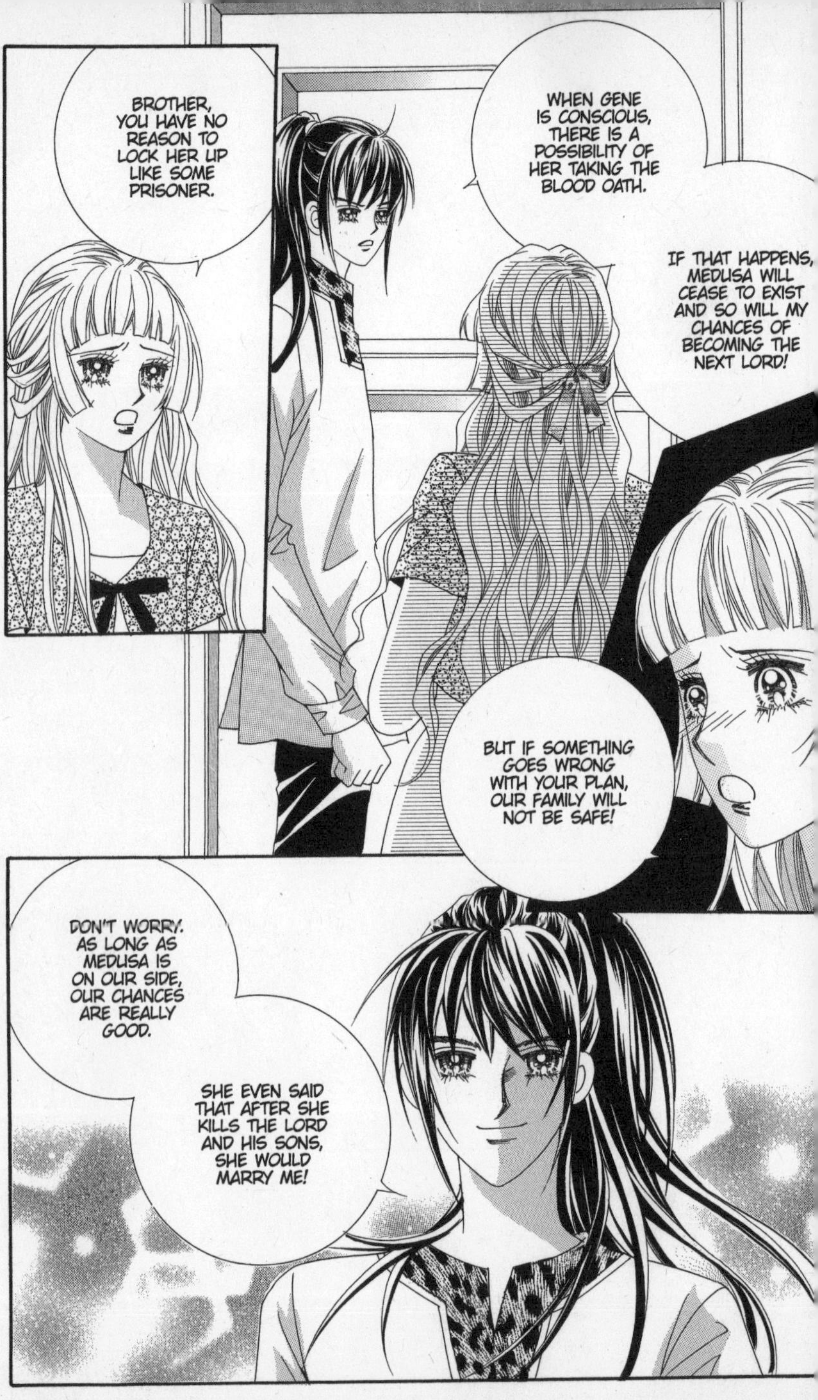
BROTHER, YOU HAVE NO REASON TO LOCK HER UP LIKE SOME PRISONER.
WHEN GENE IS CONSCIOUS, THERE IS A POSSIBILITY OF HER TAKING THE BLOOD OATH.
IF THAT HAPPENS, MEDUSA WILL CEASE TO EXIST AND SO WILL MY CHANCES OF BECOMING THE NEXT LORD!
BUT IF SOMETHING GOES WRONG WITH YOUR PLAN, OUR FAMILY WILL NOT BE SAFE!
DON'T WORRY. AS LONG AS MEDUSA IS ON OUR SIDE, OUR CHANCES ARE REALLY GOOD.
SHE EVEN SAID THAT AFTER SHE KILLS THE LORD AND HIS SONS, SHE WOULD MARRY ME!

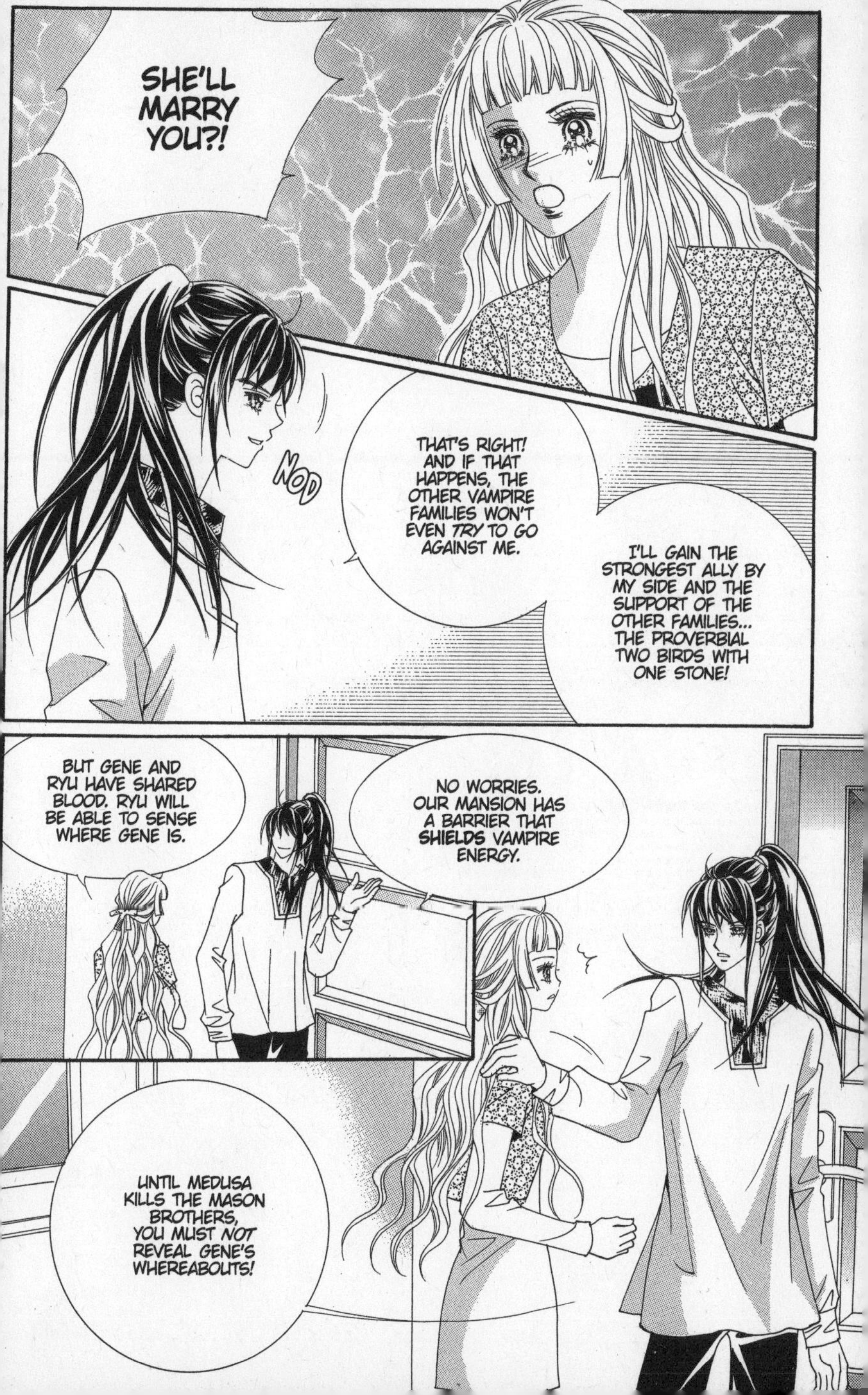
SHE'LL MARRY YOU?!
NOD
THAT'S RIGHT! AND IF THAT HAPPENS, THE OTHER VAMPIRE FAMILIES WON'T EVEN *TRY* TO GO AGAINST ME.
I'LL GAIN THE STRONGEST ALLY BY MY SIDE AND THE SUPPORT OF THE OTHER FAMILIES... THE PROVERBIAL TWO BIRDS WITH ONE STONE!
BUT GENE AND RYU HAVE SHARED BLOOD. RYU WILL BE ABLE TO SENSE WHERE GENE IS.
NO WORRIES. OUR MANSION HAS A BARRIER THAT **SHIELDS VAMPIRE** ENERGY.
UNTIL MEDUSA KILLS THE MASON BROTHERS, YOU MUST *NOT* REVEAL GENE'S WHEREABOUTS!

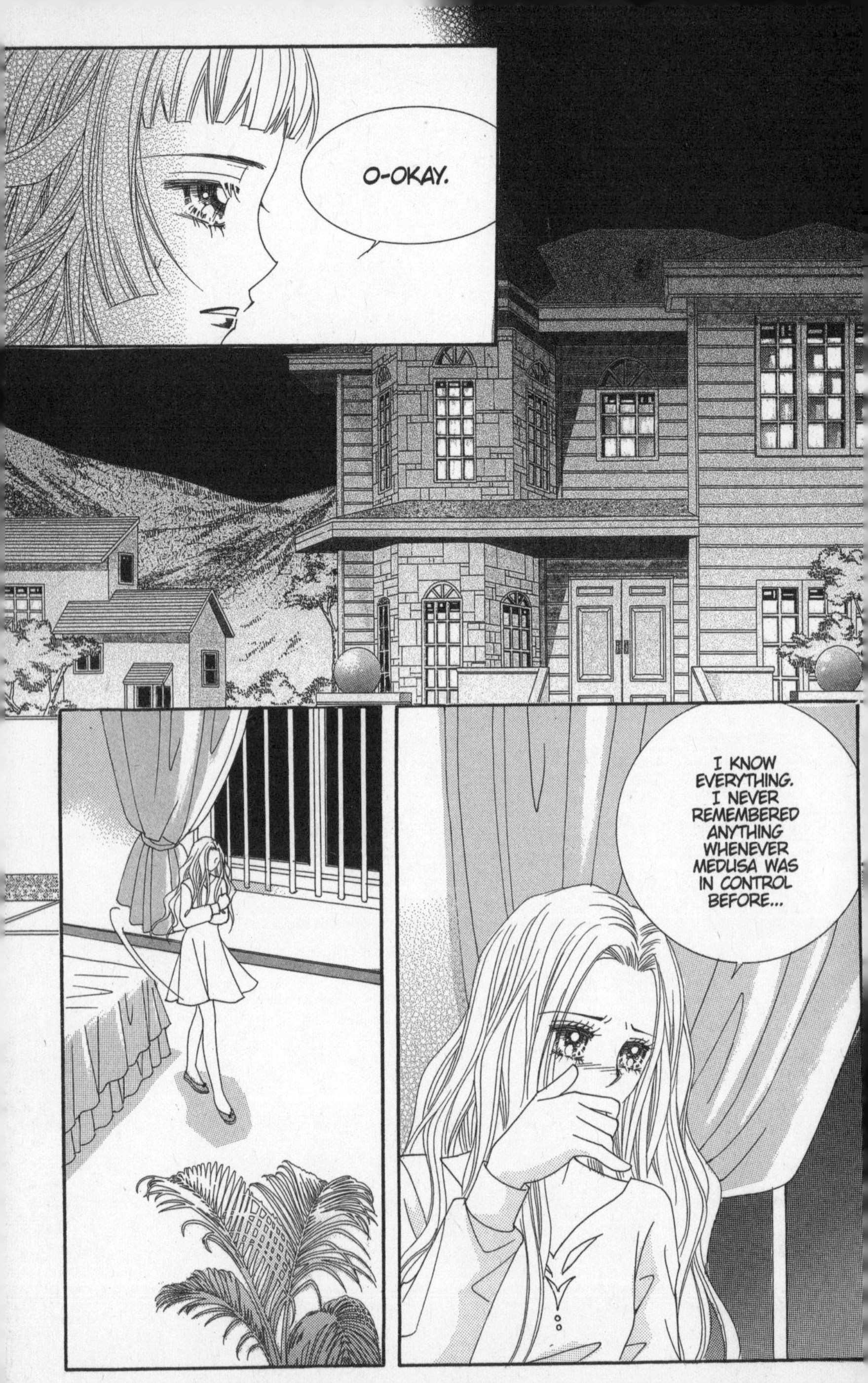
O-OKAY.
I KNOW EVERYTHING. I NEVER REMEMBERED ANYTHING WHENEVER MEDUSA WAS IN CONTROL BEFORE...

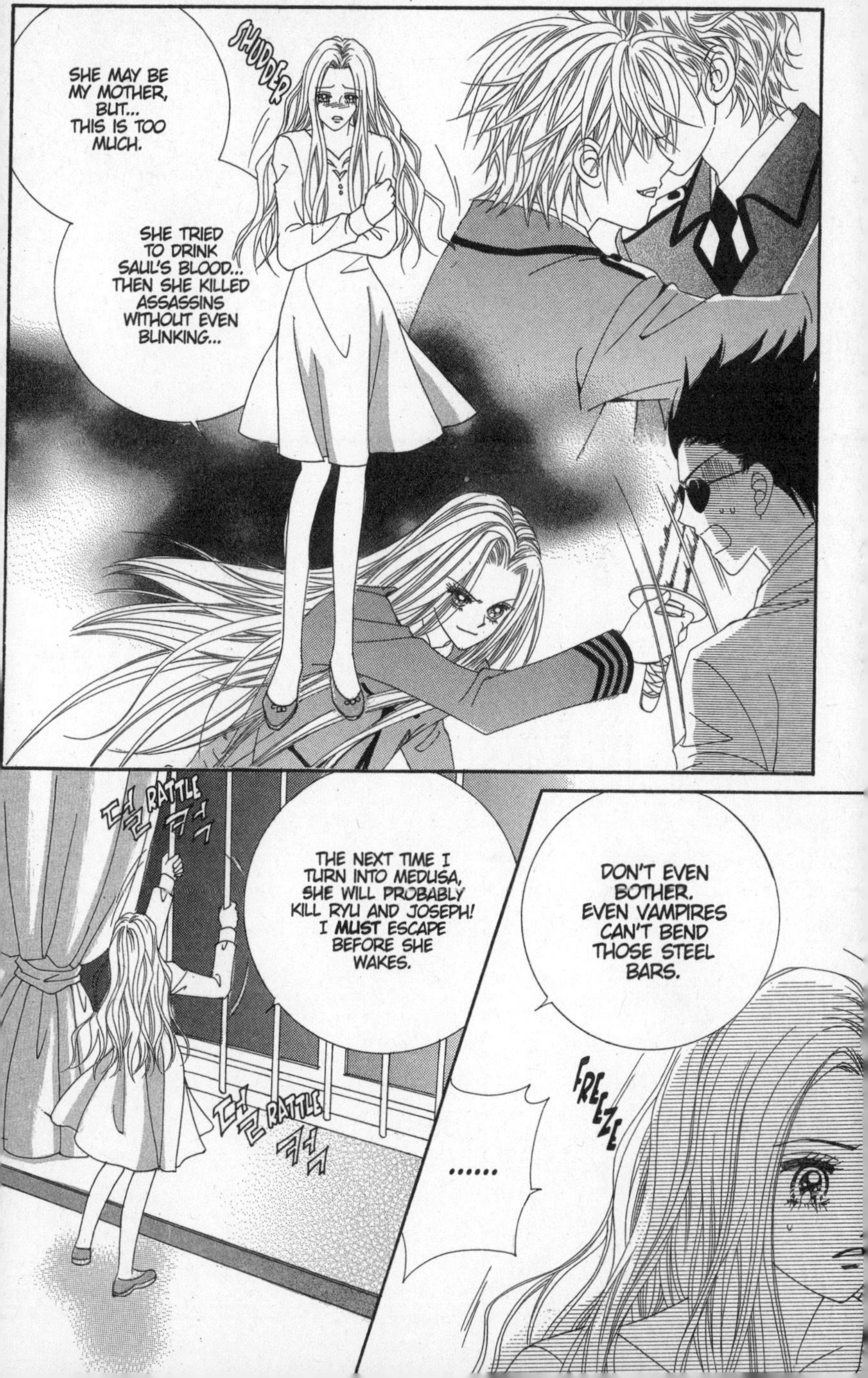
SHUDDER
SHE MAY BE MY MOTHER, BUT... THIS IS TOO MUCH.
SHE TRIED TO DRINK SAUL'S BLOOD... THEN SHE KILLED ASSASSINS WITHOUT EVEN BLINKING...
RATTLE
THE NEXT TIME I TURN INTO MEDUSA, SHE WILL PROBABLY KILL RYU AND JOSEPH! I MUST ESCAPE BEFORE SHE WAKES.
RATTLE
DON'T EVEN BOTHER. EVEN VAMPIRES CAN'T BEND THOSE STEEL BARS.
FREEZE
......

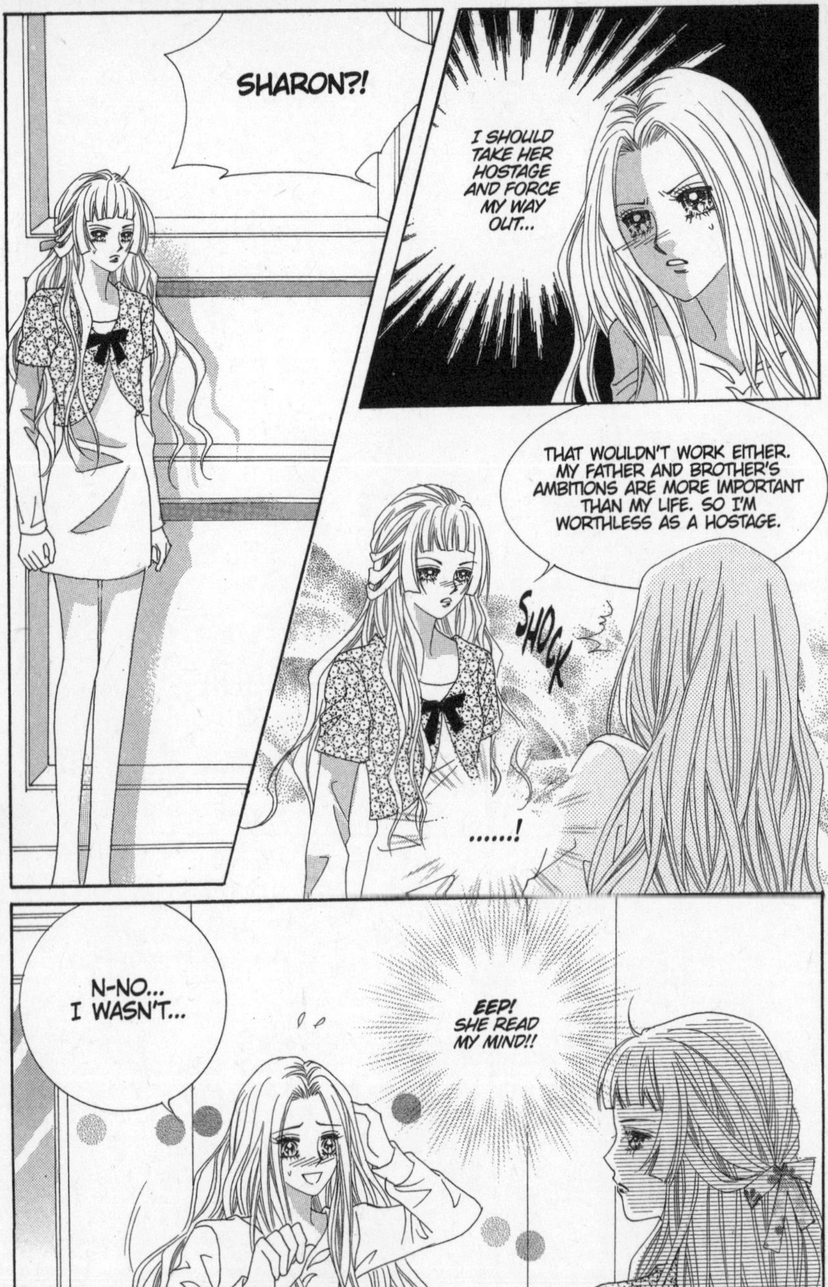
SHARON?!
I SHOULD TAKE HER HOSTAGE AND FORCE MY WAY OUT...
THAT WOULDN'T WORK EITHER. MY FATHER AND BROTHER'S AMBITIONS ARE MORE IMPORTANT THAN MY LIFE. SO I'M WORTHLESS AS A HOSTAGE.
SHOCK
......!
N-NO... I WASN'T...
EEP! SHE READ MY MIND!!

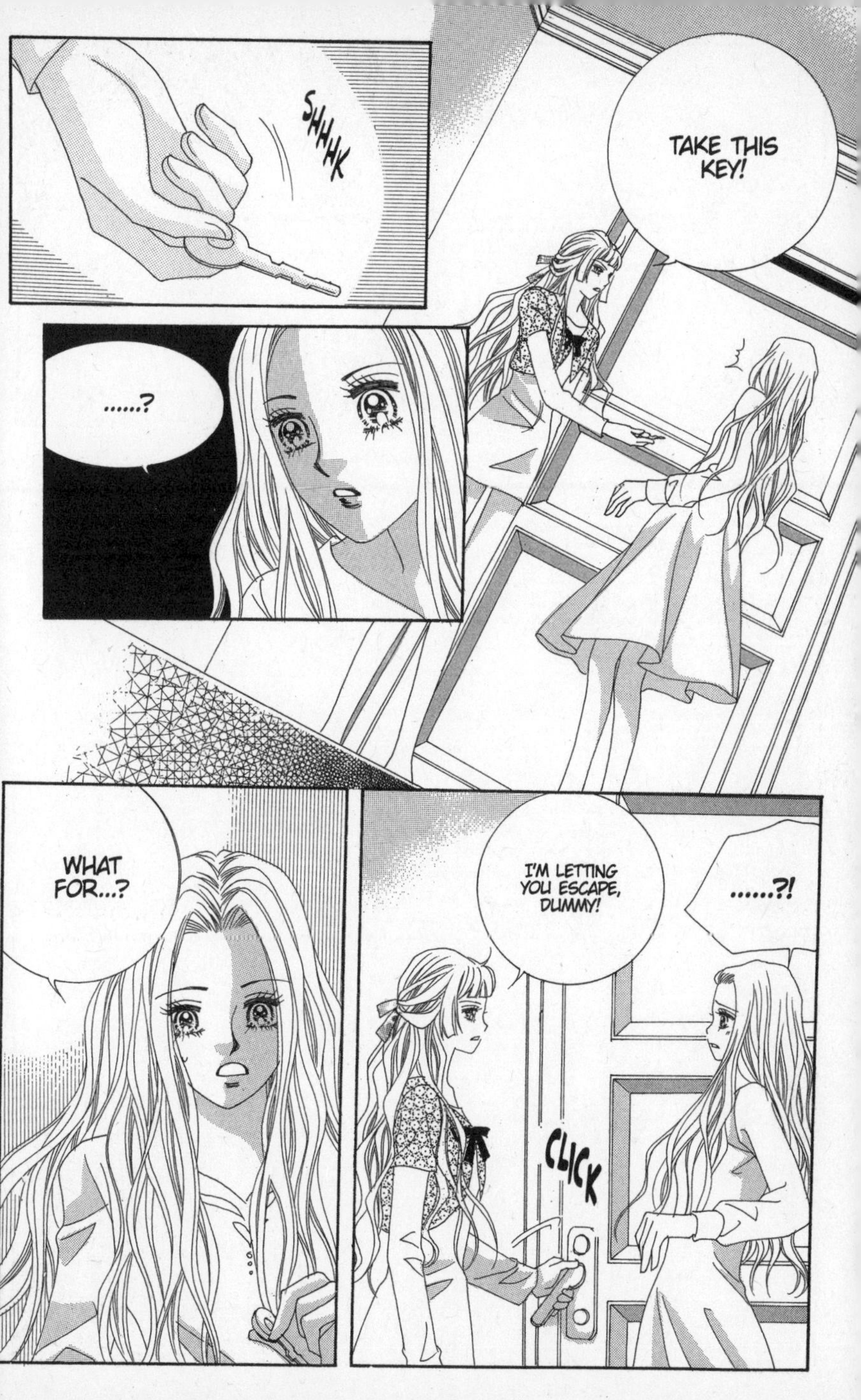
SHHHK
TAKE THIS KEY!
......?
WHAT FOR...?
I'M LETTING YOU ESCAPE, DUMMY!
CLICK
......?!

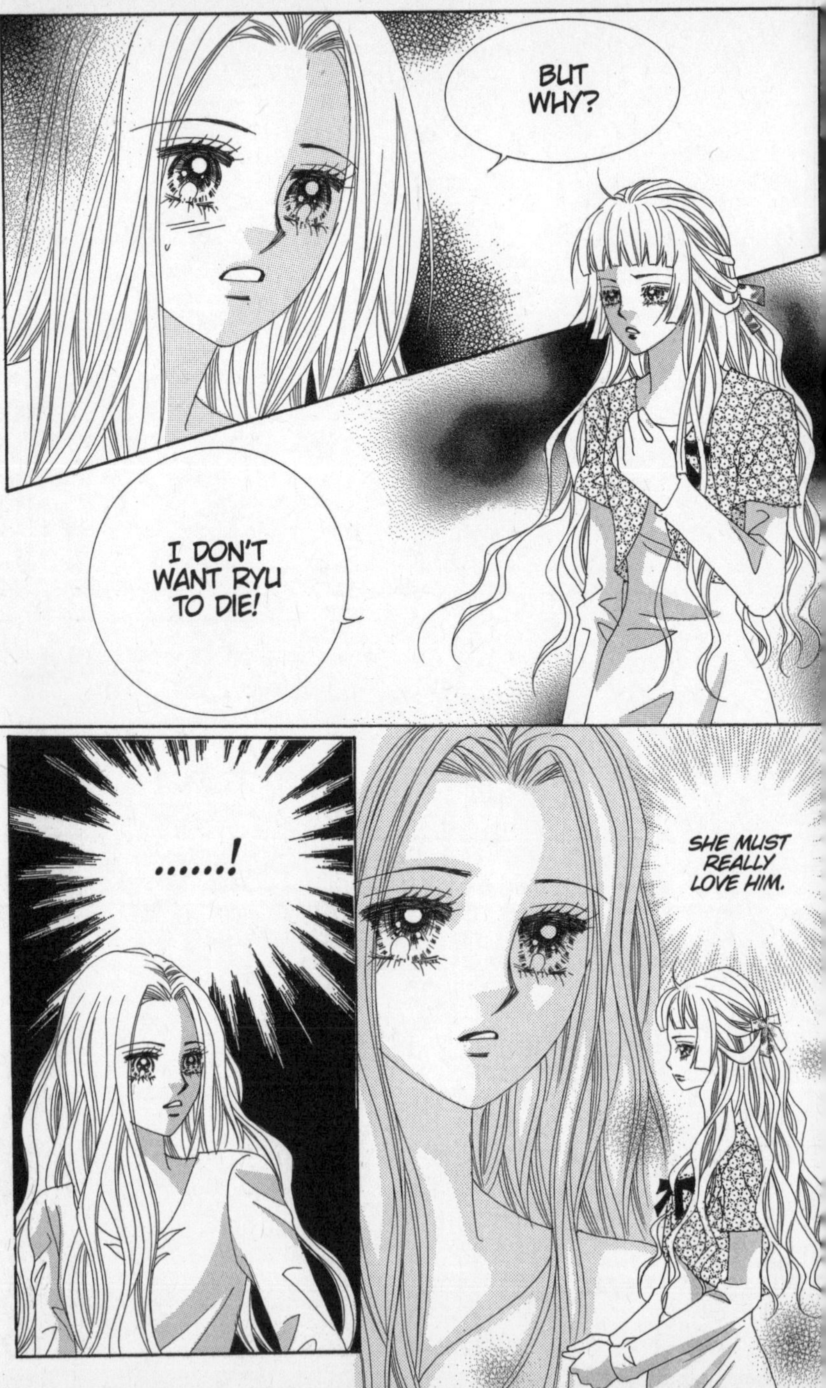
BUT WHY?
I DON'T WANT RYU TO DIE!
......!
SHE MUST REALLY LOVE HIM.

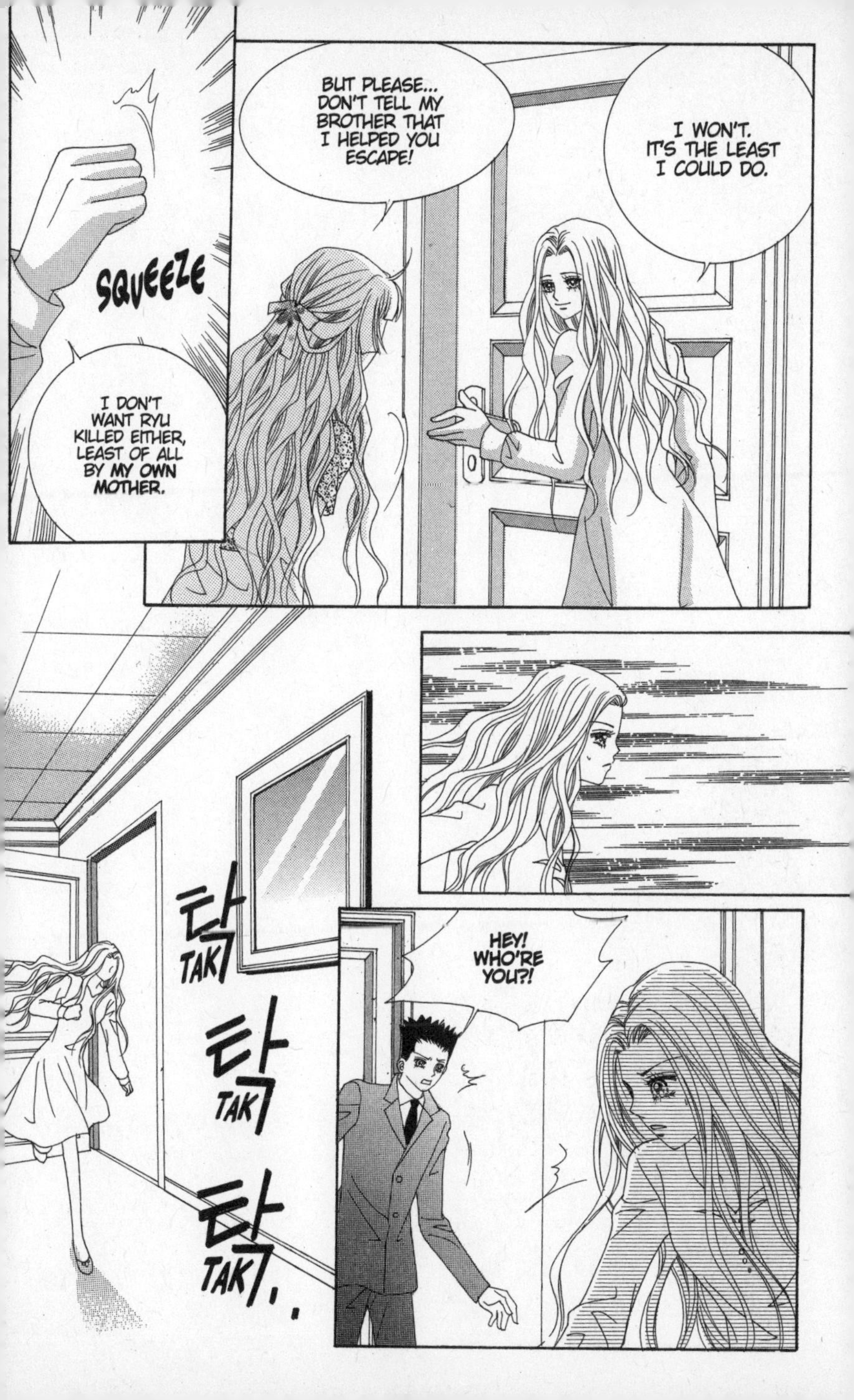
SQUEEZE
I DON'T WANT RYU KILLED EITHER, LEAST OF ALL BY MY OWN MOTHER.
BUT PLEASE... DON'T TELL MY BROTHER THAT I HELPED YOU ESCAPE!
I WON'T. IT'S THE LEAST I COULD DO.
탁
TAK
탁
TAK
탁
TAK..
HEY! WHO'RE YOU?!

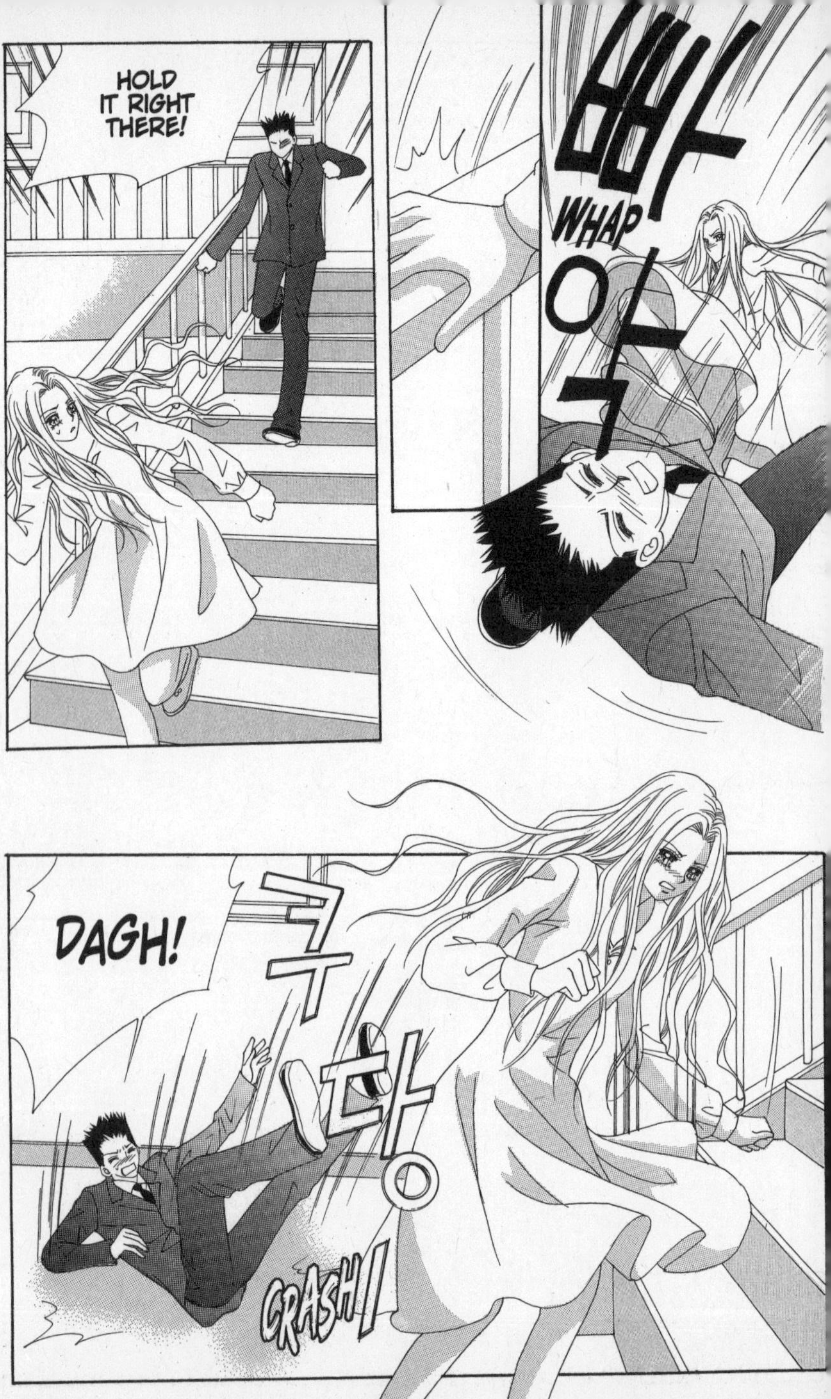
HOLD IT RIGHT THERE!
빠악
WHAP
DAGH!
쿠당
CRASH!

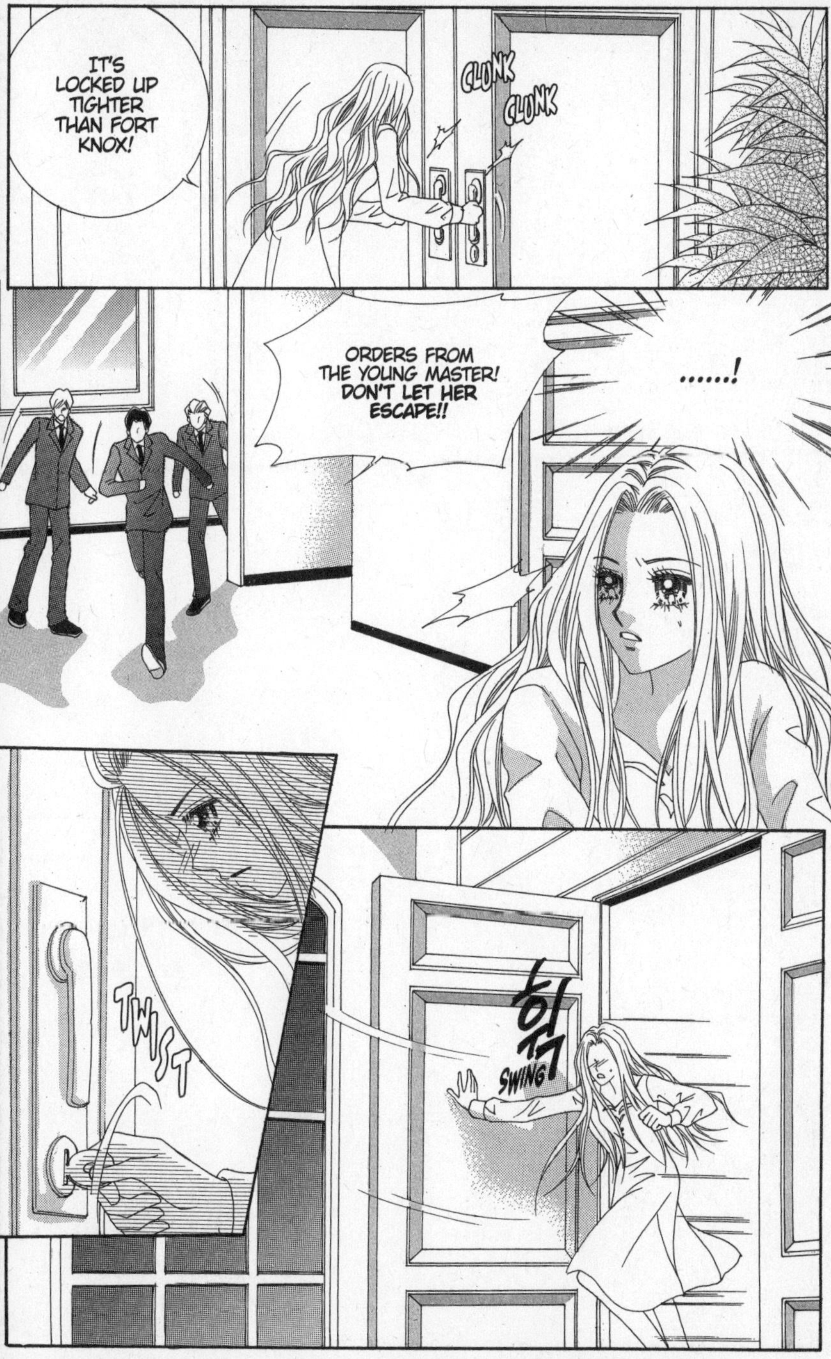

IT'S LOCKED UP TIGHTER THAN FORT KNOX!
CLUNK
CLUNK
ORDERS FROM THE YOUNG MASTER! DON'T LET HER ESCAPE!!
......!
TWIST
휘익
SWING

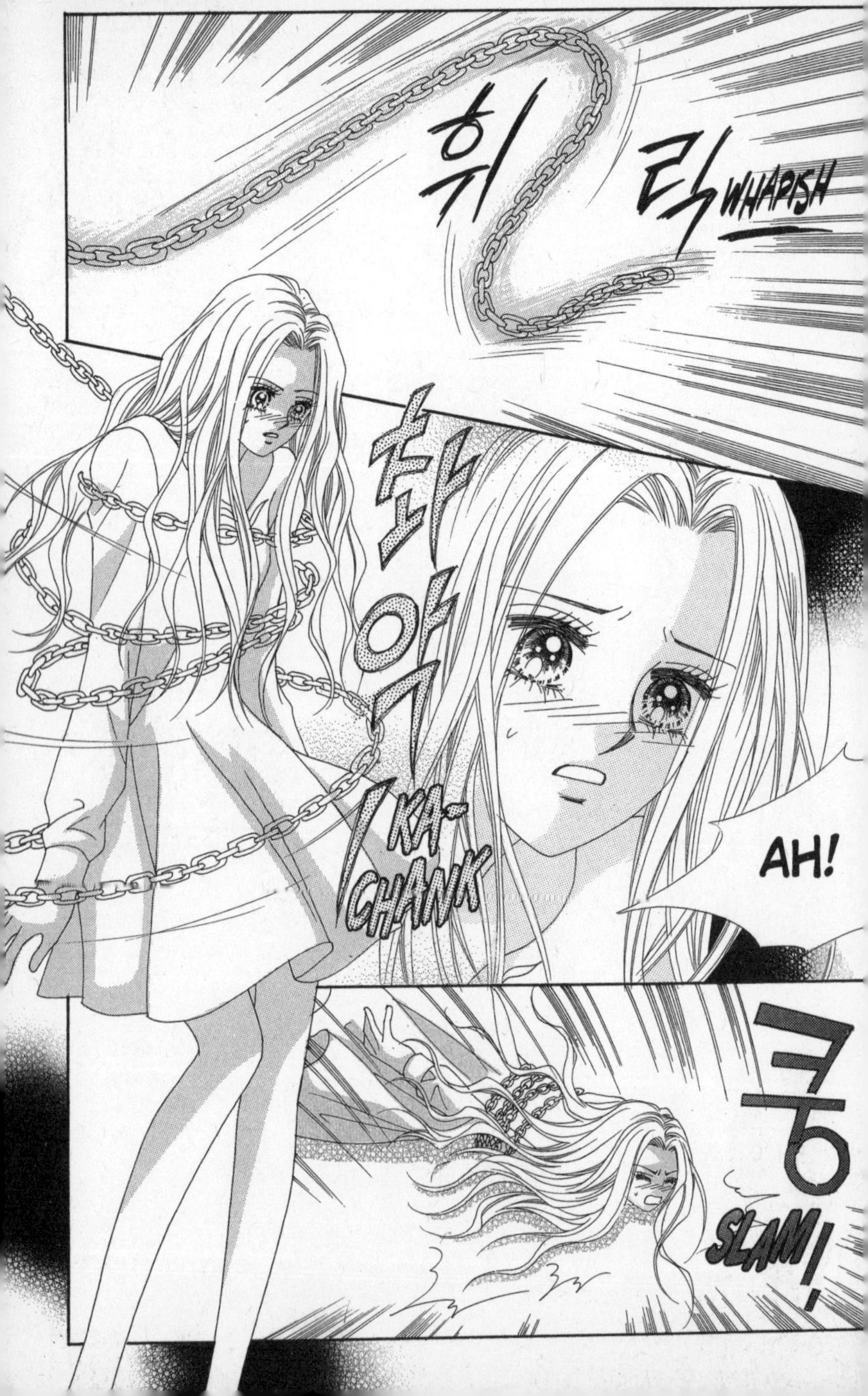
휘릭
WHARISH
촤악
KA-CHANK
AH!
쿵
SLAM!

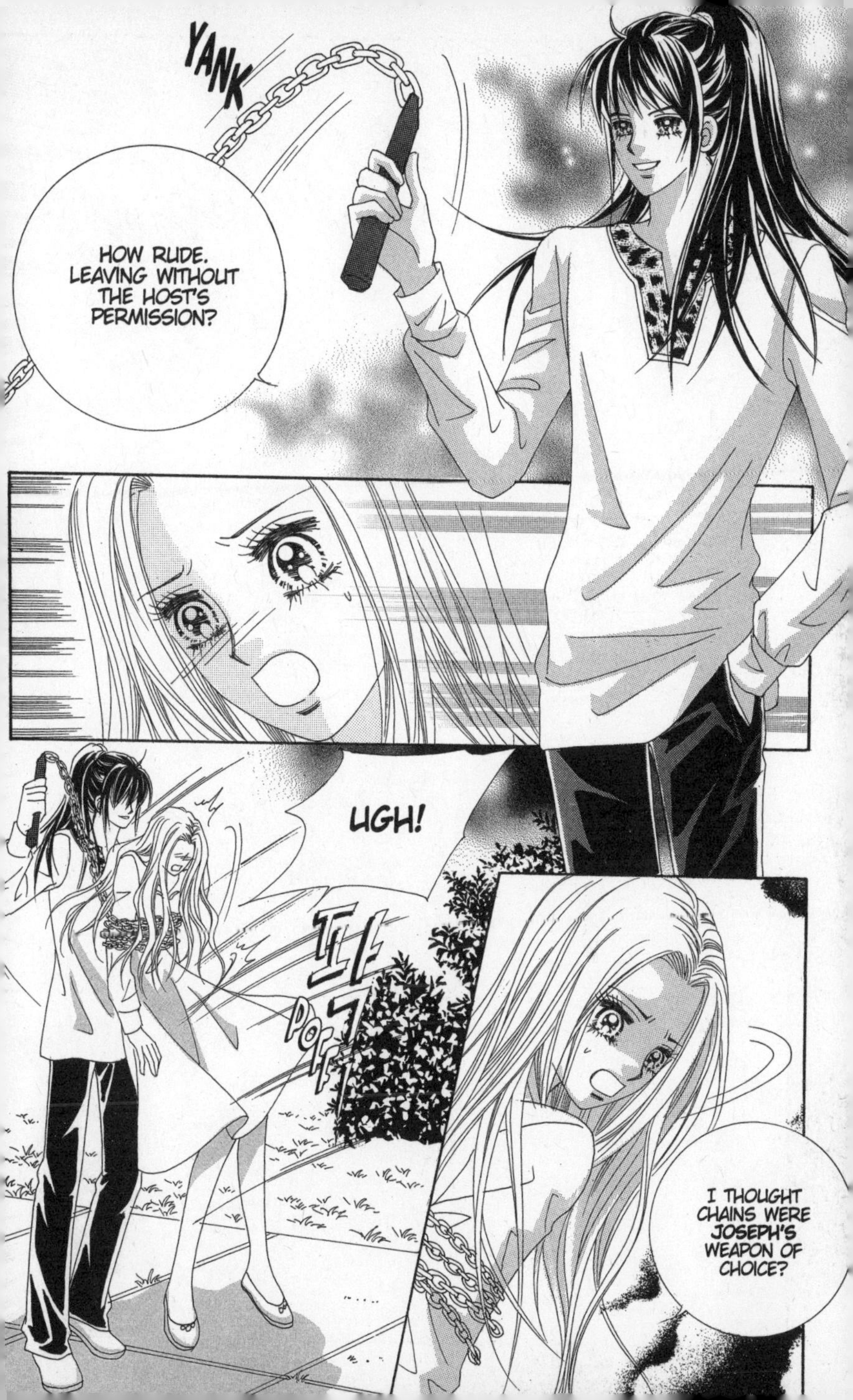
YANK
HOW RUDE. LEAVING WITHOUT THE HOST'S PERMISSION?
UGH!
POFF
......
I THOUGHT CHAINS WERE JOSEPH'S WEAPON OF CHOICE?

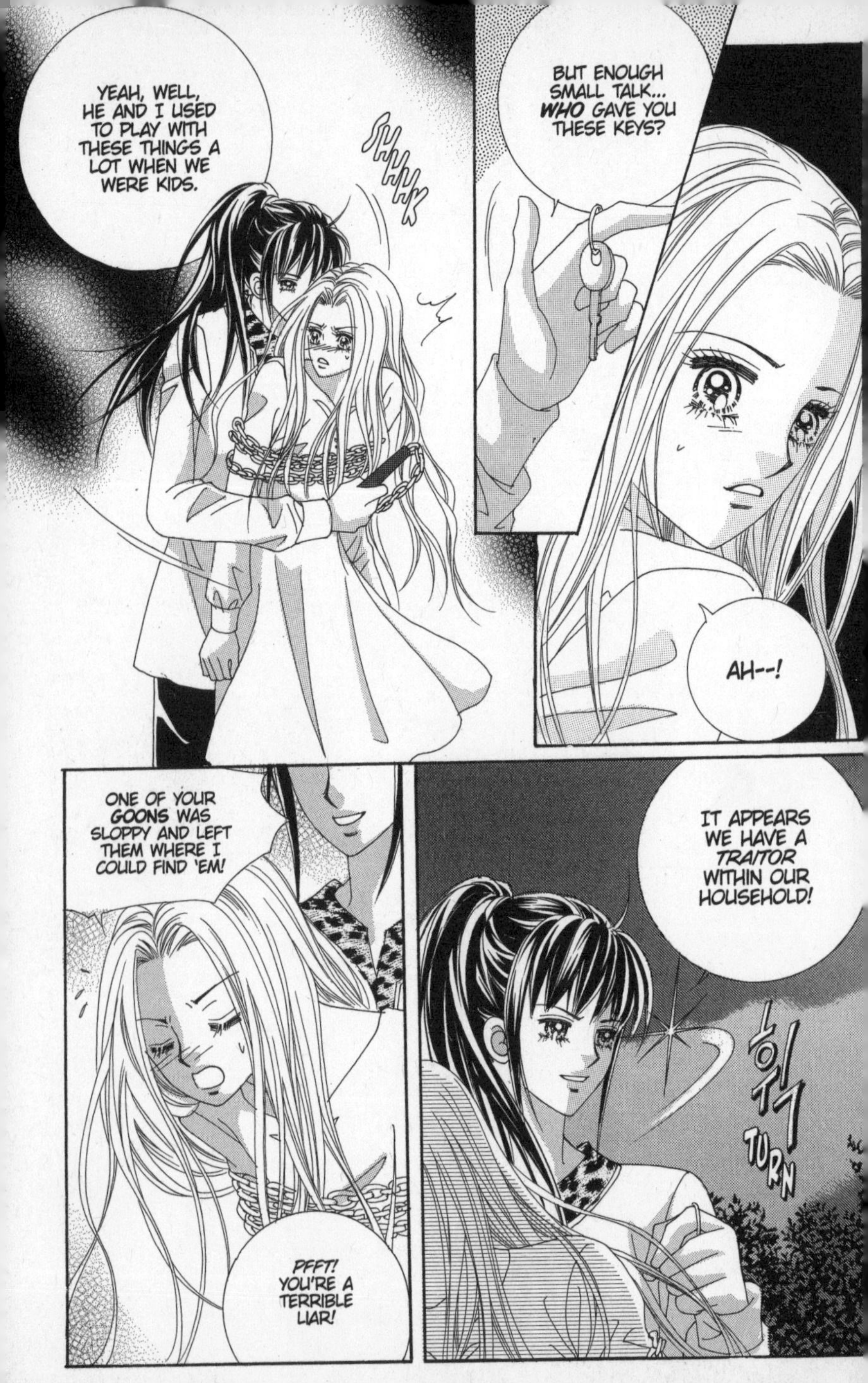
YEAH, WELL, HE AND I USED TO PLAY WITH THESE THINGS A LOT WHEN WE WERE KIDS.
SHHHK
BUT ENOUGH SMALL TALK... *WHO* GAVE YOU THESE KEYS?
AH--!
ONE OF YOUR GOONS WAS SLOPPY AND LEFT THEM WHERE I COULD FIND 'EM!
PFFT! YOU'RE A TERRIBLE LIAR!
IT APPEARS WE HAVE A *TRAITOR* WITHIN OUR HOUSEHOLD!
TURN

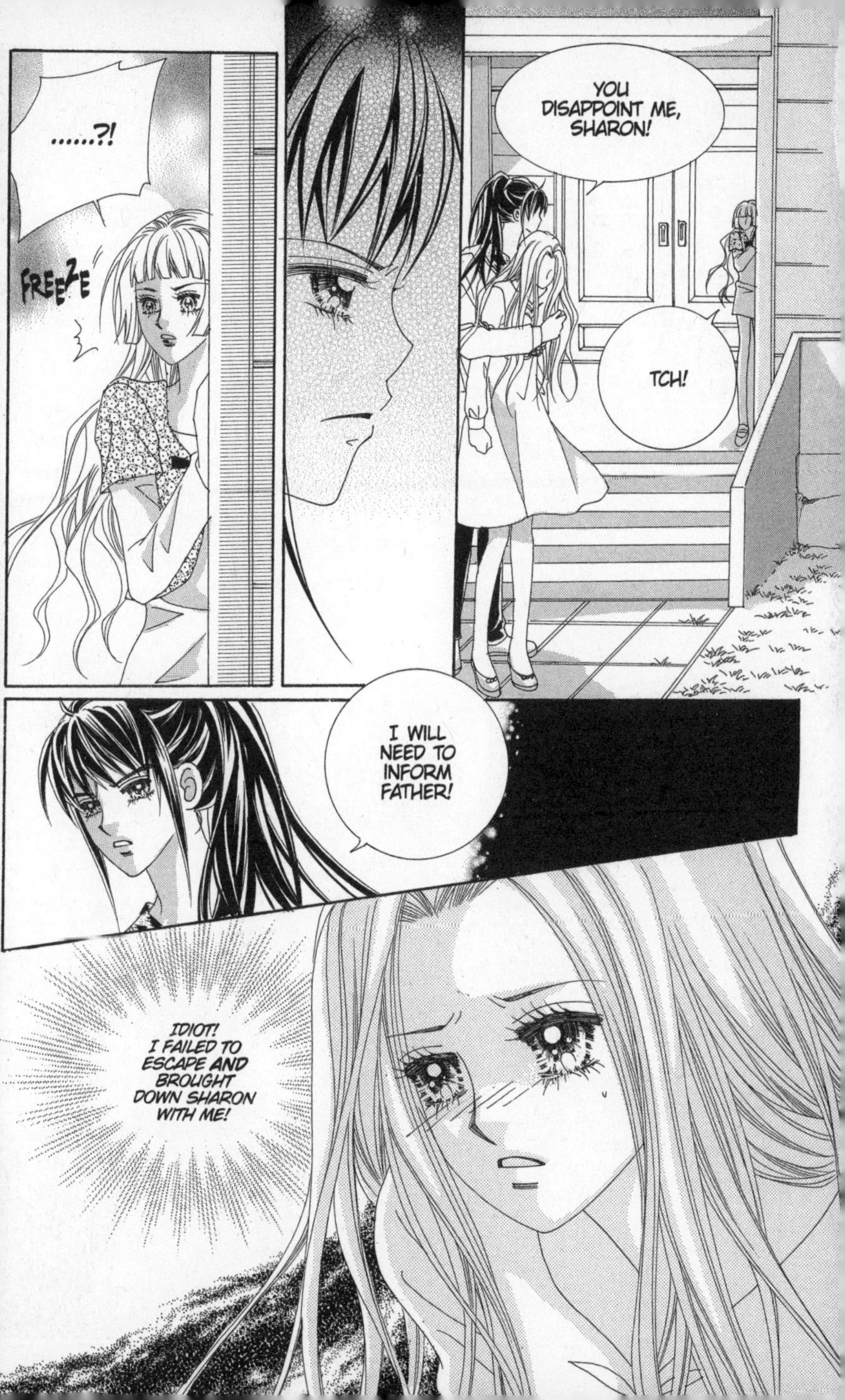
......?!
FREEZE
YOU DISAPPOINT ME, SHARON!
TCH!
I WILL NEED TO INFORM FATHER!
IDIOT! I FAILED TO ESCAPE AND BROUGHT DOWN SHARON WITH ME!

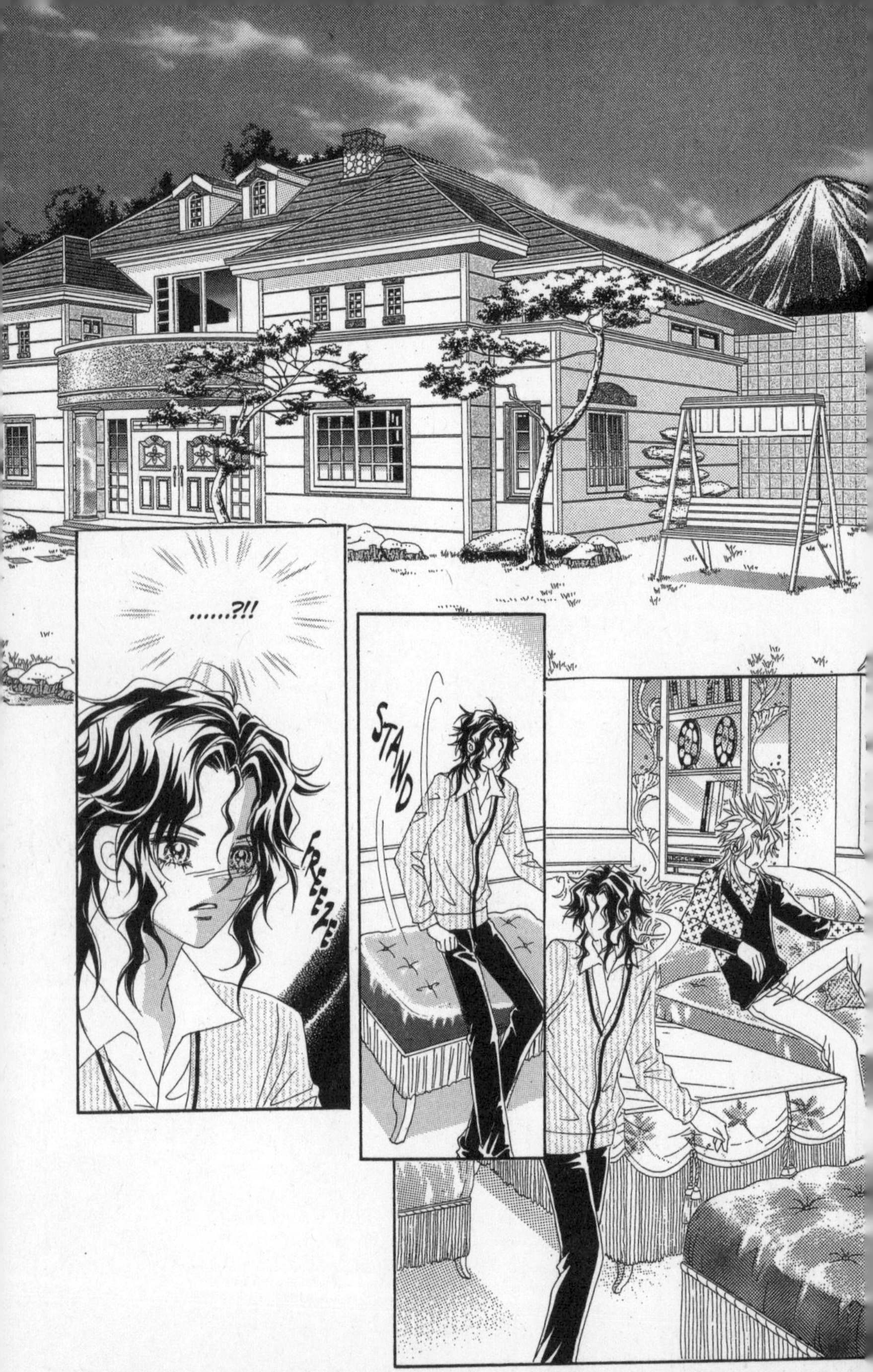
......?!!
FREEZE
STAND

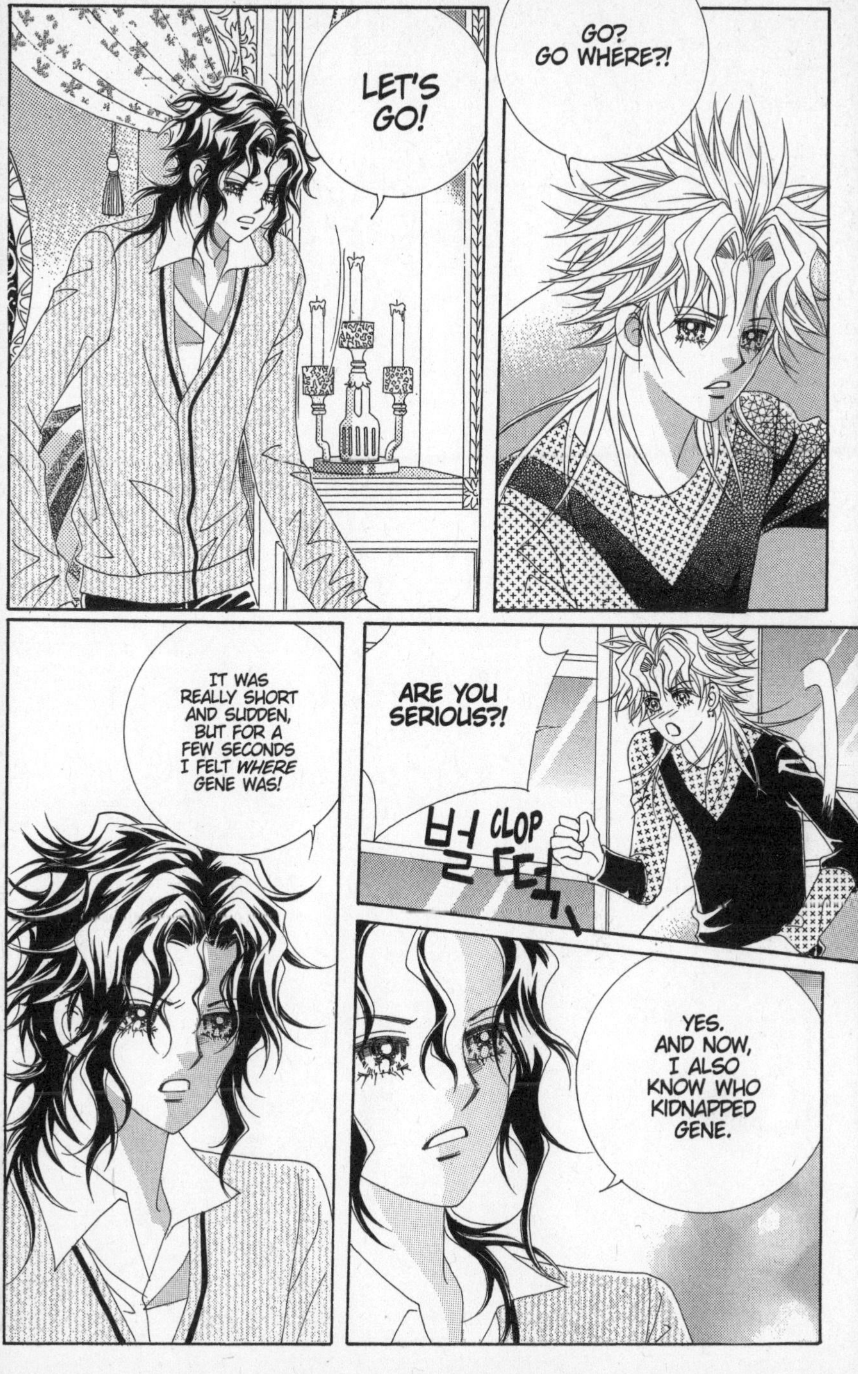
LET'S GO!
GO? GO WHERE?!
IT WAS REALLY SHORT AND SUDDEN, BUT FOR A FEW SECONDS I FELT *WHERE* GENE WAS!
ARE YOU SERIOUS?!
CLOP
YES. AND NOW, I ALSO KNOW WHO KIDNAPPED GENE.

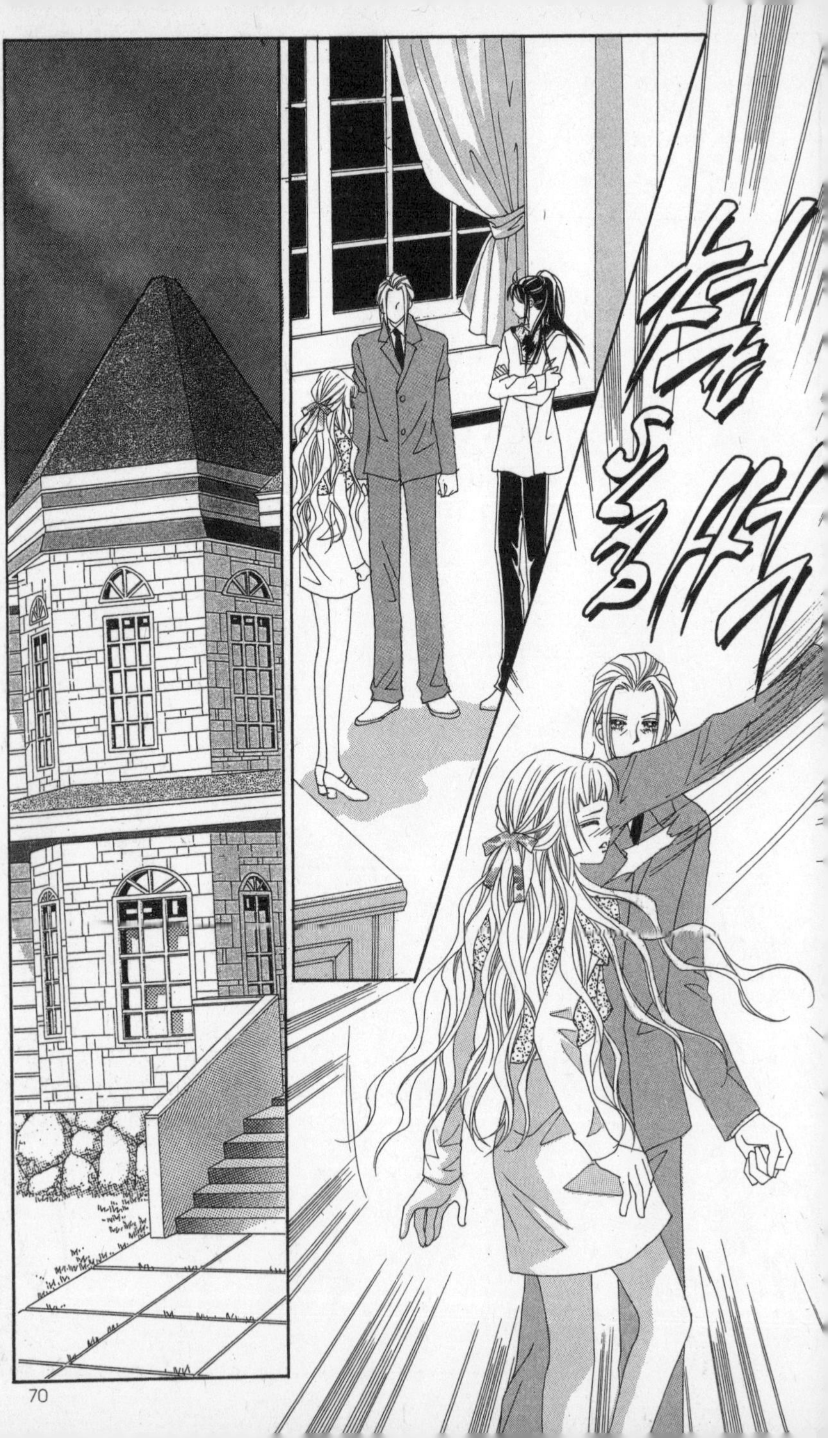

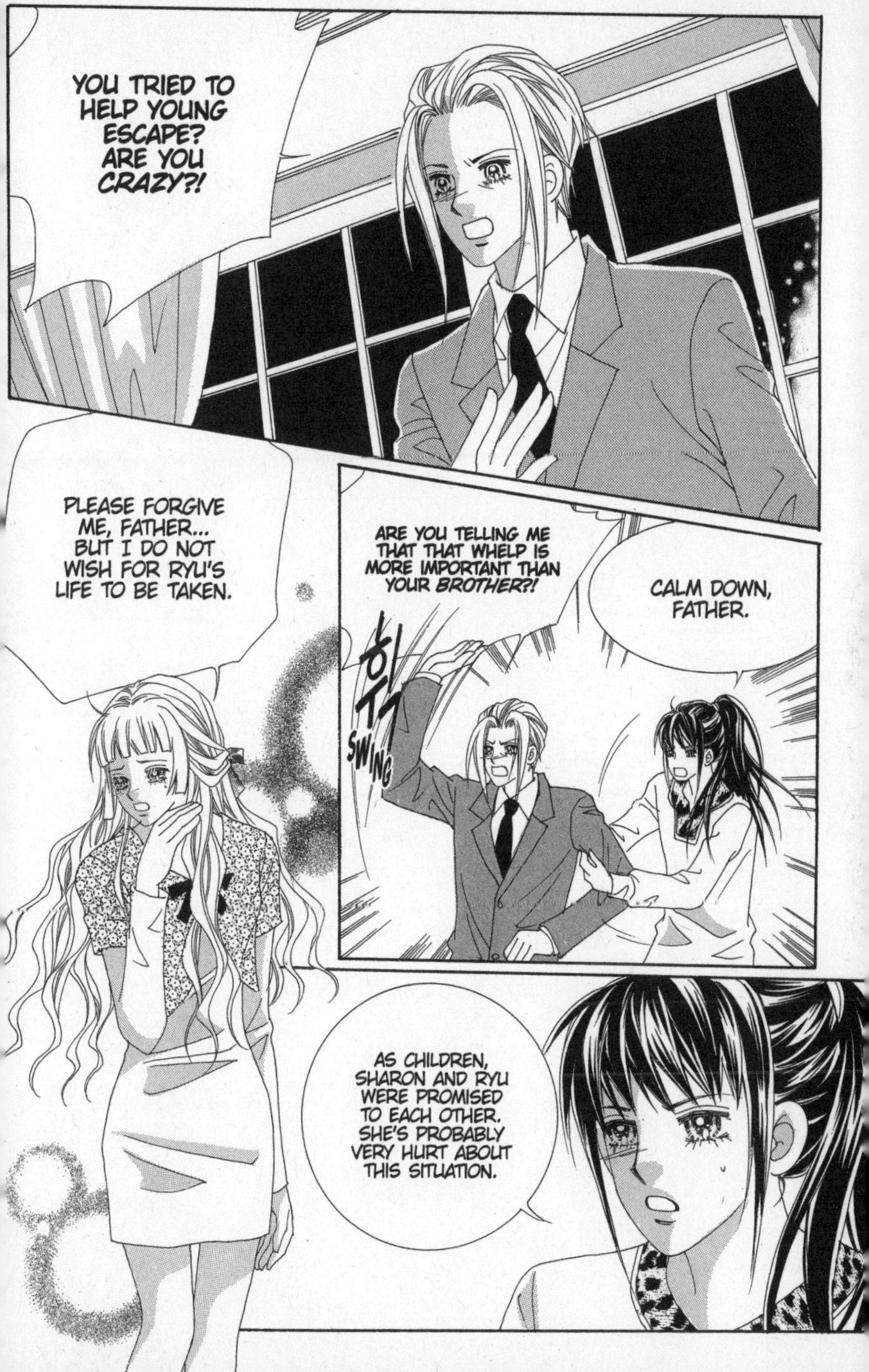
YOU TRIED TO HELP YOUNG ESCAPE? ARE YOU CRAZY?!
PLEASE FORGIVE ME, FATHER... BUT I DO NOT WISH FOR RYU'S LIFE TO BE TAKEN.
ARE YOU TELLING ME THAT THAT WHELP IS MORE IMPORTANT THAN YOUR BROTHER?!
SWING
CALM DOWN, FATHER.
AS CHILDREN, SHARON AND RYU WERE PROMISED TO EACH OTHER. SHE'S PROBABLY VERY HURT ABOUT THIS SITUATION.

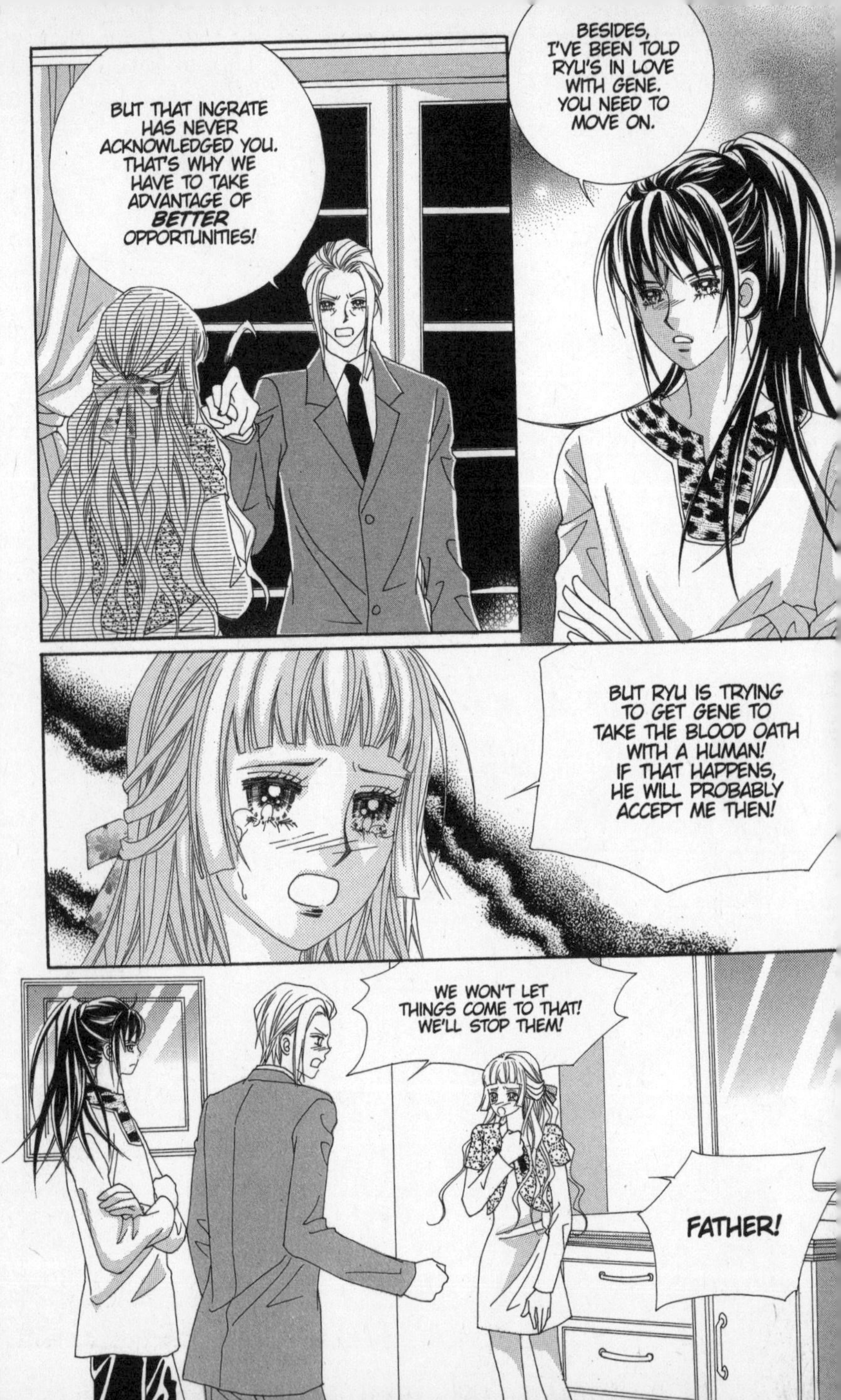
BUT THAT INGRATE HAS NEVER ACKNOWLEDGED YOU. THAT'S WHY WE HAVE TO TAKE ADVANTAGE OF ***BETTER*** OPPORTUNITIES!
BESIDES, I'VE BEEN TOLD RYU'S IN LOVE WITH GENE. YOU NEED TO MOVE ON.
BUT RYU IS TRYING TO GET GENE TO TAKE THE BLOOD OATH WITH A HUMAN! IF THAT HAPPENS, HE WILL PROBABLY ACCEPT ME THEN!
WE WON'T LET THINGS COME TO THAT! WE'LL STOP THEM!
FATHER!

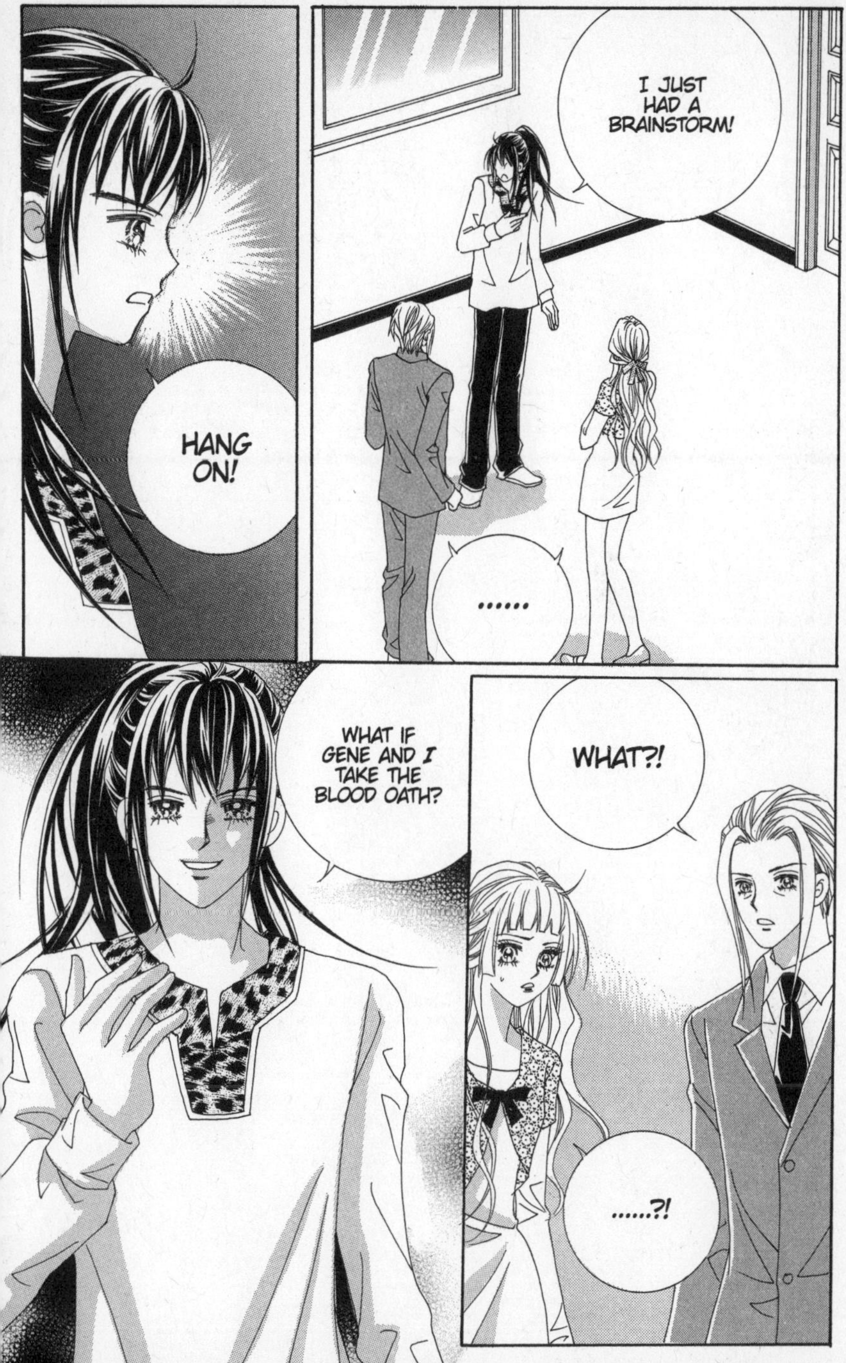
HANG ON!
I JUST HAD A BRAINSTORM!
......
WHAT IF GENE AND I TAKE THE BLOOD OATH?
WHAT?!
......?!

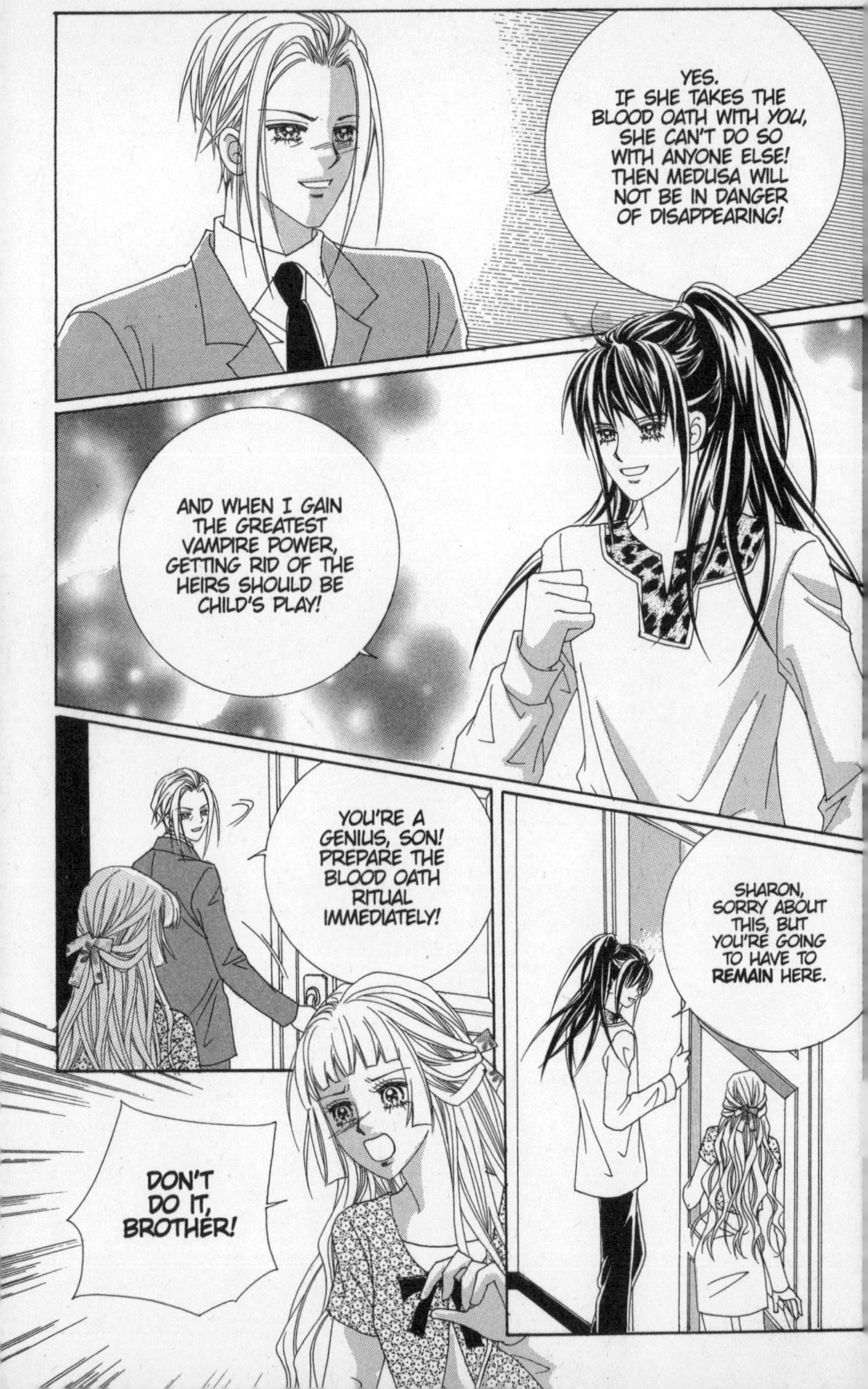
YES. IF SHE TAKES THE BLOOD OATH WITH *YOU*, SHE CAN'T DO SO WITH ANYONE ELSE! THEN MEDUSA WILL NOT BE IN DANGER OF DISAPPEARING!
AND WHEN I GAIN THE GREATEST VAMPIRE POWER, GETTING RID OF THE HEIRS SHOULD BE CHILD'S PLAY!
YOU'RE A GENIUS, SON! PREPARE THE BLOOD OATH RITUAL IMMEDIATELY!
DON'T DO IT, BROTHER!
SHARON, SORRY ABOUT THIS, BUT YOU'RE GOING TO HAVE TO REMAIN HERE.

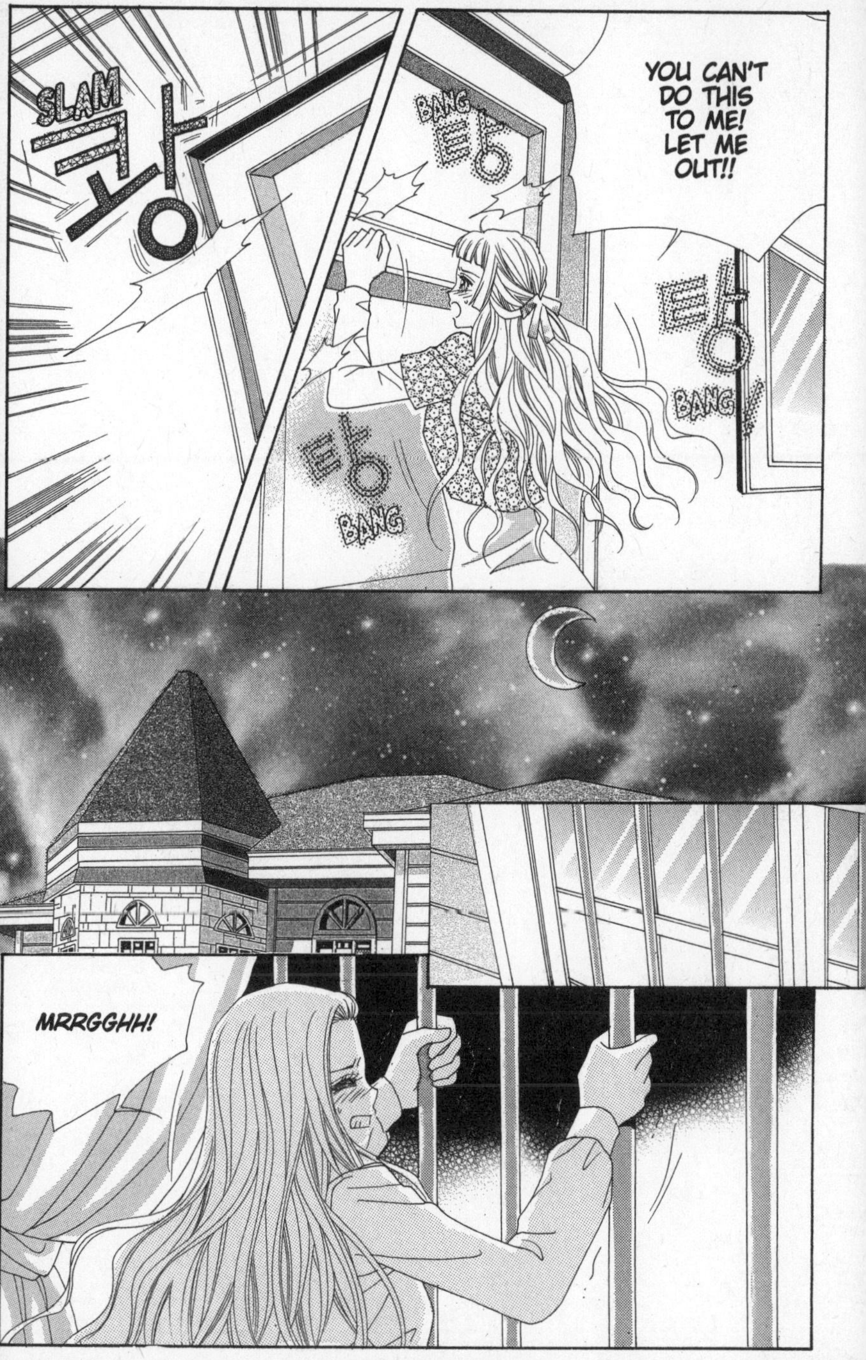
SLAM
쾅
BANG
탕
YOU CAN'T DO THIS TO ME! LET ME OUT!!
탕
BANG
탕
BANG
MRRGGHH!

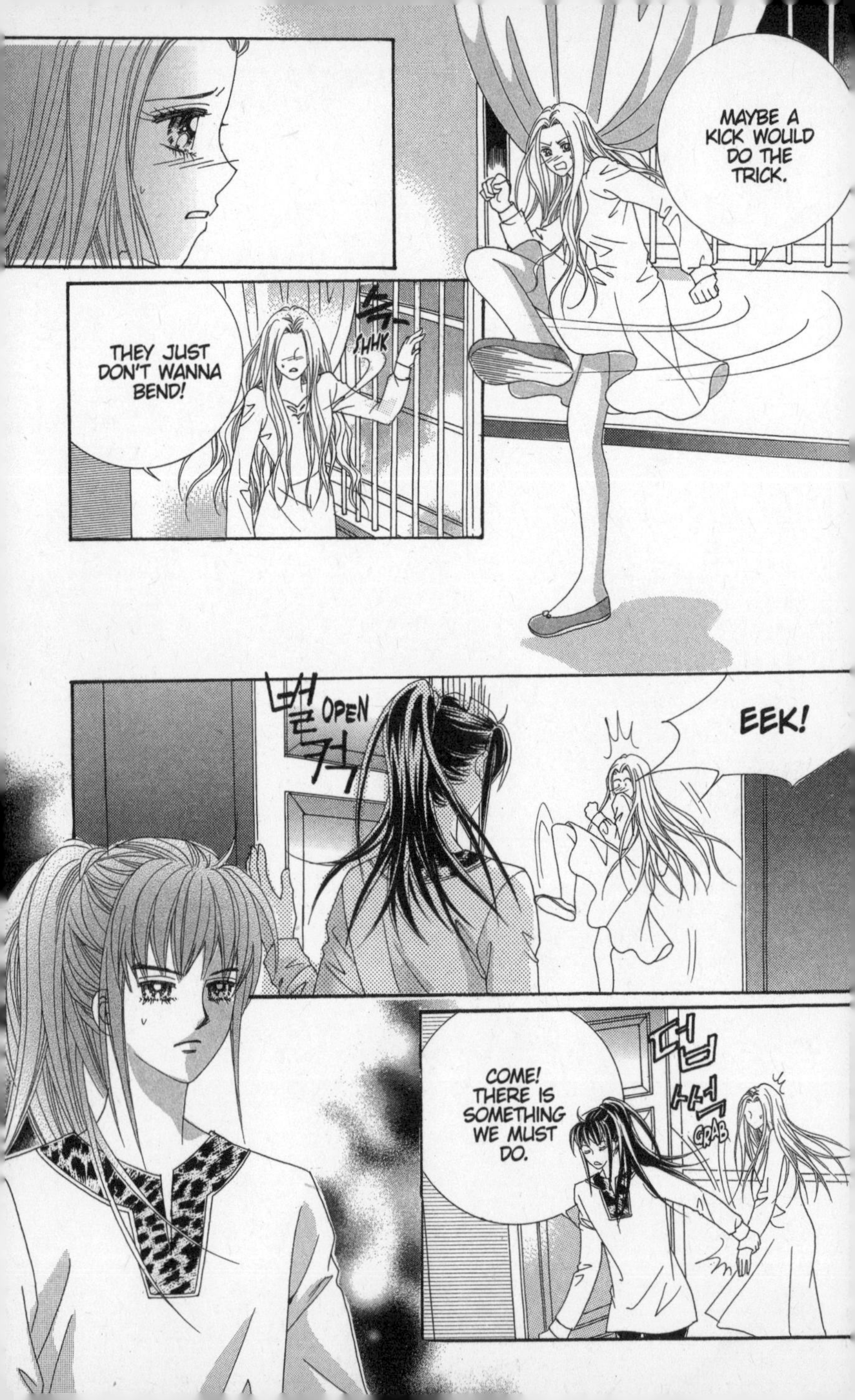
SHHK
THEY JUST DON'T WANNA BEND!
MAYBE A KICK WOULD DO THE TRICK.
OPEN
EEK!
COME! THERE IS SOMETHING WE MUST DO.
GRAB

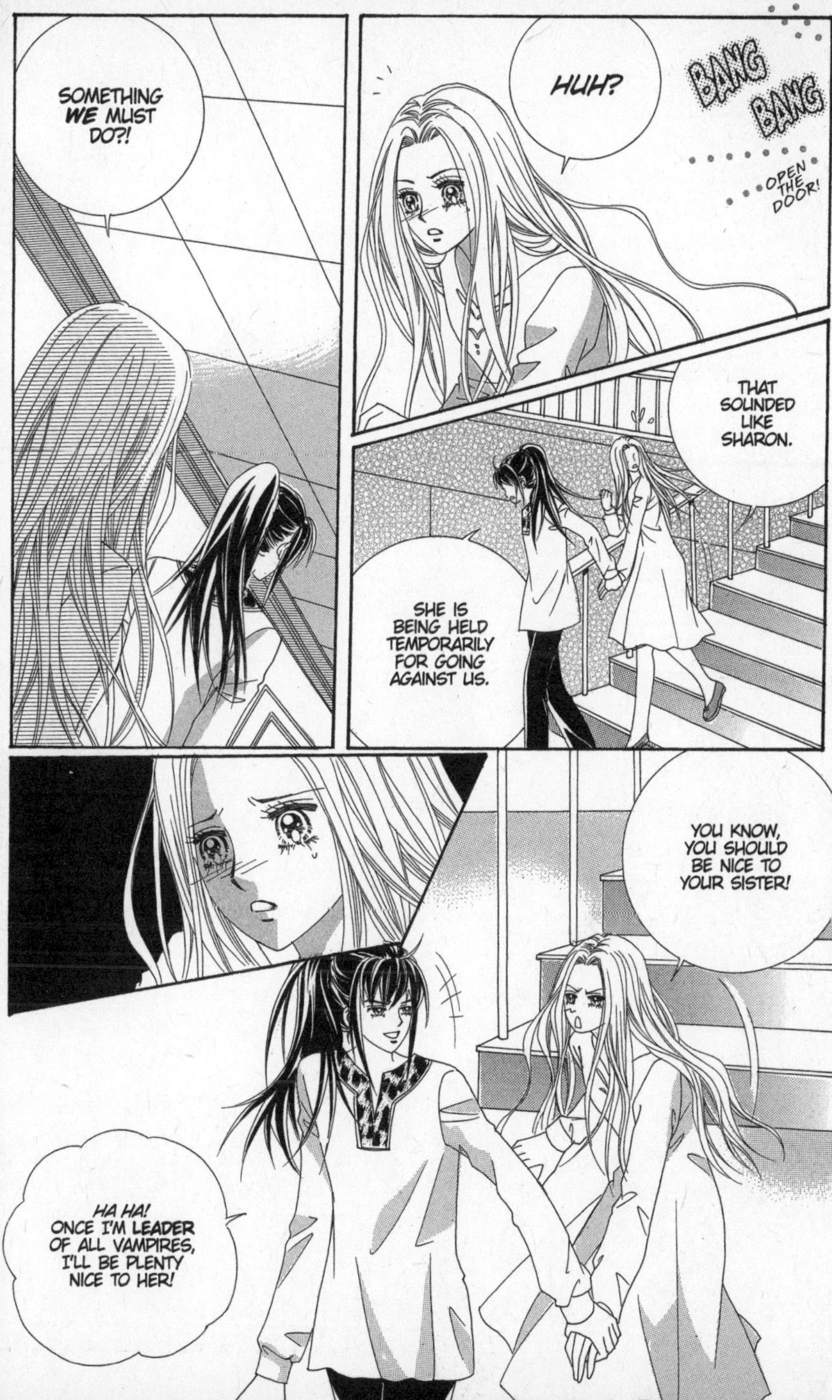
SOMETHING WE MUST DO?!
HUH?
BANG BANG
OPEN THE DOOR!
THAT SOUNDED LIKE SHARON.
SHE IS BEING HELD TEMPORARILY FOR GOING AGAINST US.
YOU KNOW, YOU SHOULD BE NICE TO YOUR SISTER!
HA HA! ONCE I'M LEADER OF ALL VAMPIRES, I'LL BE PLENTY NICE TO HER!

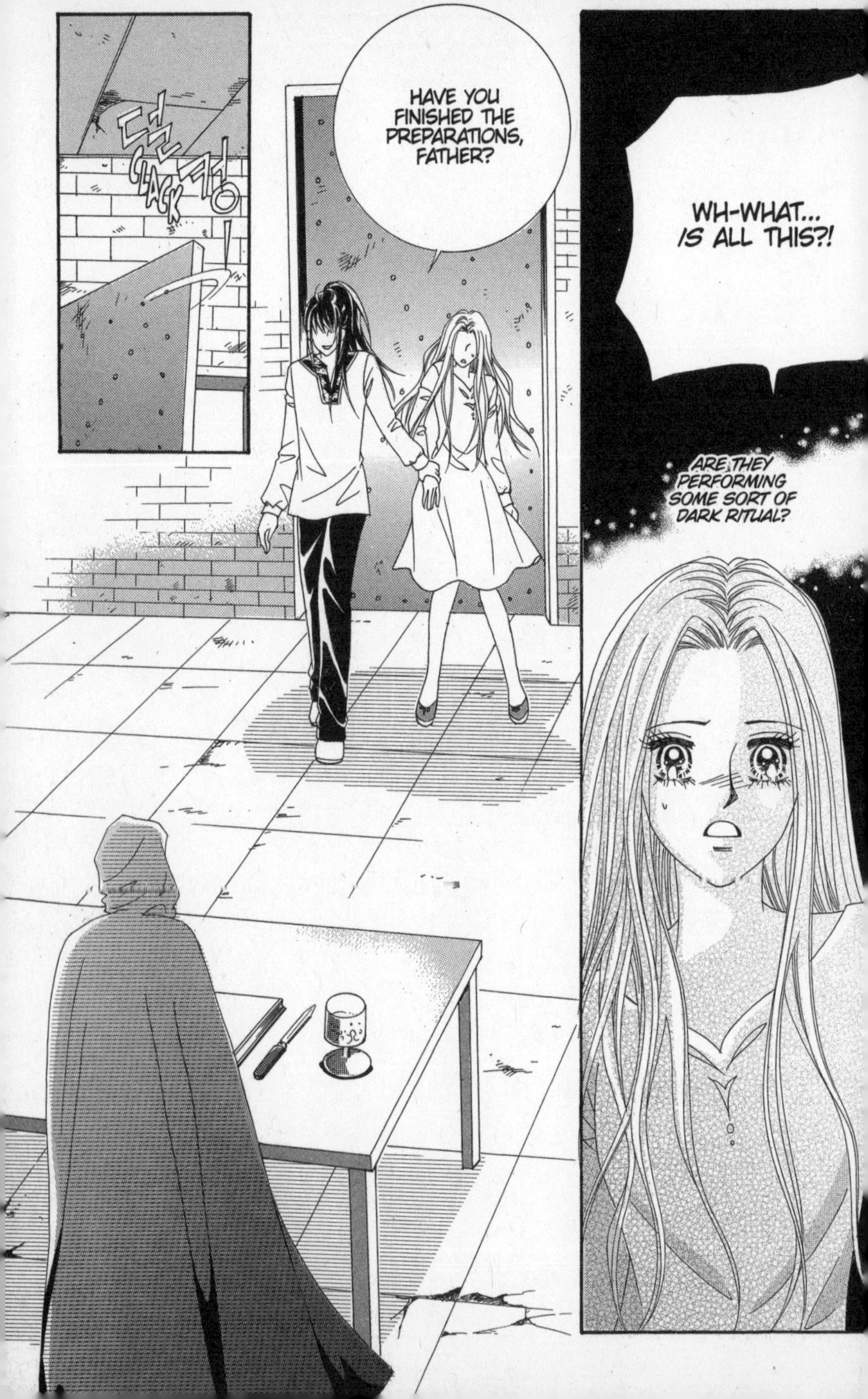
CLACK
HAVE YOU FINISHED THE PREPARATIONS, FATHER?
WH-WHAT... IS ALL THIS?!
ARE THEY PERFORMING SOME SORT OF DARK RITUAL?

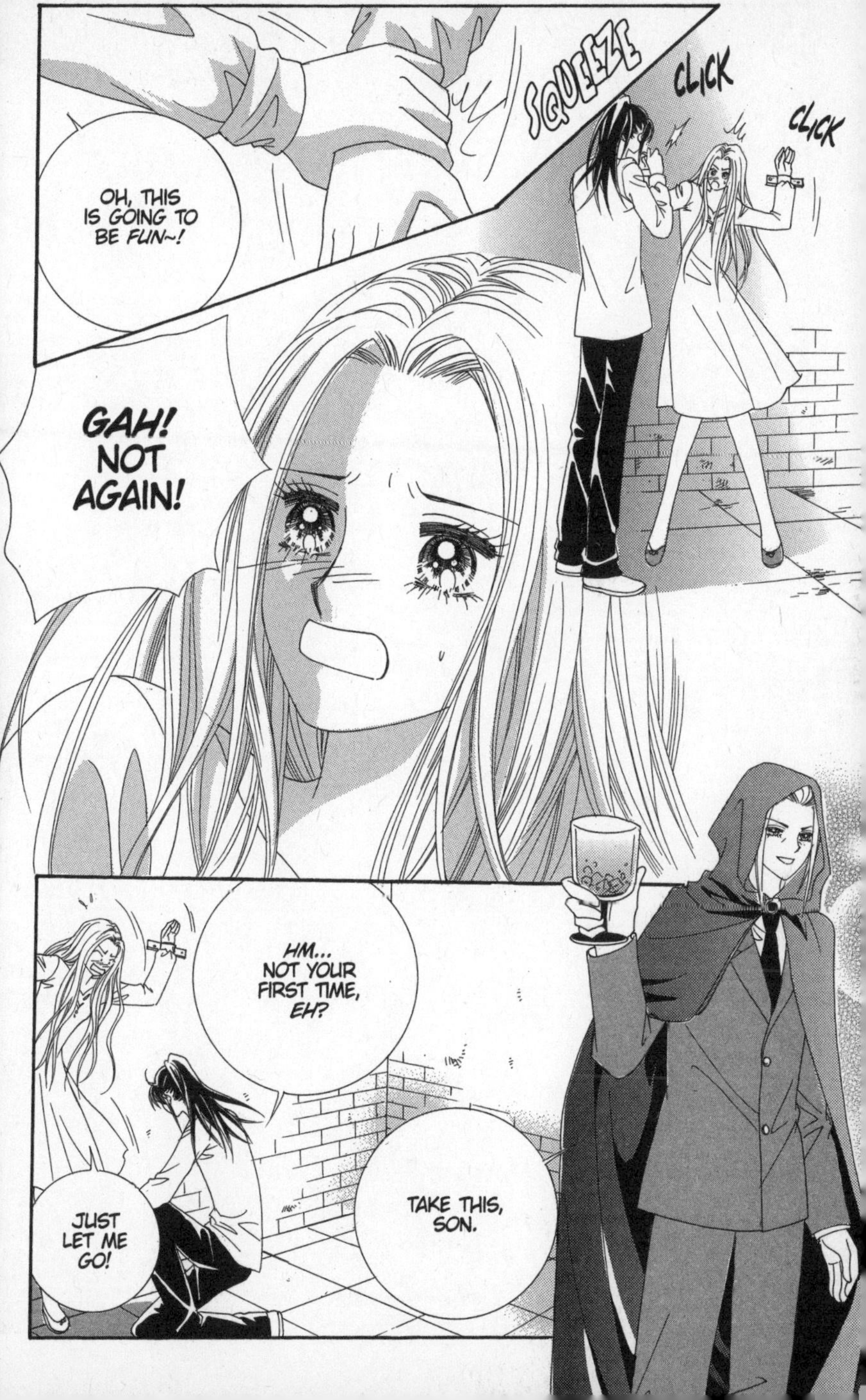
OH, THIS IS GOING TO BE FUN~!
SQUEEZE
CLICK
CLICK
GAH! NOT AGAIN!
HM... NOT YOUR FIRST TIME, EH?
JUST LET ME GO!
TAKE THIS, SON.

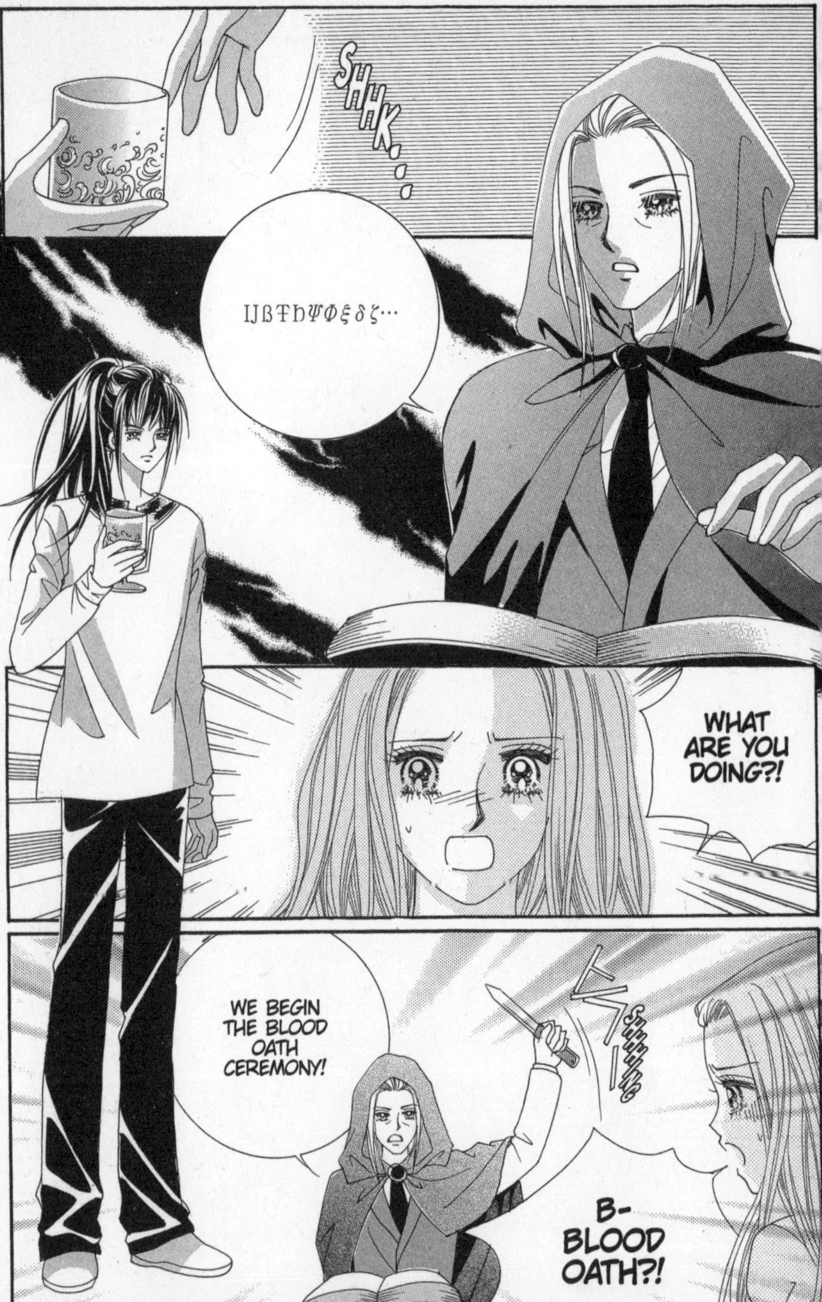
SHHK
ĲßŦҺΨΦξδζ…
WHAT ARE YOU DOING?!
WE BEGIN THE BLOOD OATH CEREMONY!
B-BLOOD OATH?!

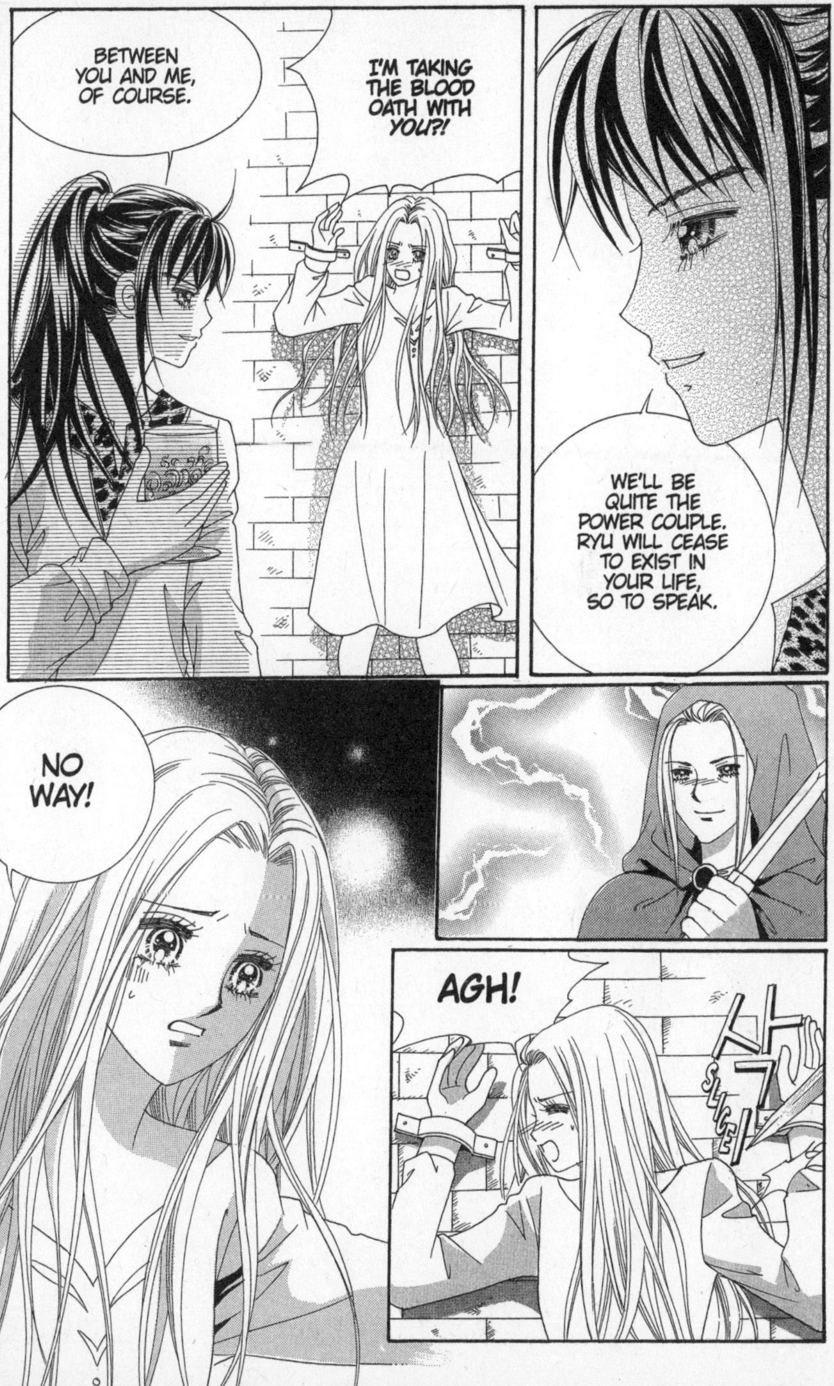

BETWEEN YOU AND ME, OF COURSE.
I'M TAKING THE BLOOD OATH WITH *YOU?!*
WE'LL BE QUITE THE POWER COUPLE. RYU WILL CEASE TO EXIST IN YOUR LIFE, SO TO SPEAK.
NO WAY!
AGH!
SLICE!

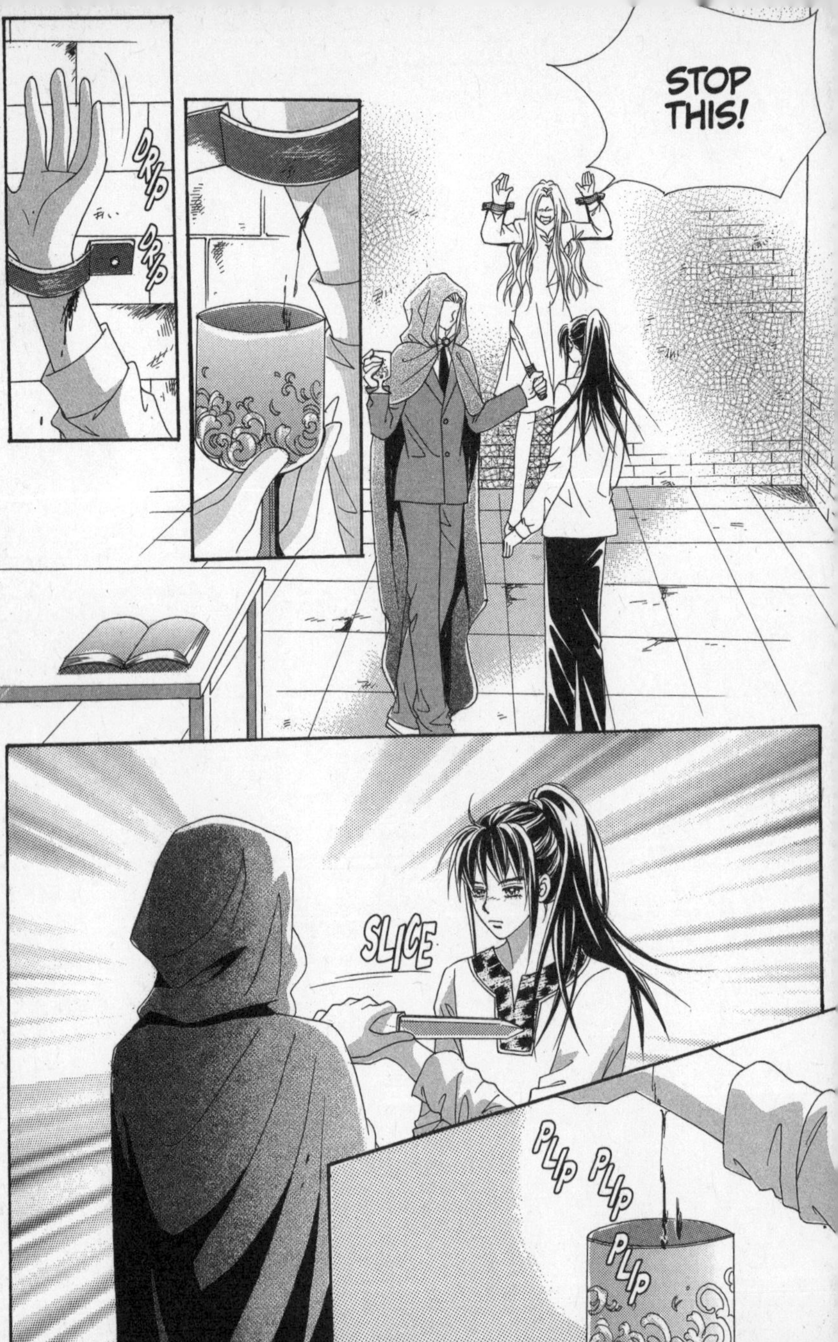
DRIP
DRIP
STOP THIS!
SLICE
PLIP PLIP
PLIP

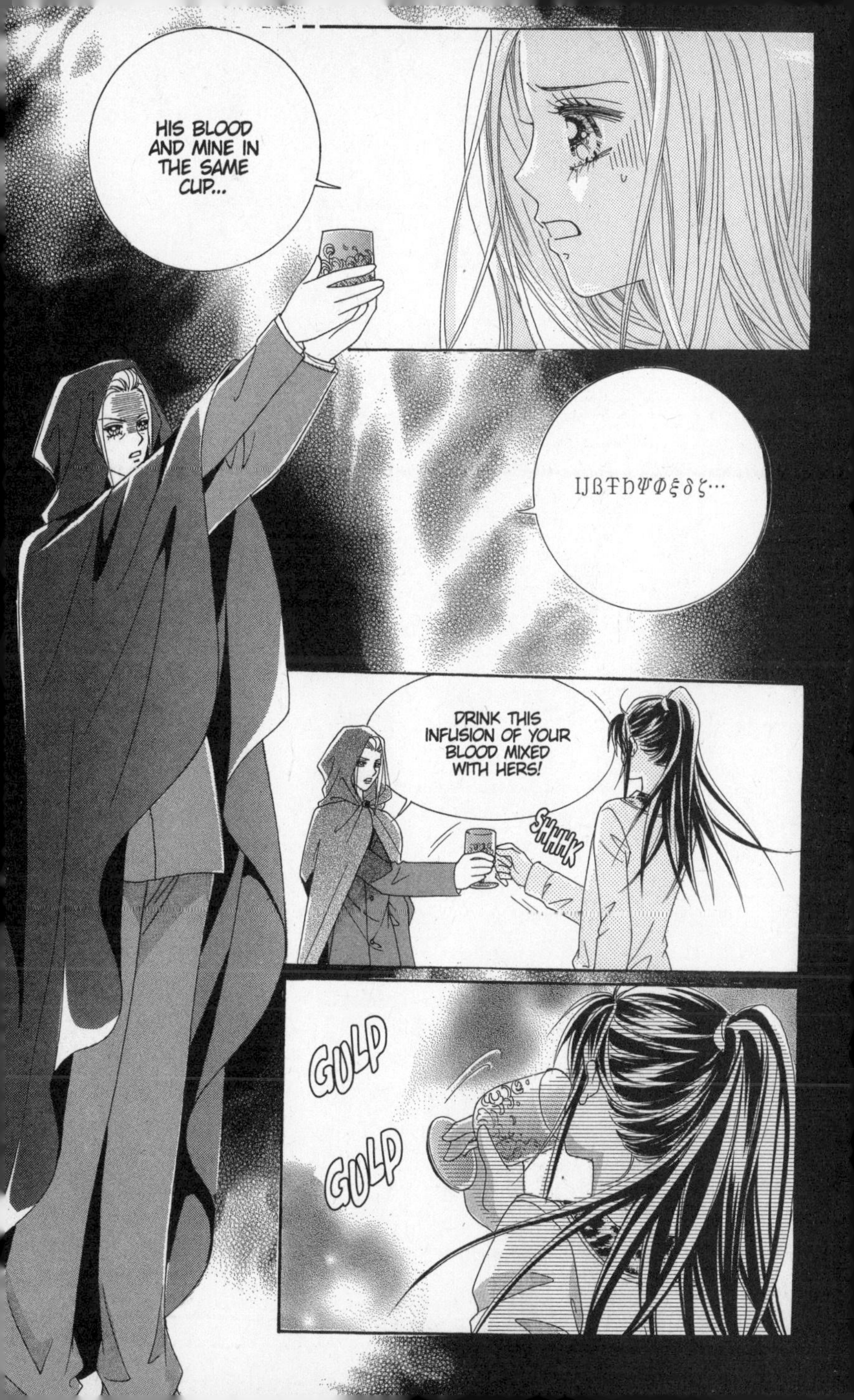
HIS BLOOD AND MINE IN THE SAME CUP...
IJßŦħΨΦξδζ…
DRINK THIS INFUSION OF YOUR BLOOD MIXED WITH HERS!
SHHHK
GULP
GULP

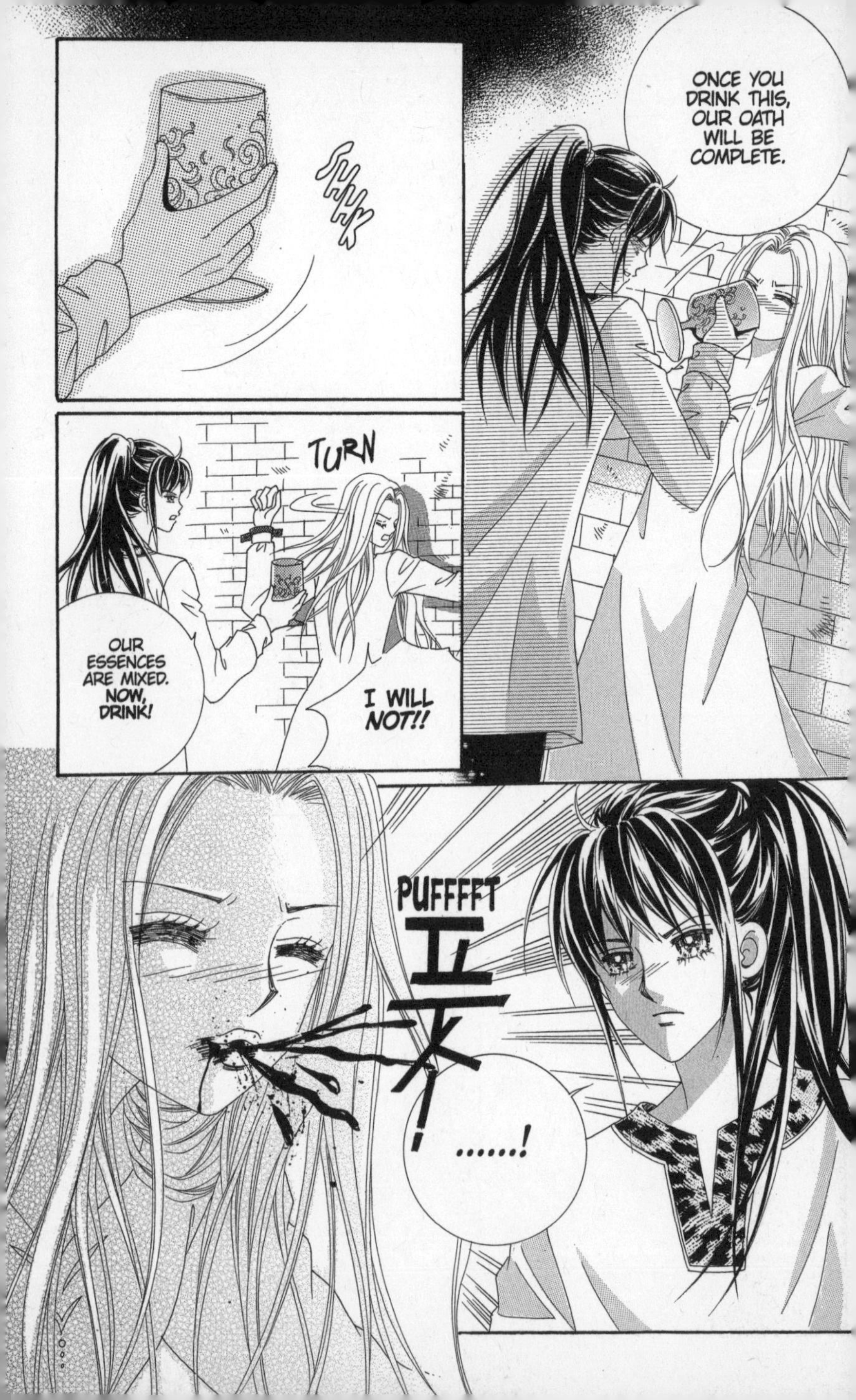
SHHK
TURN
OUR ESSENCES ARE MIXED. NOW, DRINK!
I WILL NOT!!
ONCE YOU DRINK THIS, OUR OATH WILL BE COMPLETE.
PUFFFFT
......!

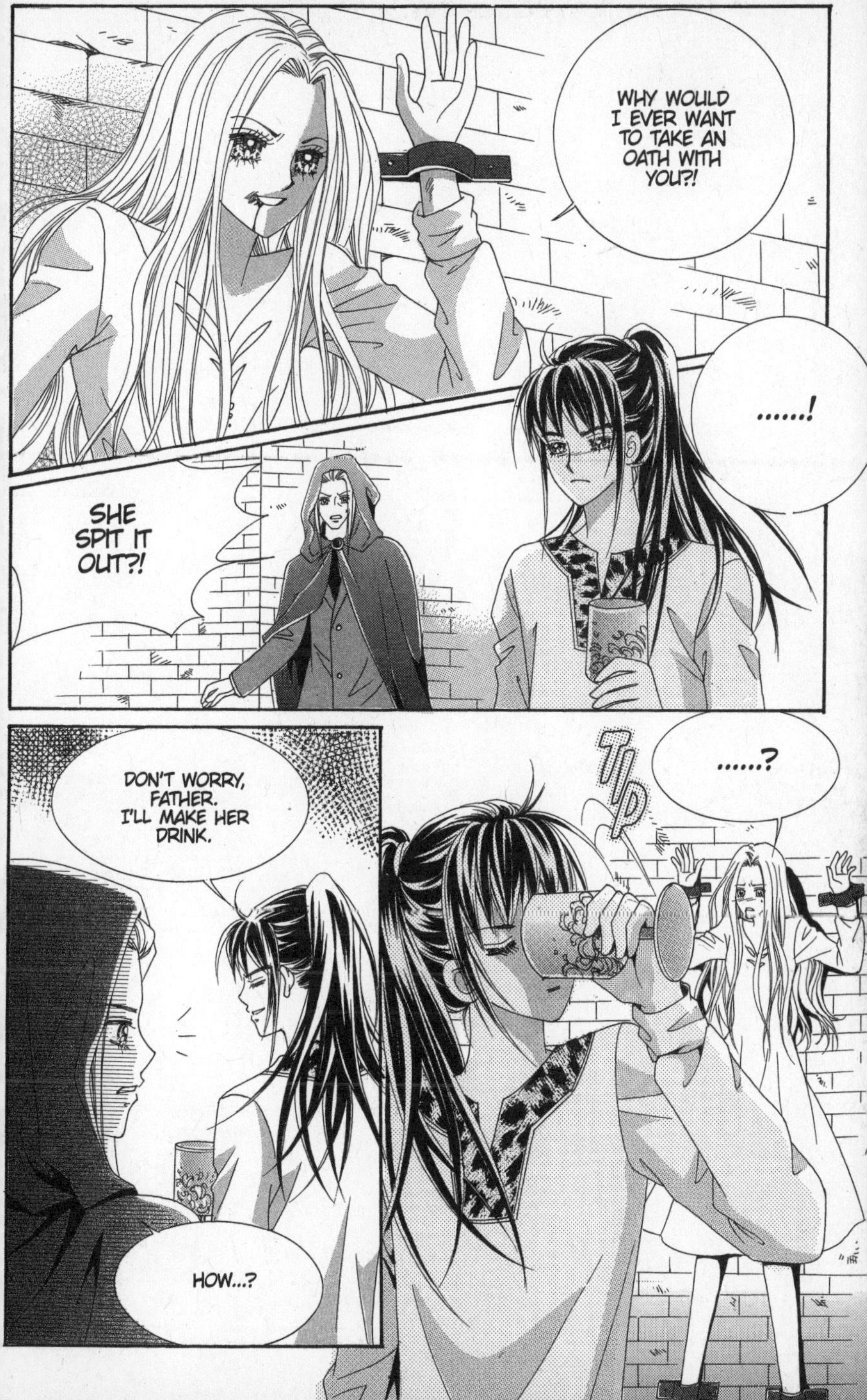

WHY WOULD I EVER WANT TO TAKE AN OATH WITH YOU?!
......!
SHE SPIT IT OUT?!
DON'T WORRY, FATHER. I'LL MAKE HER DRINK.
HOW...?
TIP
......?

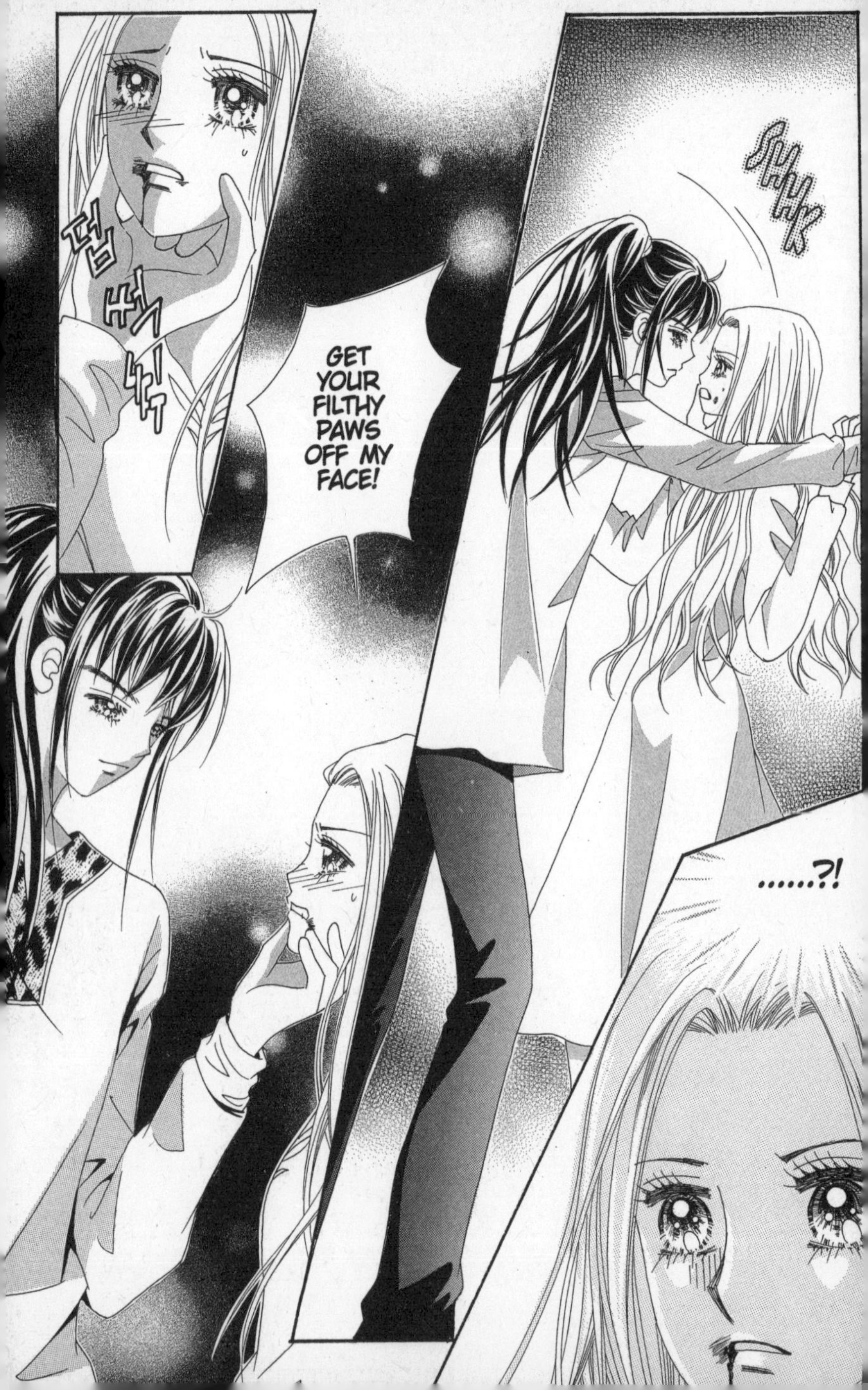
GET YOUR FILTHY PAWS OFF MY FACE!
SHHK
......?!

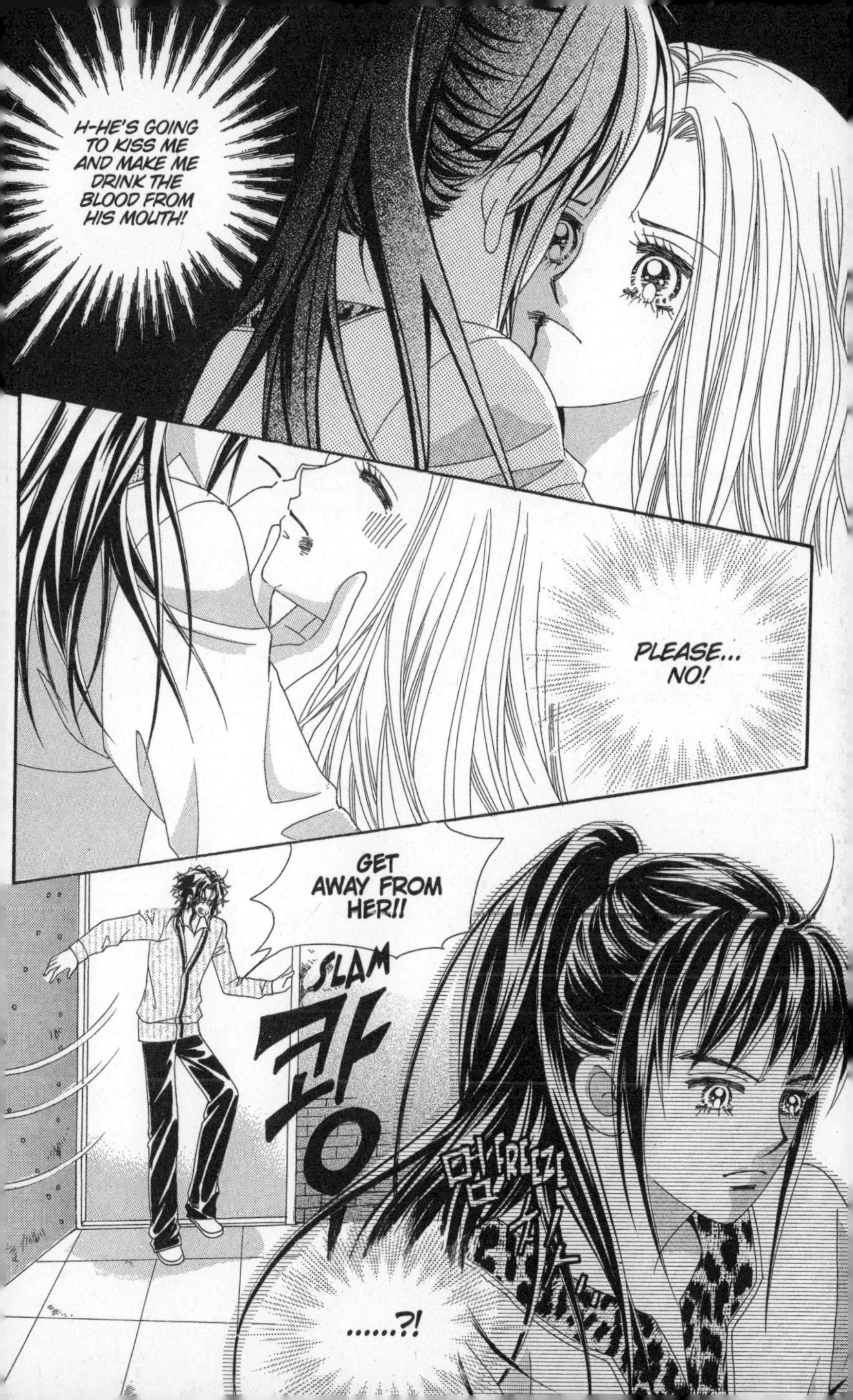
H-HE'S GOING TO KISS ME AND MAKE ME DRINK THE BLOOD FROM HIS MOUTH!
PLEASE... NO!
GET AWAY FROM HER!!
SLAM
쾅
멈칫
......?!

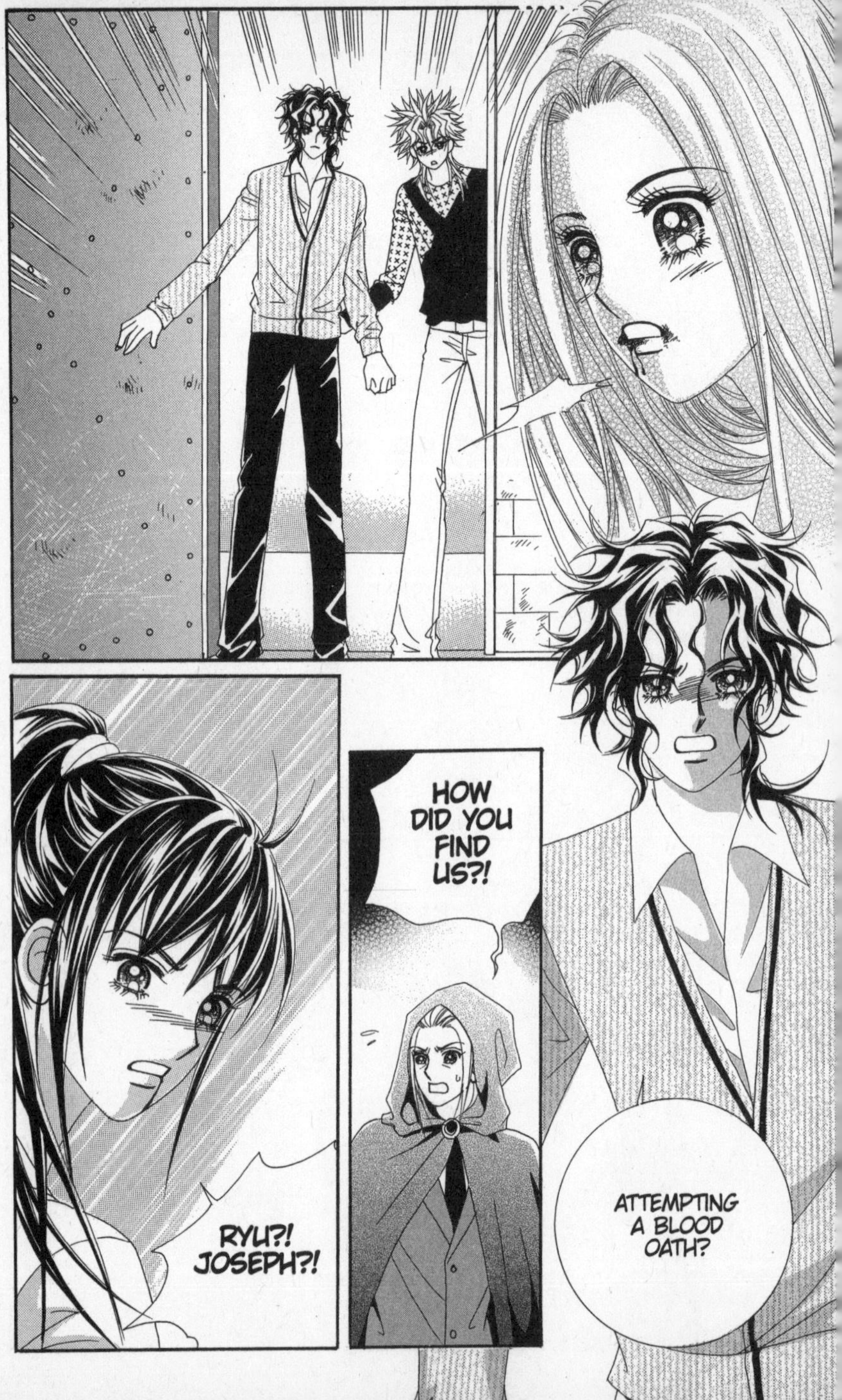
RYU?! JOSEPH?!
HOW DID YOU FIND US?!
ATTEMPTING A BLOOD OATH?

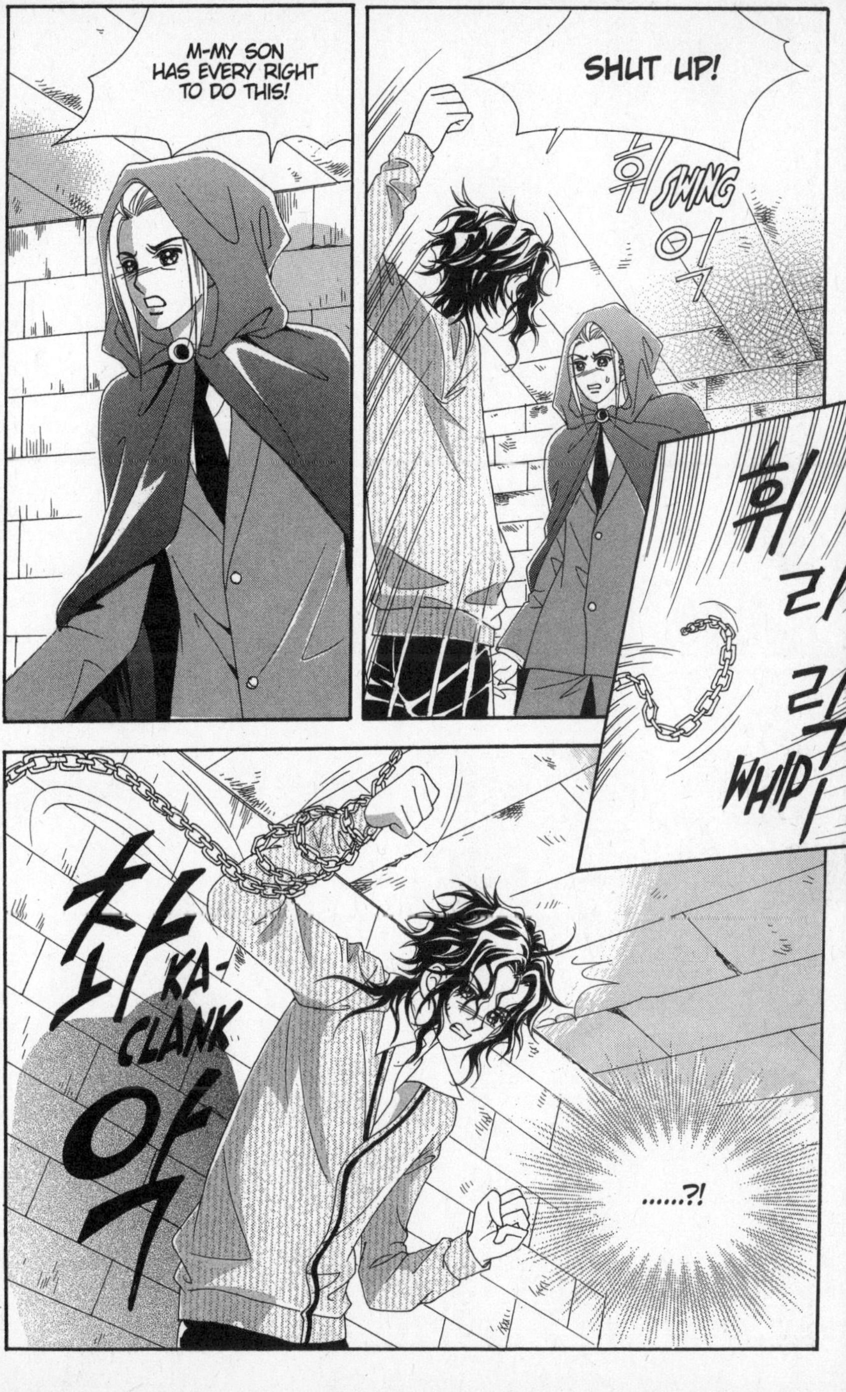
M-MY SON HAS EVERY RIGHT TO DO THIS!
SHUT UP!
휘익
SWING
휘리릭
WHIP
차악
KA-CLANK
......?!

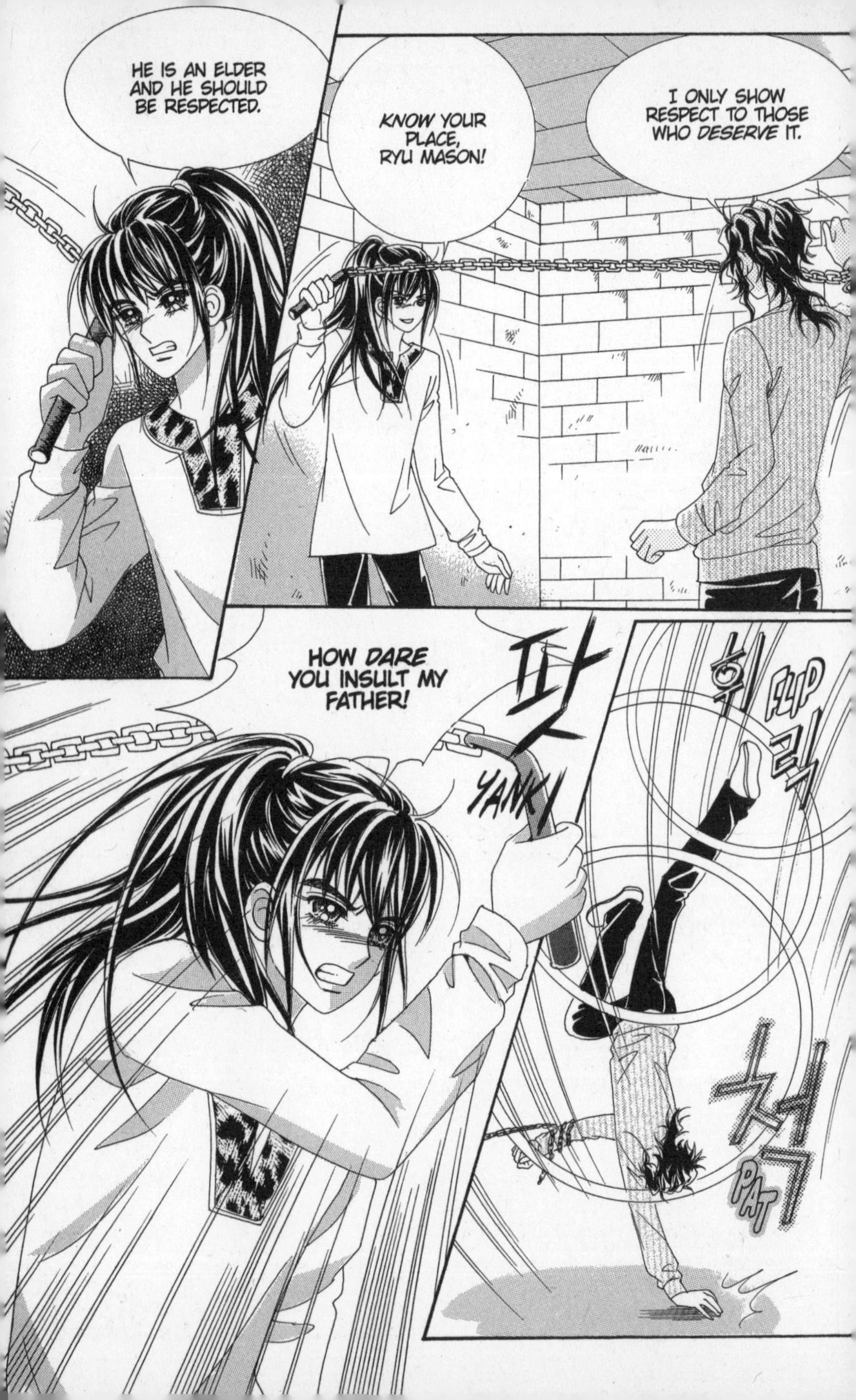
HE IS AN ELDER AND HE SHOULD BE RESPECTED.
KNOW YOUR PLACE, RYU MASON!
I ONLY SHOW RESPECT TO THOSE WHO DESERVE IT.
HOW DARE YOU INSULT MY FATHER!
YANK!
FLIP
PAT

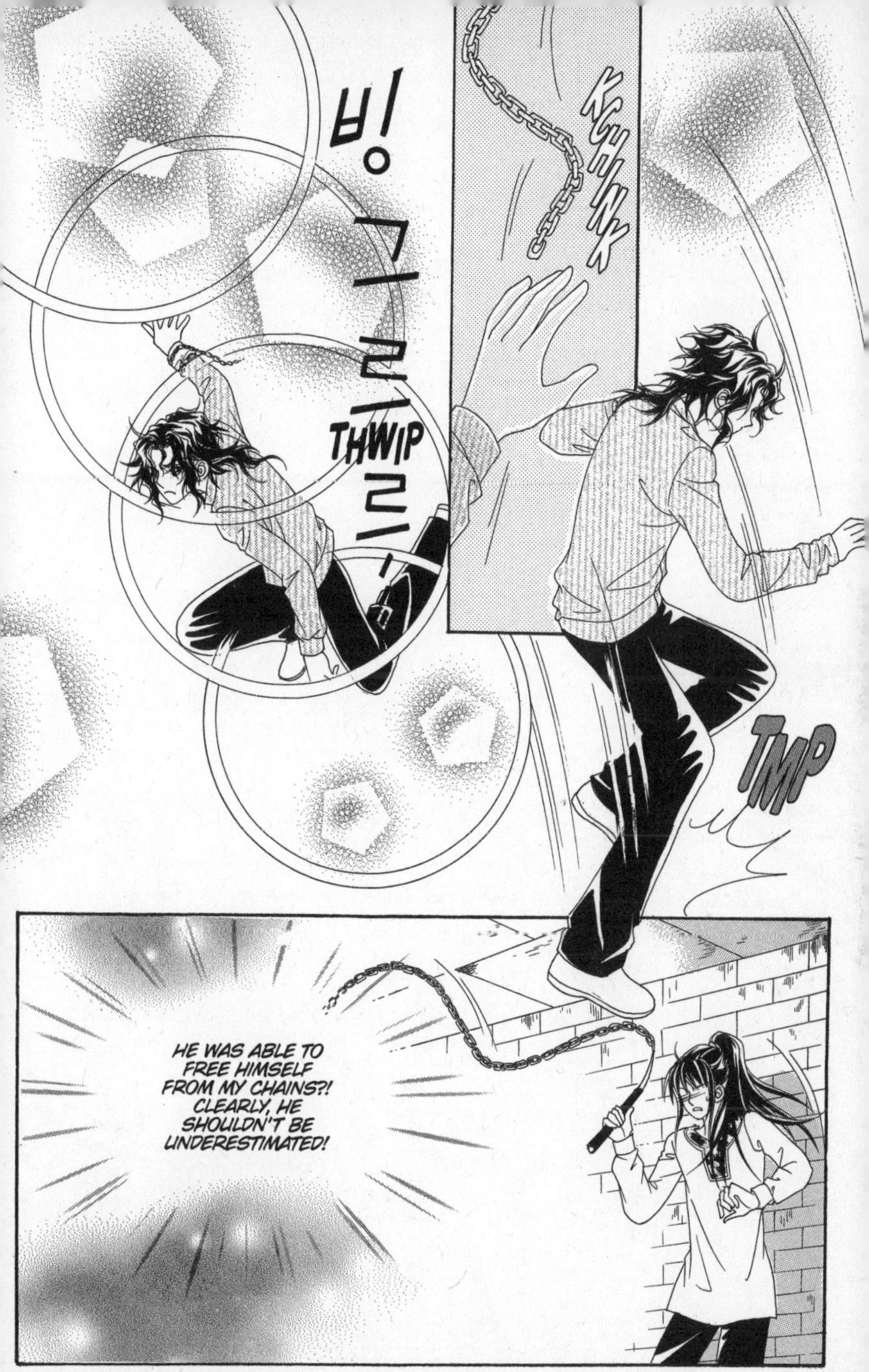
THWIP
KCHINK
TMP
HE WAS ABLE TO FREE HIMSELF FROM MY CHAINS?! CLEARLY, HE SHOULDN'T BE UNDERESTIMATED!

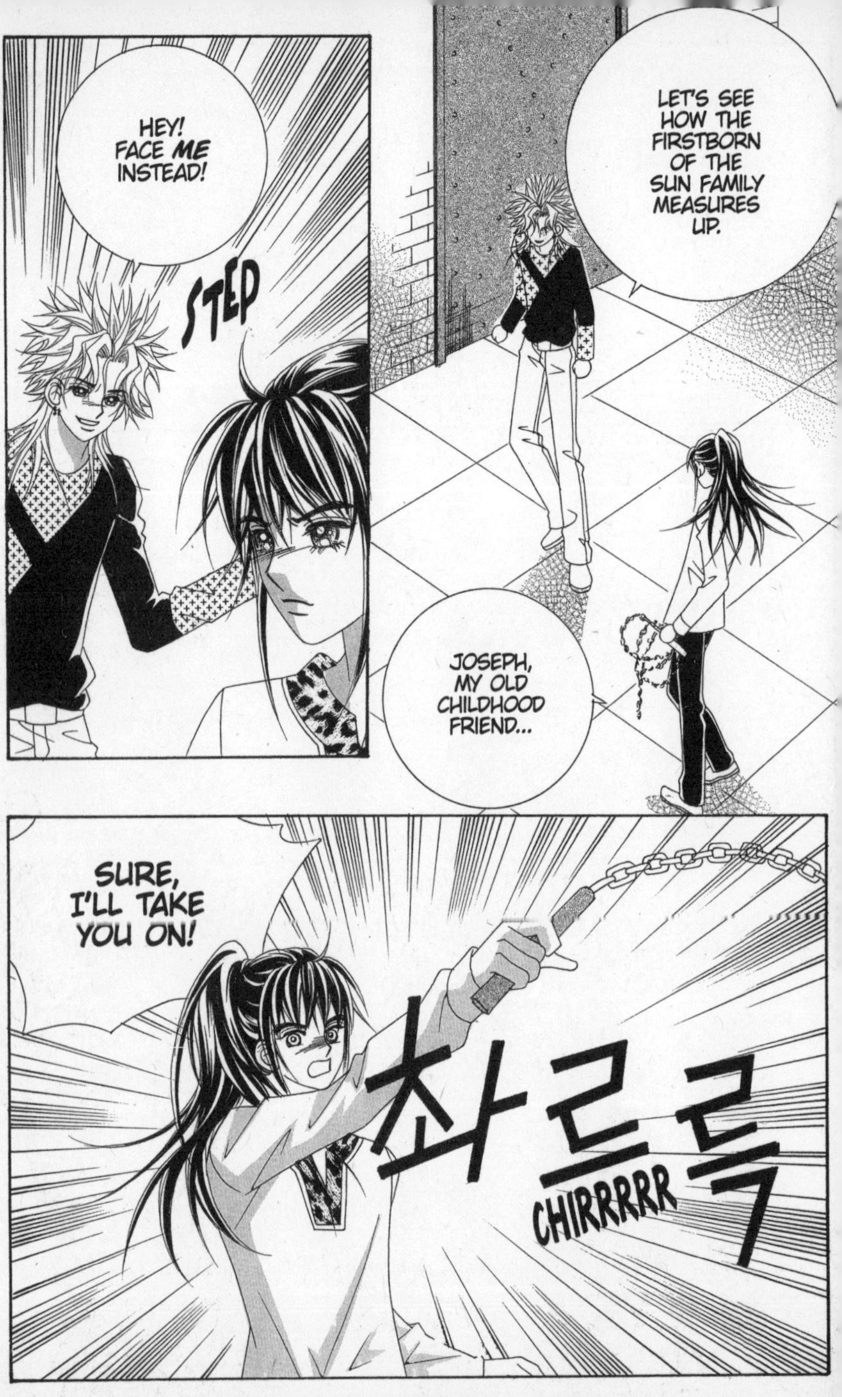
HEY! FACE ME INSTEAD!
STEP
LET'S SEE HOW THE FIRSTBORN OF THE SUN FAMILY MEASURES UP.
JOSEPH, MY OLD CHILDHOOD FRIEND...
SURE, I'LL TAKE YOU ON!
촤르륵
CHIRRRRR

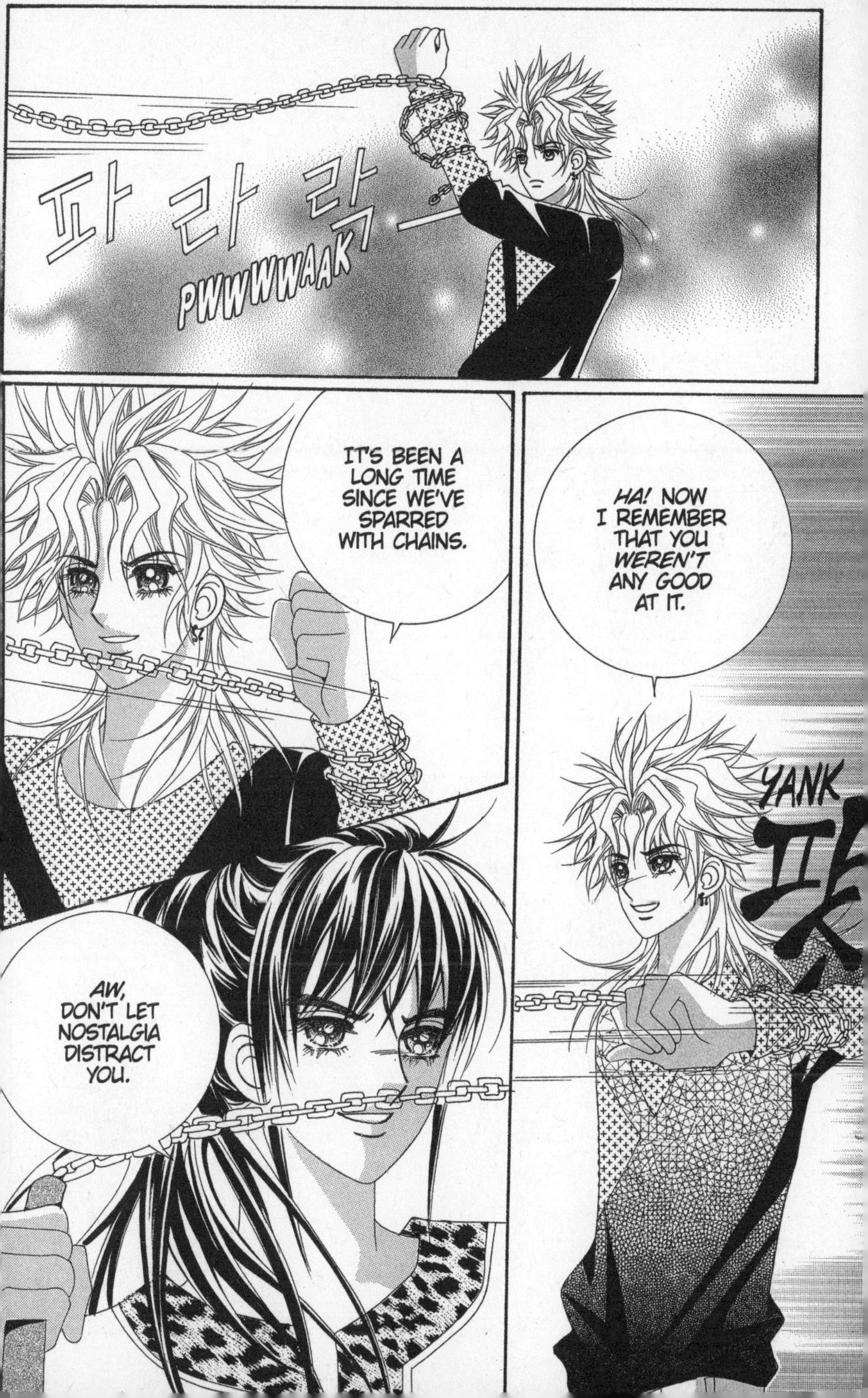

파라락
PWWWWAAK
IT'S BEEN A LONG TIME SINCE WE'VE SPARRED WITH CHAINS.
AW, DON'T LET NOSTALGIA DISTRACT YOU.
HA! NOW I REMEMBER THAT YOU WEREN'T ANY GOOD AT IT.
YANK

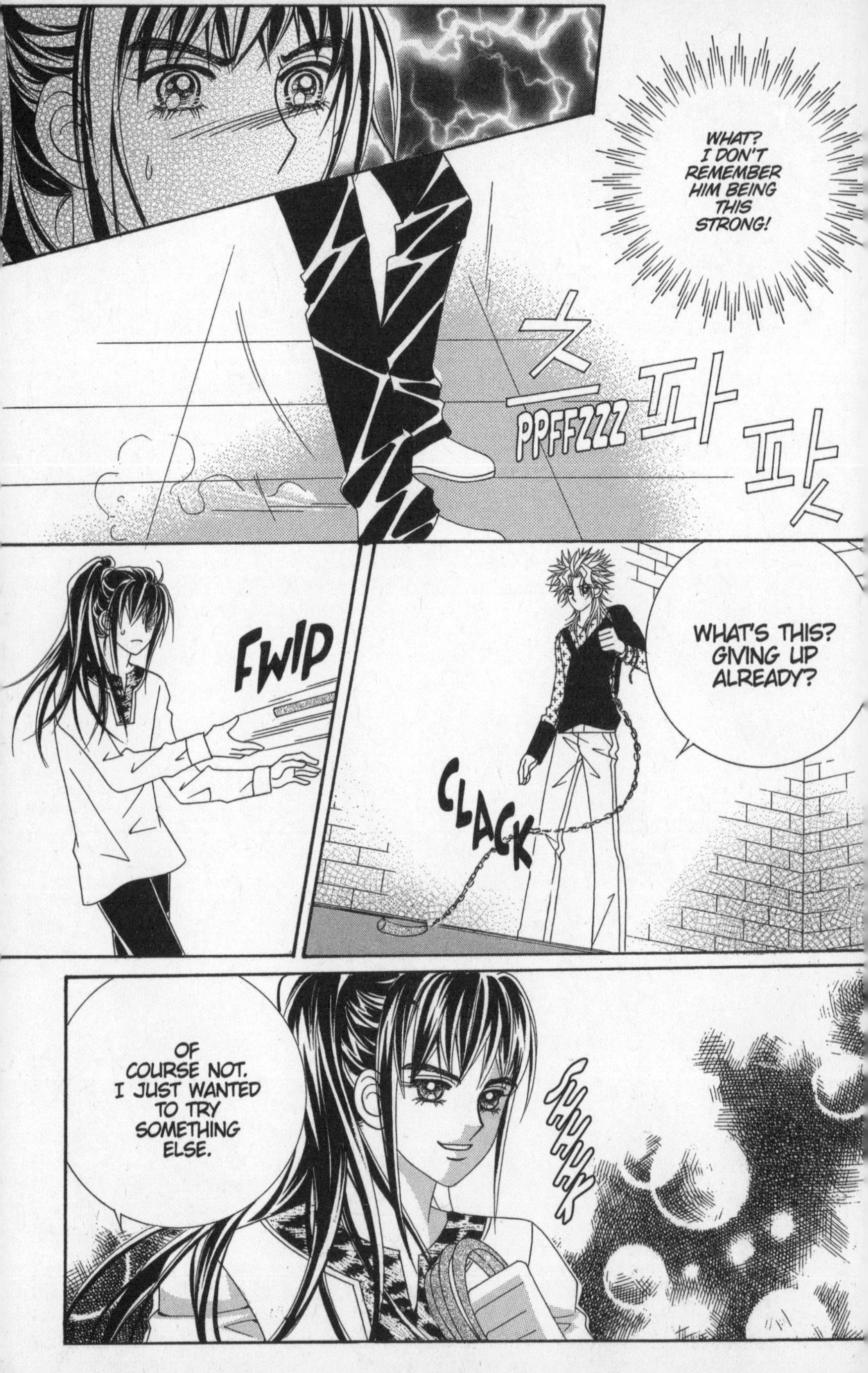
WHAT? I DON'T REMEMBER HIM BEING THIS STRONG!
PPFFZZZ
츠
파
팟
FWIP
CLACK
WHAT'S THIS? GIVING UP ALREADY?
OF COURSE NOT. I JUST WANTED TO TRY SOMETHING ELSE.

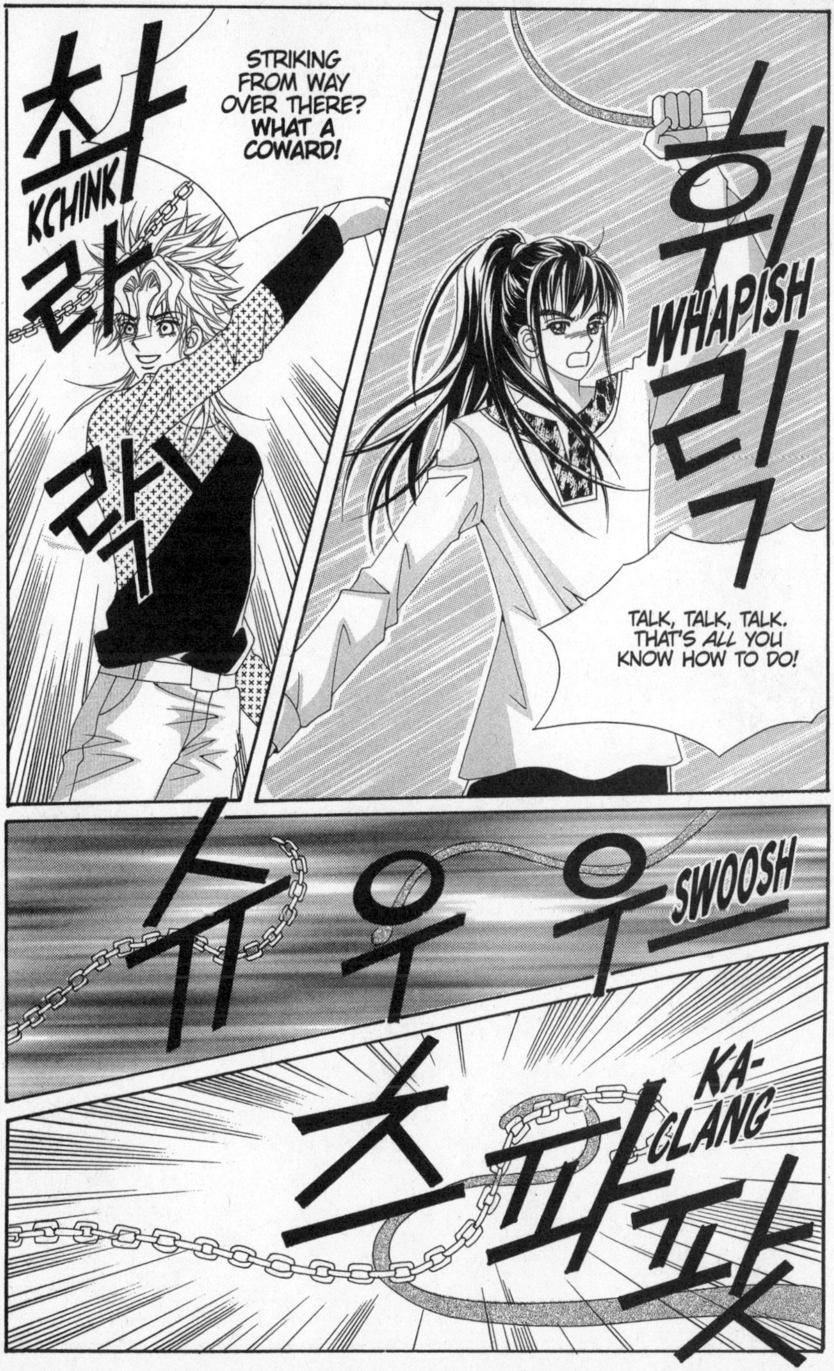
STRIKING FROM WAY OVER THERE? WHAT A COWARD!
KCHINK
WHAPISH
TALK, TALK, TALK. THAT'S ALL YOU KNOW HOW TO DO!
SWOOSH
KA-CLANG

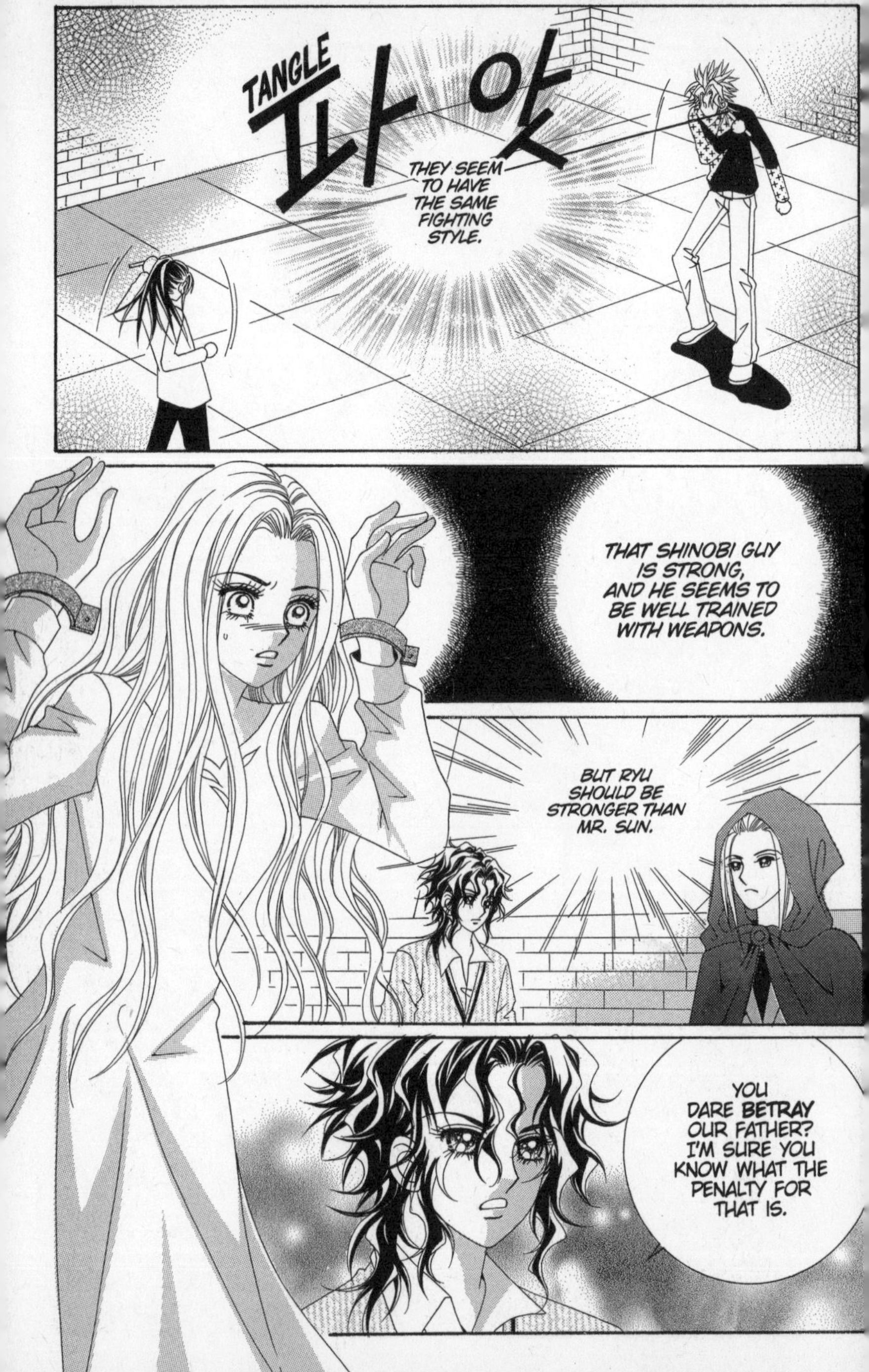
TANGLE
파앗
THEY SEEM TO HAVE THE SAME FIGHTING STYLE.
THAT SHINOBI GUY IS STRONG, AND HE SEEMS TO BE WELL TRAINED WITH WEAPONS.
BUT RYU SHOULD BE STRONGER THAN MR. SUN.
YOU DARE BETRAY OUR FATHER? I'M SURE YOU KNOW WHAT THE PENALTY FOR THAT IS.

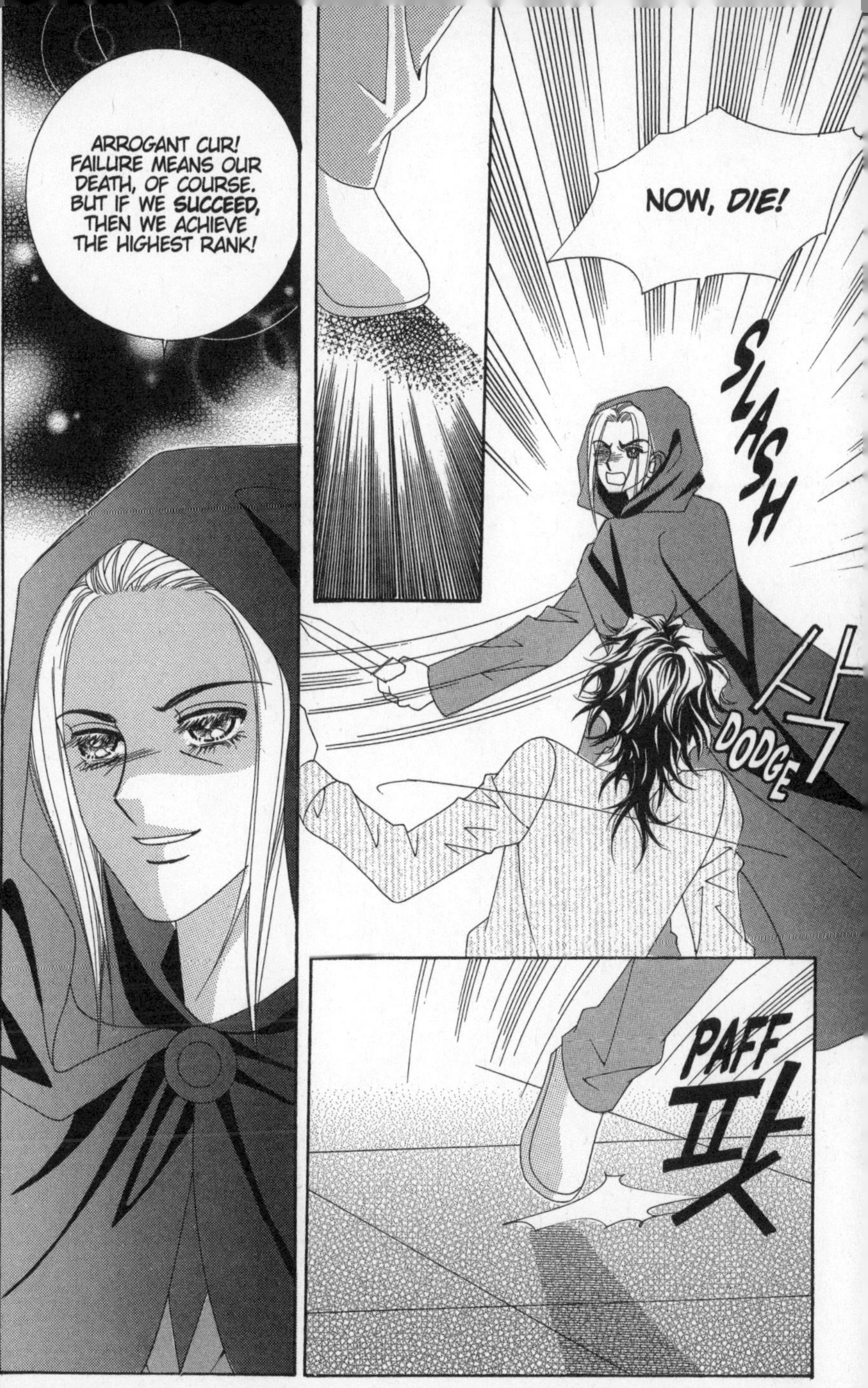
ARROGANT CUR! FAILURE MEANS OUR DEATH, OF COURSE. BUT IF WE **SUCCEED**, THEN WE ACHIEVE THE HIGHEST RANK!
NOW, *DIE!*
SLASH
DODGE
PAFF

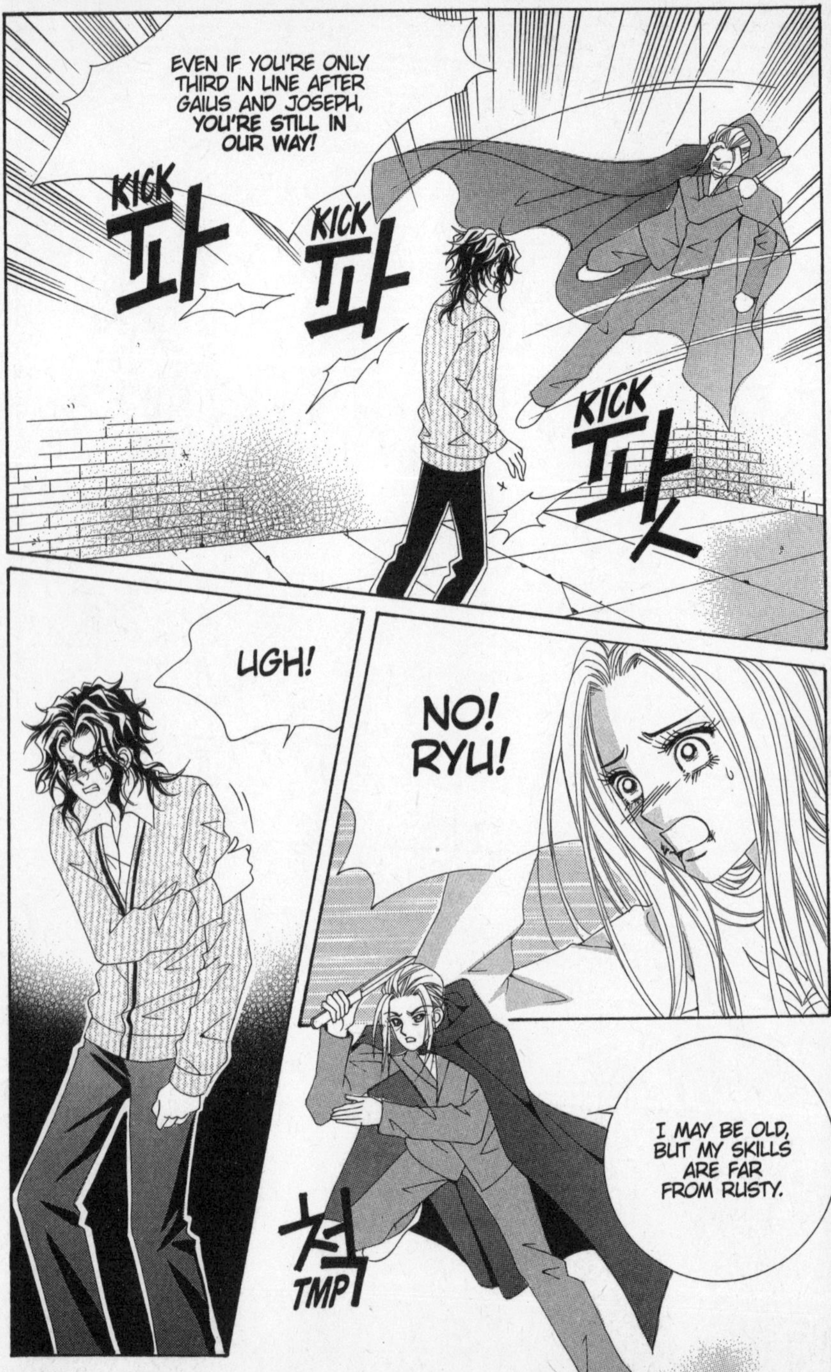
EVEN IF YOU'RE ONLY THIRD IN LINE AFTER GAIUS AND JOSEPH, YOU'RE STILL IN OUR WAY!
KICK
파
KICK
파
KICK
팟
UGH!
NO! RYU!
I MAY BE OLD, BUT MY SKILLS ARE FAR FROM RUSTY.
척
TMP

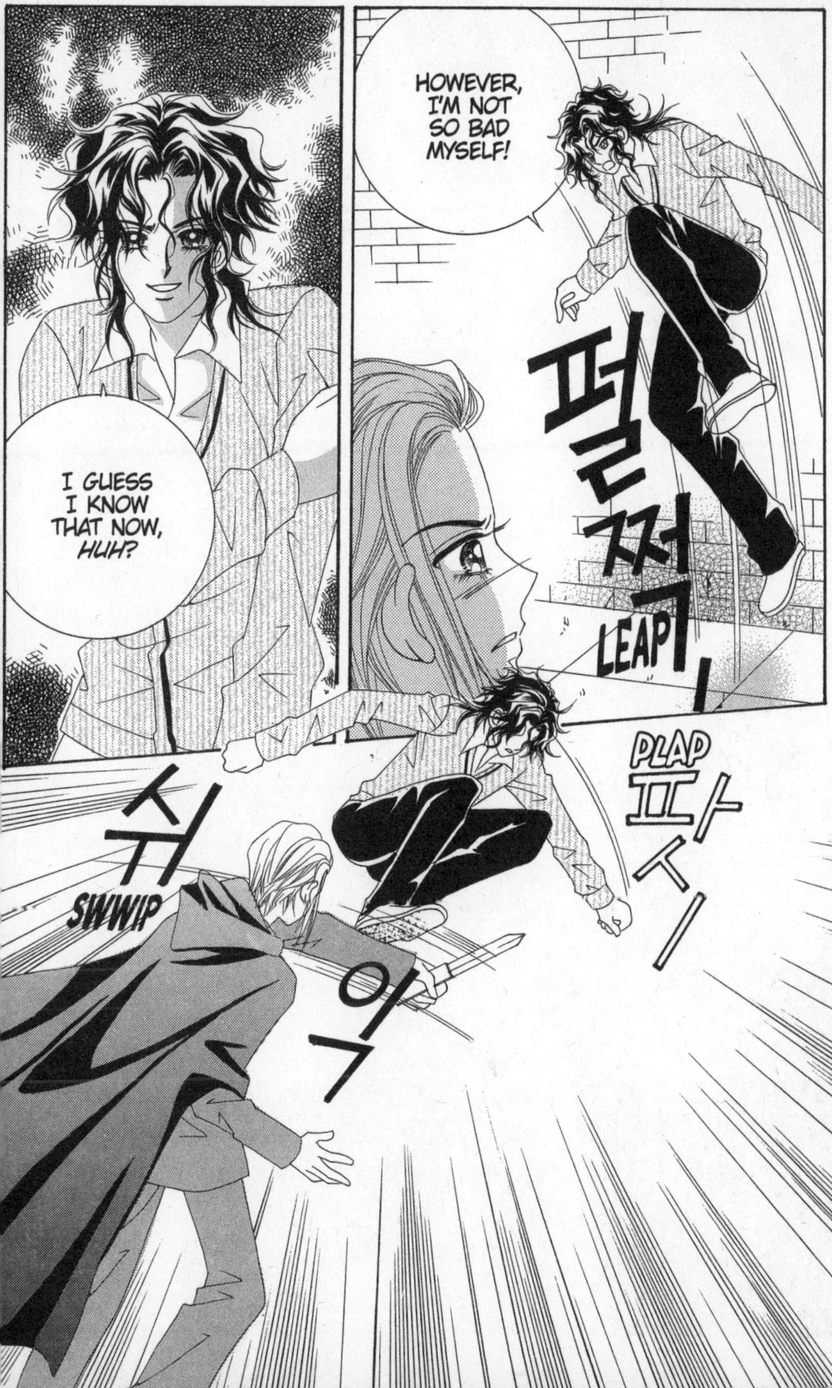

I GUESS I KNOW THAT NOW, *HUH?*
HOWEVER, I'M NOT SO BAD MYSELF!
펄쩍
LEAP
PLAP
SWWIP

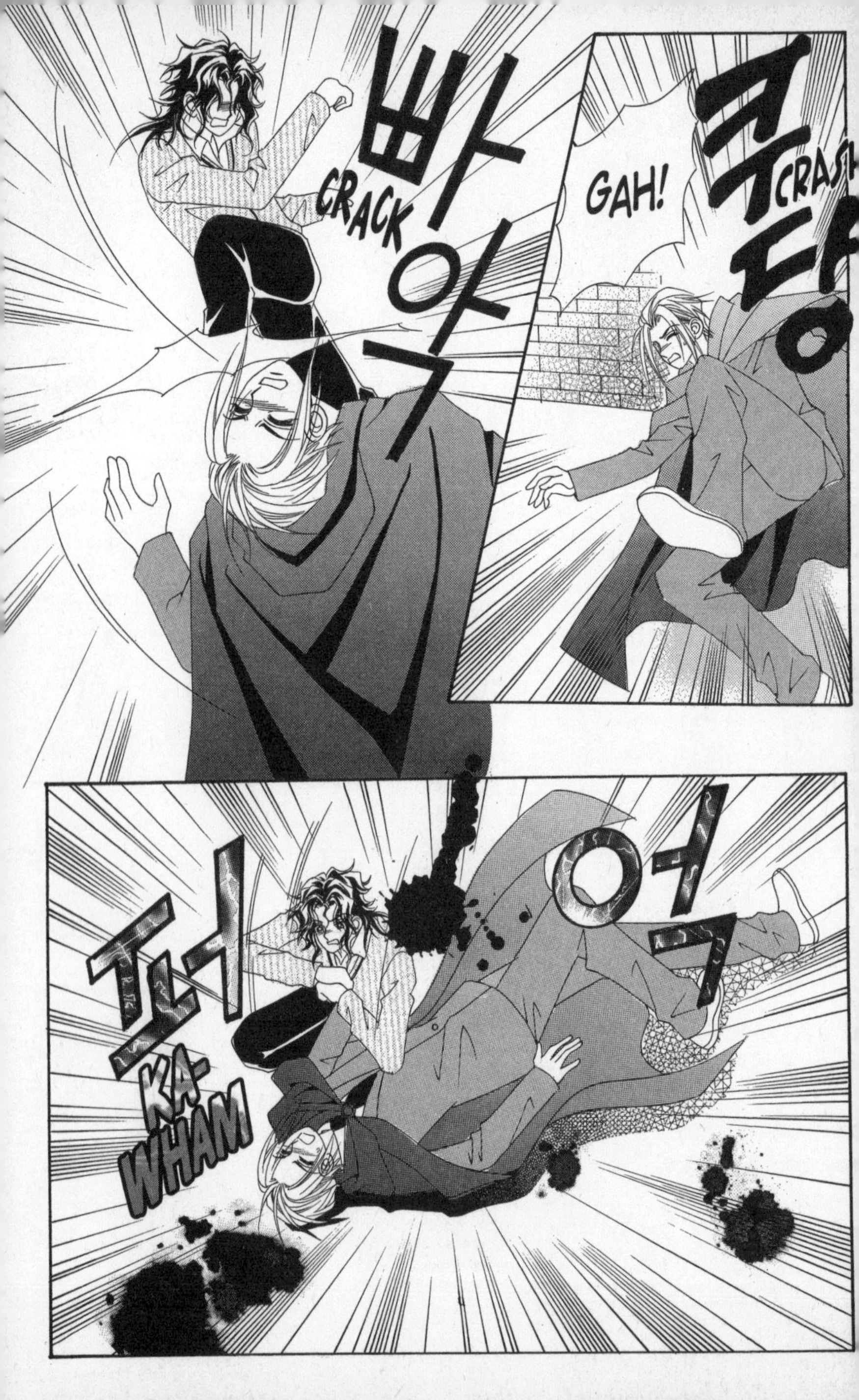
빠악
CRACK
GAH!
CRAS
KA-
WHAM

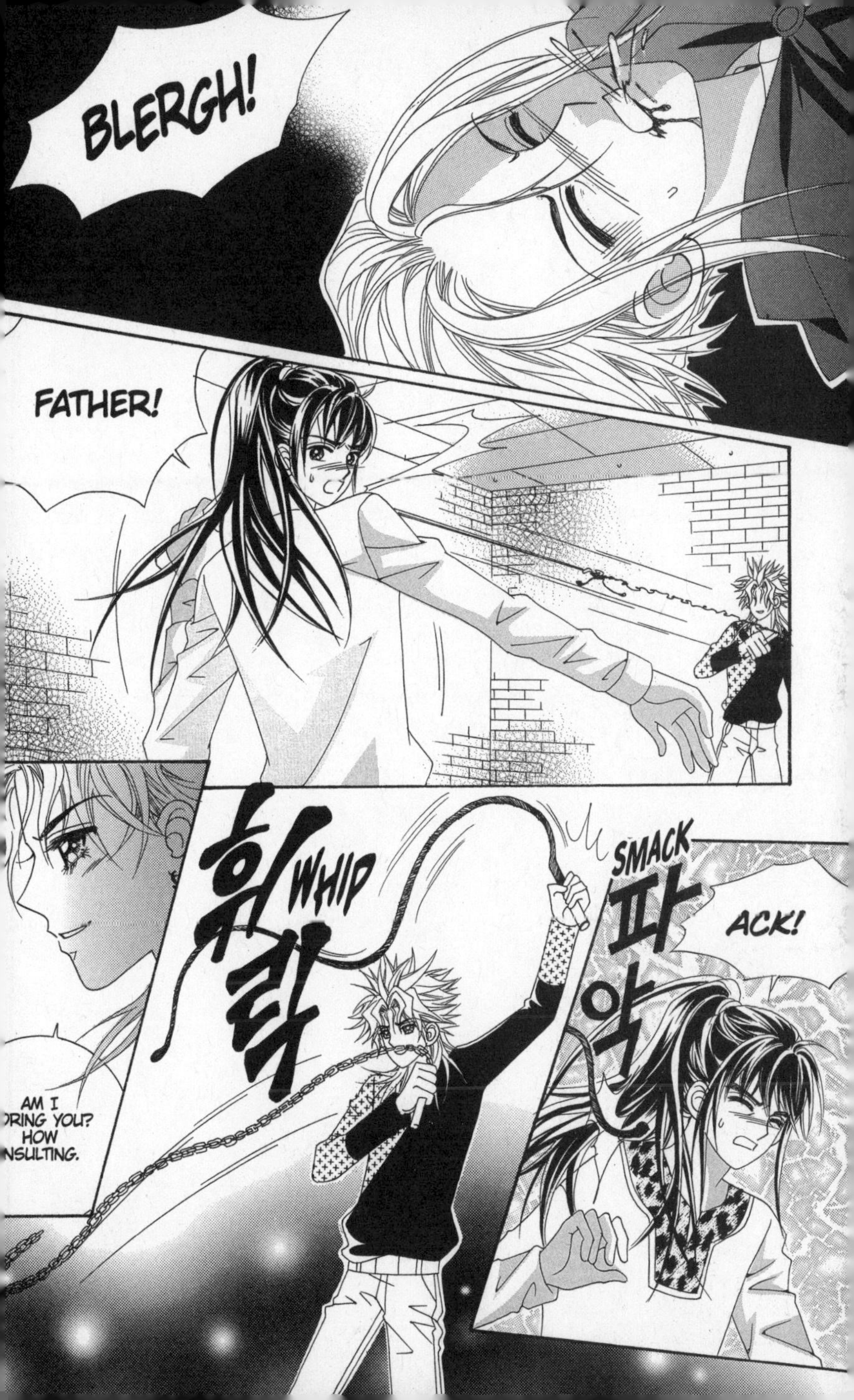
BLERGH!
FATHER!
AM I
ORING YOU?
HOW
NSULTING.
휘릭
WHIP
SMACK
파악
ACK!

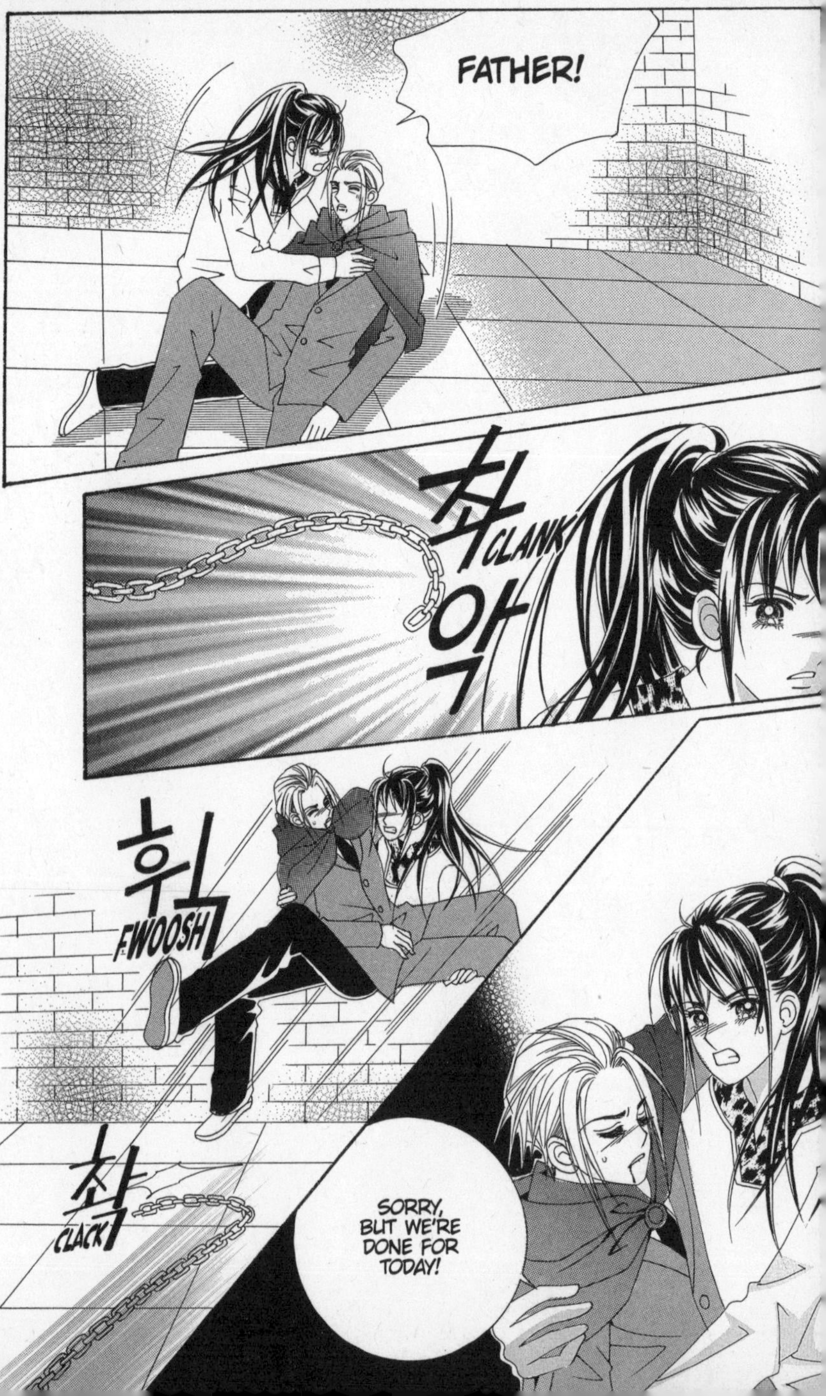
FATHER!
촤아악
CLANK
휘
FWOOSH
촤
CLACK
SORRY, BUT WE'RE DONE FOR TODAY!

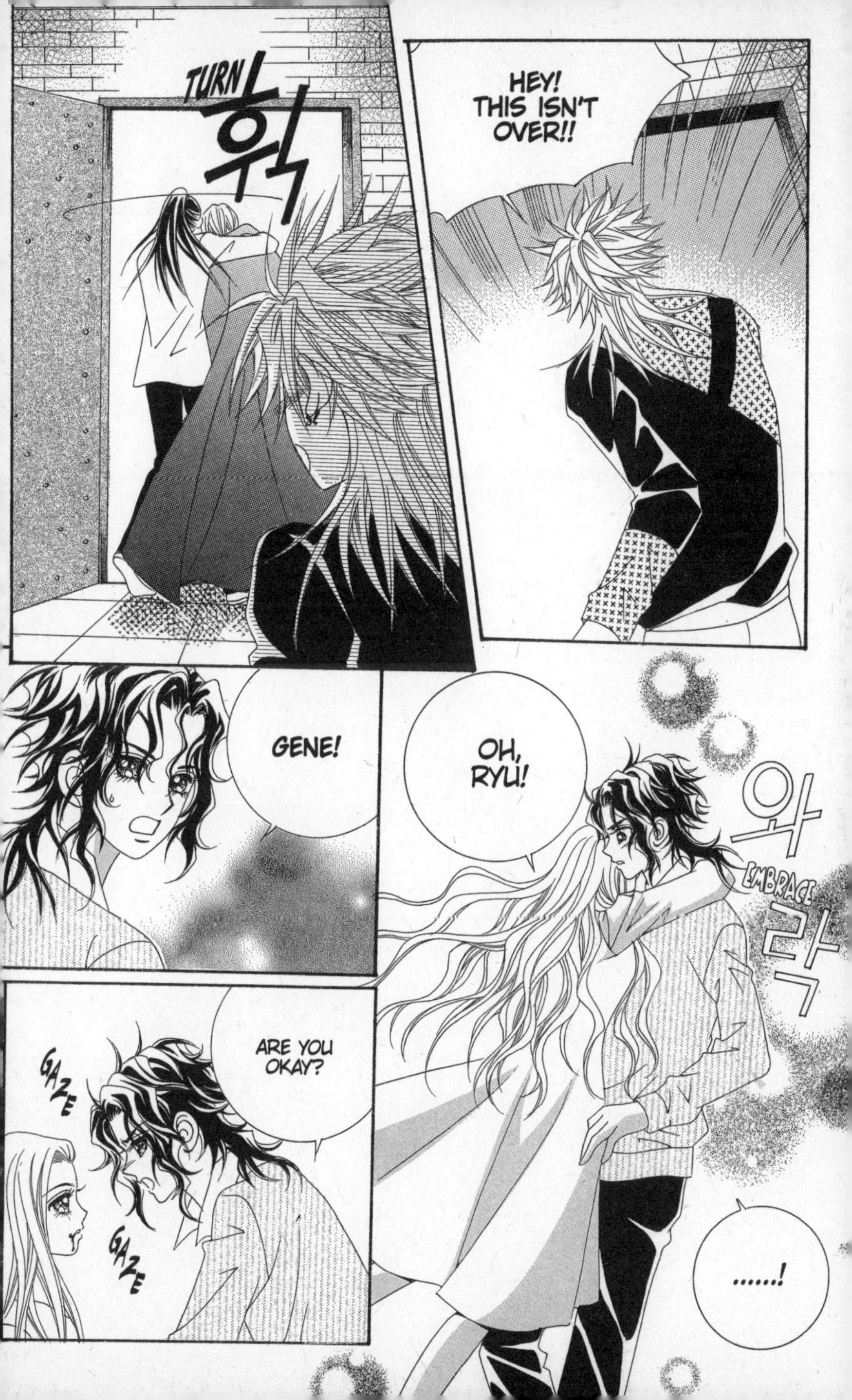
TURN
훅
HEY! THIS ISN'T OVER!!
GENE!
OH, RYU!
와락
EMBRACE
ARE YOU OKAY?
GAZE
GAZE
......!

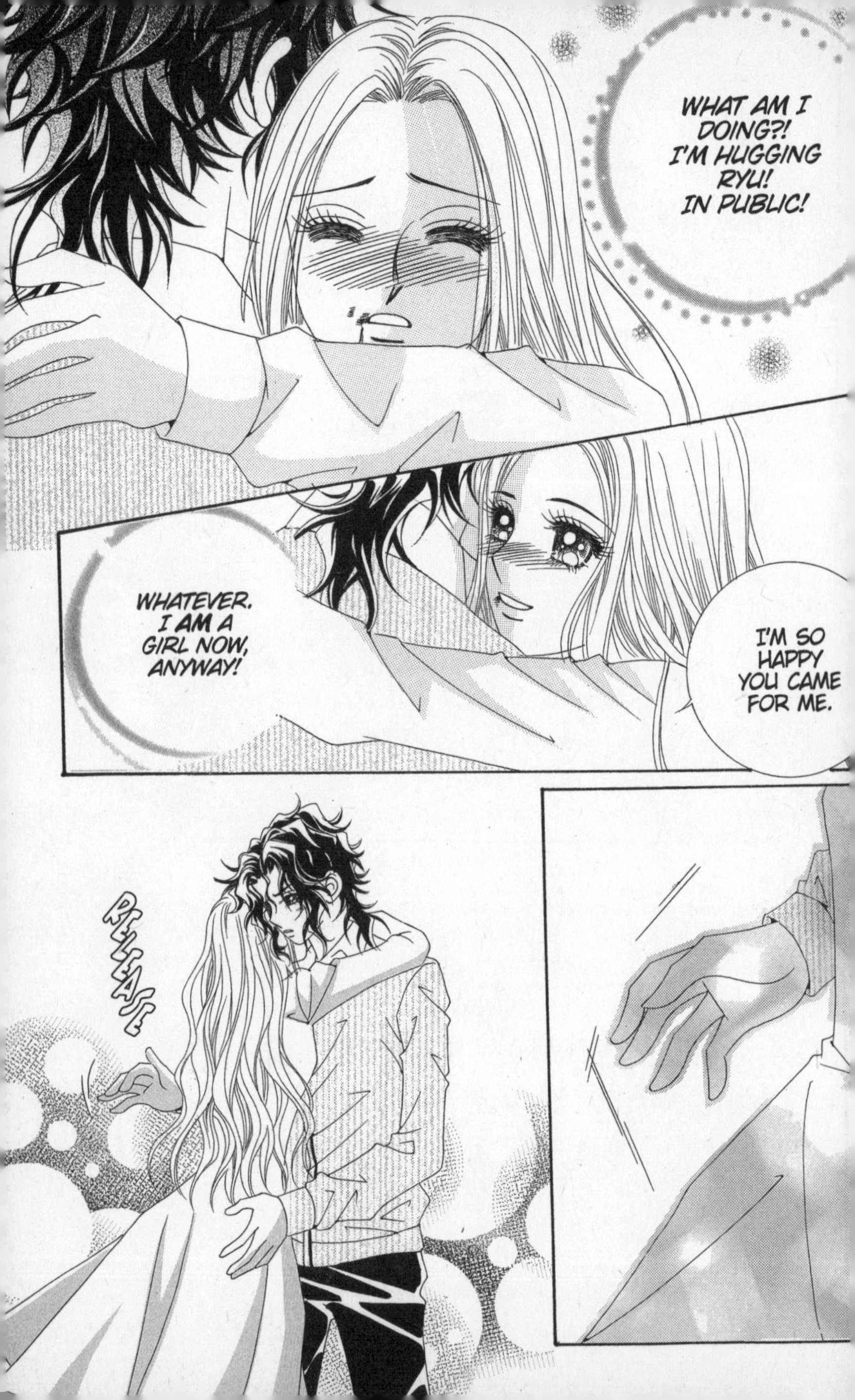
WHAT AM I DOING?! I'M HUGGING RYU! IN PUBLIC!
WHATEVER. I AM A GIRL NOW, ANYWAY!
I'M SO HAPPY YOU CAME FOR ME.
RELEASE

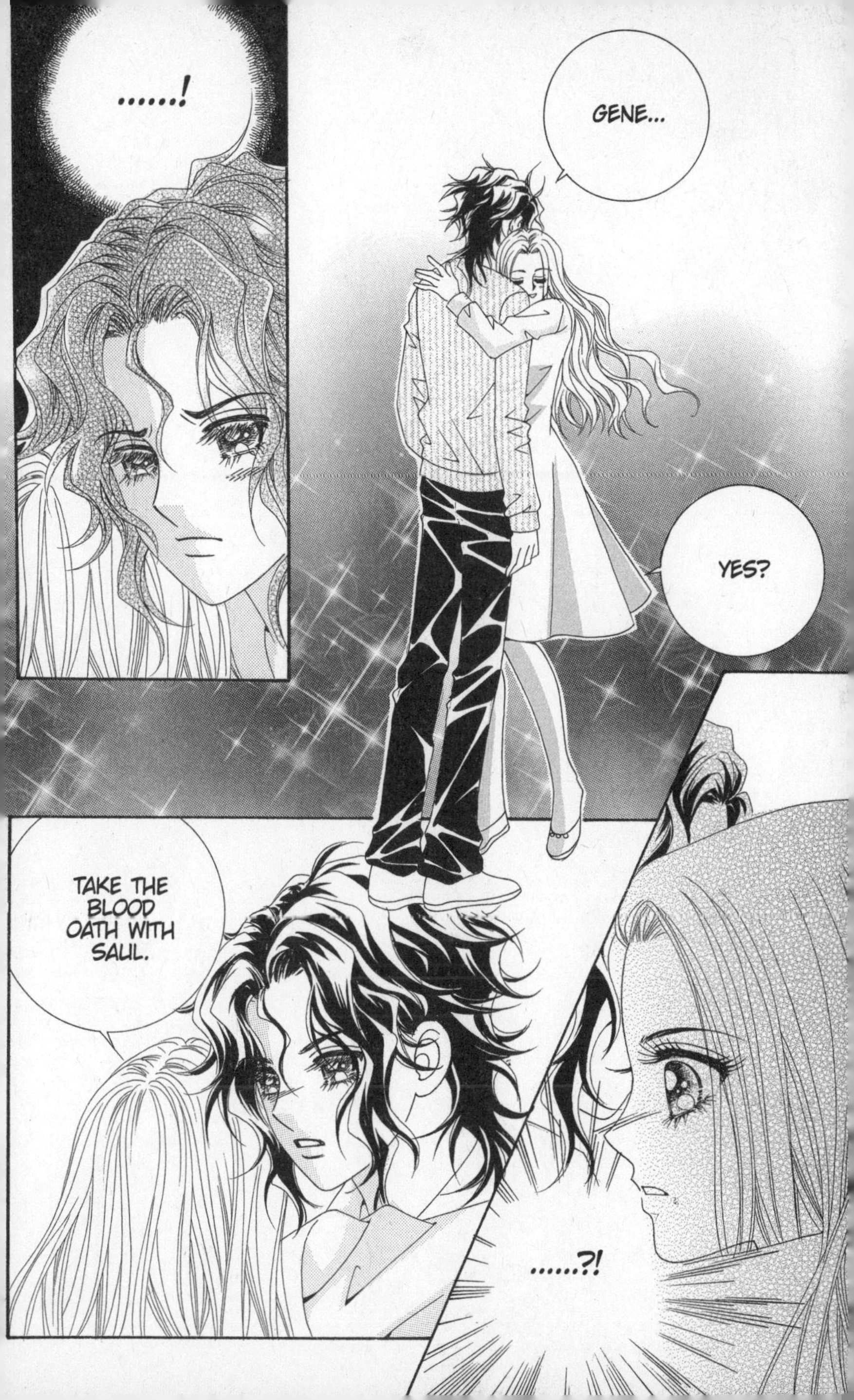
......!
GENE...
YES?
TAKE THE BLOOD OATH WITH SAUL.
......?!

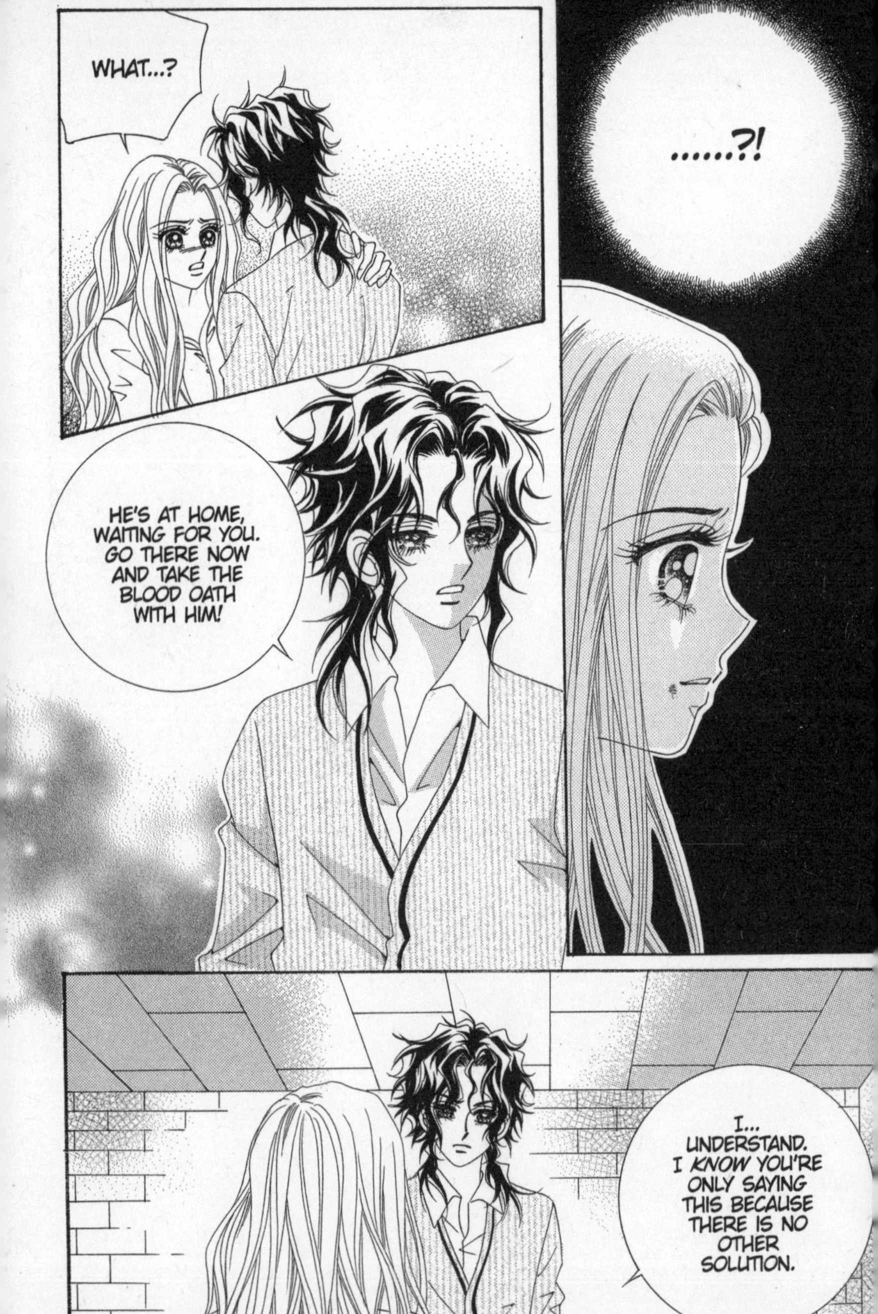
WHAT...?
......?!
HE'S AT HOME, WAITING FOR YOU. GO THERE NOW AND TAKE THE BLOOD OATH WITH HIM!
I... UNDERSTAND. I *KNOW* YOU'RE ONLY SAYING THIS BECAUSE THERE IS NO OTHER SOLUTION.

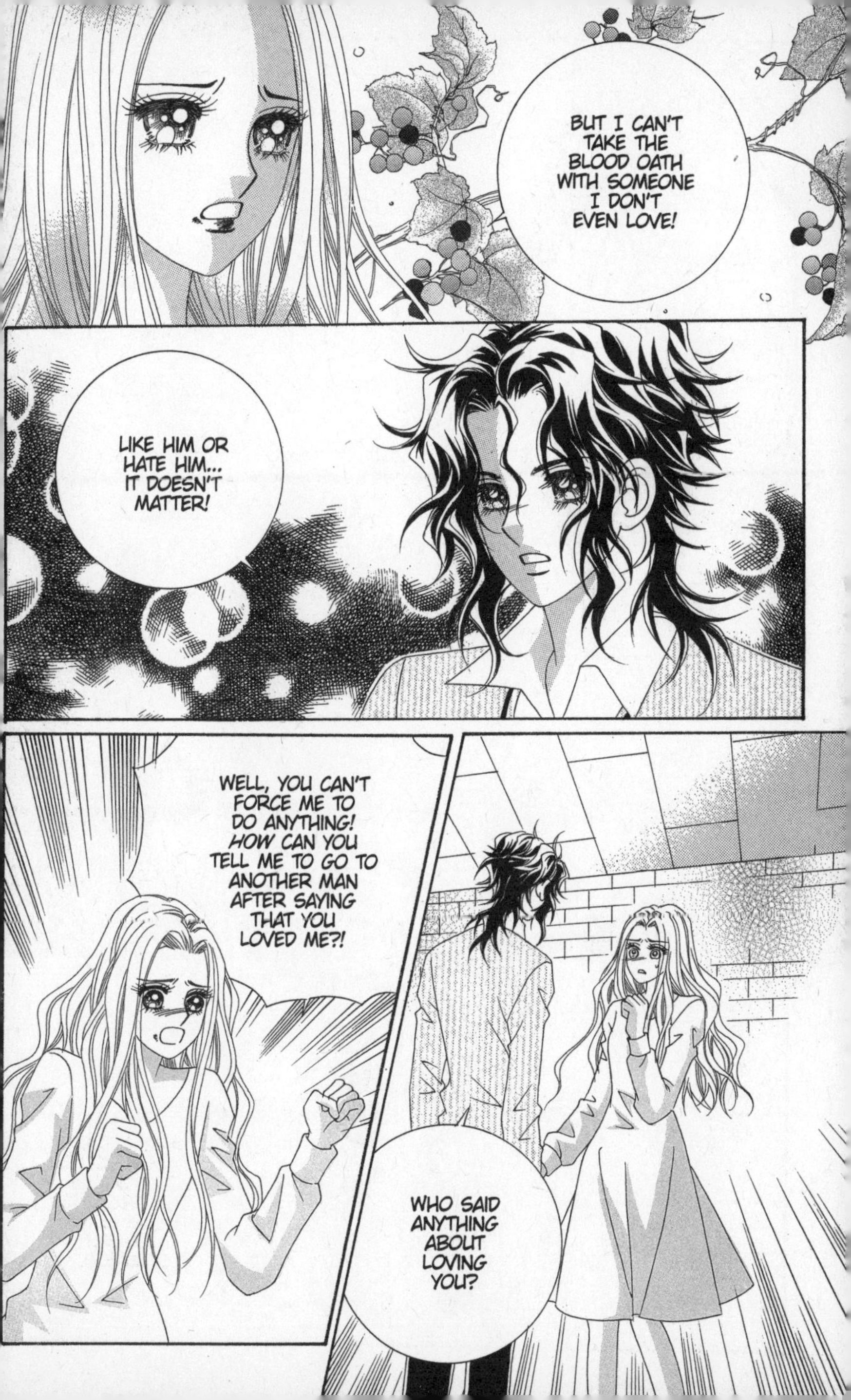
BUT I CAN'T TAKE THE BLOOD OATH WITH SOMEONE I DON'T EVEN LOVE!
LIKE HIM OR HATE HIM... IT DOESN'T MATTER!
WELL, YOU CAN'T FORCE ME TO DO ANYTHING! *HOW* CAN YOU TELL ME TO GO TO ANOTHER MAN AFTER SAYING THAT YOU LOVED ME?!
WHO SAID ANYTHING ABOUT LOVING YOU?

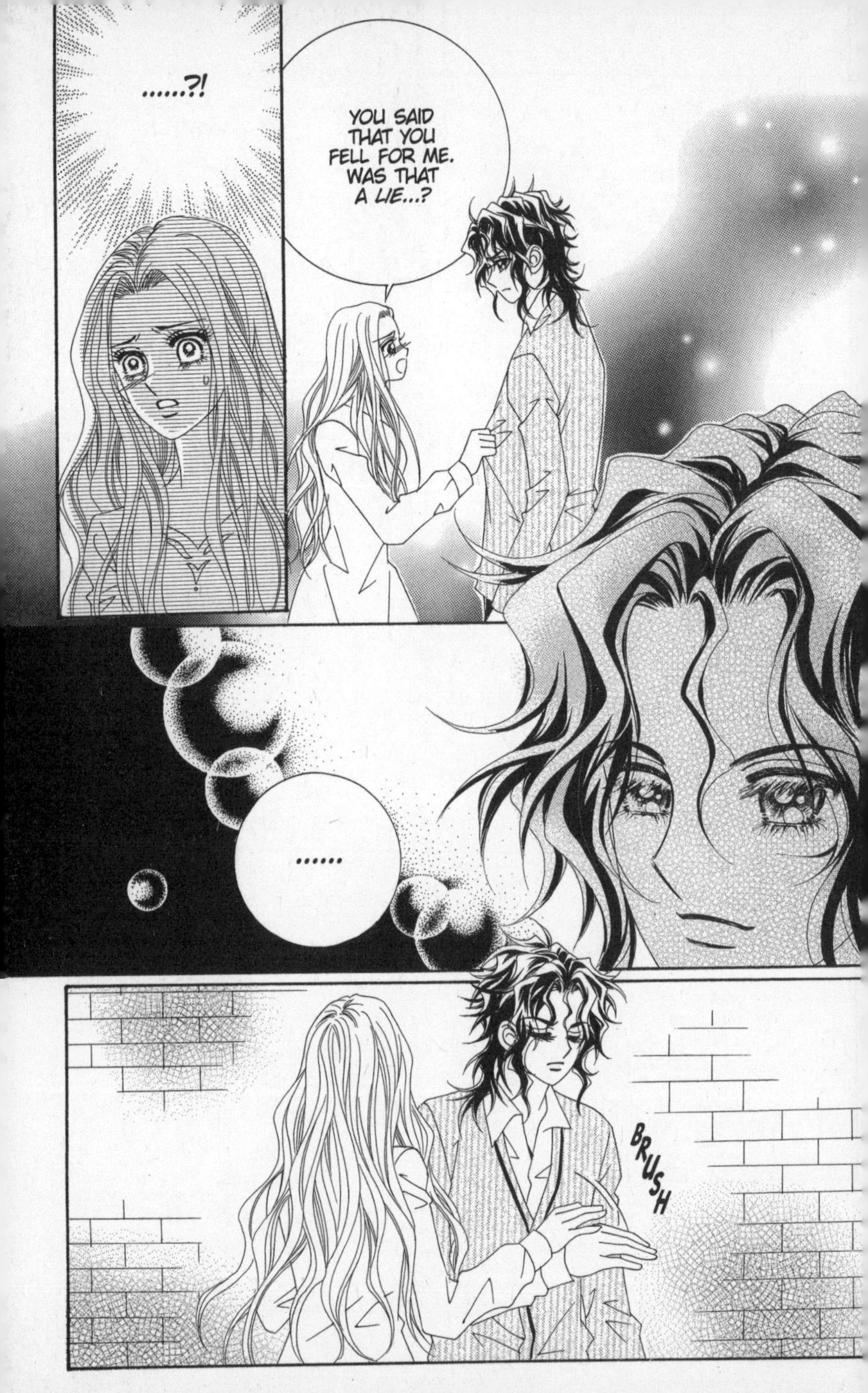
......?!
YOU SAID THAT YOU FELL FOR ME. WAS THAT A LIE...?
......
BRUSH

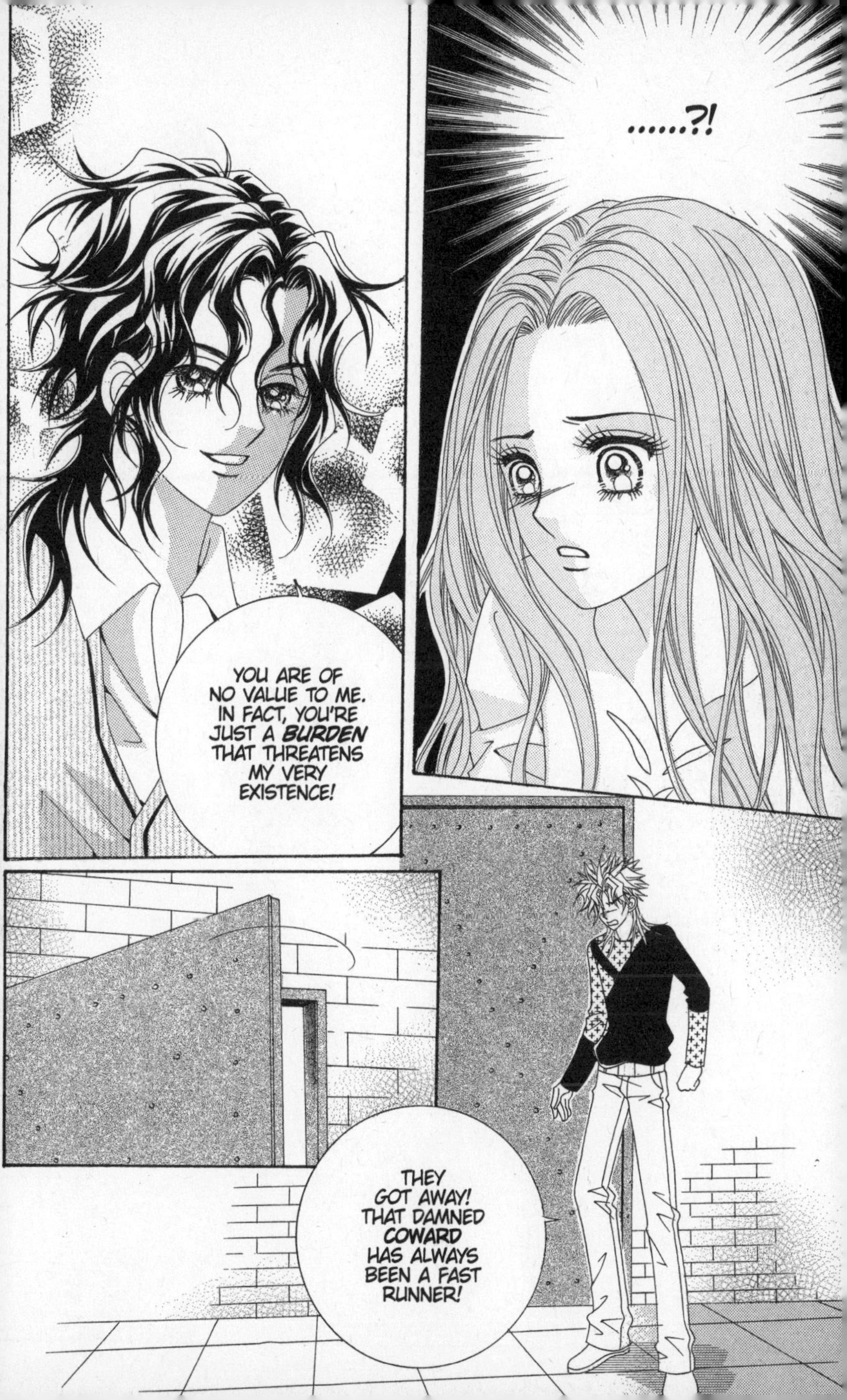
YOU ARE OF NO VALUE TO ME. IN FACT, YOU'RE JUST A **BURDEN** THAT THREATENS MY VERY EXISTENCE!
......?!
THEY GOT AWAY! THAT DAMNED COWARD HAS ALWAYS BEEN A FAST RUNNER!

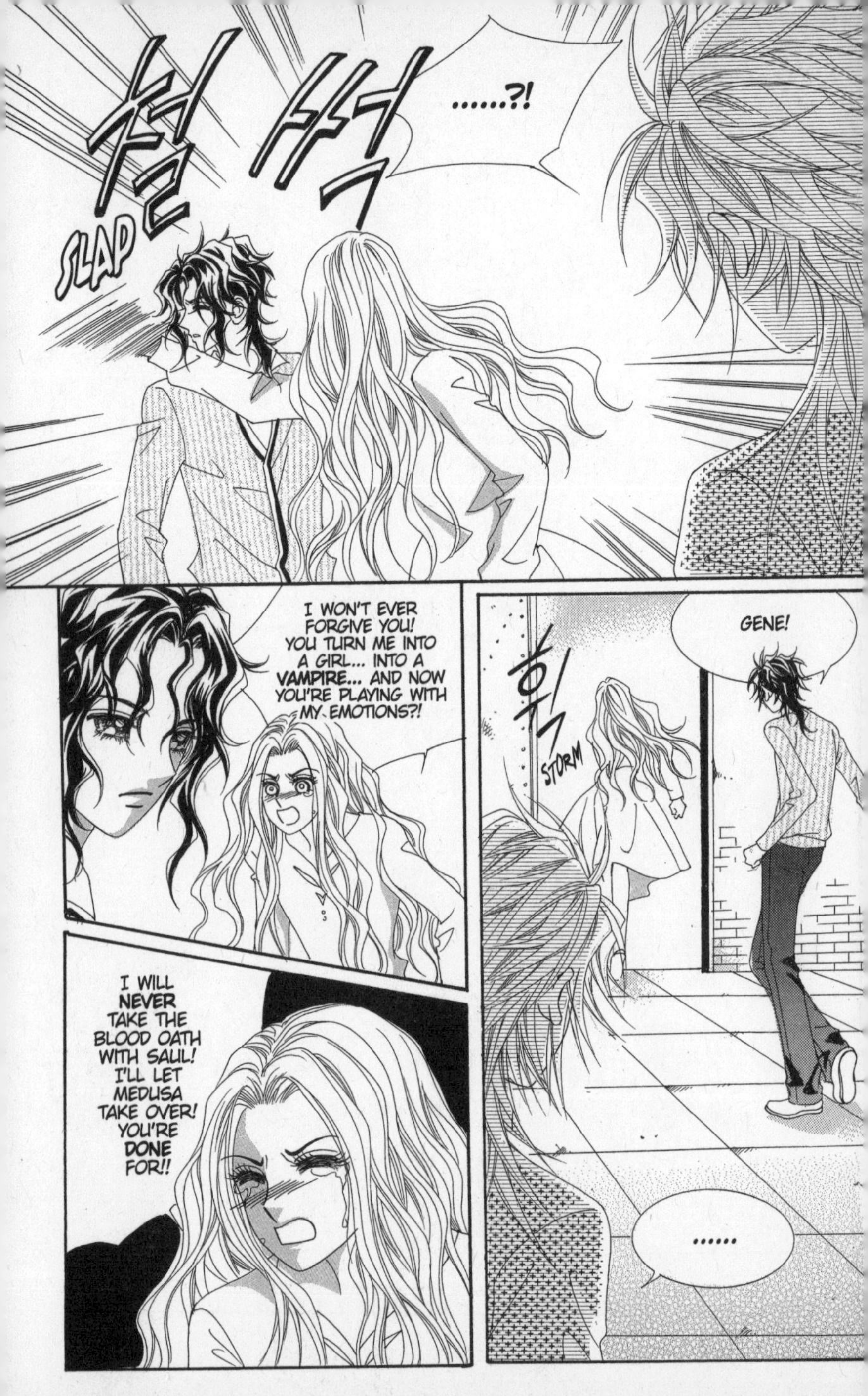

철썩
SLAP
......?!
I WON'T EVER FORGIVE YOU! YOU TURN ME INTO A GIRL... INTO A VAMPIRE... AND NOW YOU'RE PLAYING WITH MY EMOTIONS?!
I WILL NEVER TAKE THE BLOOD OATH WITH SAUL! I'LL LET MEDUSA TAKE OVER! YOU'RE DONE FOR!!
GENE!
STORM
......

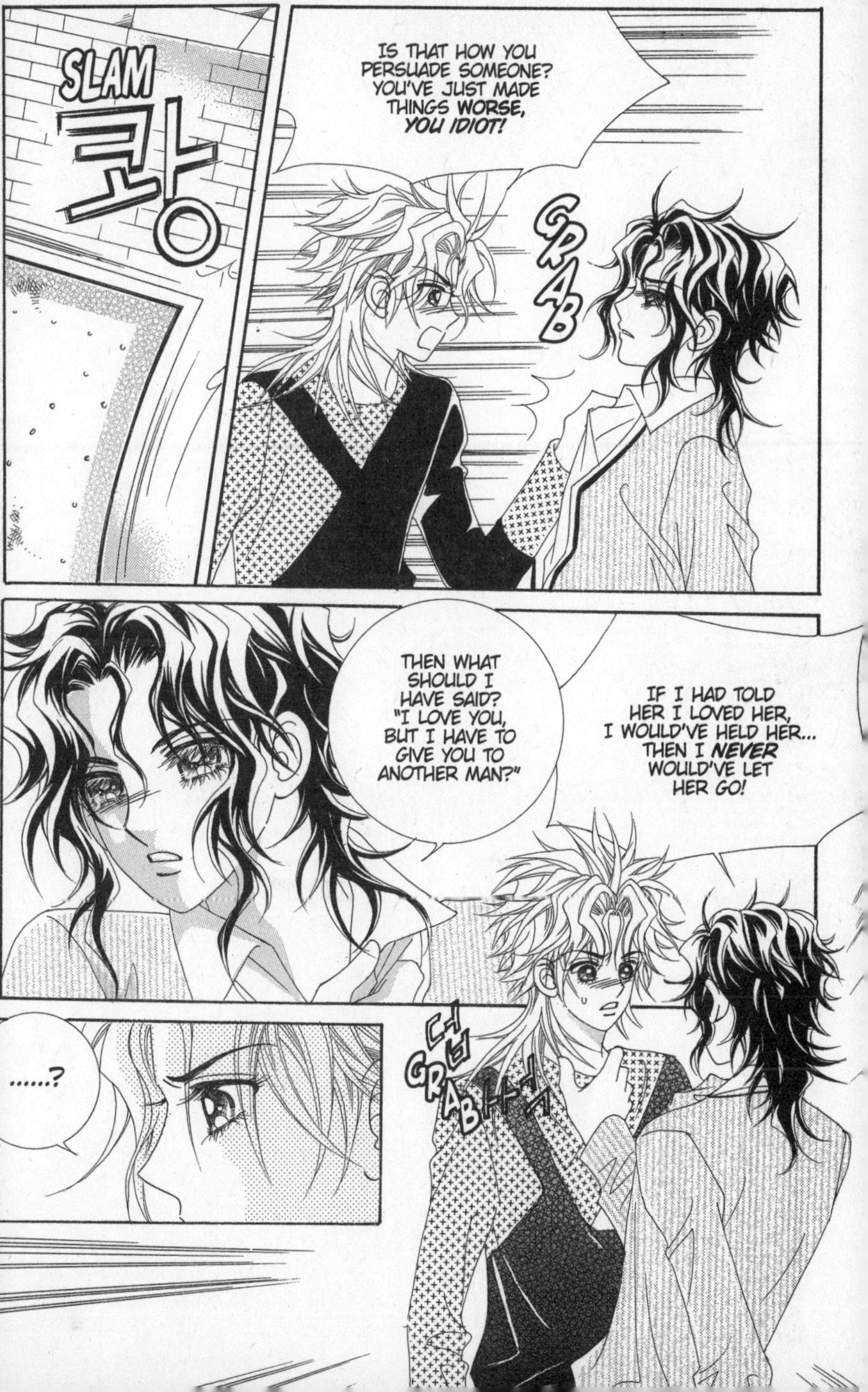
SLAM
쾅
IS THAT HOW YOU PERSUADE SOMEONE? YOU'VE JUST MADE THINGS WORSE, YOU IDIOT!
GRAB
THEN WHAT SHOULD I HAVE SAID? "I LOVE YOU, BUT I HAVE TO GIVE YOU TO ANOTHER MAN?"
IF I HAD TOLD HER I LOVED HER, I WOULD'VE HELD HER... THEN I NEVER WOULD'VE LET HER GO!
......?
GRAB
덥석

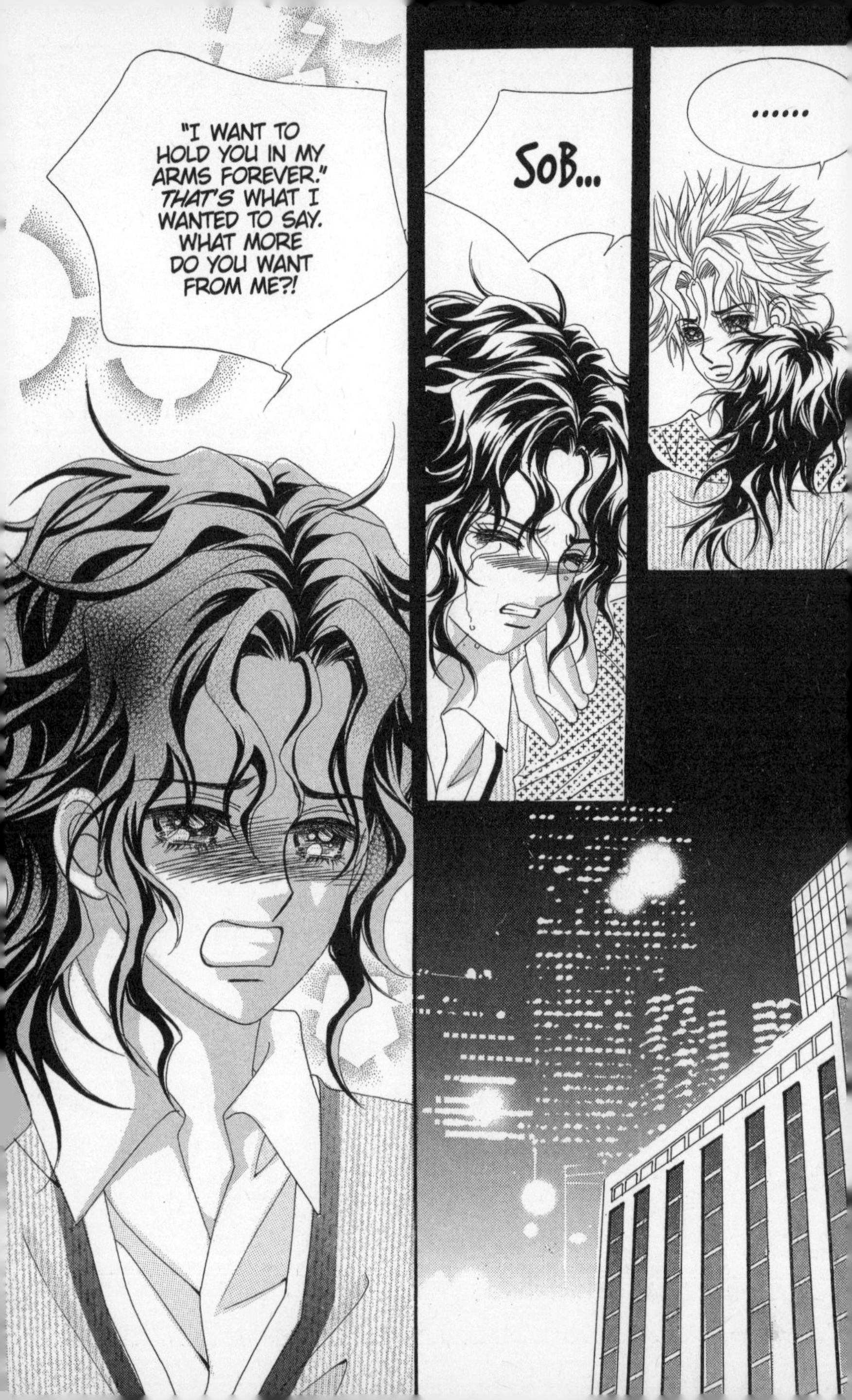
"I WANT TO HOLD YOU IN MY ARMS FOREVER." *THAT'S* WHAT I WANTED TO SAY. WHAT MORE DO YOU WANT FROM ME?!
SOB...
......

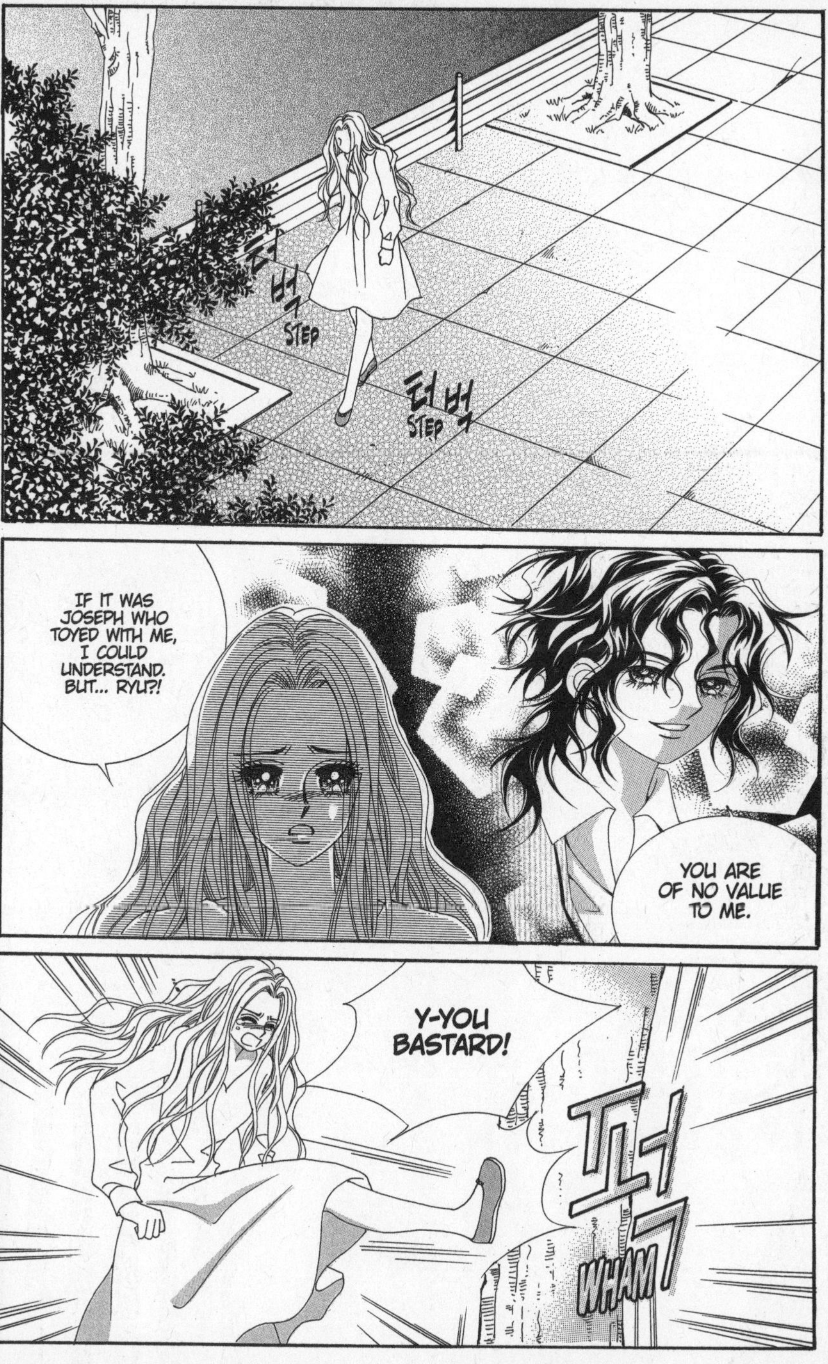
터벅
STEP
터벅
STEP
IF IT WAS JOSEPH WHO TOYED WITH ME, I COULD UNDERSTAND. BUT... RYU?!
YOU ARE OF NO VALUE TO ME.
Y-YOU BASTARD!
퍽
WHAM

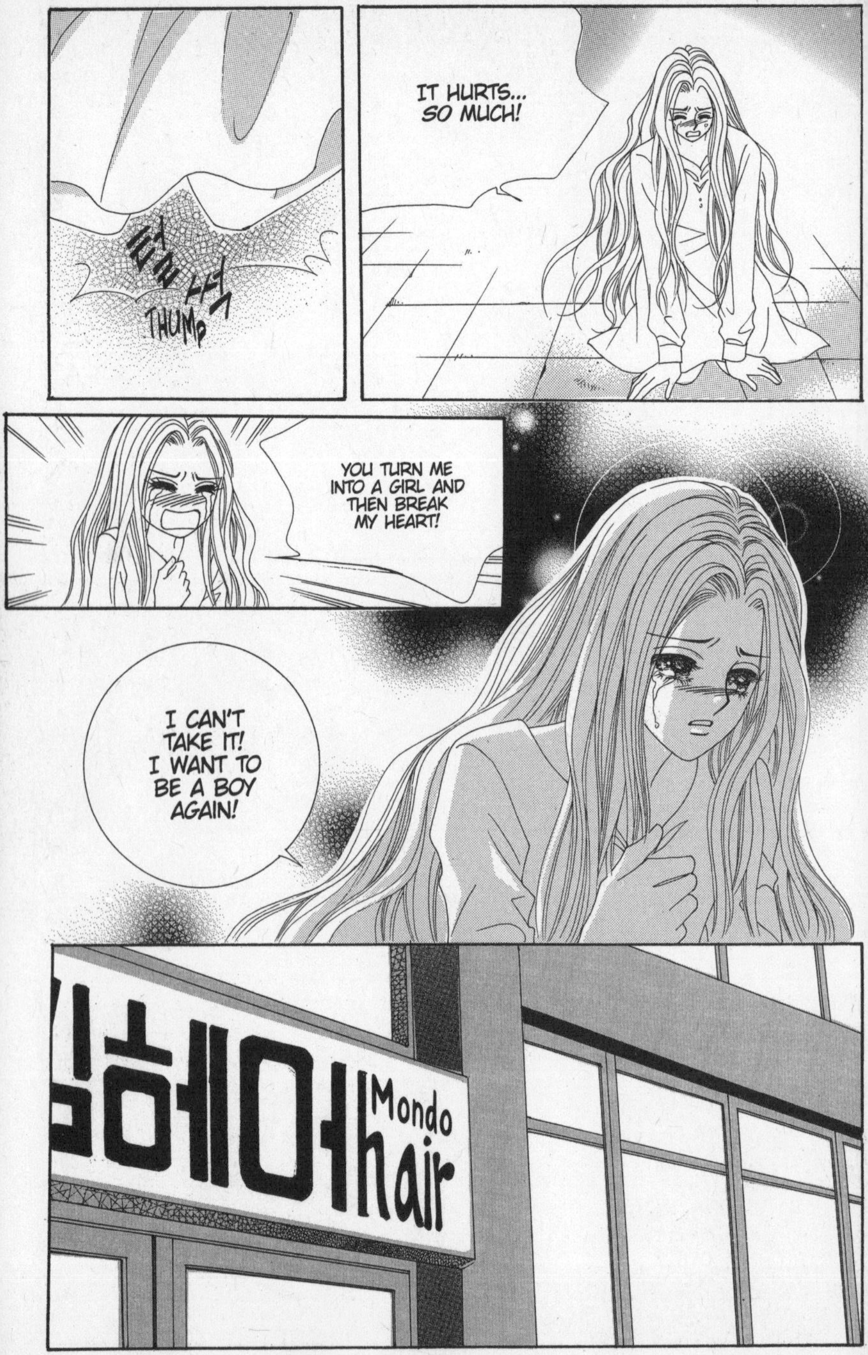
THUMP
IT HURTS... SO MUCH!
YOU TURN ME INTO A GIRL AND THEN BREAK MY HEART!
I CAN'T TAKE IT! I WANT TO BE A BOY AGAIN!
Mondo hair

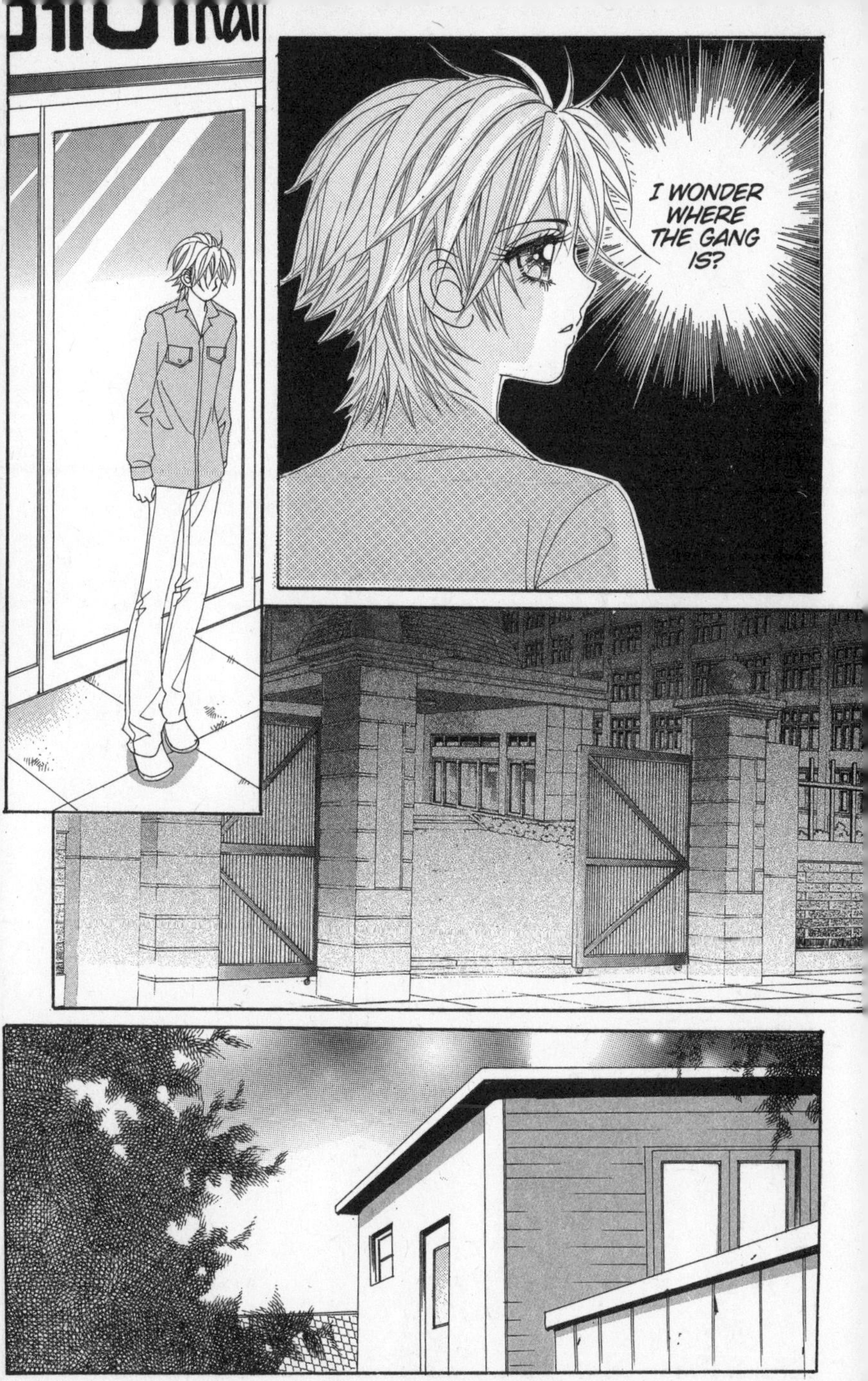
I WONDER WHERE THE GANG IS?

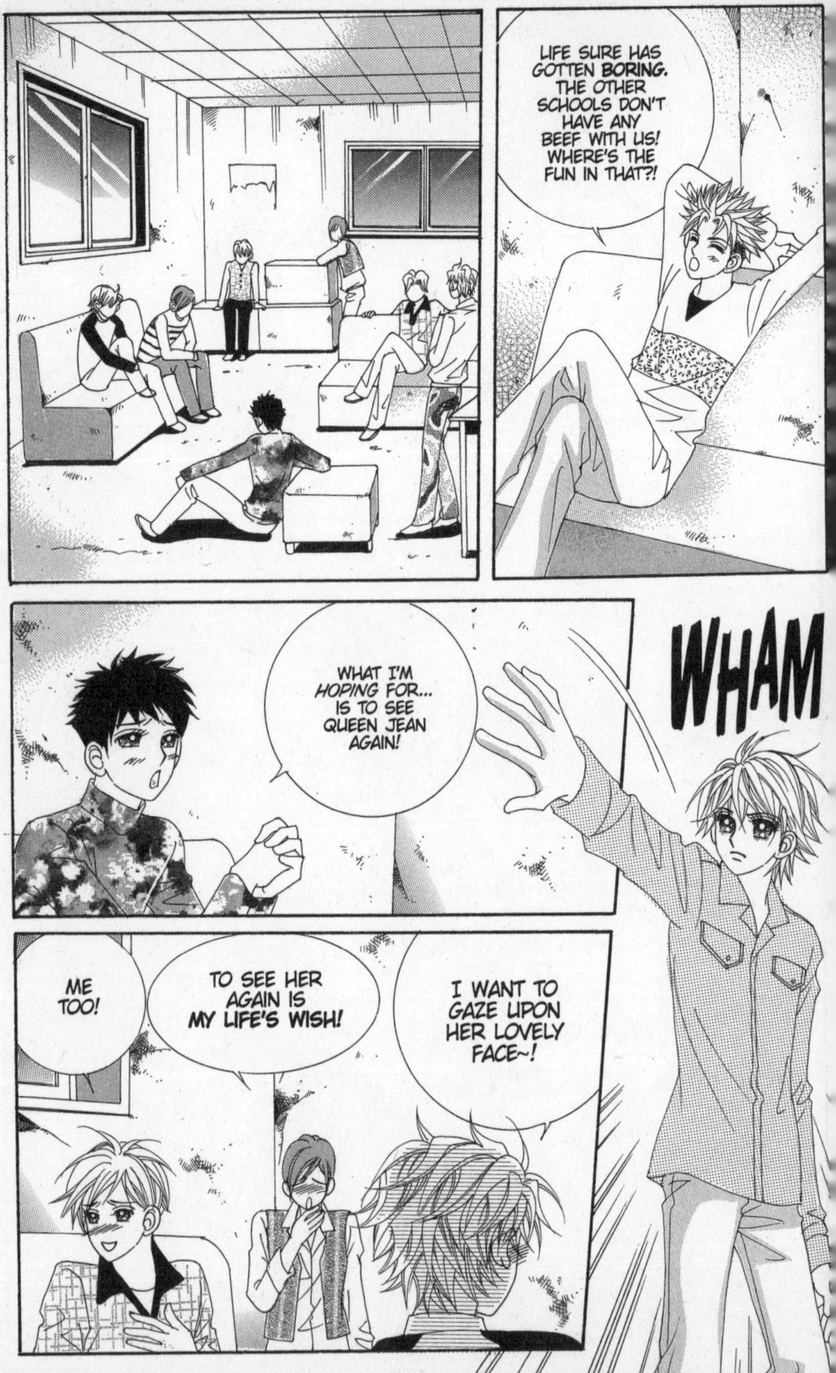
LIFE SURE HAS GOTTEN BORING. THE OTHER SCHOOLS DON'T HAVE ANY BEEF WITH US! WHERE'S THE FUN IN THAT?!
WHAT I'M HOPING FOR... IS TO SEE QUEEN JEAN AGAIN!
WHAM
ME TOO!
TO SEE HER AGAIN IS MY LIFE'S WISH!
I WANT TO GAZE UPON HER LOVELY FACE~!

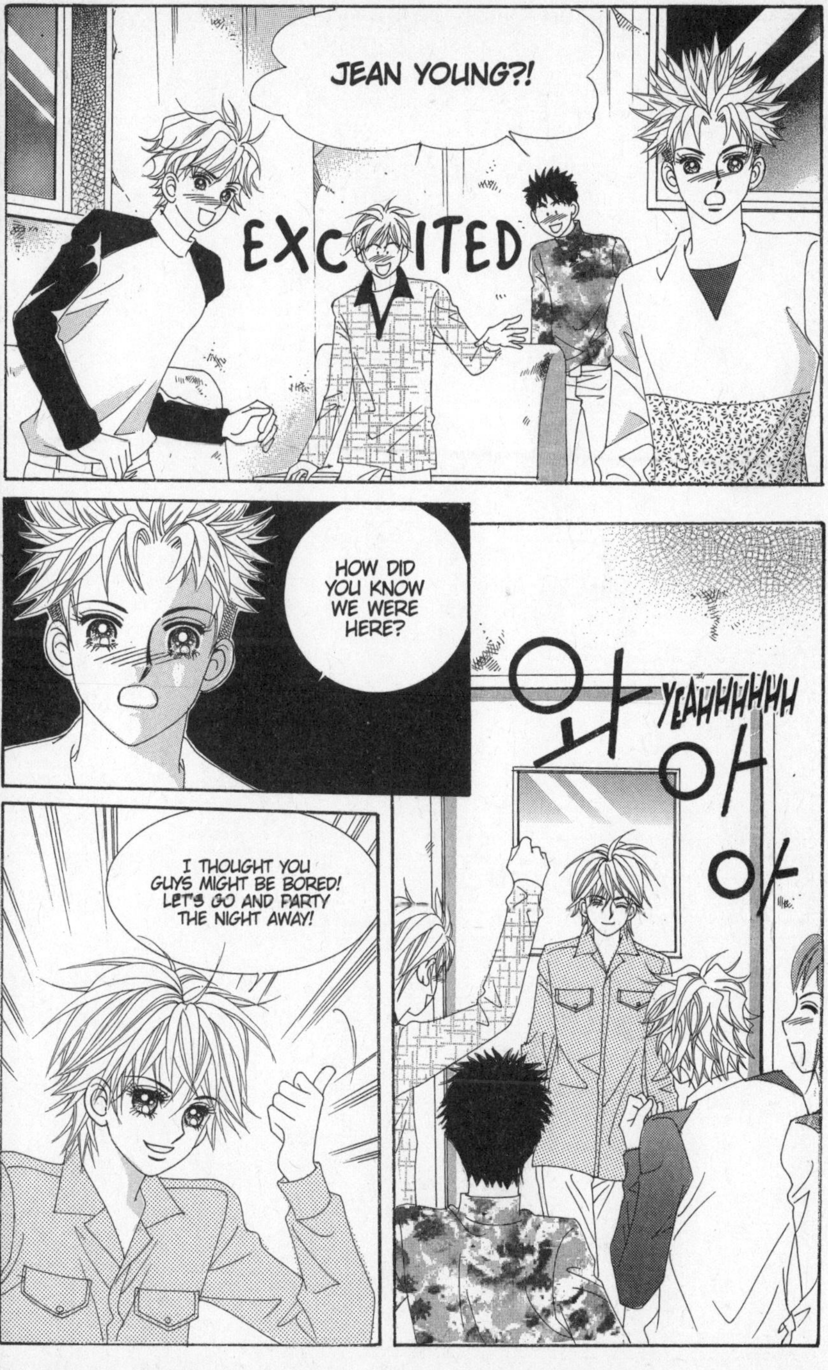
JEAN YOUNG?!
EXCITED
HOW DID YOU KNOW WE WERE HERE?
I THOUGHT YOU GUYS MIGHT BE BORED! LET'S GO AND PARTY THE NIGHT AWAY!
와아아
YEAHHHHHH

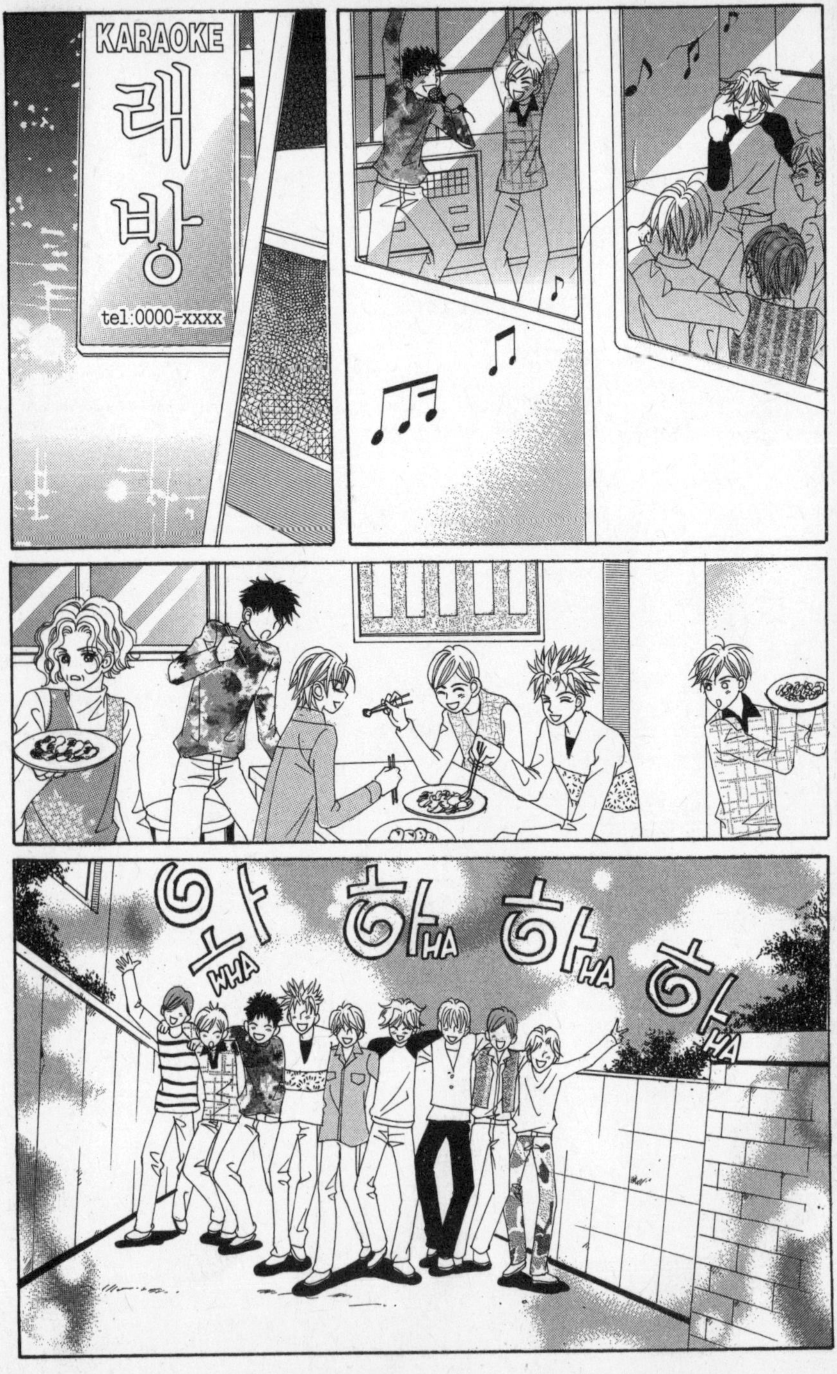
KARAOKE
래방
tel:0000-xxxx
와 WHA
하 HA
하 HA
하 HA

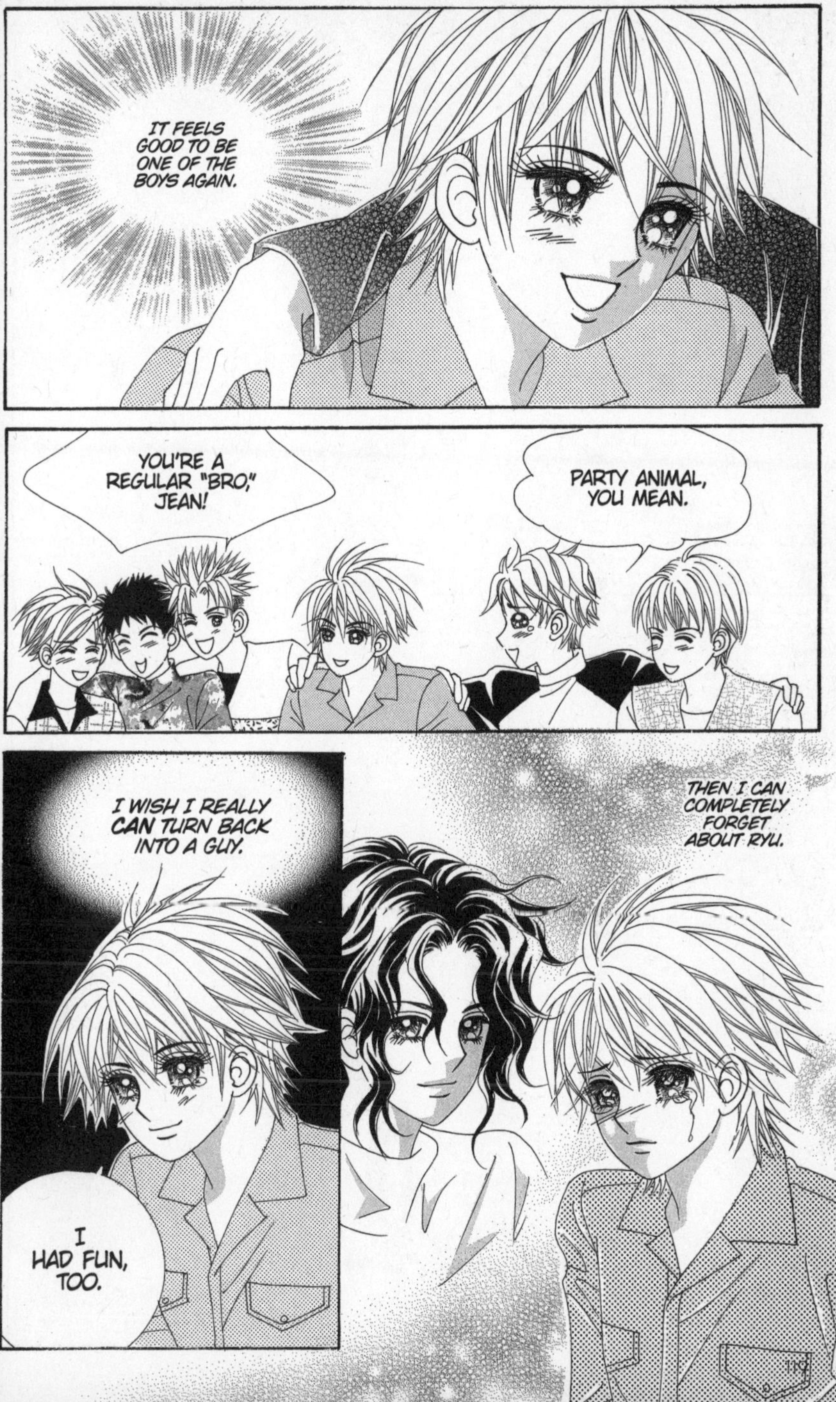
IT FEELS GOOD TO BE ONE OF THE BOYS AGAIN.
YOU'RE A REGULAR "BRO," JEAN!
PARTY ANIMAL, YOU MEAN.
I WISH I REALLY CAN TURN BACK INTO A GUY.
I HAD FUN, TOO.
THEN I CAN COMPLETELY FORGET ABOUT RYU.

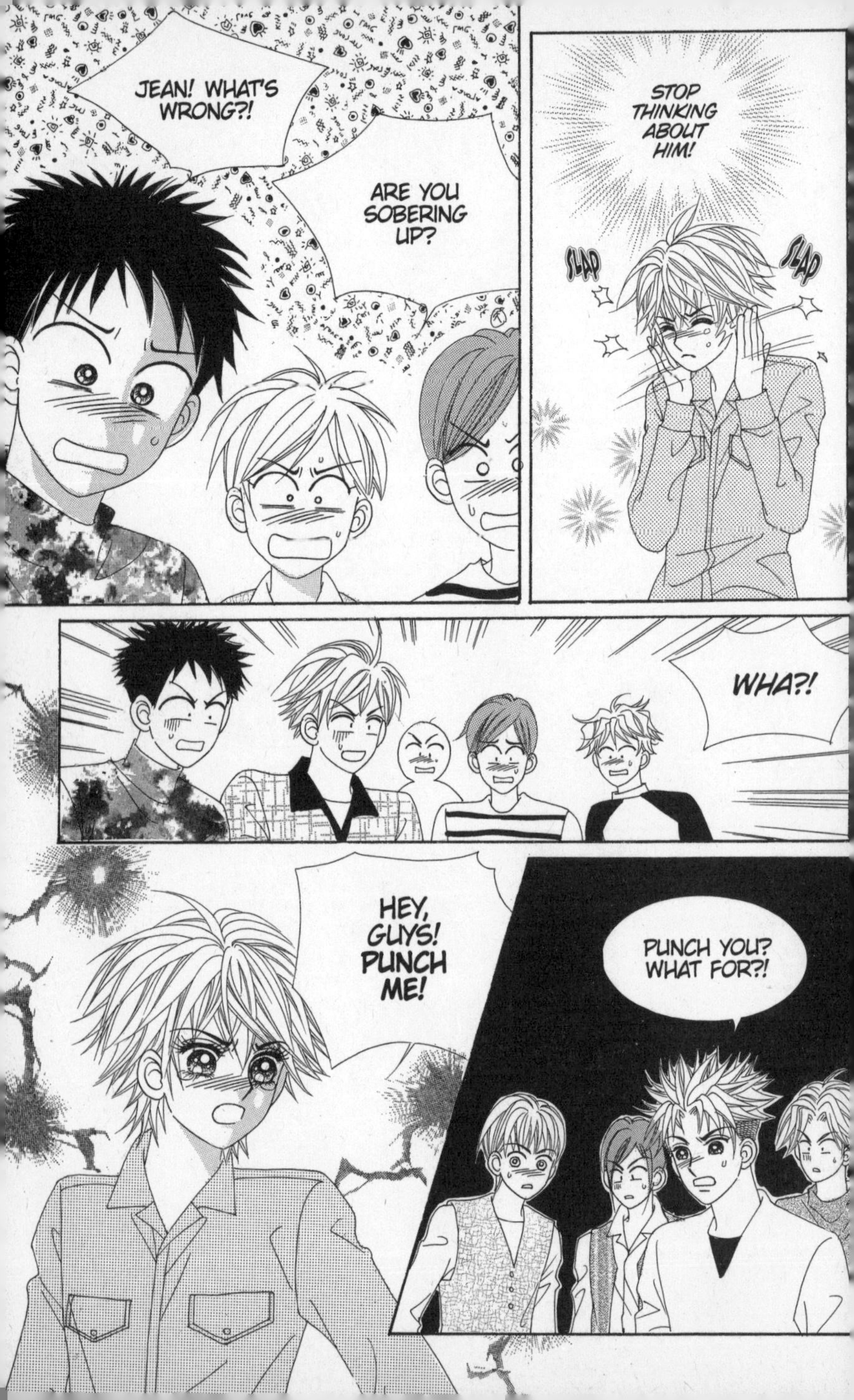
JEAN! WHAT'S WRONG?!
ARE YOU SOBERING UP?
STOP THINKING ABOUT HIM!
SLAP
SLAP
WHA?!
HEY, GUYS! PUNCH ME!
PUNCH YOU? WHAT FOR?!

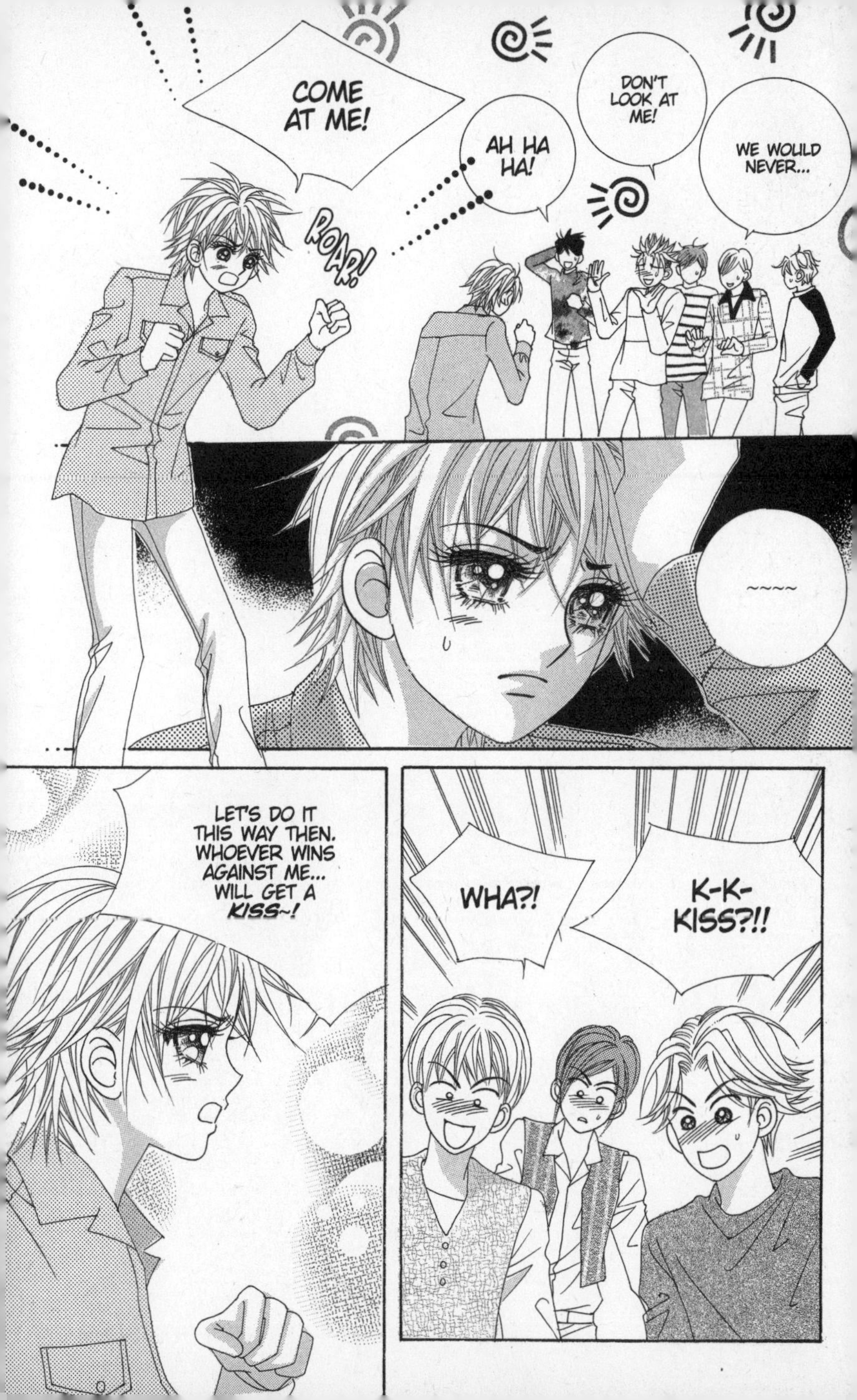
COME AT ME!
ROAR!
AH HA HA!
DON'T LOOK AT ME!
WE WOULD NEVER...
~~~~
LET'S DO IT THIS WAY THEN. WHOEVER WINS AGAINST ME... WILL GET A KISS~!
WHA?!
K-K-KISS?!!
~~~~

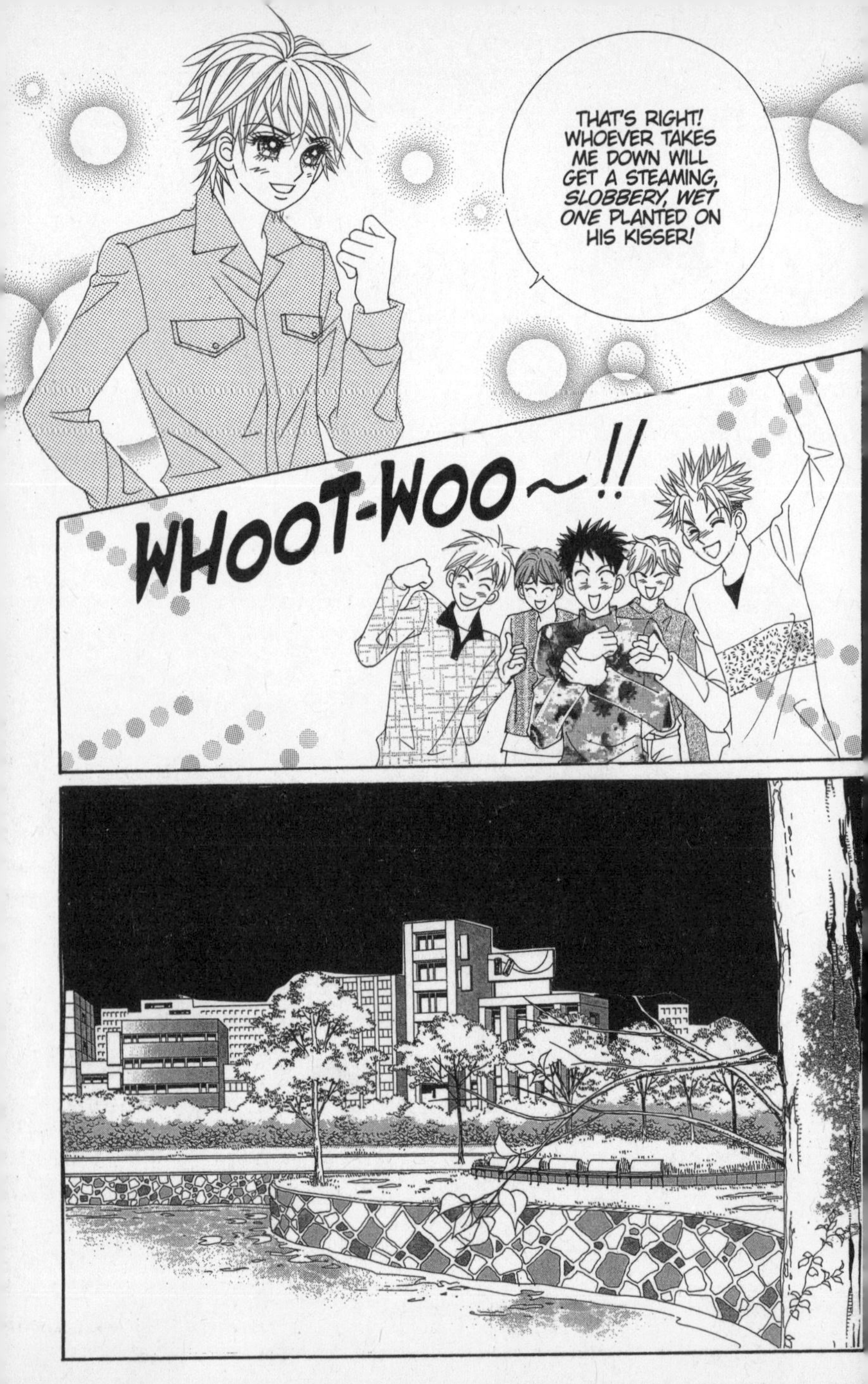
THAT'S RIGHT! WHOEVER TAKES ME DOWN WILL GET A STEAMING, *SLOBBERY, WET* ONE PLANTED ON HIS KISSER!
WHOOT-WOO~!!

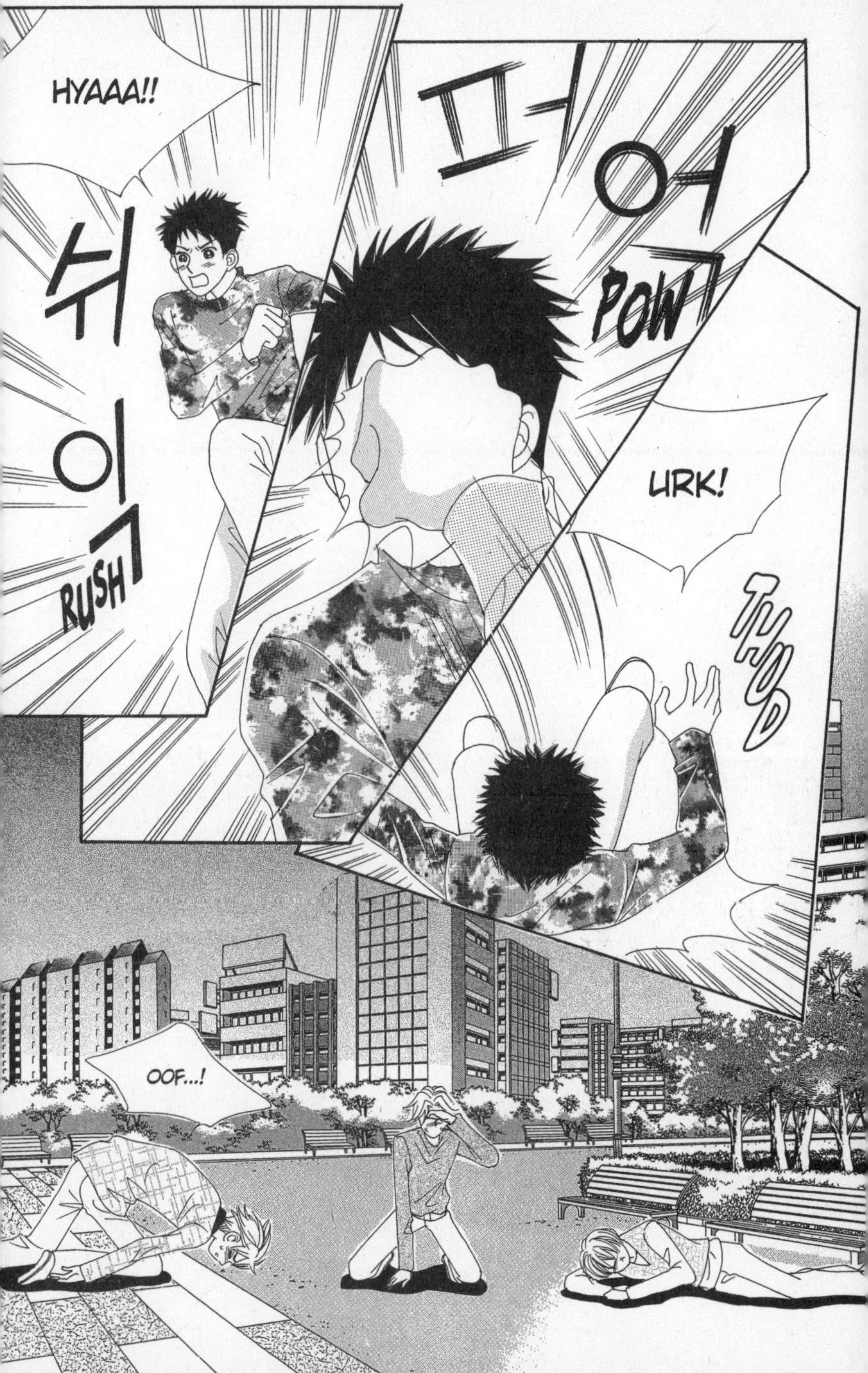
HYAAA!!
쉬익
RUSH
퍼억
POW
URK!
THUD
OOF...!

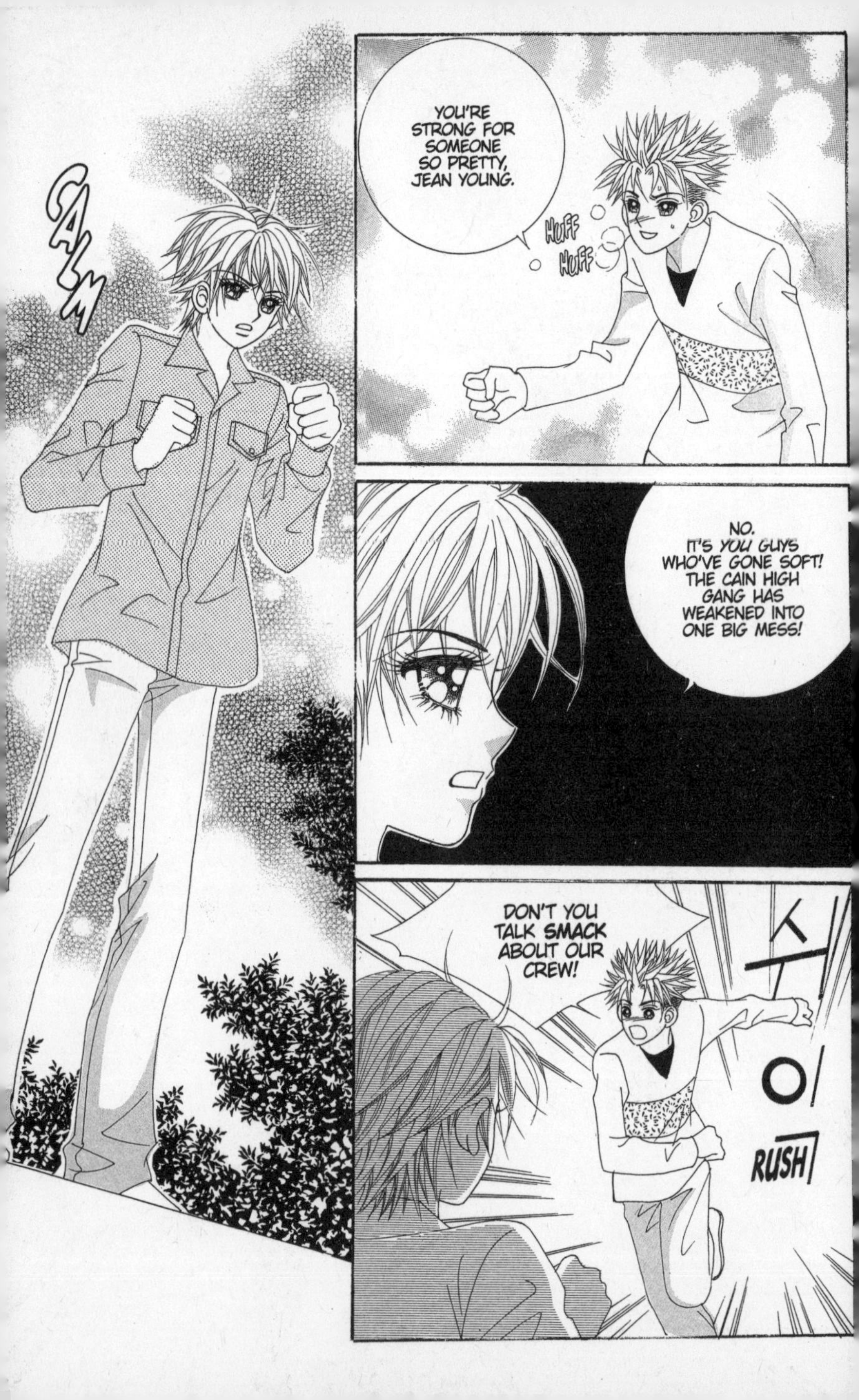
CALM
YOU'RE STRONG FOR SOMEONE SO PRETTY, JEAN YOUNG.
HUFF HUFF
NO. IT'S *YOU* GUYS WHO'VE GONE SOFT! THE CAIN HIGH GANG HAS WEAKENED INTO ONE BIG MESS!
DON'T YOU TALK **SMACK** ABOUT OUR CREW!
RUSH

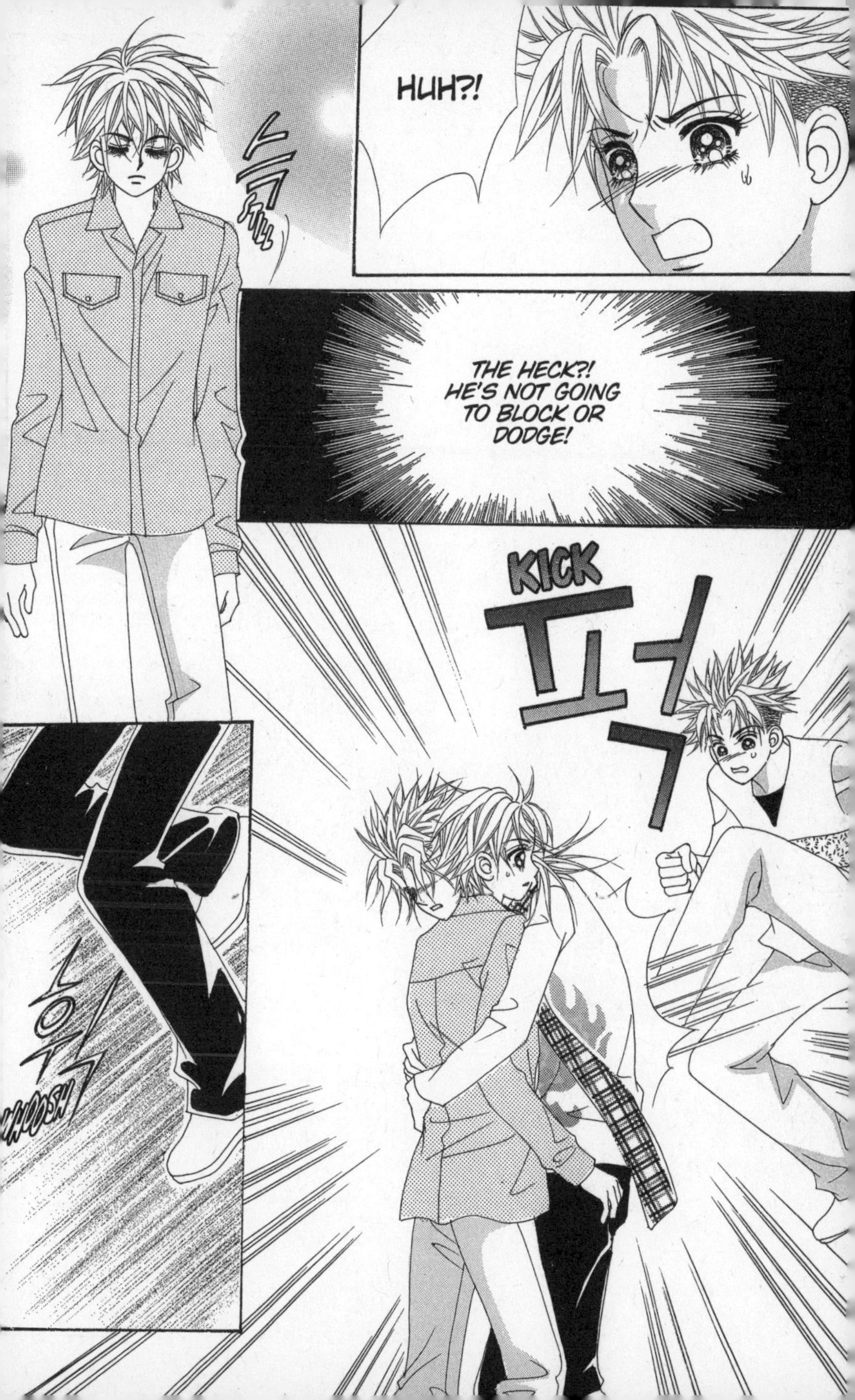

HUH?!
THE HECK?! HE'S NOT GOING TO BLOCK OR DODGE!
KICK
WHOOSH

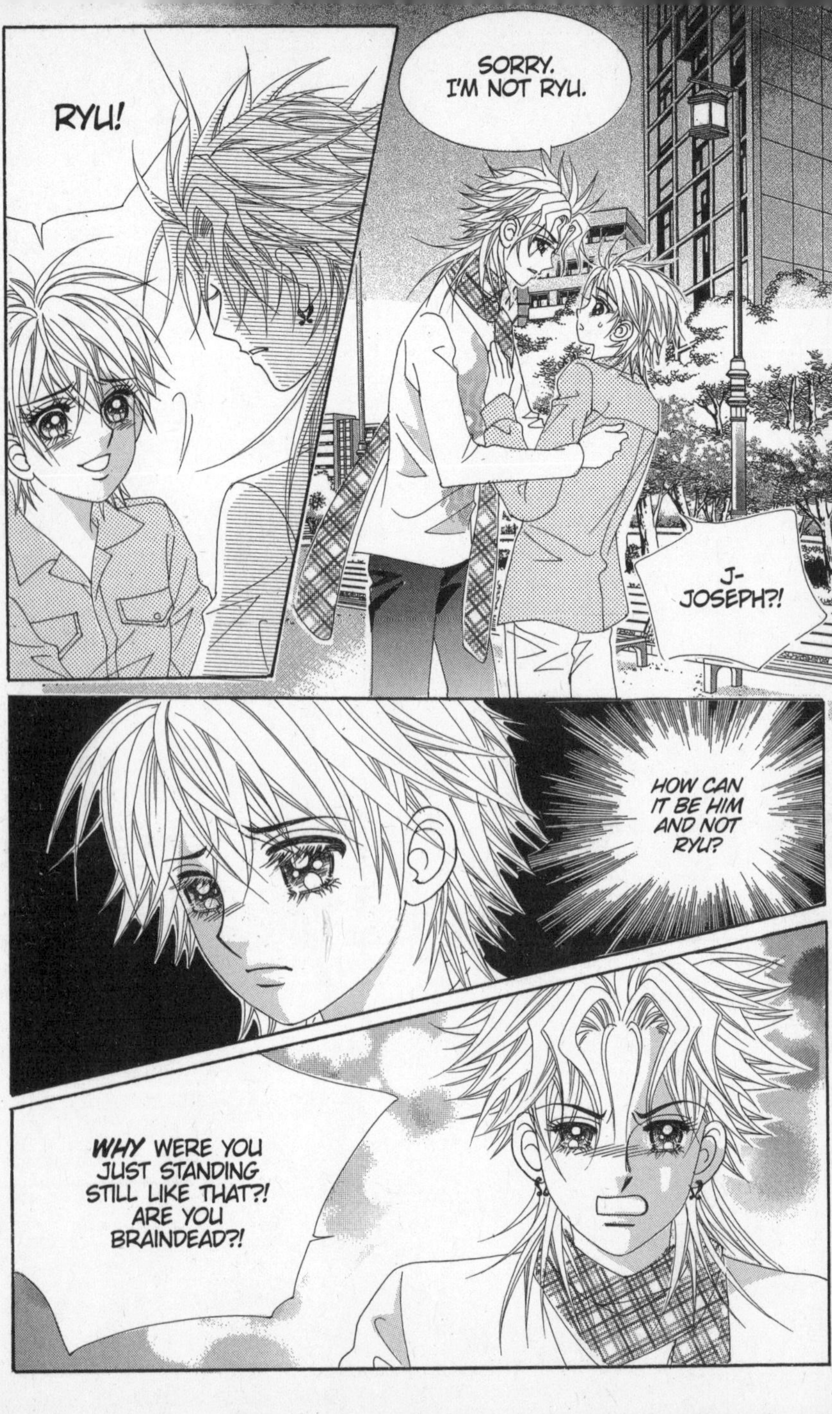
RYU!
SORRY. I'M NOT RYU.
J-JOSEPH?!
HOW CAN IT BE HIM AND NOT RYU?
WHY WERE YOU JUST STANDING STILL LIKE THAT?! ARE YOU BRAINDEAD?!

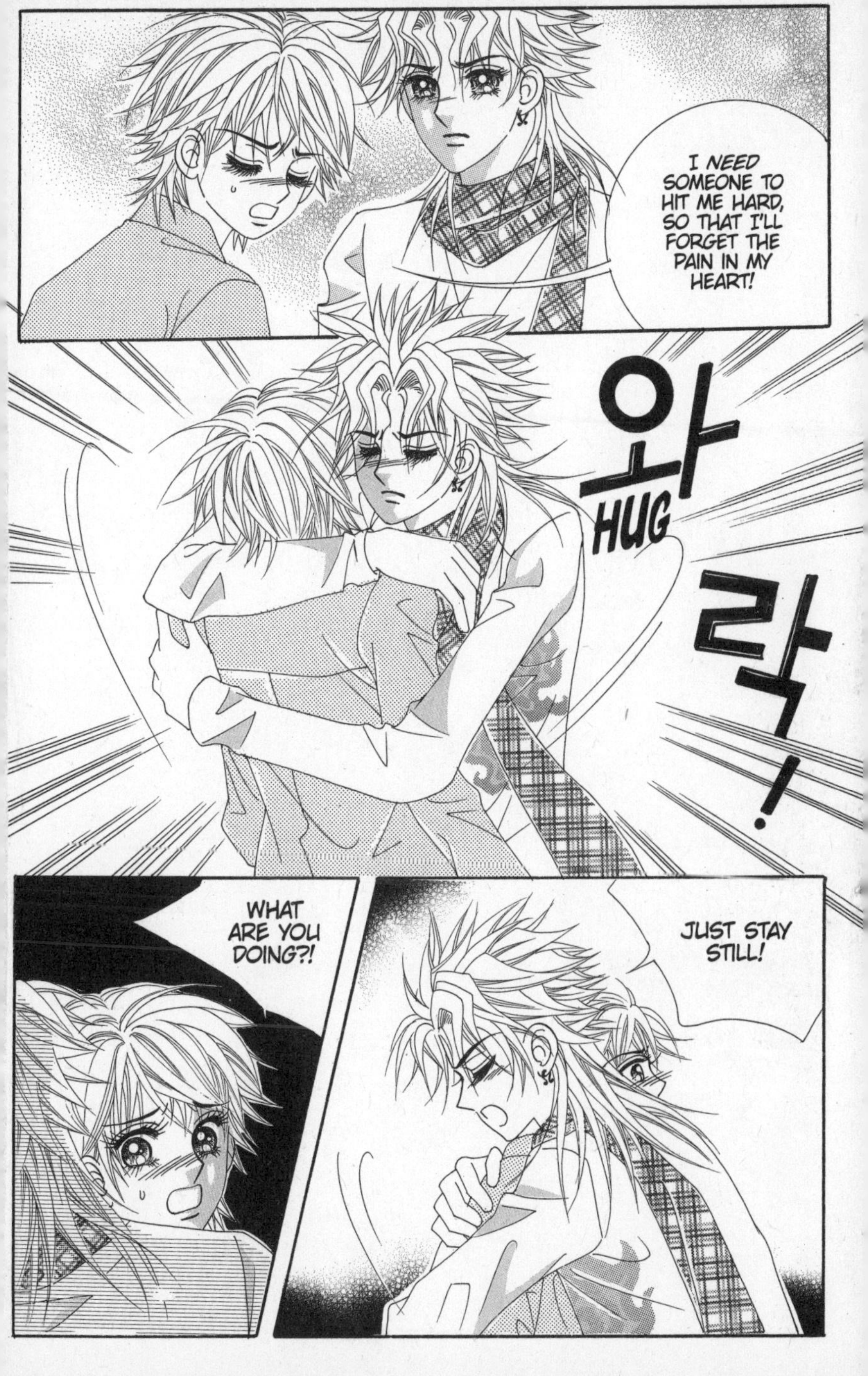
I NEED SOMEONE TO HIT ME HARD, SO THAT I'LL FORGET THE PAIN IN MY HEART!
와락!
HUG
WHAT ARE YOU DOING?!
JUST STAY STILL!

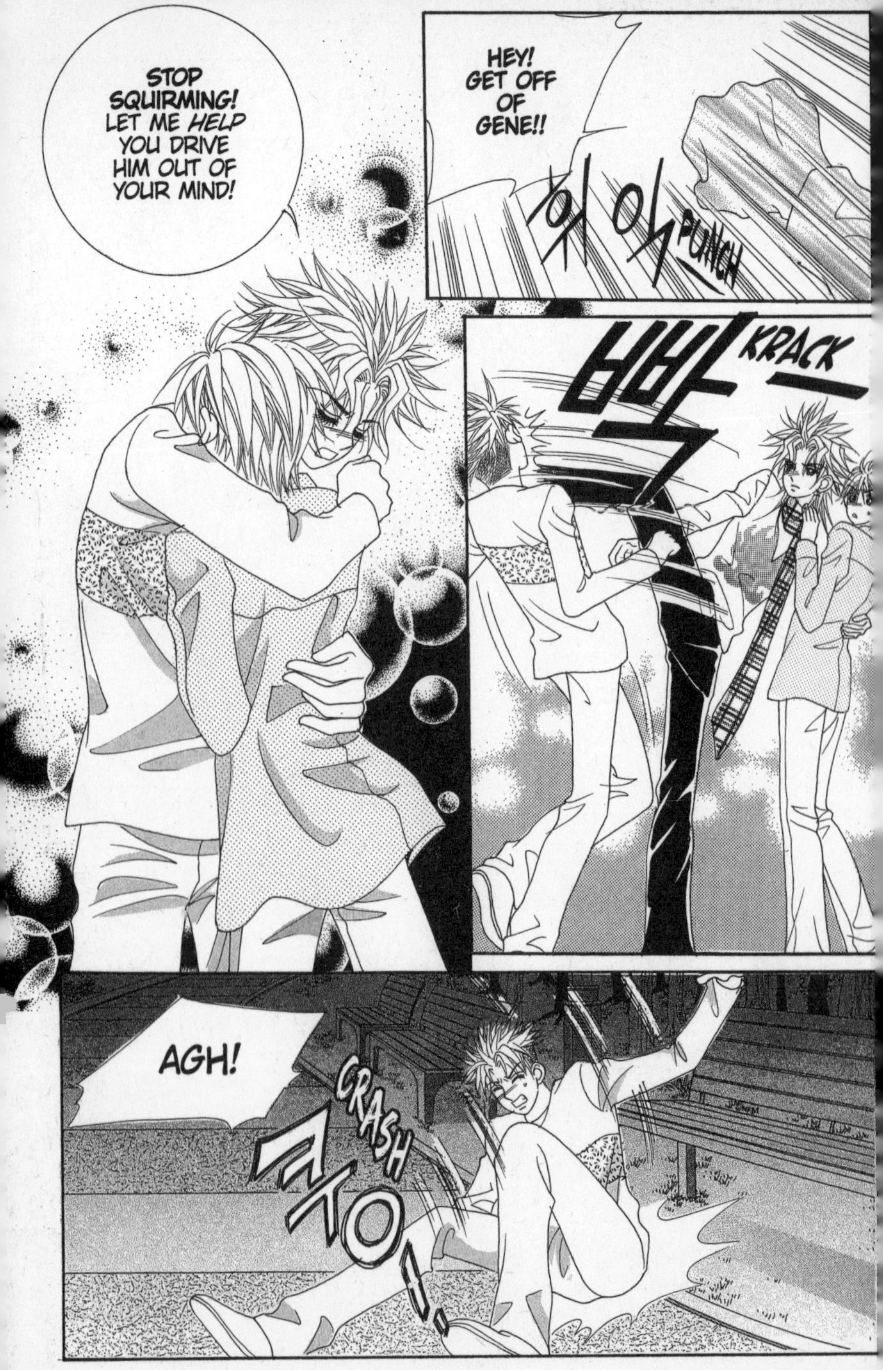
STOP SQUIRMING! LET ME *HELP* YOU DRIVE HIM OUT OF YOUR MIND!
HEY! GET OFF OF GENE!!
PUNCH
KRACK
AGH!
CRASH

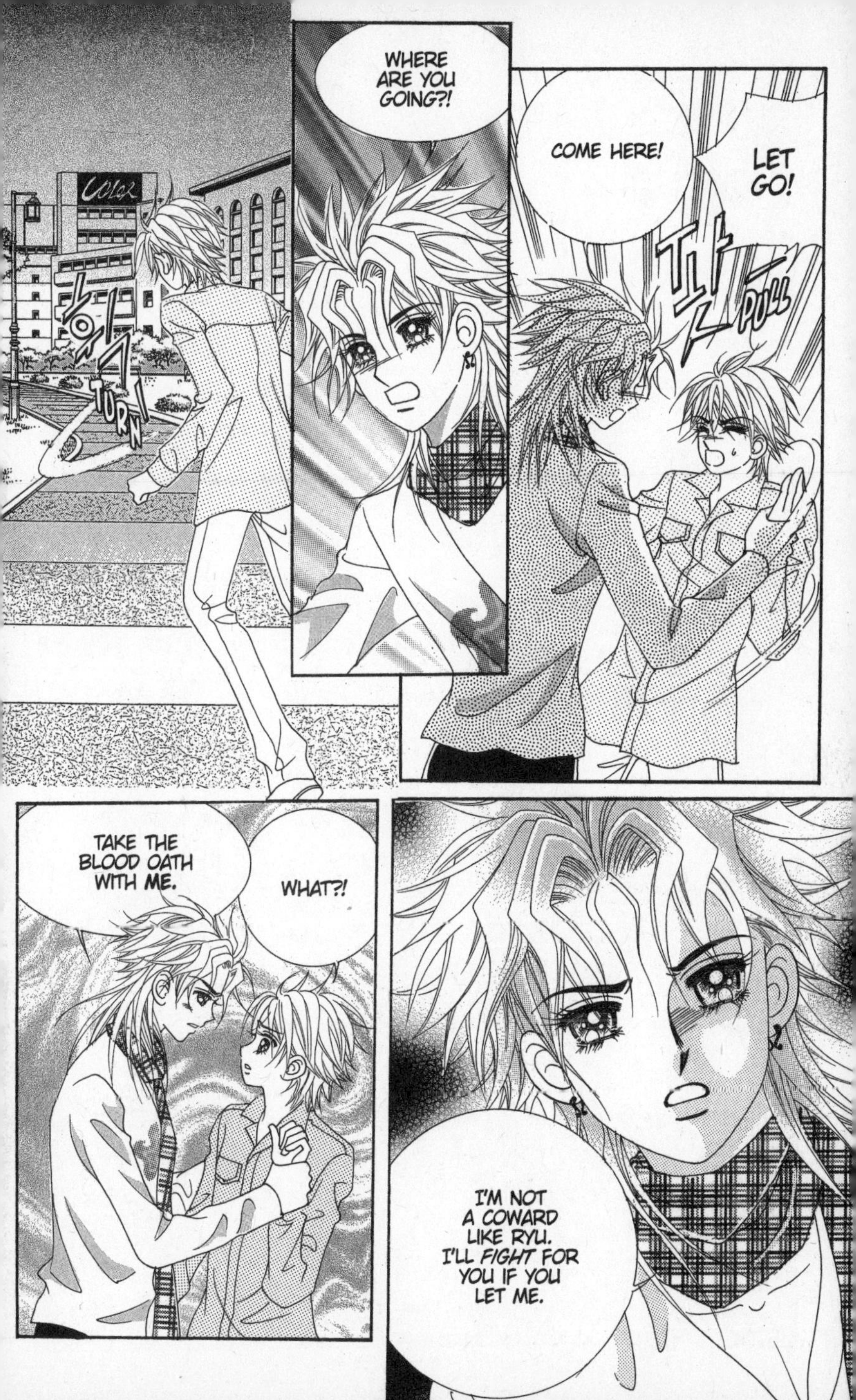
TURN!
WHERE ARE YOU GOING?!
COME HERE!
LET GO!
PULL
TAKE THE BLOOD OATH WITH ME.
WHAT?!
I'M NOT A COWARD LIKE RYU. I'LL *FIGHT* FOR YOU IF YOU LET ME.

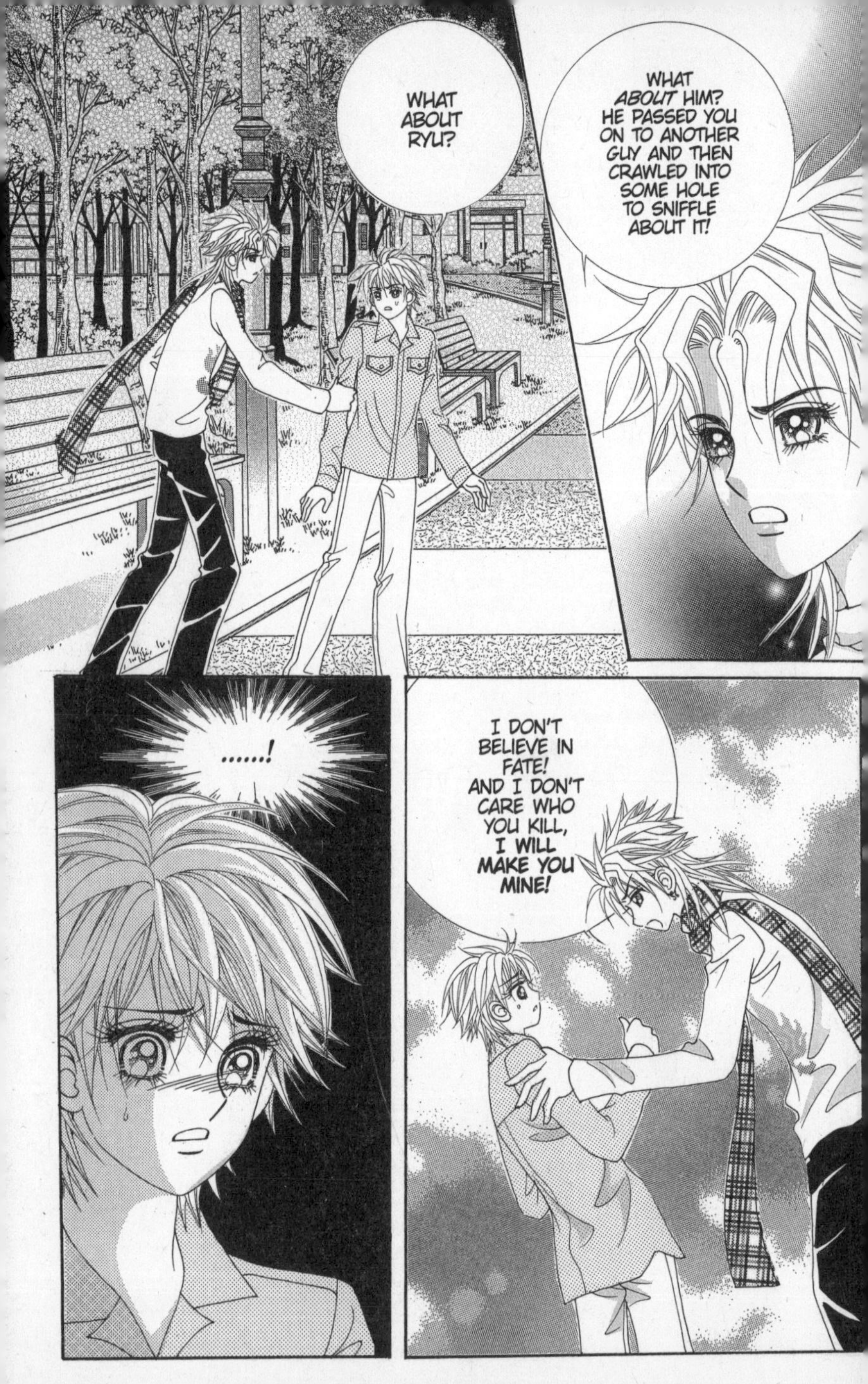
WHAT ABOUT RYU?
WHAT *ABOUT* HIM? HE PASSED YOU ON TO ANOTHER GUY AND THEN CRAWLED INTO SOME HOLE TO SNIFFLE ABOUT IT!
......!
I DON'T BELIEVE IN FATE! AND I DON'T CARE WHO YOU KILL, **I WILL MAKE YOU MINE!**

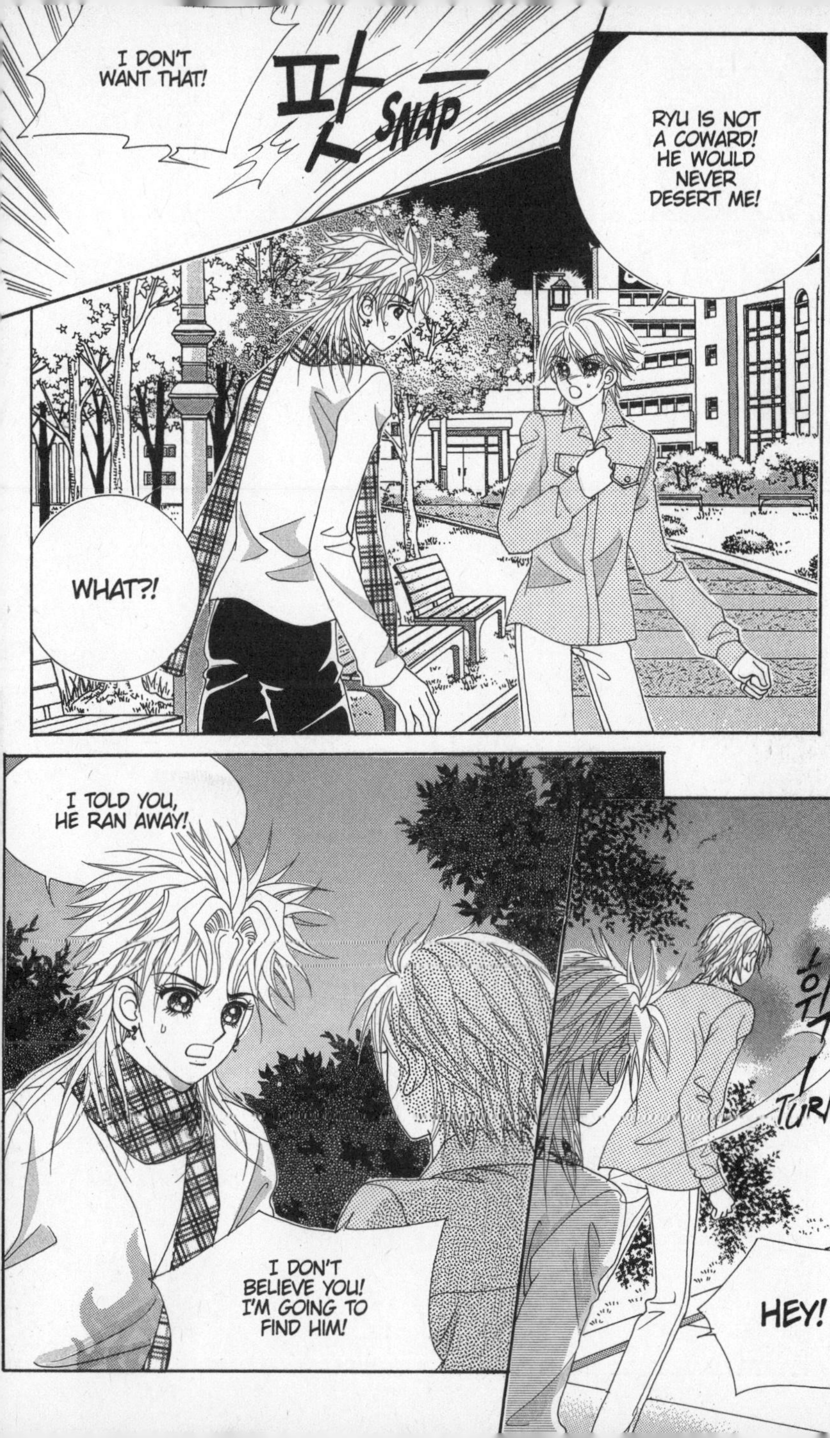
I DON'T WANT THAT!
팍
SNAP
RYU IS NOT A COWARD! HE WOULD NEVER DESERT ME!
WHAT?!
I TOLD YOU, HE RAN AWAY!
I DON'T BELIEVE YOU! I'M GOING TO FIND HIM!
TURN
HEY!

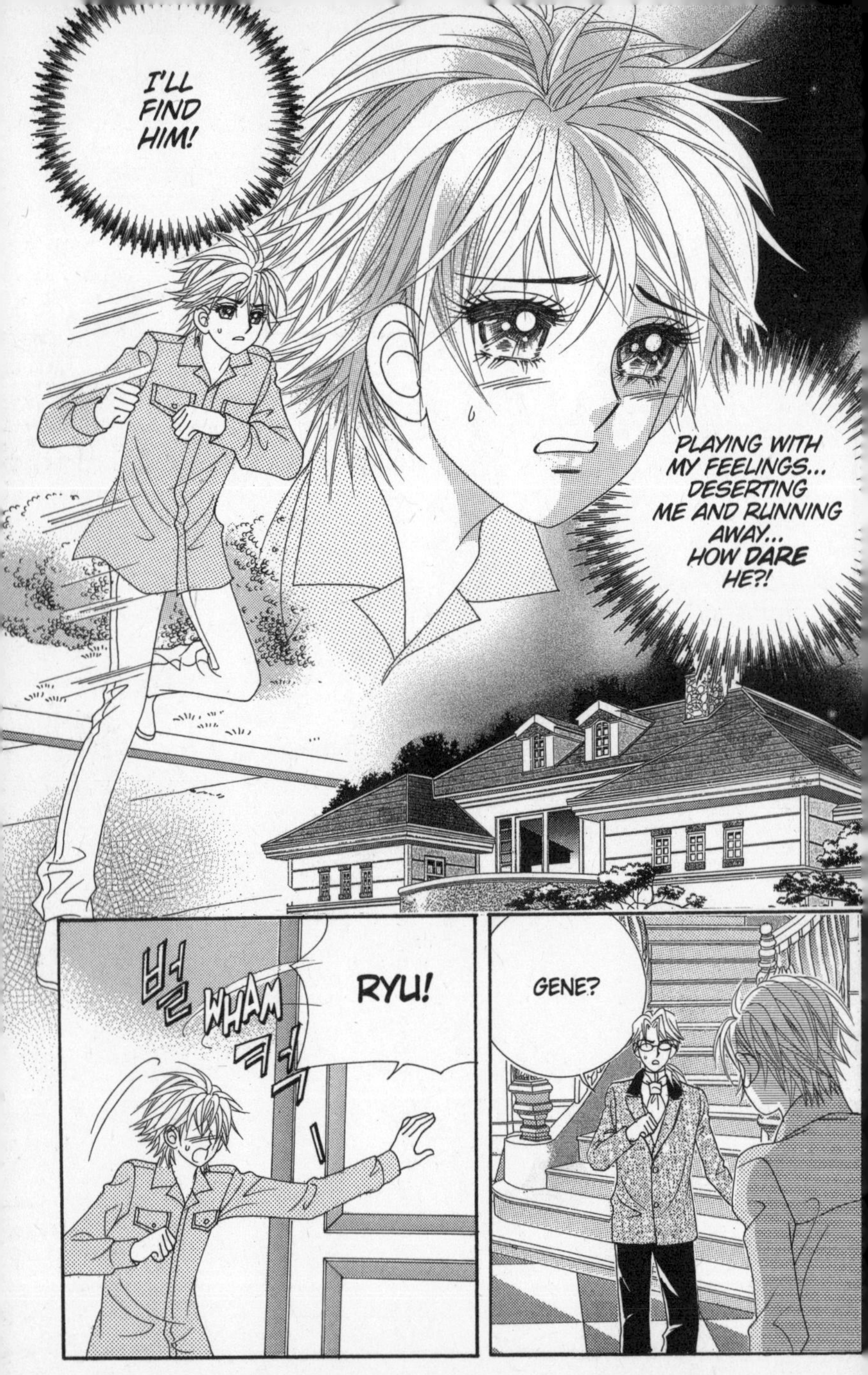
I'LL FIND HIM!
PLAYING WITH MY FEELINGS... DESERTING ME AND RUNNING AWAY... HOW DARE HE?!
WHAM
RYU!
GENE?

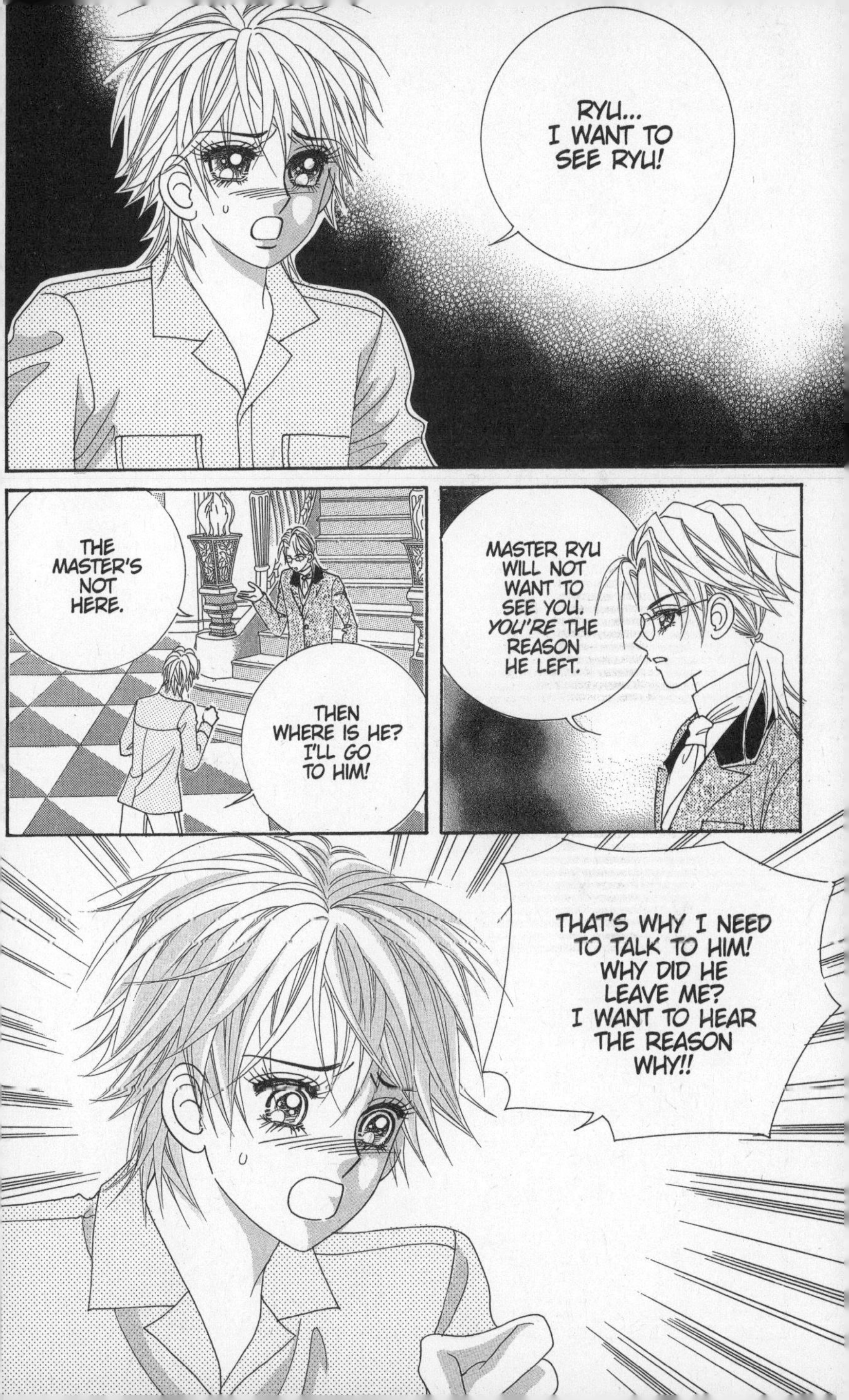
RYU... I WANT TO SEE RYU!
THE MASTER'S NOT HERE.
THEN WHERE IS HE? I'LL GO TO HIM!
MASTER RYU WILL NOT WANT TO SEE YOU. *YOU'RE* THE REASON HE LEFT.
THAT'S WHY I NEED TO TALK TO HIM! WHY DID HE LEAVE ME? I WANT TO HEAR THE REASON WHY!!

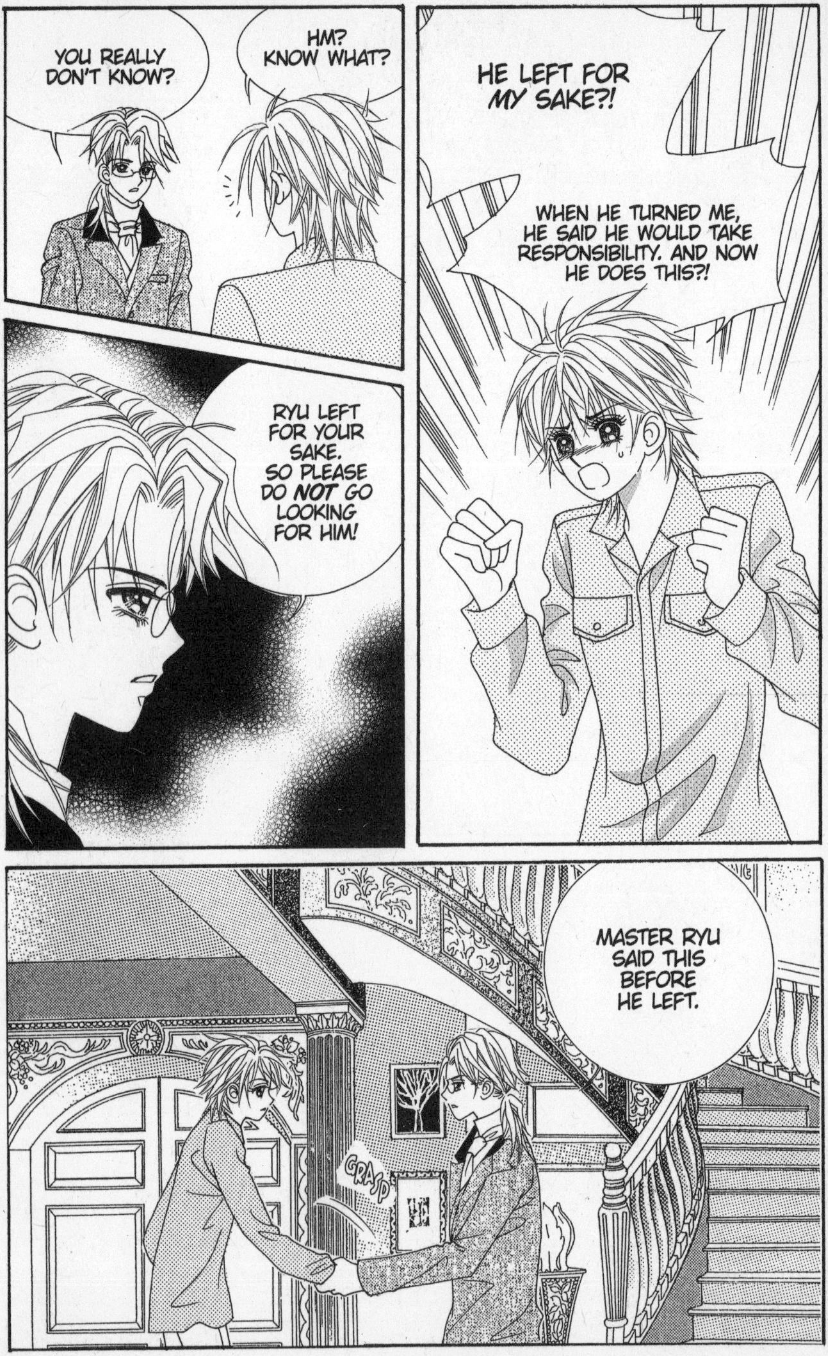
YOU REALLY DON'T KNOW?
HM? KNOW WHAT?
RYU LEFT FOR YOUR SAKE. SO PLEASE DO **NOT** GO LOOKING FOR HIM!
HE LEFT FOR *MY* SAKE?!
WHEN HE TURNED ME, HE SAID HE WOULD TAKE RESPONSIBILITY. AND NOW HE DOES THIS?!
MASTER RYU SAID THIS BEFORE HE LEFT.
GRASP

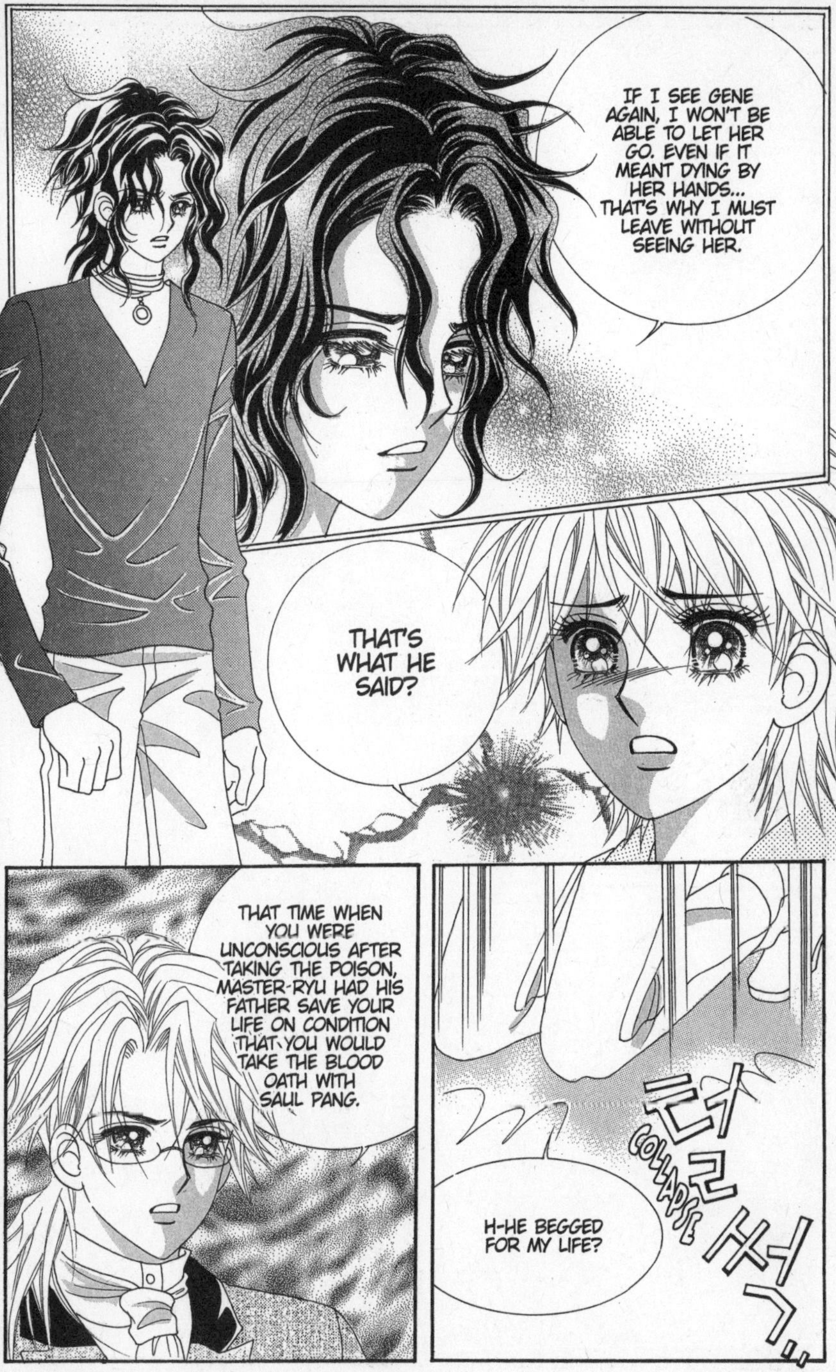
IF I SEE GENE AGAIN, I WON'T BE ABLE TO LET HER GO. EVEN IF IT MEANT DYING BY HER HANDS... THAT'S WHY I MUST LEAVE WITHOUT SEEING HER.
THAT'S WHAT HE SAID?
THAT TIME WHEN YOU WERE UNCONSCIOUS AFTER TAKING THE POISON, MASTER-RYU HAD HIS FATHER SAVE YOUR LIFE ON CONDITION THAT YOU WOULD TAKE THE BLOOD OATH WITH SAUL PANG.
COLLAPSE
H-HE BEGGED FOR MY LIFE?

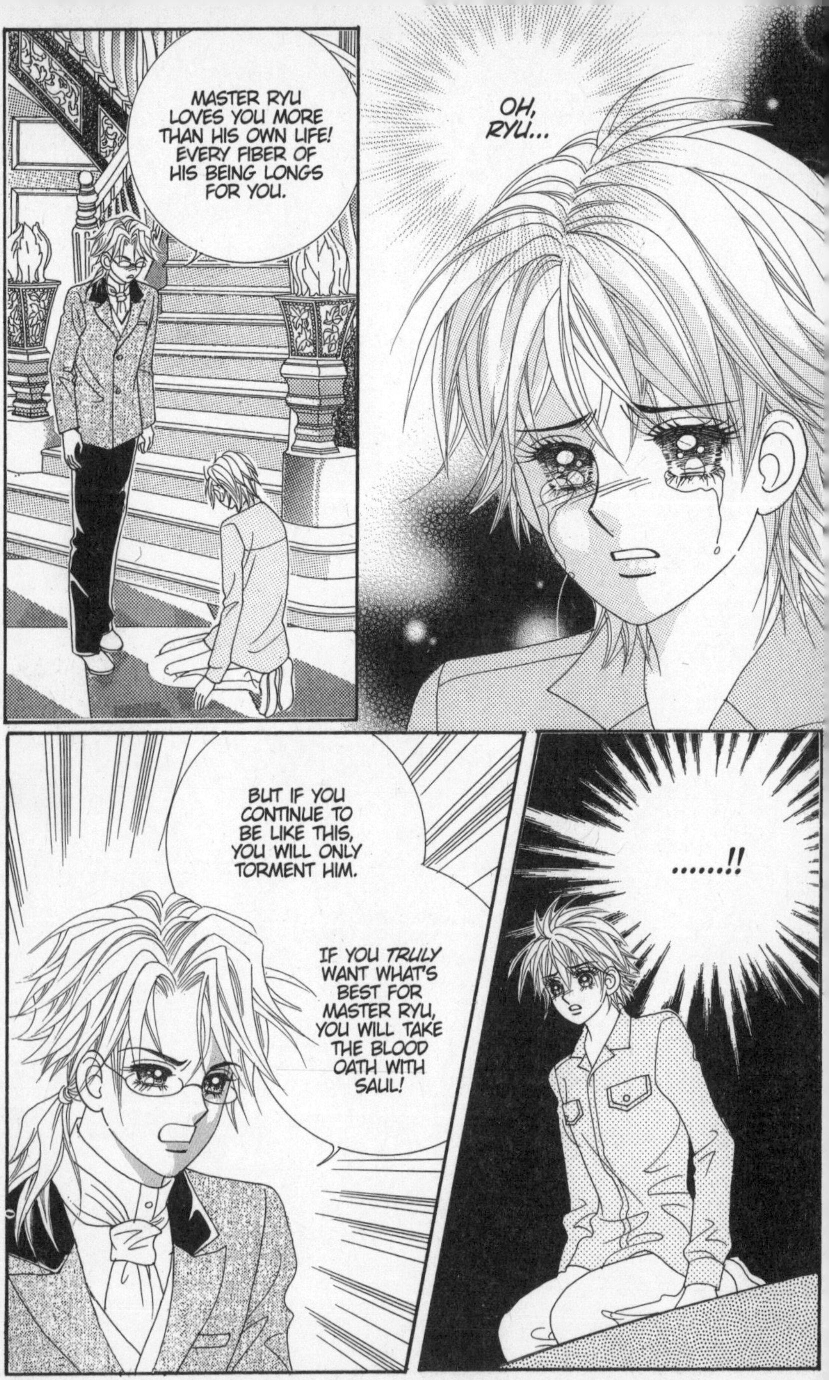
MASTER RYU LOVES YOU MORE THAN HIS OWN LIFE! EVERY FIBER OF HIS BEING LONGS FOR YOU.
OH, RYU...
BUT IF YOU CONTINUE TO BE LIKE THIS, YOU WILL ONLY TORMENT HIM.
IF YOU *TRULY* WANT WHAT'S BEST FOR MASTER RYU, YOU WILL TAKE THE BLOOD OATH WITH SAUL!
......!!

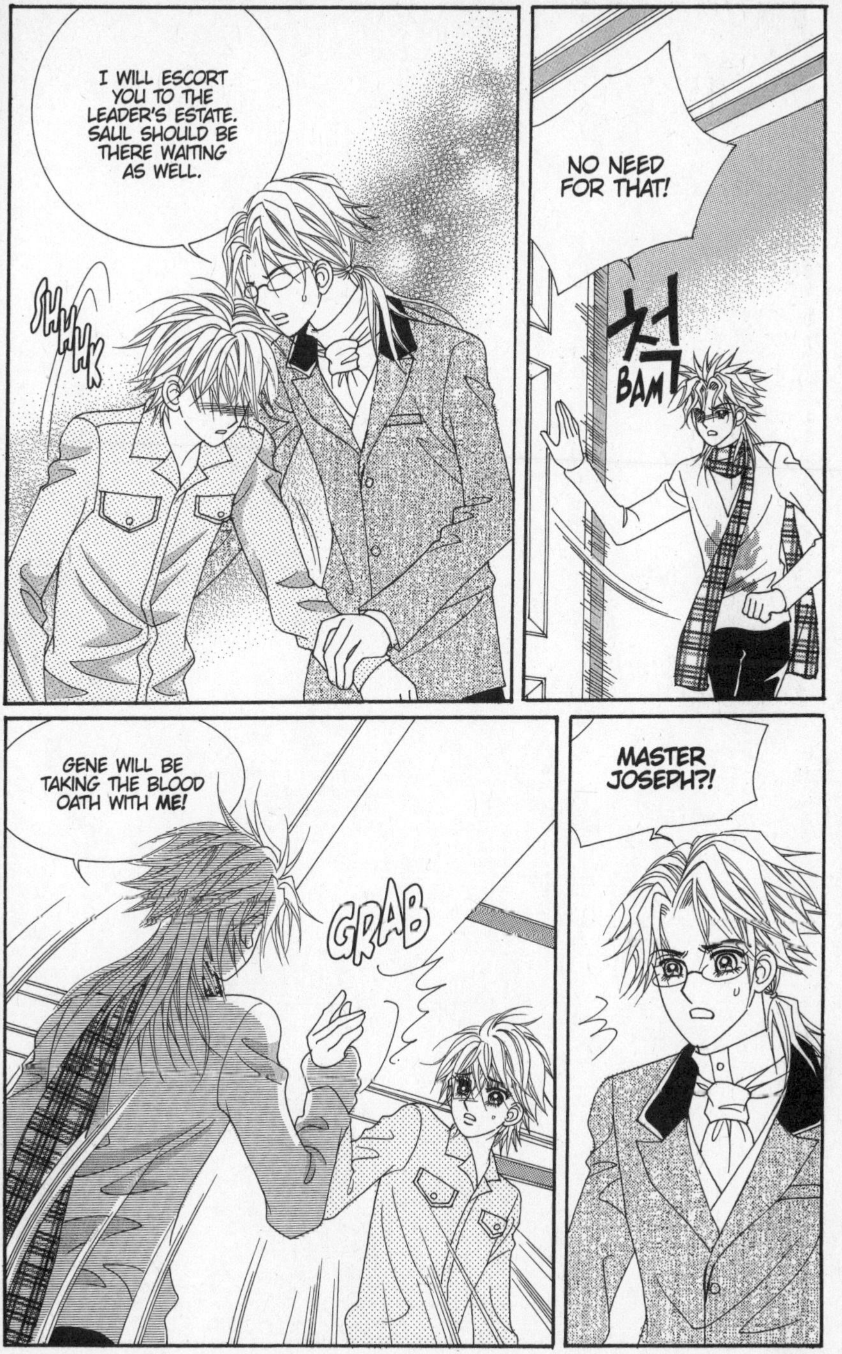
I WILL ESCORT YOU TO THE LEADER'S ESTATE. SAUL SHOULD BE THERE WAITING AS WELL.
SHHHK
NO NEED FOR THAT!
척
BAM
GENE WILL BE TAKING THE BLOOD OATH WITH ME!
GRAB
MASTER JOSEPH?!

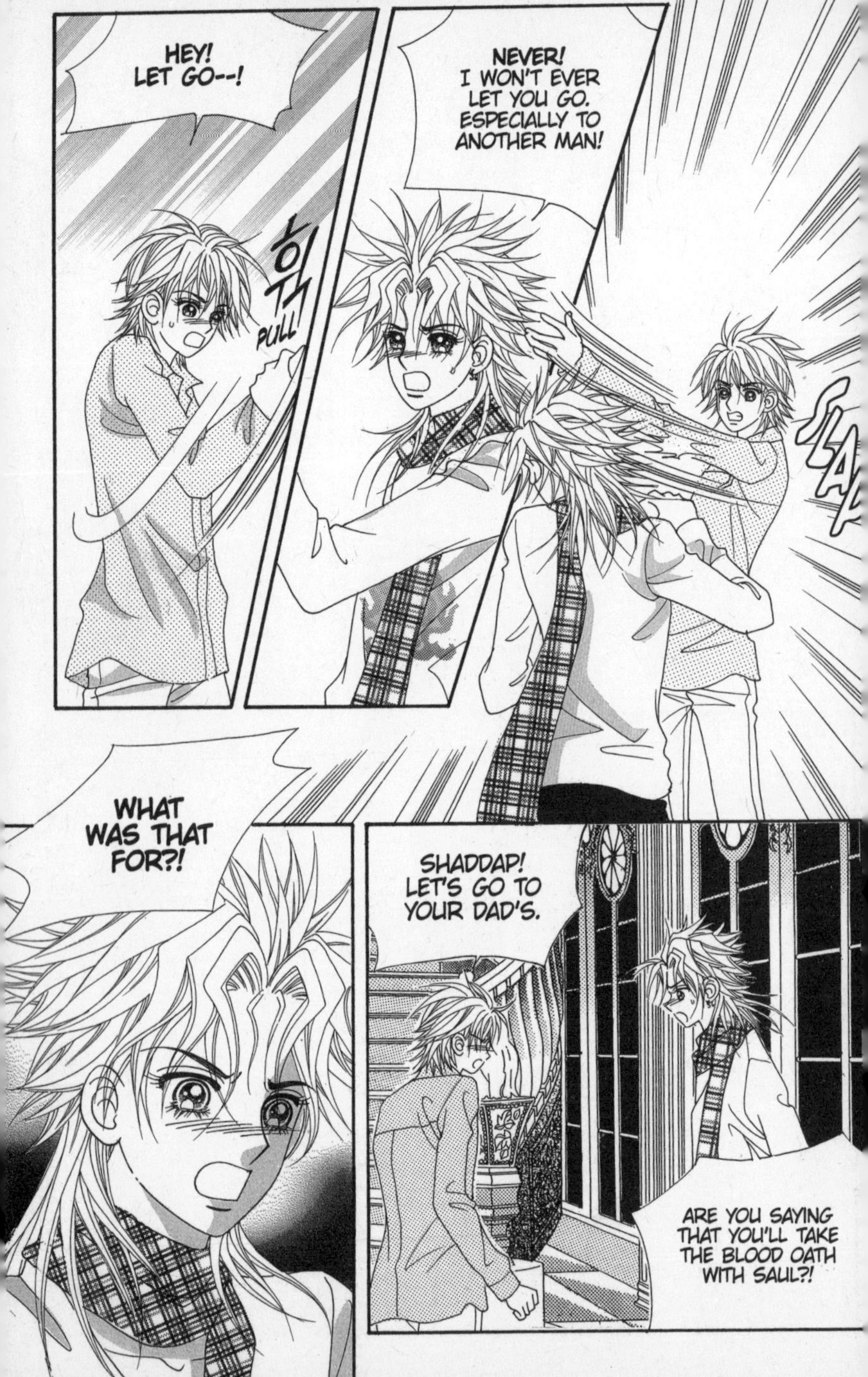
HEY! LET GO--!
PULL
NEVER! I WON'T EVER LET YOU GO. ESPECIALLY TO ANOTHER MAN!
SLAP
WHAT WAS THAT FOR?!
SHADDAP! LET'S GO TO YOUR DAD'S.
ARE YOU SAYING THAT YOU'LL TAKE THE BLOOD OATH WITH SAUL?!

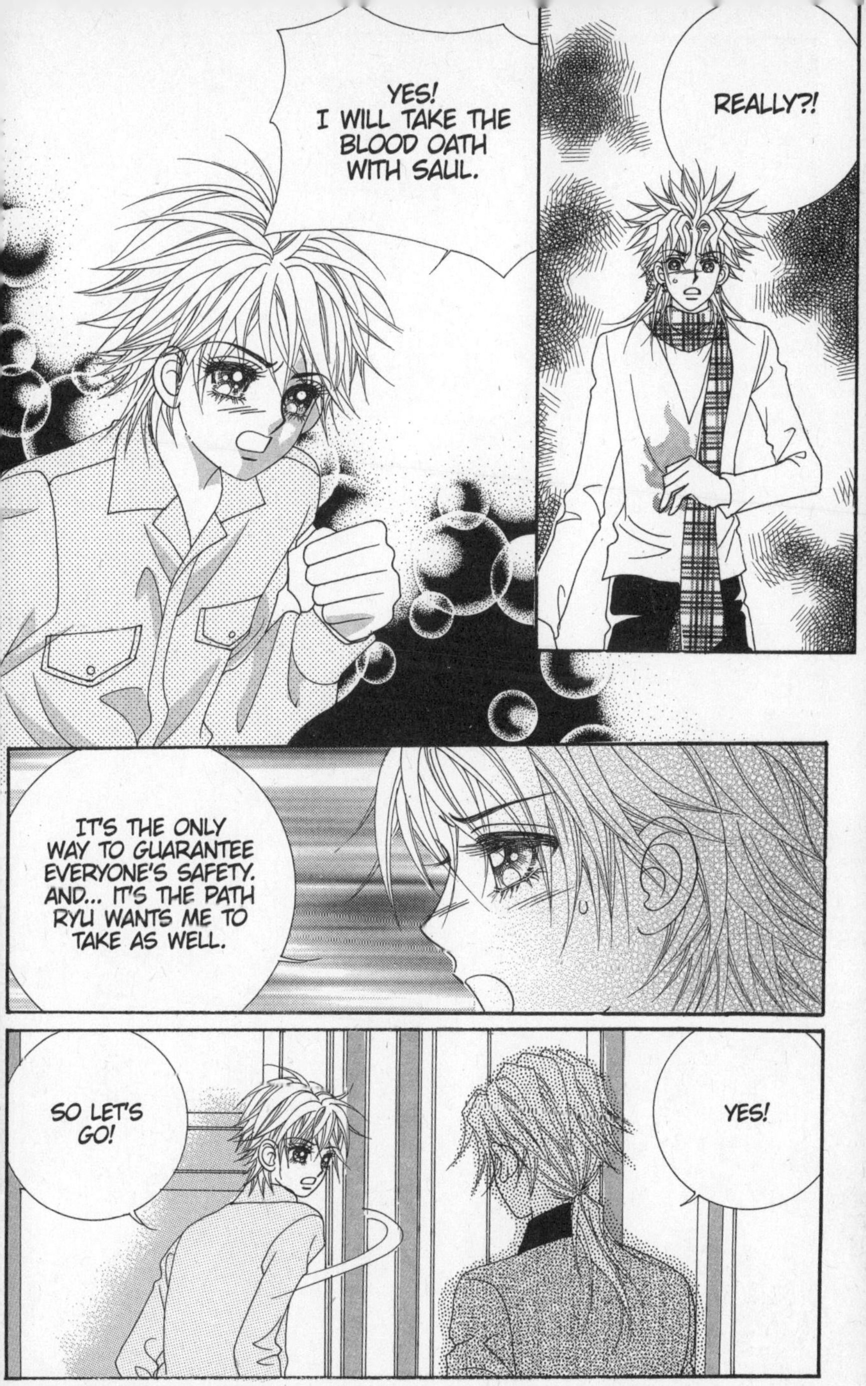
YES! I WILL TAKE THE BLOOD OATH WITH SAUL.
REALLY?!
IT'S THE ONLY WAY TO GUARANTEE EVERYONE'S SAFETY. AND... IT'S THE PATH RYU WANTS ME TO TAKE AS WELL.
SO LET'S GO!
YES!

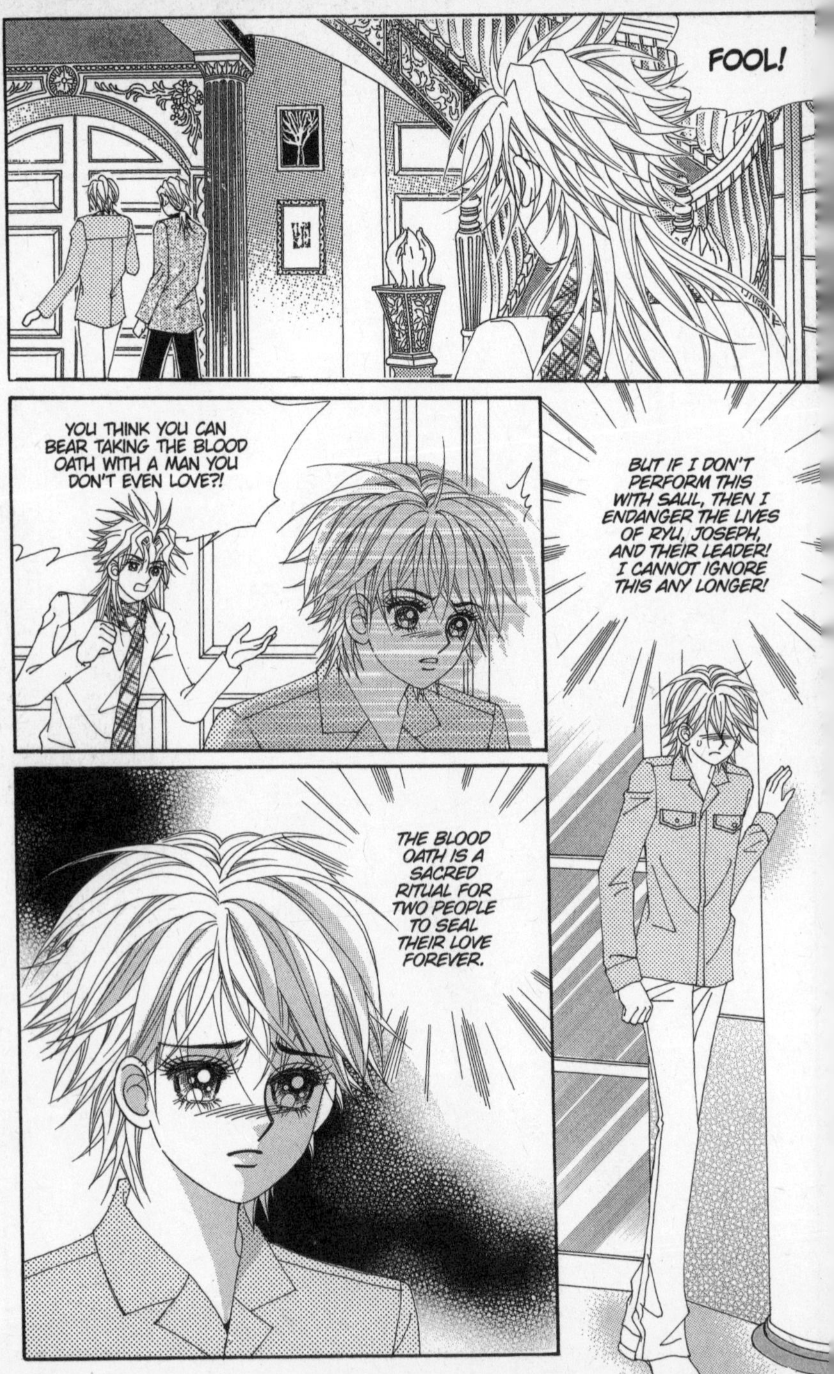
FOOL!
YOU THINK YOU CAN BEAR TAKING THE BLOOD OATH WITH A MAN YOU DON'T EVEN LOVE?!
BUT IF I DON'T PERFORM THIS WITH SAUL, THEN I ENDANGER THE LIVES OF RYU, JOSEPH, AND THEIR LEADER! I CANNOT IGNORE THIS ANY LONGER!
THE BLOOD OATH IS A SACRED RITUAL FOR TWO PEOPLE TO SEAL THEIR LOVE FOREVER.

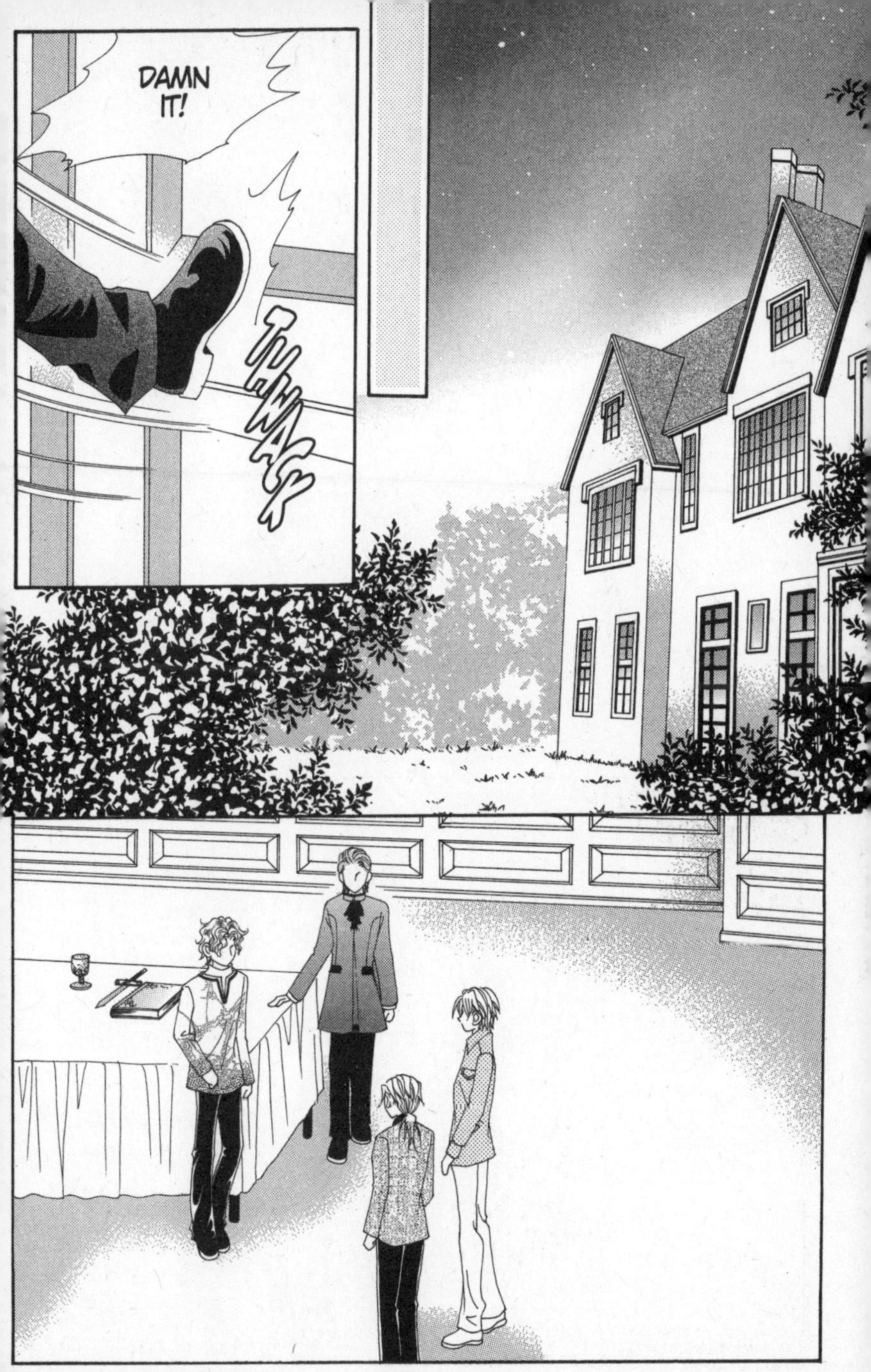
DAMN IT!
THWACK

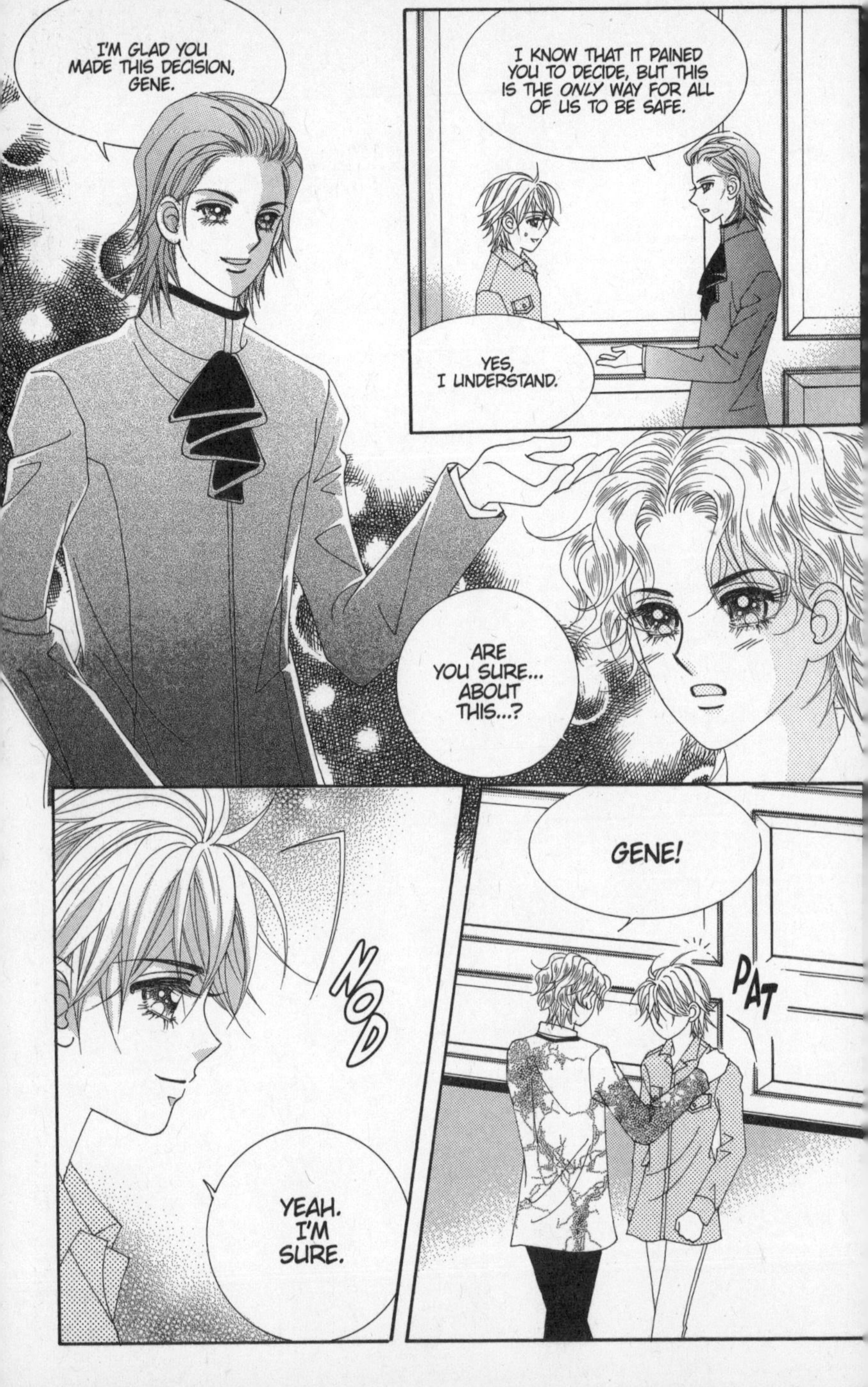
I'M GLAD YOU MADE THIS DECISION, GENE.
I KNOW THAT IT PAINED YOU TO DECIDE, BUT THIS IS THE *ONLY* WAY FOR ALL OF US TO BE SAFE.
YES, I UNDERSTAND.
ARE YOU SURE... ABOUT THIS...?
NOD
YEAH. I'M SURE.
GENE!
PAT

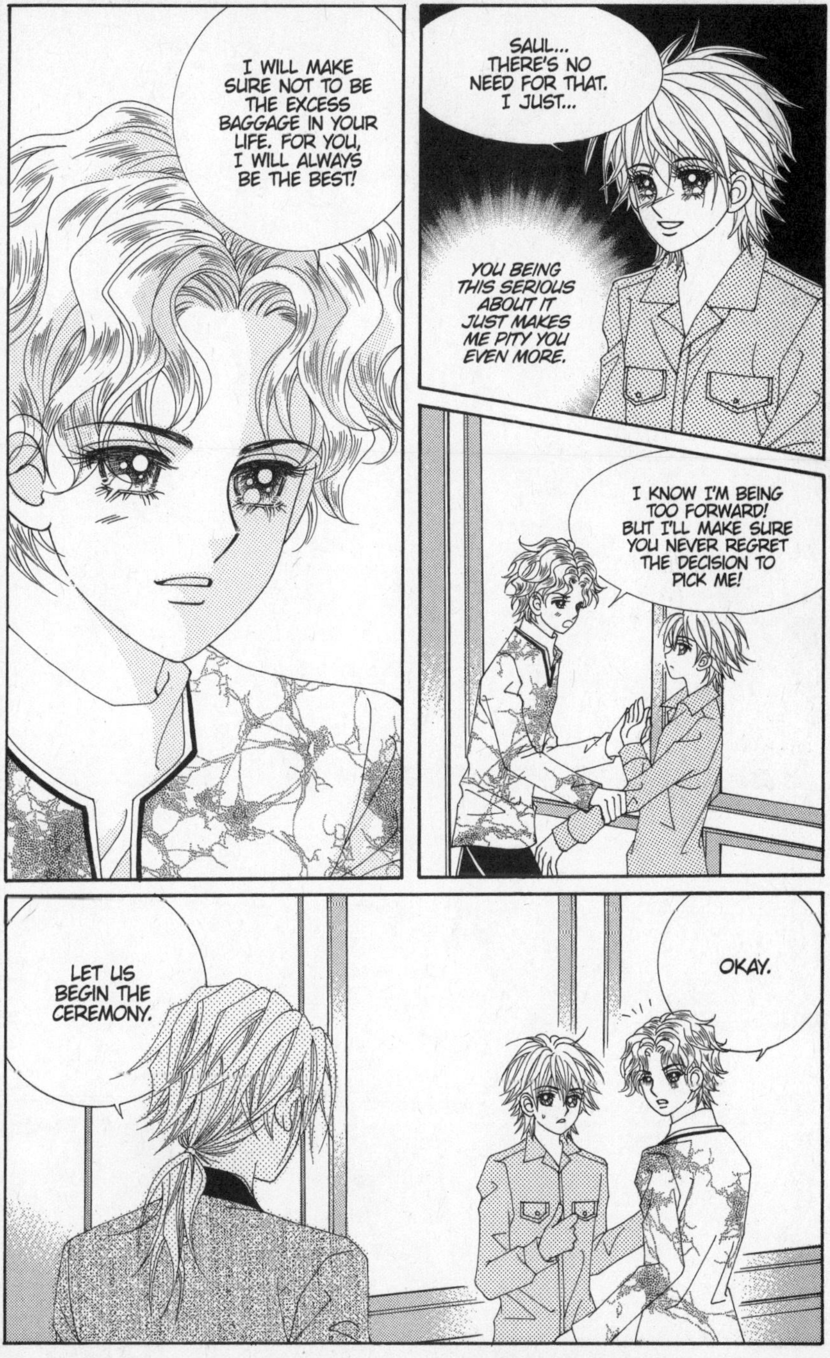
I WILL MAKE SURE NOT TO BE THE EXCESS BAGGAGE IN YOUR LIFE. FOR YOU, I WILL ALWAYS BE THE BEST!
SAUL... THERE'S NO NEED FOR THAT. I JUST...
YOU BEING THIS SERIOUS ABOUT IT JUST MAKES ME PITY YOU EVEN MORE.
I KNOW I'M BEING TOO FORWARD! BUT I'LL MAKE SURE YOU NEVER REGRET THE DECISION TO PICK ME!
LET US BEGIN THE CEREMONY.
OKAY.

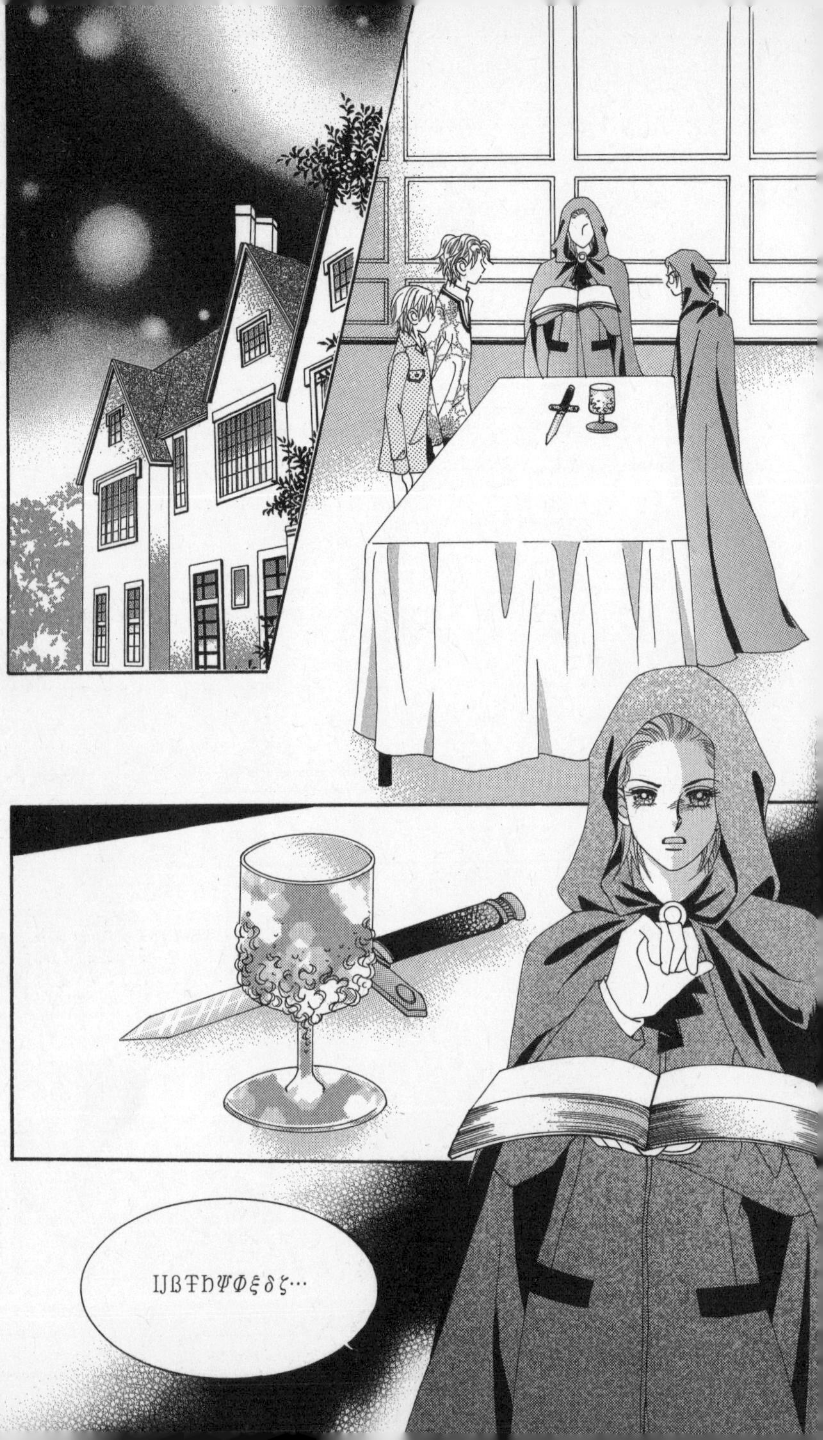
IJß∓ħΨΦξδζ…

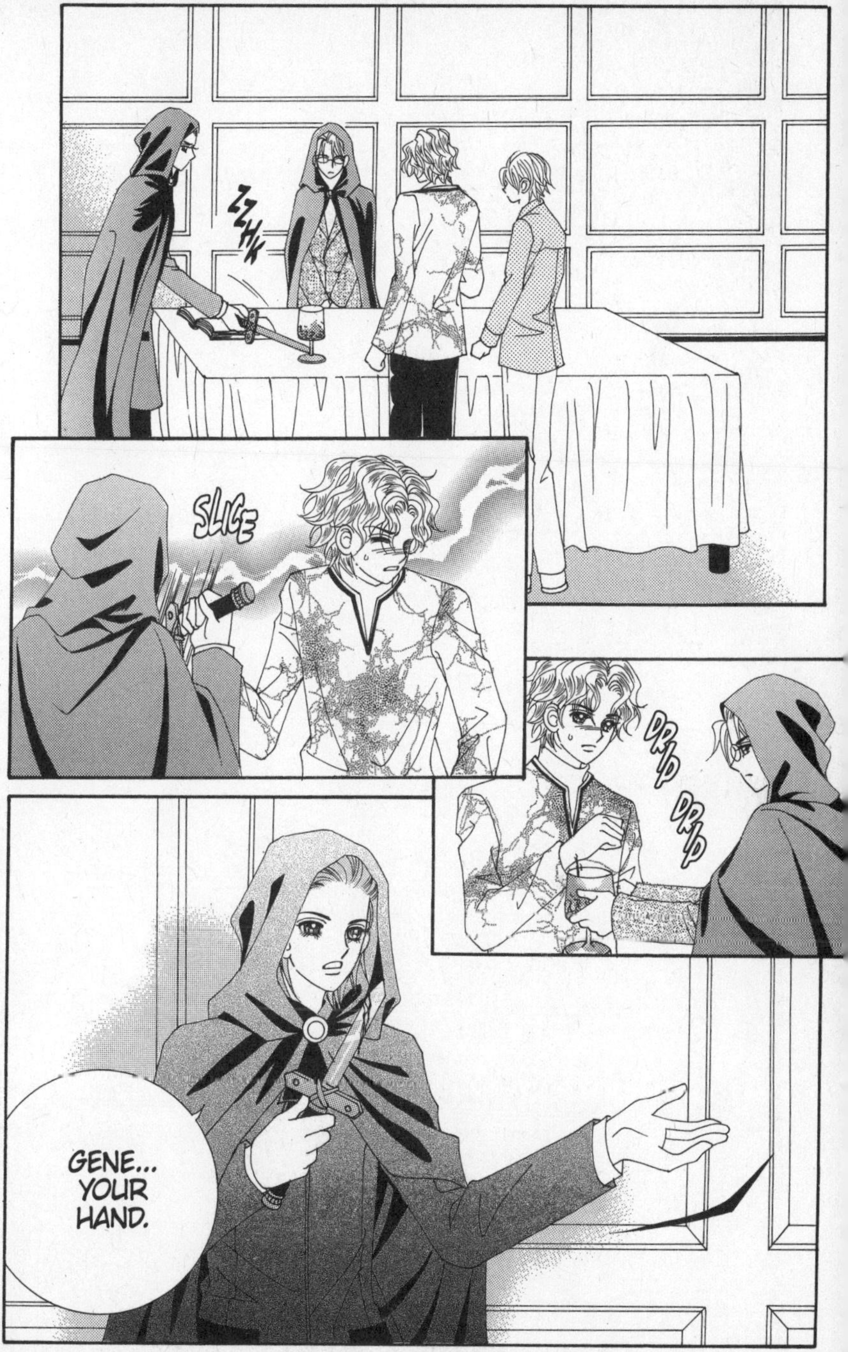
ZZHK
SLICE
DRIP
DRIP
GENE... YOUR HAND.

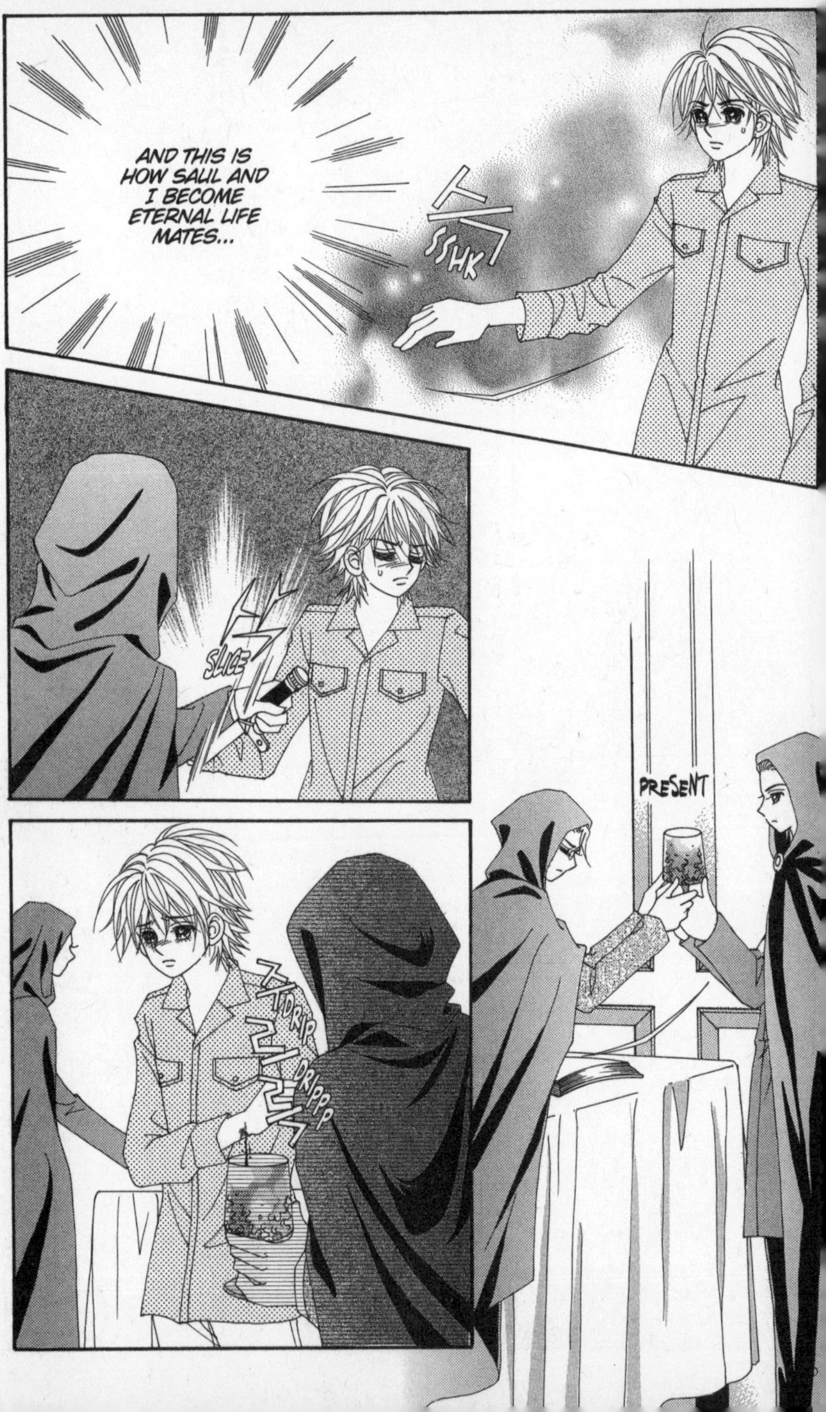
AND THIS IS HOW SAUL AND I BECOME ETERNAL LIFE MATES...
SSHK
SLICE
DRIP
DRIPPP
PRESENT

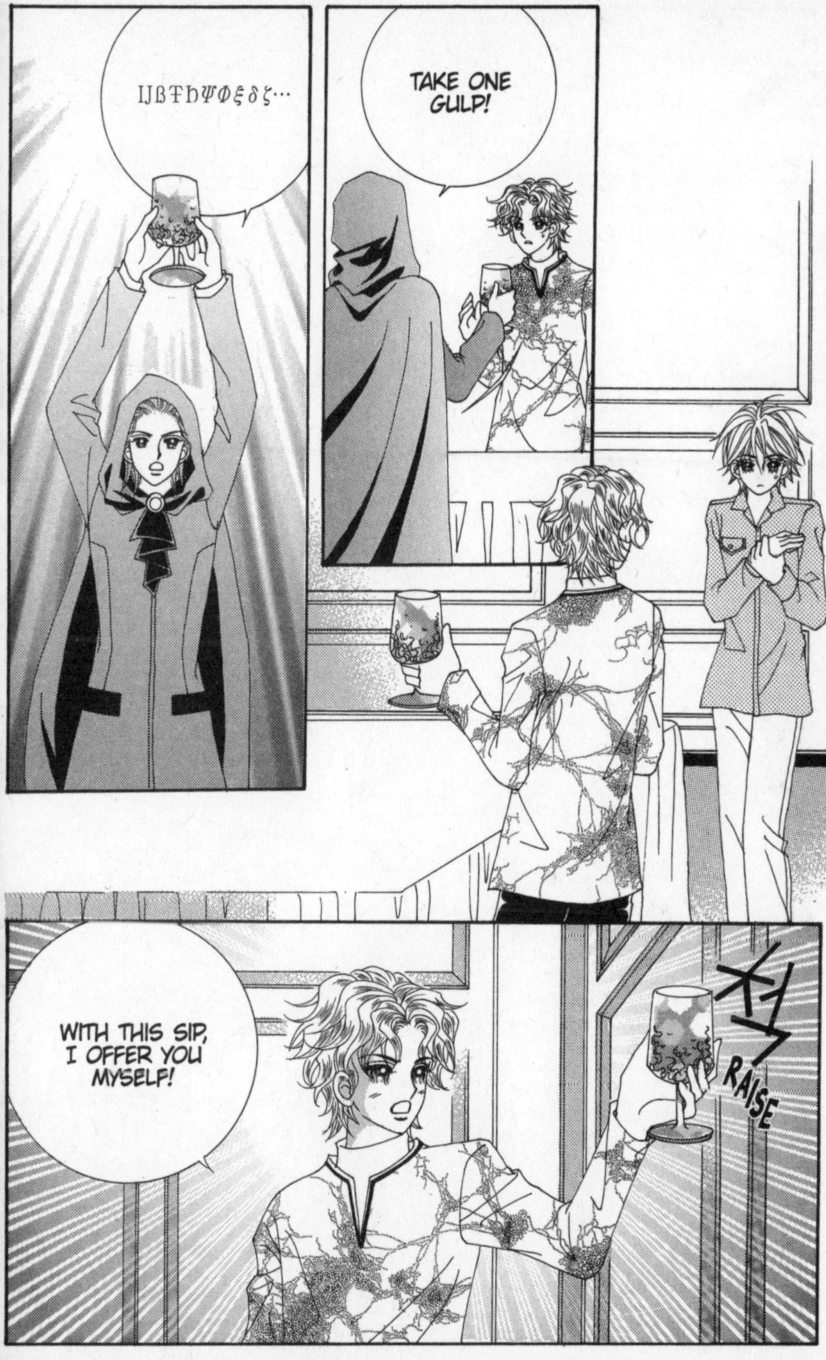
IJBŦhΨΦξδζ…
TAKE ONE GULP!
WITH THIS SIP, I OFFER YOU MYSELF!
RAISE

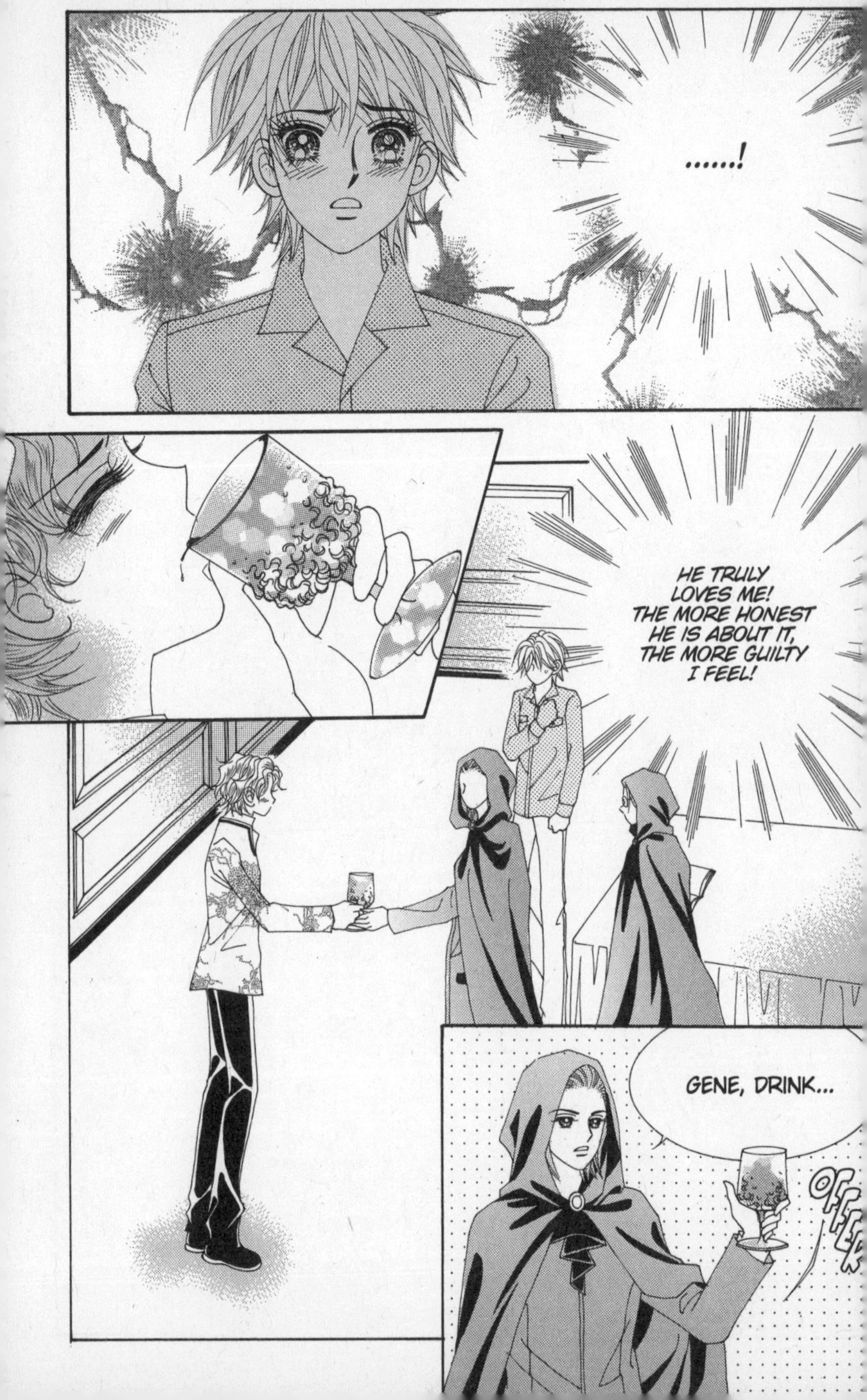
......!
HE TRULY LOVES ME! THE MORE HONEST HE IS ABOUT IT, THE MORE GUILTY I FEEL!
GENE, DRINK...
OFFER

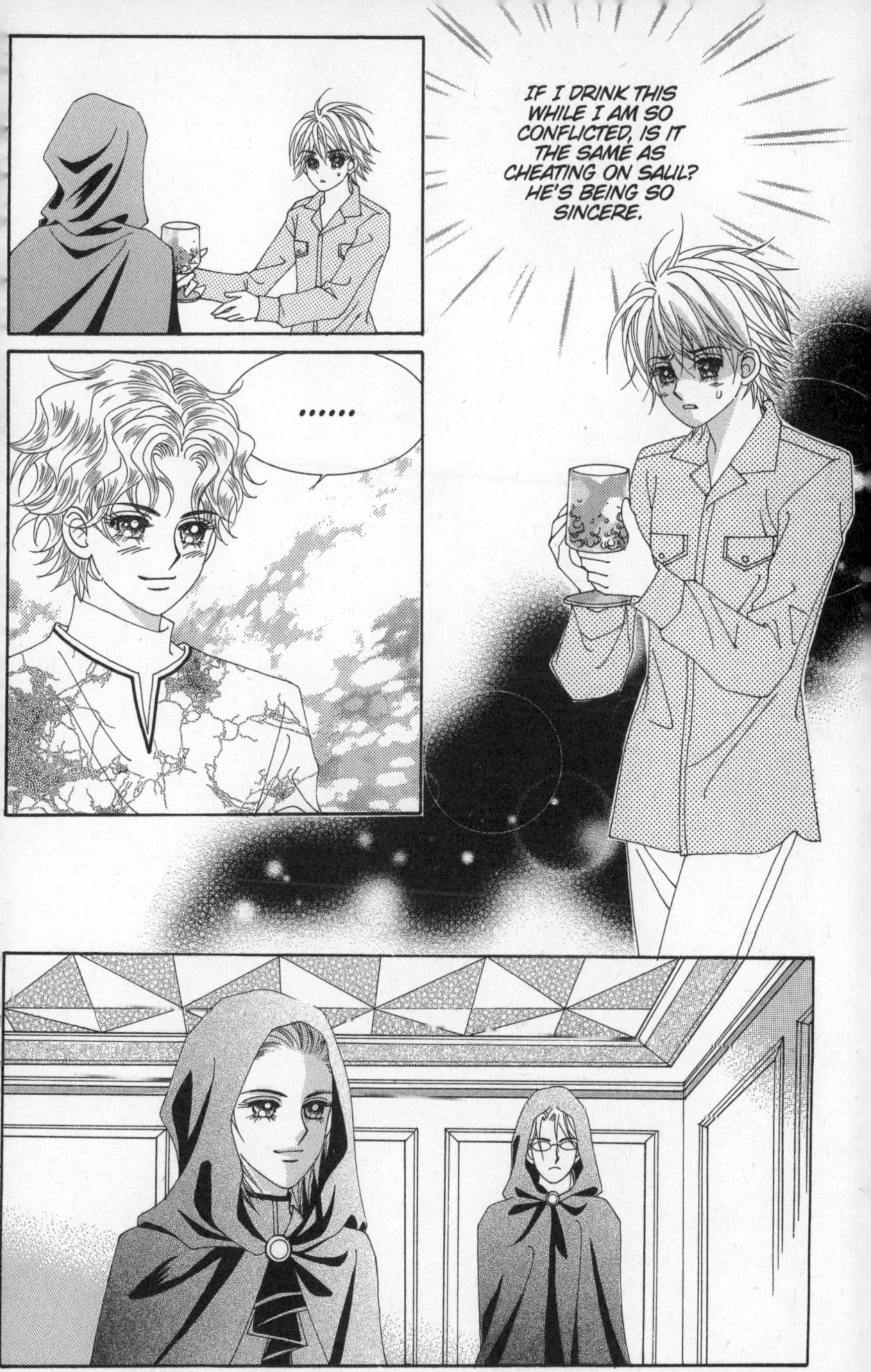
IF I DRINK THIS WHILE I AM SO CONFLICTED, IS IT THE SAME AS CHEATING ON SAUL? HE'S BEING SO SINCERE.
......

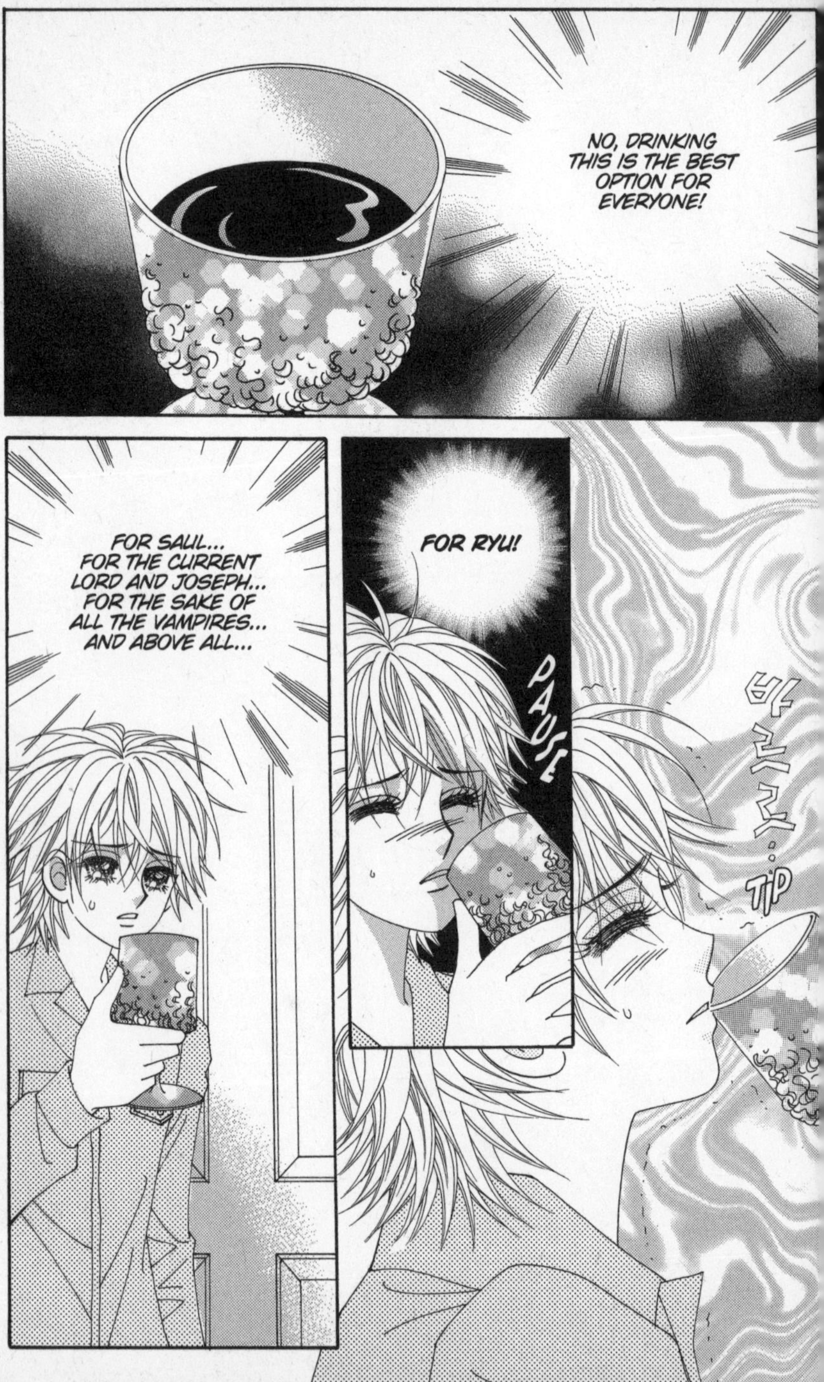
NO, DRINKING THIS IS THE BEST OPTION FOR EVERYONE!
FOR SAUL... FOR THE CURRENT LORD AND JOSEPH... FOR THE SAKE OF ALL THE VAMPIRES... AND ABOVE ALL...
FOR RYU!
PAUSE
TIP

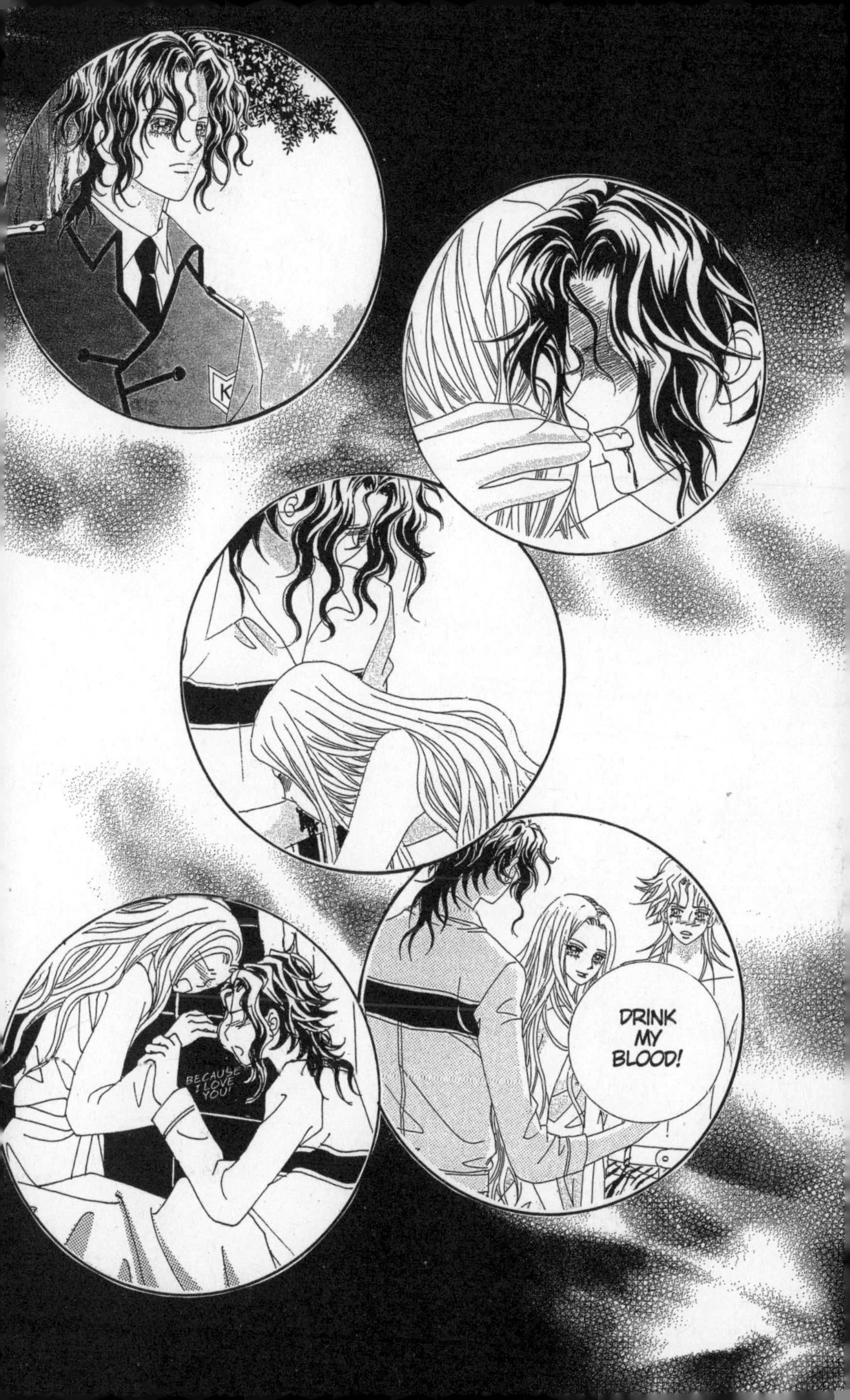
BECAUSE I LOVE YOU!
DRINK MY BLOOD!

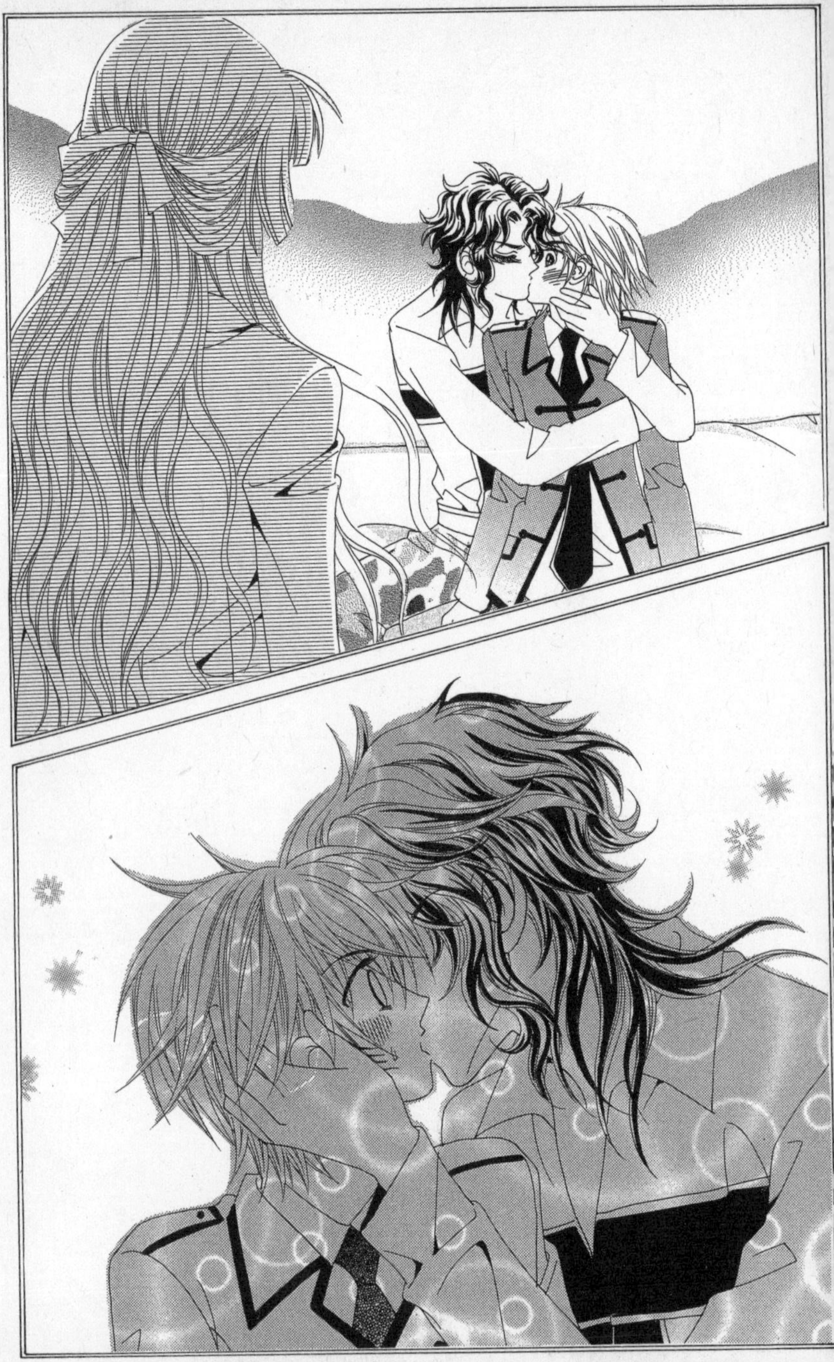

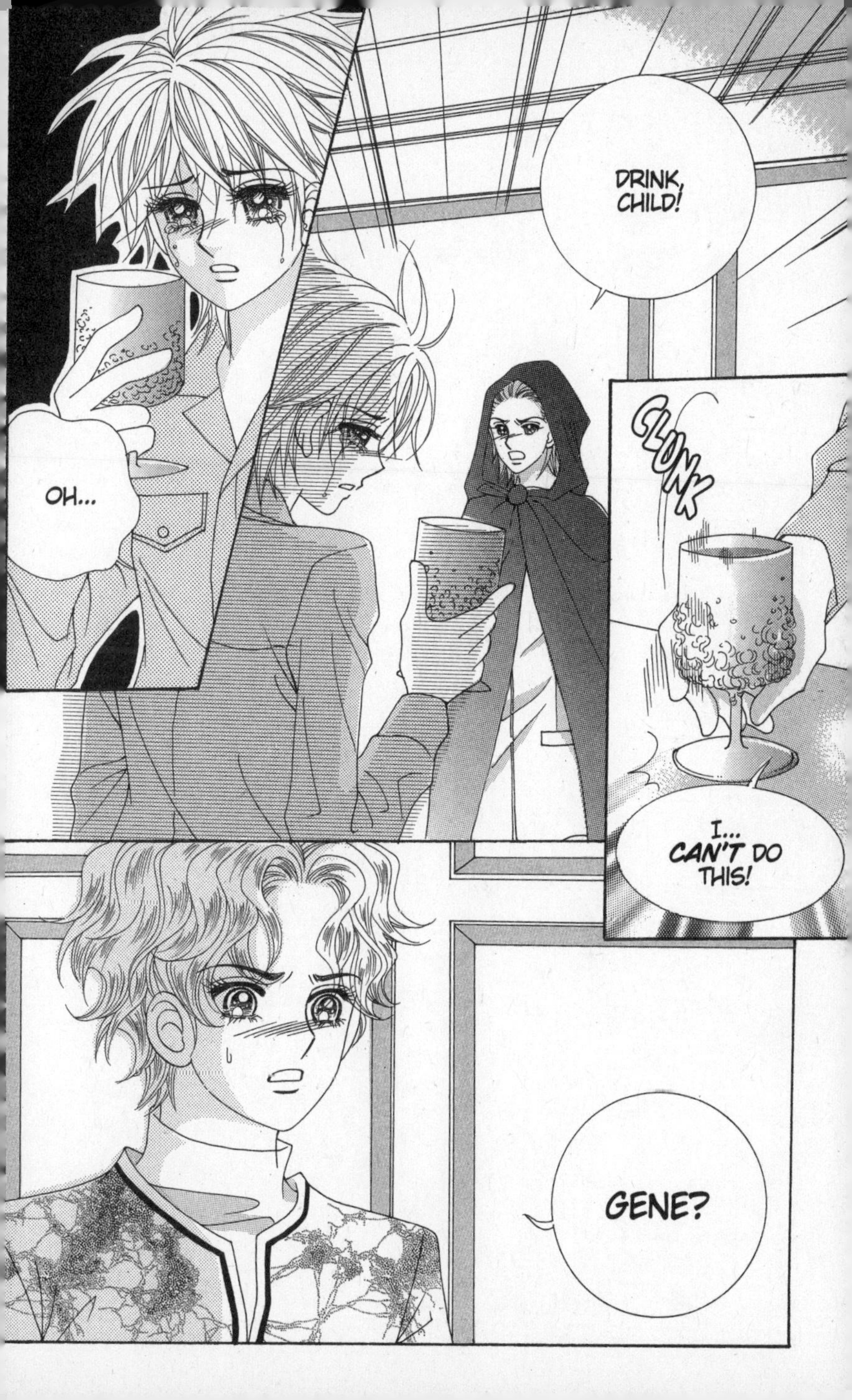
OH...
DRINK, CHILD!
CLUNK
I... CAN'T DO THIS!
GENE?

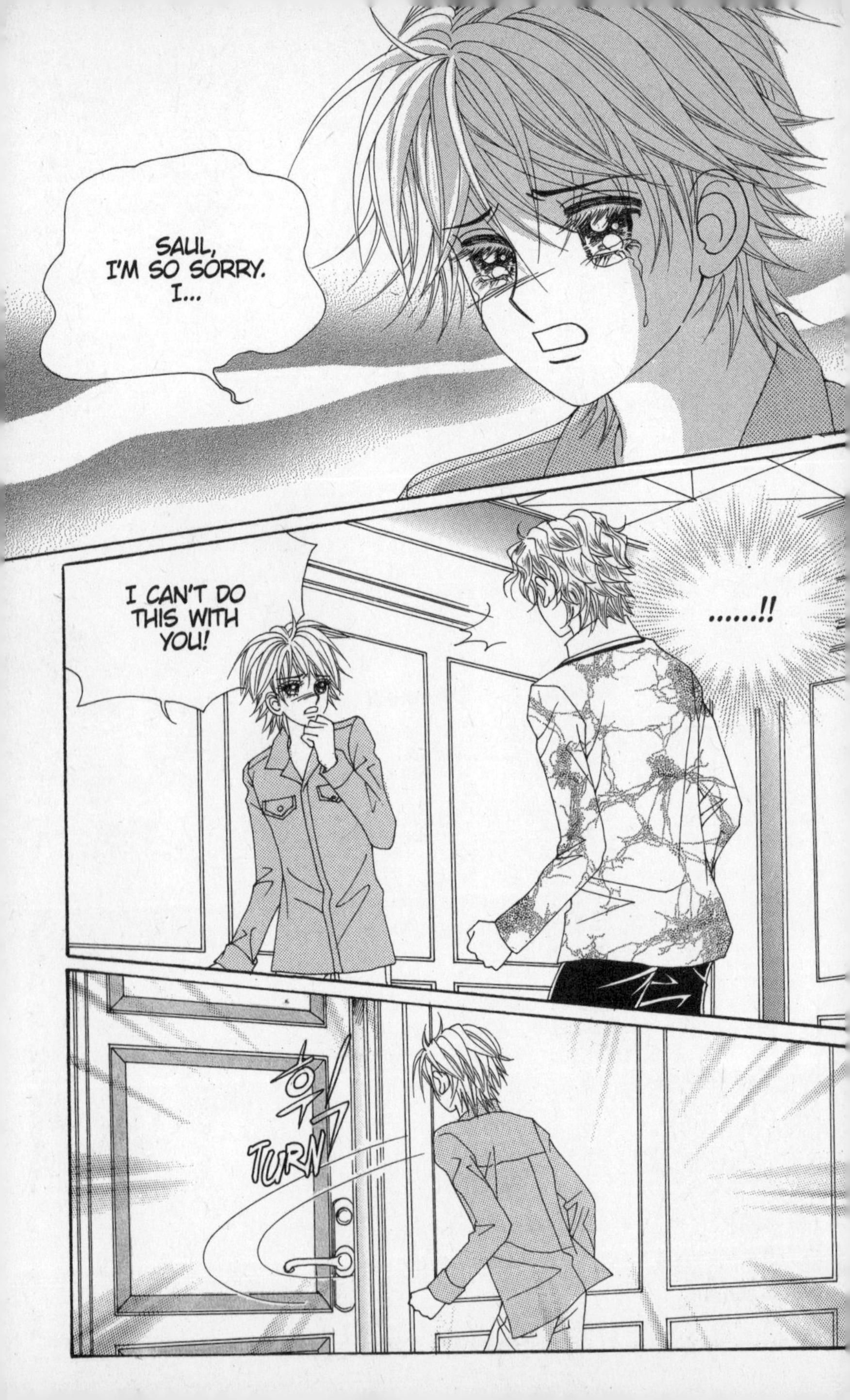
SAUL, I'M SO SORRY. I...
I CAN'T DO THIS WITH YOU!
......!!
TURN

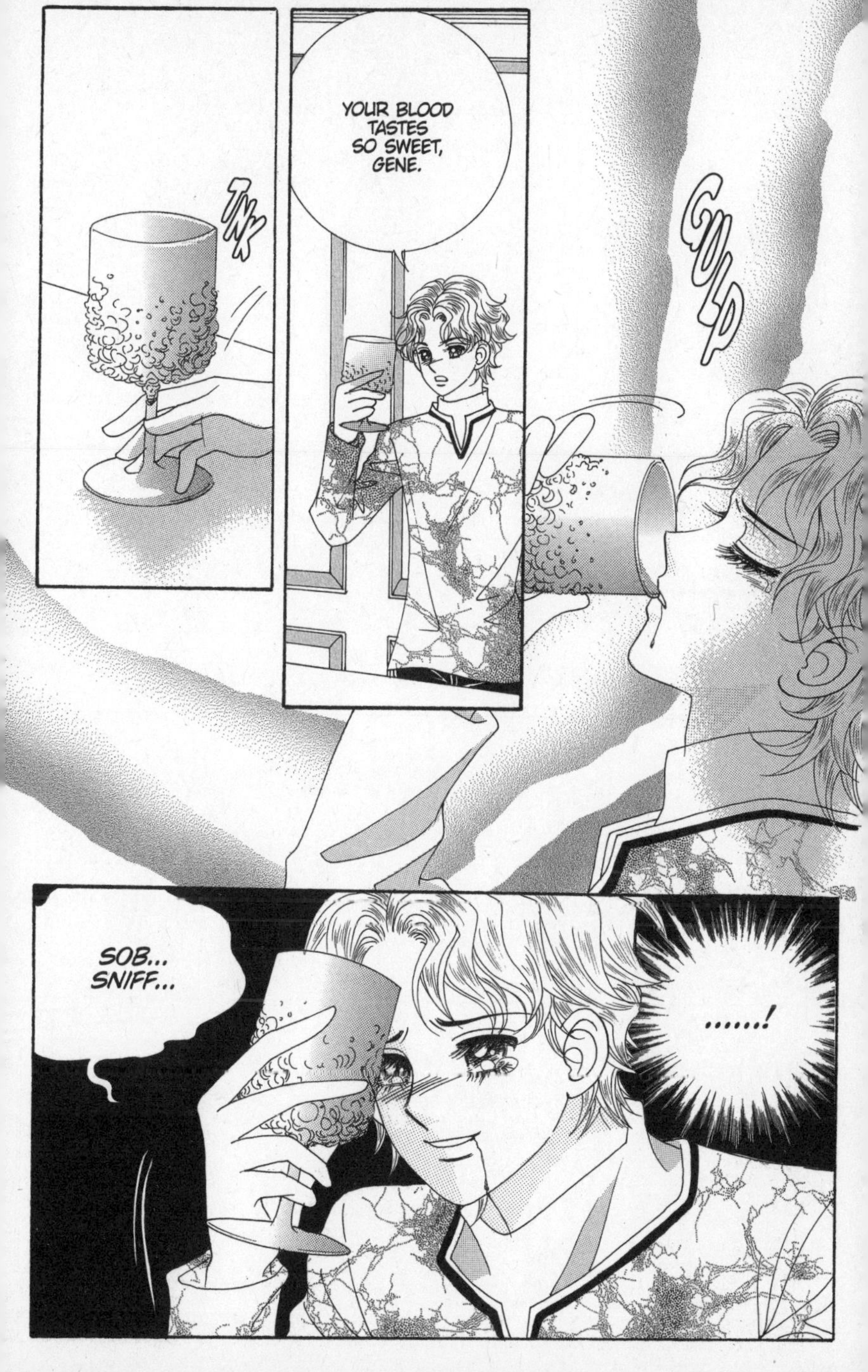
TNK
YOUR BLOOD TASTES SO SWEET, GENE.
GULP
SOB... SNIFF...
......!

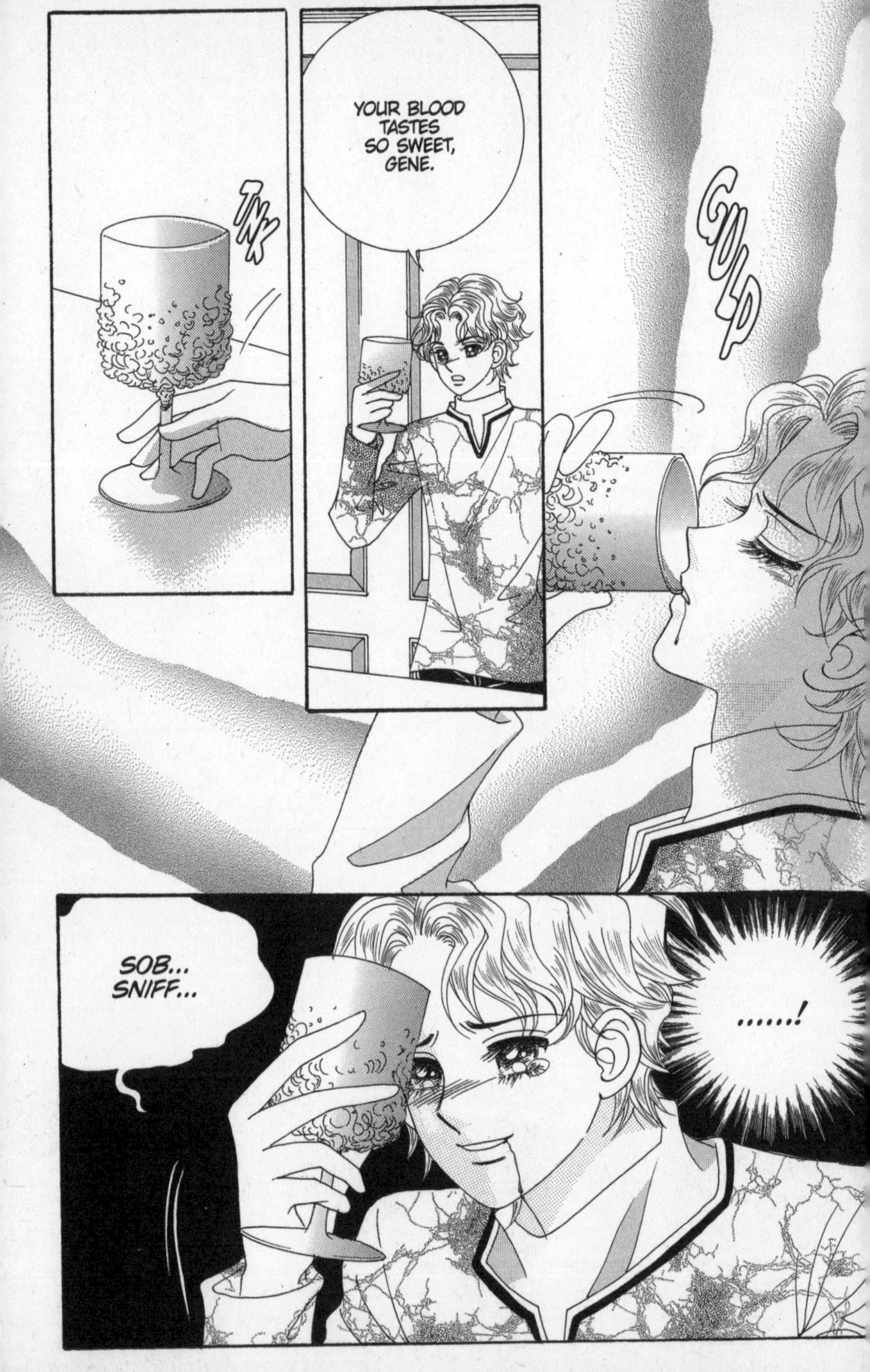
TNK
YOUR BLOOD TASTES SO SWEET, GENE.
GULP
SOB... SNIFF...
......!

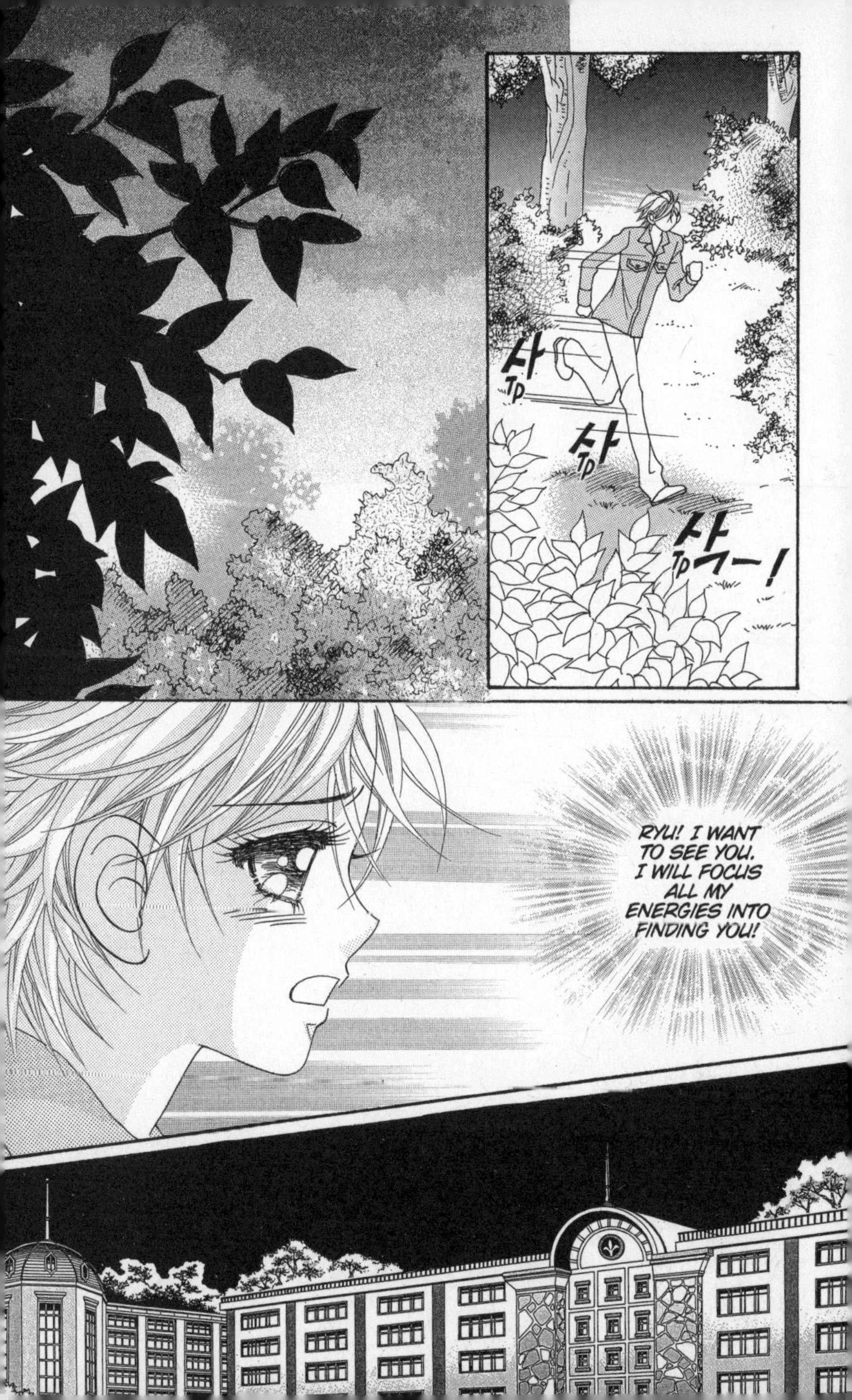

샤 TP
샤 TP
샥~! TP
RYU! I WANT TO SEE YOU. I WILL FOCUS ALL MY ENERGIES INTO FINDING YOU!

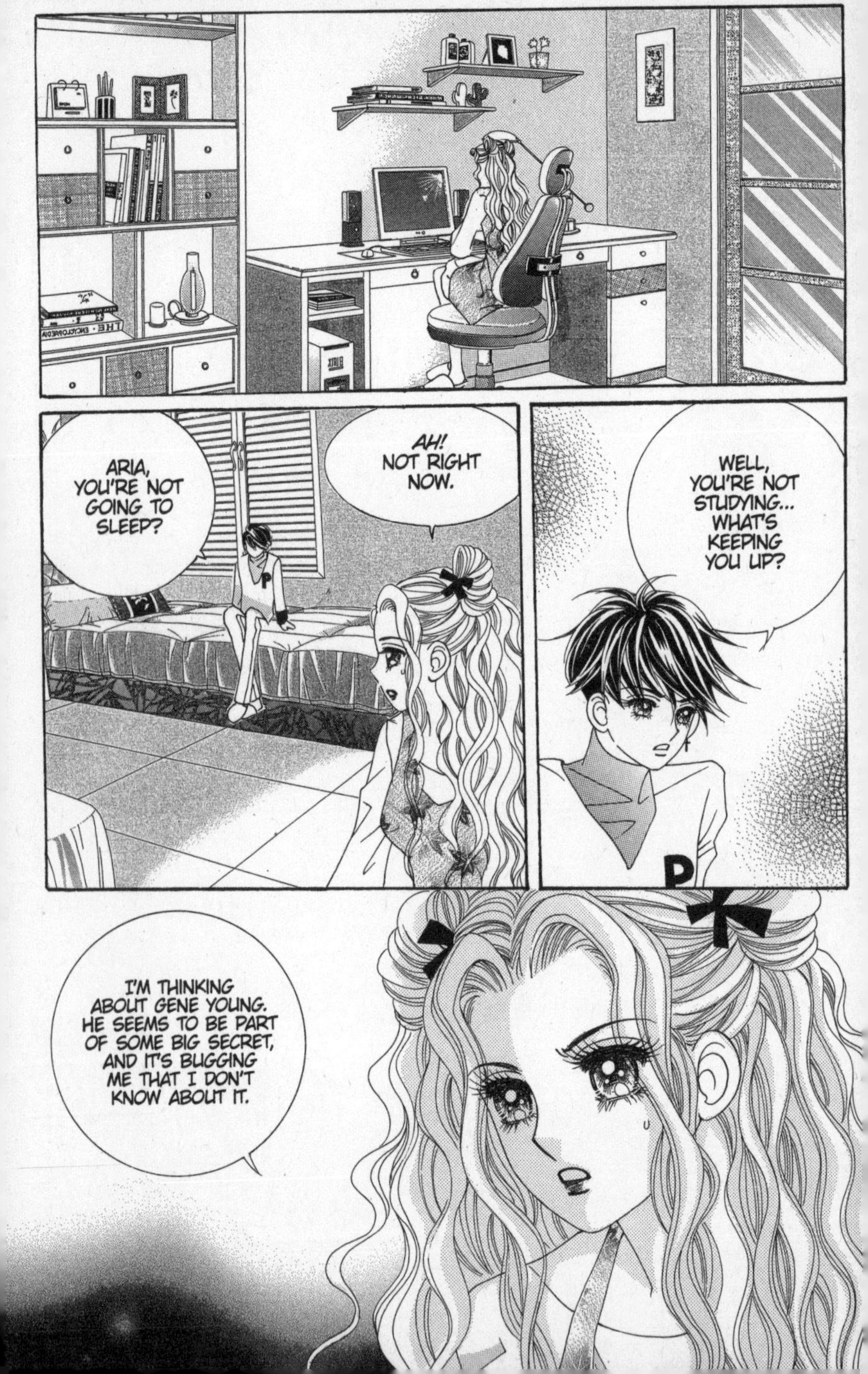
ARIA, YOU'RE NOT GOING TO SLEEP?
AH! NOT RIGHT NOW.
WELL, YOU'RE NOT STUDYING... WHAT'S KEEPING YOU UP?
I'M THINKING ABOUT GENE YOUNG. HE SEEMS TO BE PART OF SOME BIG SECRET, AND IT'S BUGGING ME THAT I DON'T KNOW ABOUT IT.

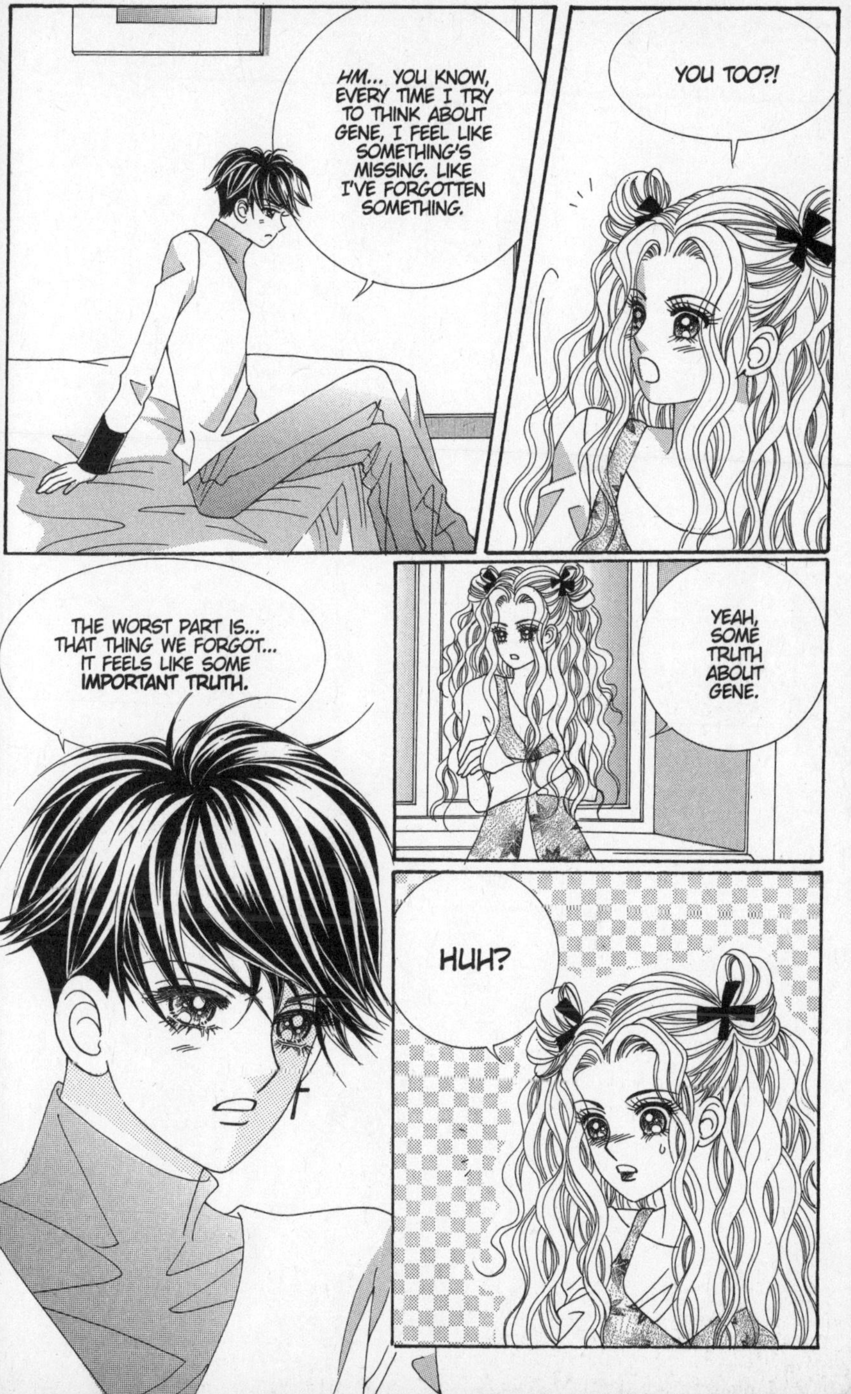
HM... YOU KNOW, EVERY TIME I TRY TO THINK ABOUT GENE, I FEEL LIKE SOMETHING'S MISSING. LIKE I'VE FORGOTTEN SOMETHING.
YOU TOO?!
THE WORST PART IS... THAT THING WE FORGOT... IT FEELS LIKE SOME IMPORTANT TRUTH.
YEAH, SOME TRUTH ABOUT GENE.
HUH?

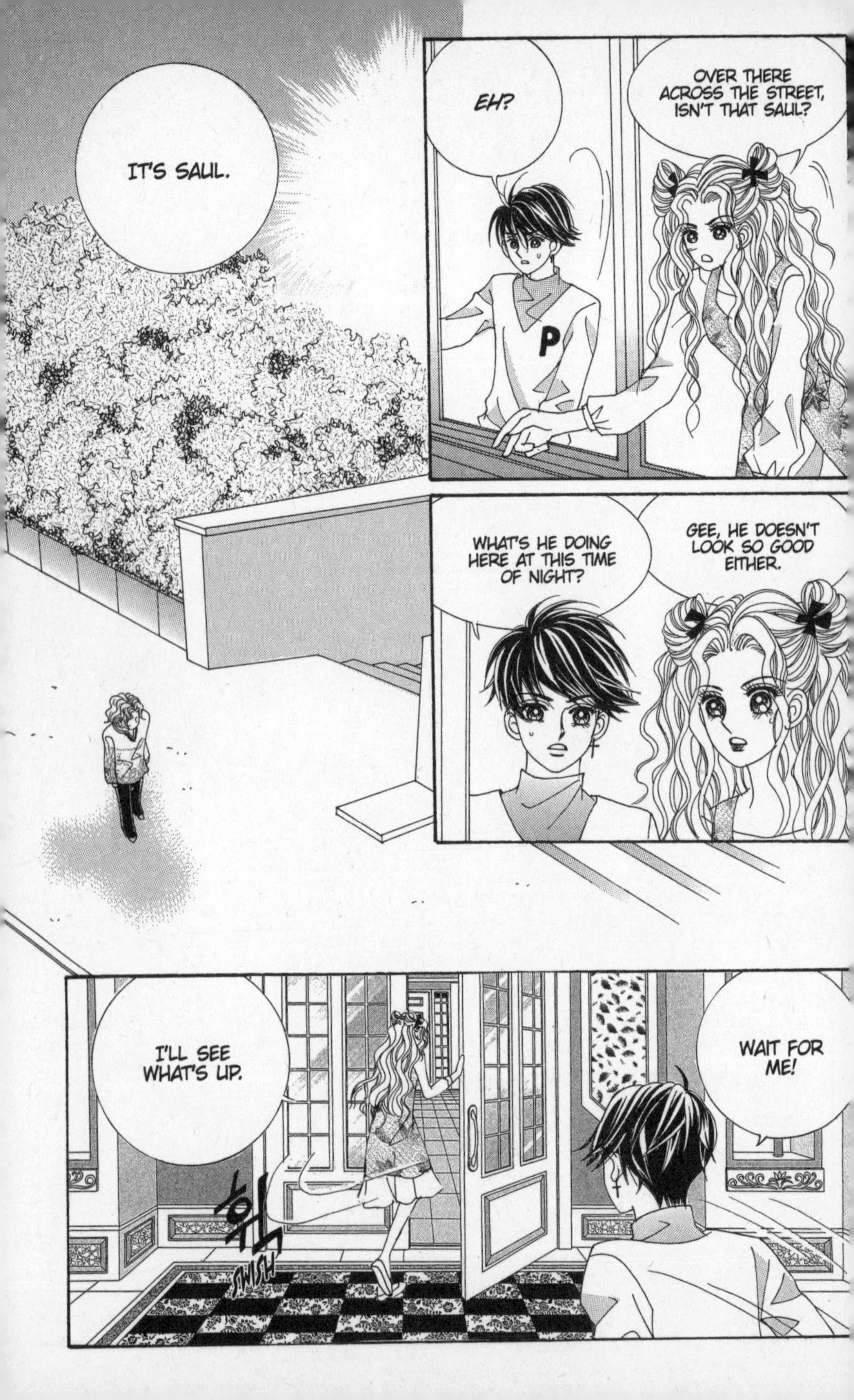
IT'S SAUL.
EH?
OVER THERE ACROSS THE STREET, ISN'T THAT SAUL?
WHAT'S HE DOING HERE AT THIS TIME OF NIGHT?
GEE, HE DOESN'T LOOK SO GOOD EITHER.
I'LL SEE WHAT'S UP.
SWISH
WAIT FOR ME!

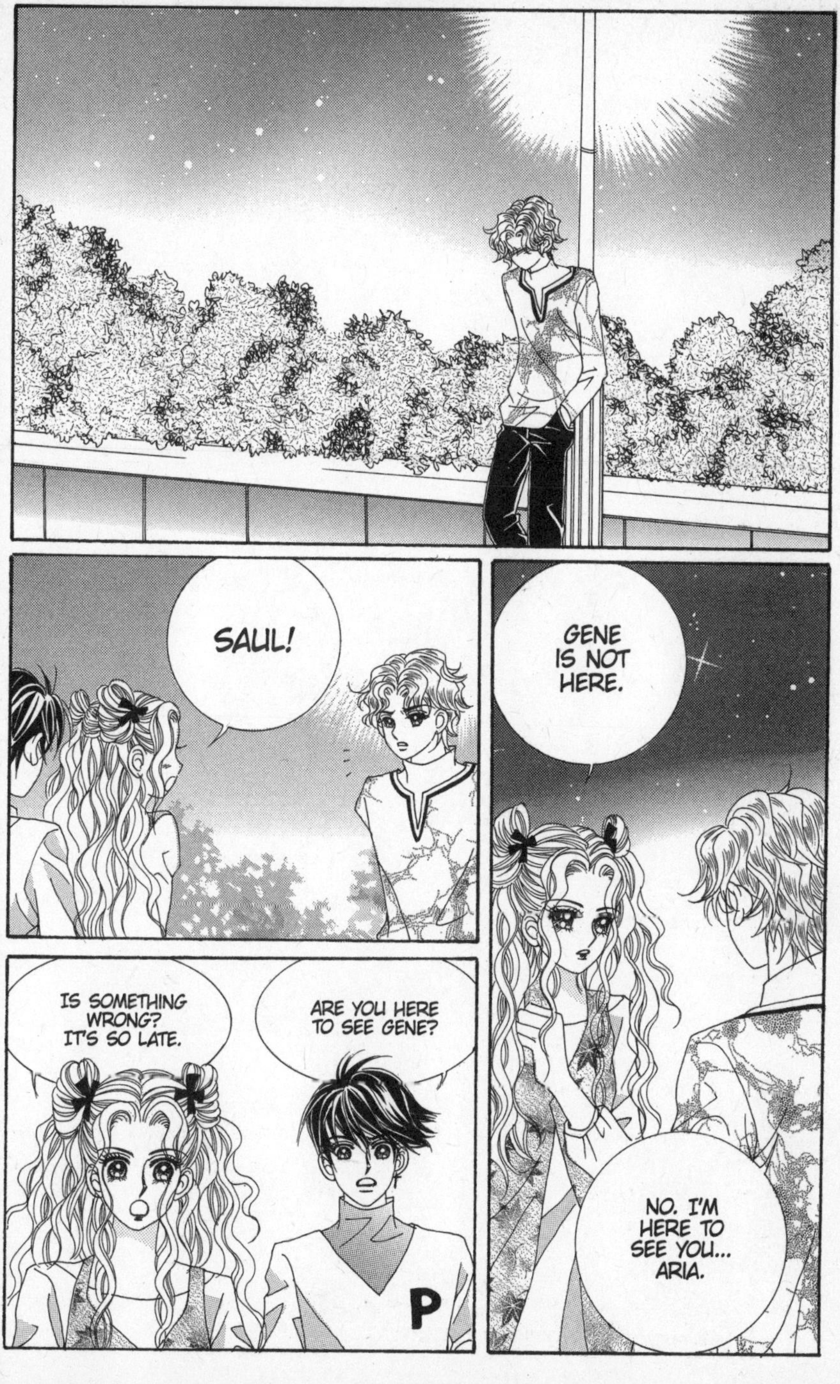
SAUL!
IS SOMETHING WRONG? IT'S SO LATE.
ARE YOU HERE TO SEE GENE?
GENE IS NOT HERE.
NO. I'M HERE TO SEE YOU... ARIA.

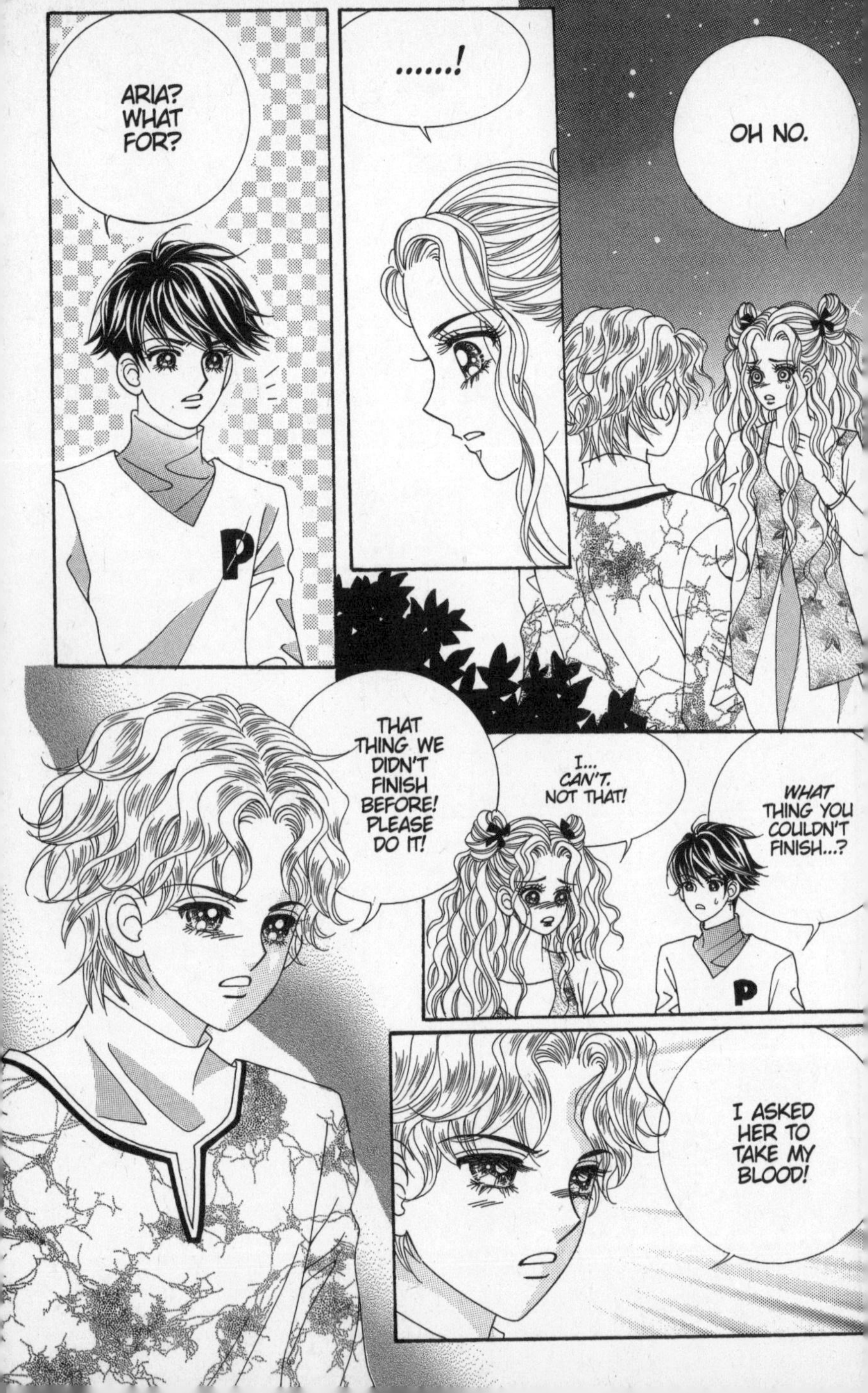
ARIA? WHAT FOR?
......!
OH NO.
THAT THING WE DIDN'T FINISH BEFORE! PLEASE DO IT!
I... CAN'T. NOT THAT!
WHAT THING YOU COULDN'T FINISH...?
I ASKED HER TO TAKE MY BLOOD!

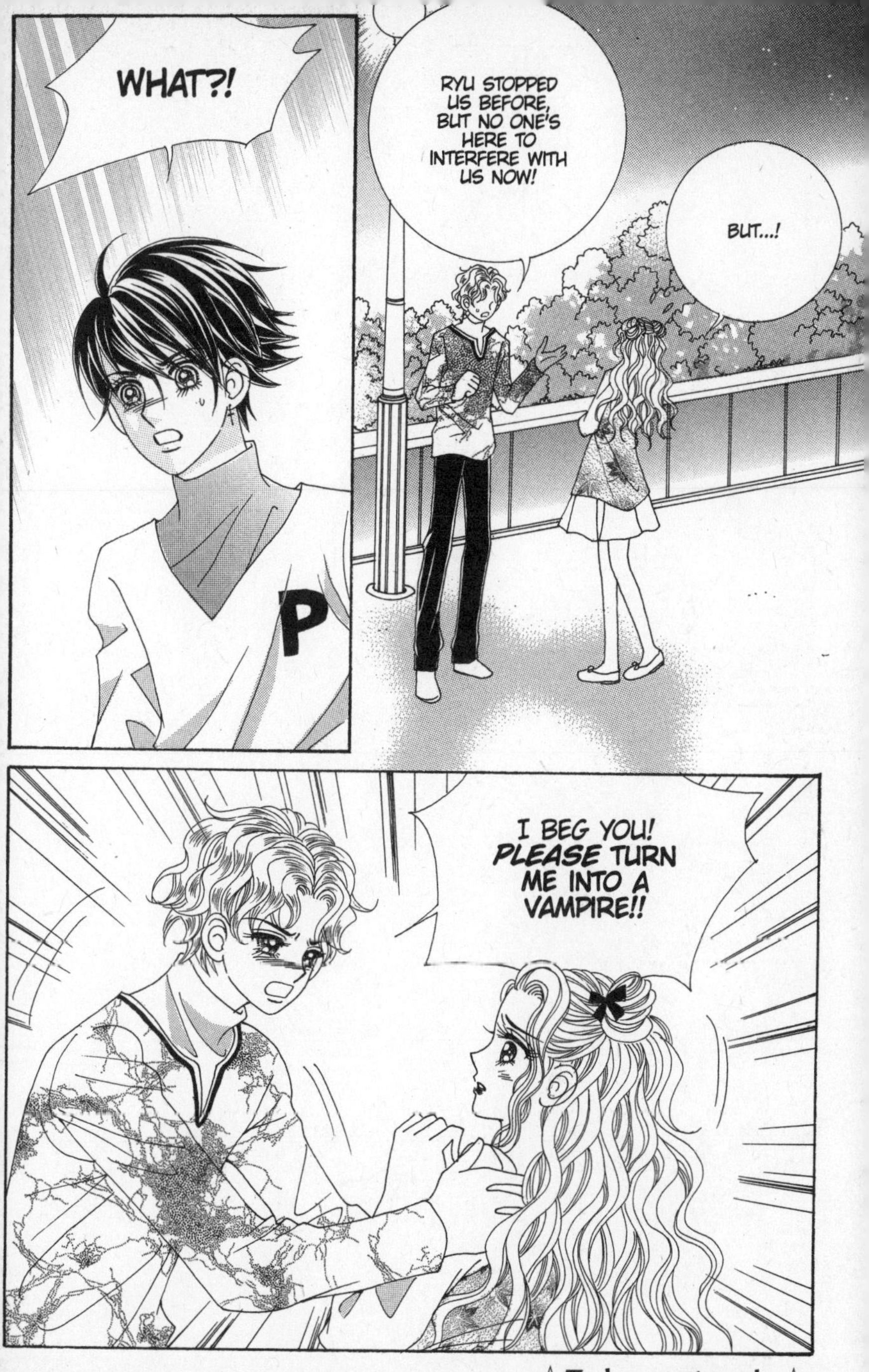
WHAT?!
RYU STOPPED US BEFORE, BUT NO ONE'S HERE TO INTERFERE WITH US NOW!
BUT...!
...
I BEG YOU! *PLEASE* TURN ME INTO A VAMPIRE!!

☆To be continued...☆

My Boyfriend is a

VAMPIRE

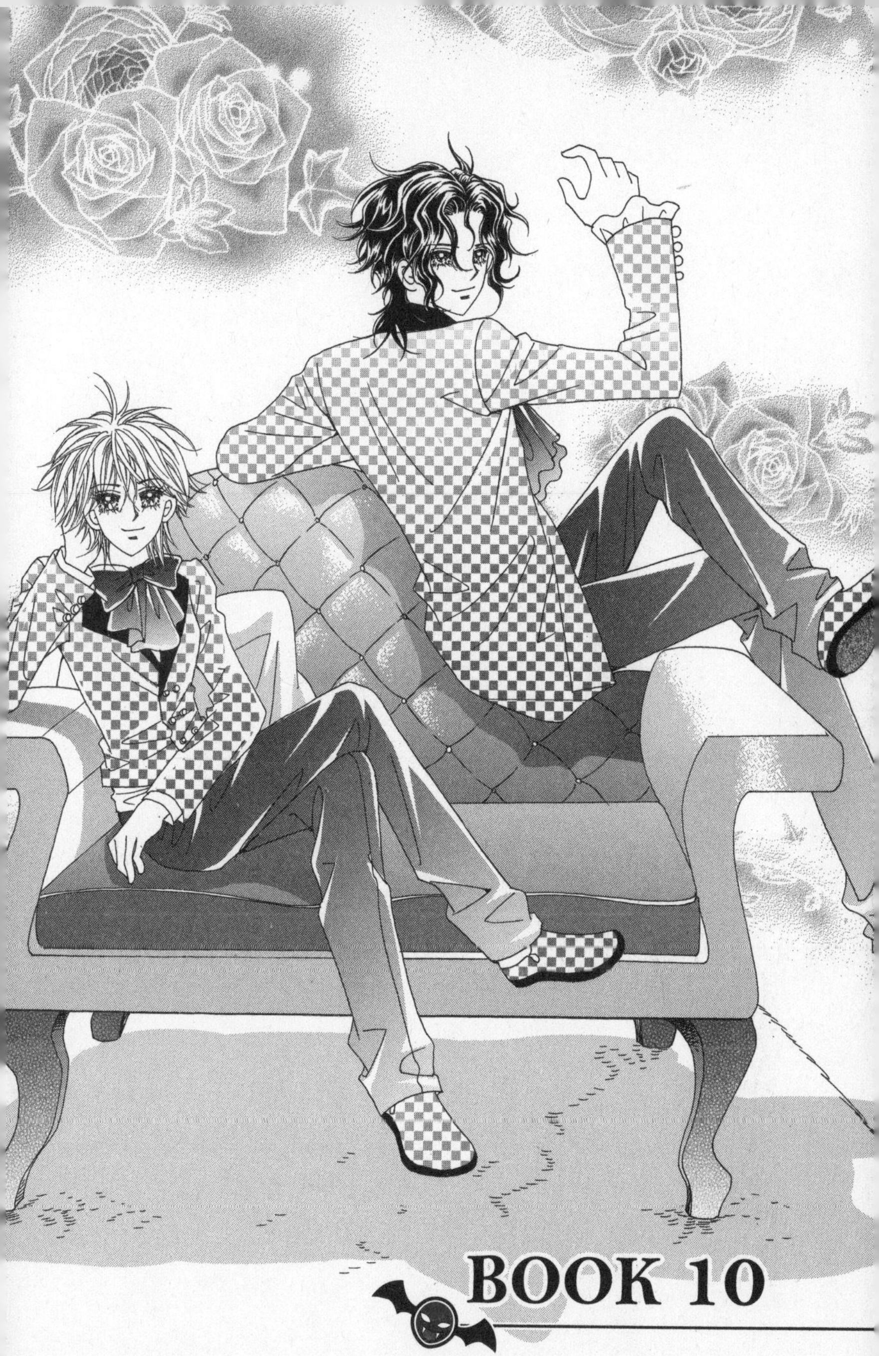

BOOK 10

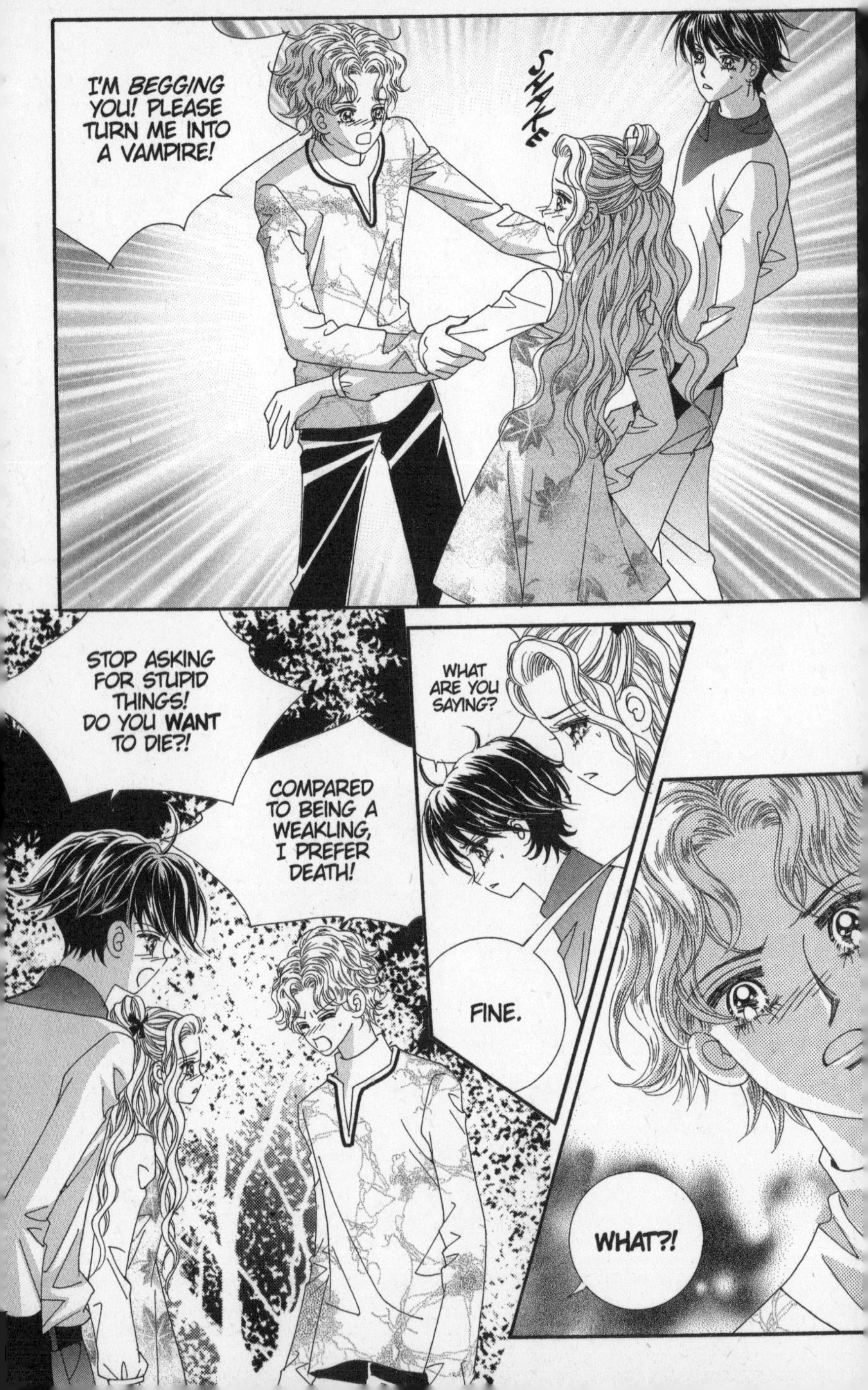
I'M *BEGGING* YOU! PLEASE TURN ME INTO A VAMPIRE!
SHAKE
STOP ASKING FOR STUPID THINGS! DO YOU WANT TO DIE?!
COMPARED TO BEING A WEAKLING, I PREFER DEATH!
WHAT ARE YOU SAYING?
FINE.
WHAT?!

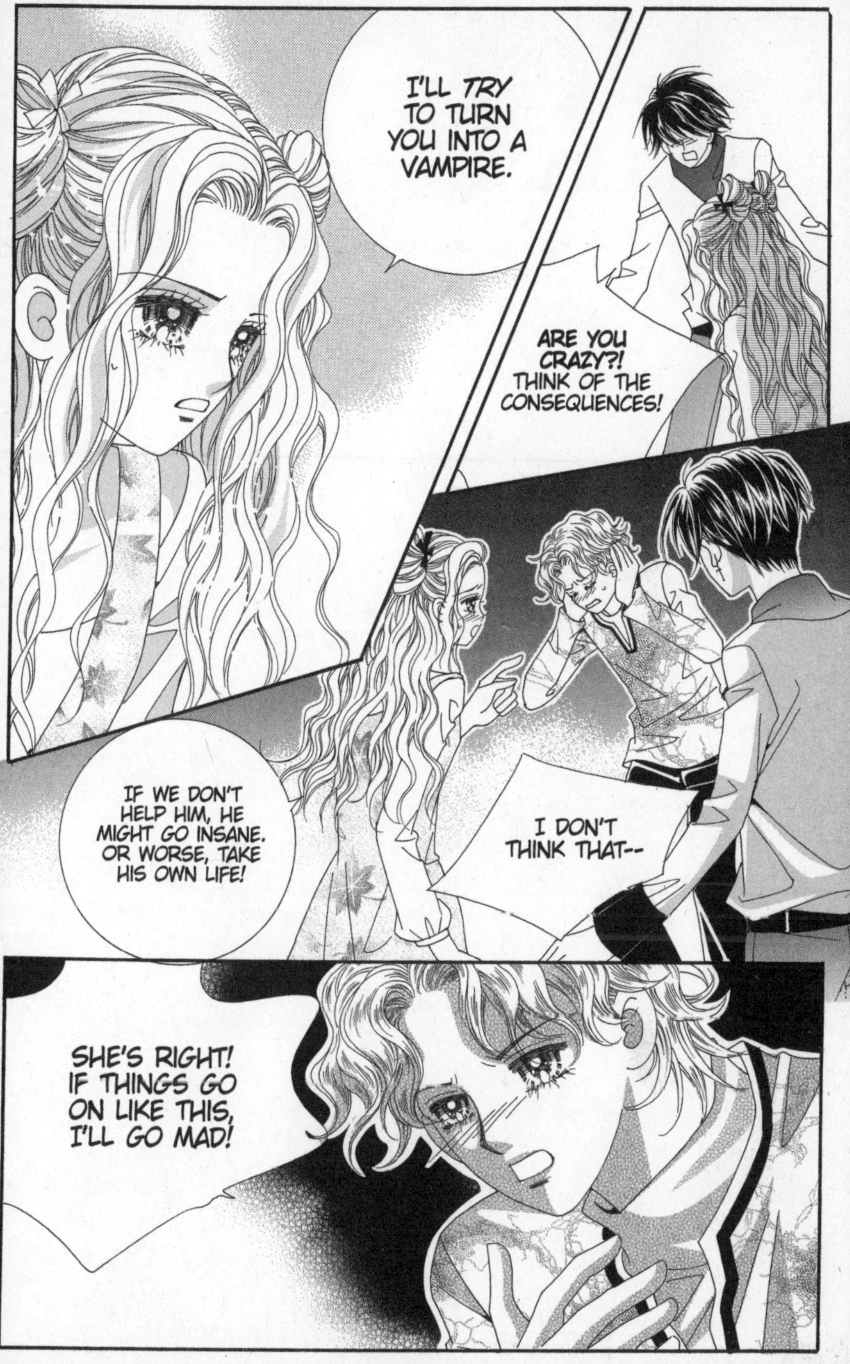
I'LL *TRY* TO TURN YOU INTO A VAMPIRE.
ARE YOU CRAZY?! THINK OF THE CONSEQUENCES!
IF WE DON'T HELP HIM, HE MIGHT GO INSANE. OR WORSE, TAKE HIS OWN LIFE!
I DON'T THINK THAT--
SHE'S RIGHT! IF THINGS GO ON LIKE THIS, I'LL GO MAD!

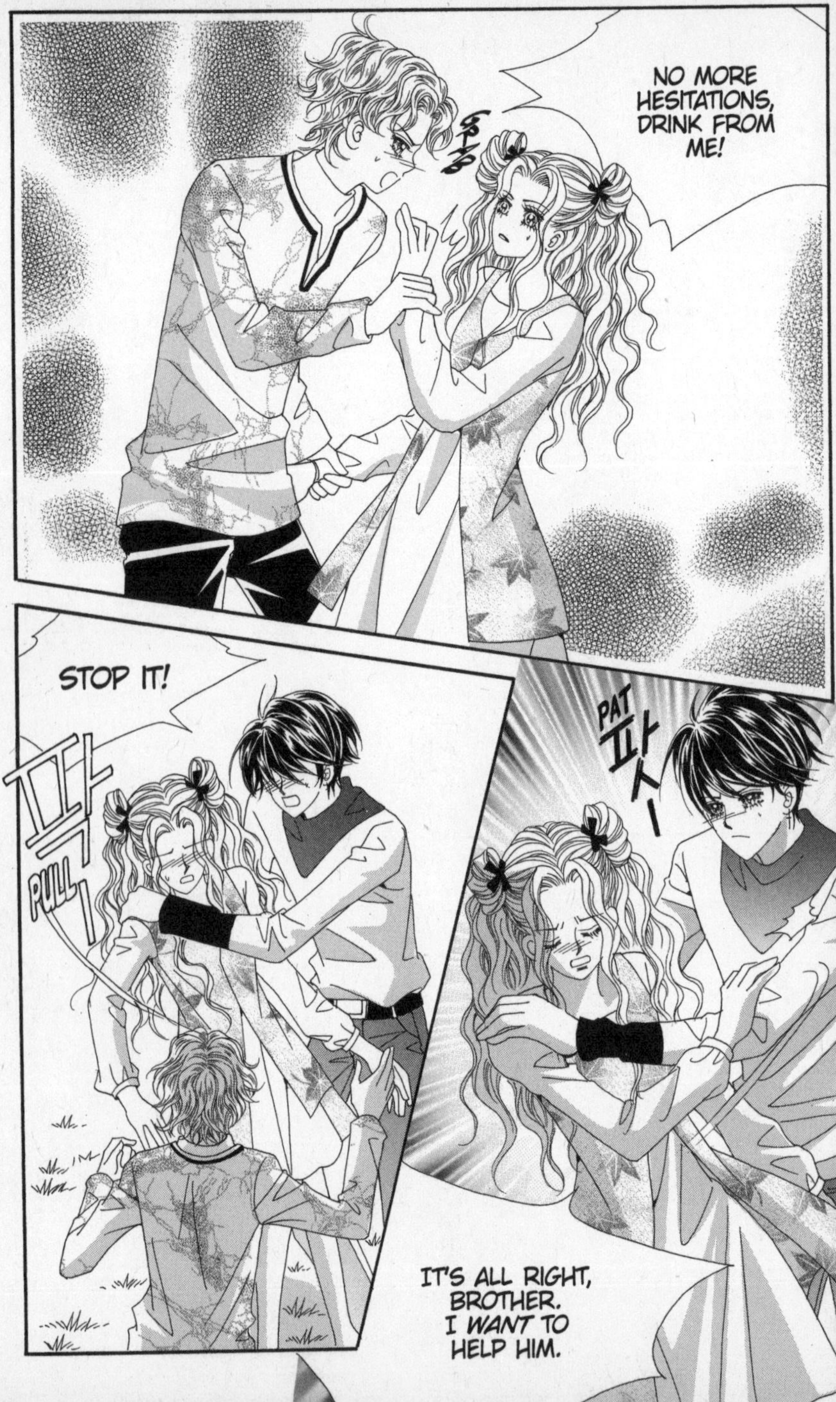
GRAB
NO MORE HESITATIONS, DRINK FROM ME!
STOP IT!
PULL
PAT
IT'S ALL RIGHT, BROTHER. I *WANT* TO HELP HIM.

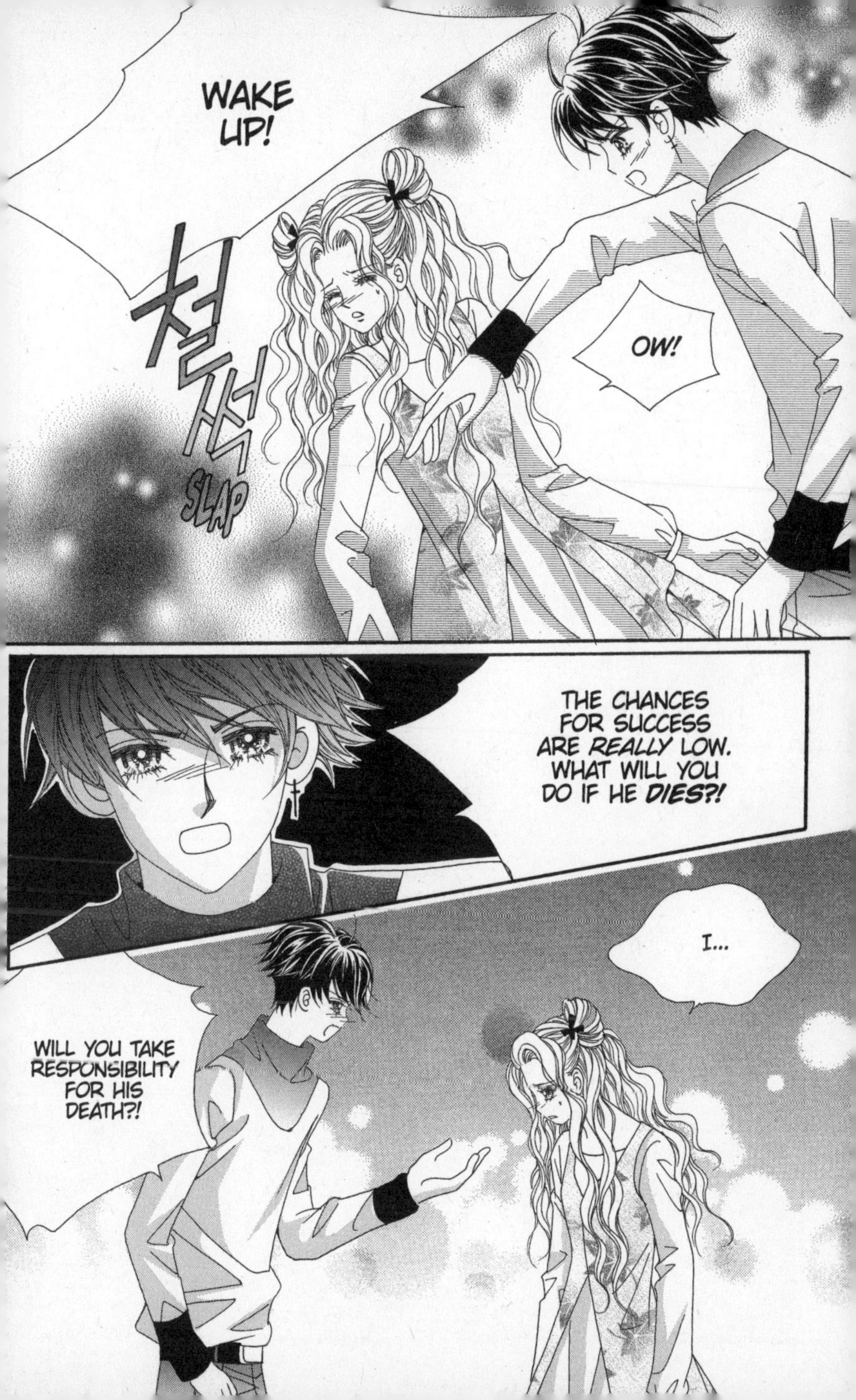
WAKE UP!
철썩
SLAP
OW!
THE CHANCES FOR SUCCESS ARE *REALLY* LOW. WHAT WILL YOU DO IF HE ***DIES***?!
WILL YOU TAKE RESPONSIBILITY FOR HIS DEATH?!
I...

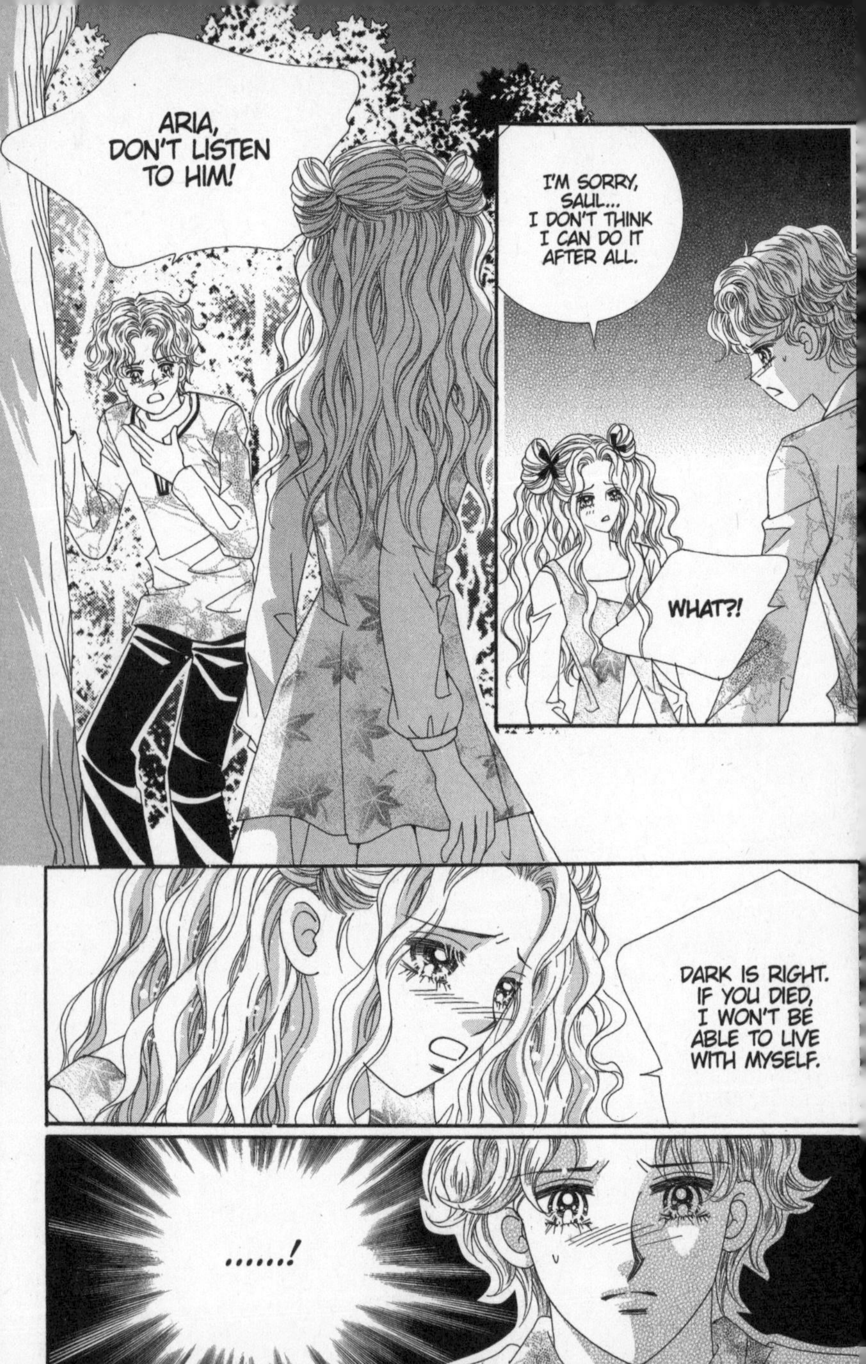
ARIA, DON'T LISTEN TO HIM!
I'M SORRY, SAUL... I DON'T THINK I CAN DO IT AFTER ALL.
WHAT?!
DARK IS RIGHT. IF YOU DIED, I WON'T BE ABLE TO LIVE WITH MYSELF.
......!

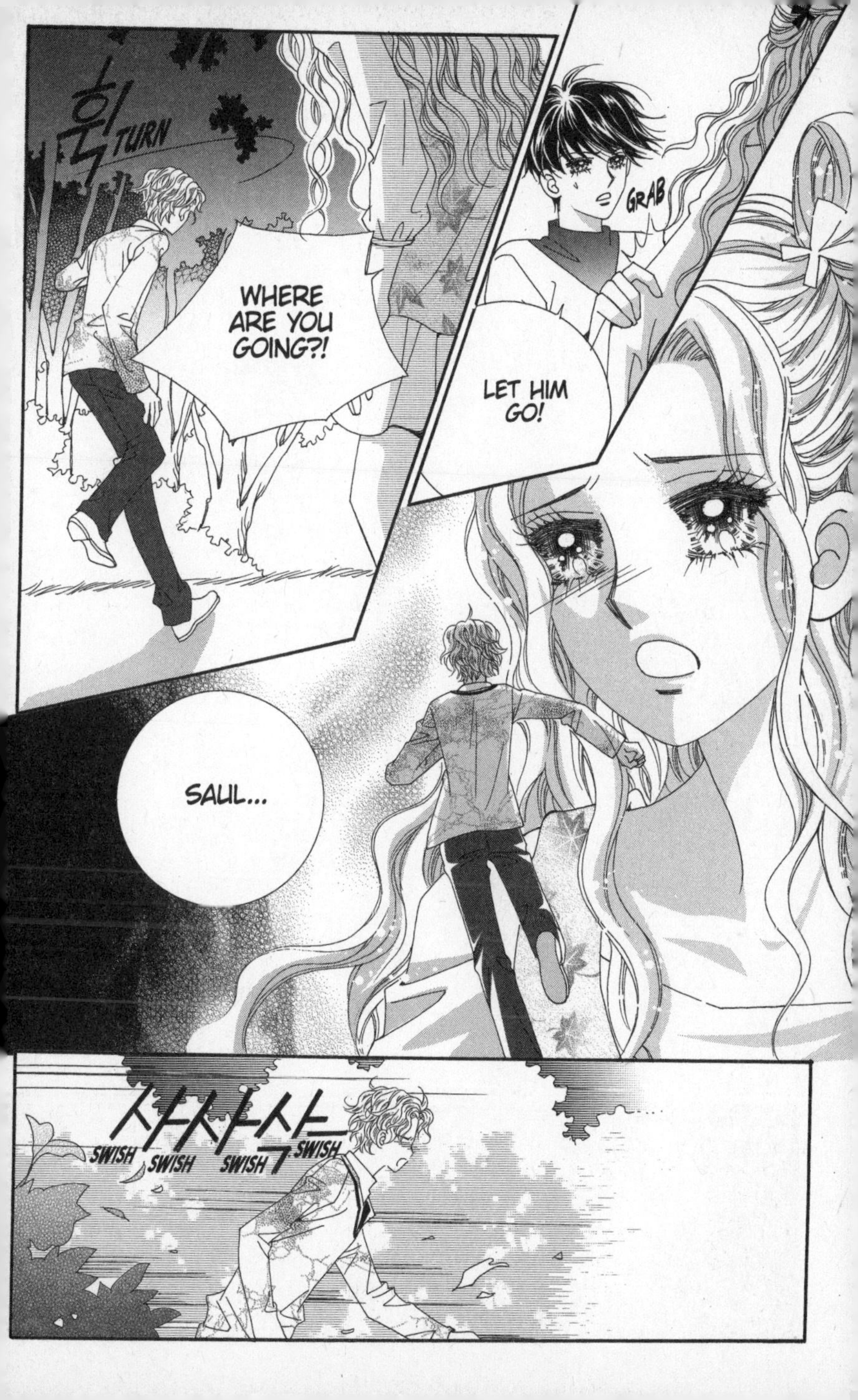

훽
TURN
WHERE ARE YOU GOING?!
GRAB
LET HIM GO!
SAUL...
사사사삭
SWISH SWISH SWISH SWISH

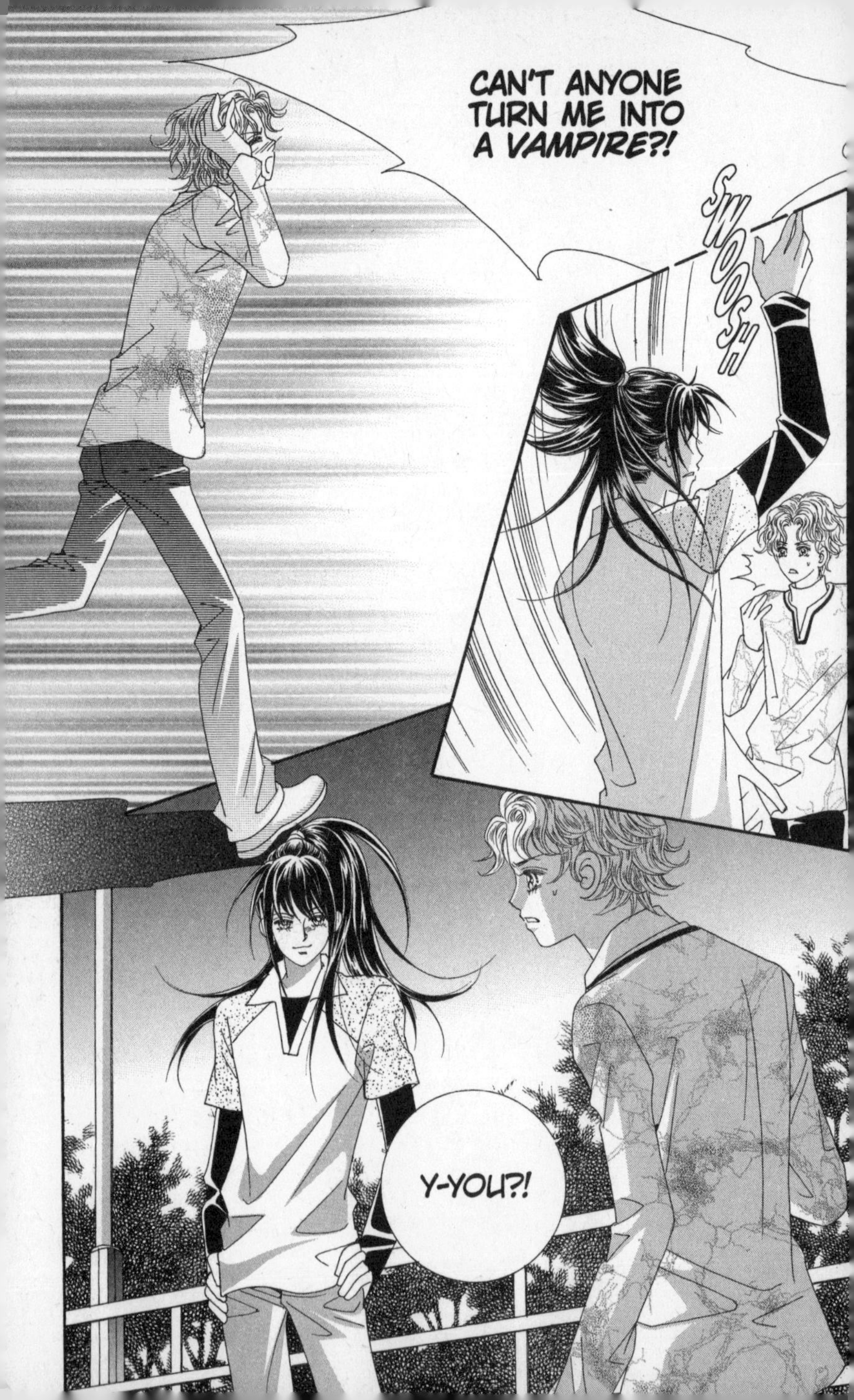
CAN'T ANYONE TURN ME INTO A VAMPIRE?!
SWOOSH
Y-YOU?!

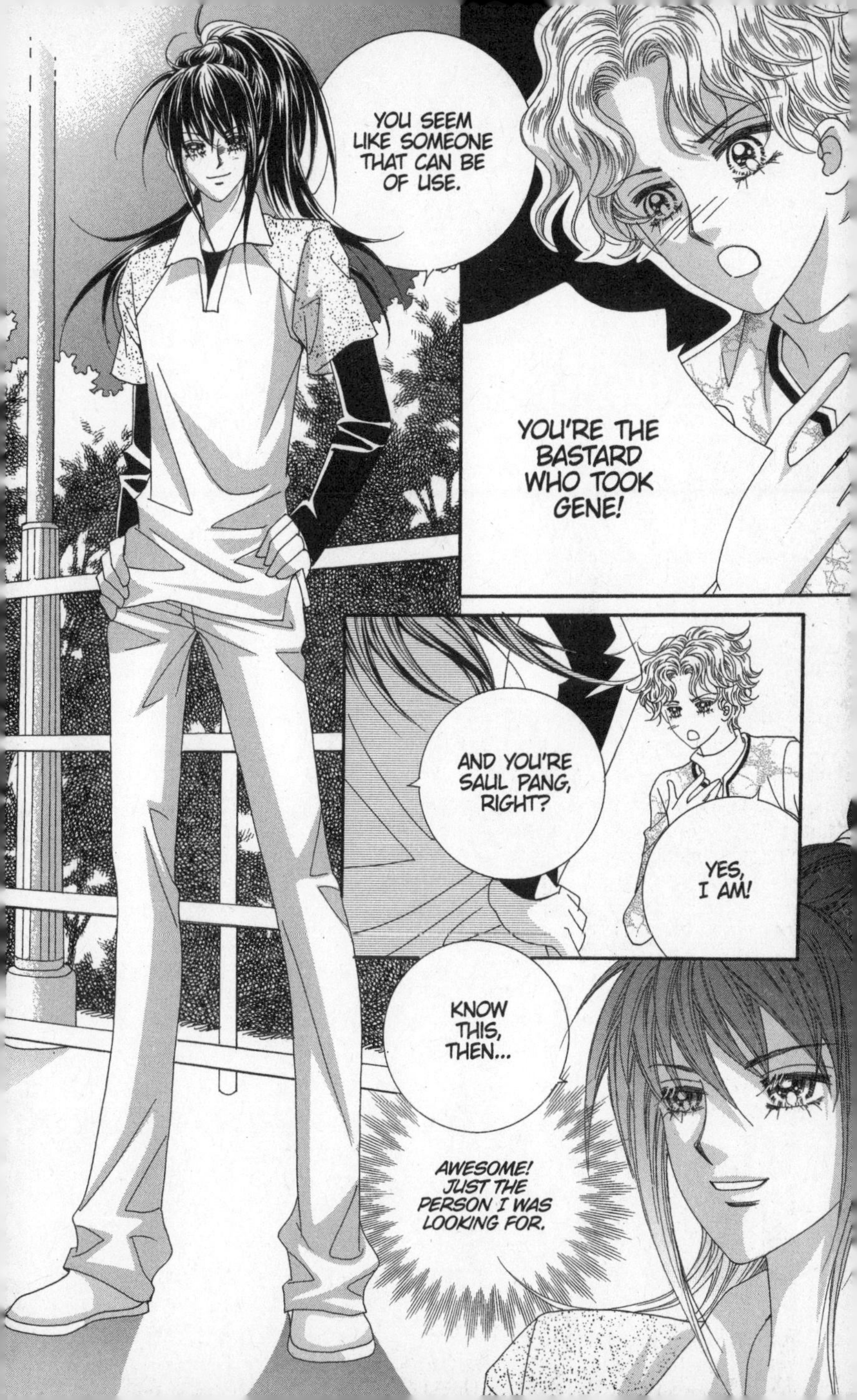
YOU SEEM LIKE SOMEONE THAT CAN BE OF USE.
YOU'RE THE BASTARD WHO TOOK GENE!
AND YOU'RE SAUL PANG, RIGHT?
YES, I AM!
KNOW THIS, THEN...
AWESOME! JUST THE PERSON I WAS LOOKING FOR.

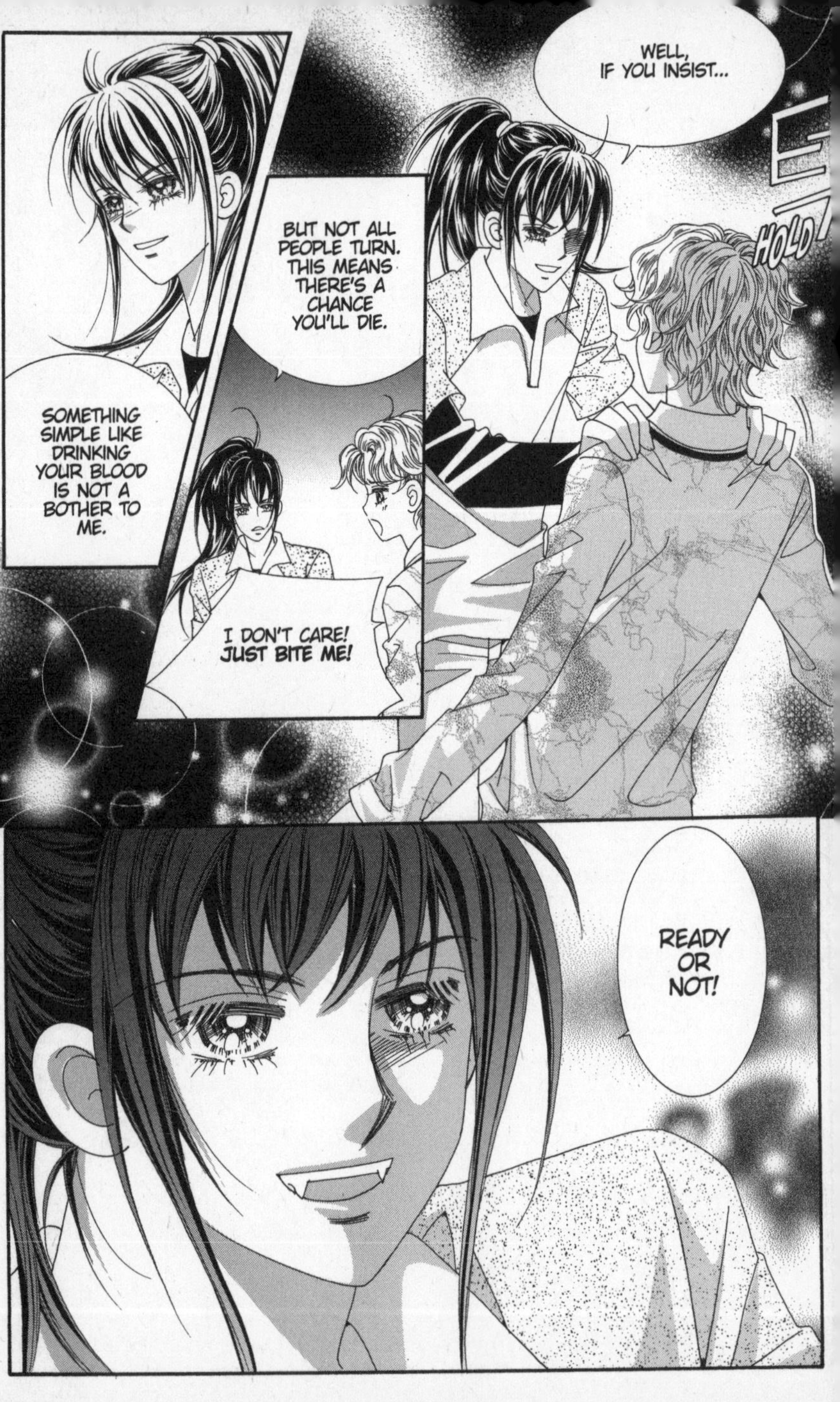
SOMETHING SIMPLE LIKE DRINKING YOUR BLOOD IS NOT A BOTHER TO ME.
BUT NOT ALL PEOPLE TURN. THIS MEANS THERE'S A CHANCE YOU'LL DIE.
I DON'T CARE! JUST BITE ME!
WELL, IF YOU INSIST...
HOLD
READY OR NOT!

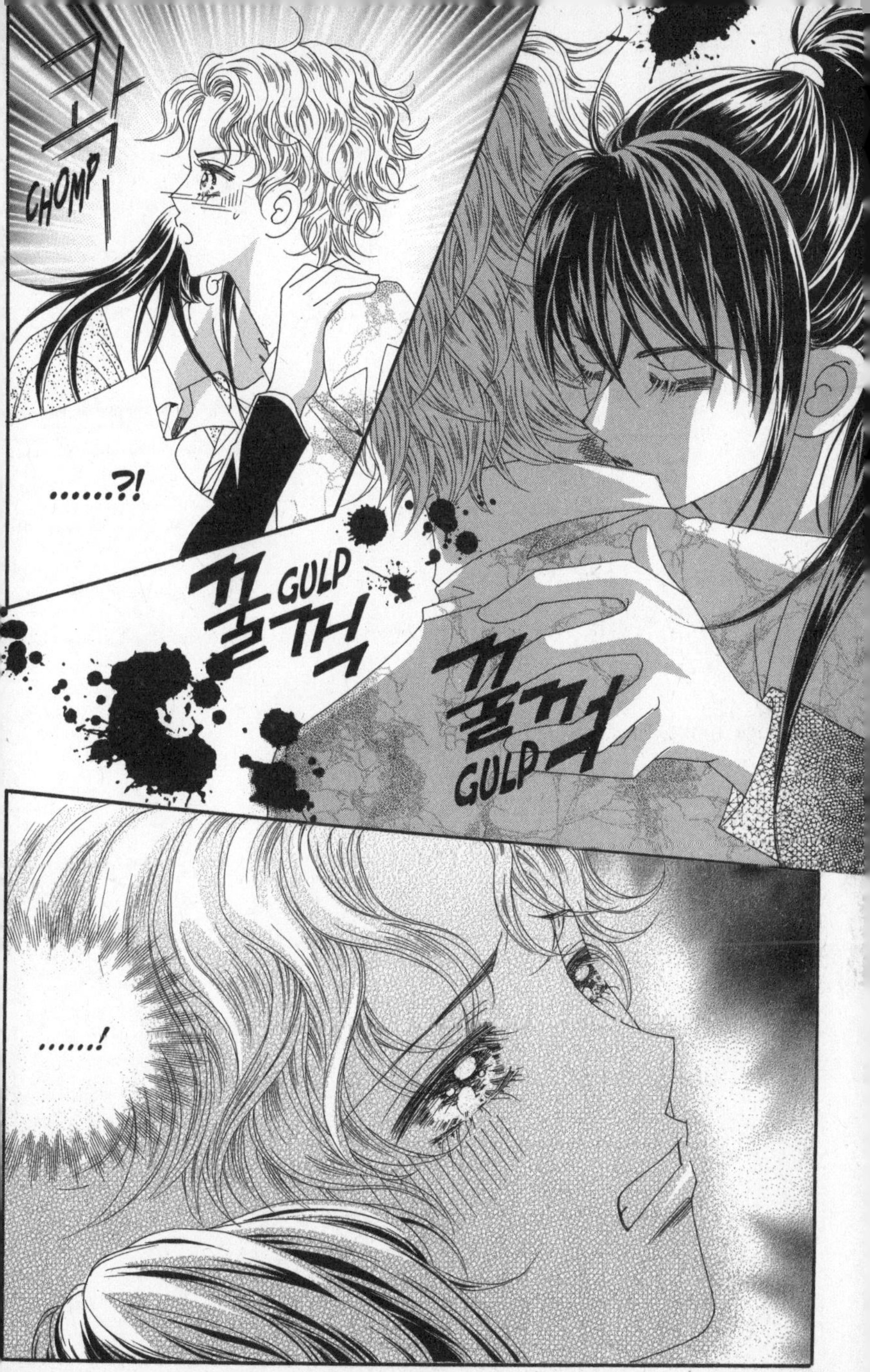
콱
CHOMP
......?!
꿀꺽
GULP
꿀꺽
GULP
......!

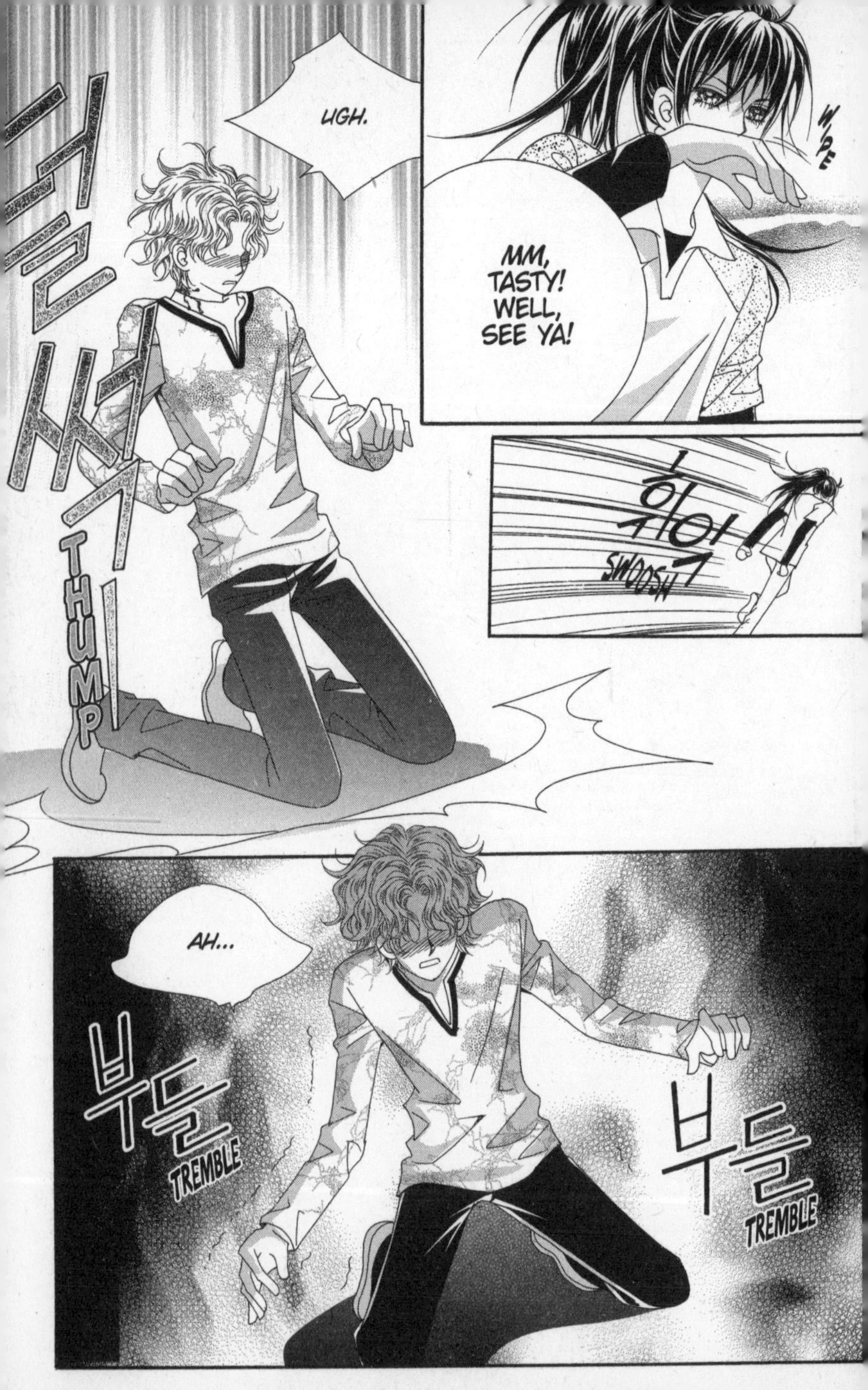
UGH.
THUMP
WIPE
MM, TASTY! WELL, SEE YA!
SWOOSH
AH...
부들
TREMBLE
부들
TREMBLE

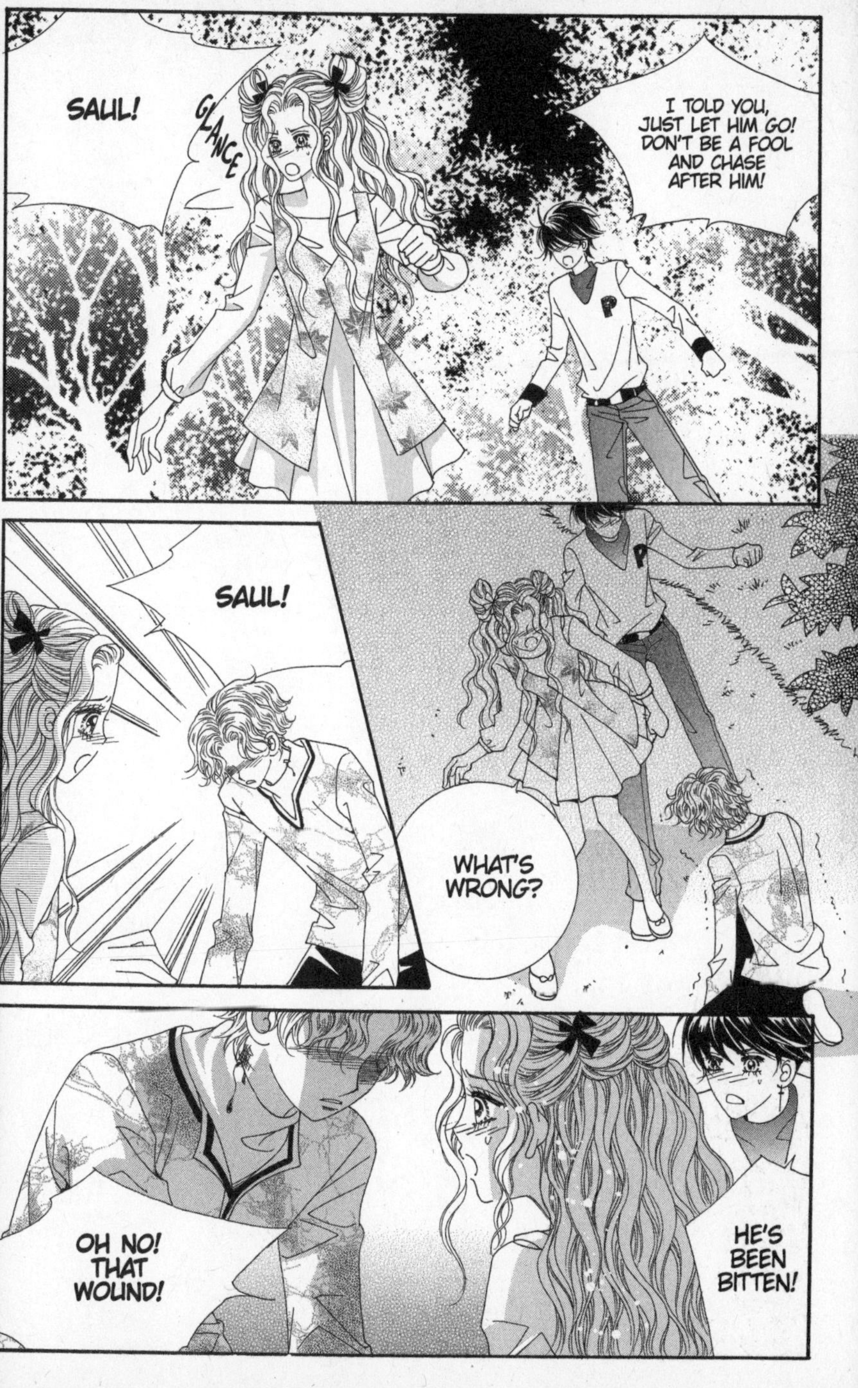
SAUL!
GLANCE
I TOLD YOU, JUST LET HIM GO! DON'T BE A FOOL AND CHASE AFTER HIM!
SAUL!
WHAT'S WRONG?
OH NO! THAT WOUND!
HE'S BEEN BITTEN!

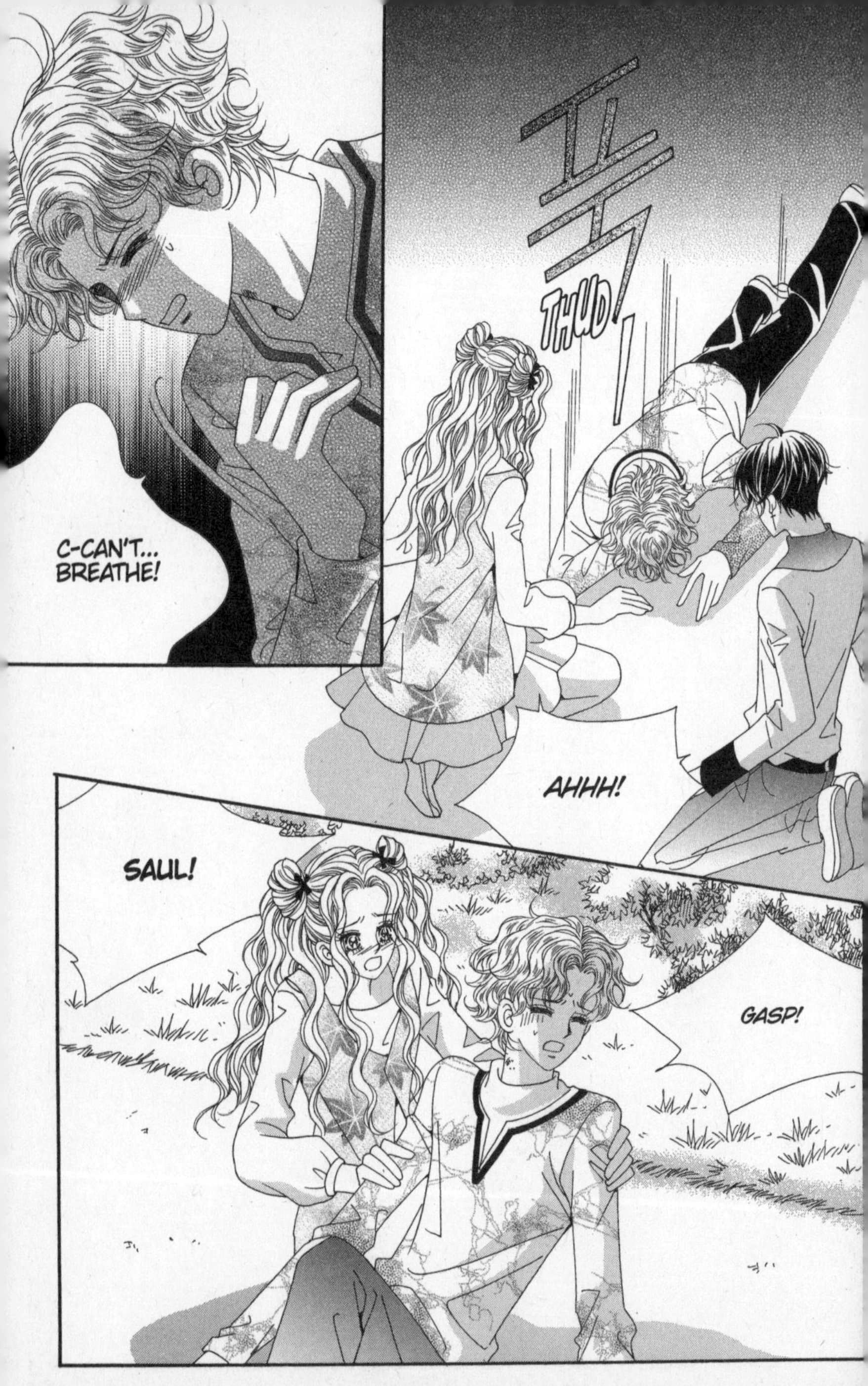
C-CAN'T...
BREATHE!
THUD
AHHH!
SAUL!
GASP!

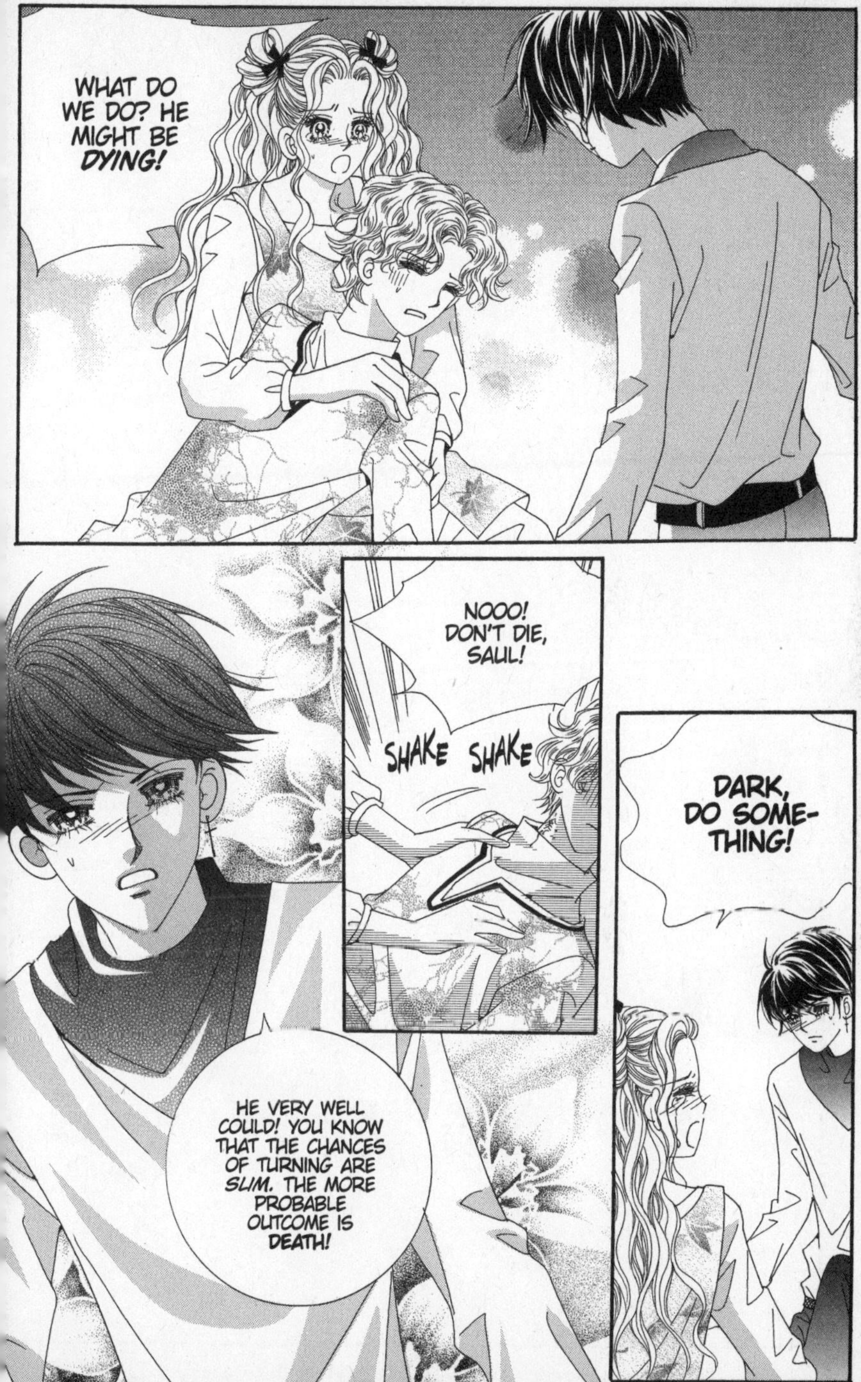
WHAT DO WE DO? HE MIGHT BE *DYING!*
HE VERY WELL COULD! YOU KNOW THAT THE CHANCES OF TURNING ARE *SLIM.* THE MORE PROBABLE OUTCOME IS DEATH!
NOOO! DON'T DIE, SAUL!
SHAKE SHAKE
DARK, DO SOME-THING!

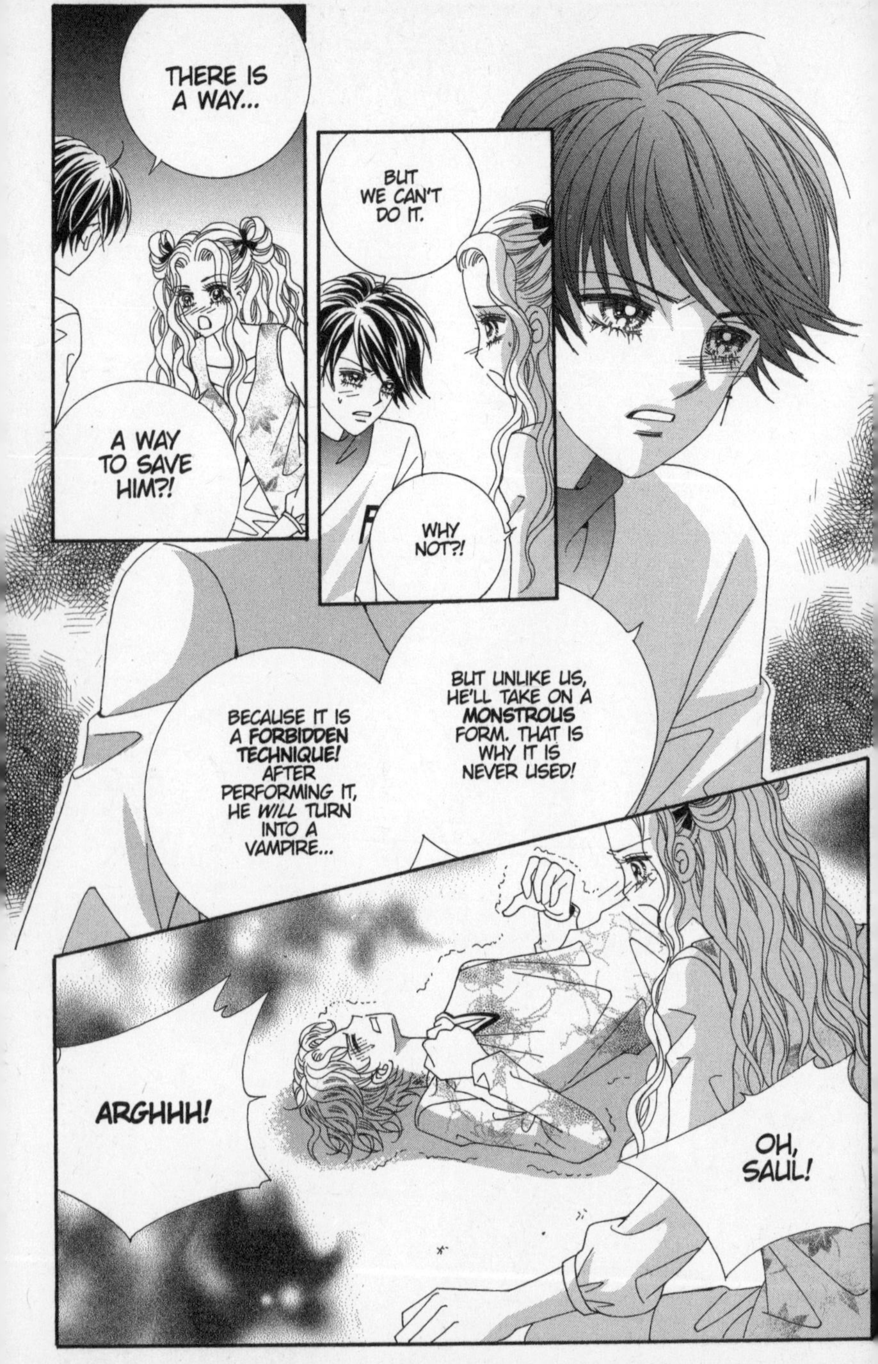
THERE IS A WAY...
A WAY TO SAVE HIM?!
BUT WE CAN'T DO IT.
WHY NOT?!
BECAUSE IT IS A **FORBIDDEN TECHNIQUE!** AFTER PERFORMING IT, HE *WILL* TURN INTO A VAMPIRE...
BUT UNLIKE US, HE'LL TAKE ON A **MONSTROUS** FORM. THAT IS WHY IT IS NEVER USED!
ARGHHH!
OH, SAUL!

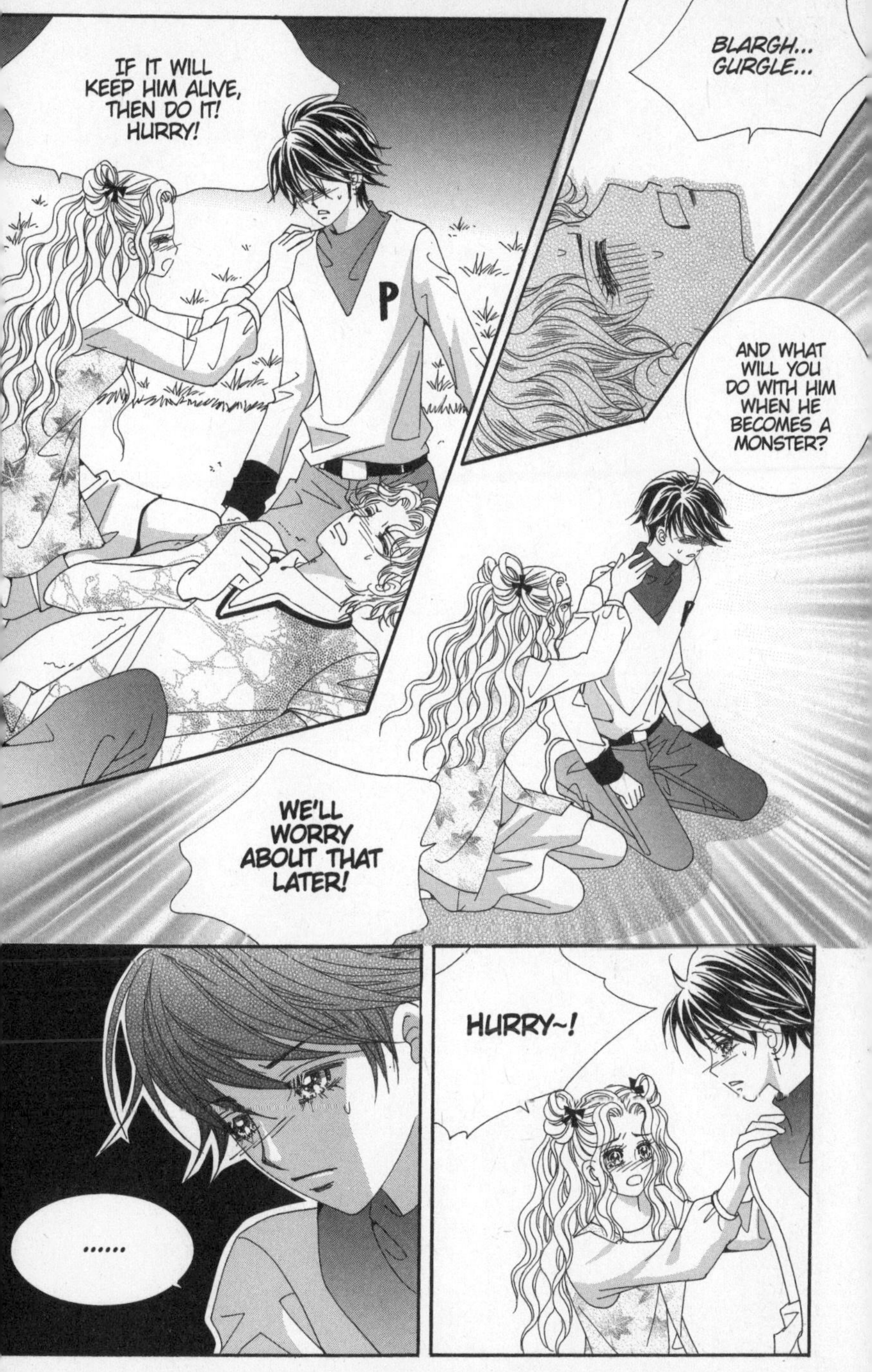
IF IT WILL KEEP HIM ALIVE, THEN DO IT! HURRY!
BLARGH... GURGLE...
AND WHAT WILL YOU DO WITH HIM WHEN HE BECOMES A MONSTER?
WE'LL WORRY ABOUT THAT LATER!
......
HURRY~!

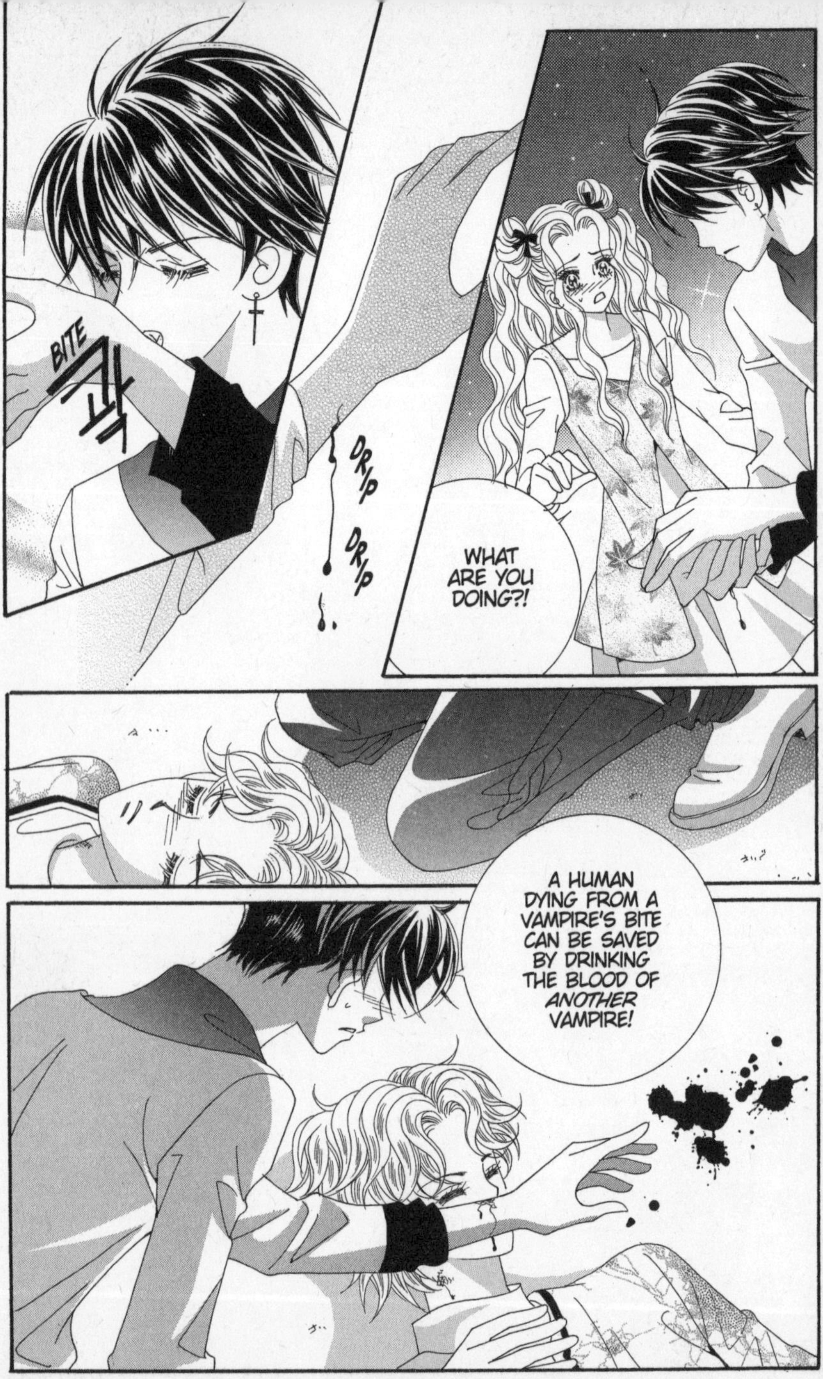

BITE
DRIP DRIP
WHAT ARE YOU DOING?!
A HUMAN DYING FROM A VAMPIRE'S BITE CAN BE SAVED BY DRINKING THE BLOOD OF *ANOTHER* VAMPIRE!

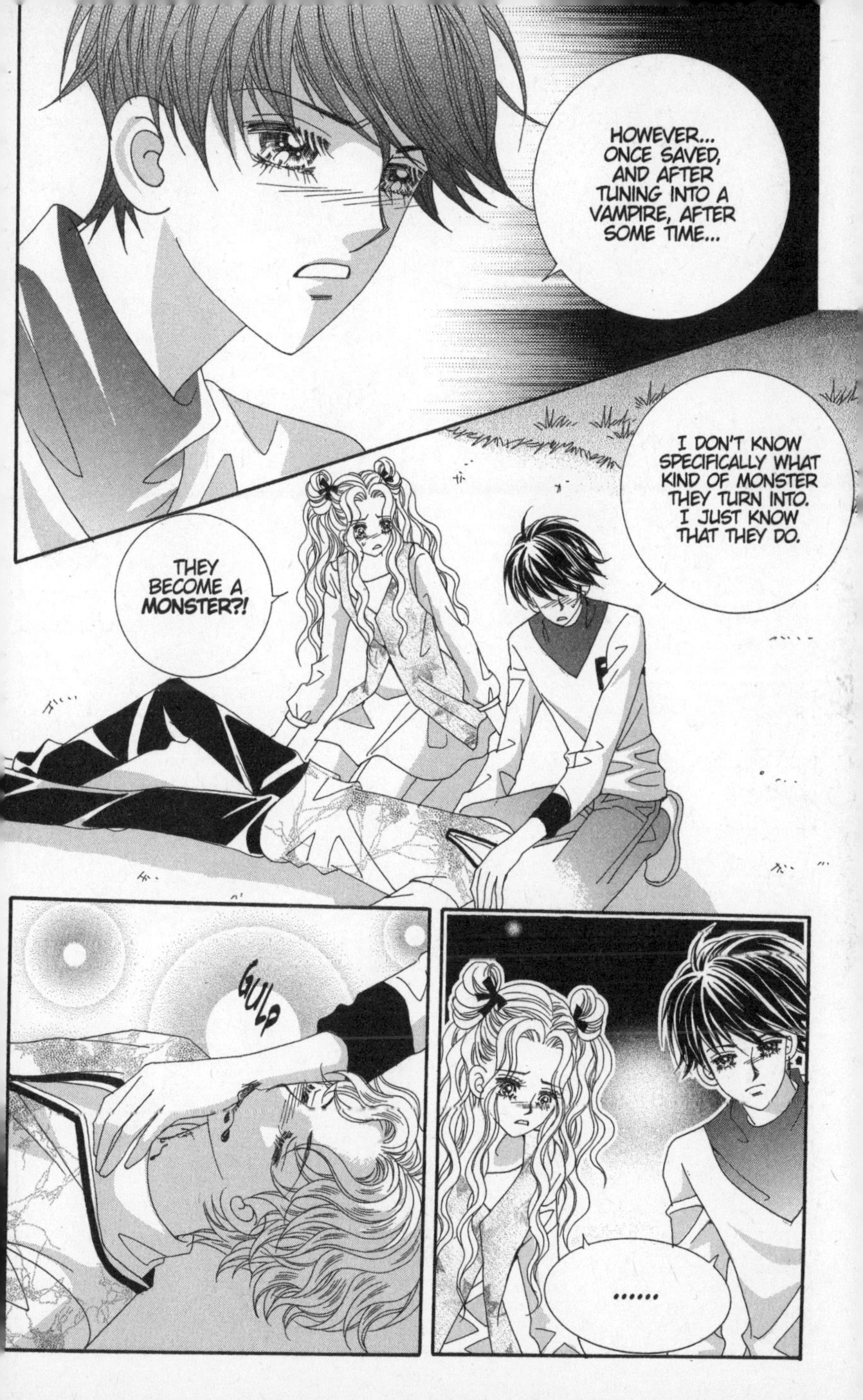
HOWEVER... ONCE SAVED, AND AFTER TUNING INTO A VAMPIRE, AFTER SOME TIME...
THEY BECOME A MONSTER?!
I DON'T KNOW SPECIFICALLY WHAT KIND OF MONSTER THEY TURN INTO. I JUST KNOW THAT THEY DO.
GULP
......

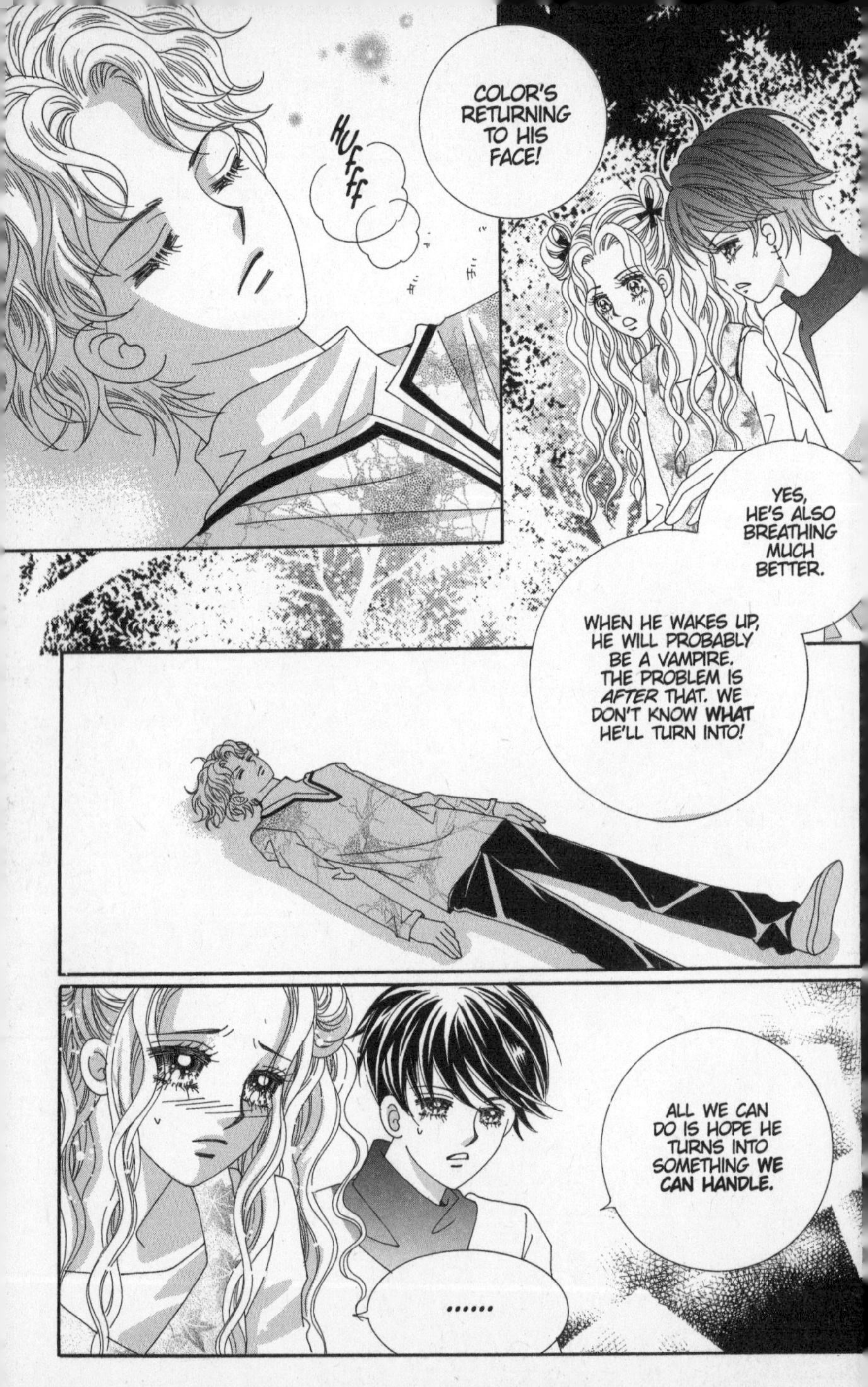
HUFFF
COLOR'S RETURNING TO HIS FACE!
YES, HE'S ALSO BREATHING MUCH BETTER.
WHEN HE WAKES UP, HE WILL PROBABLY BE A VAMPIRE. THE PROBLEM IS *AFTER* THAT. WE DON'T KNOW WHAT HE'LL TURN INTO!
ALL WE CAN DO IS HOPE HE TURNS INTO SOMETHING WE CAN HANDLE.
......

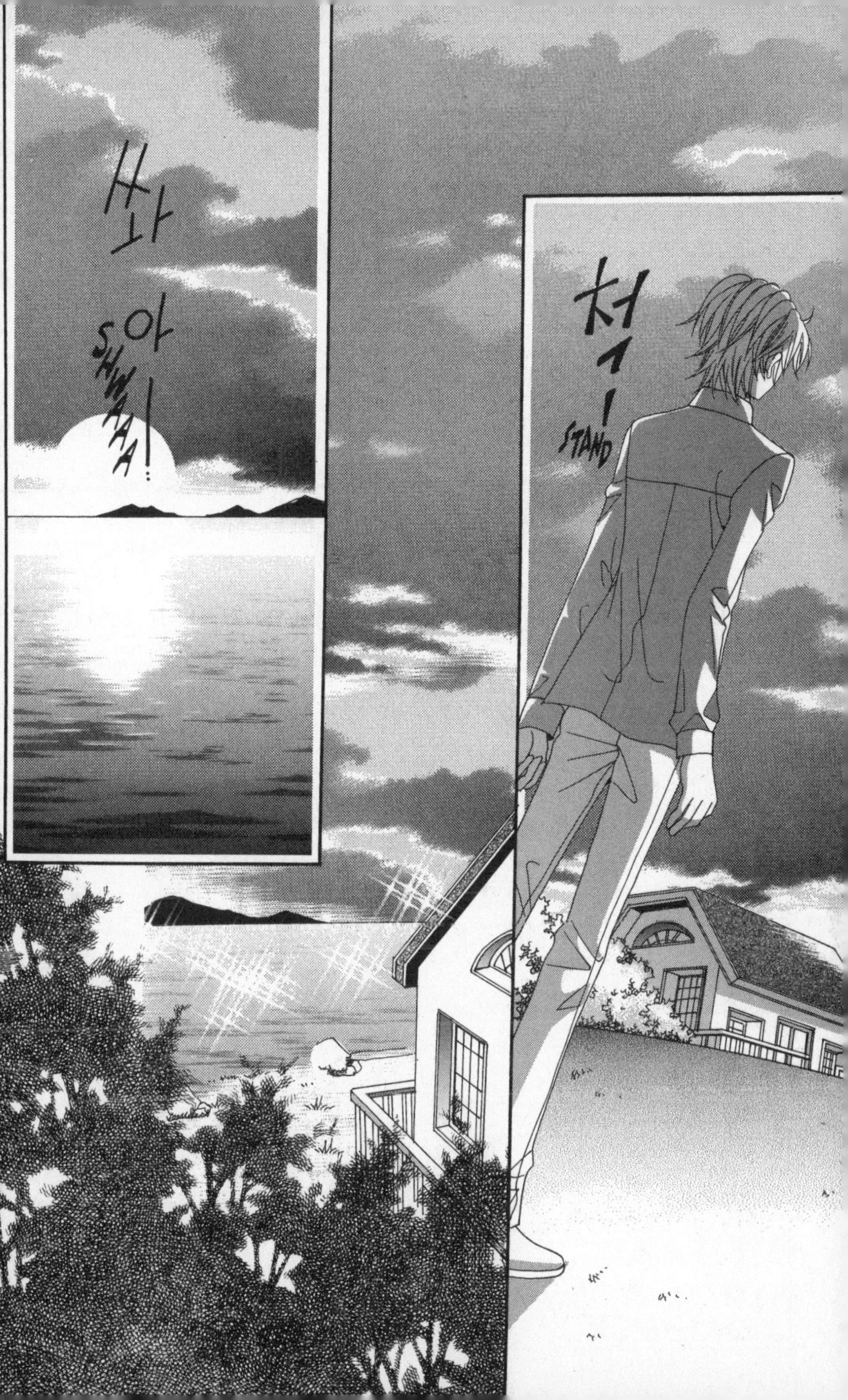
쏴아
SHWAAA!
척
STAND

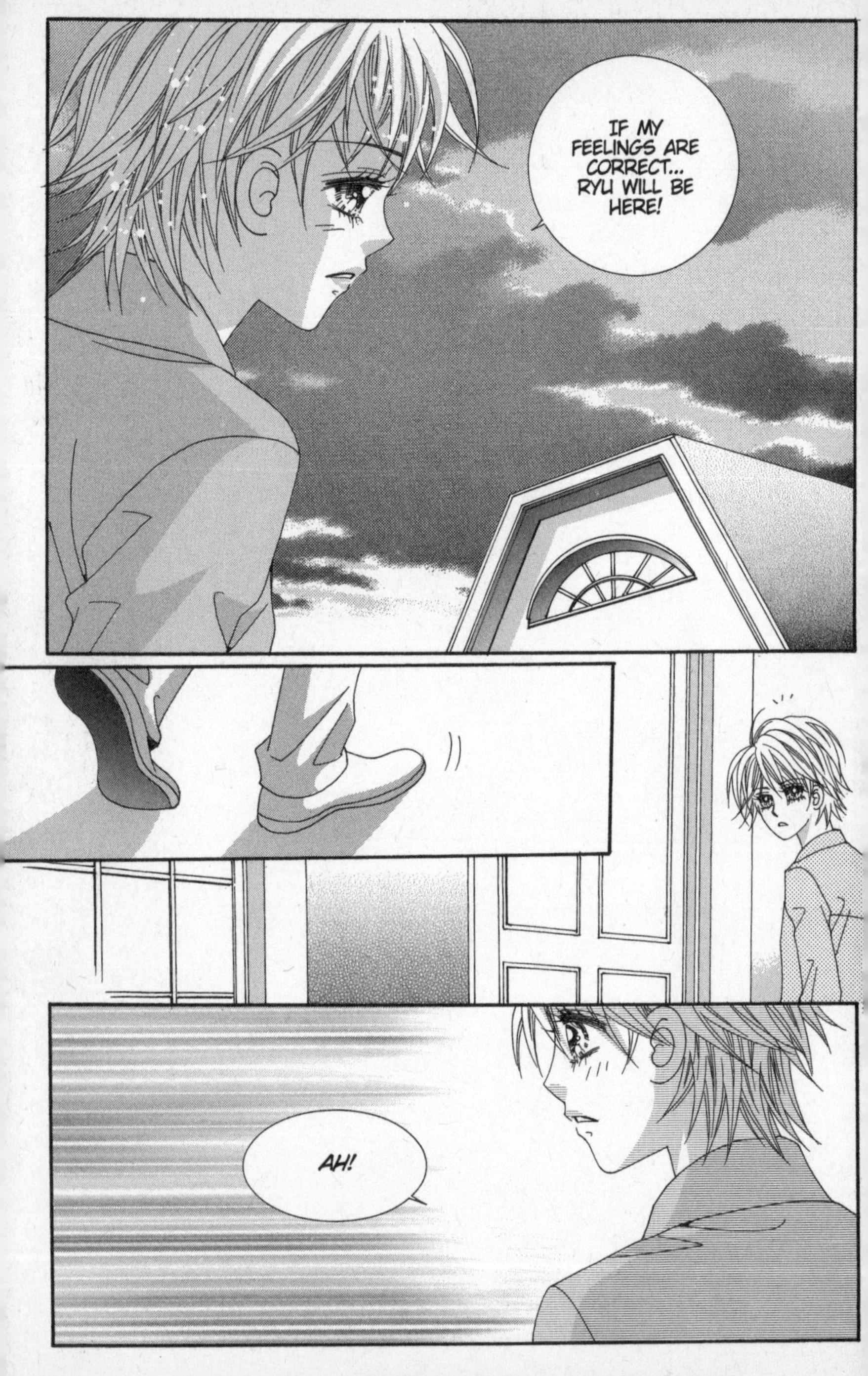
IF MY FEELINGS ARE CORRECT... RYU WILL BE HERE!
AH!

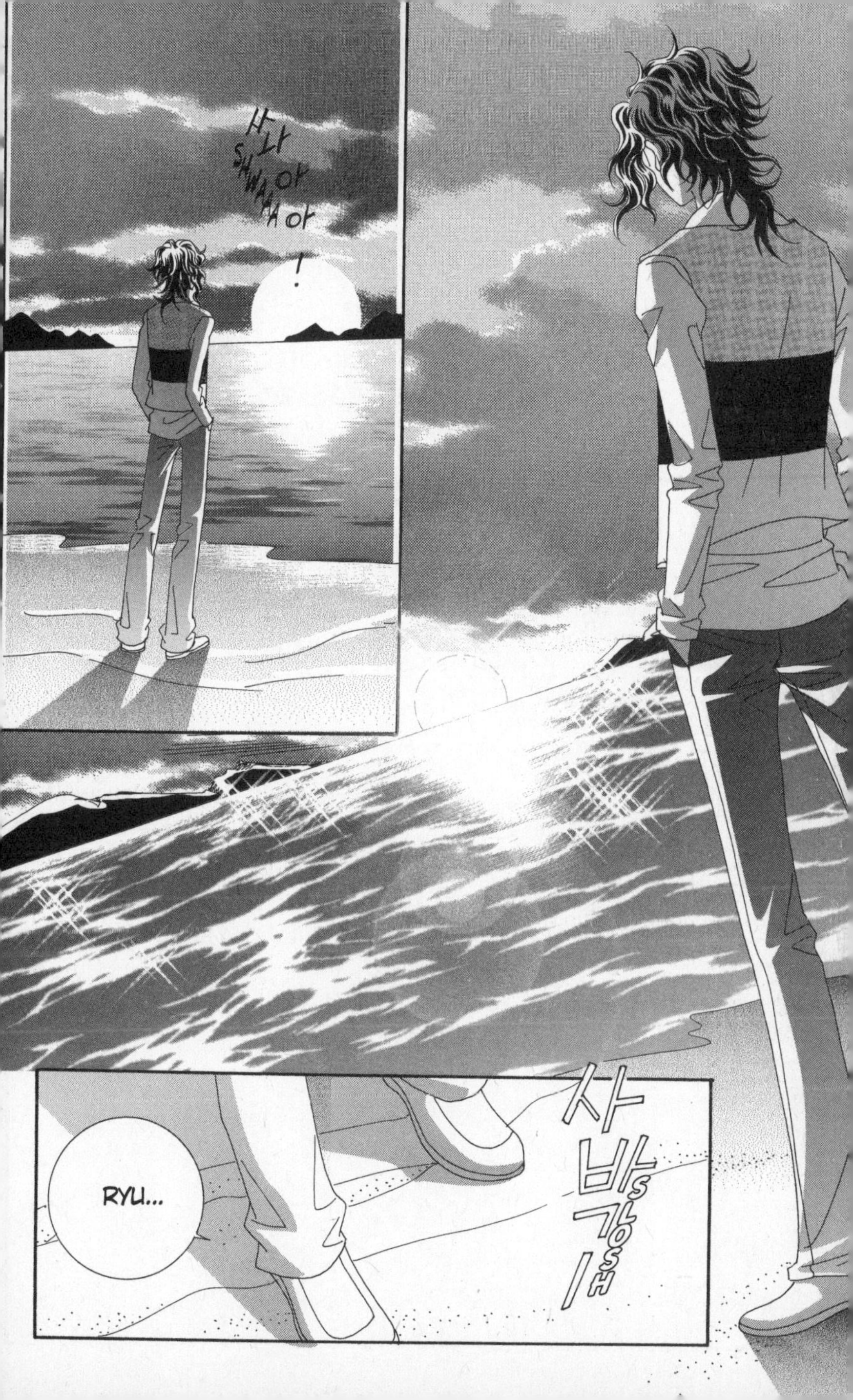

SHWAAA!
RYU...
SLOSH

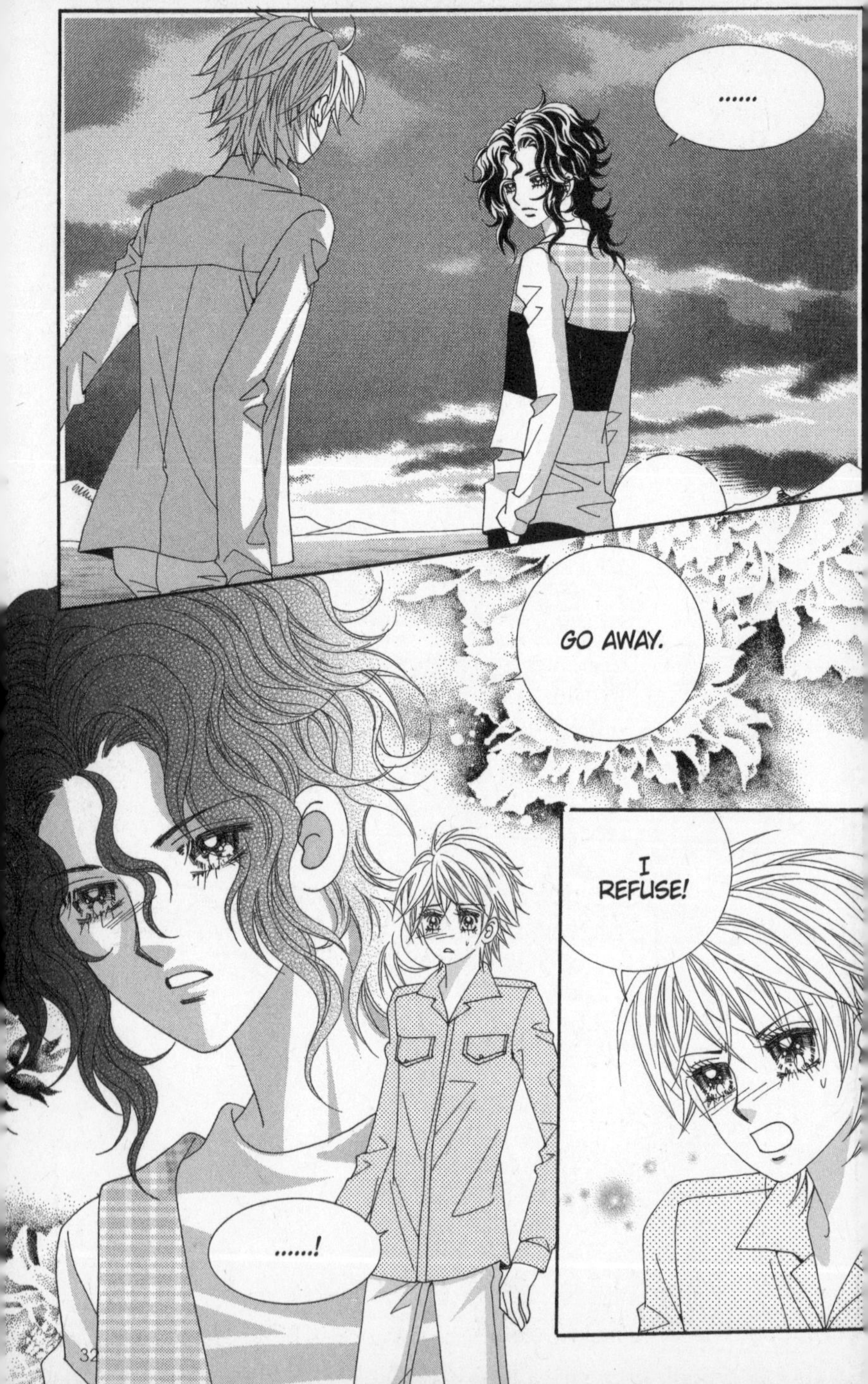
......
GO AWAY.
I REFUSE!
......!

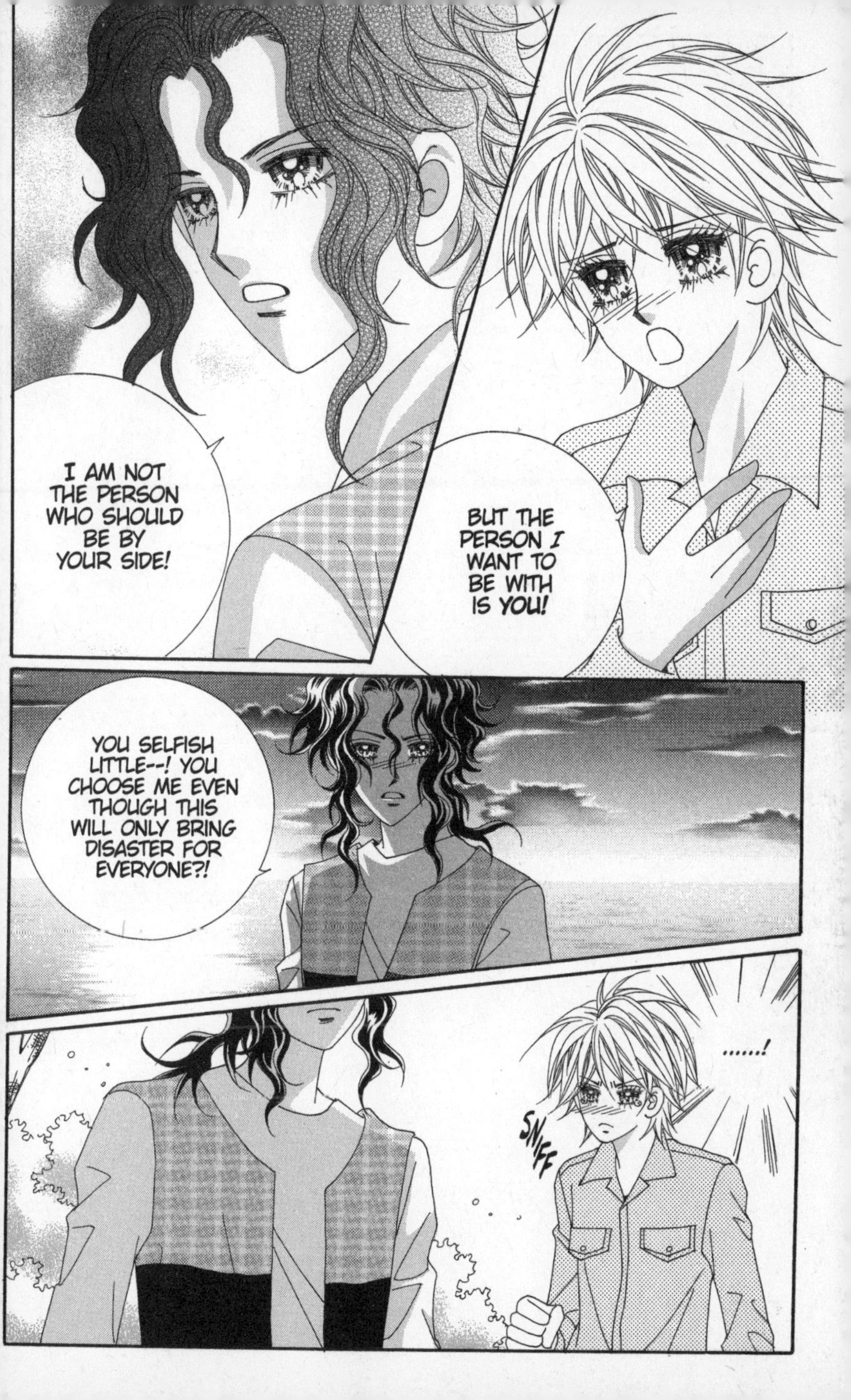
I AM NOT THE PERSON WHO SHOULD BE BY YOUR SIDE!
BUT THE PERSON I WANT TO BE WITH IS YOU!
YOU SELFISH LITTLE--! YOU CHOOSE ME EVEN THOUGH THIS WILL ONLY BRING DISASTER FOR EVERYONE?!
SNIFF
......!

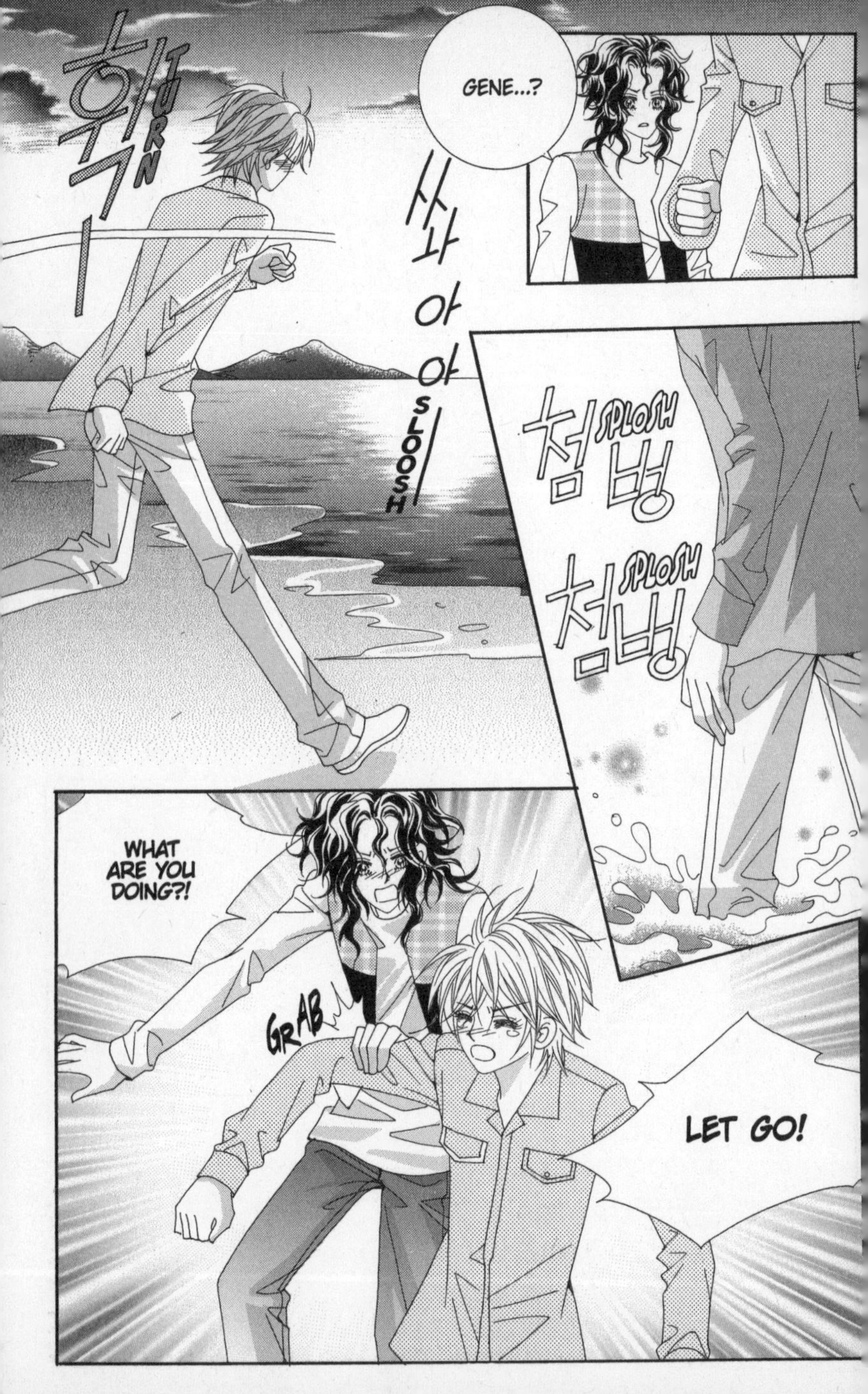
TURN
SLOOSH
GENE...?
SPLOSH
SPLOSH
WHAT ARE YOU DOING?!
GRAB
LET GO!

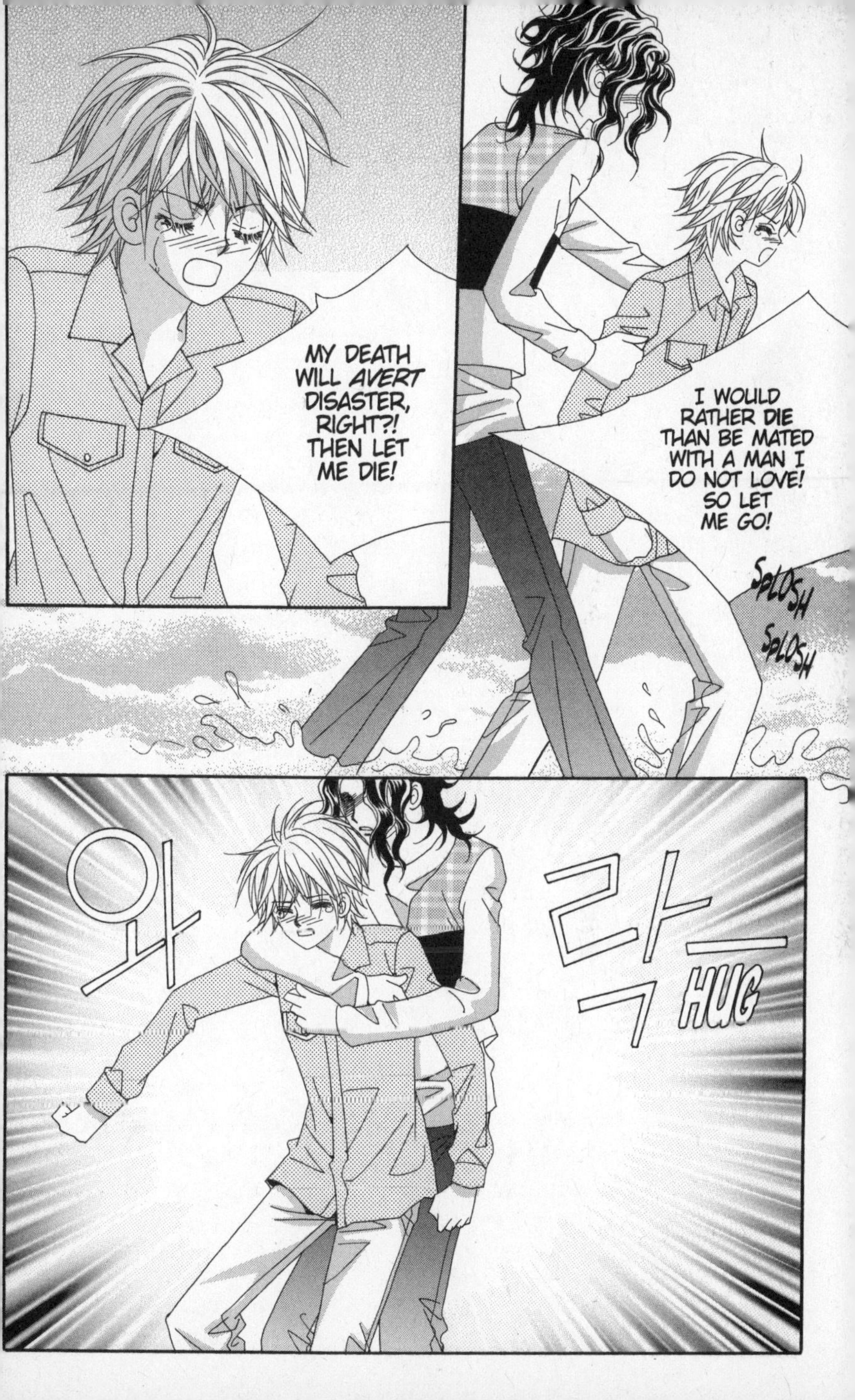
MY DEATH WILL *AVERT* DISASTER, RIGHT?! THEN LET ME DIE!
I WOULD RATHER DIE THAN BE MATED WITH A MAN I DO NOT LOVE! SO LET ME GO!
SPLOSH
SPLOSH
와락
HUG

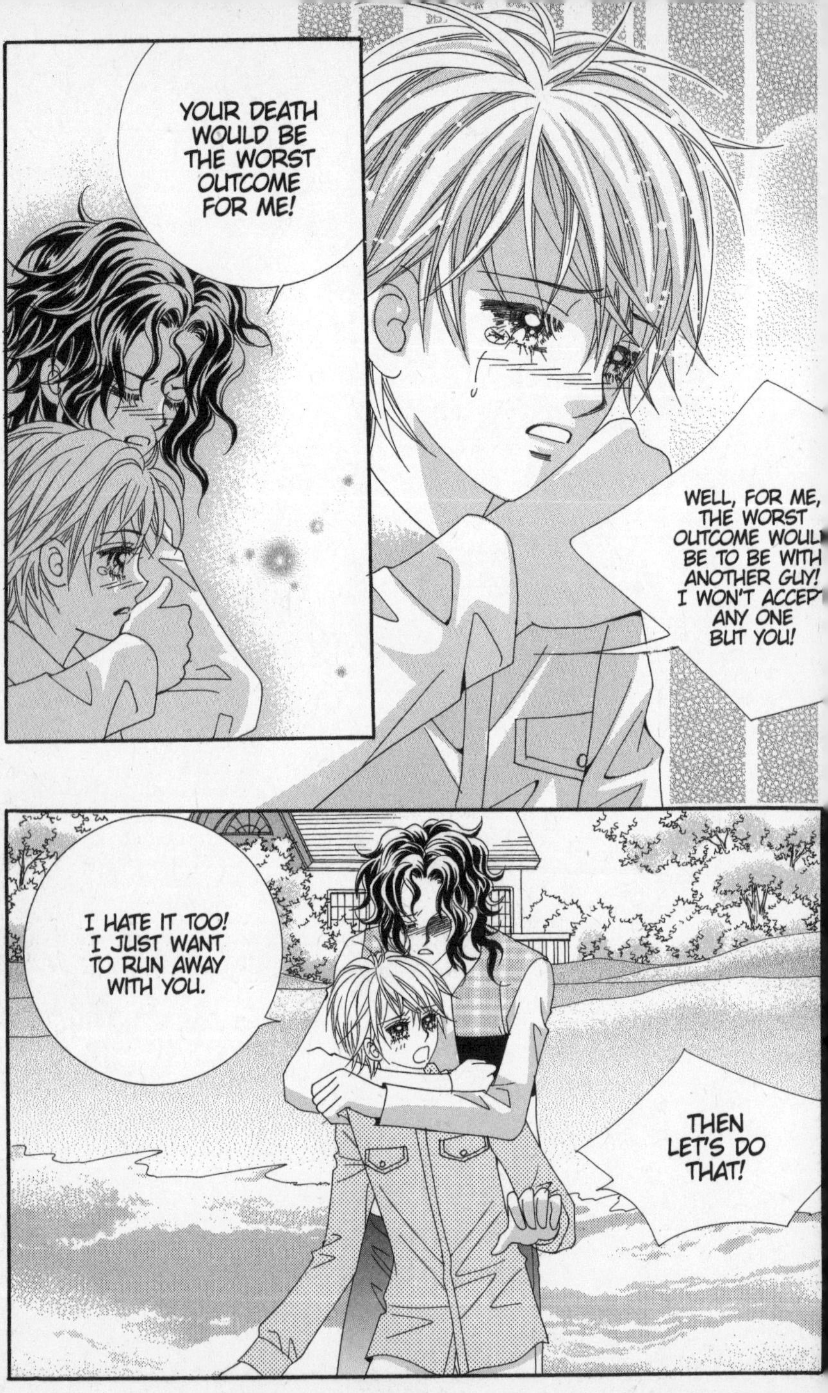
YOUR DEATH WOULD BE THE WORST OUTCOME FOR ME!
WELL, FOR ME, THE WORST OUTCOME WOULD BE TO BE WITH ANOTHER GUY! I WON'T ACCEP ANY ONE BUT YOU!
I HATE IT TOO! I JUST WANT TO RUN AWAY WITH YOU.
THEN LET'S DO THAT!

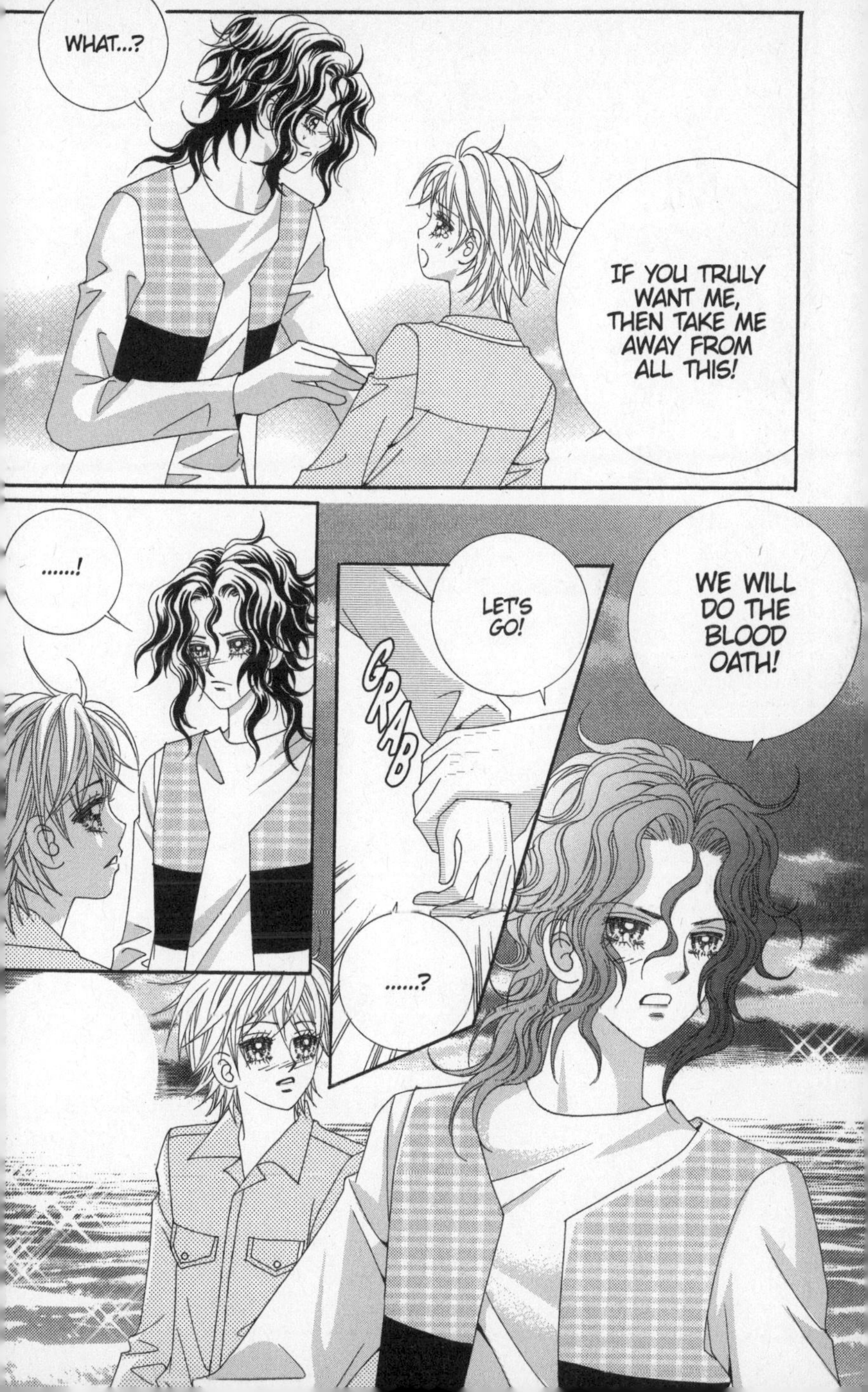
WHAT...?
IF YOU TRULY WANT ME, THEN TAKE ME AWAY FROM ALL THIS!
......!
LET'S GO!
GRAB
WE WILL DO THE BLOOD OATH!
......?

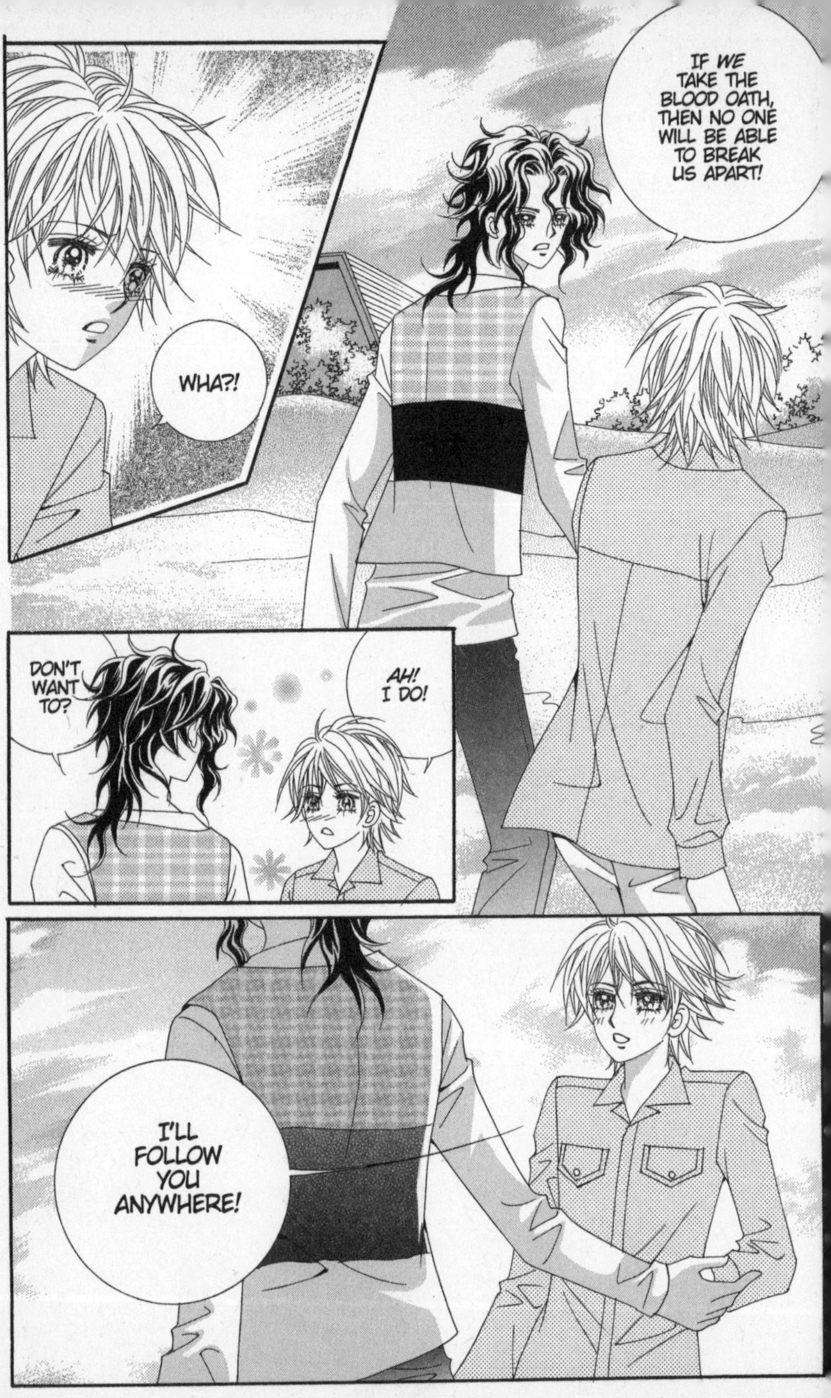
WHA?!
DON'T WANT TO?
AH! I DO!
IF *WE* TAKE THE BLOOD OATH, THEN NO ONE WILL BE ABLE TO BREAK US APART!
I'LL FOLLOW YOU ANYWHERE!

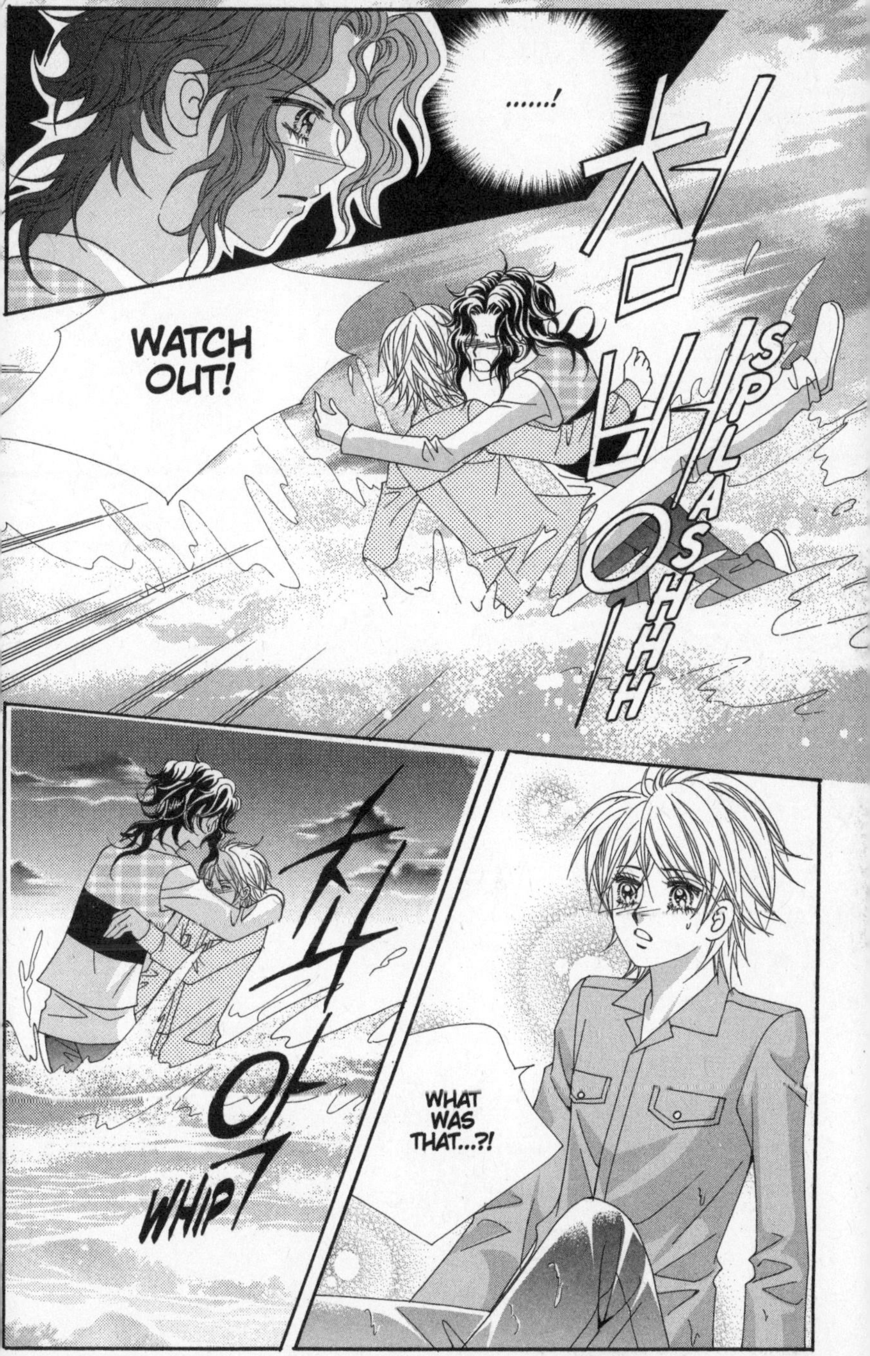
......!
첨벙-
WATCH OUT!
SPLASHHHH
WHIP
WHAT WAS THAT...?!

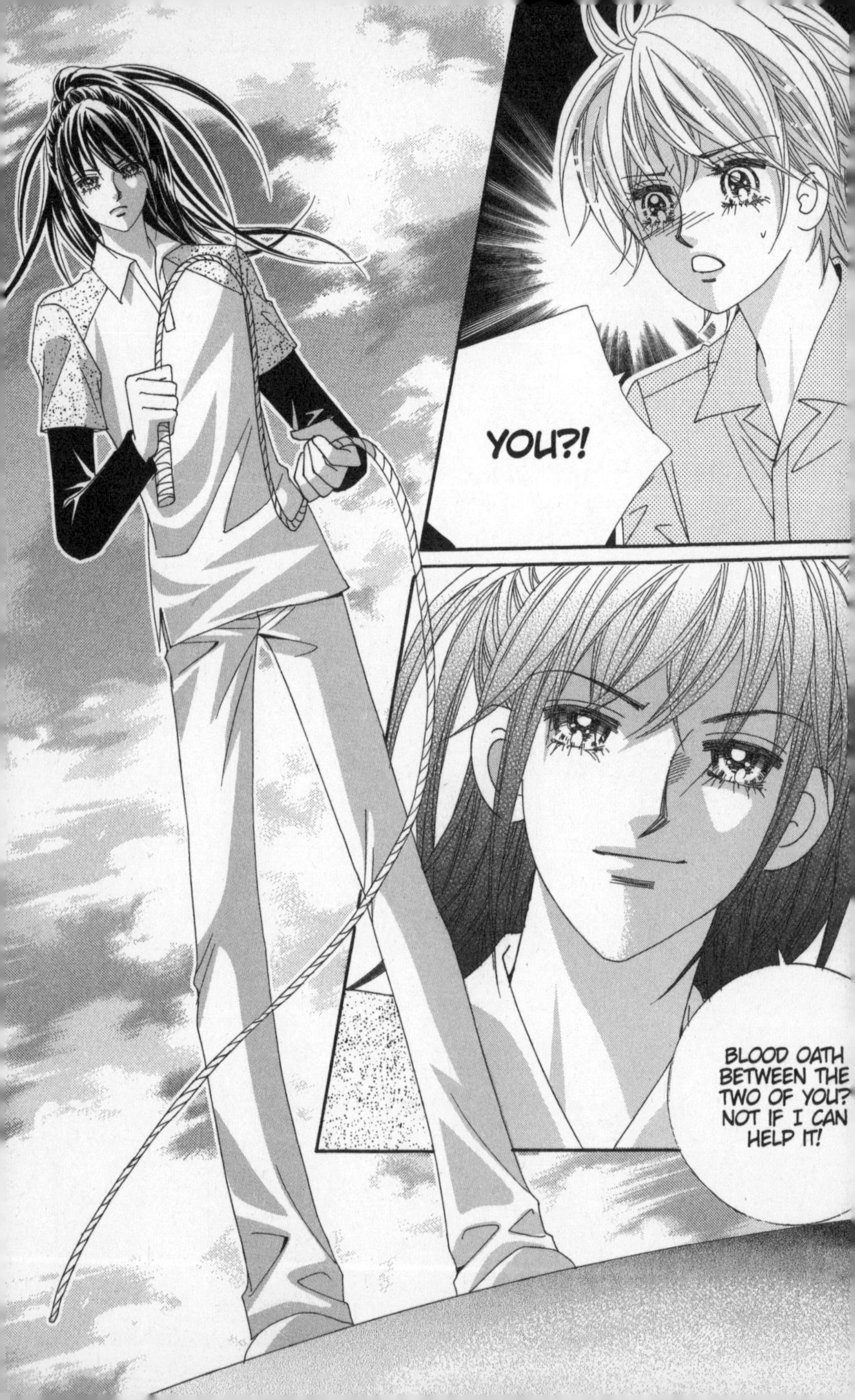
YOU?!
BLOOD OATH BETWEEN THE TWO OF YOU? NOT IF I CAN HELP IT!

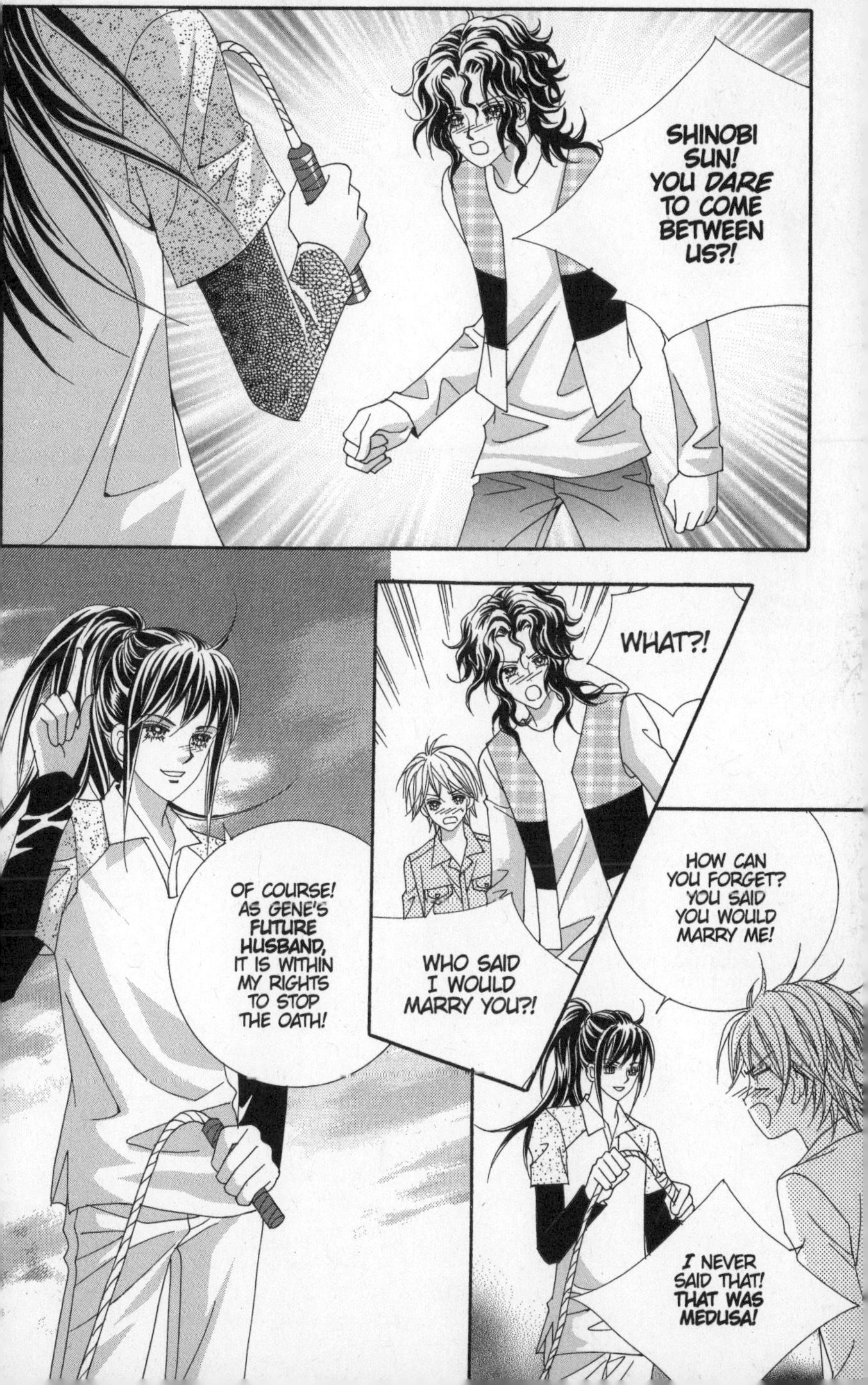
SHINOBI SUN! YOU DARE TO COME BETWEEN US?!
OF COURSE! AS GENE'S FUTURE HUSBAND, IT IS WITHIN MY RIGHTS TO STOP THE OATH!
WHAT?!
WHO SAID I WOULD MARRY YOU?!
HOW CAN YOU FORGET? YOU SAID YOU WOULD MARRY ME!
I NEVER SAID THAT! THAT WAS MEDUSA!

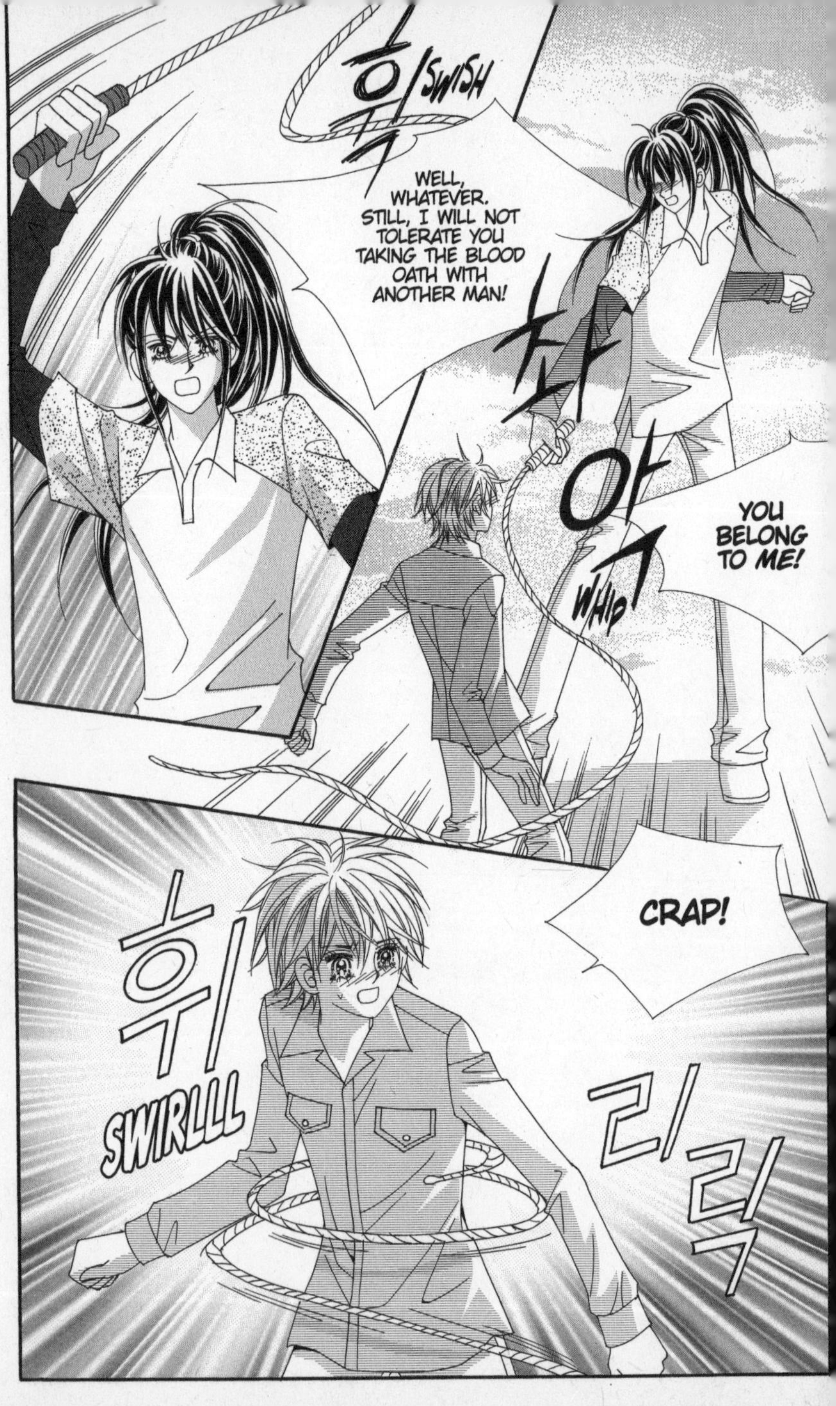
SWISH
WELL, WHATEVER. STILL, I WILL NOT TOLERATE YOU TAKING THE BLOOD OATH WITH ANOTHER MAN!
YOU BELONG TO ME!
WHIP
CRAP!
SWIRLLL

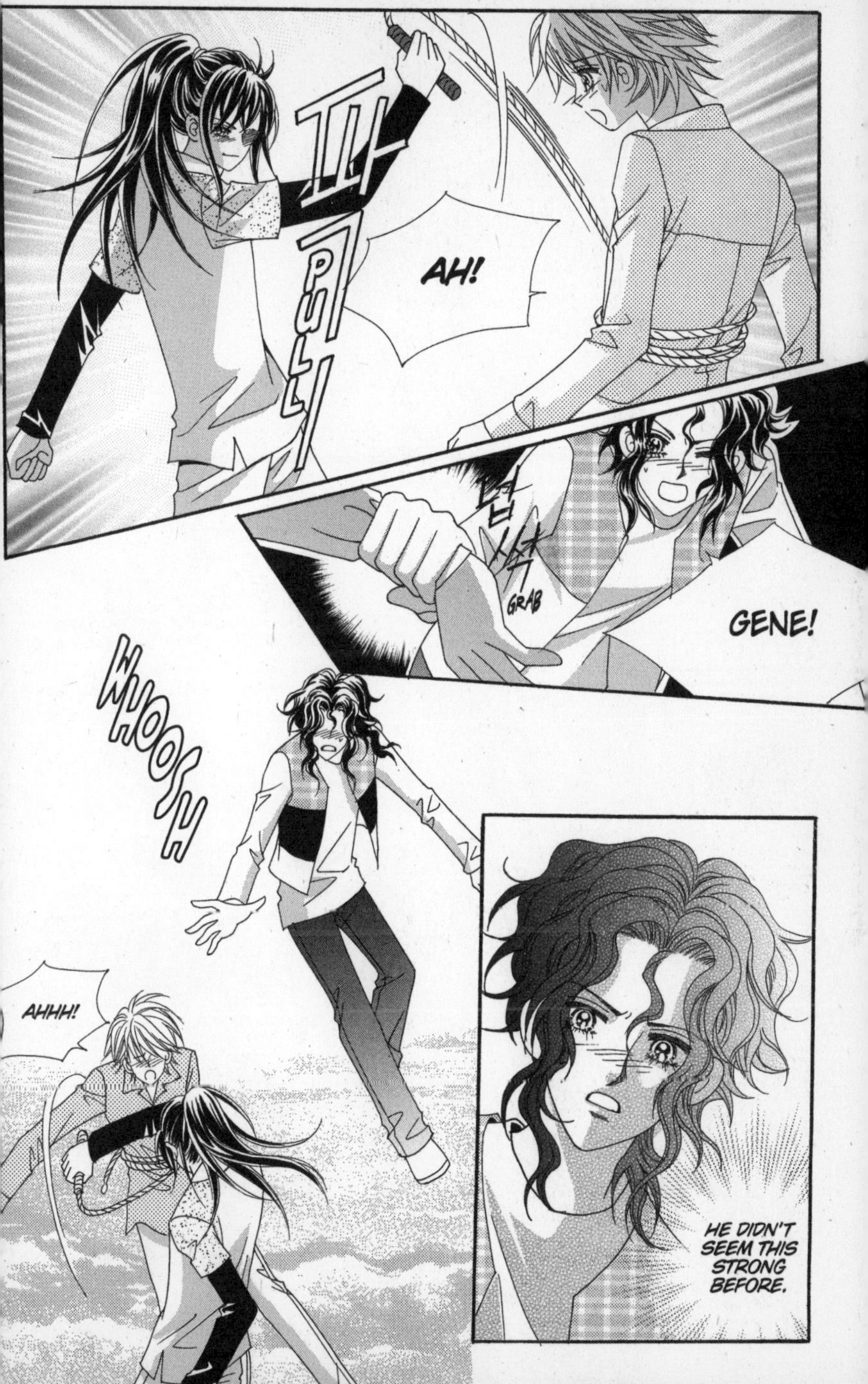
PULL
AH!
GRAB
GENE!
WHOOSH
AHHH!
HE DIDN'T SEEM THIS STRONG BEFORE.

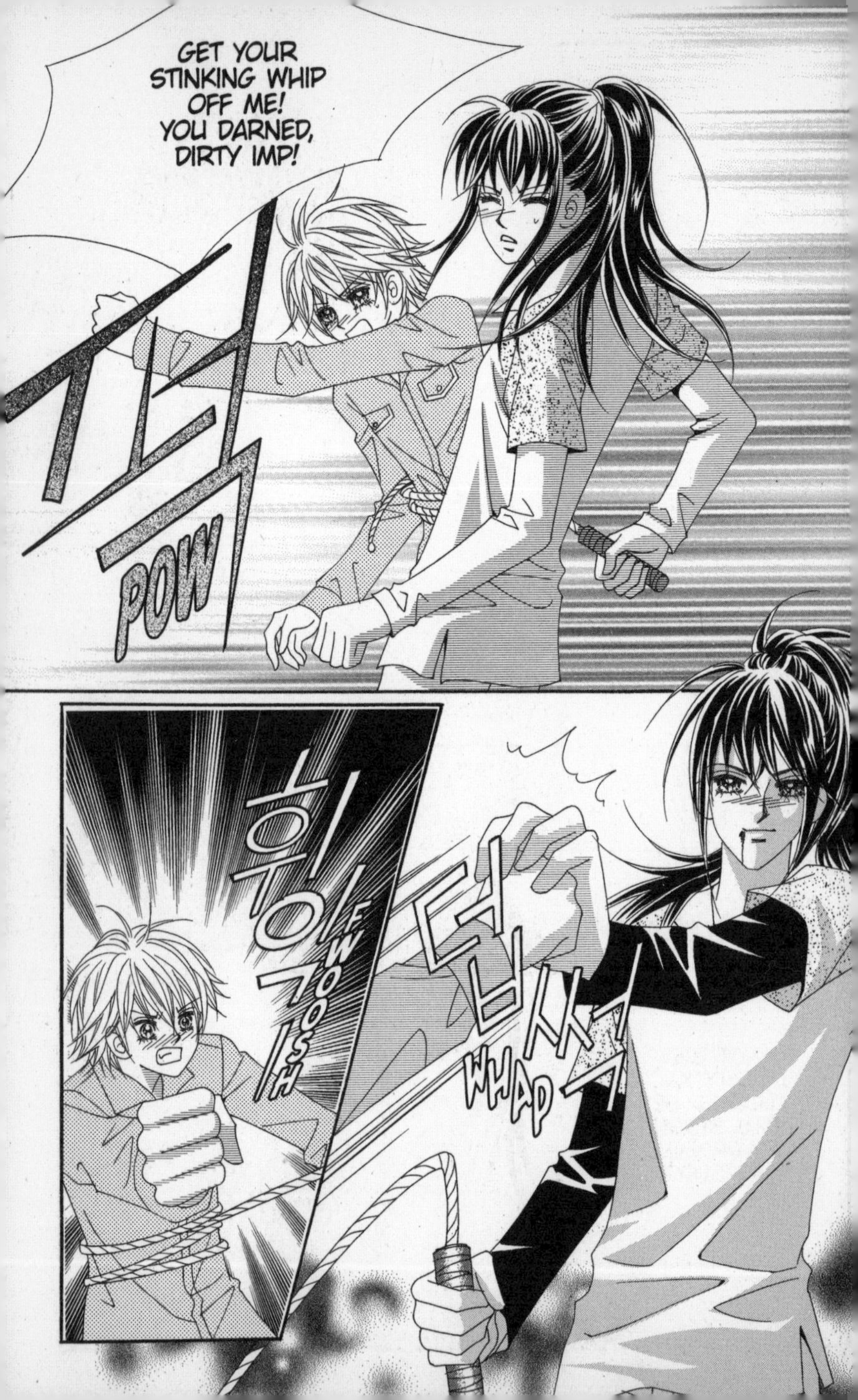
GET YOUR STINKING WHIP OFF ME! YOU DARNED, DIRTY IMP!
POW
FWOOSH
WHAP

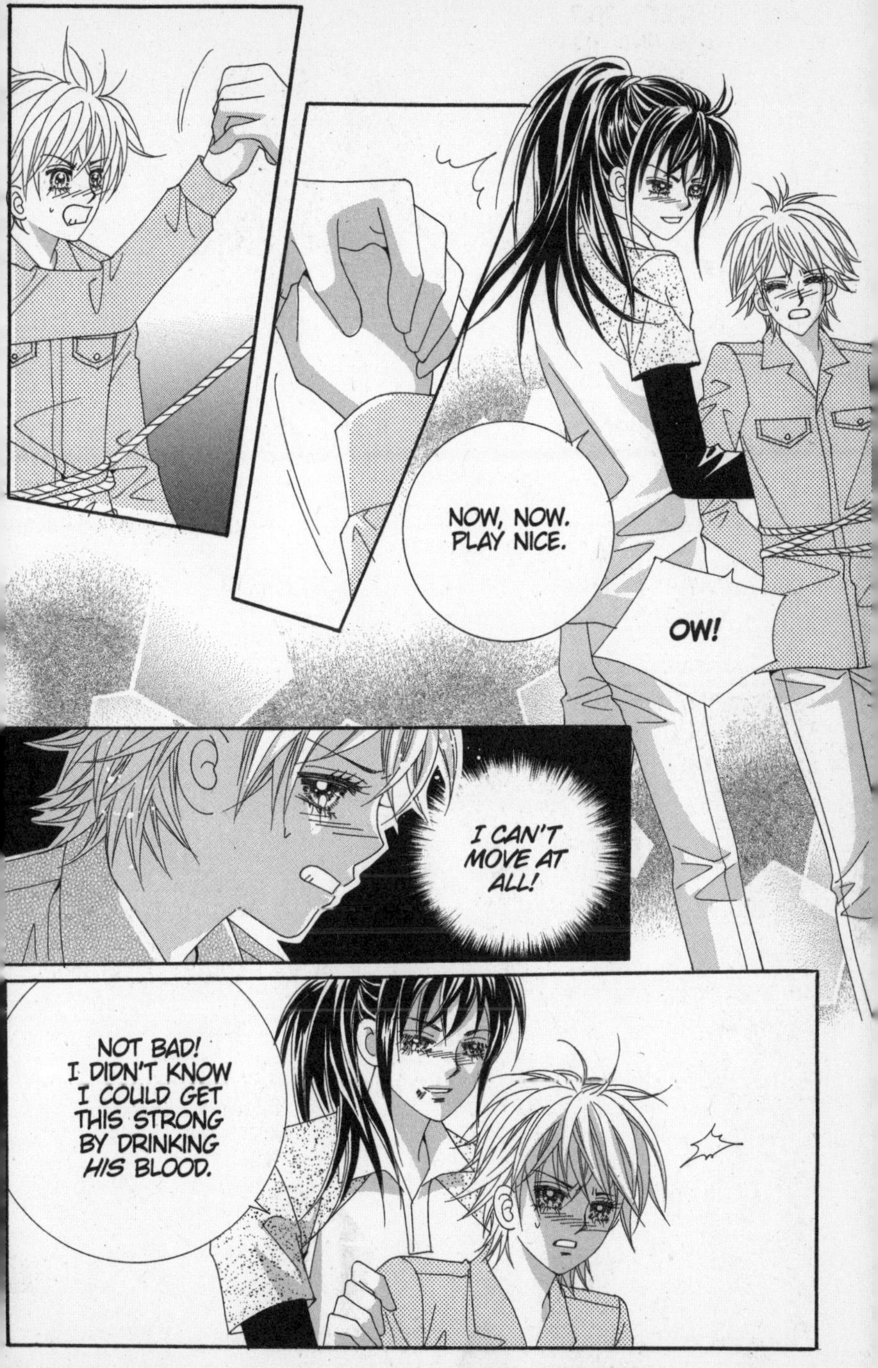
NOW, NOW. PLAY NICE.
OW!
I CAN'T MOVE AT ALL!
NOT BAD! I DIDN'T KNOW I COULD GET THIS STRONG BY DRINKING *HIS* BLOOD.

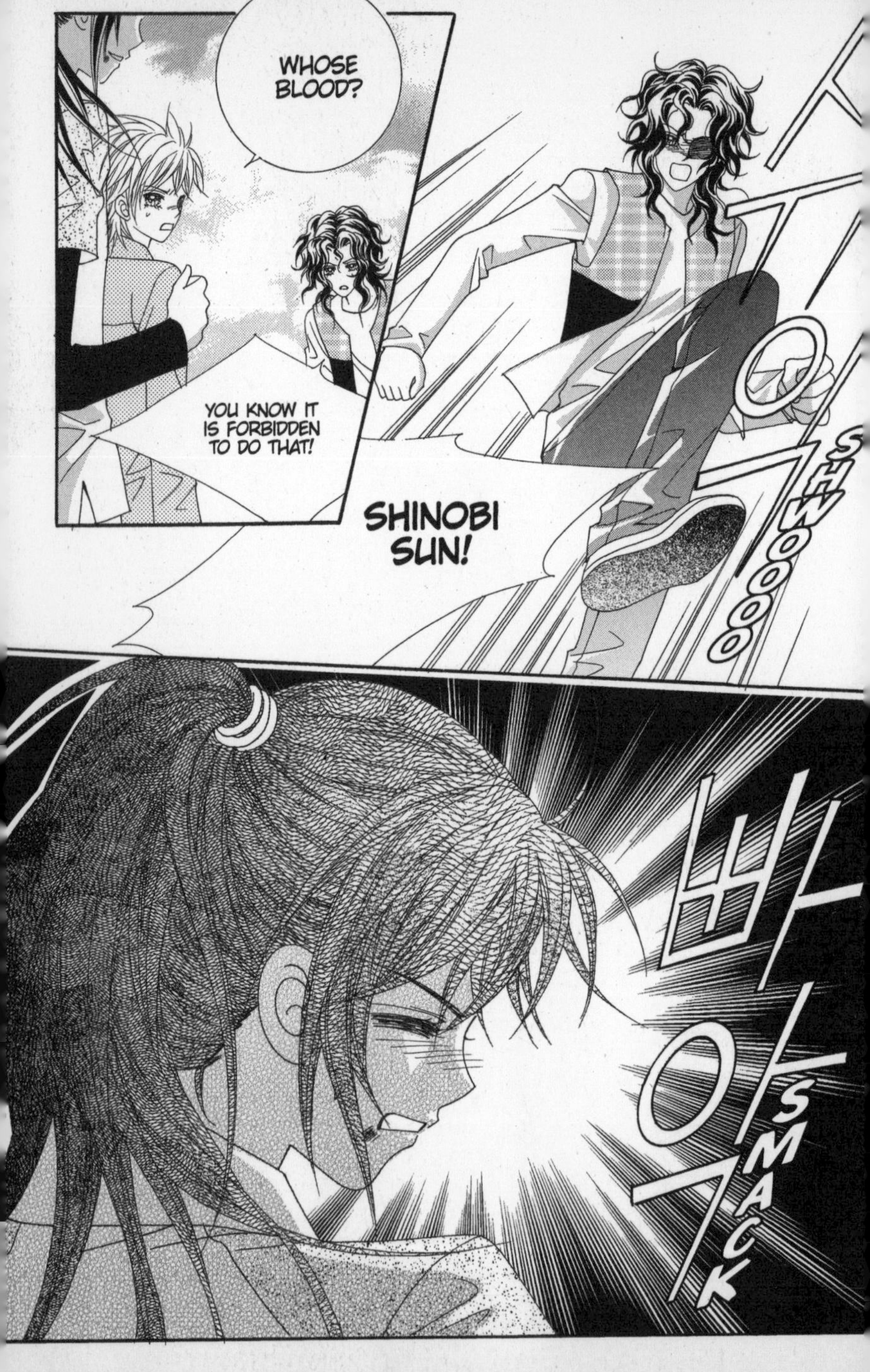
WHOSE BLOOD?
YOU KNOW IT IS FORBIDDEN TO DO THAT!
SHINOBI SUN!
SHWOOOOOO
SMACK

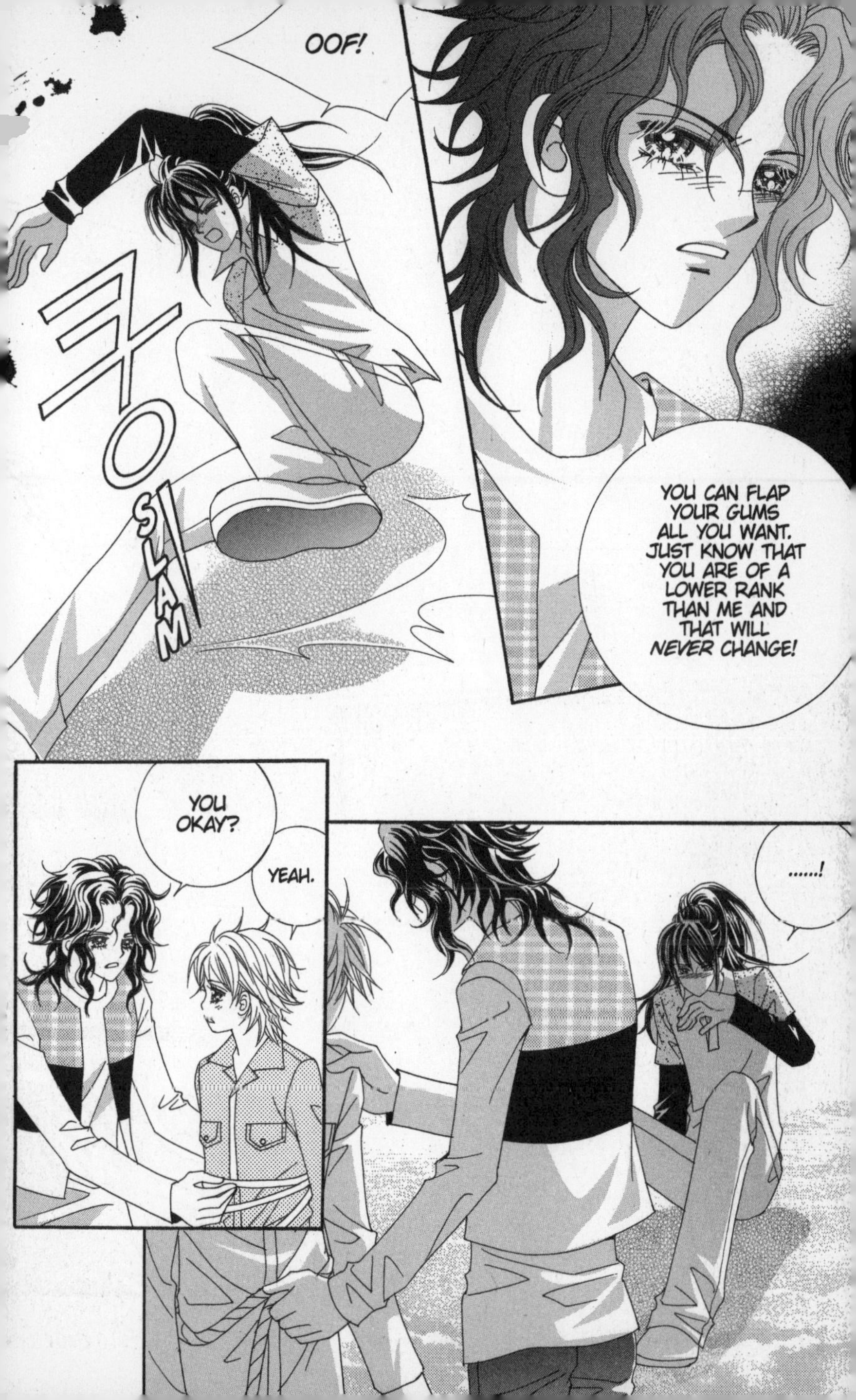
OOF!
SLAM
YOU CAN FLAP YOUR GUMS ALL YOU WANT. JUST KNOW THAT YOU ARE OF A LOWER RANK THAN ME AND THAT WILL *NEVER* CHANGE!
YOU OKAY?
YEAH.
......!

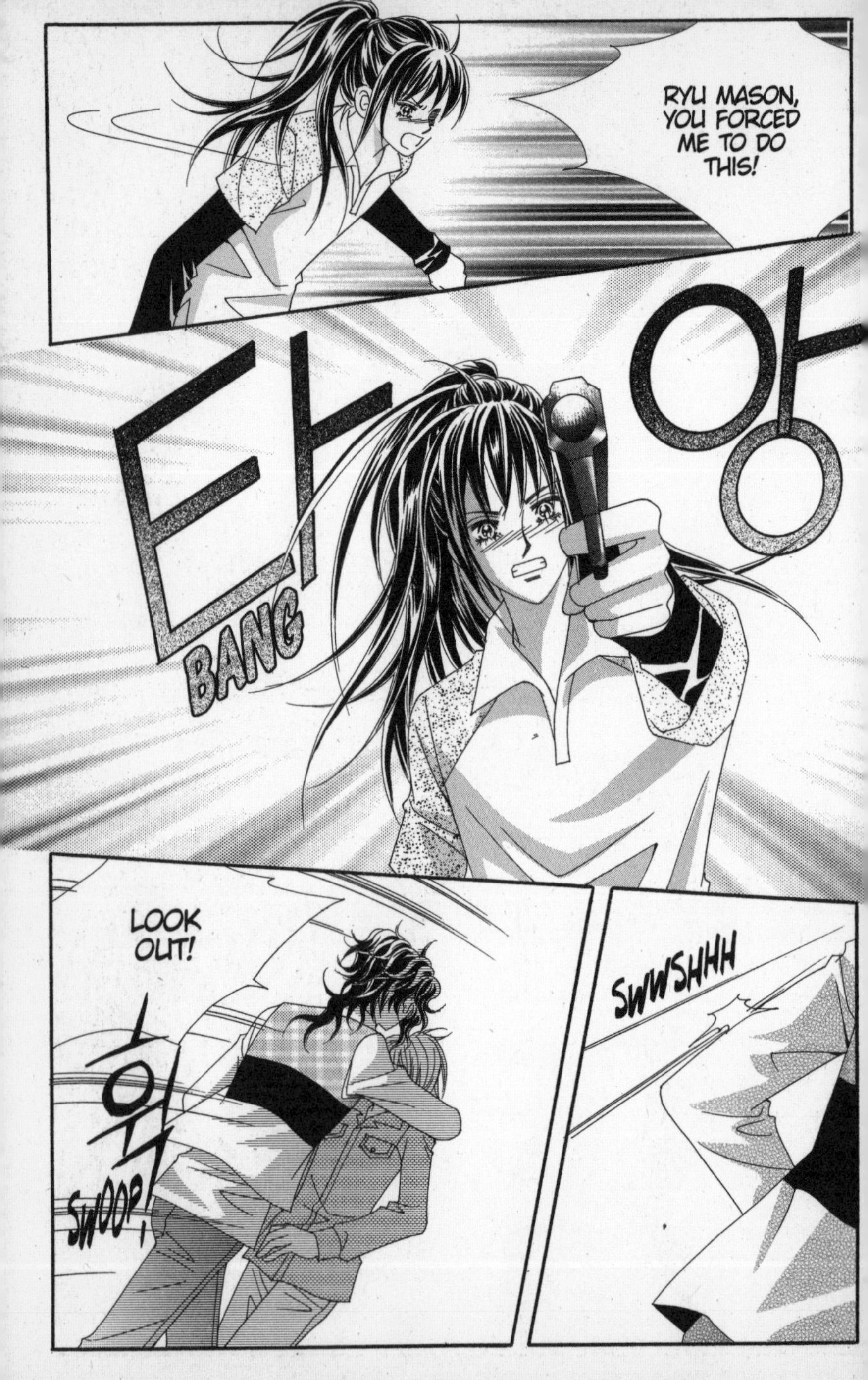
RYU MASON, YOU FORCED ME TO DO THIS!
타앙
BANG
LOOK OUT!
SWOOP!
SWWSHHH

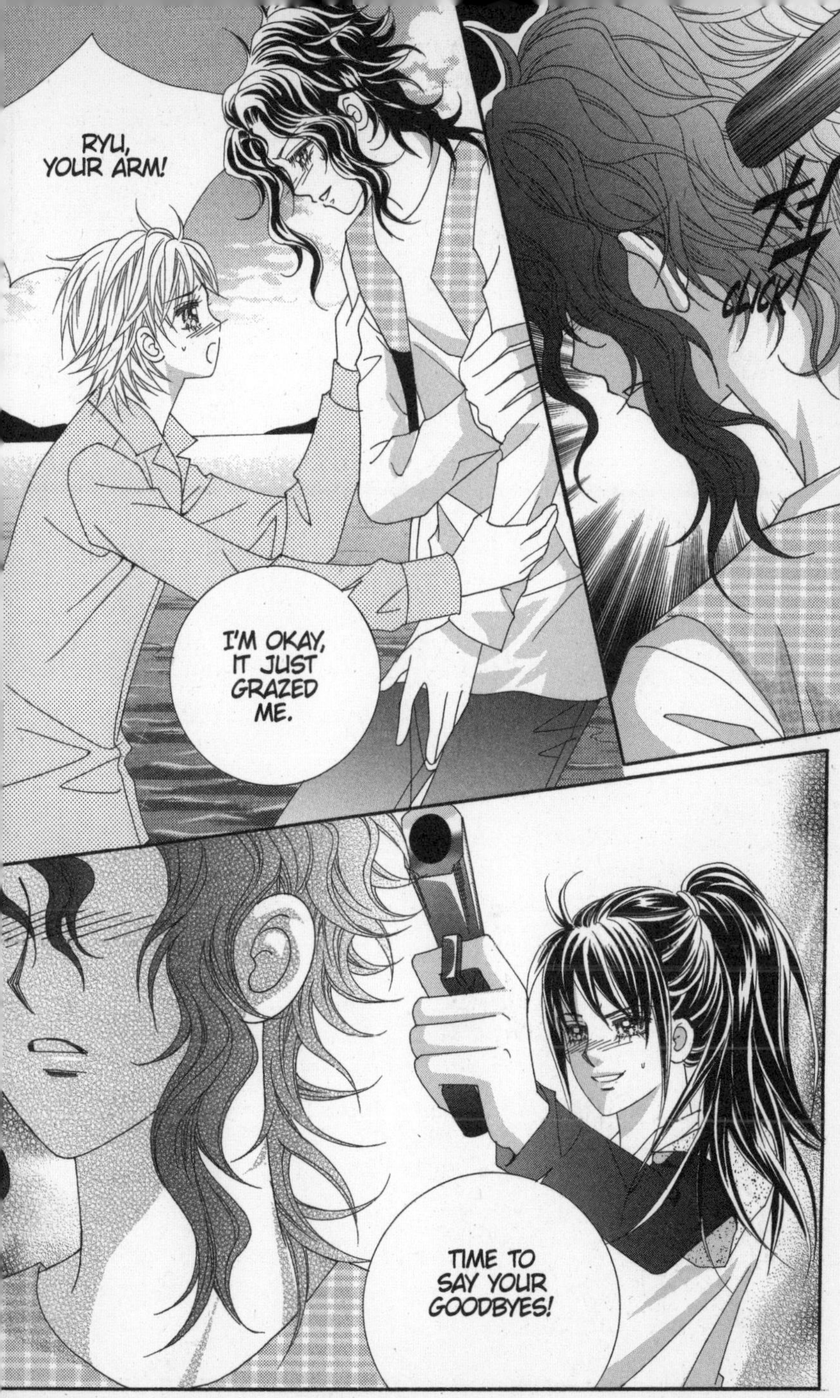
RYU, YOUR ARM!
I'M OKAY, IT JUST GRAZED ME.
CLICK
TIME TO SAY YOUR GOODBYES!

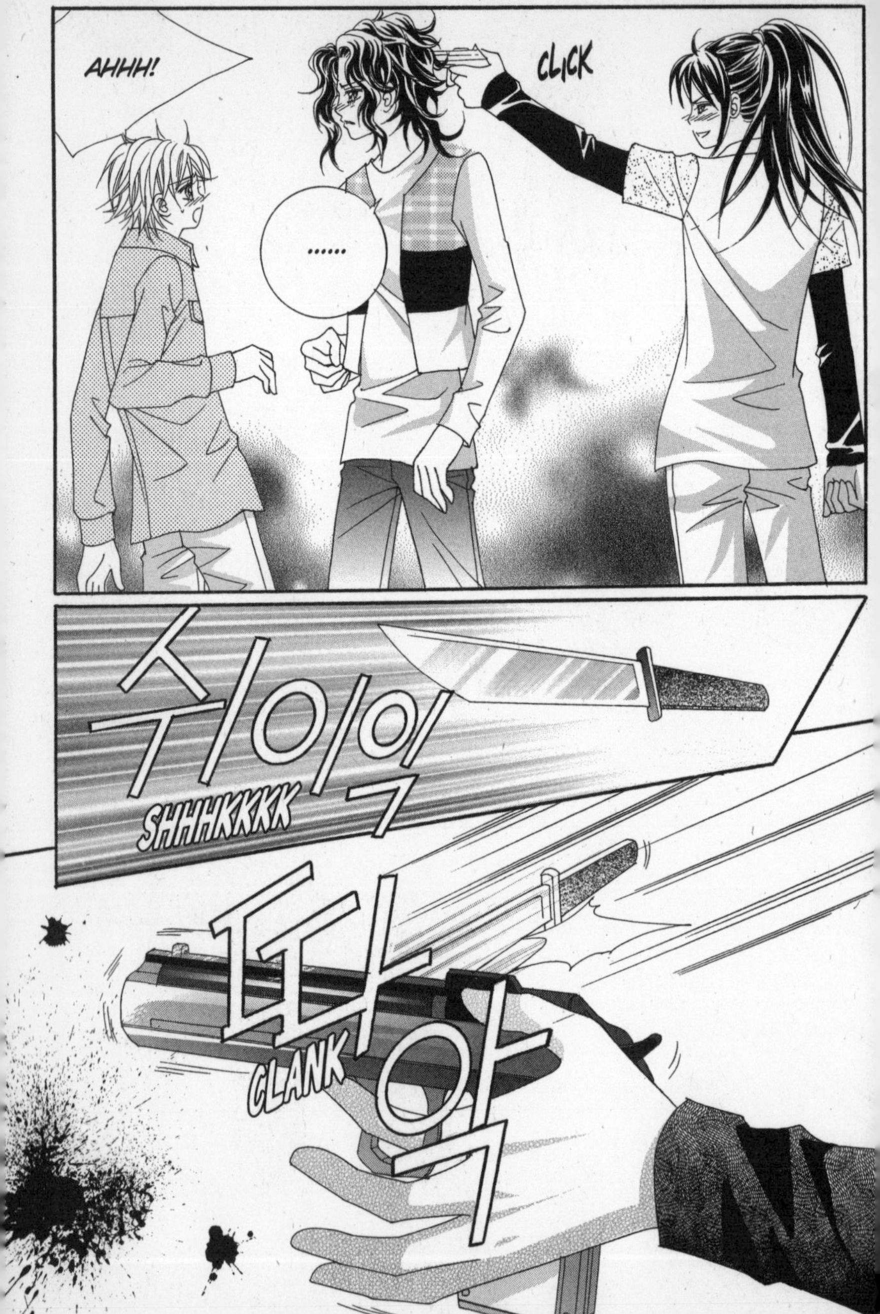
AHHH!
CLICK
......
쉬이익
SHHHKKKK
따악
CLANK

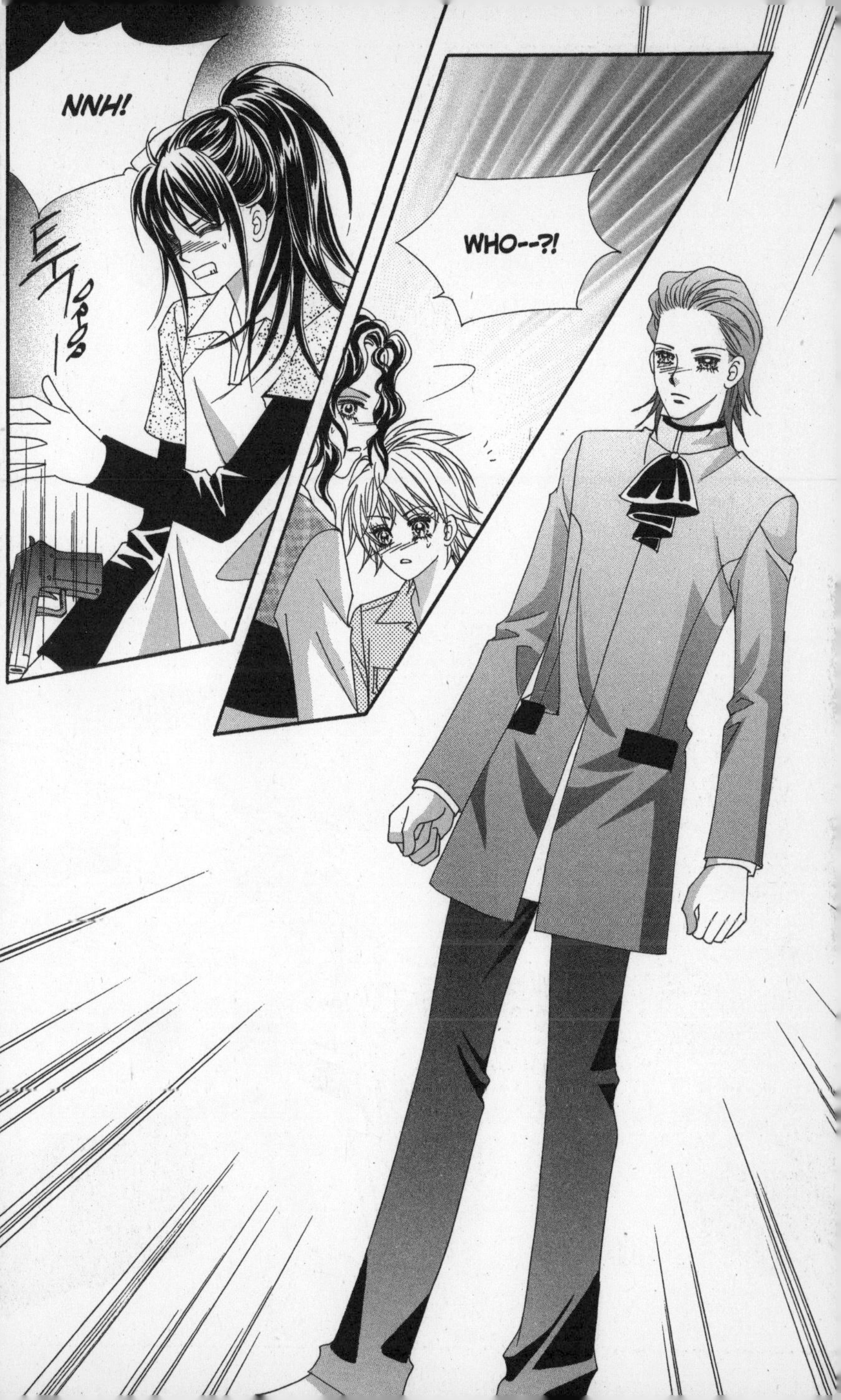
NNH!
툭
DROP
WHO--?!

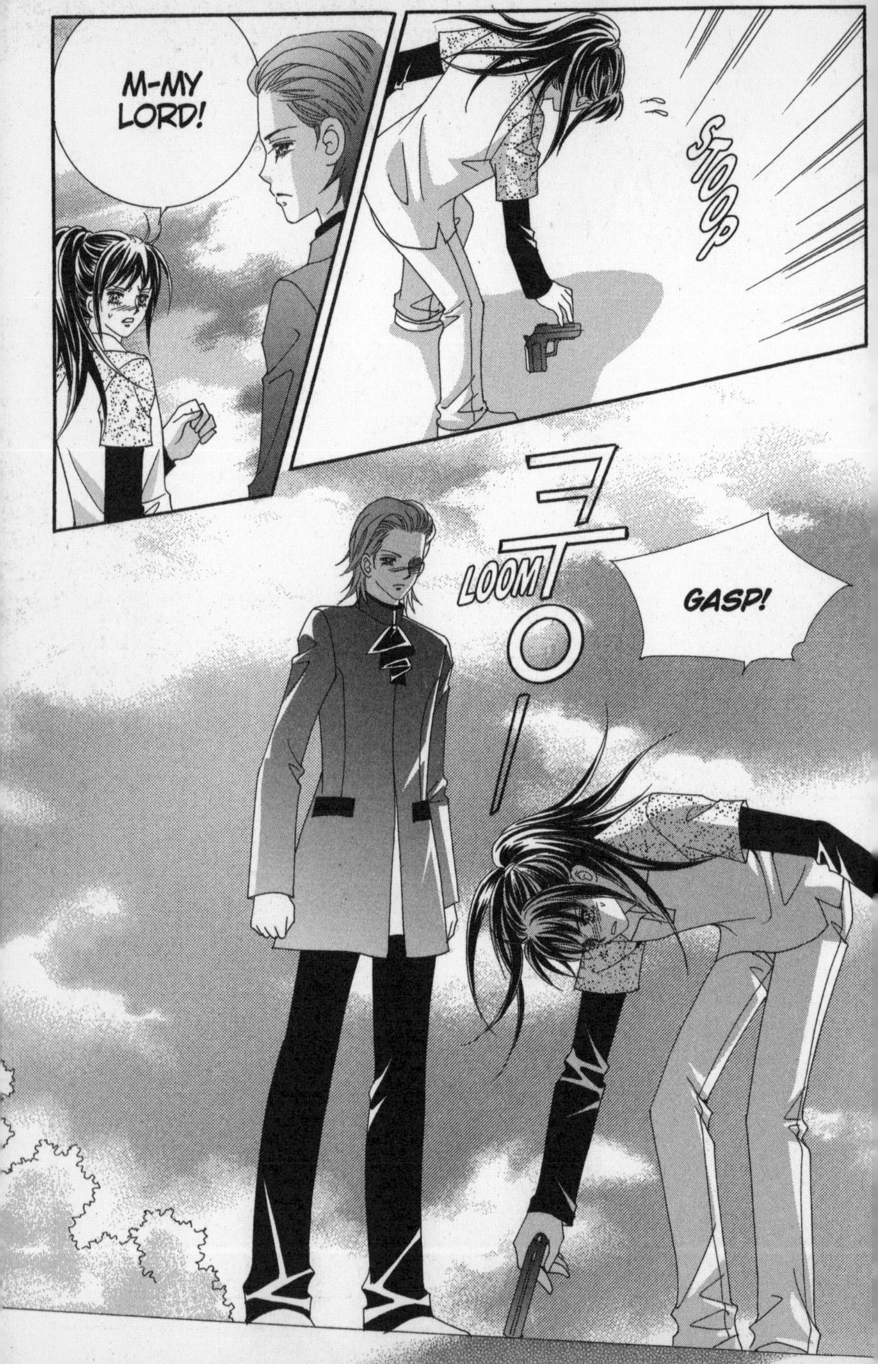
M-MY LORD!
STOOP
LOOM
GASP!

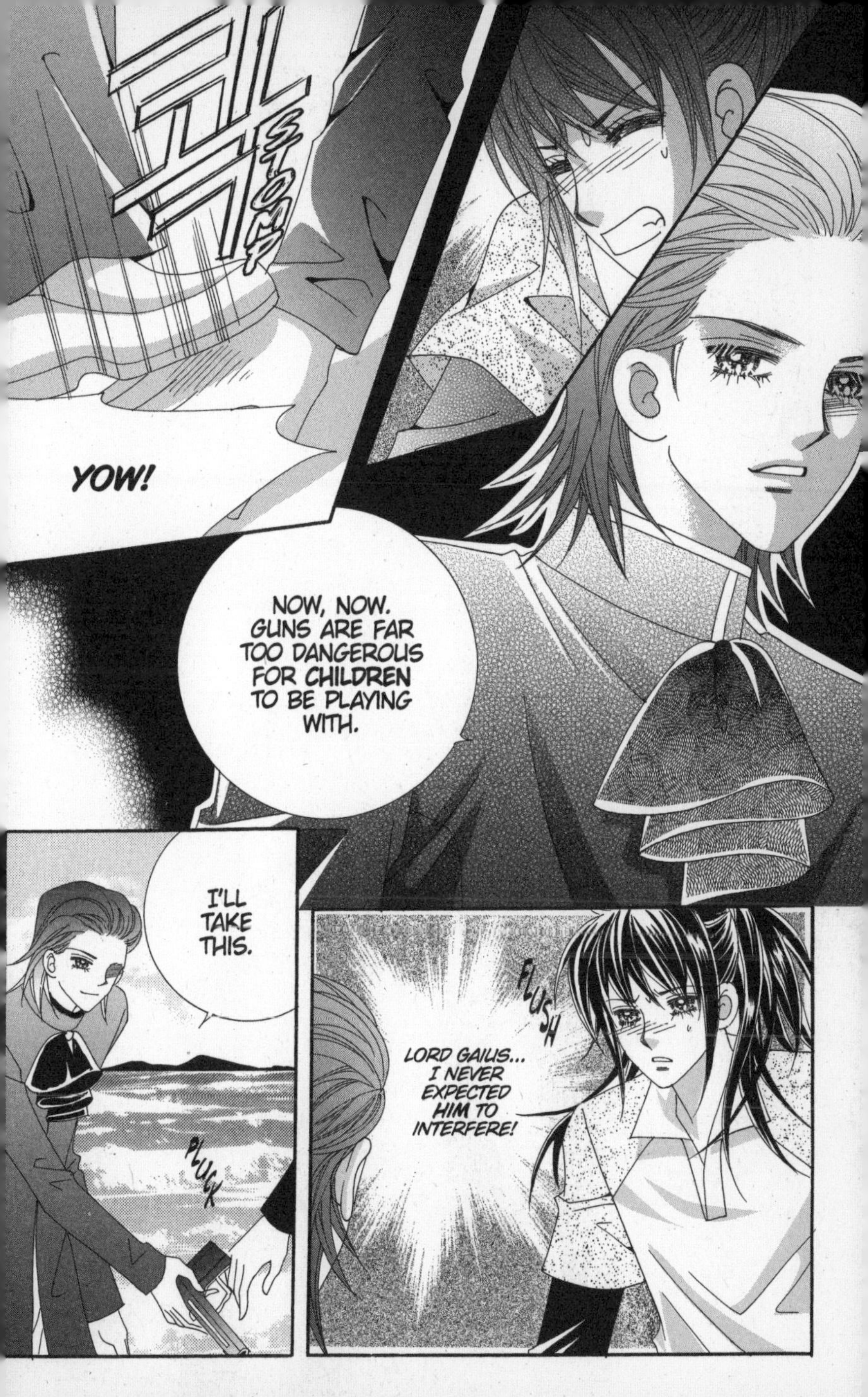
STOMP
YOW!
NOW, NOW. GUNS ARE FAR TOO DANGEROUS FOR CHILDREN TO BE PLAYING WITH.
I'LL TAKE THIS.
PLUCK
FLUSH
LORD GAIUS... I NEVER EXPECTED HIM TO INTERFERE!

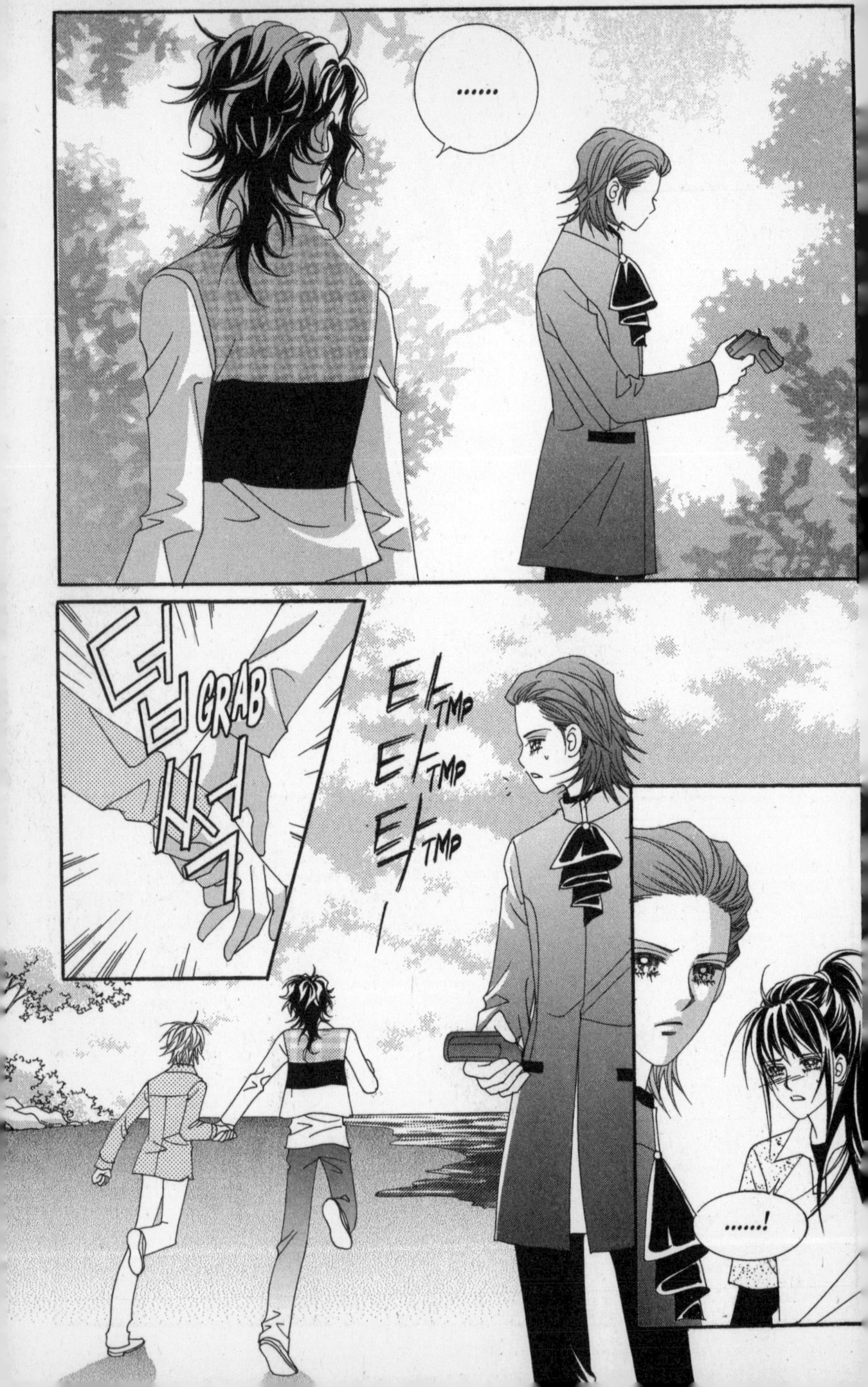

......
덥석
GRAB
타 TMP
타 TMP
타 TMP
......!

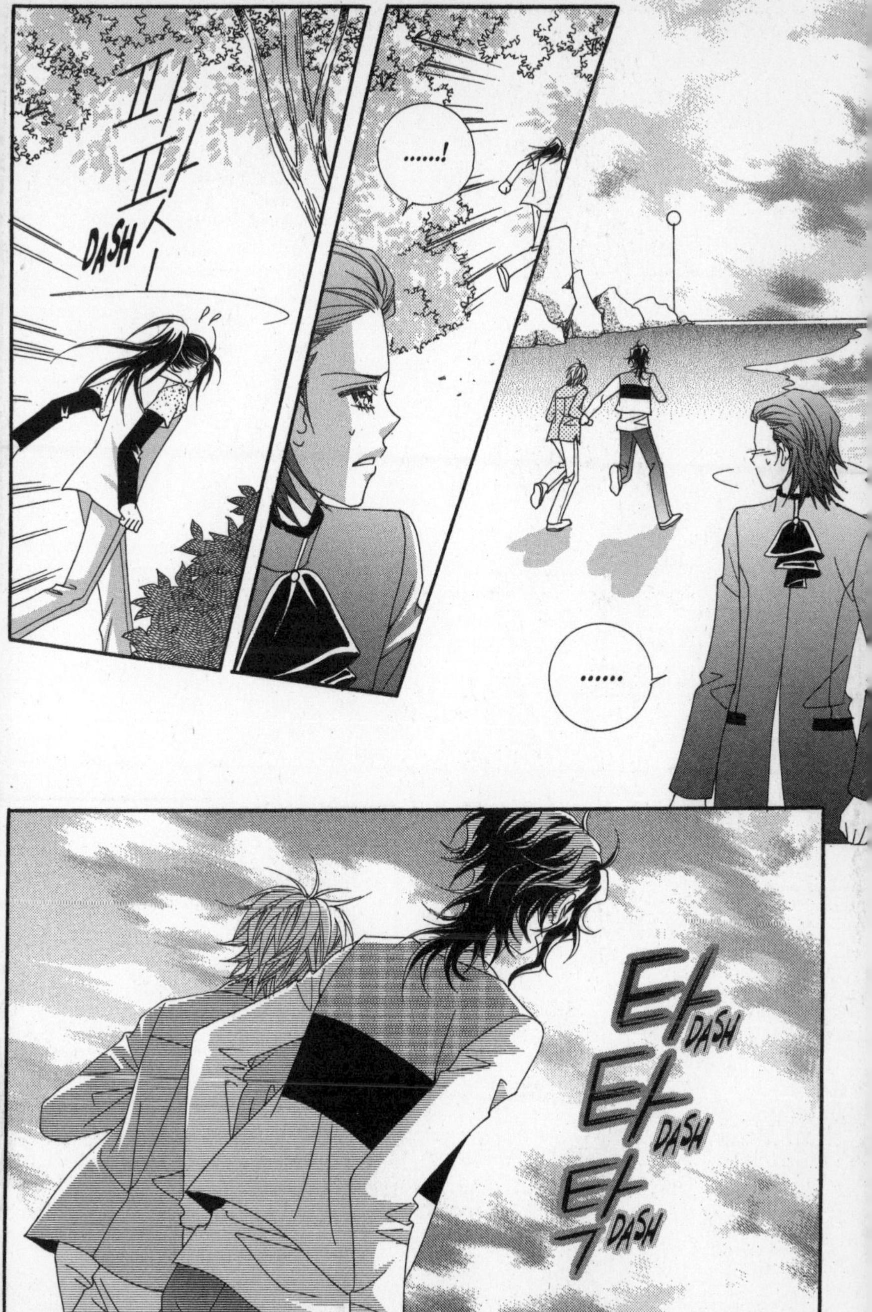
파팟!
DASH
......!
......
타
DASH
타
DASH
탁
DASH

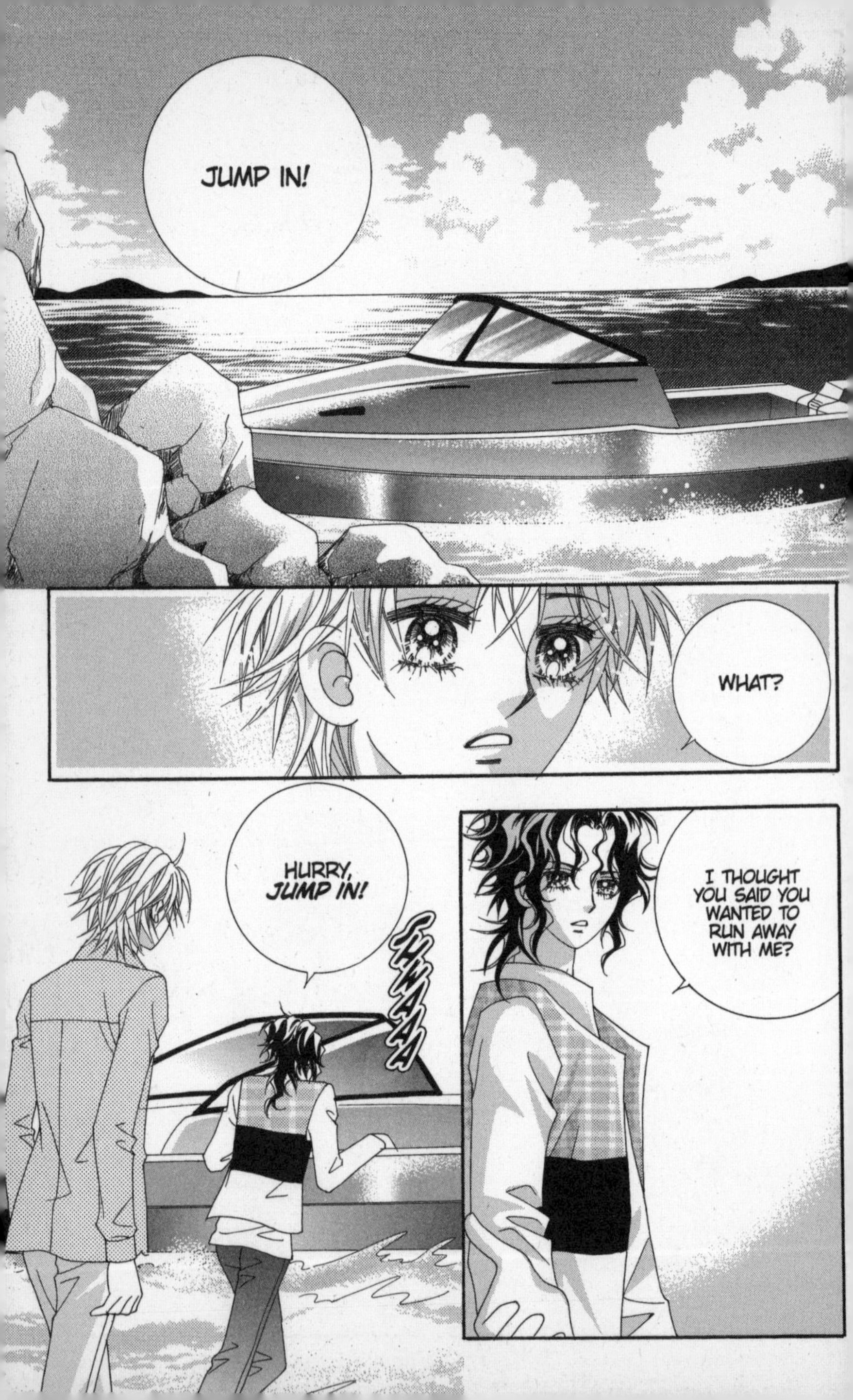
JUMP IN!
WHAT?
HURRY, JUMP IN!
CHWAAAA
I THOUGHT YOU SAID YOU WANTED TO RUN AWAY WITH ME?

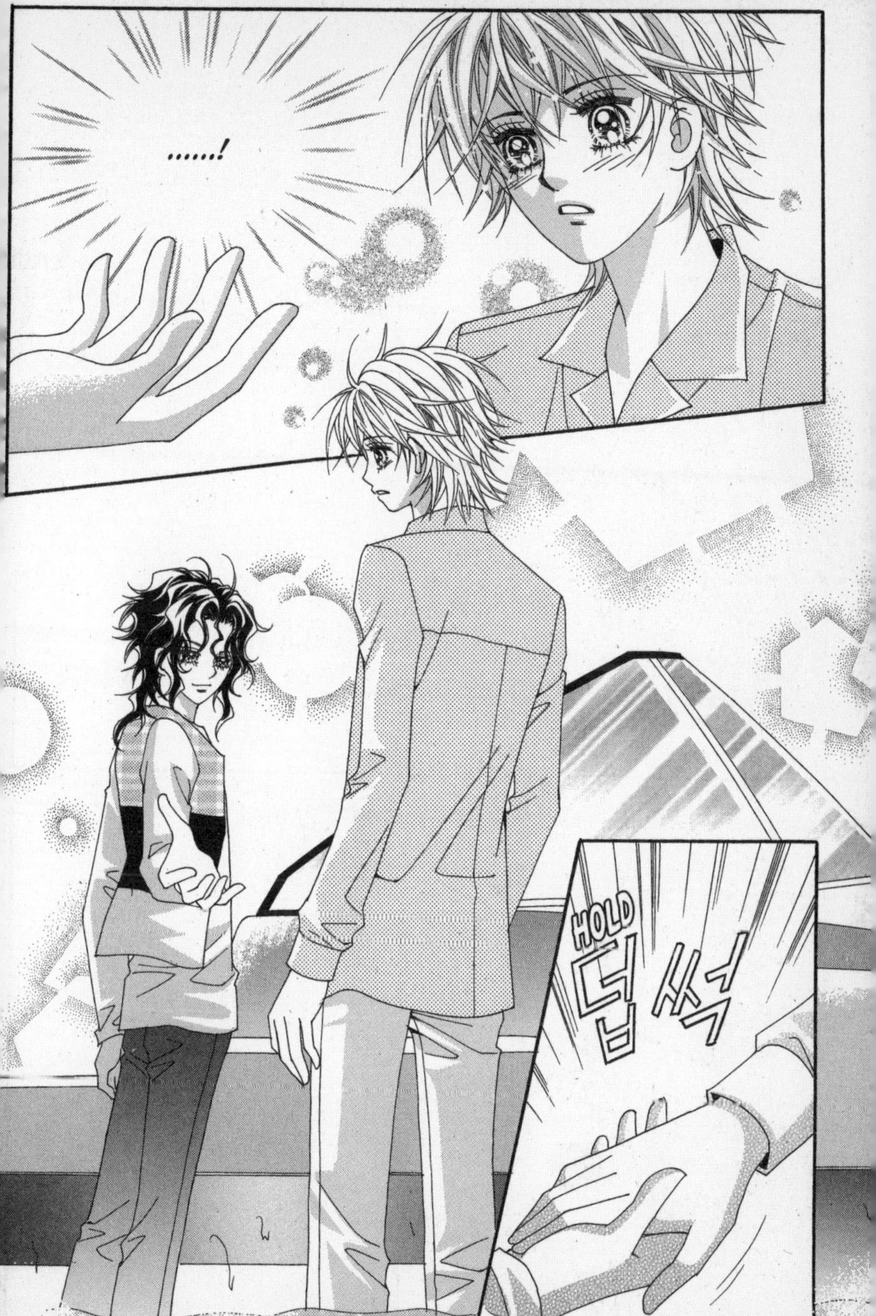
......!
HOLD
덥석

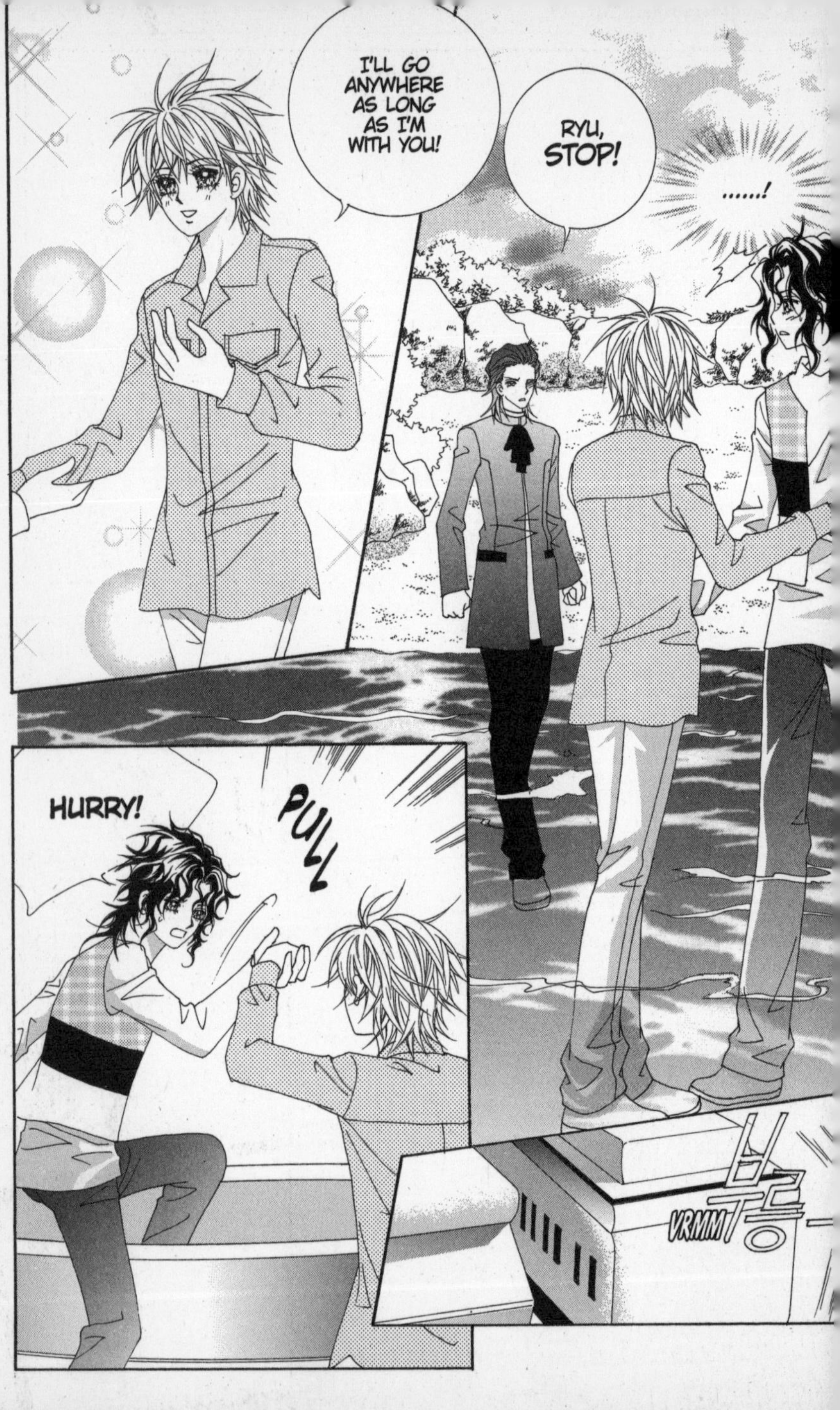
I'LL GO ANYWHERE AS LONG AS I'M WITH YOU!
RYU, STOP!
......!
HURRY!
PULL
VRMM
부릉-

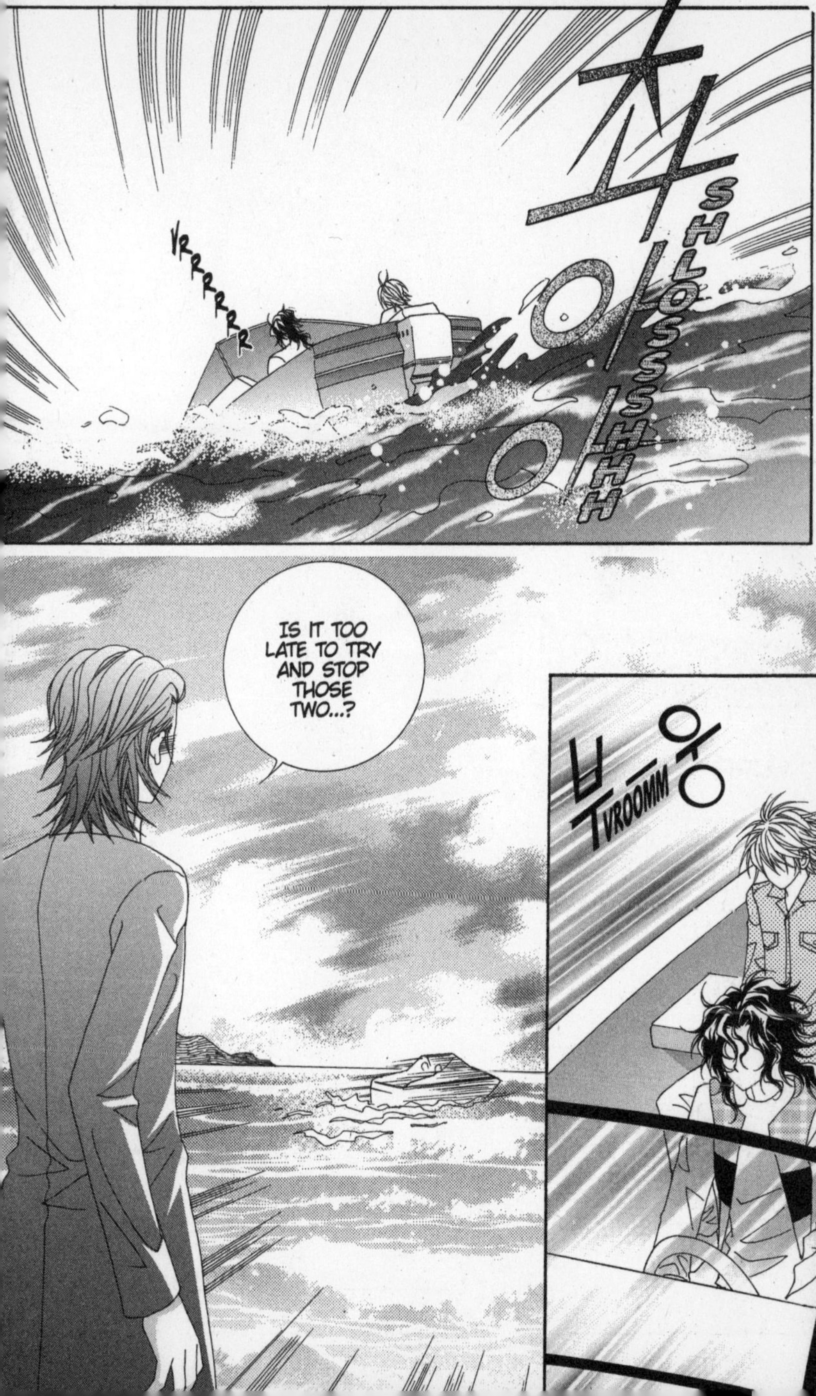
VRRRRRRRR
촤아아
SHLOSSSHHH
IS IT TOO LATE TO TRY AND STOP THOSE TWO...?
부우웅
VROOMM

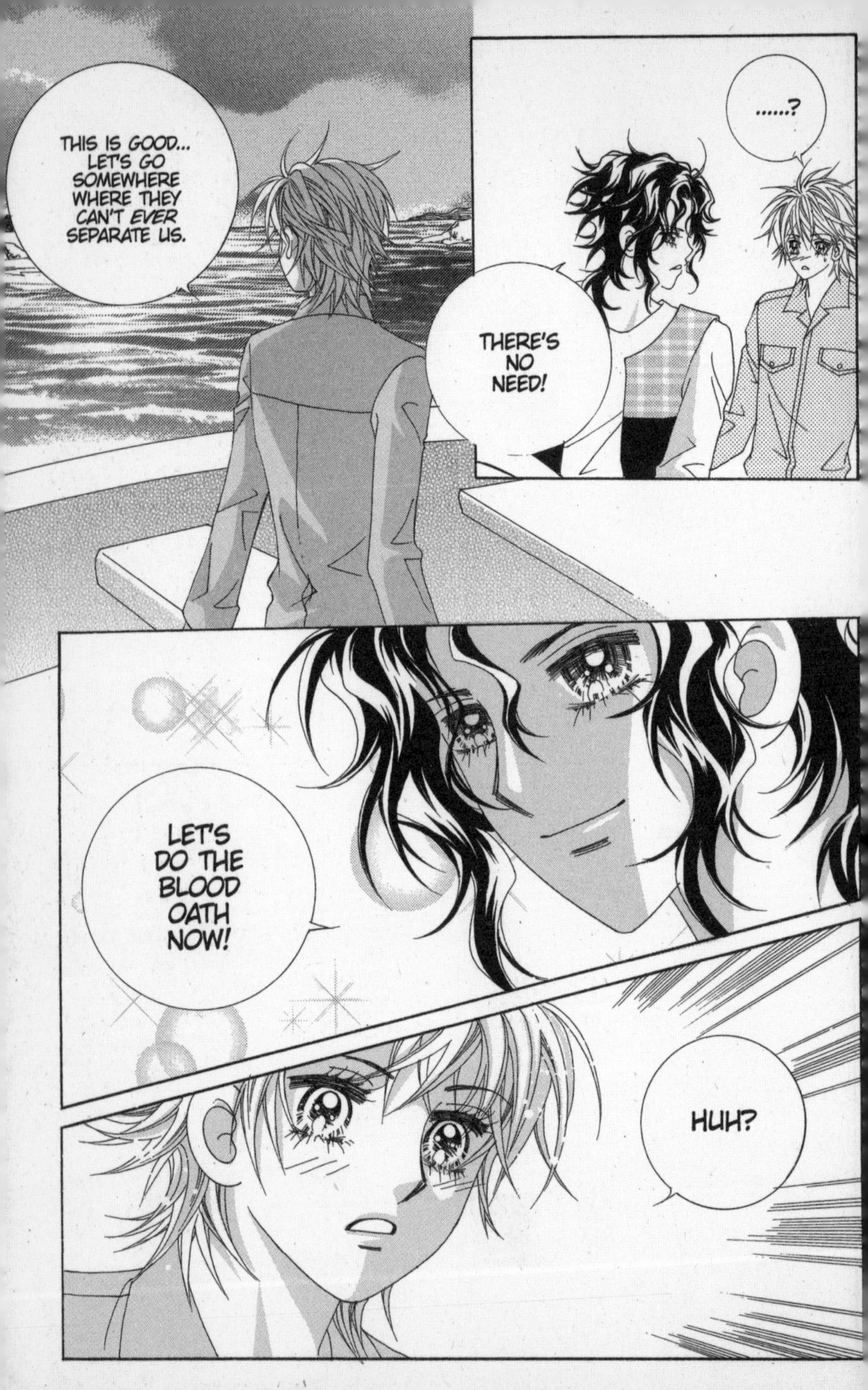
THIS IS GOOD... LET'S GO SOMEWHERE WHERE THEY CAN'T *EVER* SEPARATE US.
......?
THERE'S NO NEED!
LET'S DO THE BLOOD OATH NOW!
HUH?

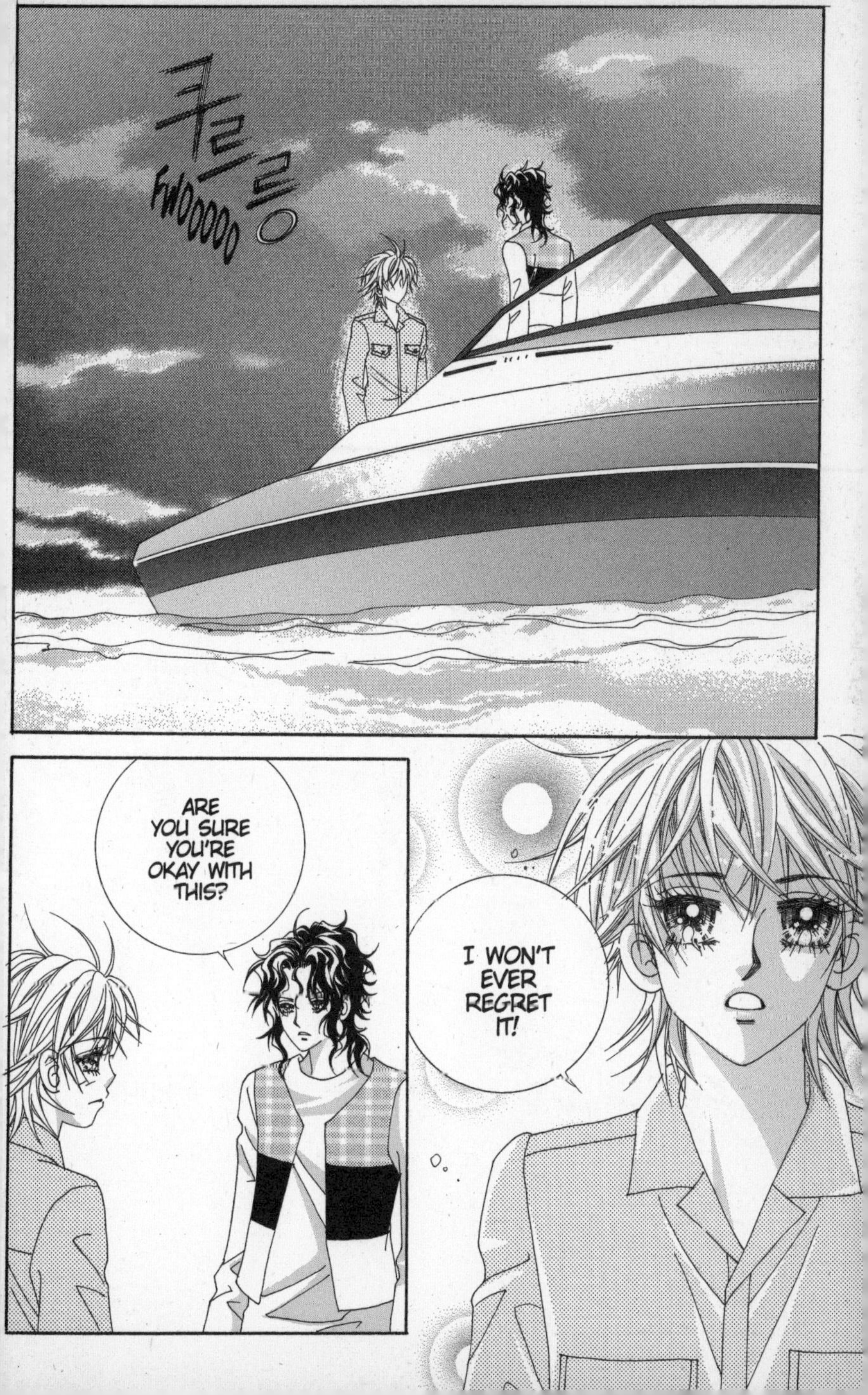
크르릉
FWOOOOO
ARE YOU SURE YOU'RE OKAY WITH THIS?
I WON'T EVER REGRET IT!

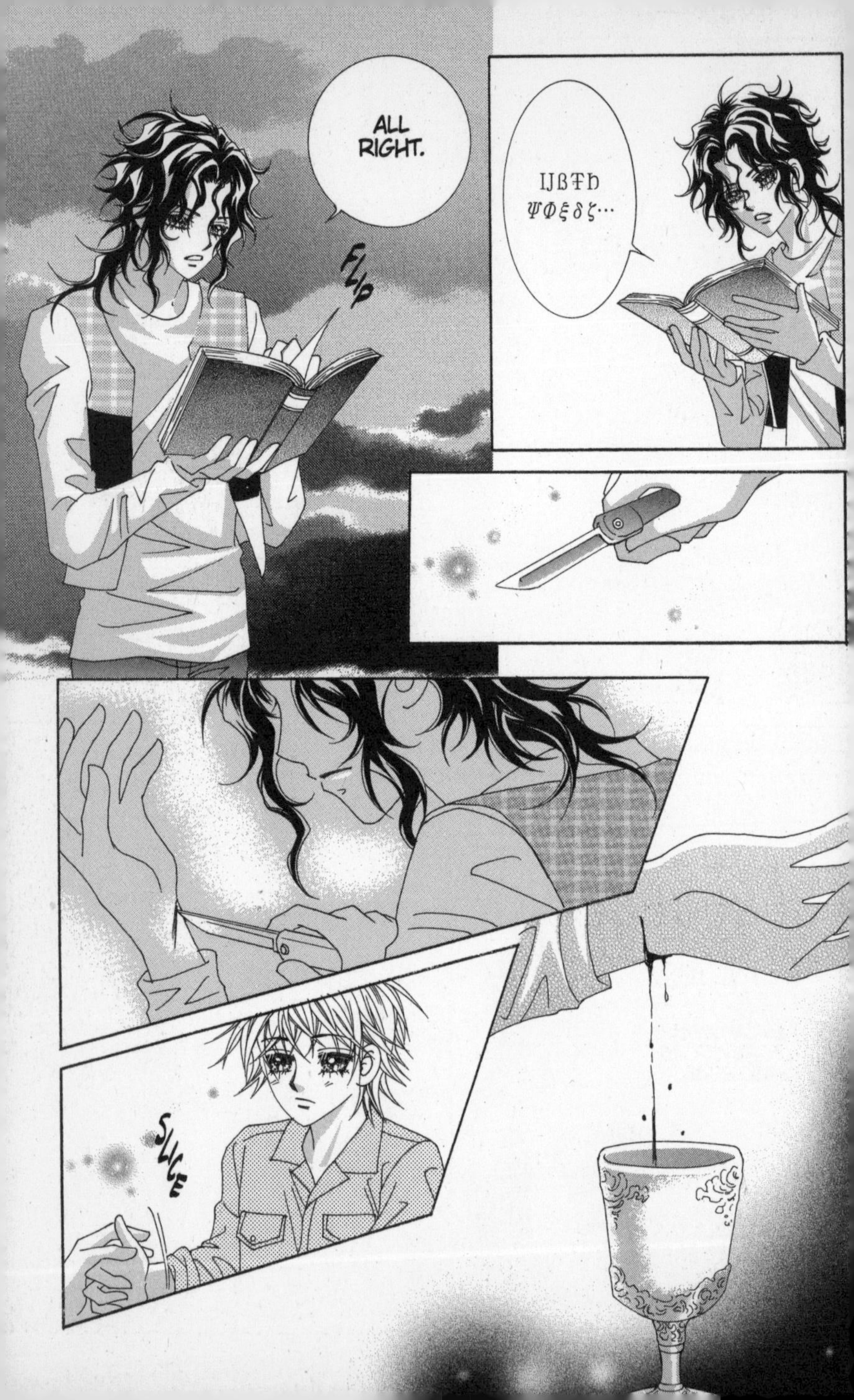
ALL RIGHT.
FLIP
IJßŦh ΨΦξδζ…
SLICE

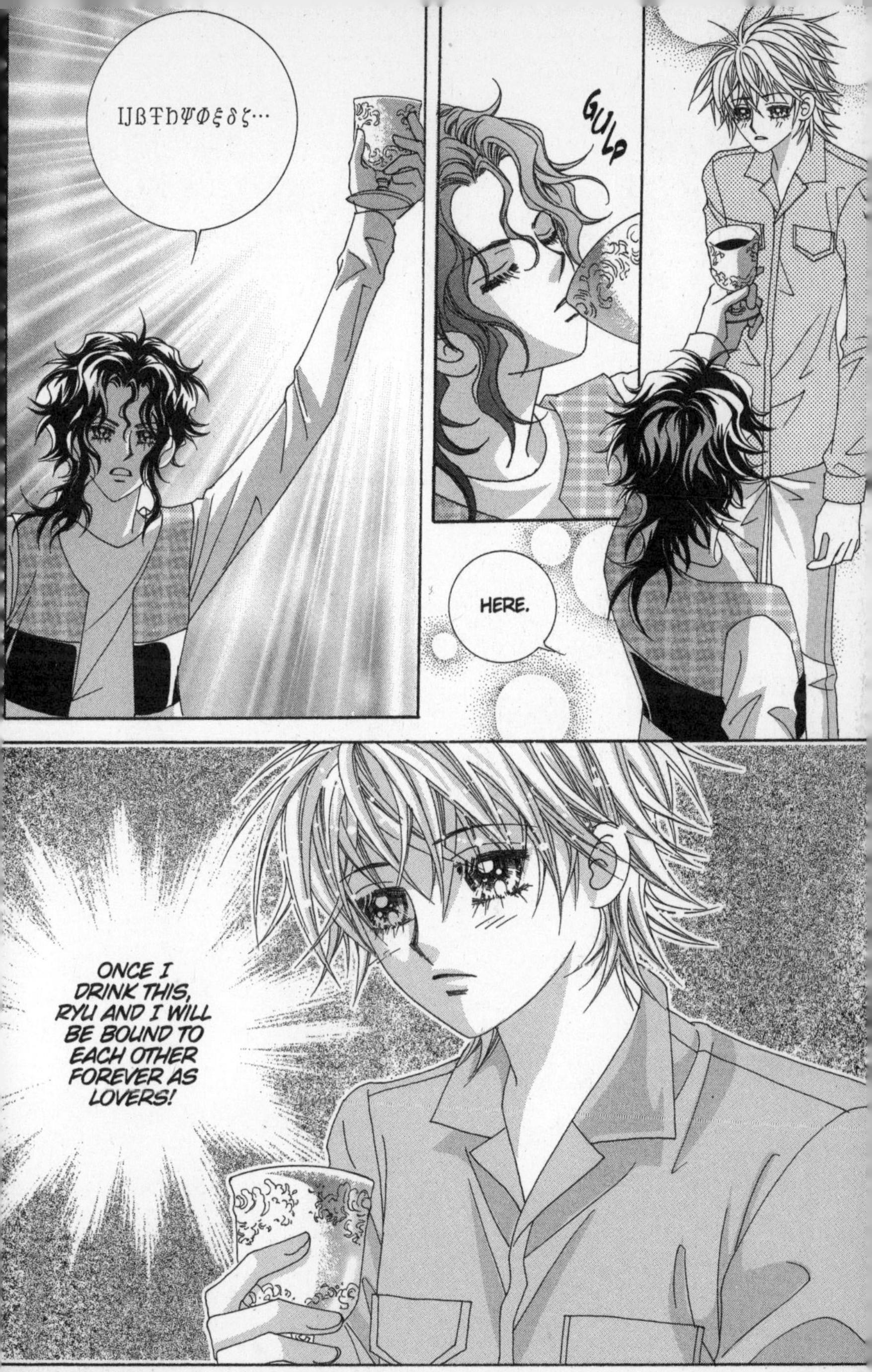
IJBŦƕΨΦξδζ…
GULP
HERE.
ONCE I DRINK THIS, RYU AND I WILL BE BOUND TO EACH OTHER FOREVER AS LOVERS!

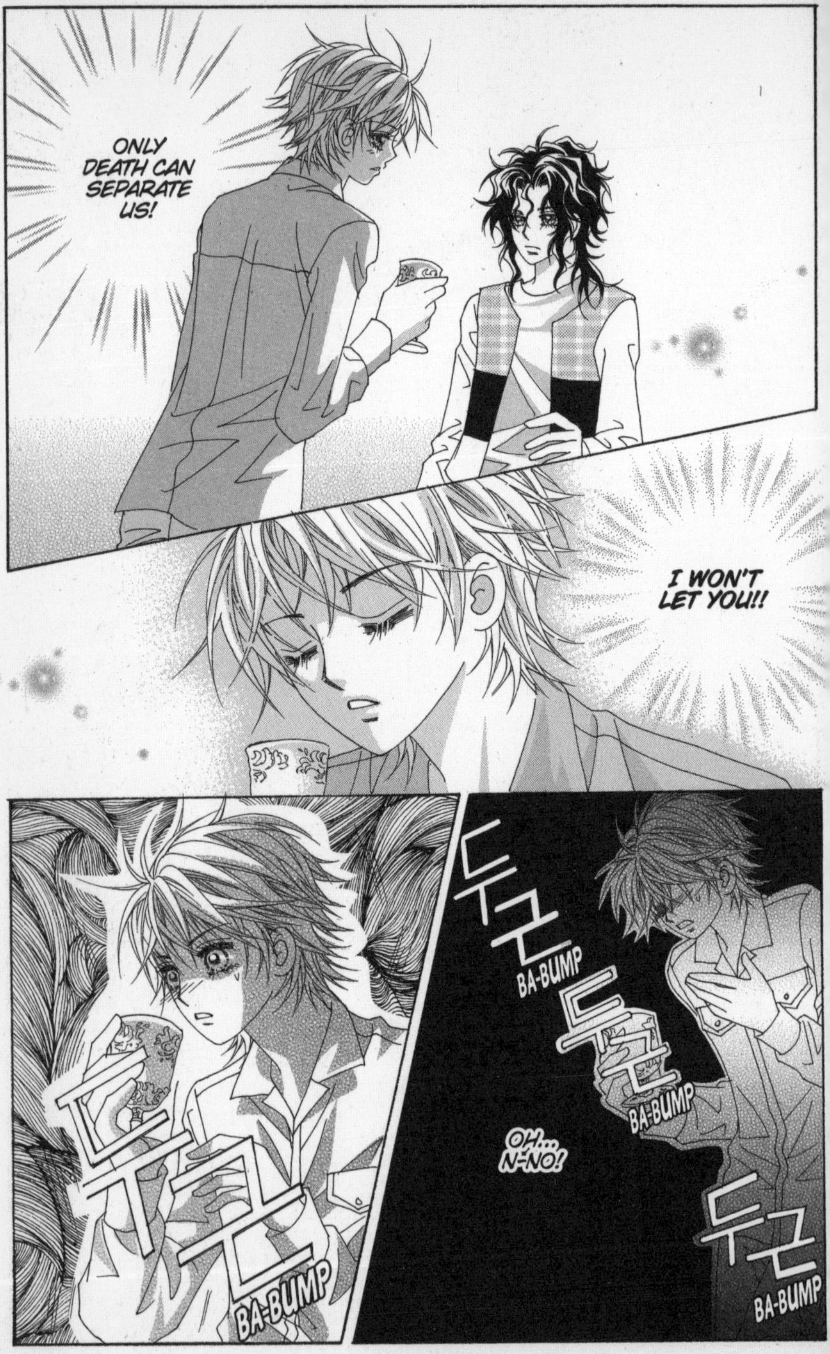
ONLY DEATH CAN SEPARATE US!
I WON'T LET YOU!!
BA-BUMP
BA-BUMP
BA-BUMP
OH... N-NO!
BA-BUMP

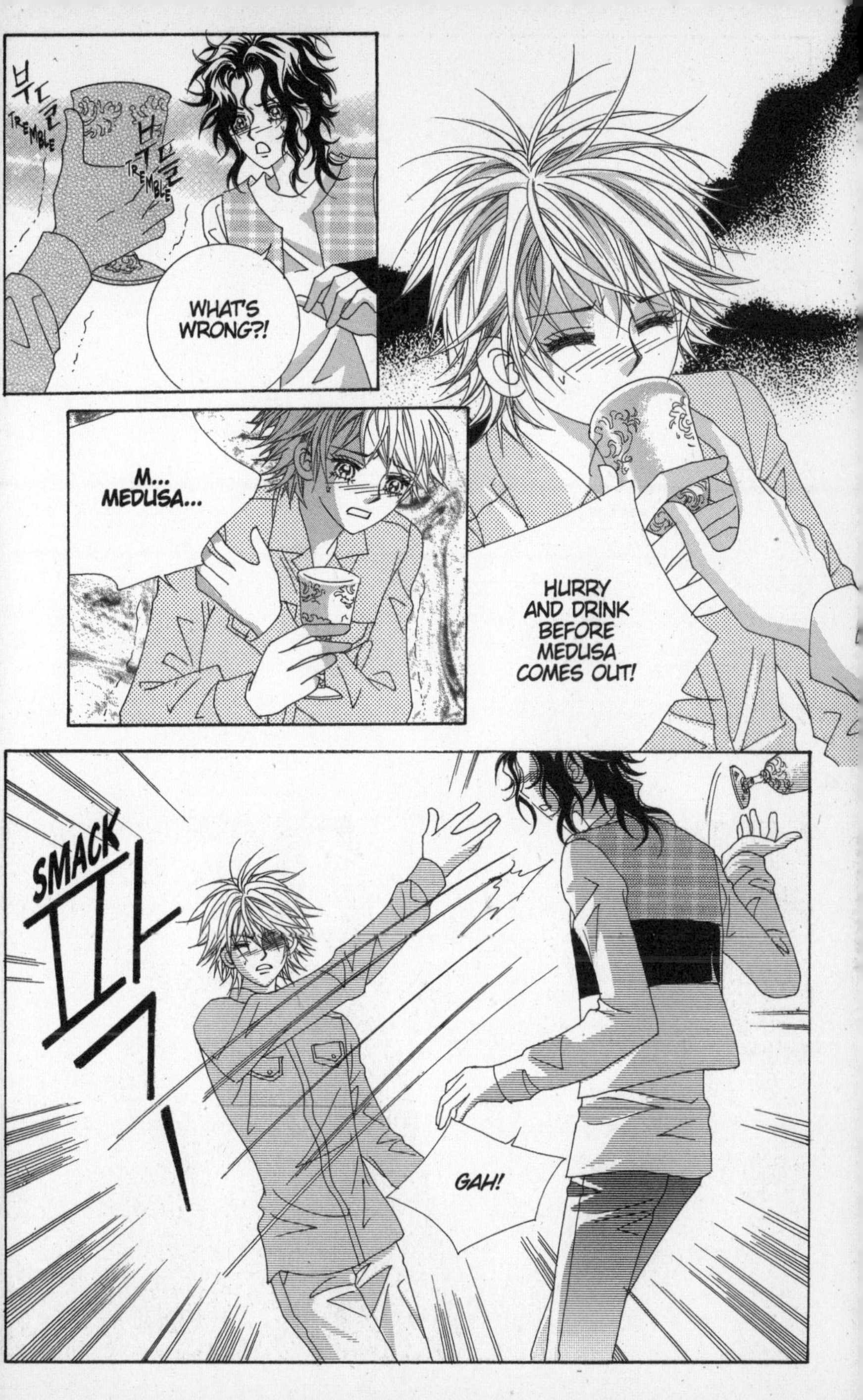
부들
TREMBLE
부들
TREMBLE
WHAT'S WRONG?!
M... MEDUSA...
HURRY AND DRINK BEFORE MEDUSA COMES OUT!
SMACK
GAH!

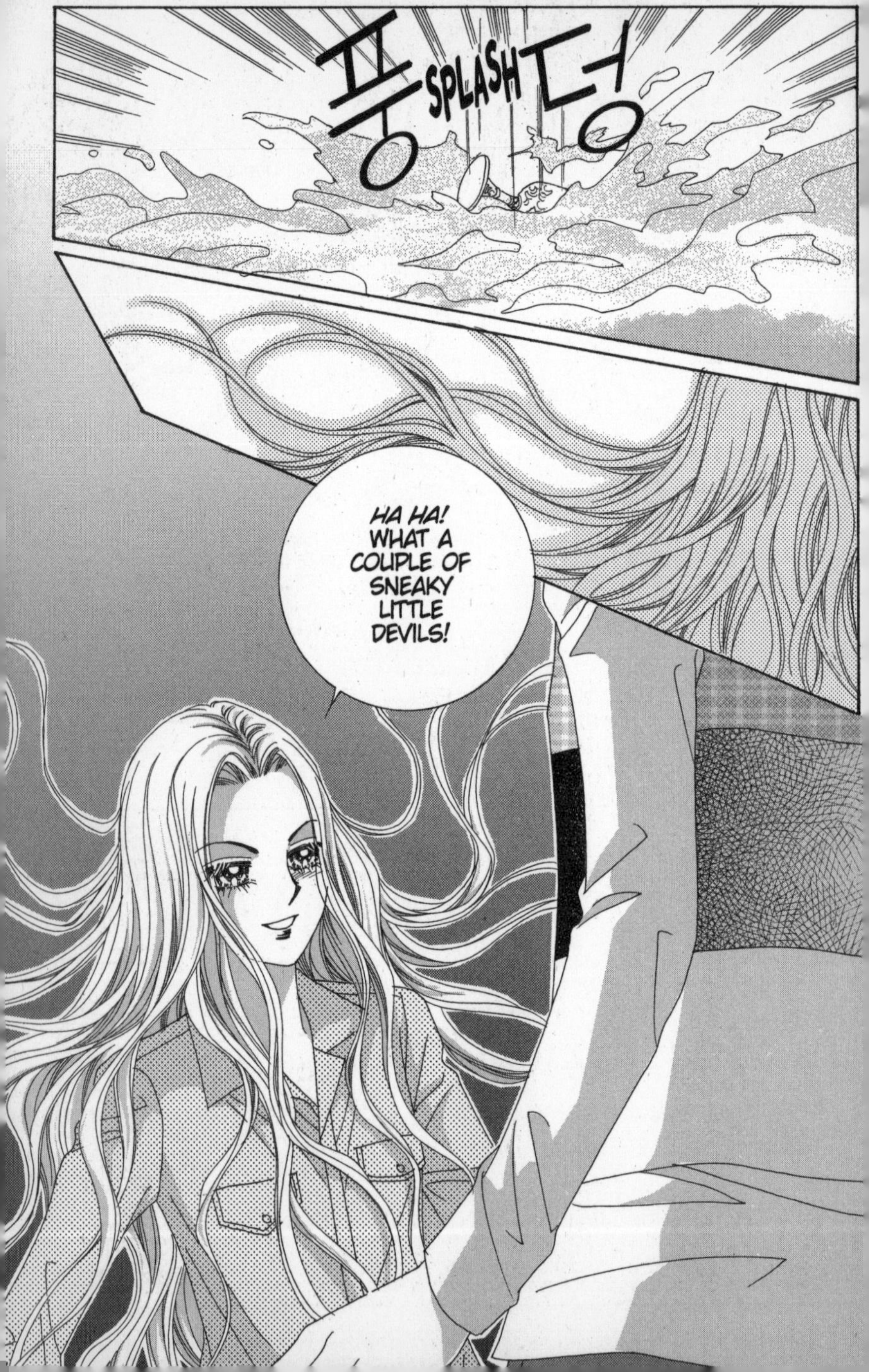
풍덩
SPLASH
HA HA! WHAT A COUPLE OF SNEAKY LITTLE DEVILS!

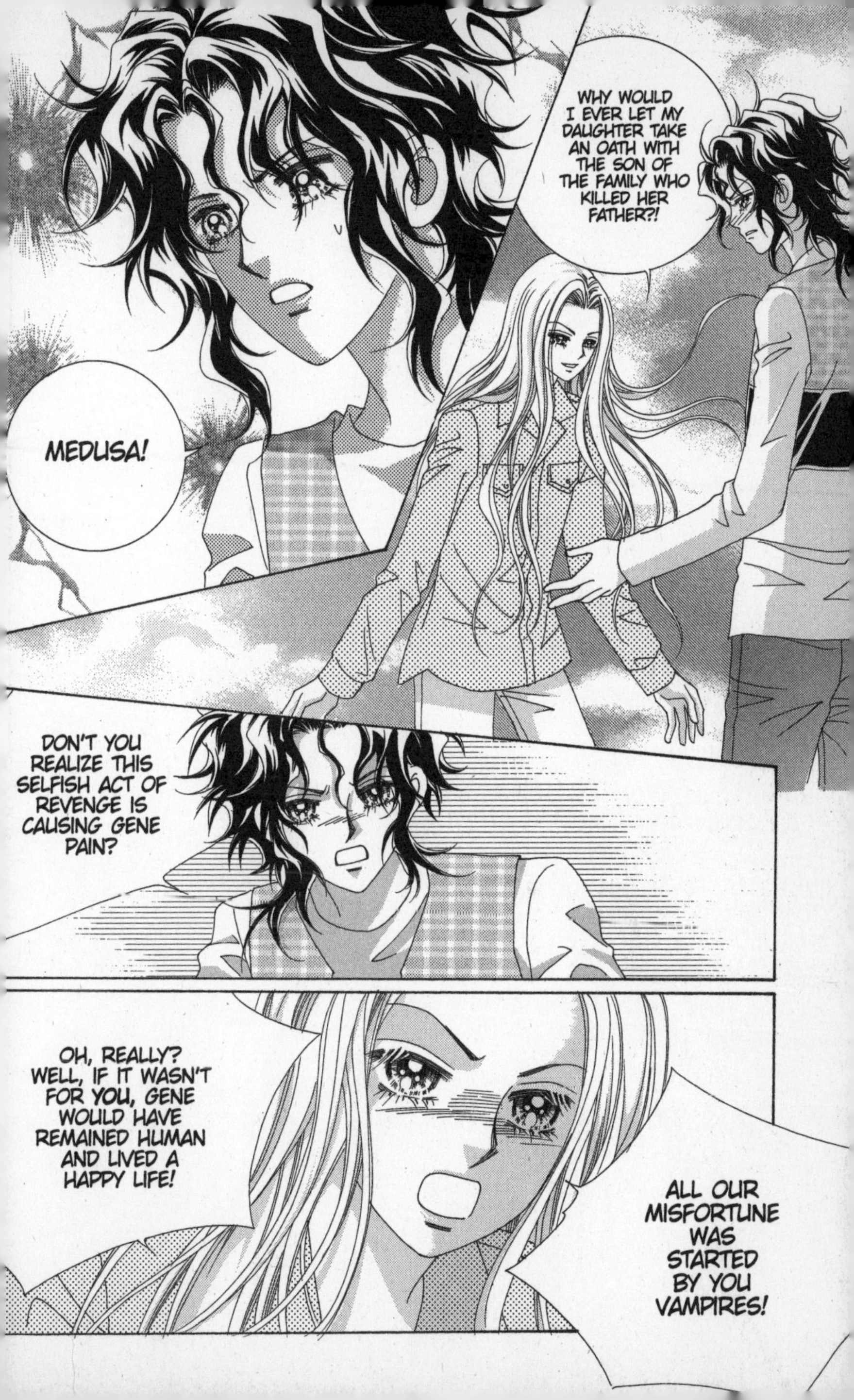
MEDUSA!
WHY WOULD I EVER LET MY DAUGHTER TAKE AN OATH WITH THE SON OF THE FAMILY WHO KILLED HER FATHER?!
DON'T YOU REALIZE THIS SELFISH ACT OF REVENGE IS CAUSING GENE PAIN?
OH, REALLY? WELL, IF IT WASN'T FOR YOU, GENE WOULD HAVE REMAINED HUMAN AND LIVED A HAPPY LIFE!
ALL OUR MISFORTUNE WAS STARTED BY YOU VAMPIRES!

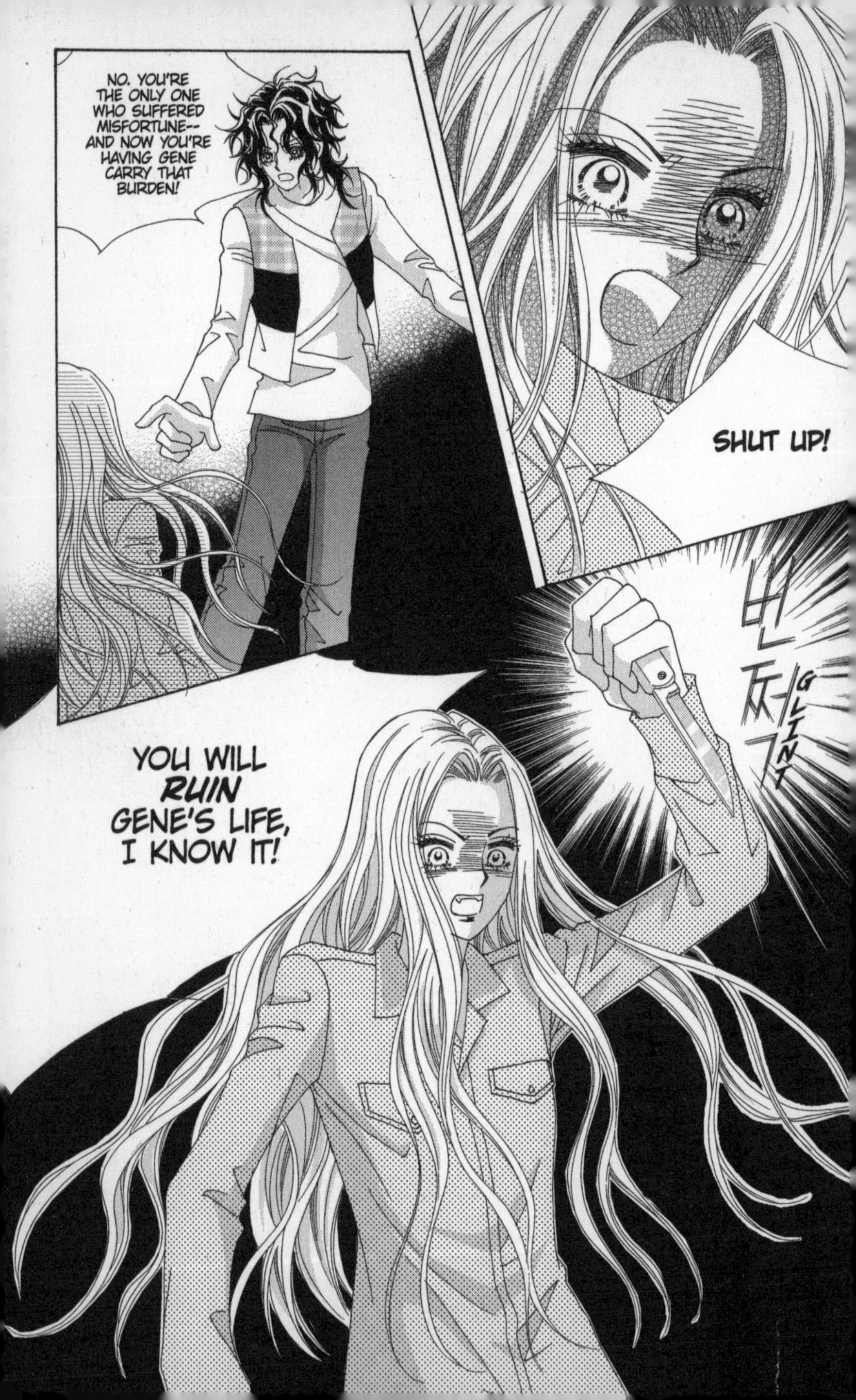
NO. YOU'RE THE ONLY ONE WHO SUFFERED MISFORTUNE-- AND NOW YOU'RE HAVING GENE CARRY THAT BURDEN!
SHUT UP!
YOU WILL RUIN GENE'S LIFE, I KNOW IT!
번쩍
GLINT

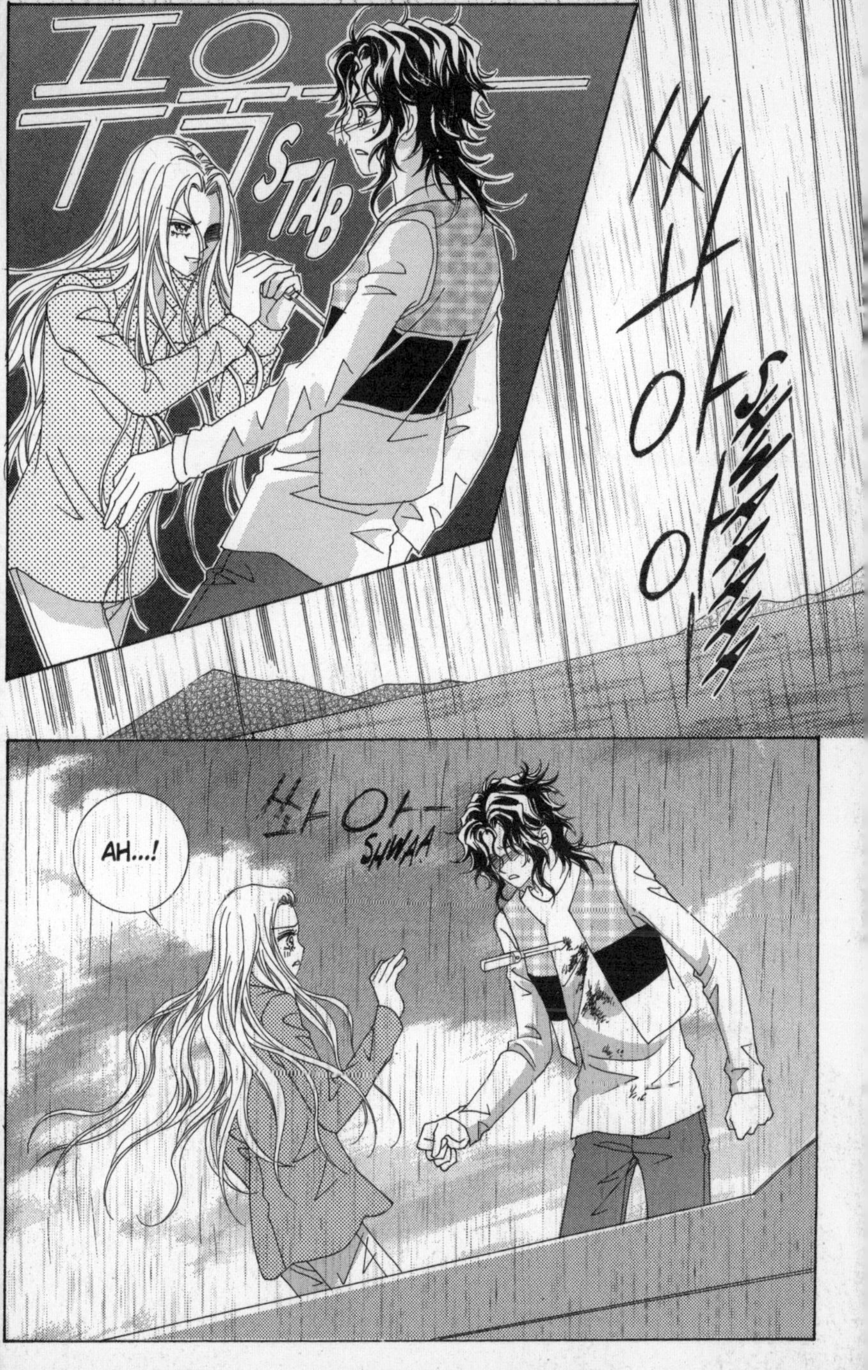
STAB
쏴아아!
SHWAAAAAAA
AH...!
쏴아—
SHWAA

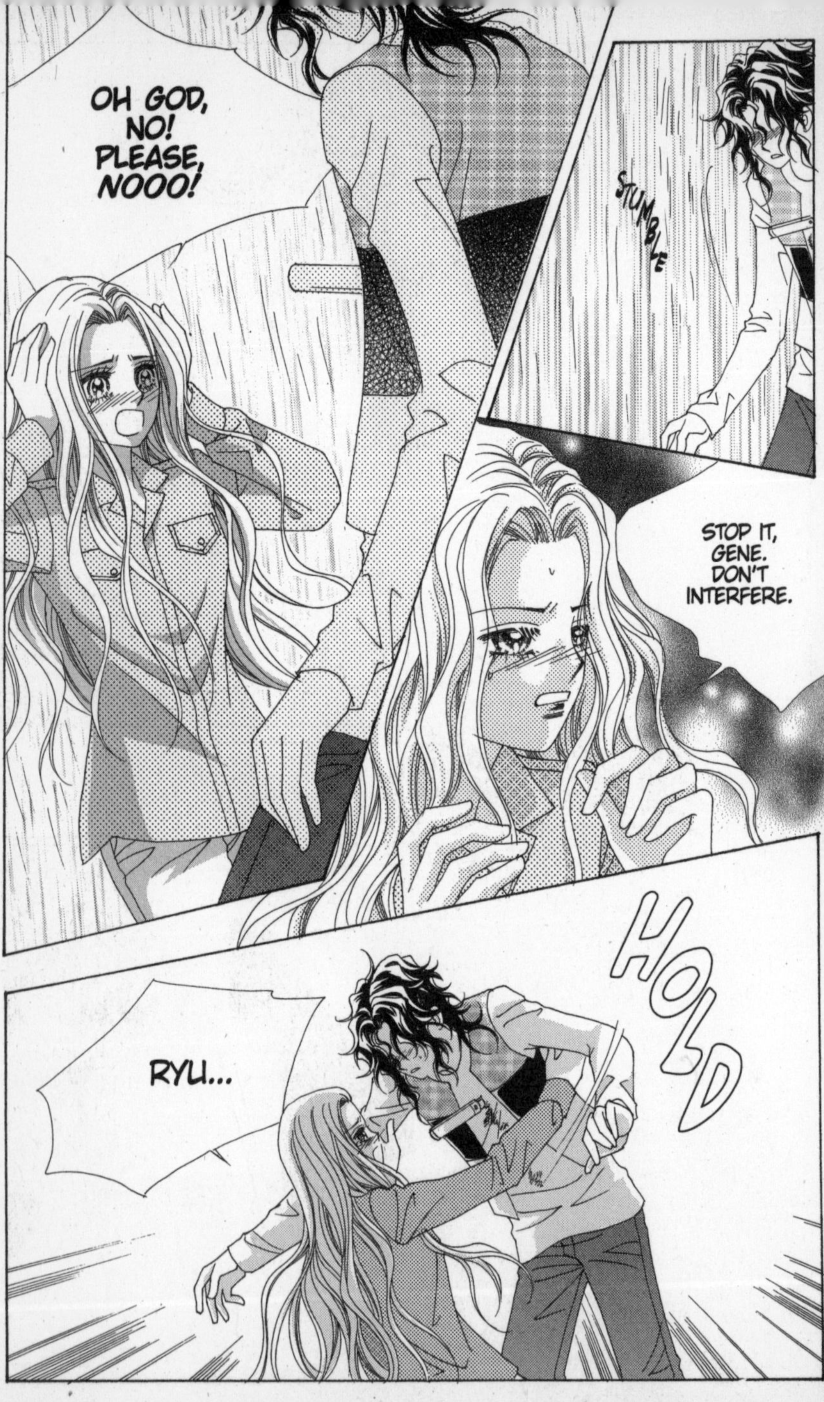
OH GOD, NO! PLEASE, NOOO!
STUMBLE
STOP IT, GENE. DON'T INTERFERE.
RYU...
HOLD

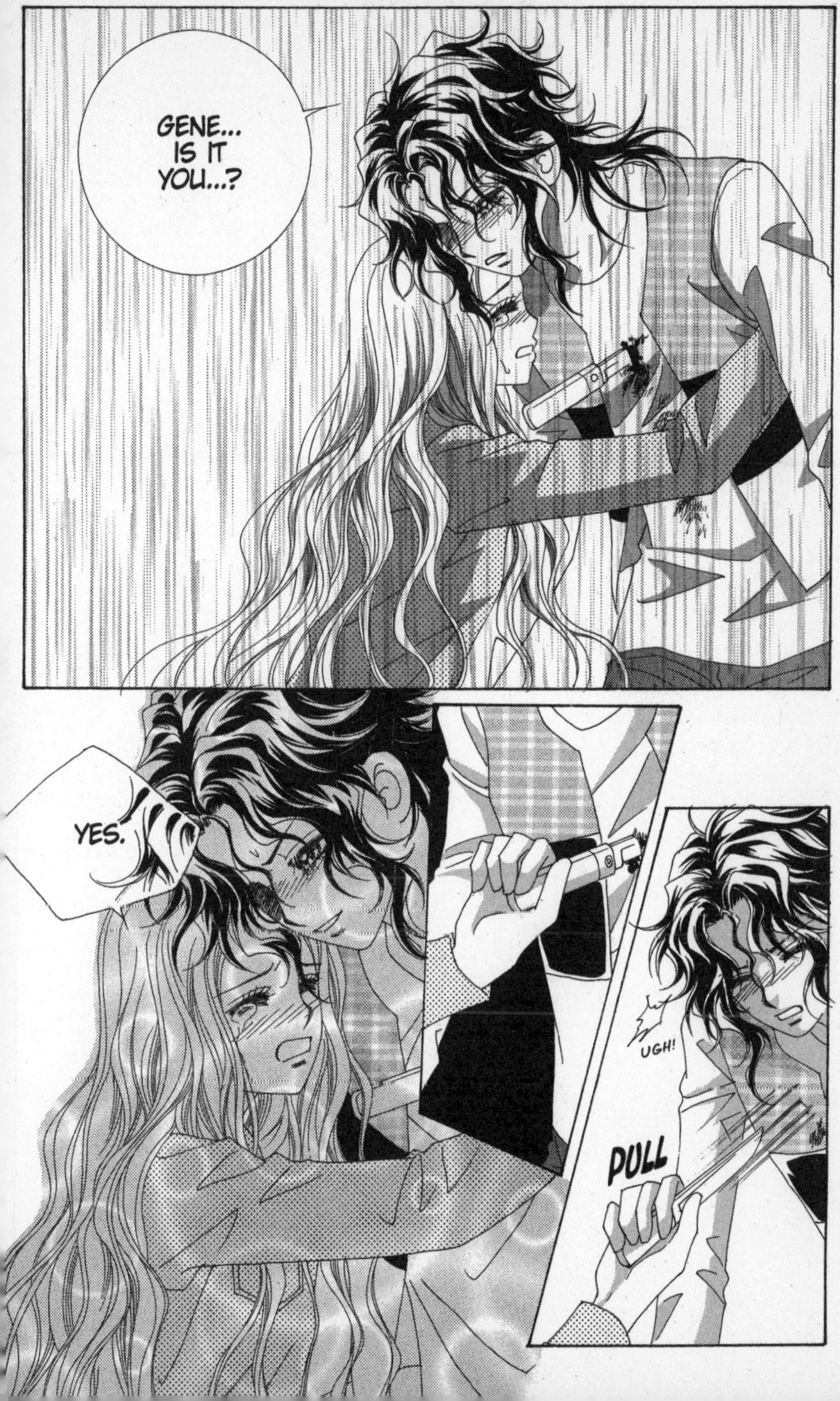
GENE... IS IT YOU...?
YES.
UGH!
PULL

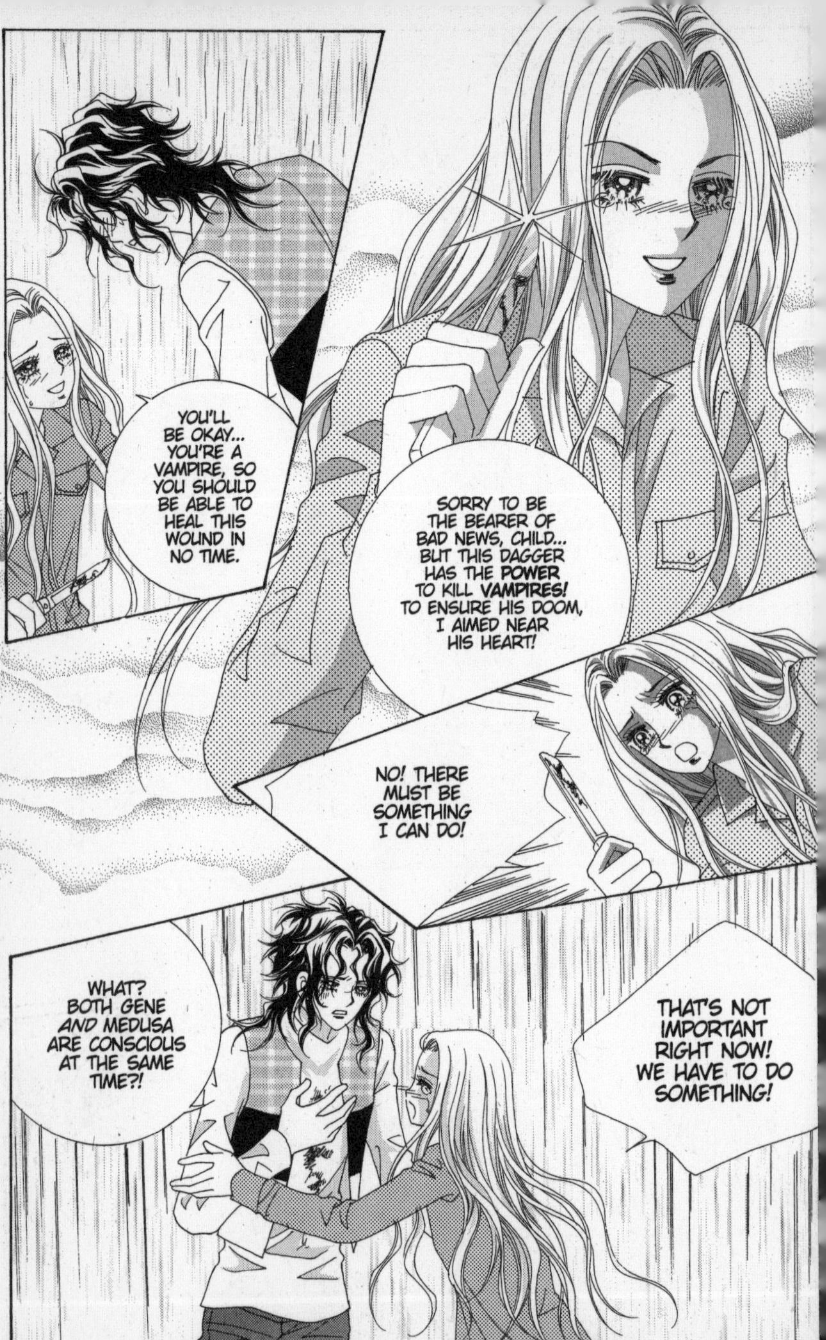
YOU'LL BE OKAY... YOU'RE A VAMPIRE, SO YOU SHOULD BE ABLE TO HEAL THIS WOUND IN NO TIME.
SORRY TO BE THE BEARER OF BAD NEWS, CHILD... BUT THIS DAGGER HAS THE POWER TO KILL VAMPIRES! TO ENSURE HIS DOOM, I AIMED NEAR HIS HEART!
NO! THERE MUST BE SOMETHING I CAN DO!
WHAT? BOTH GENE AND MEDUSA ARE CONSCIOUS AT THE SAME TIME?!
THAT'S NOT IMPORTANT RIGHT NOW! WE HAVE TO DO SOMETHING!

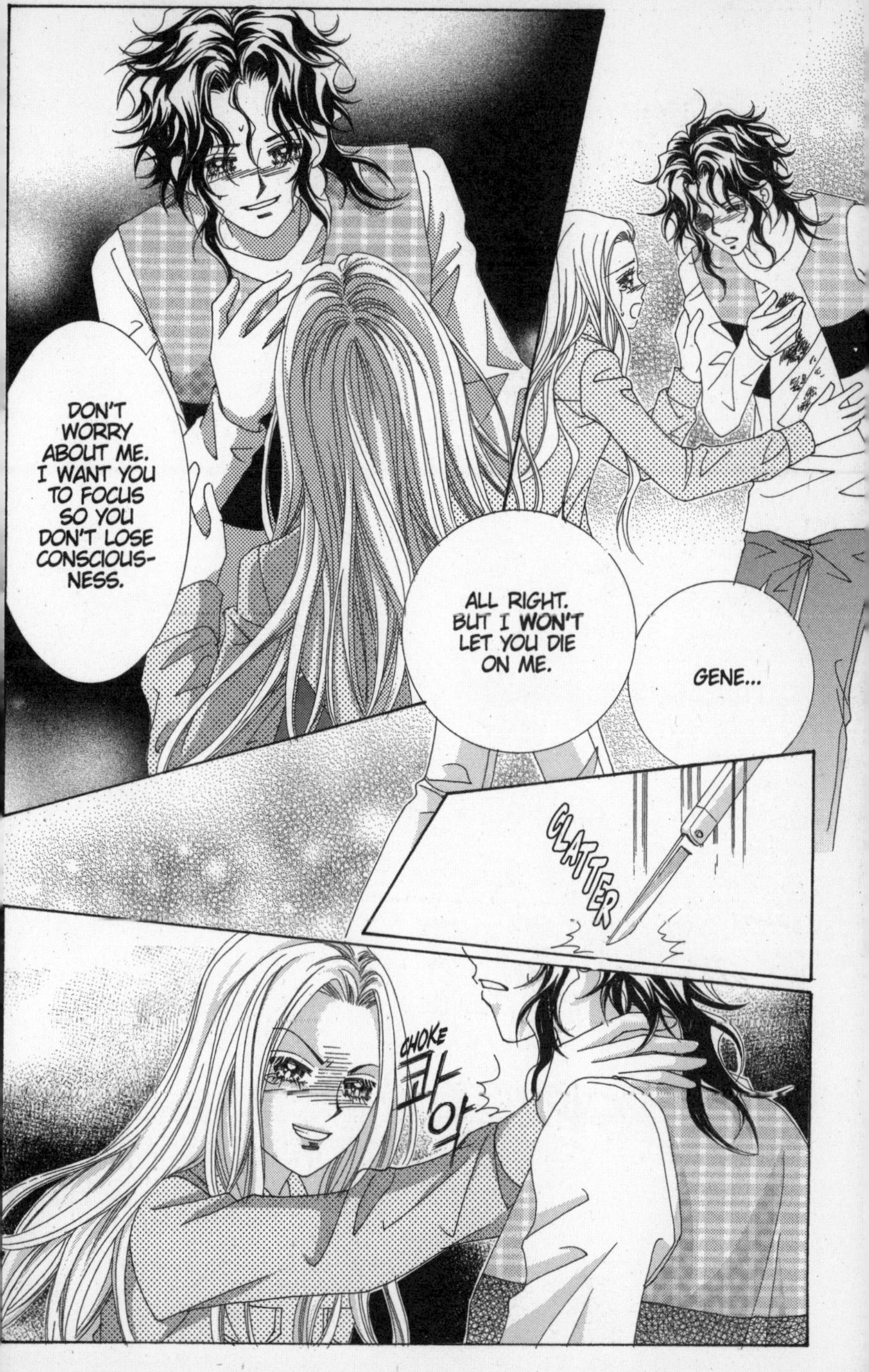
DON'T WORRY ABOUT ME. I WANT YOU TO FOCUS SO YOU DON'T LOSE CONSCIOUSNESS.
ALL RIGHT. BUT I WON'T LET YOU DIE ON ME.
GENE...
CLATTER
CHOKE

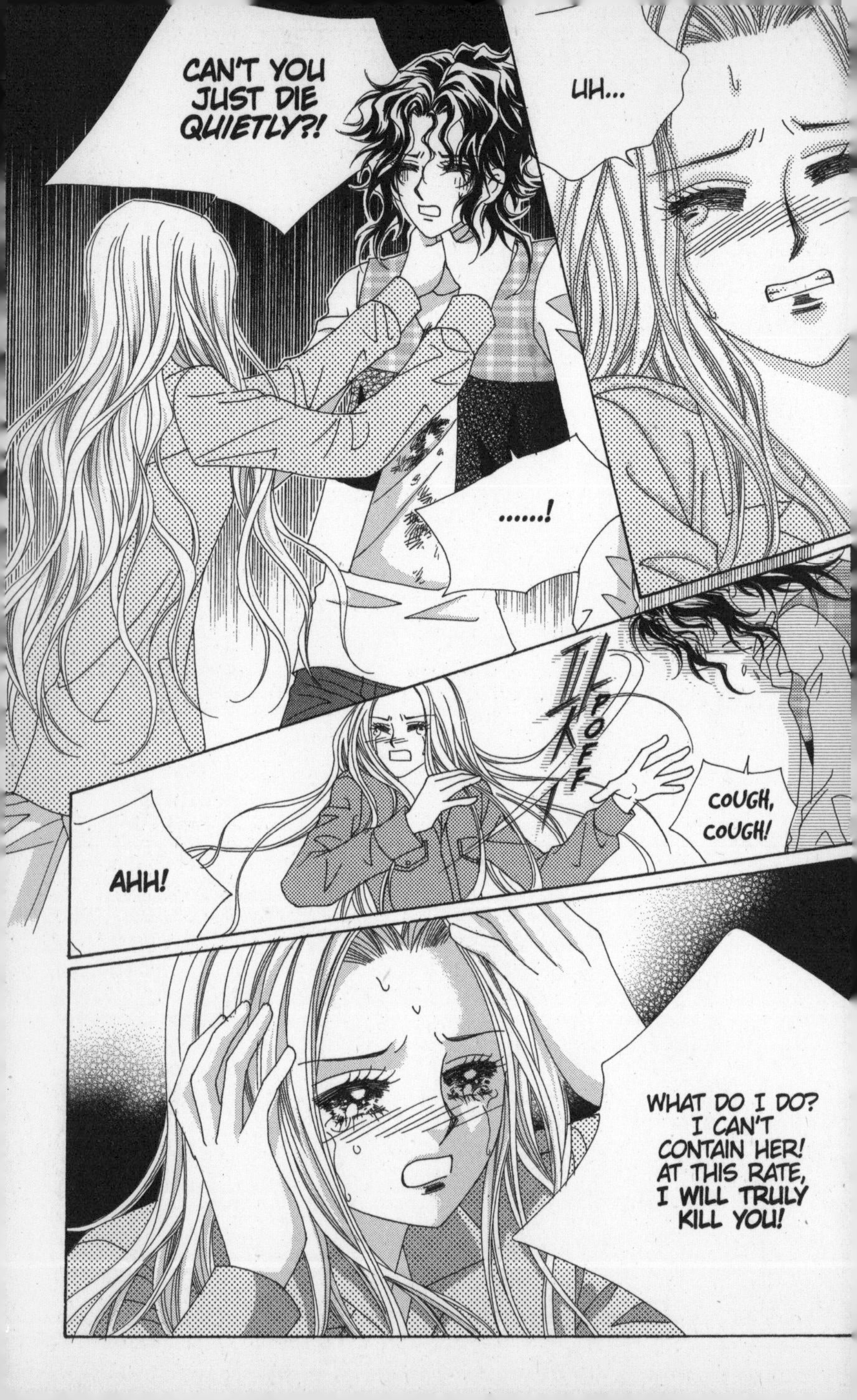
CAN'T YOU JUST DIE QUIETLY?!
UH...
......!
AHH!
POFF
COUGH, COUGH!
WHAT DO I DO? I CAN'T CONTAIN HER! AT THIS RATE, I WILL TRULY KILL YOU!

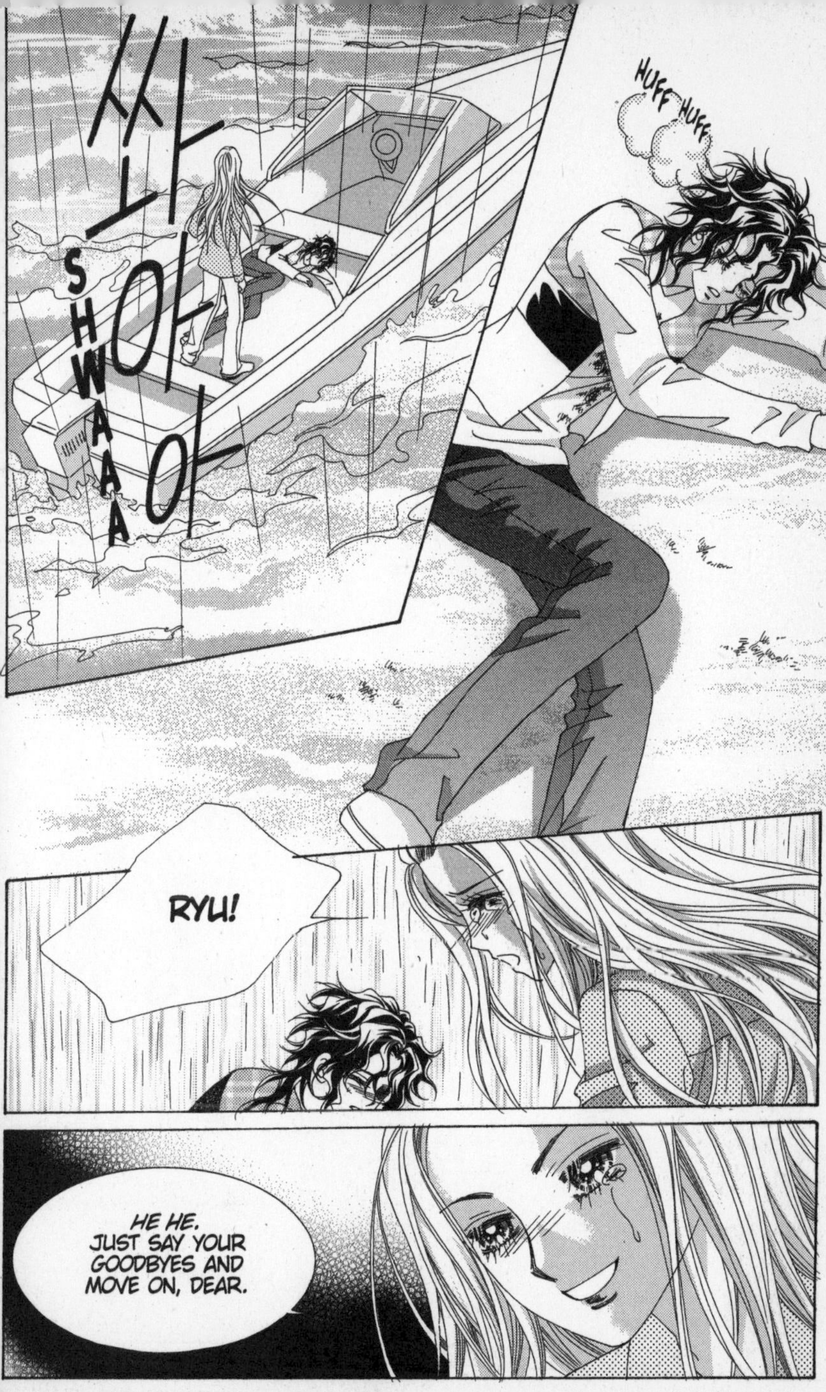
쏴아아
SHWAAAA
HUFF HUFF
RYU!
HE HE.
JUST SAY YOUR GOODBYES AND MOVE ON, DEAR.

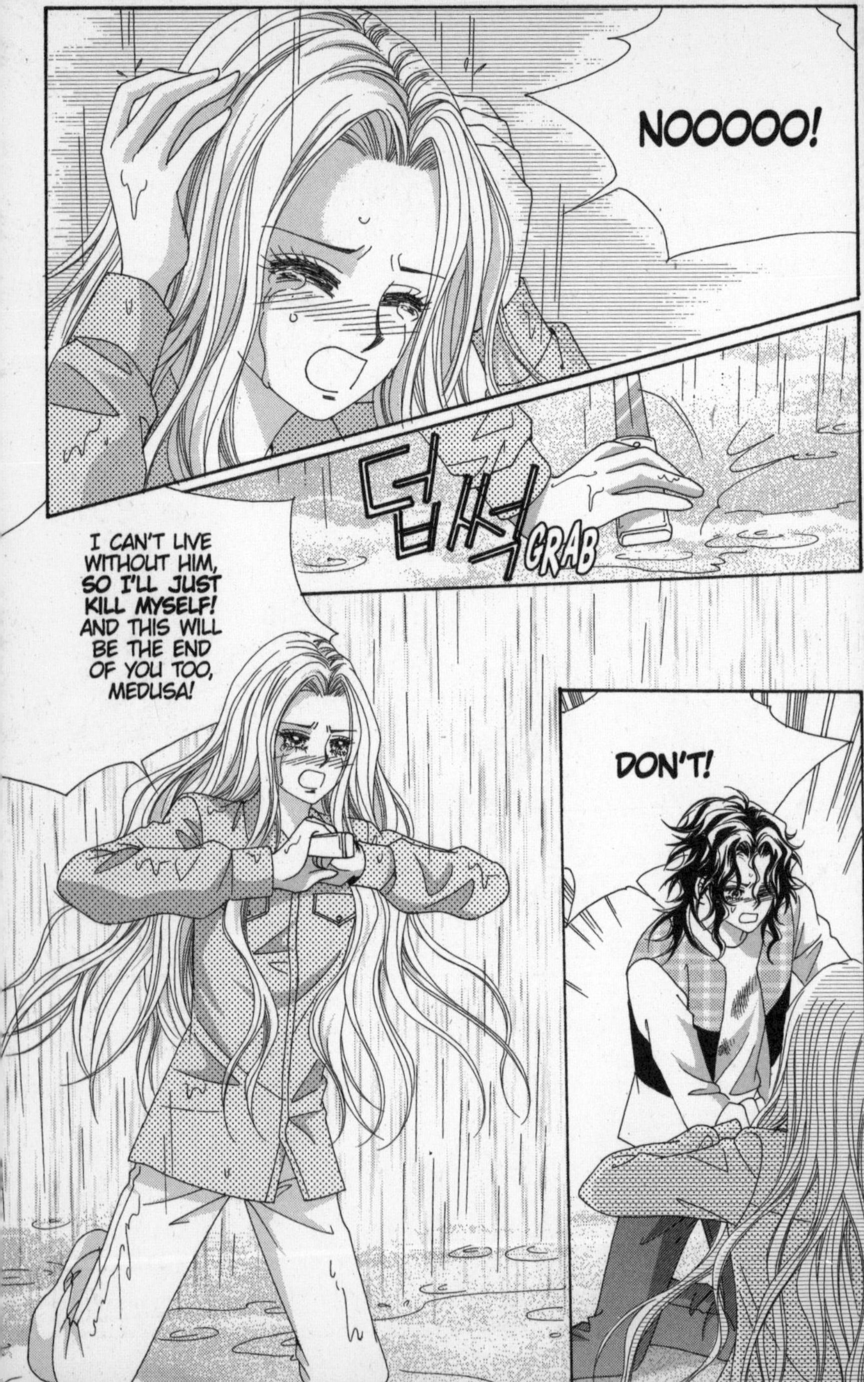
NOOOOO!
덥썩
GRAB
I CAN'T LIVE WITHOUT HIM, SO I'LL JUST KILL MYSELF! AND THIS WILL BE THE END OF YOU TOO, MEDUSA!
DON'T!

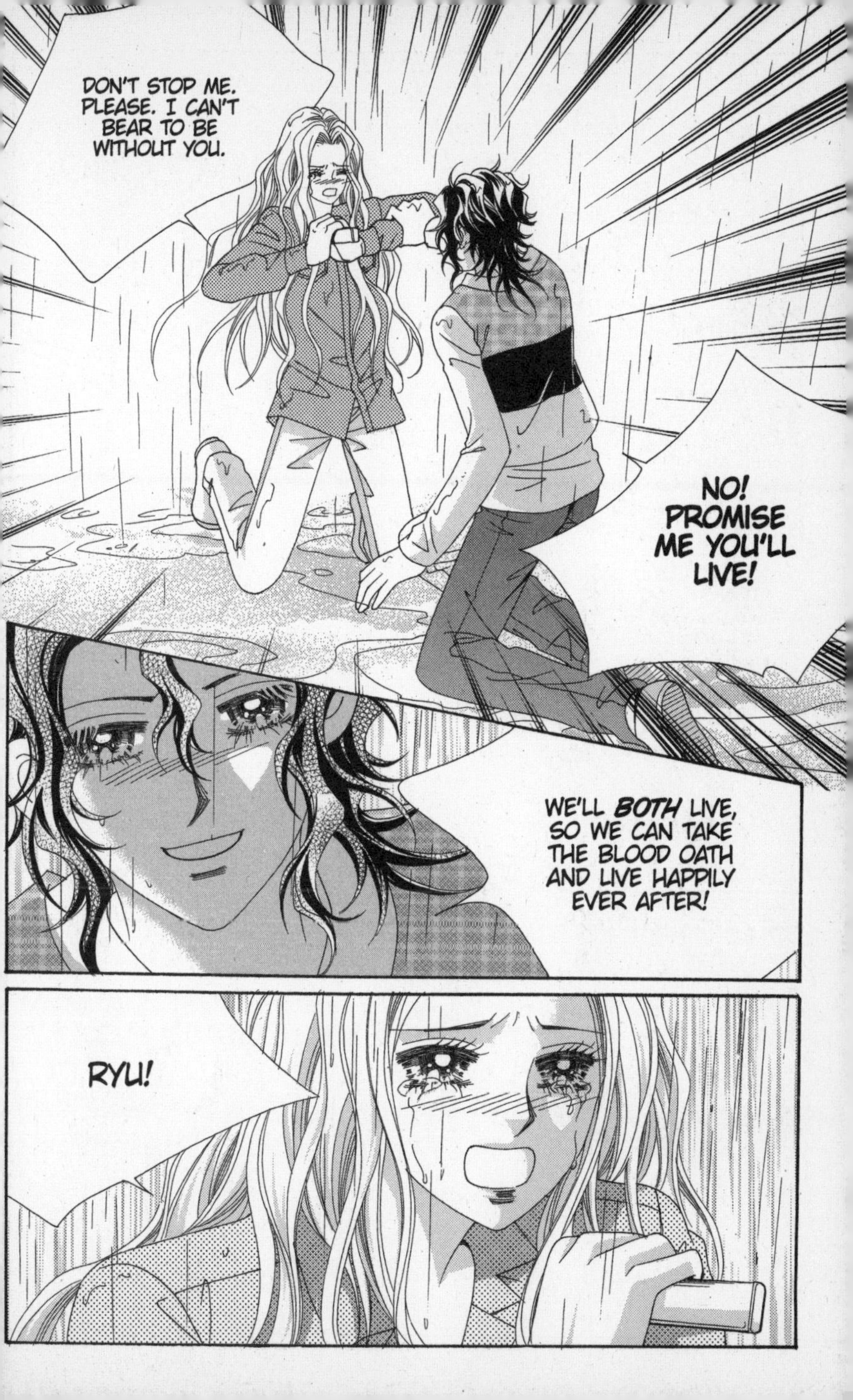
DON'T STOP ME. PLEASE. I CAN'T BEAR TO BE WITHOUT YOU.
NO! PROMISE ME YOU'LL LIVE!
WE'LL *BOTH* LIVE, SO WE CAN TAKE THE BLOOD OATH AND LIVE HAPPILY EVER AFTER!
RYU!

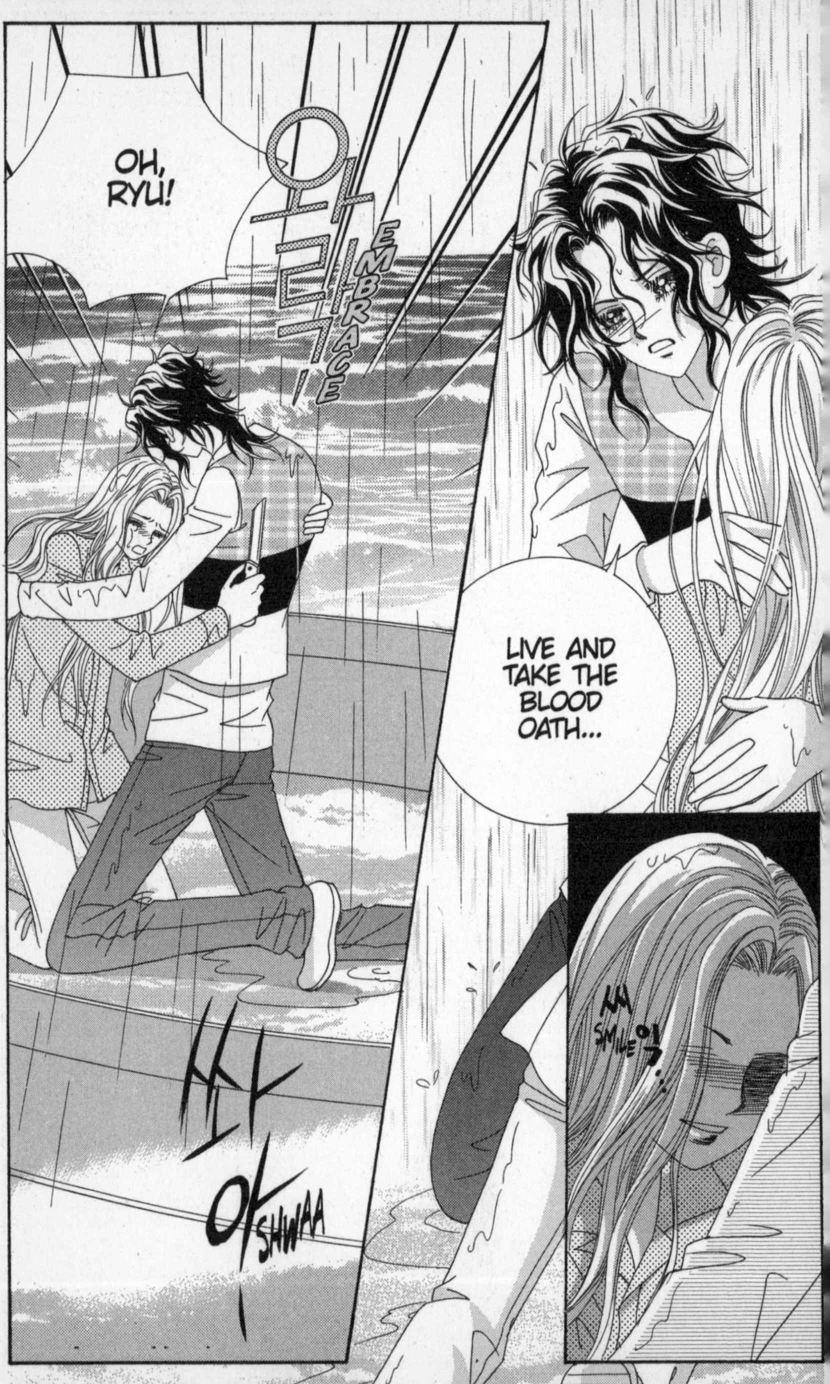

OH, RYU!
와락
EMBRACE!
쏴아
SHWAA
LIVE AND TAKE THE BLOOD OATH...
씨익
SMILE

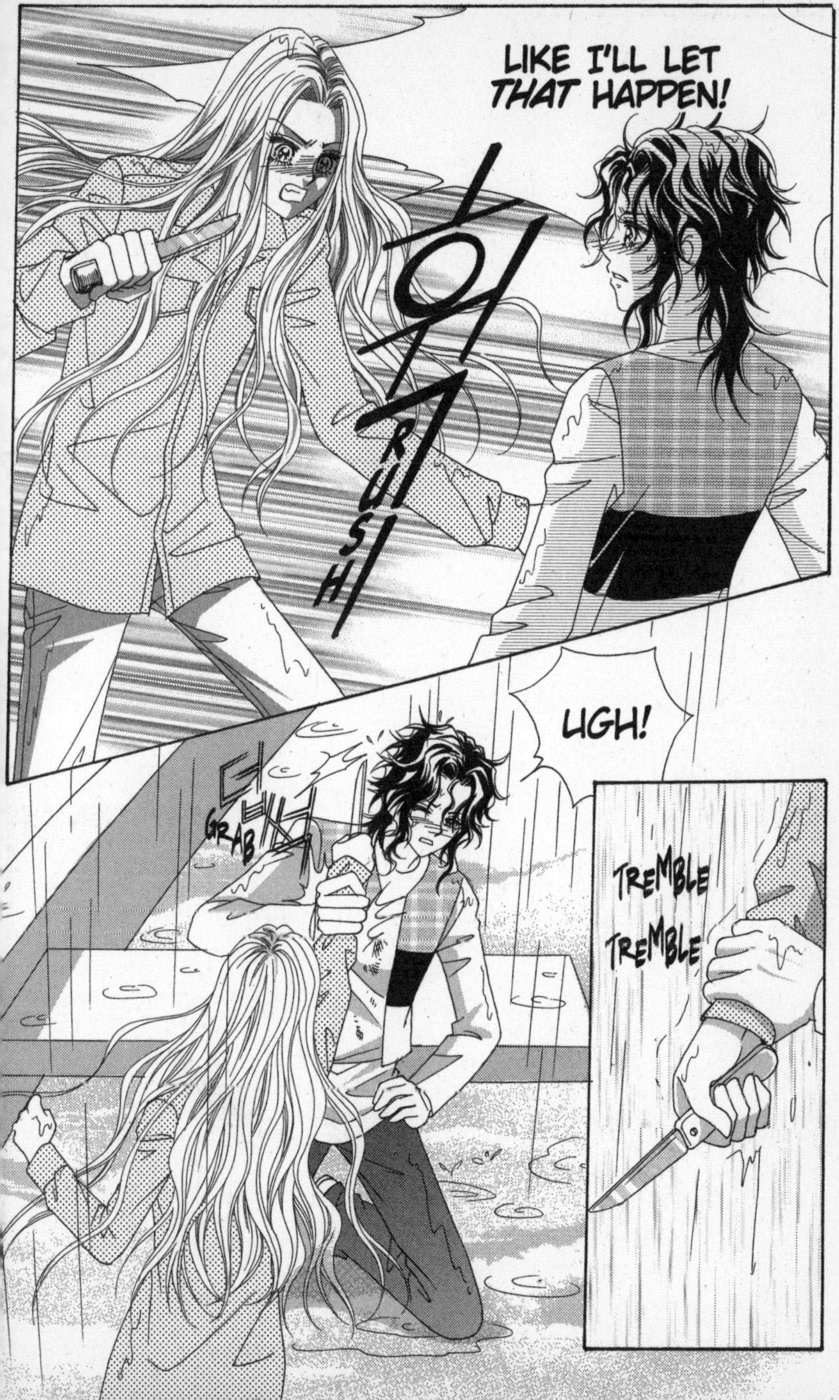
LIKE I'LL LET *THAT* HAPPEN!
RUSH
UGH!
GRAB
TREMBLE
TREMBLE

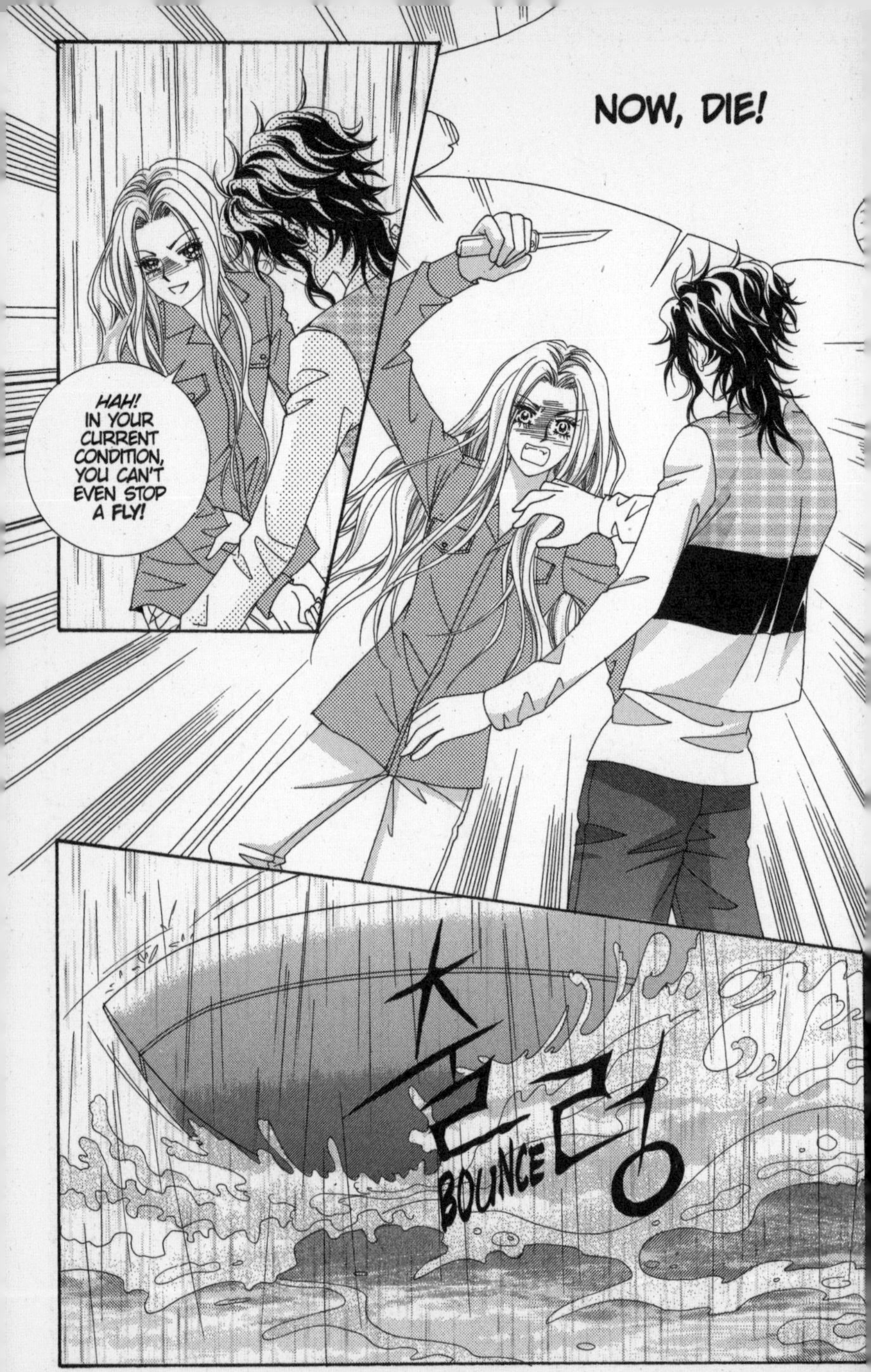
HAH! IN YOUR CURRENT CONDITION, YOU CAN'T EVEN STOP A FLY!
NOW, DIE!
BOUNCE

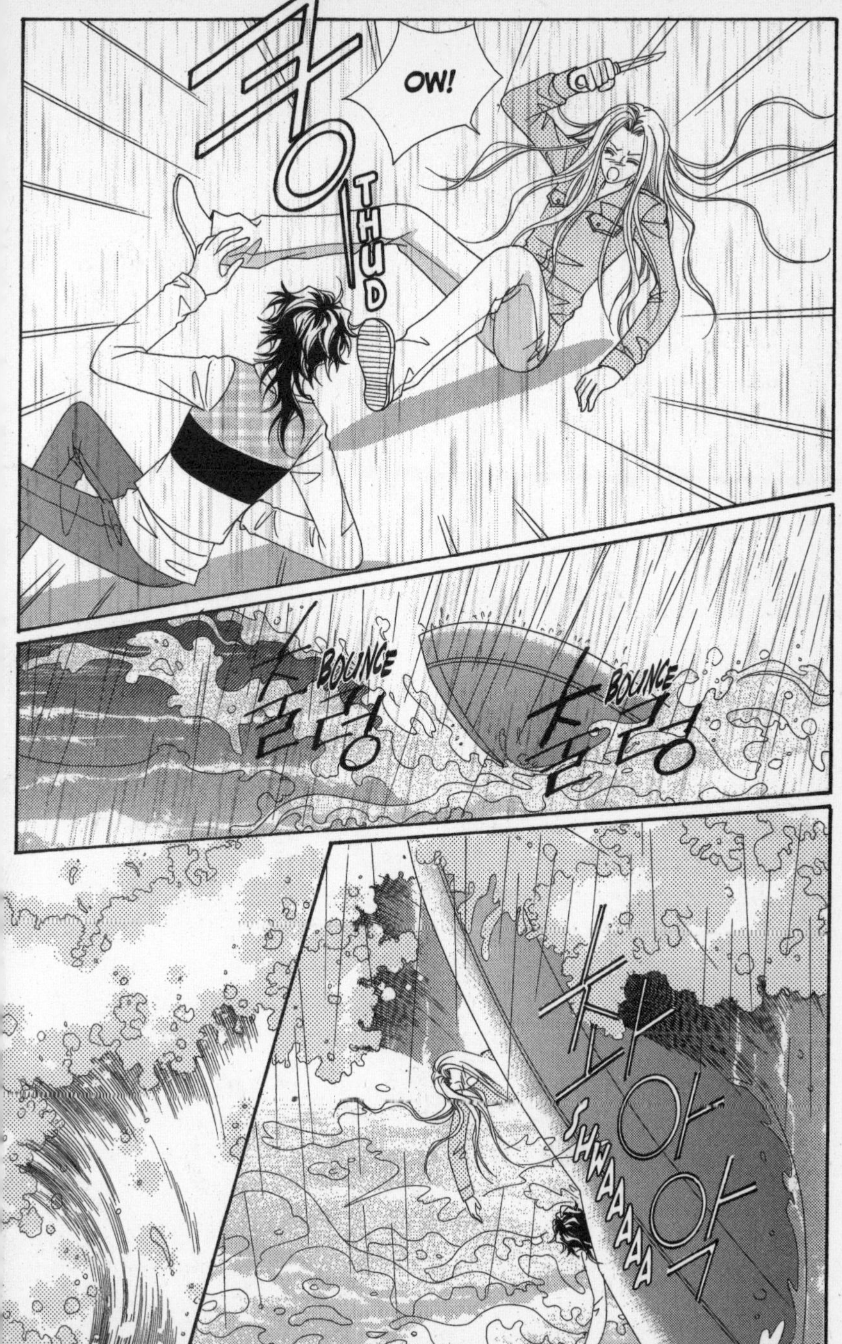
OW!
THUD
BOUNCE
출렁
BOUNCE
출렁
SHWAAAAAA

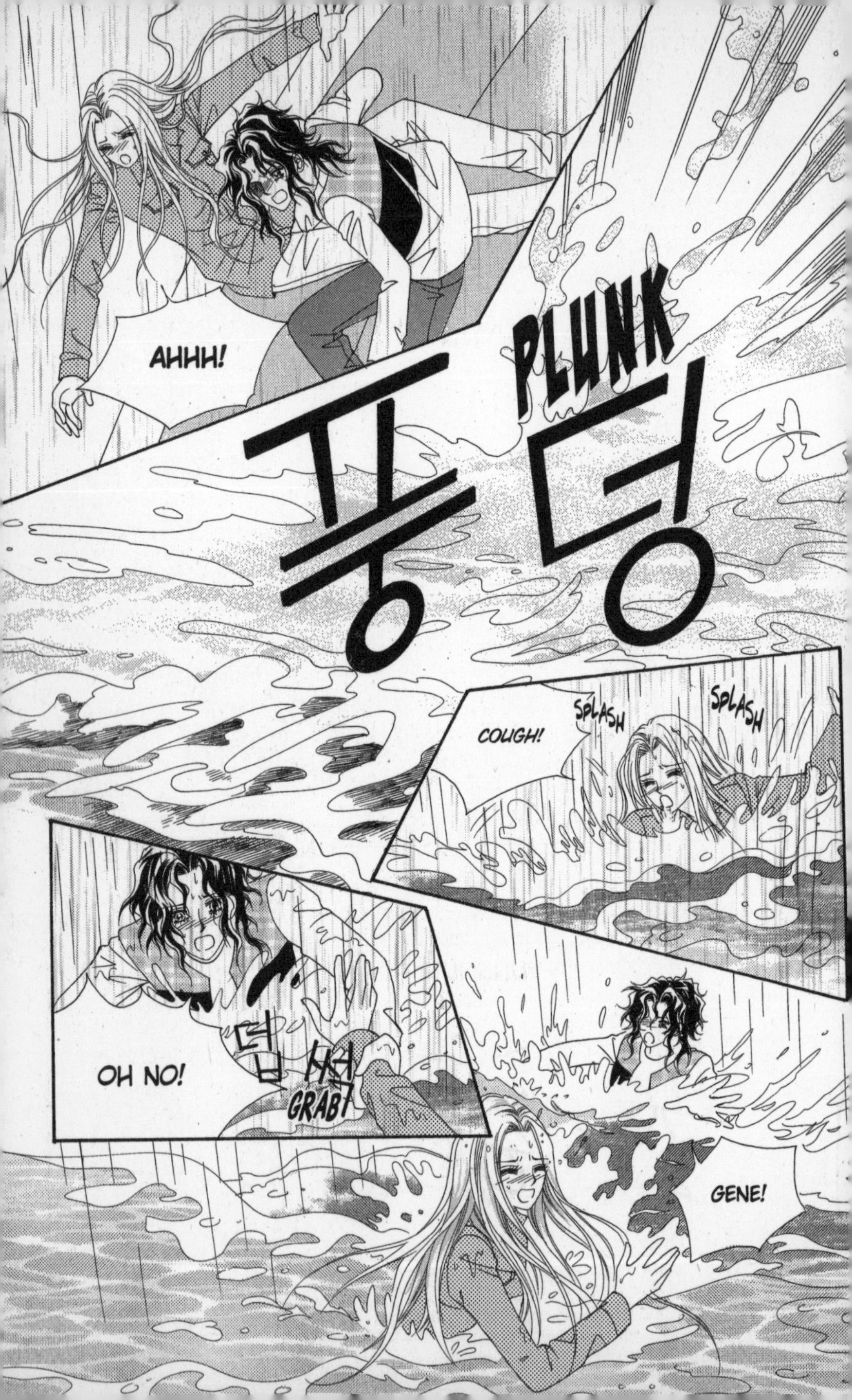
AHHH!
PLUNK
풍덩
COUGH!
SPLASH
SPLASH
OH NO!
덥석
GRAB!
GENE!

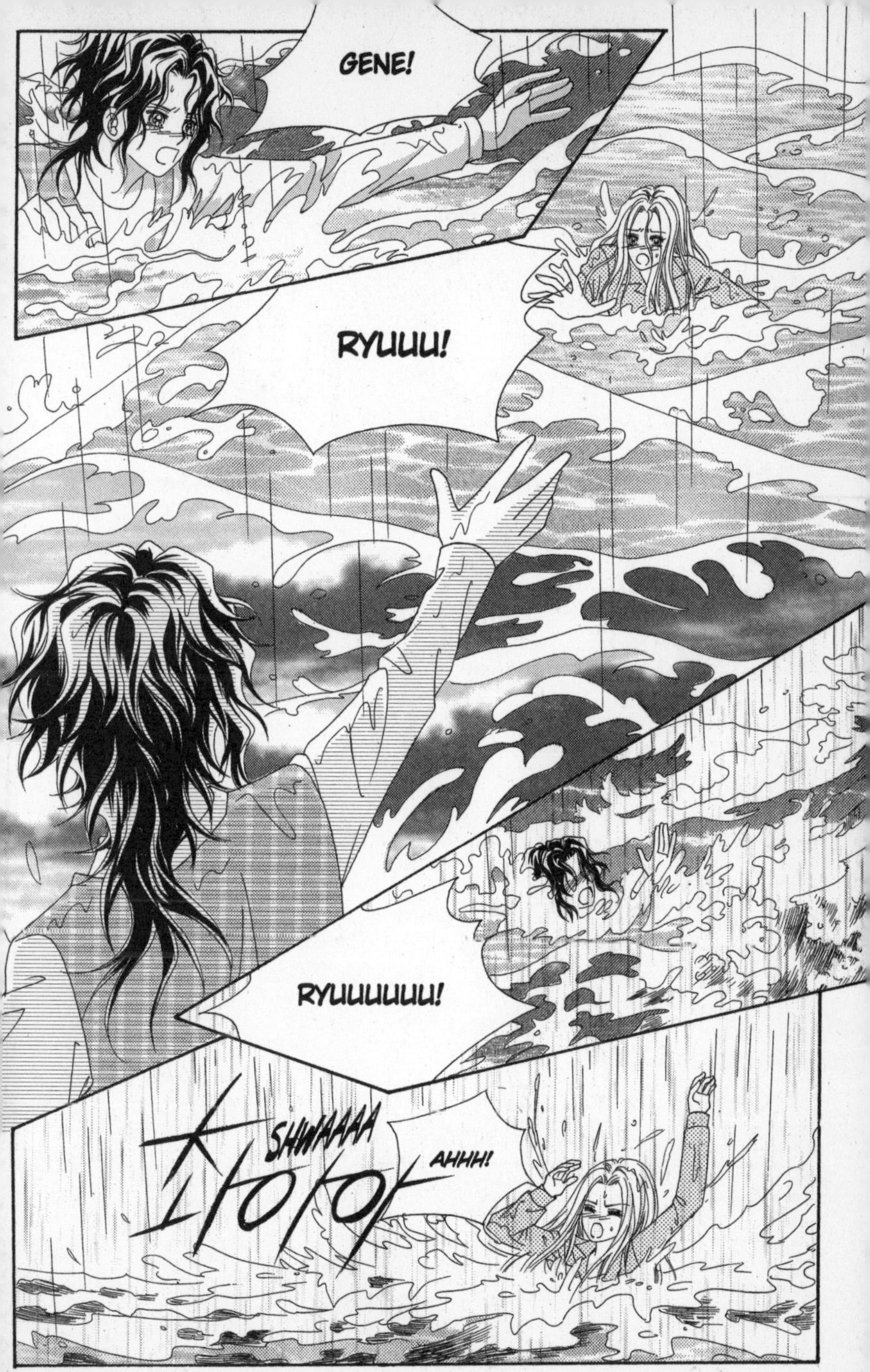
GENE!
RYUUU!
RYUUUUUU!
SHWAAAA
AHHH!

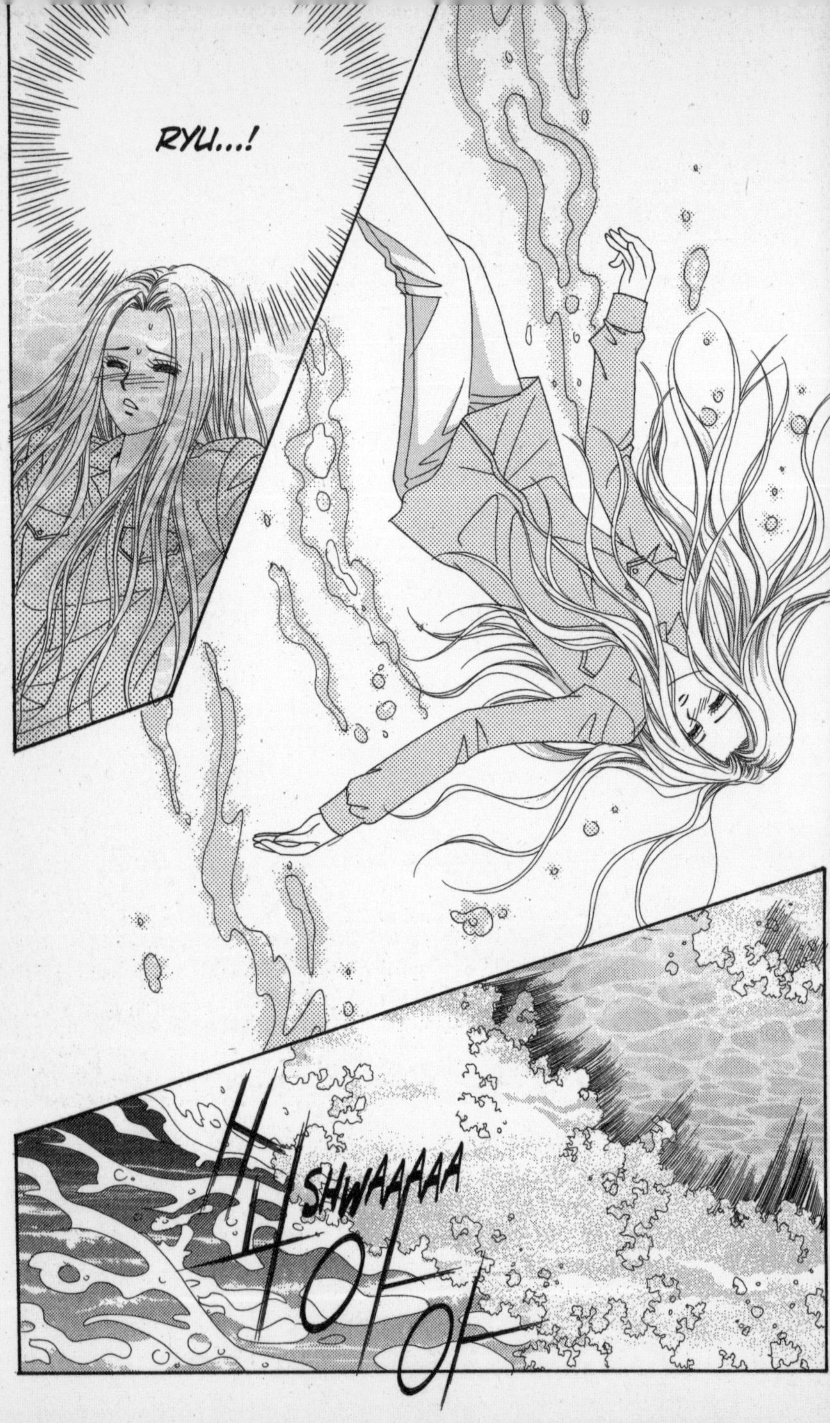
RYU...!
SHWAAAAA

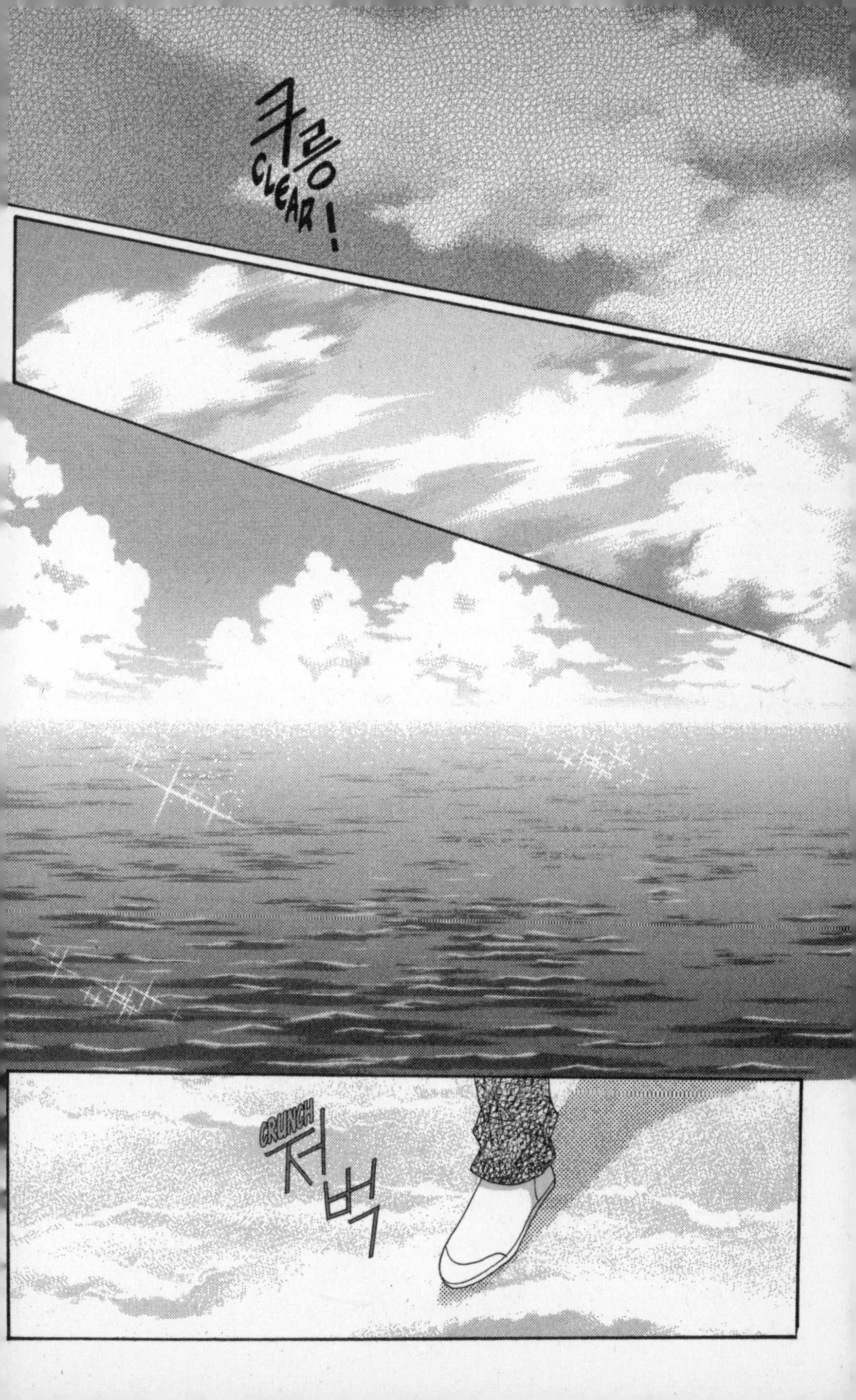

쿠릉
CLEAR!
CRUNCH
저벅

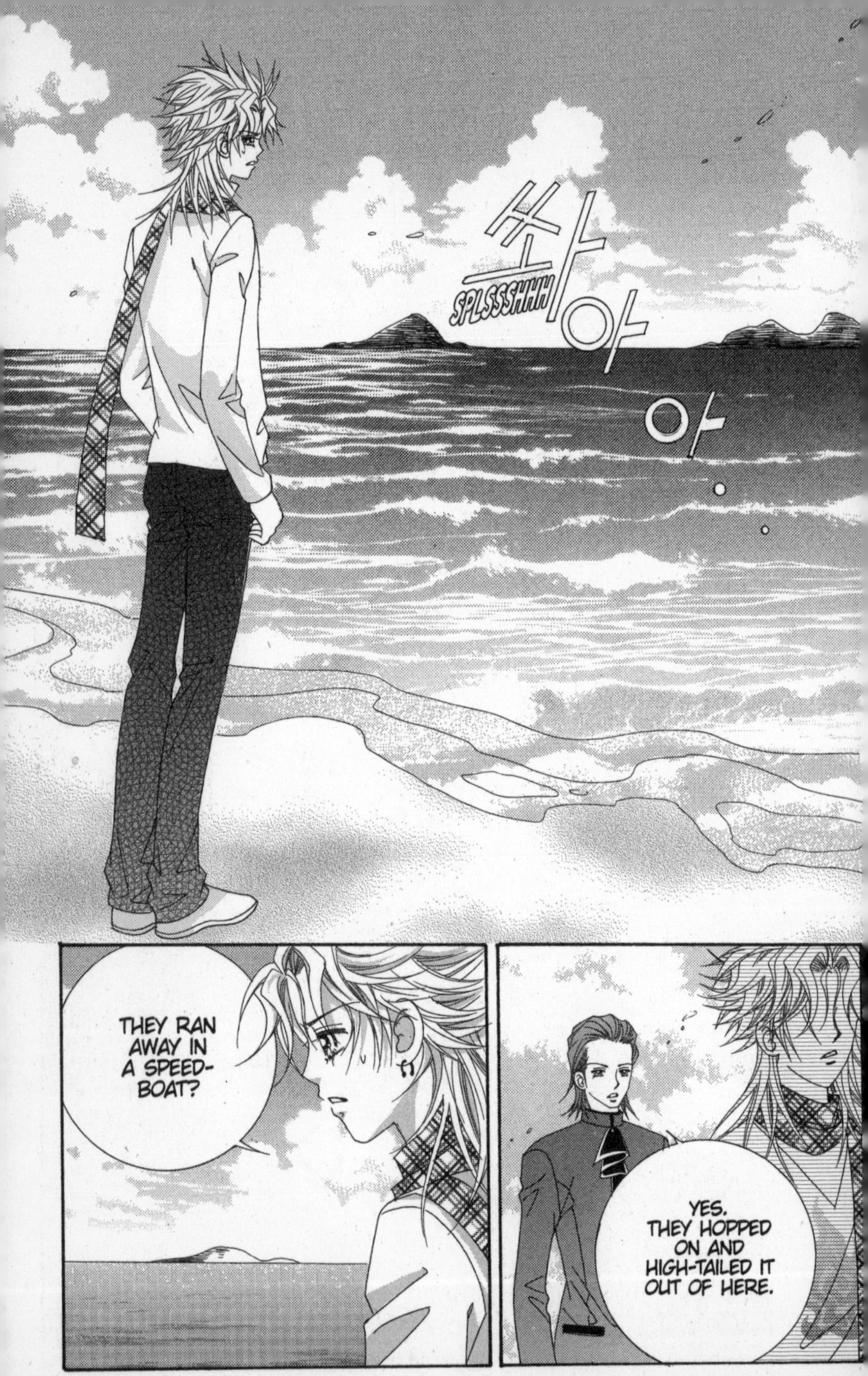
쏴아아
SPLSSSHHH
THEY RAN AWAY IN A SPEED-BOAT?
YES. THEY HOPPED ON AND HIGH-TAILED IT OUT OF HERE.

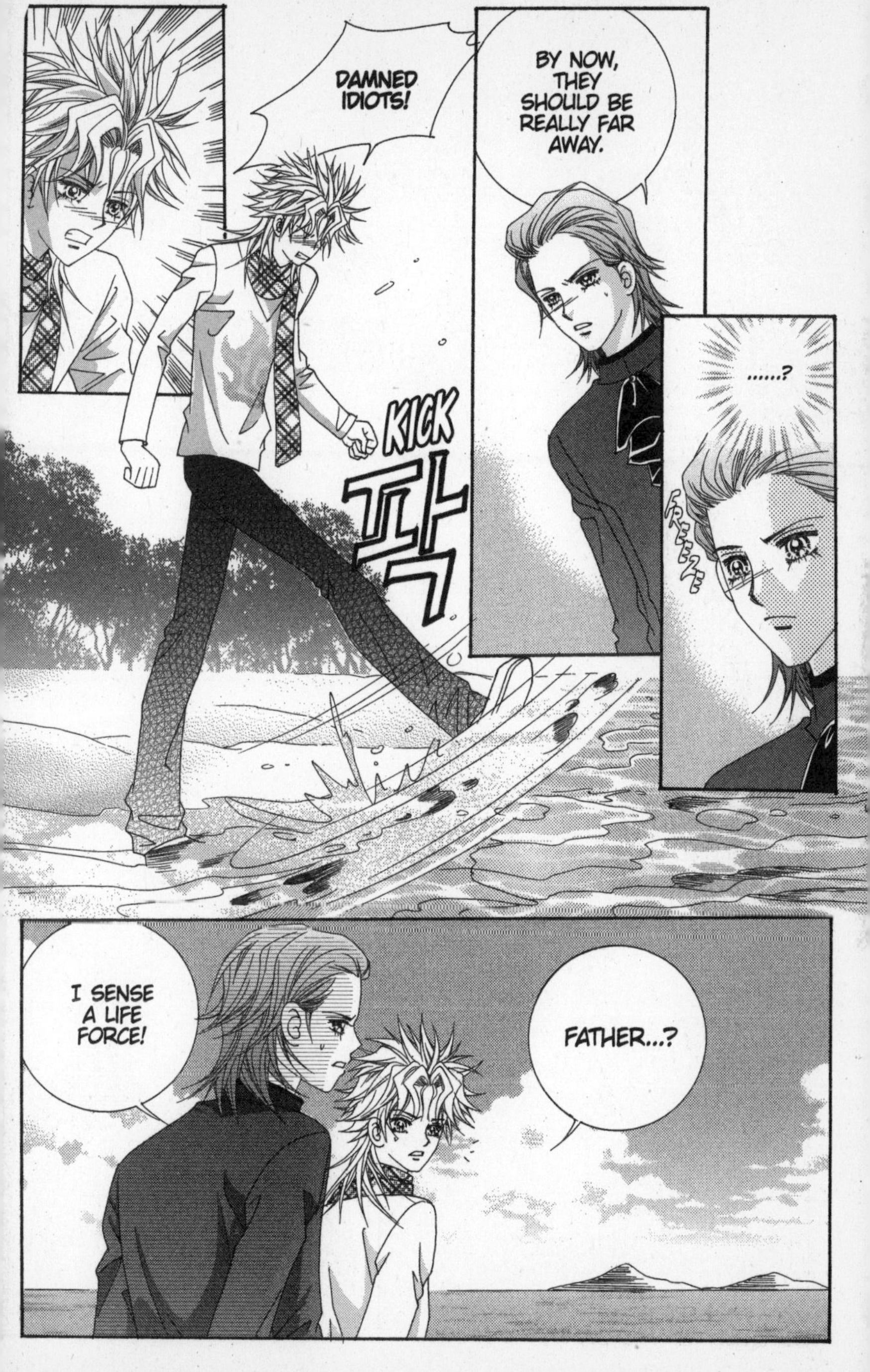
DAMNED IDIOTS!
KICK
팍
BY NOW, THEY SHOULD BE REALLY FAR AWAY.
......?
FREEZE
I SENSE A LIFE FORCE!
FATHER...?

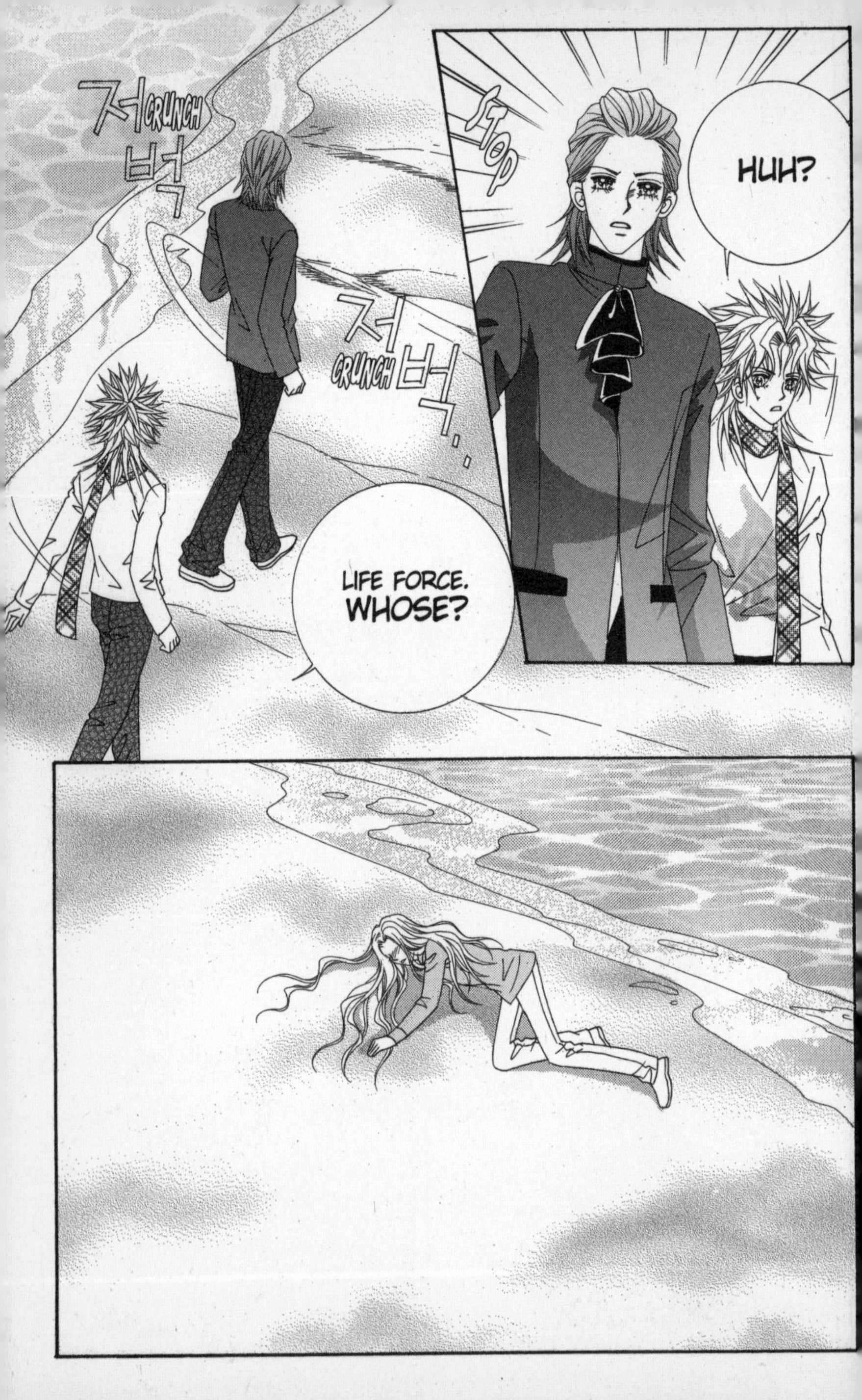

저CRUNCH 벅
저 CRUNCH 벅..
LIFE FORCE. WHOSE?
STOP
HUH?

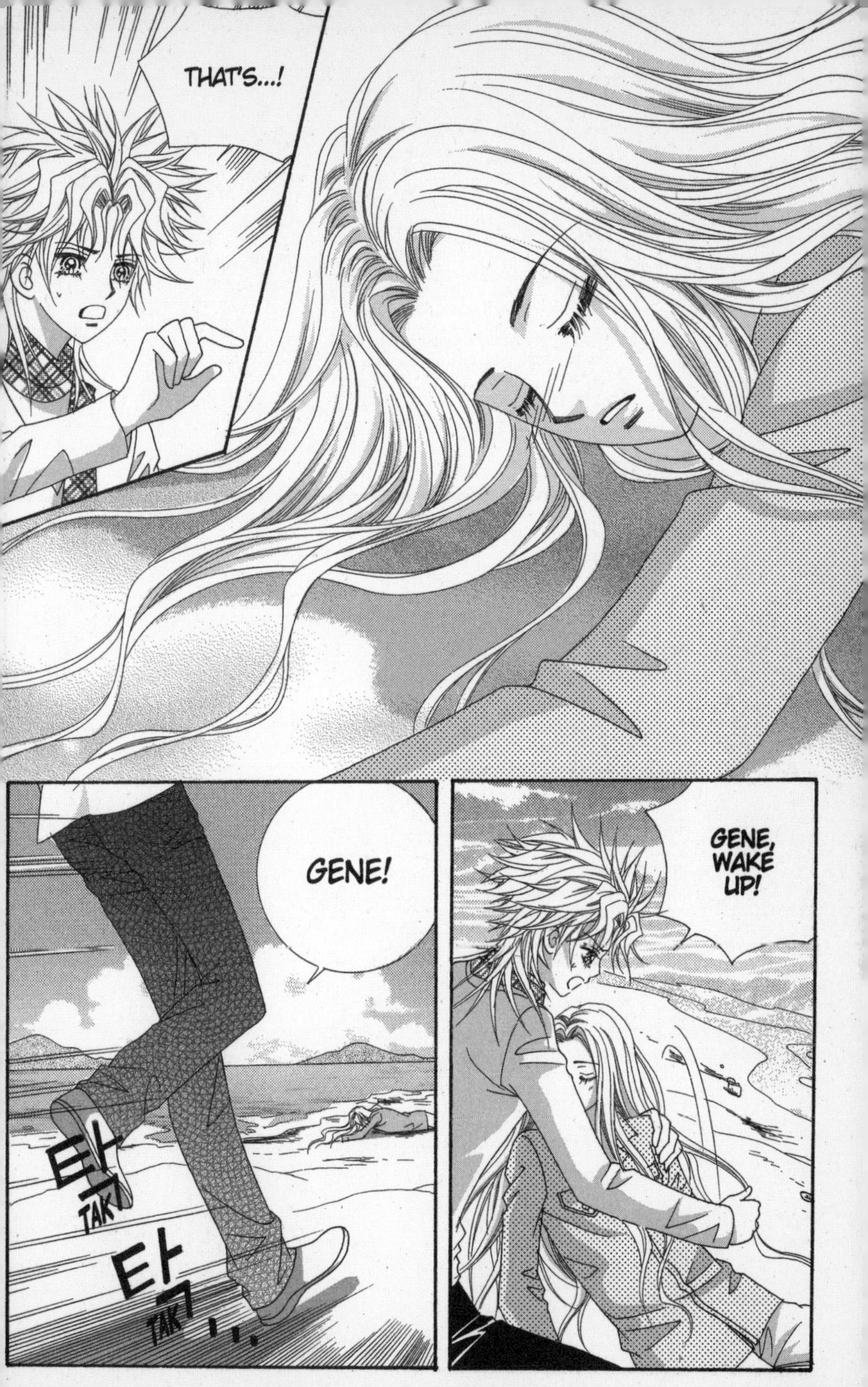

THAT'S...!
GENE!
탁
TAK
탁
TAK
GENE, WAKE UP!

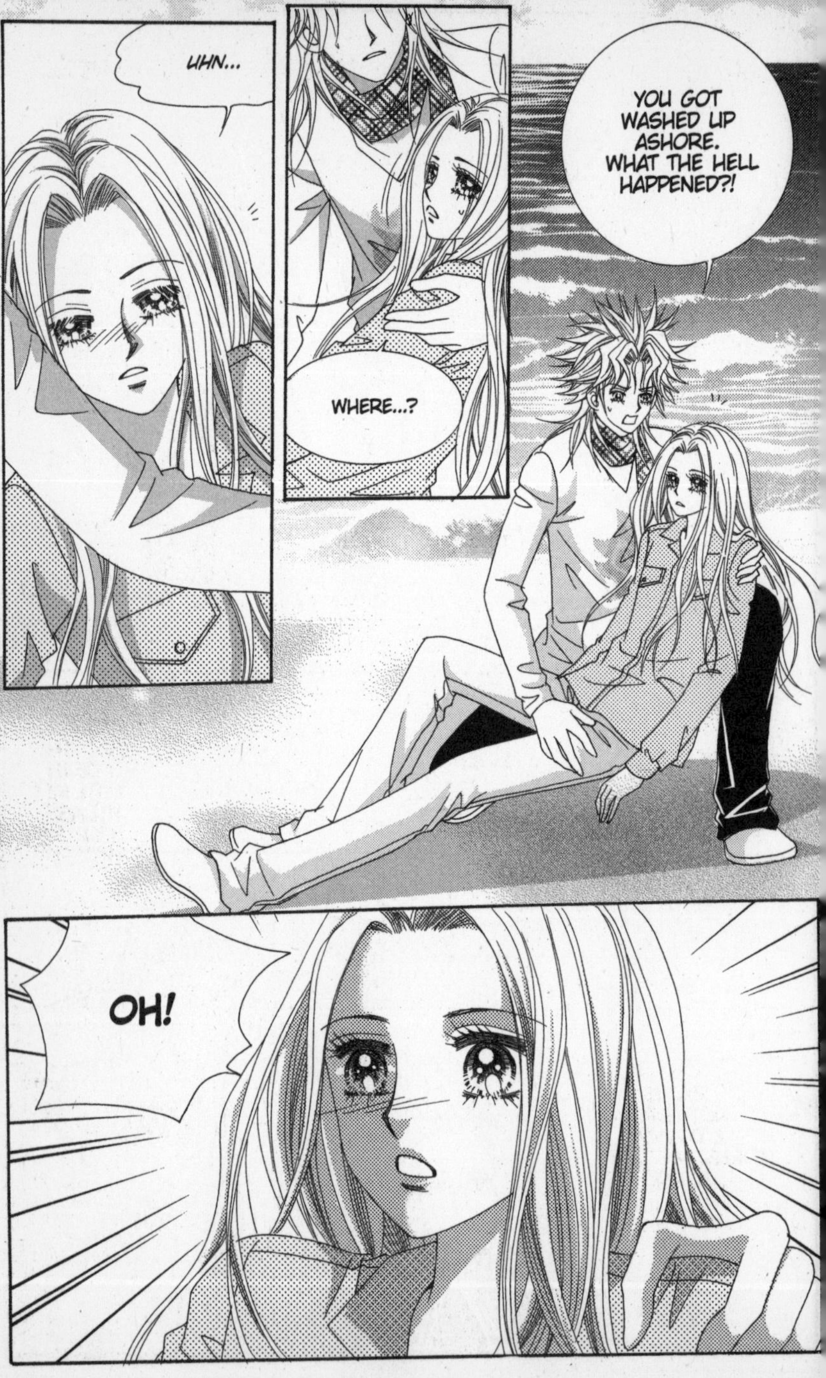
UHN...
WHERE...?
YOU GOT WASHED UP ASHORE. WHAT THE HELL HAPPENED?!
OH!

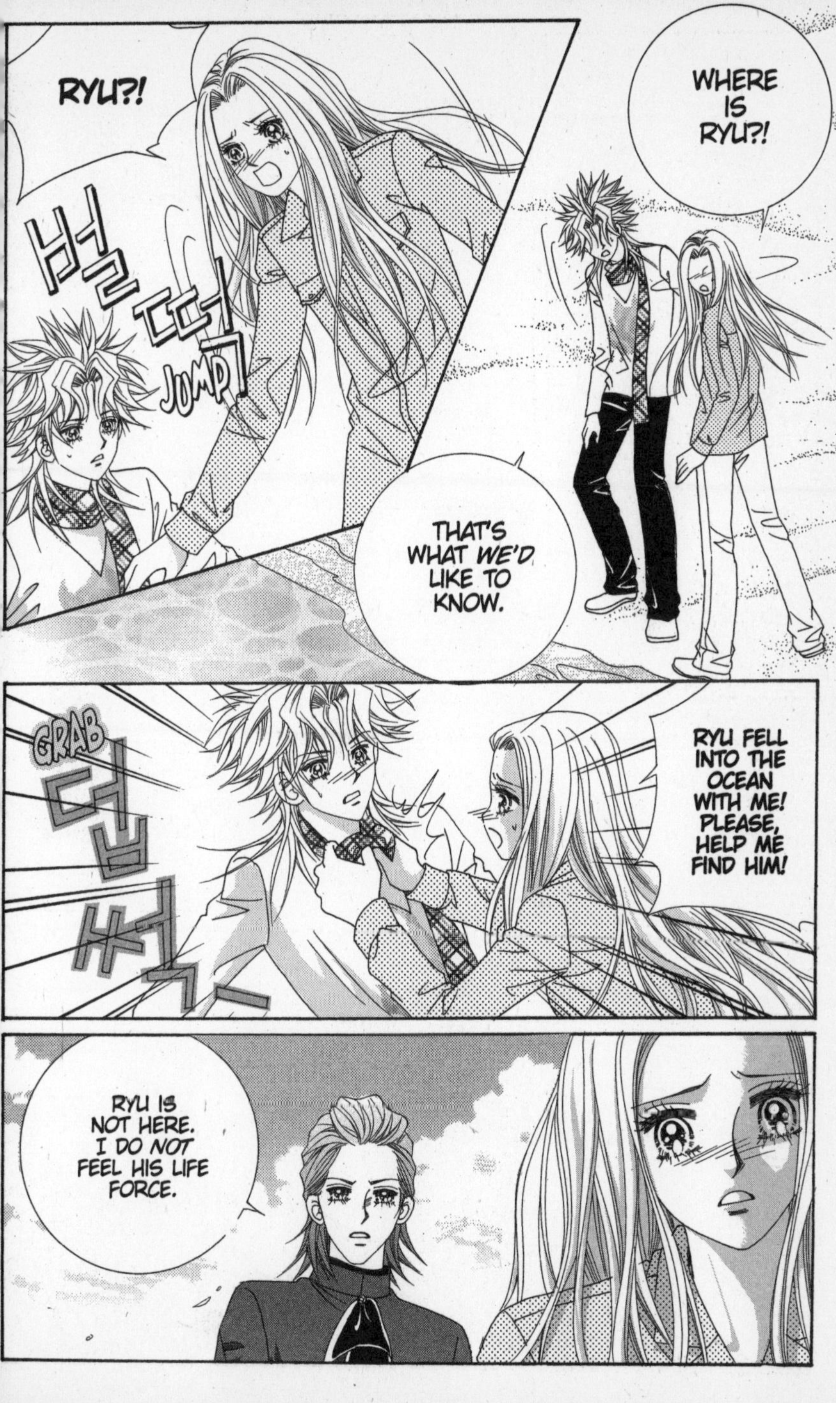
RYU?!
벌떡
JUMP
WHERE IS RYU?!
THAT'S WHAT WE'D LIKE TO KNOW.
GRAB
덥석
RYU FELL INTO THE OCEAN WITH ME! PLEASE, HELP ME FIND HIM!
RYU IS NOT HERE. I DO NOT FEEL HIS LIFE FORCE.

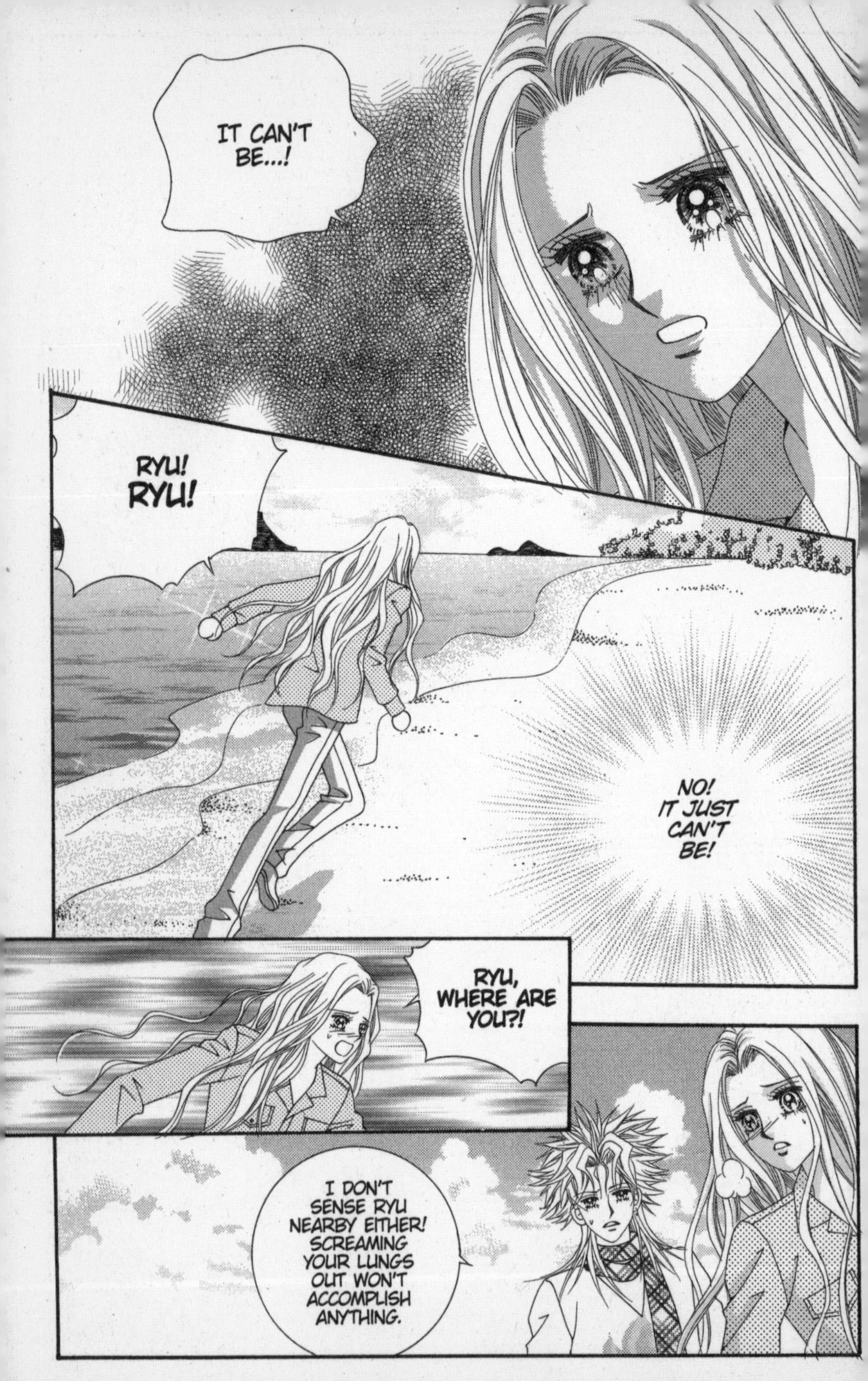
IT CAN'T BE...!
RYU! RYU!
NO! IT JUST CAN'T BE!
RYU, WHERE ARE YOU?!
I DON'T SENSE RYU NEARBY EITHER! SCREAMING YOUR LUNGS OUT WON'T ACCOMPLISH ANYTHING.

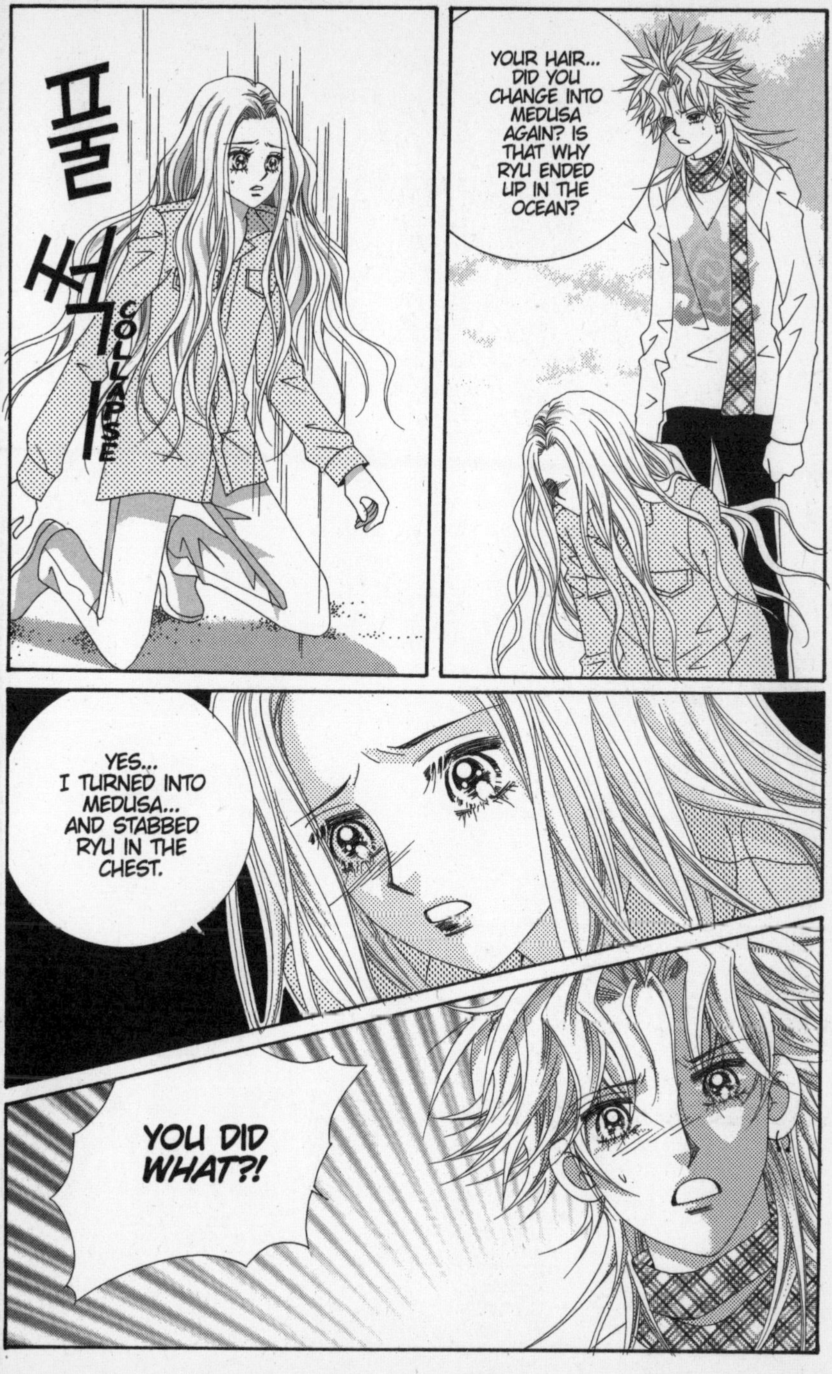

풀썩
COLLAPSE
YOUR HAIR... DID YOU CHANGE INTO MEDUSA AGAIN? IS THAT WHY RYU ENDED UP IN THE OCEAN?
YES... I TURNED INTO MEDUSA... AND STABBED RYU IN THE CHEST.
YOU DID WHAT?!

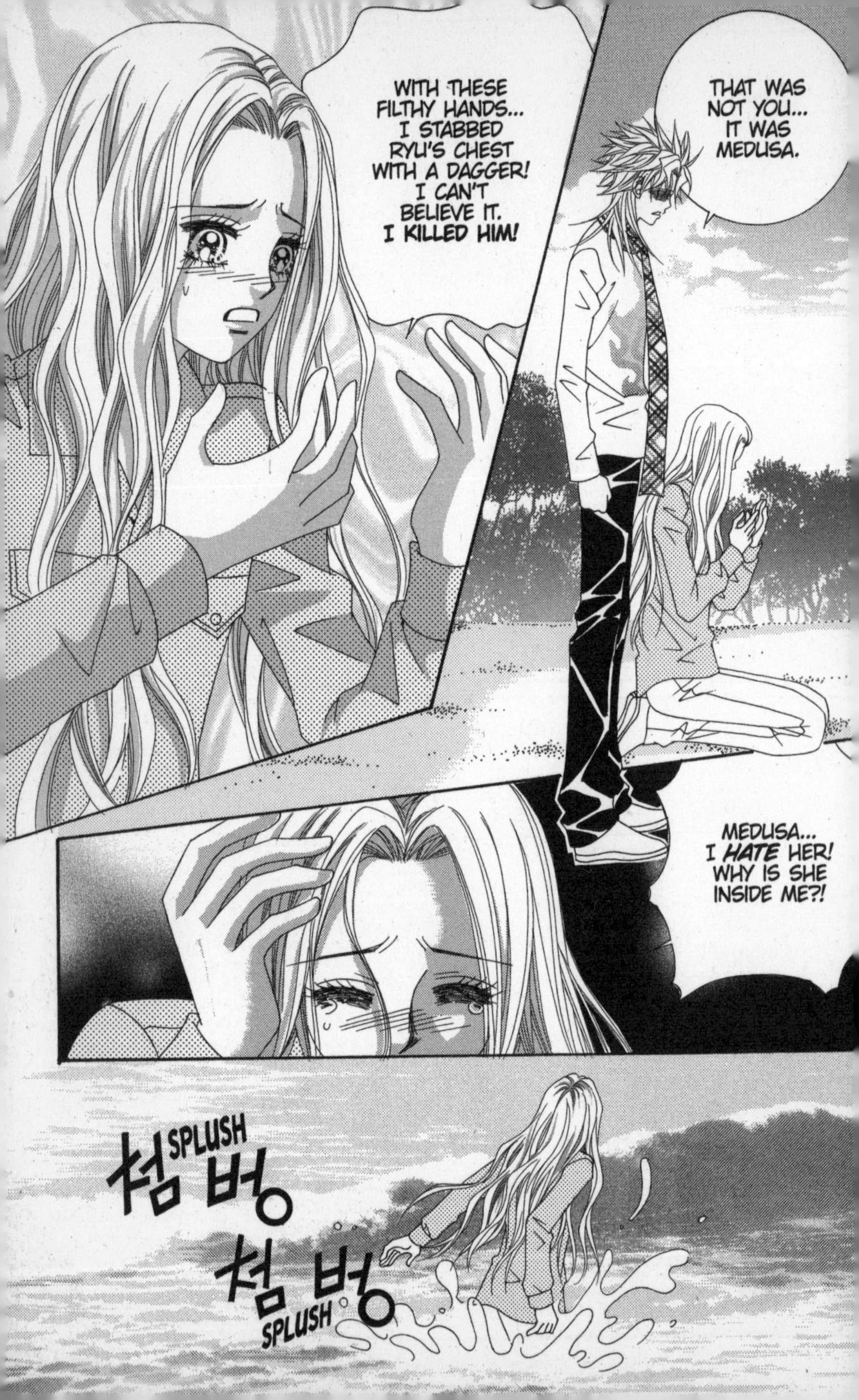
WITH THESE FILTHY HANDS... I STABBED RYU'S CHEST WITH A DAGGER! I CAN'T BELIEVE IT. I KILLED HIM!
THAT WAS NOT YOU... IT WAS MEDUSA.
MEDUSA... I HATE HER! WHY IS SHE INSIDE ME?!
첨벙 SPLUSH
첨벙 SPLUSH

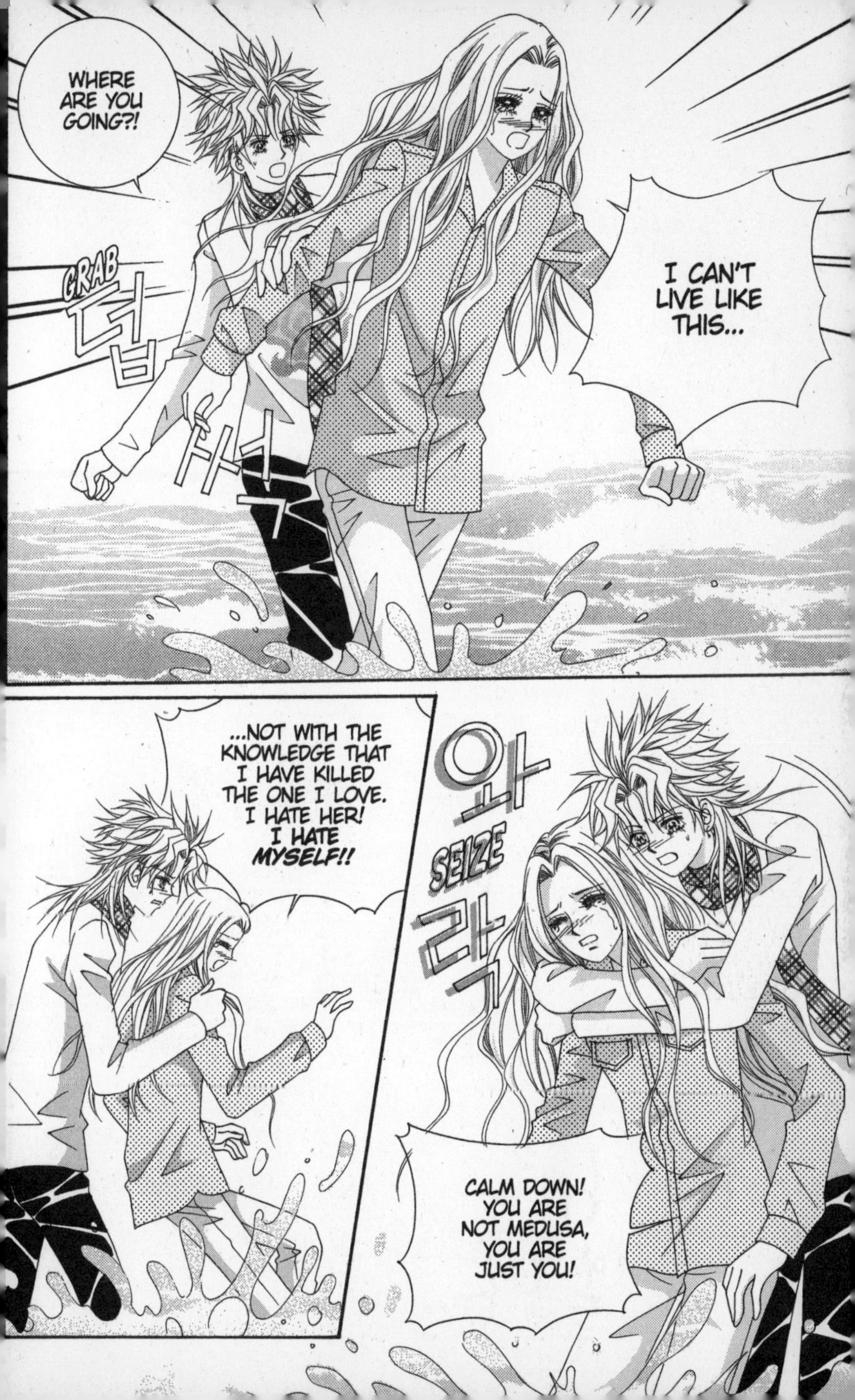
WHERE ARE YOU GOING?!
GRAB
덥
I CAN'T LIVE LIKE THIS...
...NOT WITH THE KNOWLEDGE THAT I HAVE KILLED THE ONE I LOVE. I HATE HER! I HATE *MYSELF!!*
SEIZE
CALM DOWN! YOU ARE NOT MEDUSA, YOU ARE JUST YOU!

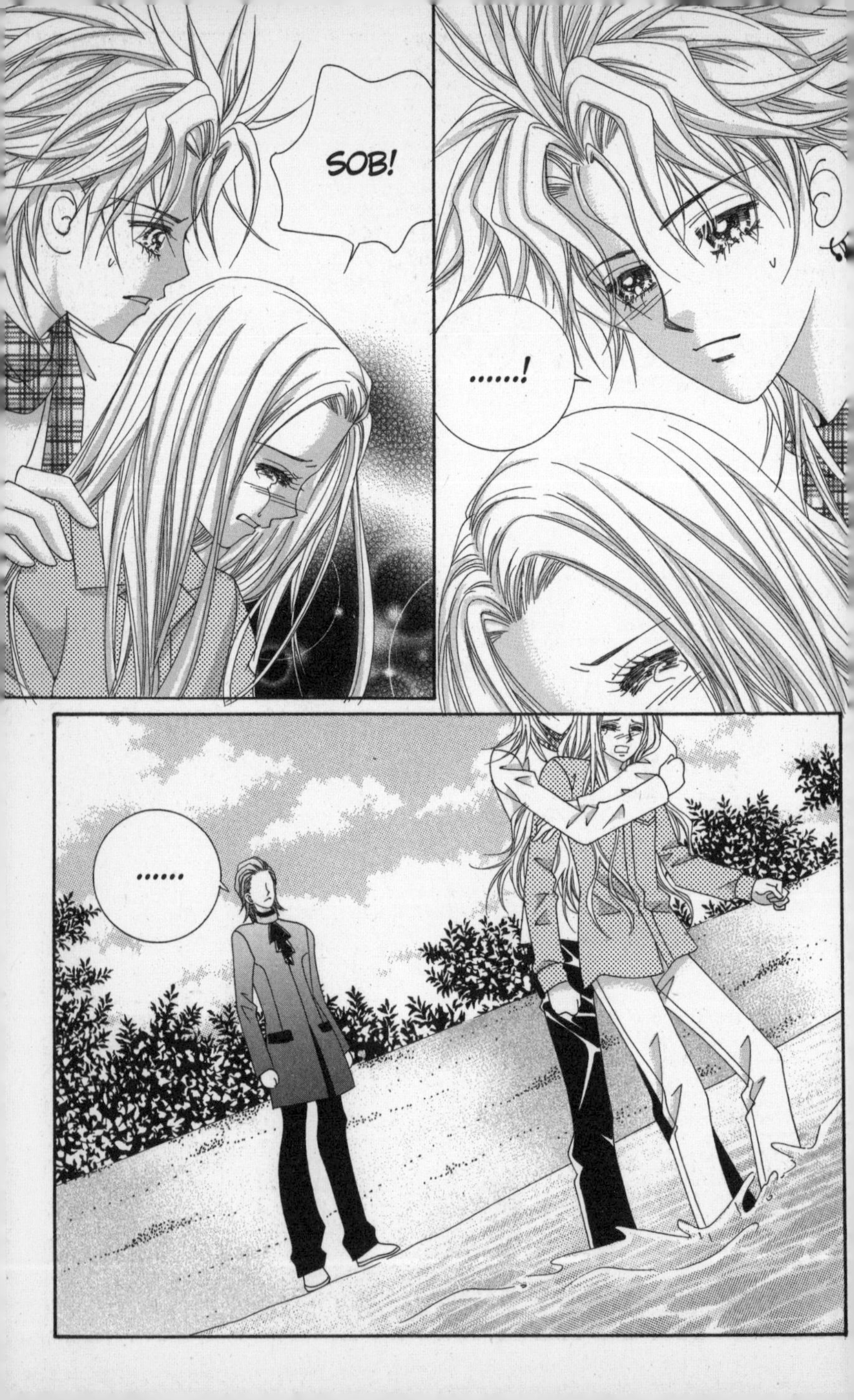
SOB!
......!
......

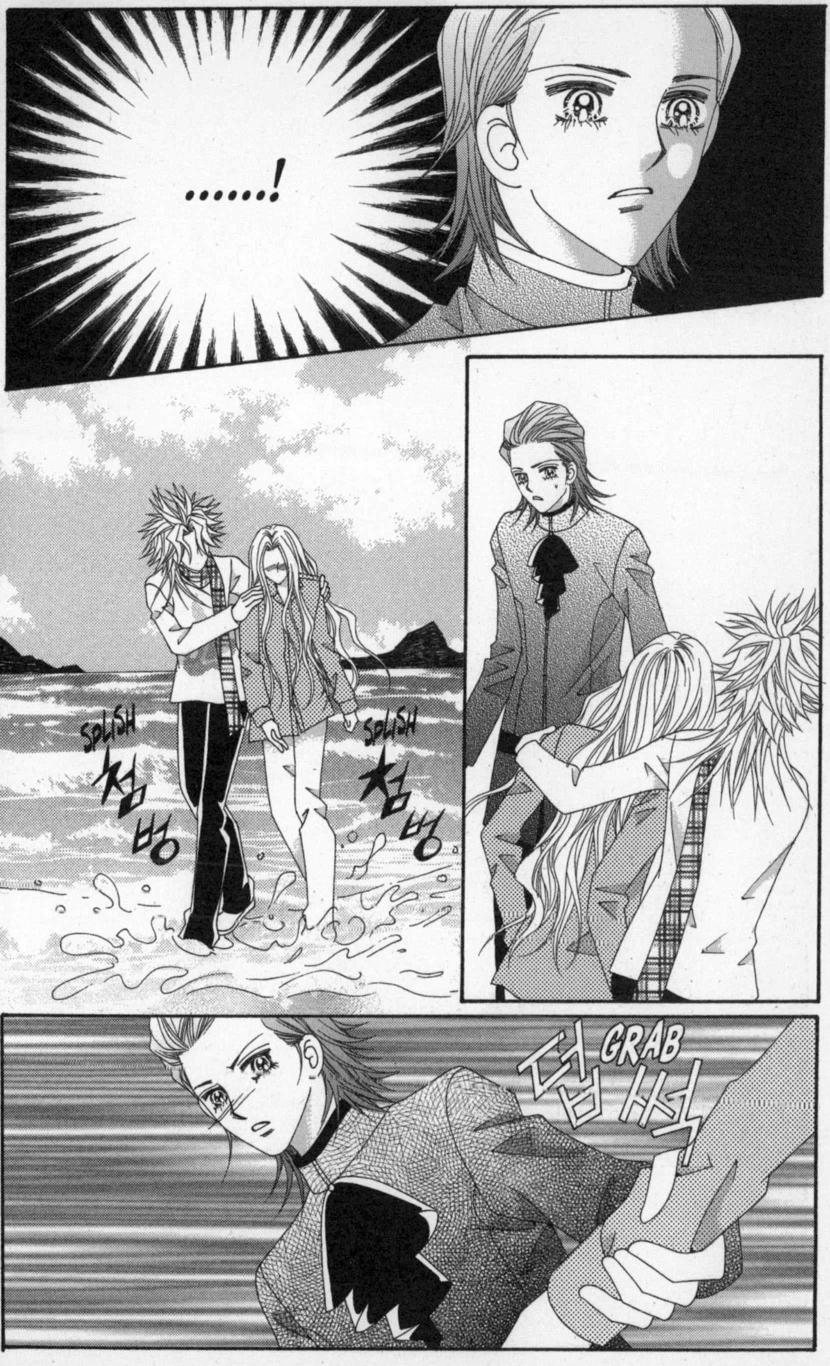
......!
SPLISH
첨벙
SPLISH
첨벙
GRAB
덥석

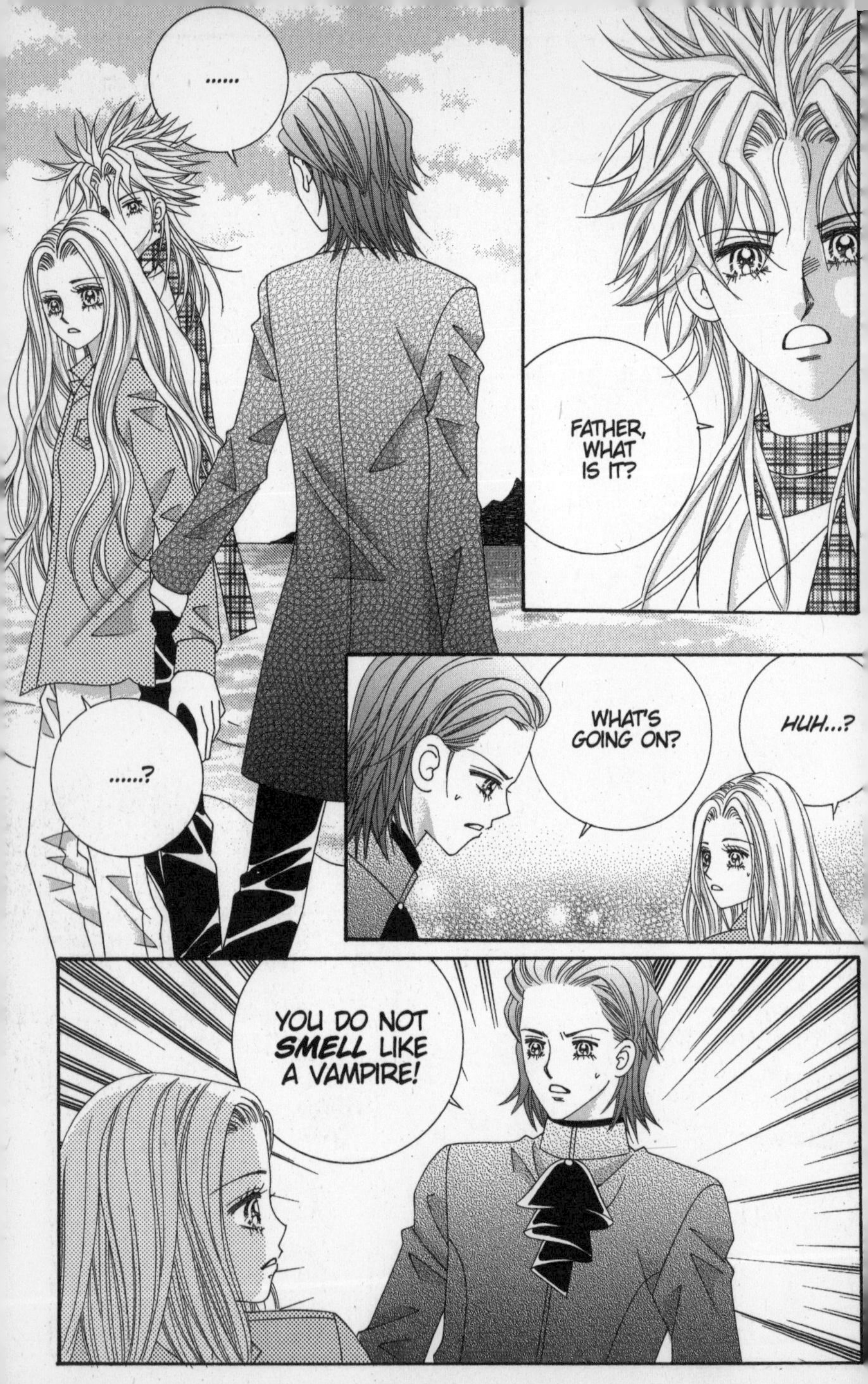
......
......?
FATHER, WHAT IS IT?
WHAT'S GOING ON?
HUH...?
YOU DO NOT SMELL LIKE A VAMPIRE!

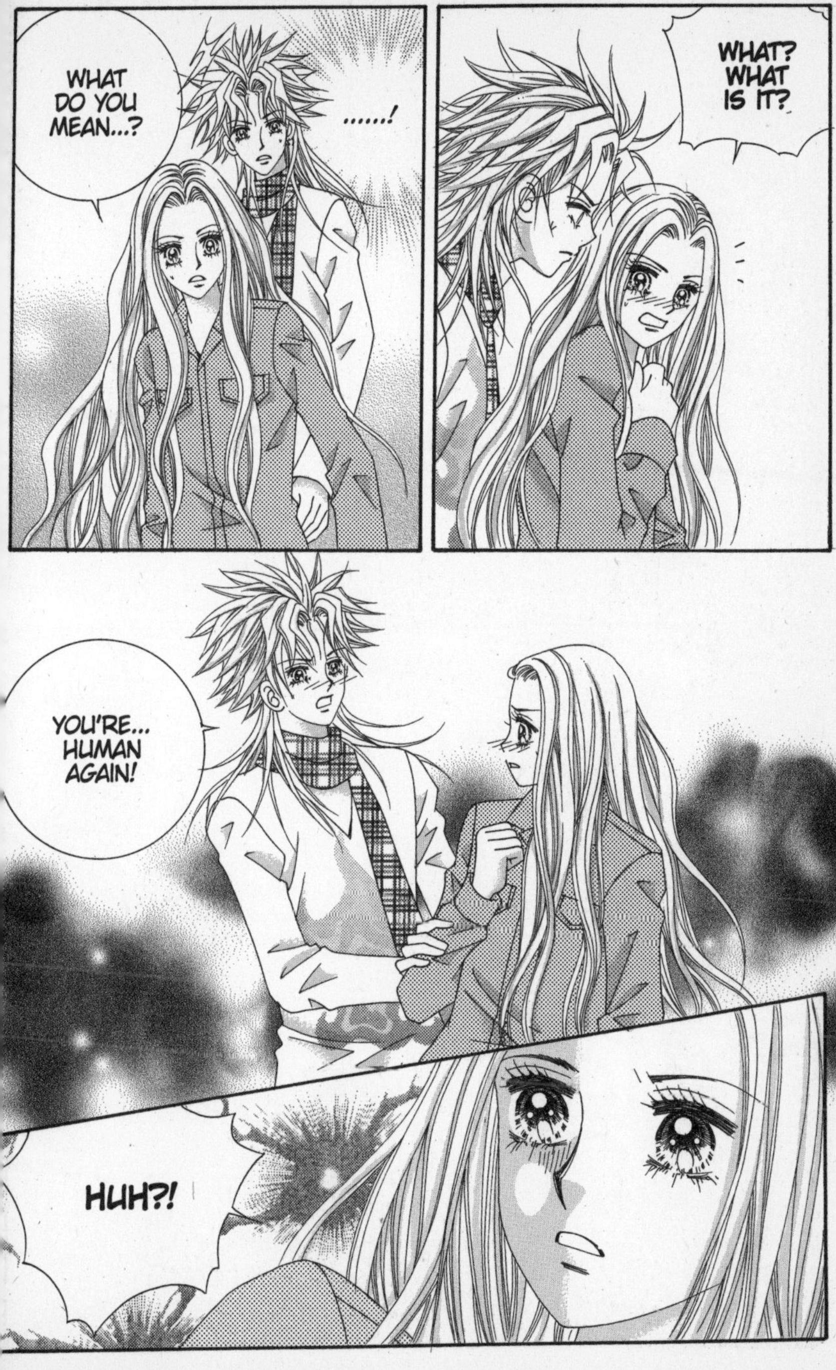
WHAT DO YOU MEAN...?
......!
WHAT? WHAT IS IT?
YOU'RE... HUMAN AGAIN!
HUH?!

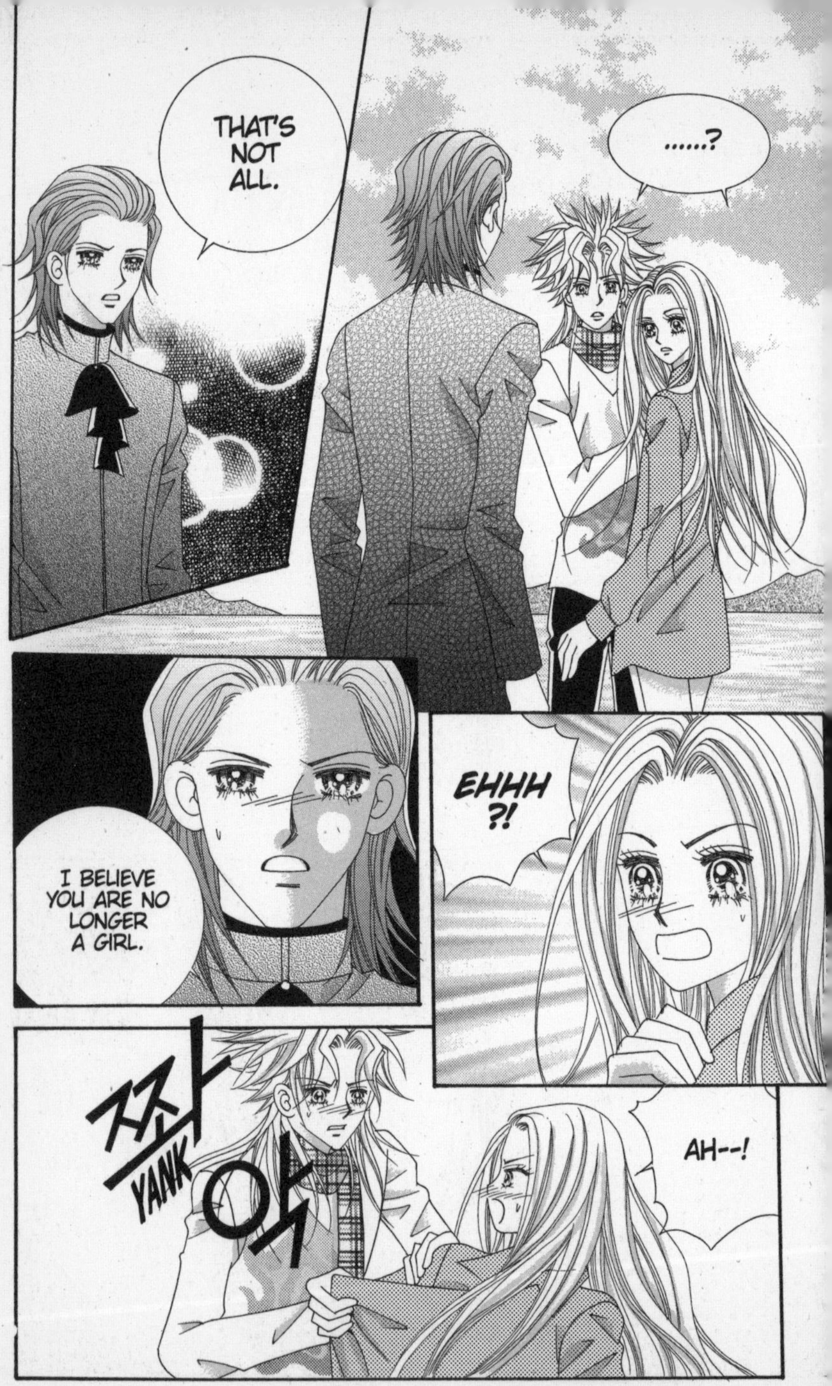
THAT'S NOT ALL.
......?
I BELIEVE YOU ARE NO LONGER A GIRL.
EHHH ?!
YANK
AH--!

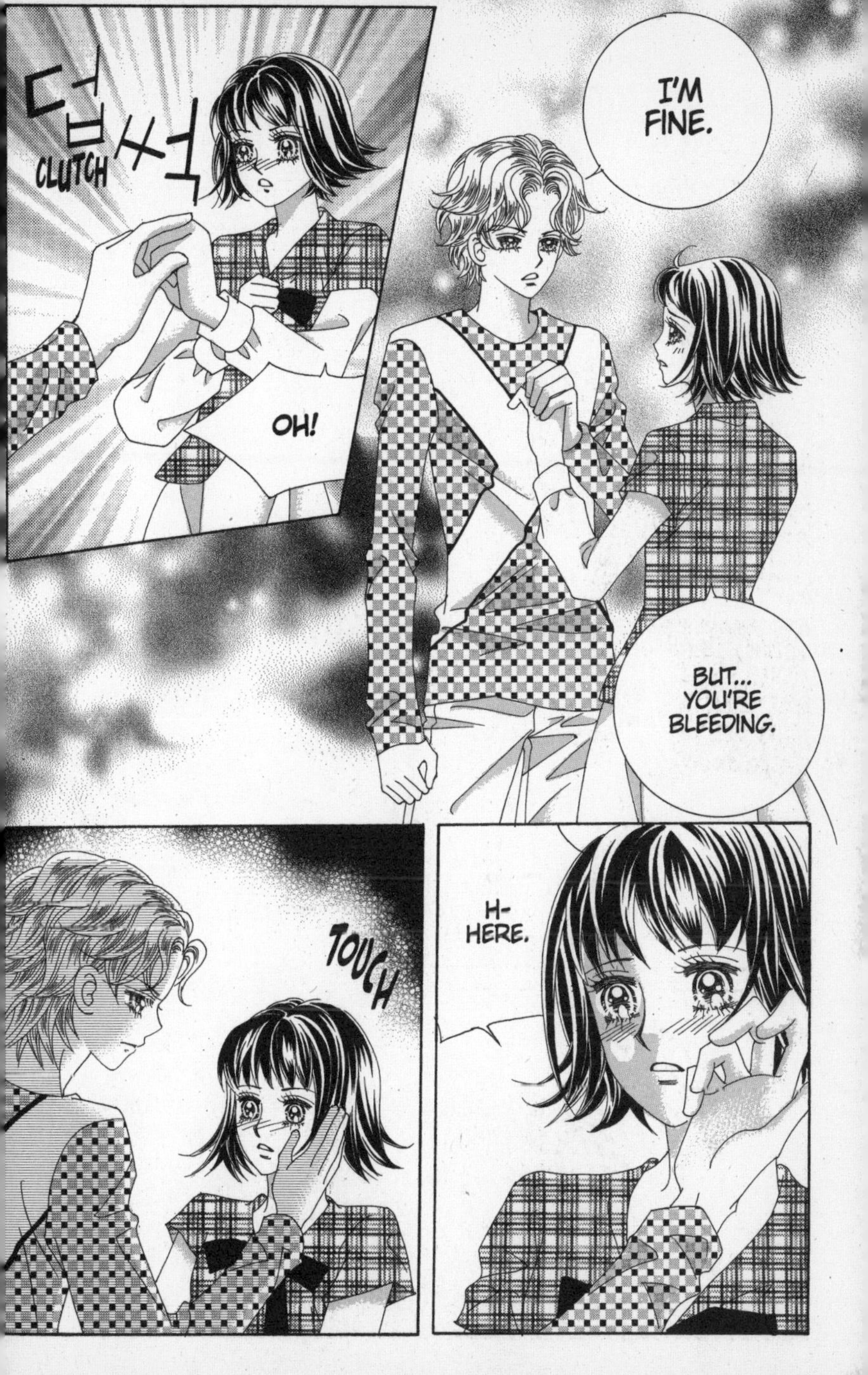
CLUTCH
OH!
I'M FINE.
BUT... YOU'RE BLEEDING.
TOUCH
H-HERE.

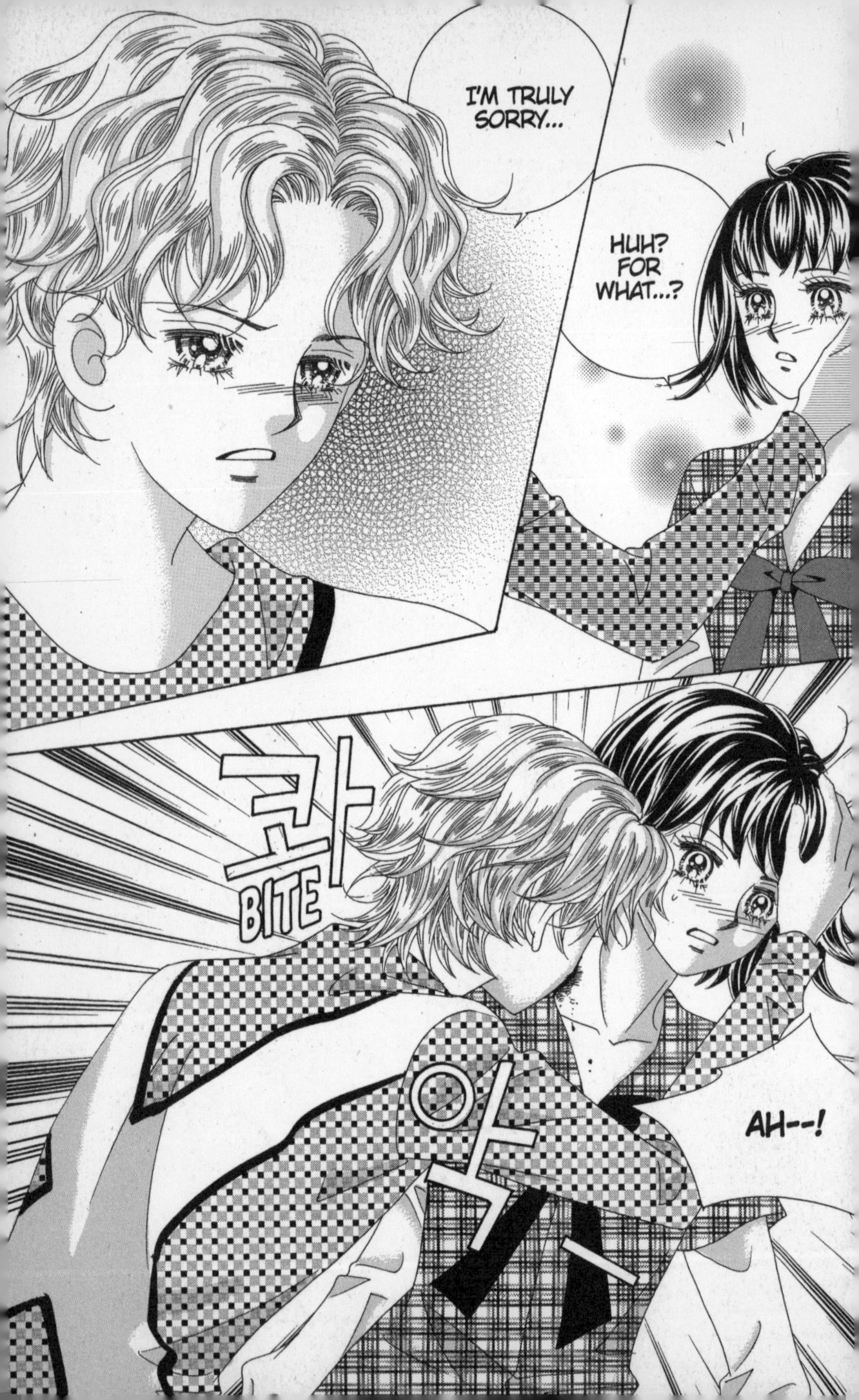
I'M TRULY SORRY...
HUH? FOR WHAT...?
BITE
AH--!

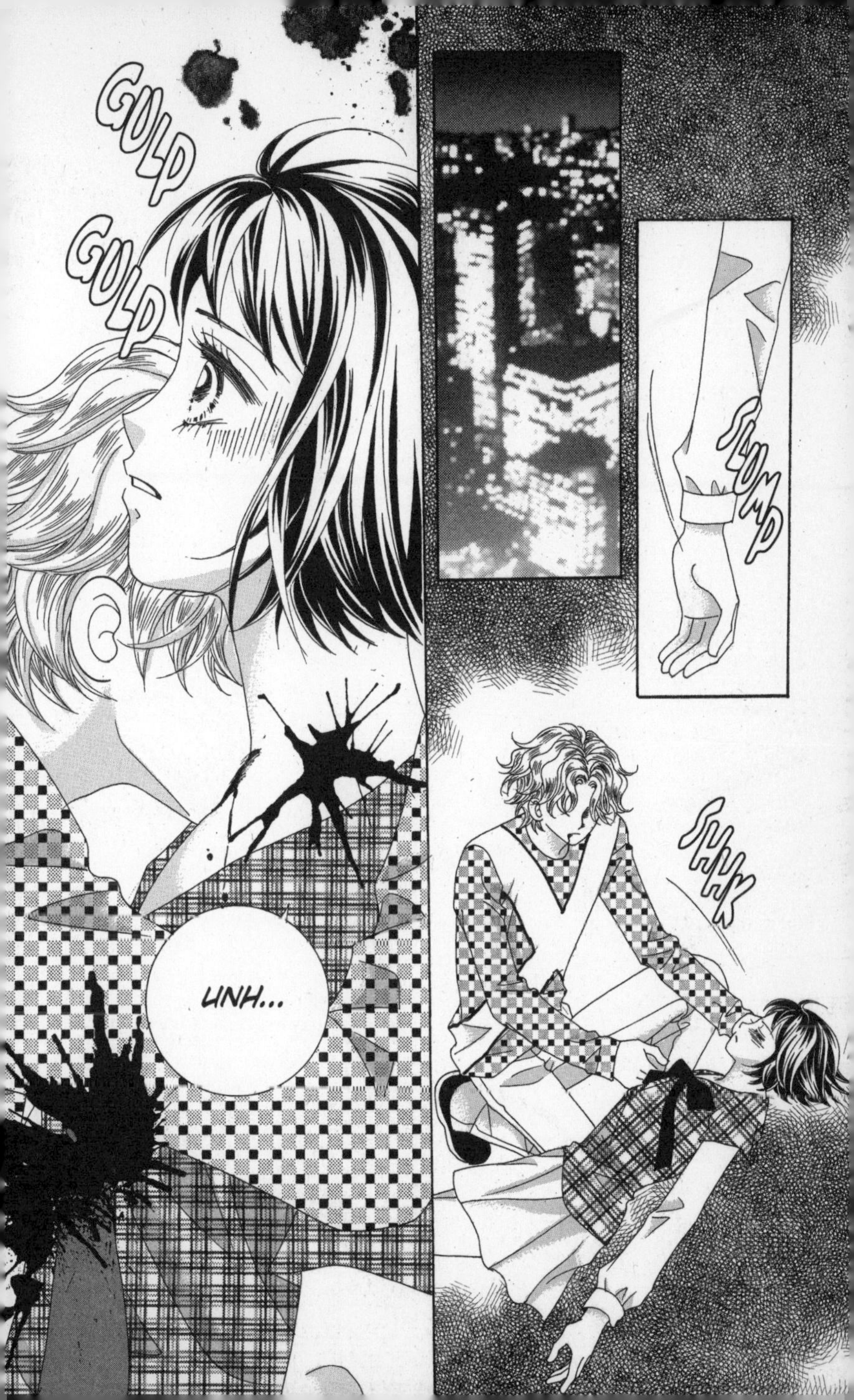
GULP
GULP
UNH...
SLUMP
SHHK

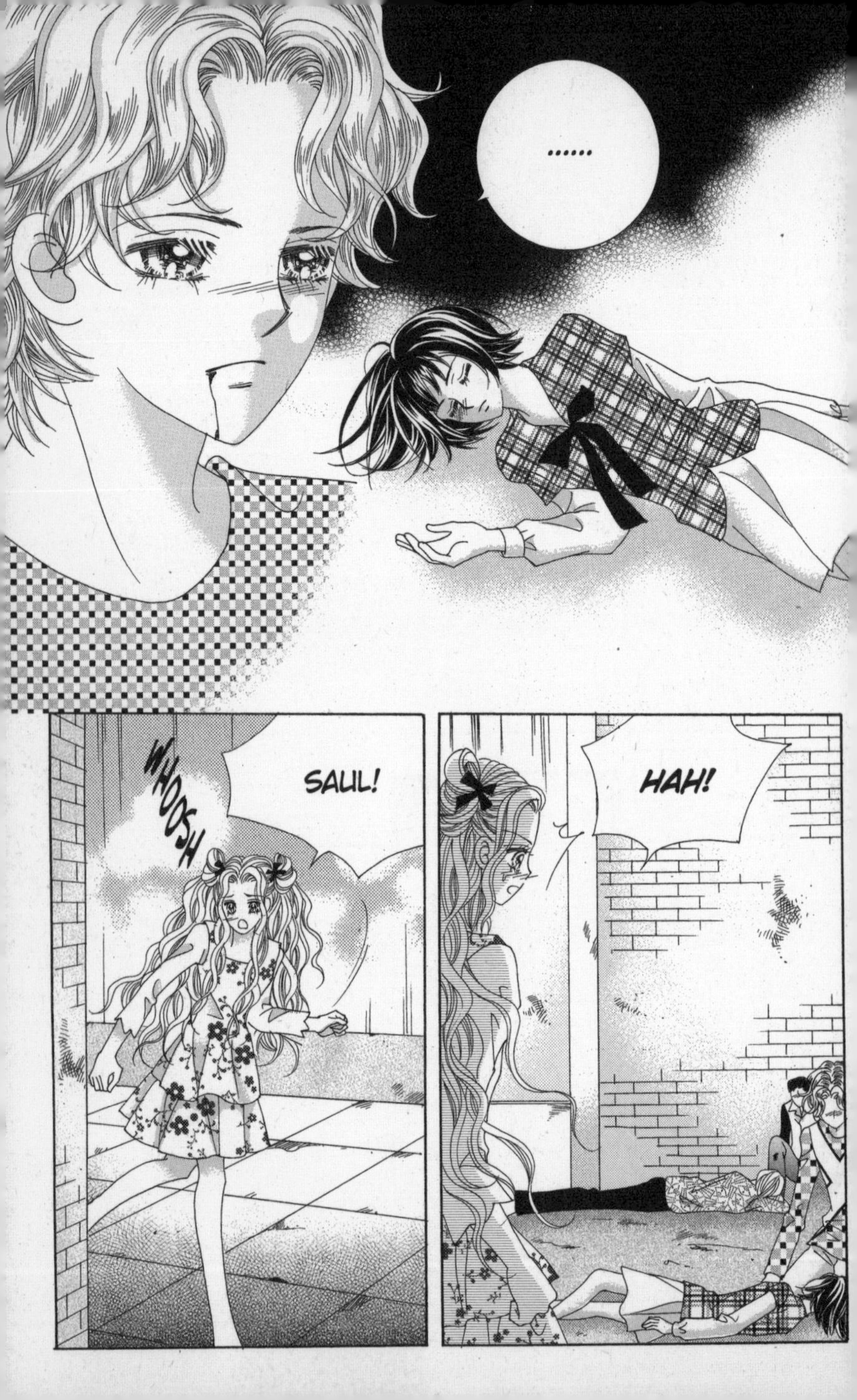
....
WHOOSH
SAUL!
HAH!

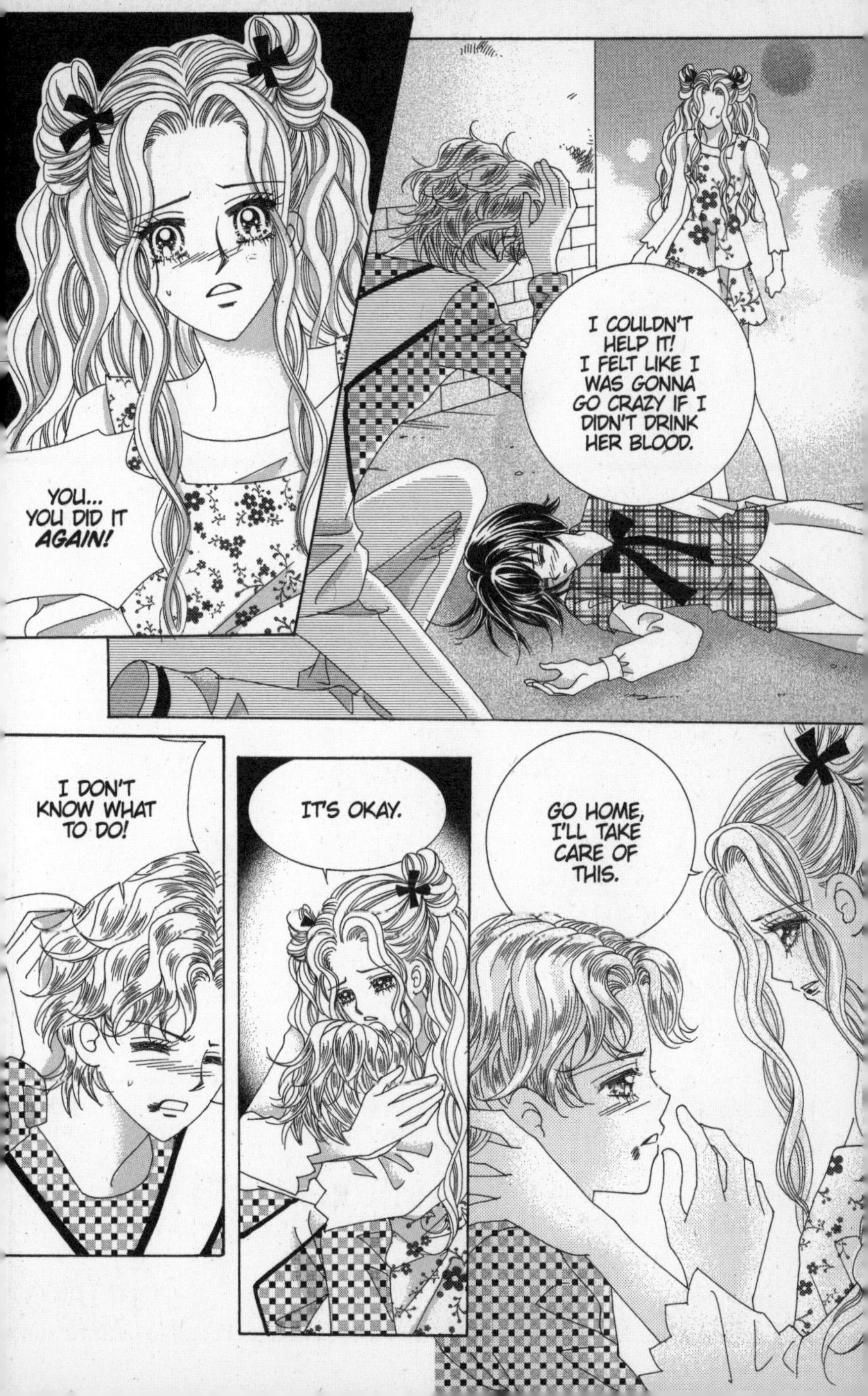
YOU... YOU DID IT AGAIN!
I COULDN'T HELP IT! I FELT LIKE I WAS GONNA GO CRAZY IF I DIDN'T DRINK HER BLOOD.
I DON'T KNOW WHAT TO DO!
IT'S OKAY.
GO HOME, I'LL TAKE CARE OF THIS.

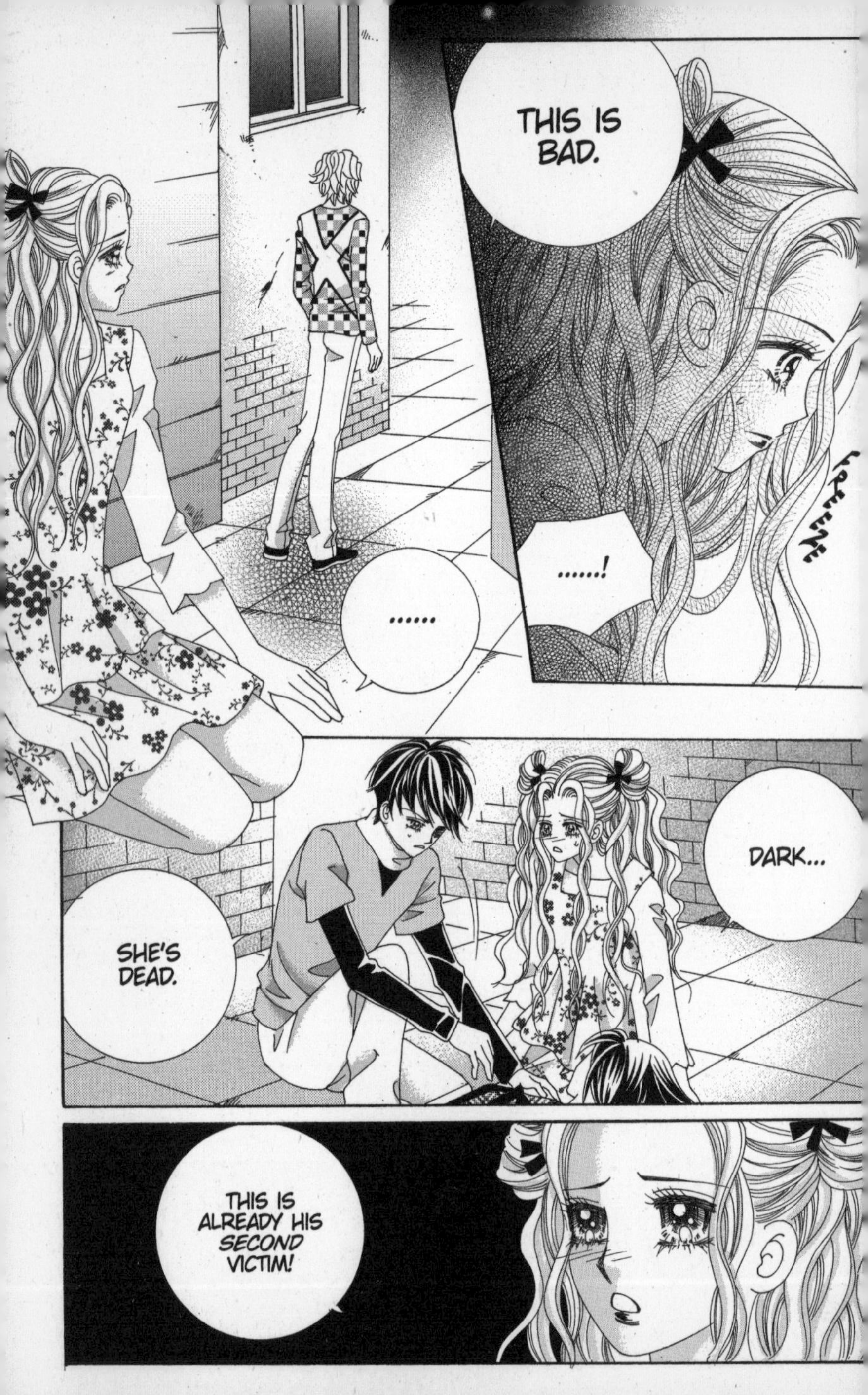
......
THIS IS BAD.
......!
SHE'S DEAD.
DARK...
THIS IS ALREADY HIS SECOND VICTIM!

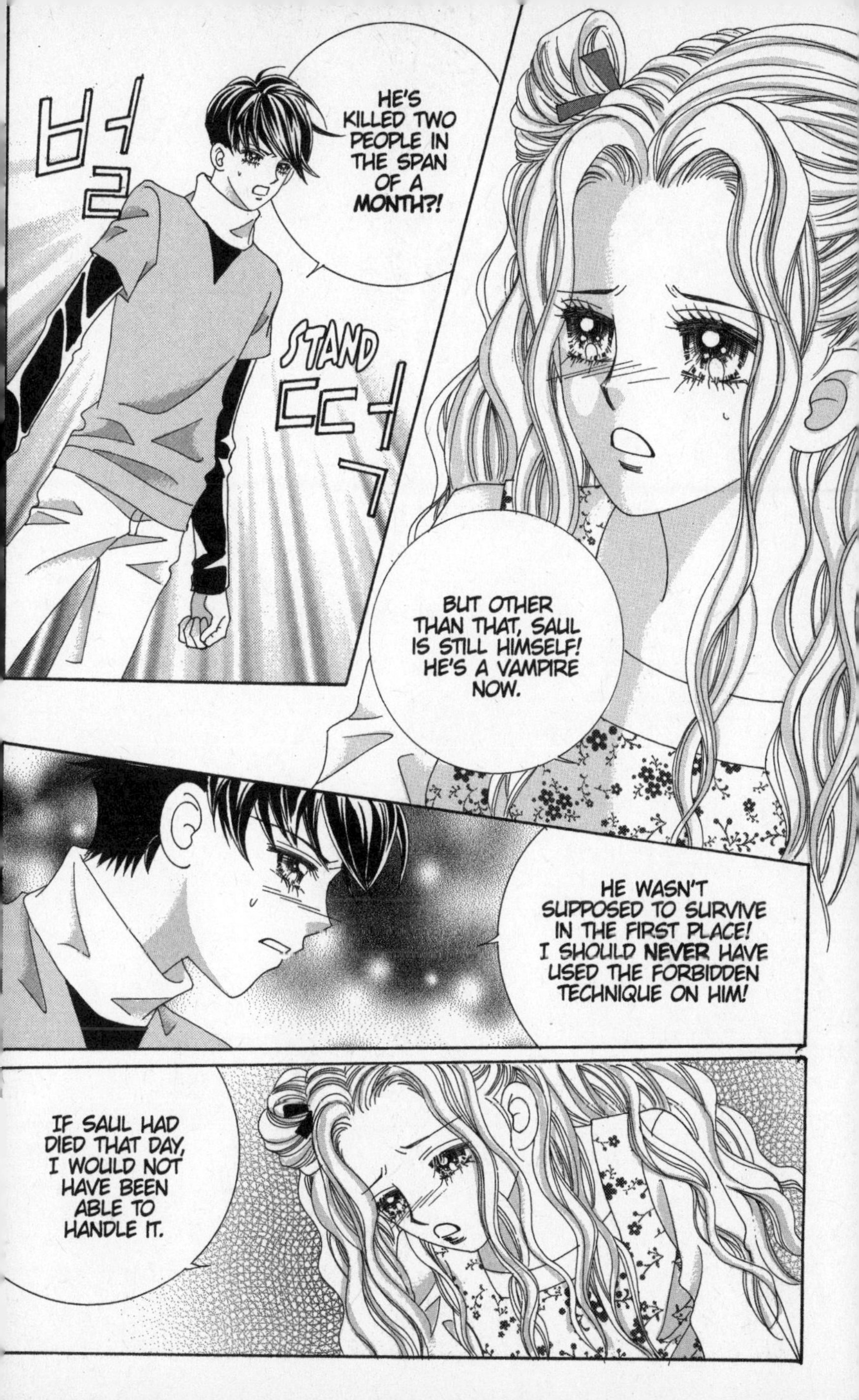
HE'S KILLED TWO PEOPLE IN THE SPAN OF A MONTH?!
STAND
BUT OTHER THAN THAT, SAUL IS STILL HIMSELF! HE'S A VAMPIRE NOW.
HE WASN'T SUPPOSED TO SURVIVE IN THE FIRST PLACE! I SHOULD NEVER HAVE USED THE FORBIDDEN TECHNIQUE ON HIM!
IF SAUL HAD DIED THAT DAY, I WOULD NOT HAVE BEEN ABLE TO HANDLE IT.

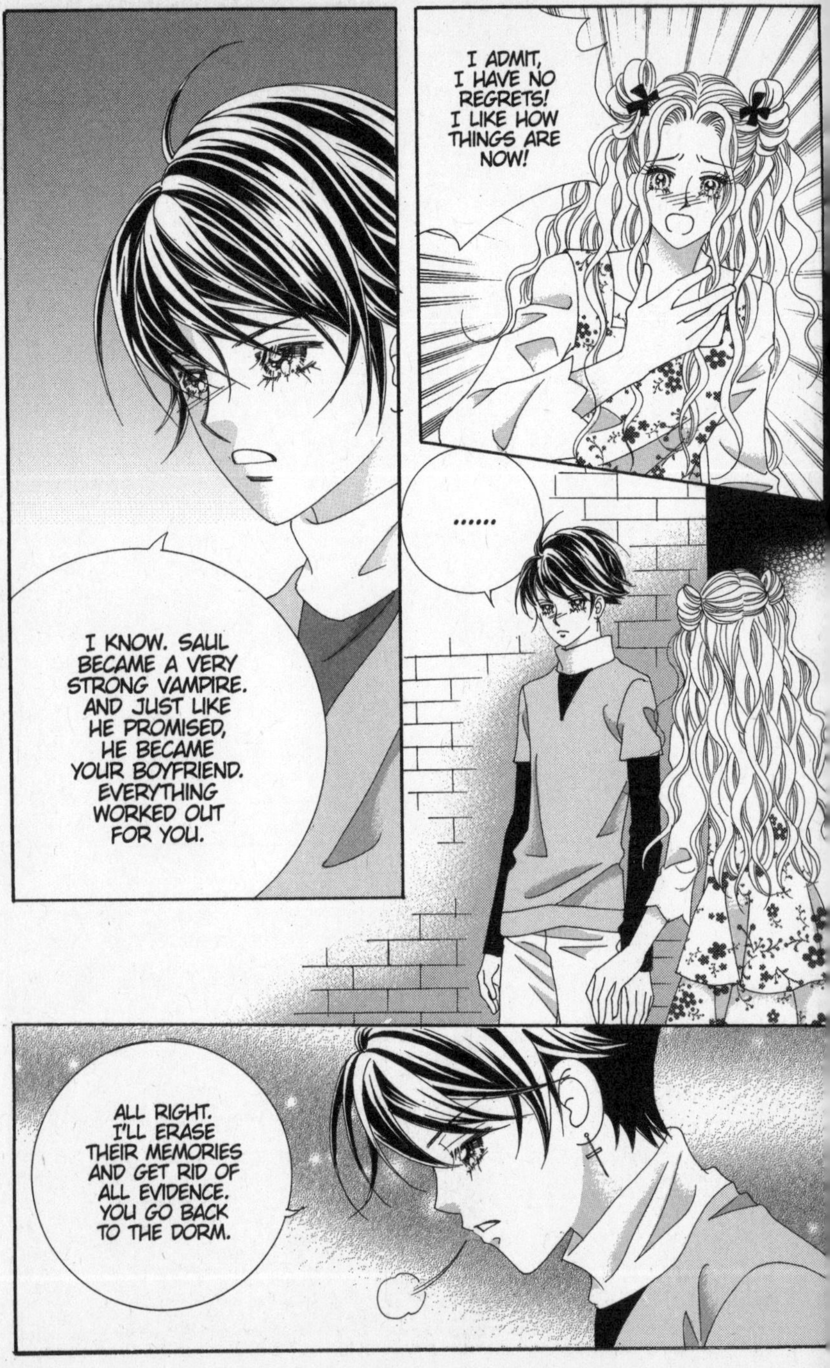
I KNOW. SAUL BECAME A VERY STRONG VAMPIRE. AND JUST LIKE HE PROMISED, HE BECAME YOUR BOYFRIEND. EVERYTHING WORKED OUT FOR YOU.
I ADMIT, I HAVE NO REGRETS! I LIKE HOW THINGS ARE NOW!
......
ALL RIGHT. I'LL ERASE THEIR MEMORIES AND GET RID OF ALL EVIDENCE. YOU GO BACK TO THE DORM.

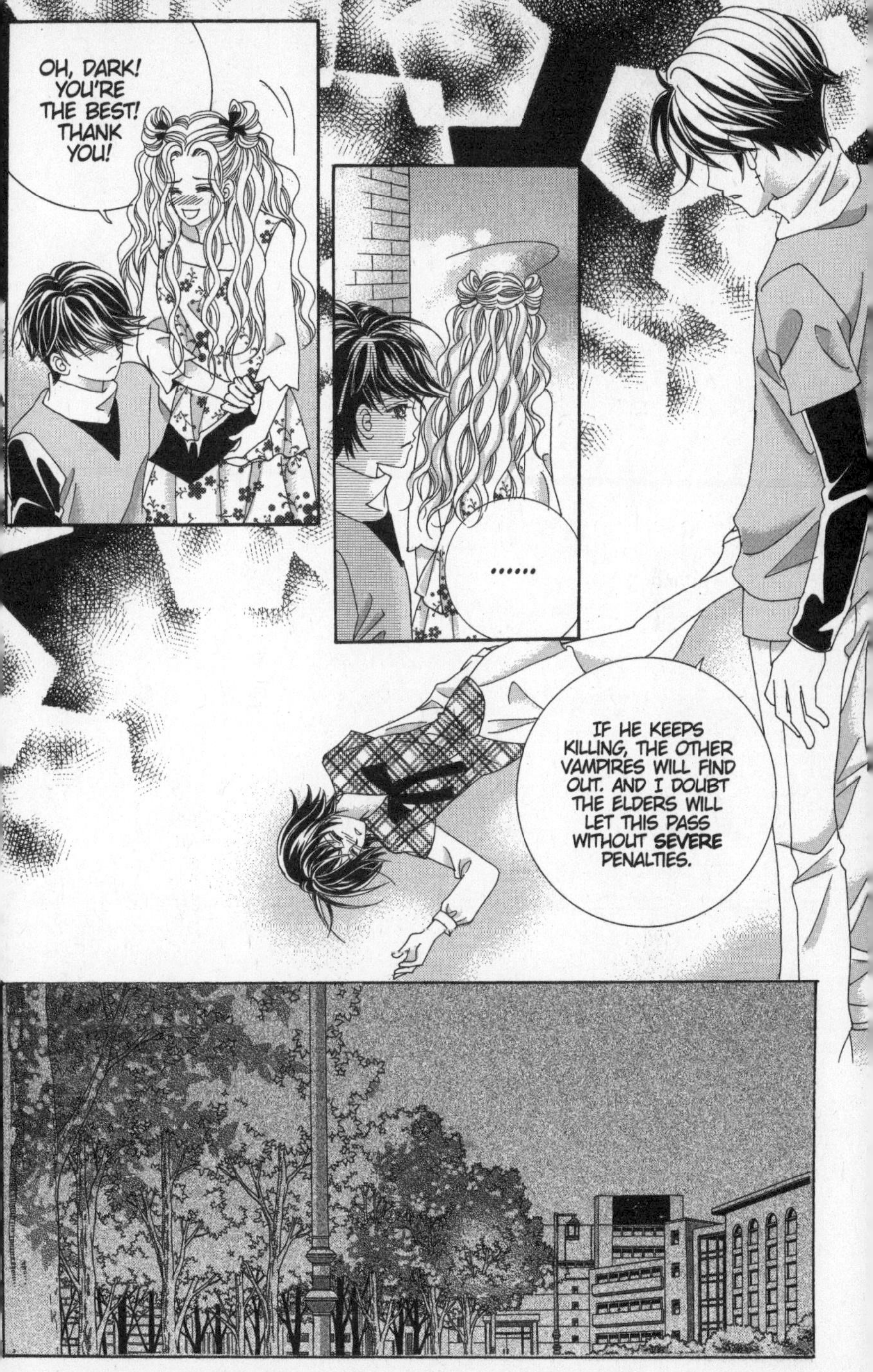
OH, DARK! YOU'RE THE BEST! THANK YOU!
......
IF HE KEEPS KILLING, THE OTHER VAMPIRES WILL FIND OUT. AND I DOUBT THE ELDERS WILL LET THIS PASS WITHOUT SEVERE PENALTIES.

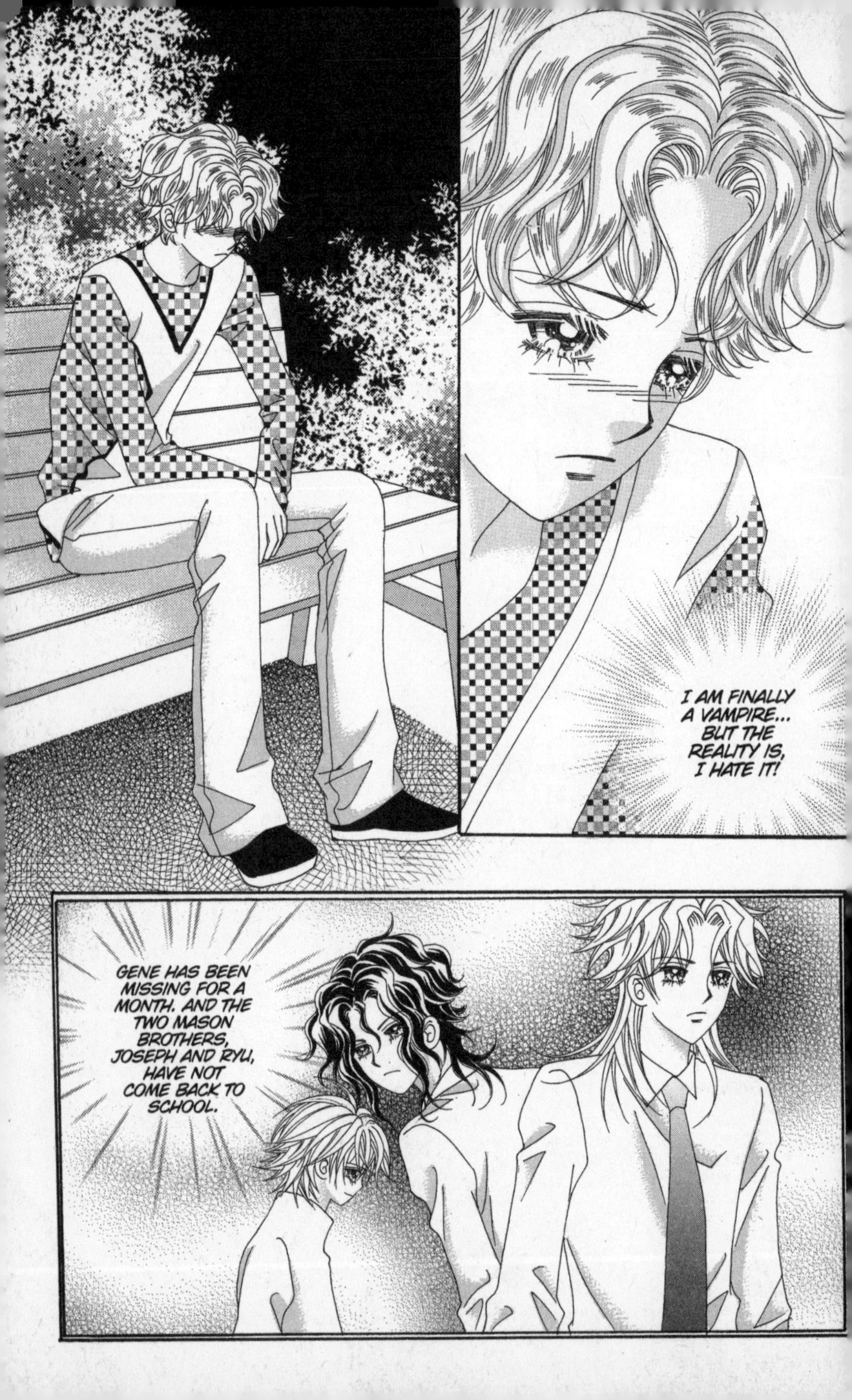
I AM FINALLY A VAMPIRE... BUT THE REALITY IS, I HATE IT!
GENE HAS BEEN MISSING FOR A MONTH. AND THE TWO MASON BROTHERS, JOSEPH AND RYU, HAVE NOT COME BACK TO SCHOOL.

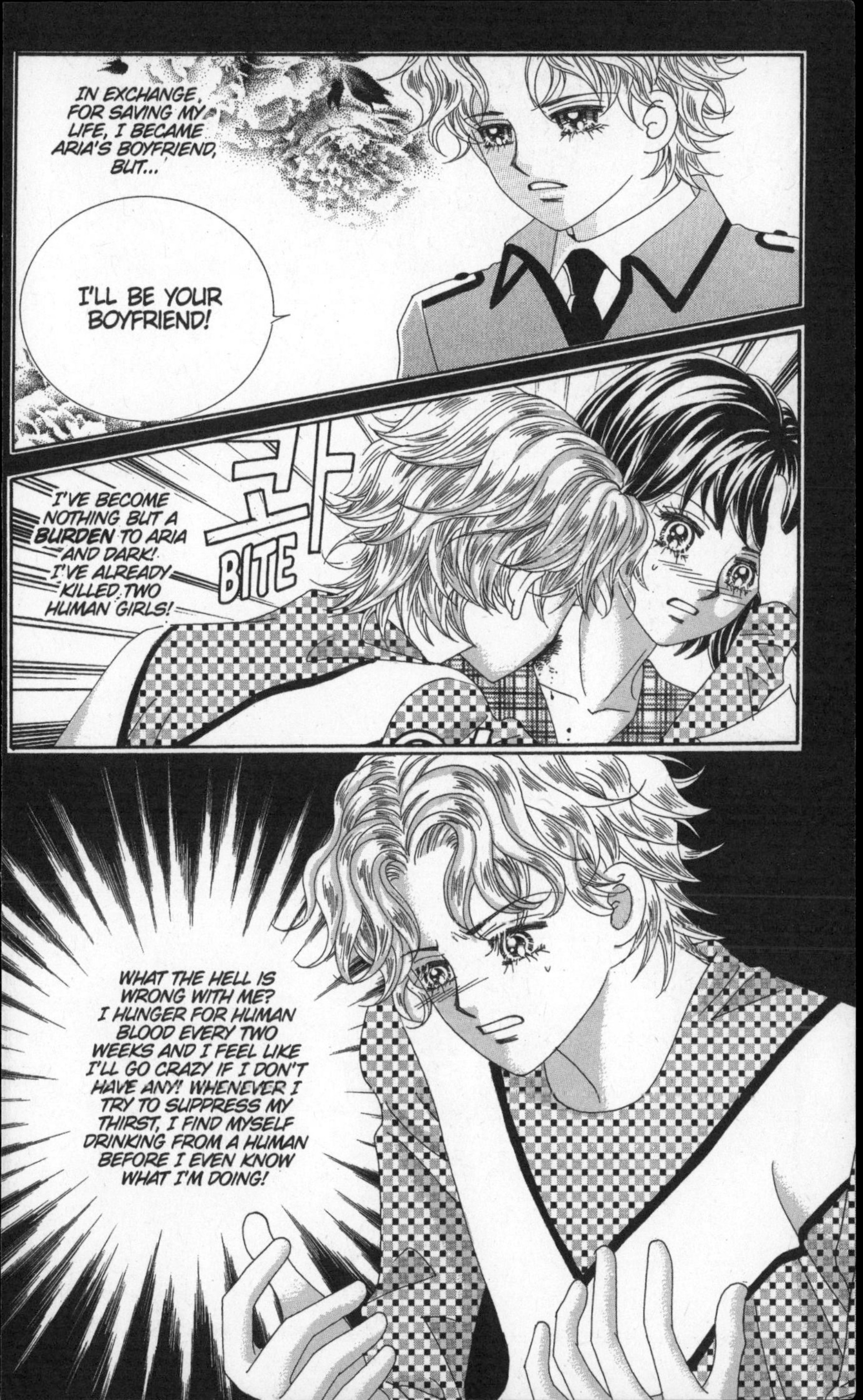
IN EXCHANGE FOR SAVING MY LIFE, I BECAME ARIA'S BOYFRIEND, BUT...
I'LL BE YOUR BOYFRIEND!
I'VE BECOME NOTHING BUT A BURDEN TO ARIA AND DARK! I'VE ALREADY KILLED TWO HUMAN GIRLS!
BITE
WHAT THE HELL IS WRONG WITH ME? I HUNGER FOR HUMAN BLOOD EVERY TWO WEEKS AND I FEEL LIKE I'LL GO CRAZY IF I DON'T HAVE ANY! WHENEVER I TRY TO SUPPRESS MY THIRST, I FIND MYSELF DRINKING FROM A HUMAN BEFORE I EVEN KNOW WHAT I'M DOING!

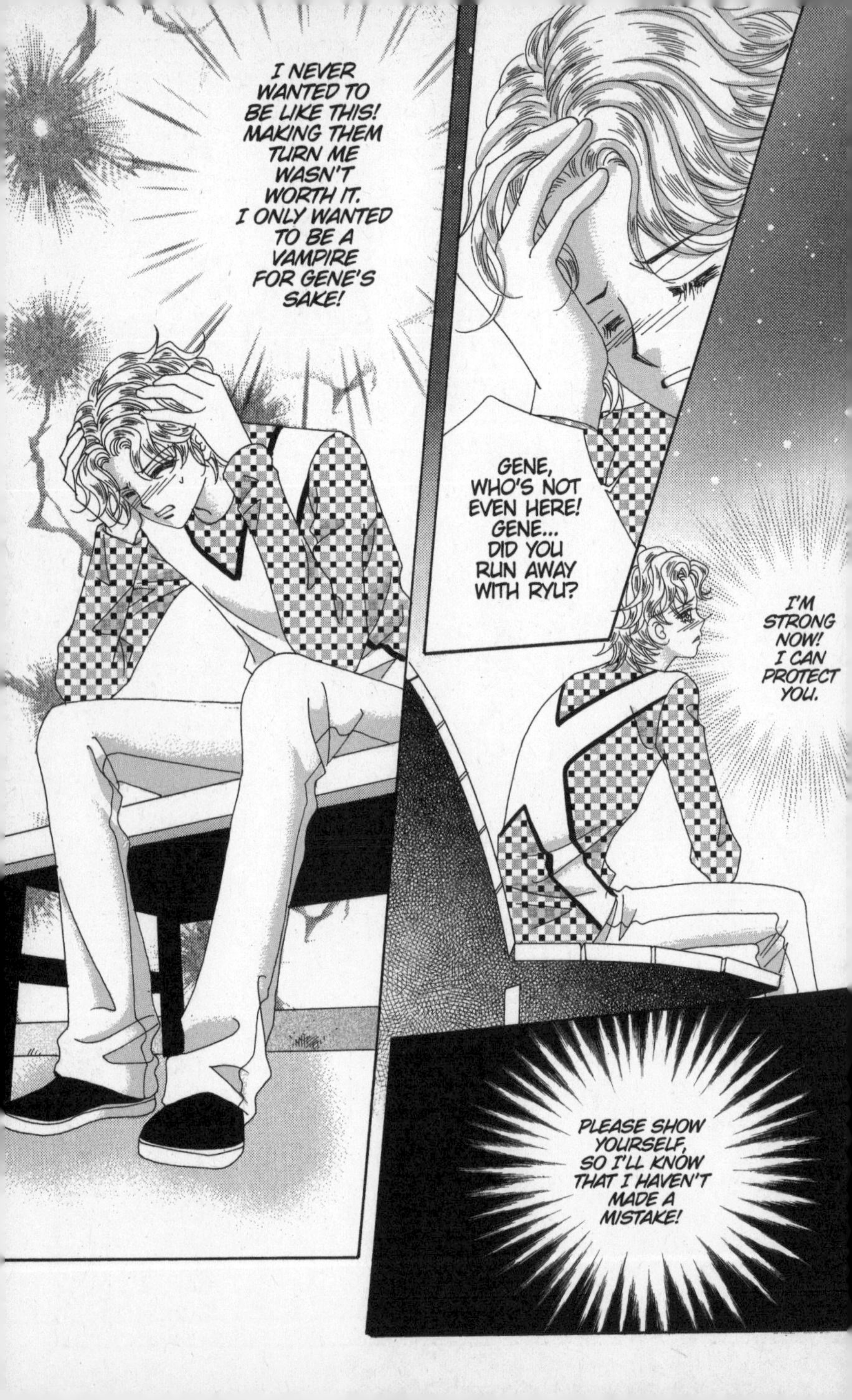
I NEVER WANTED TO BE LIKE THIS! MAKING THEM TURN ME WASN'T WORTH IT. I ONLY WANTED TO BE A VAMPIRE FOR GENE'S SAKE!
GENE, WHO'S NOT EVEN HERE! GENE... DID YOU RUN AWAY WITH RYU?
I'M STRONG NOW! I CAN PROTECT YOU.
PLEASE SHOW YOURSELF, SO I'LL KNOW THAT I HAVEN'T MADE A MISTAKE!

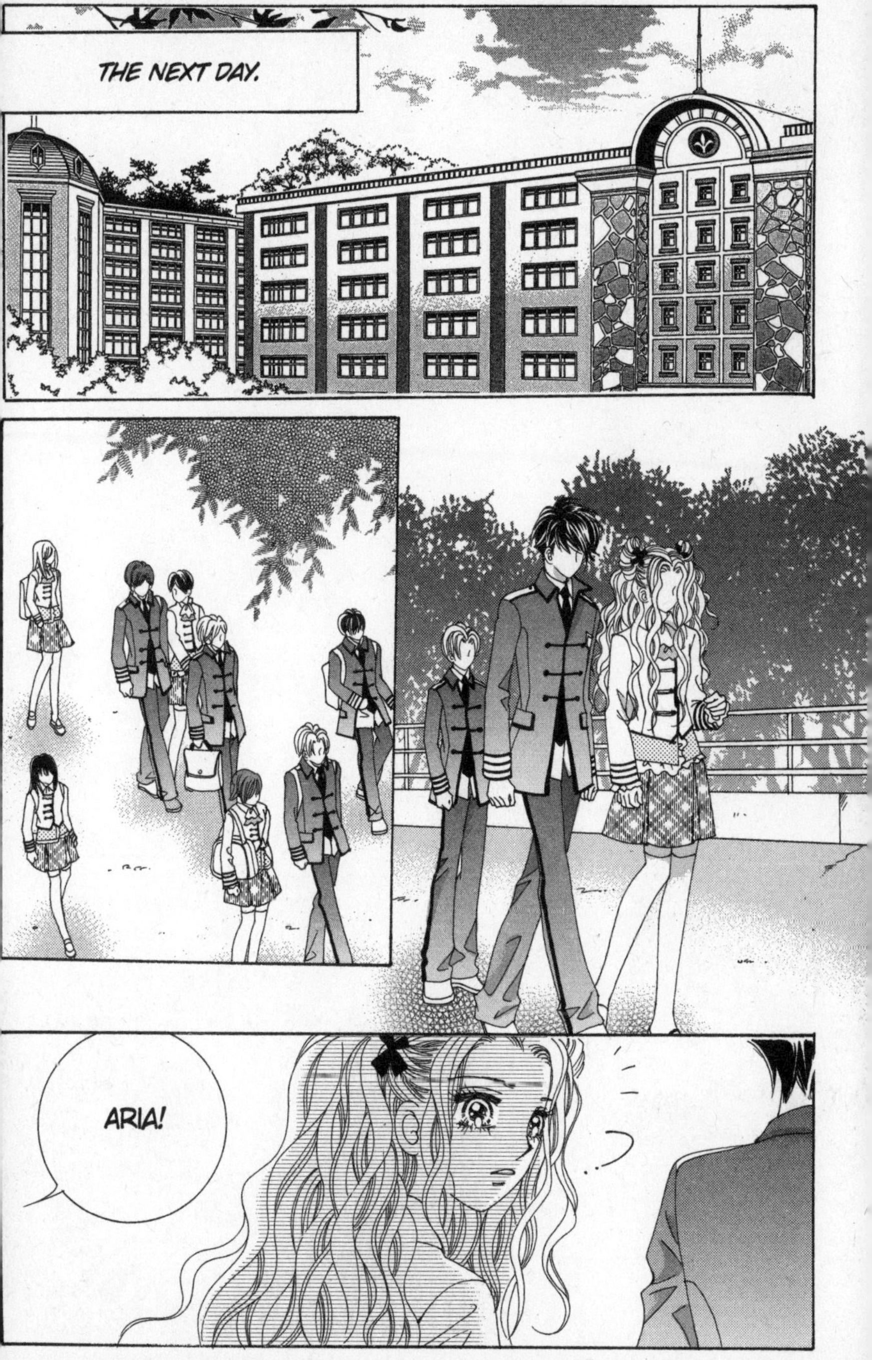
THE NEXT DAY.
ARIA!

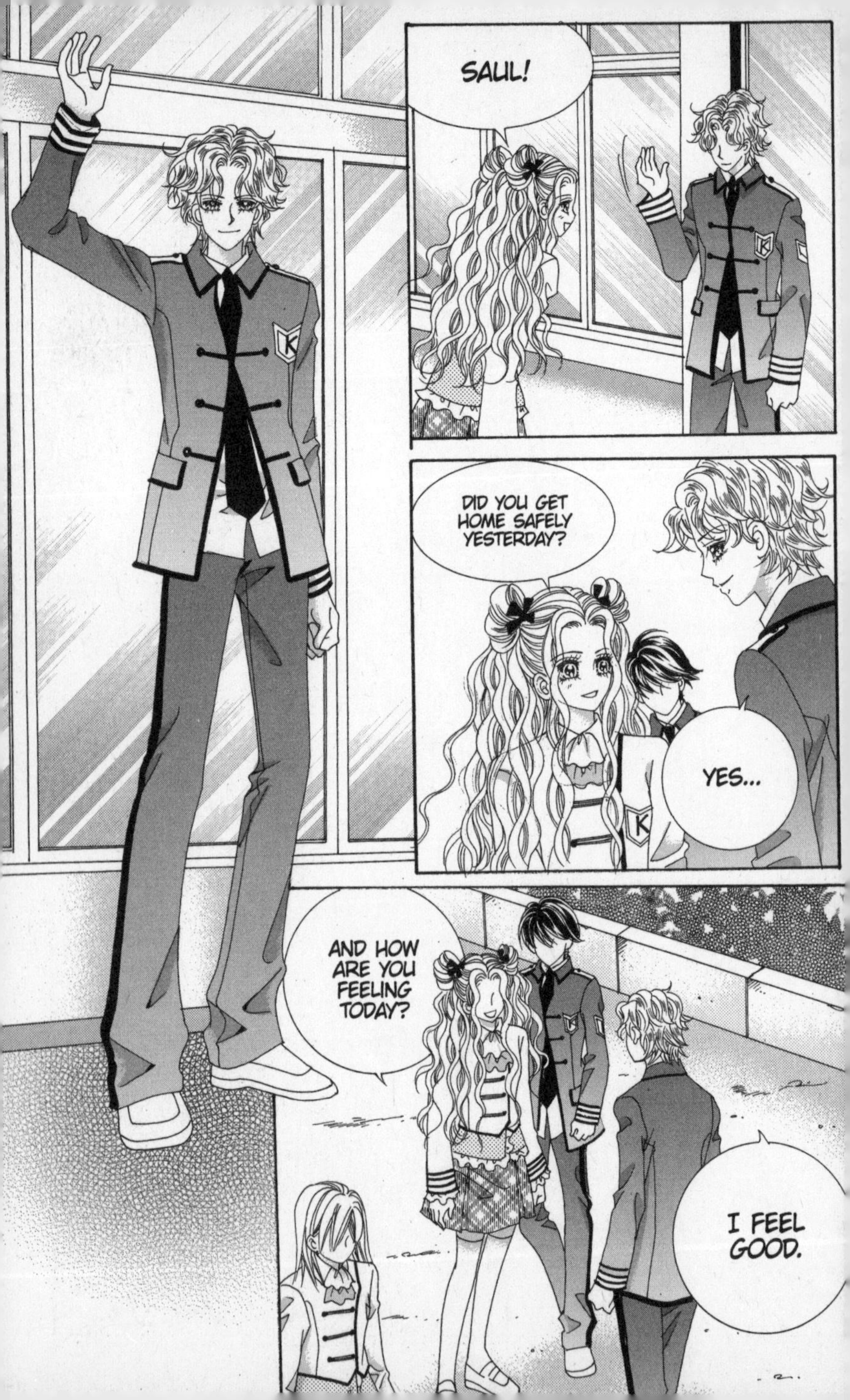
SAUL!
DID YOU GET HOME SAFELY YESTERDAY?
YES...
AND HOW ARE YOU FEELING TODAY?
I FEEL GOOD.

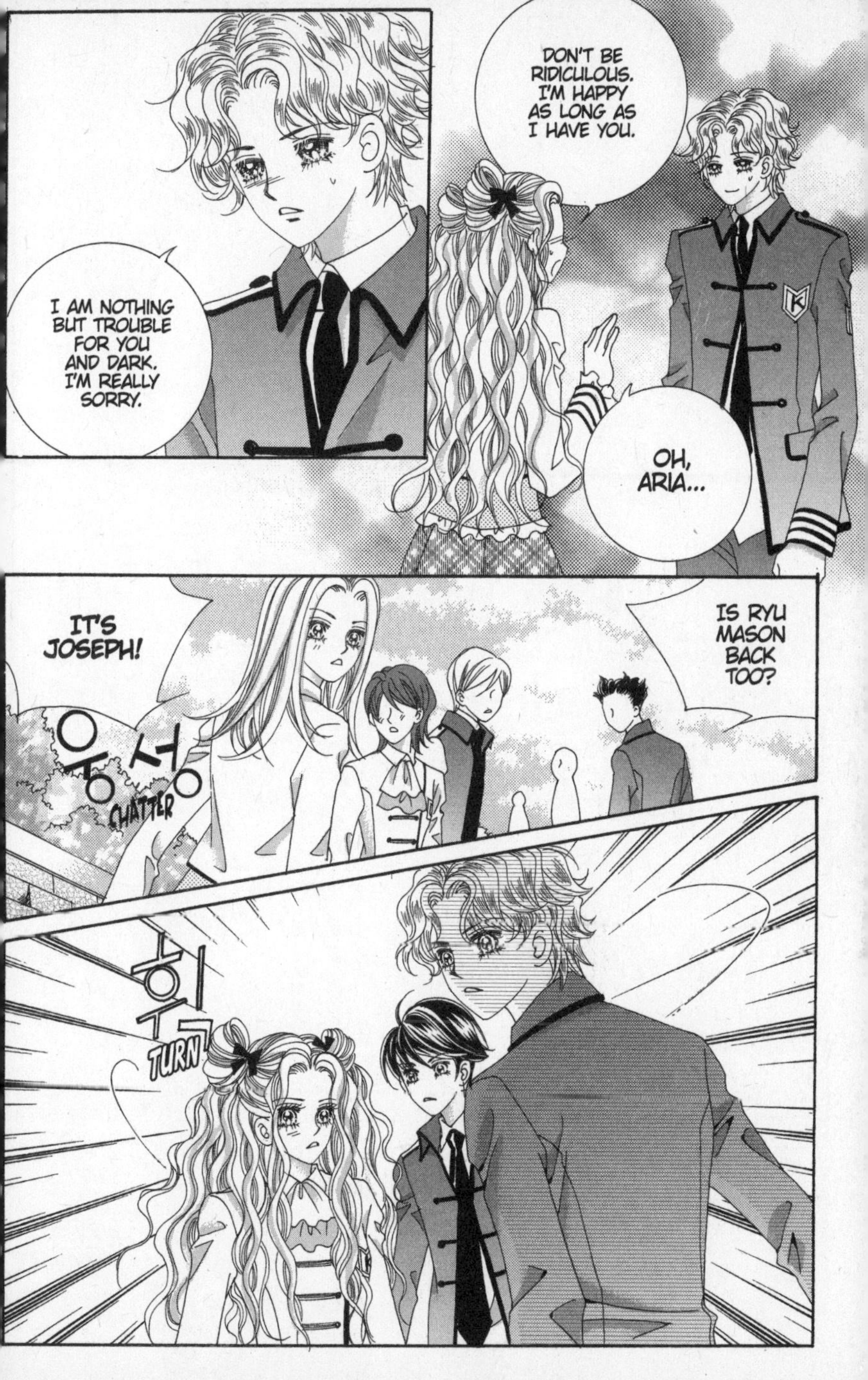
I AM NOTHING BUT TROUBLE FOR YOU AND DARK. I'M REALLY SORRY.
DON'T BE RIDICULOUS. I'M HAPPY AS LONG AS I HAVE YOU.
OH, ARIA...
IT'S JOSEPH!
CHATTER
IS RYU MASON BACK TOO?
TURN

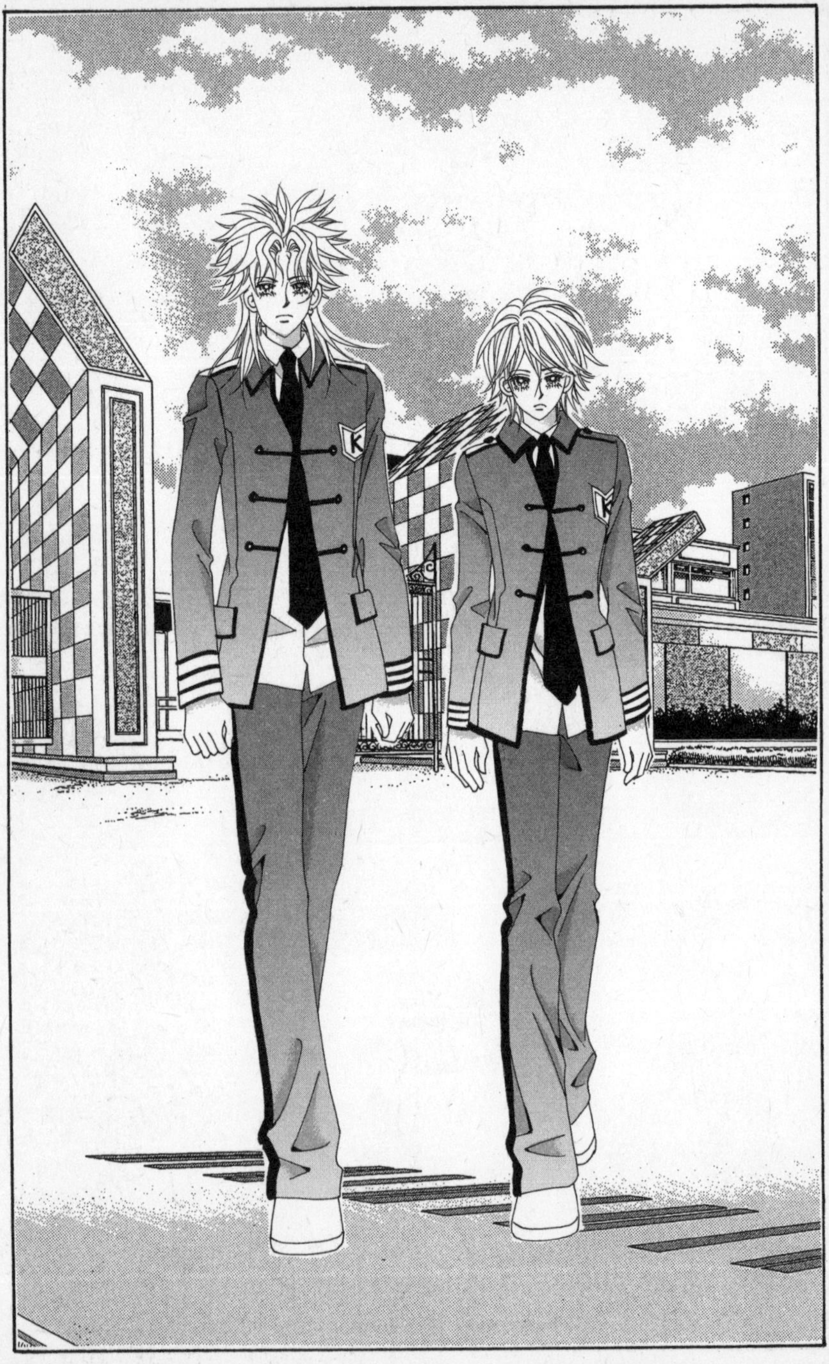

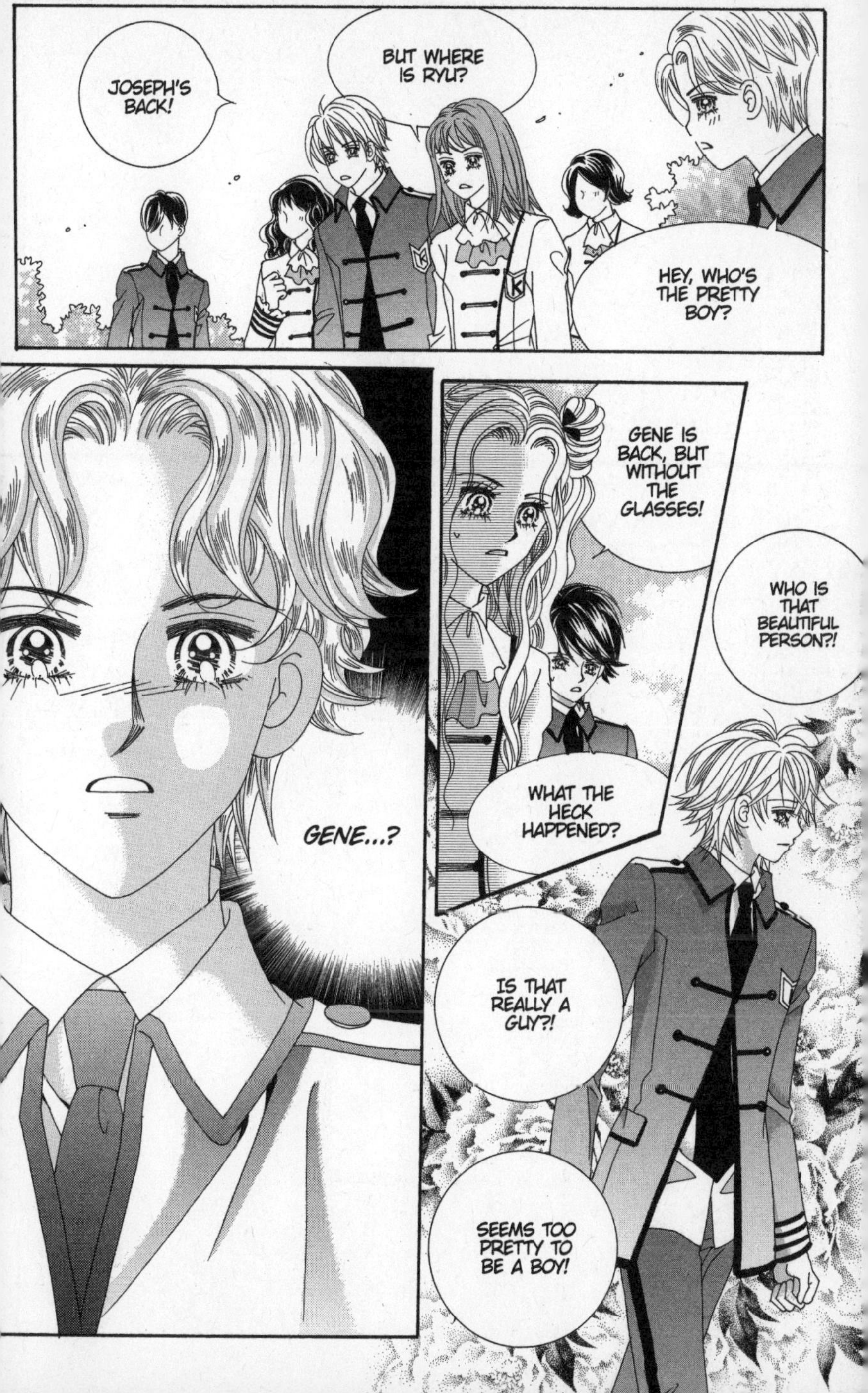
JOSEPH'S BACK!
BUT WHERE IS RYU?
HEY, WHO'S THE PRETTY BOY?
GENE...?
GENE IS BACK, BUT WITHOUT THE GLASSES!
WHO IS THAT BEAUTIFUL PERSON?!
WHAT THE HECK HAPPENED?
IS THAT REALLY A GUY?!
SEEMS TOO PRETTY TO BE A BOY!

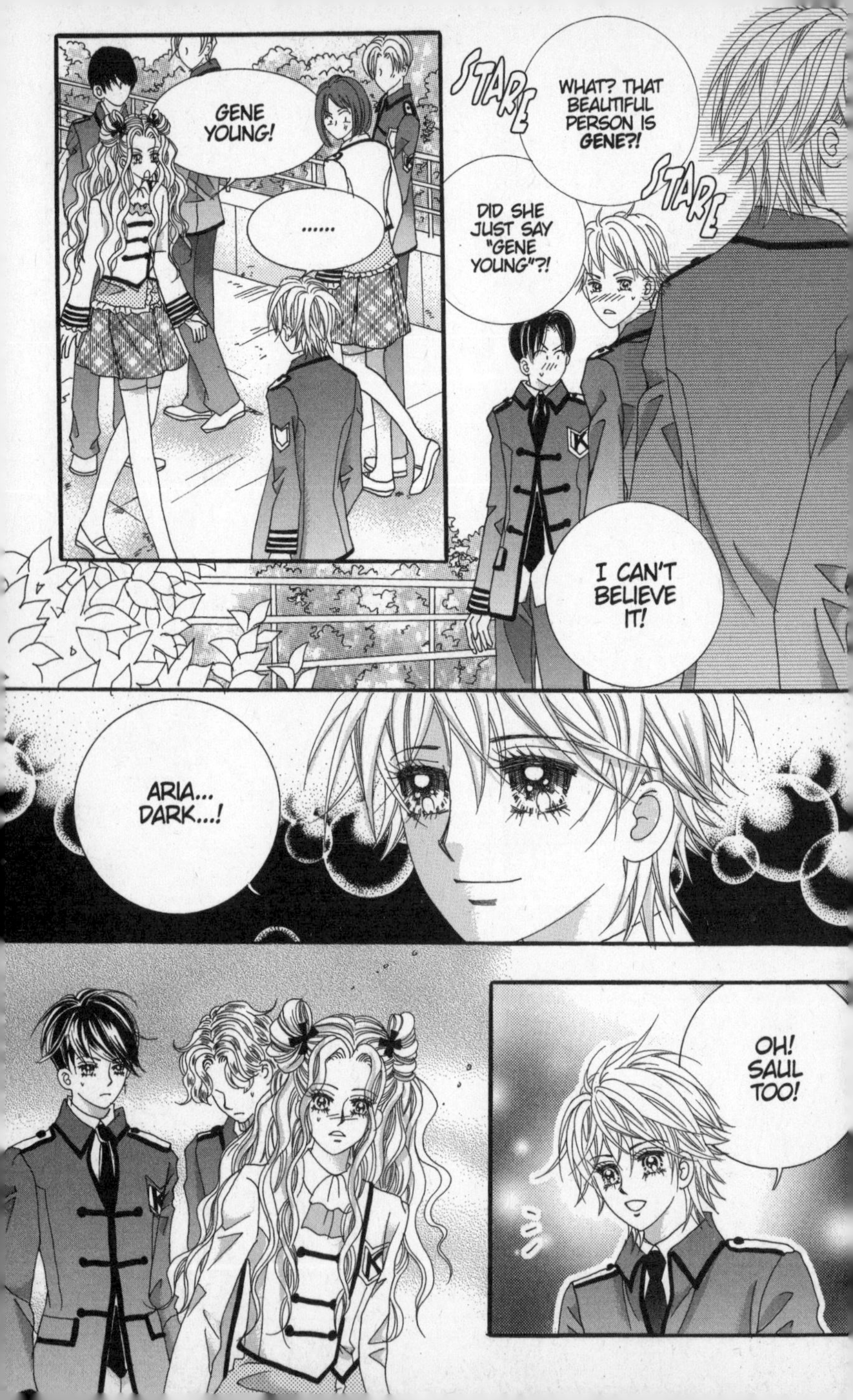
GENE YOUNG!
......
STARE
WHAT? THAT BEAUTIFUL PERSON IS GENE?!
STARE
DID SHE JUST SAY "GENE YOUNG"?!
I CAN'T BELIEVE IT!
ARIA... DARK...!
OH! SAUL TOO!

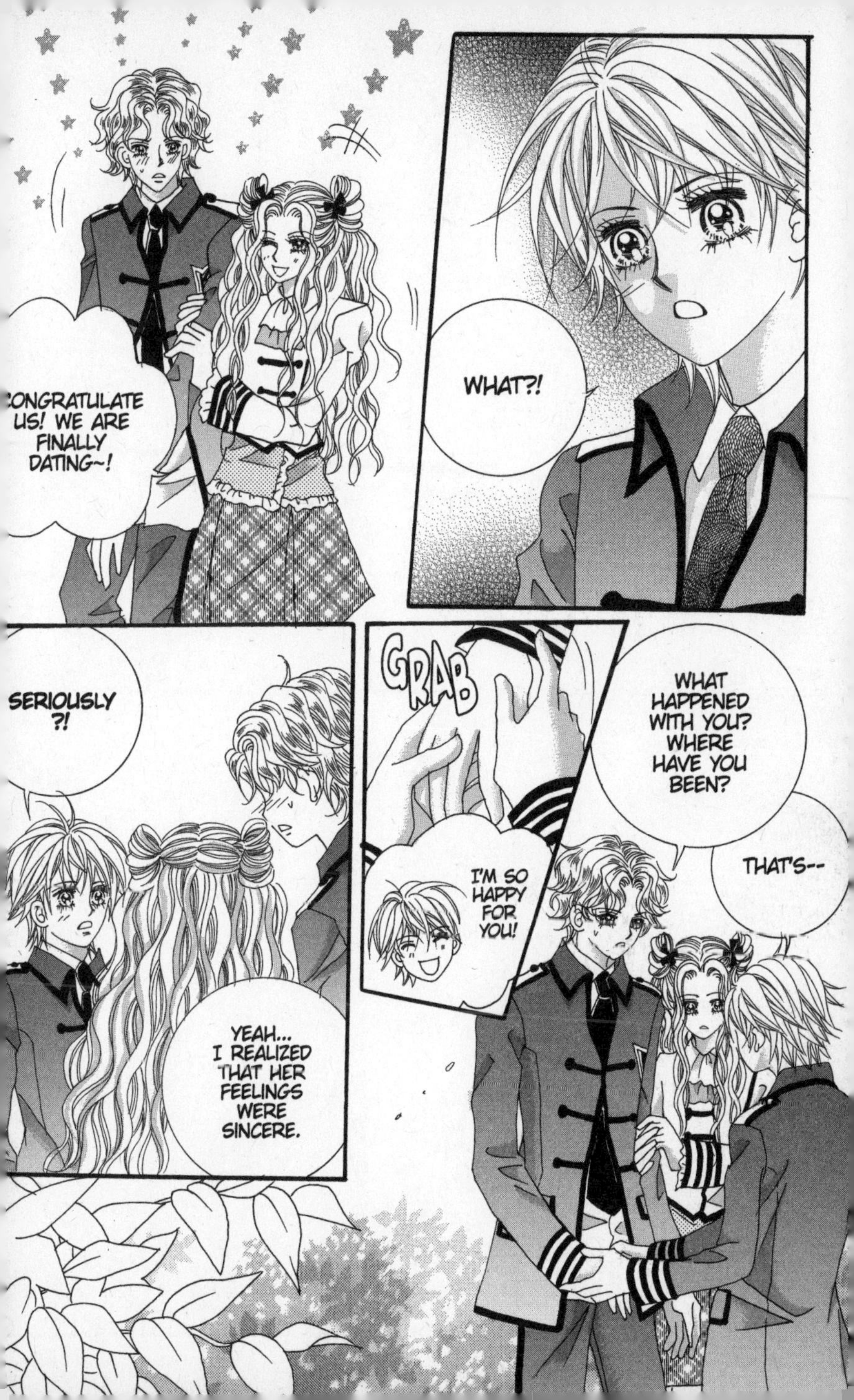
CONGRATULATE US! WE ARE FINALLY DATING~!
WHAT?!
SERIOUSLY ?!
YEAH... I REALIZED THAT HER FEELINGS WERE SINCERE.
GRAB
I'M SO HAPPY FOR YOU!
WHAT HAPPENED WITH YOU? WHERE HAVE YOU BEEN?
THAT'S--

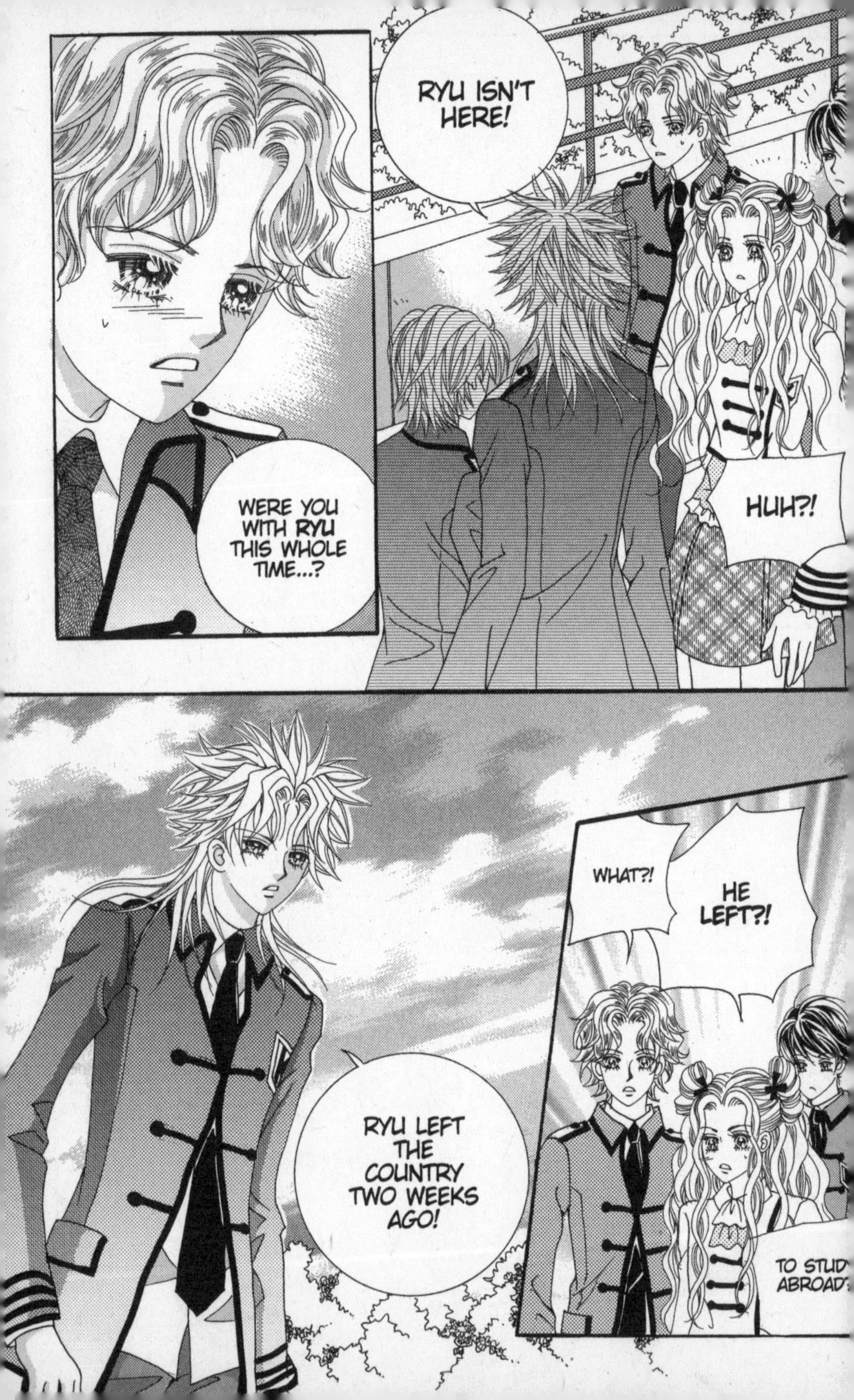
WERE YOU WITH RYU THIS WHOLE TIME...?
RYU ISN'T HERE!
HUH?!
RYU LEFT THE COUNTRY TWO WEEKS AGO!
WHAT?!
HE LEFT?!
TO STUD ABROAD

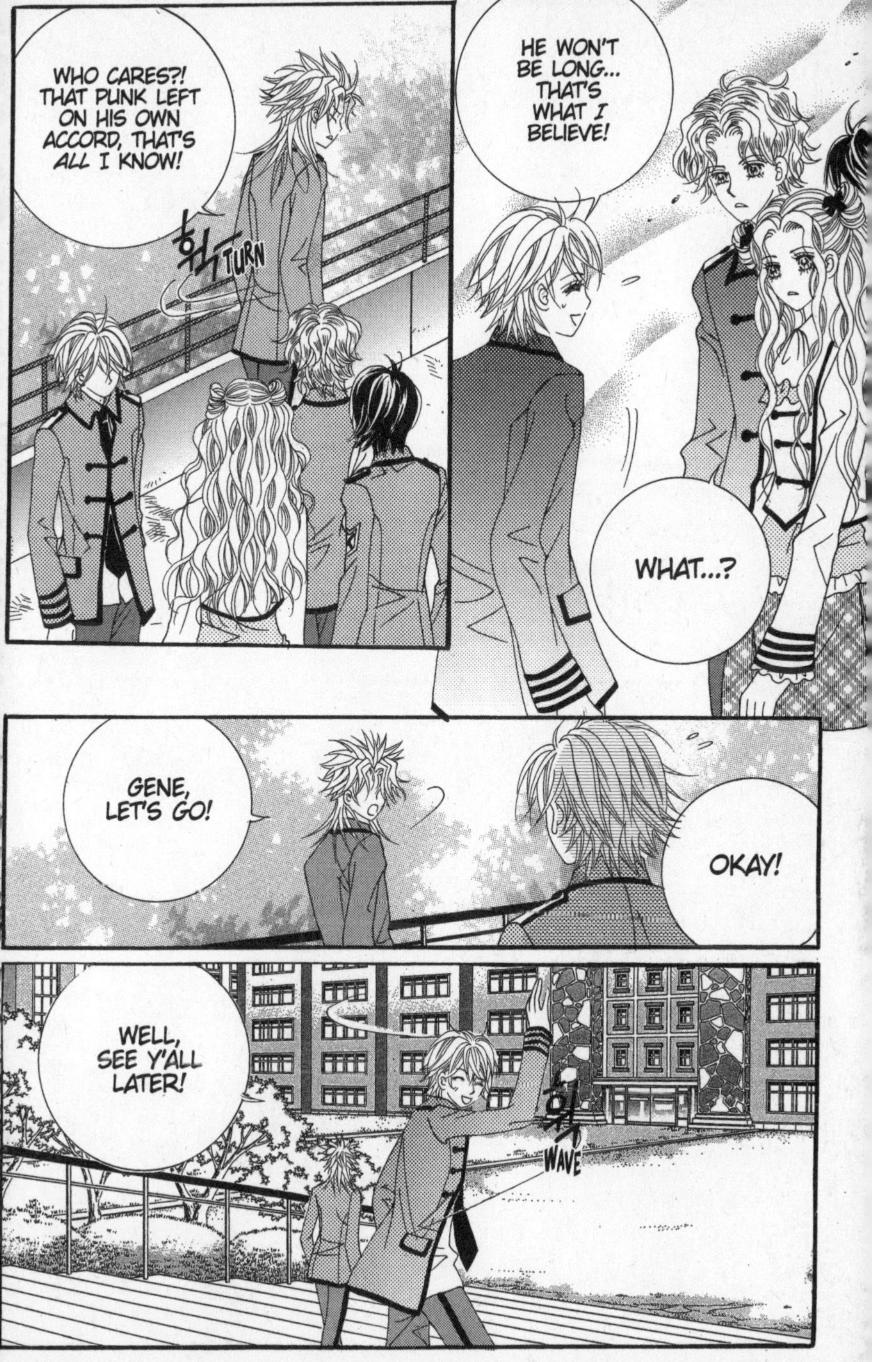
WHO CARES?! THAT PUNK LEFT ON HIS OWN ACCORD, THAT'S ALL I KNOW!
TURN
HE WON'T BE LONG... THAT'S WHAT I BELIEVE!
WHAT...?
GENE, LET'S GO!
OKAY!
WELL, SEE Y'ALL LATER!
WAVE

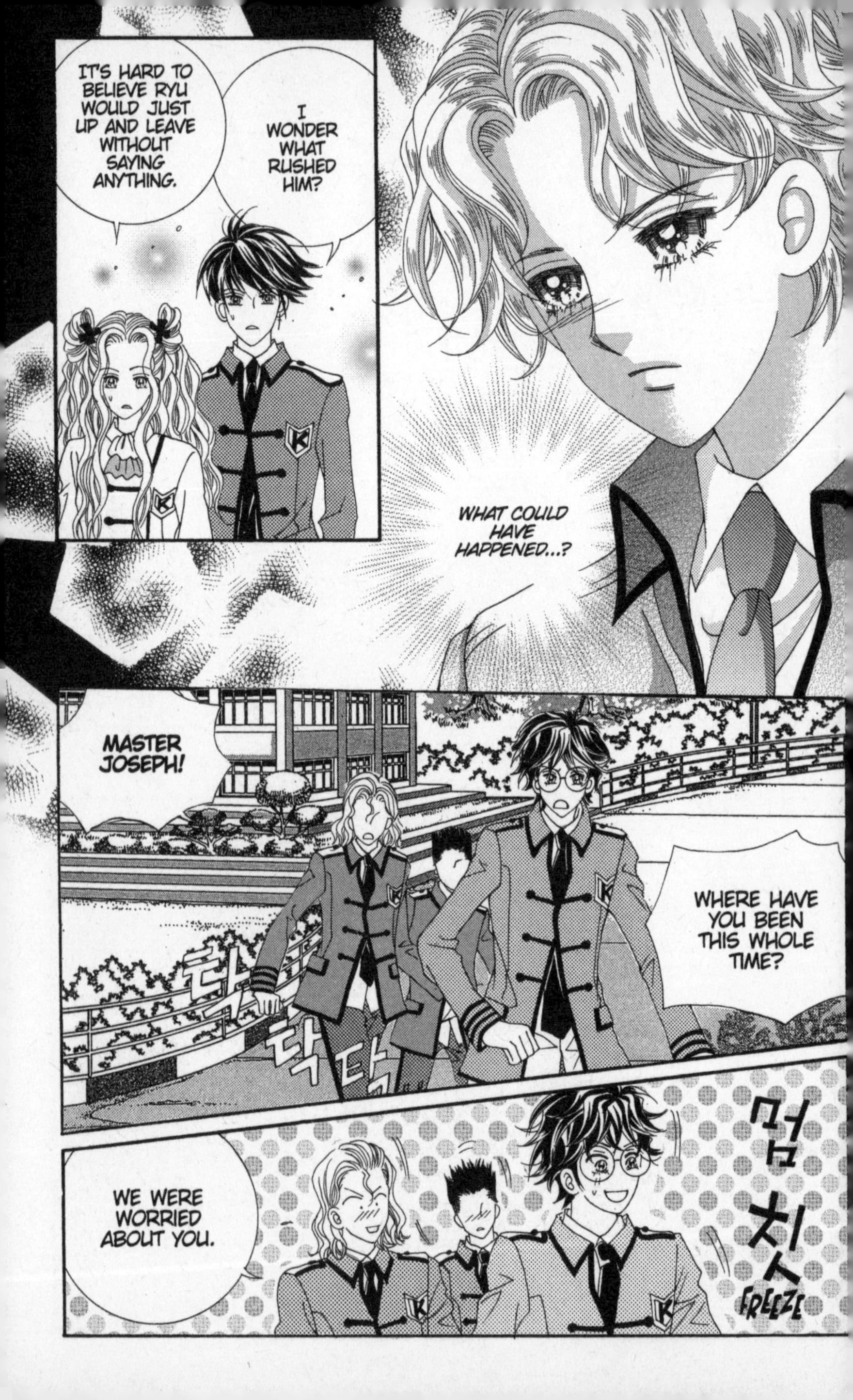
IT'S HARD TO BELIEVE RYU WOULD JUST UP AND LEAVE WITHOUT SAYING ANYTHING.
I WONDER WHAT RUSHED HIM?
WHAT COULD HAVE HAPPENED...?
MASTER JOSEPH!
탁
탁
탁
WHERE HAVE YOU BEEN THIS WHOLE TIME?
WE WERE WORRIED ABOUT YOU.
멈칫
FREEZE

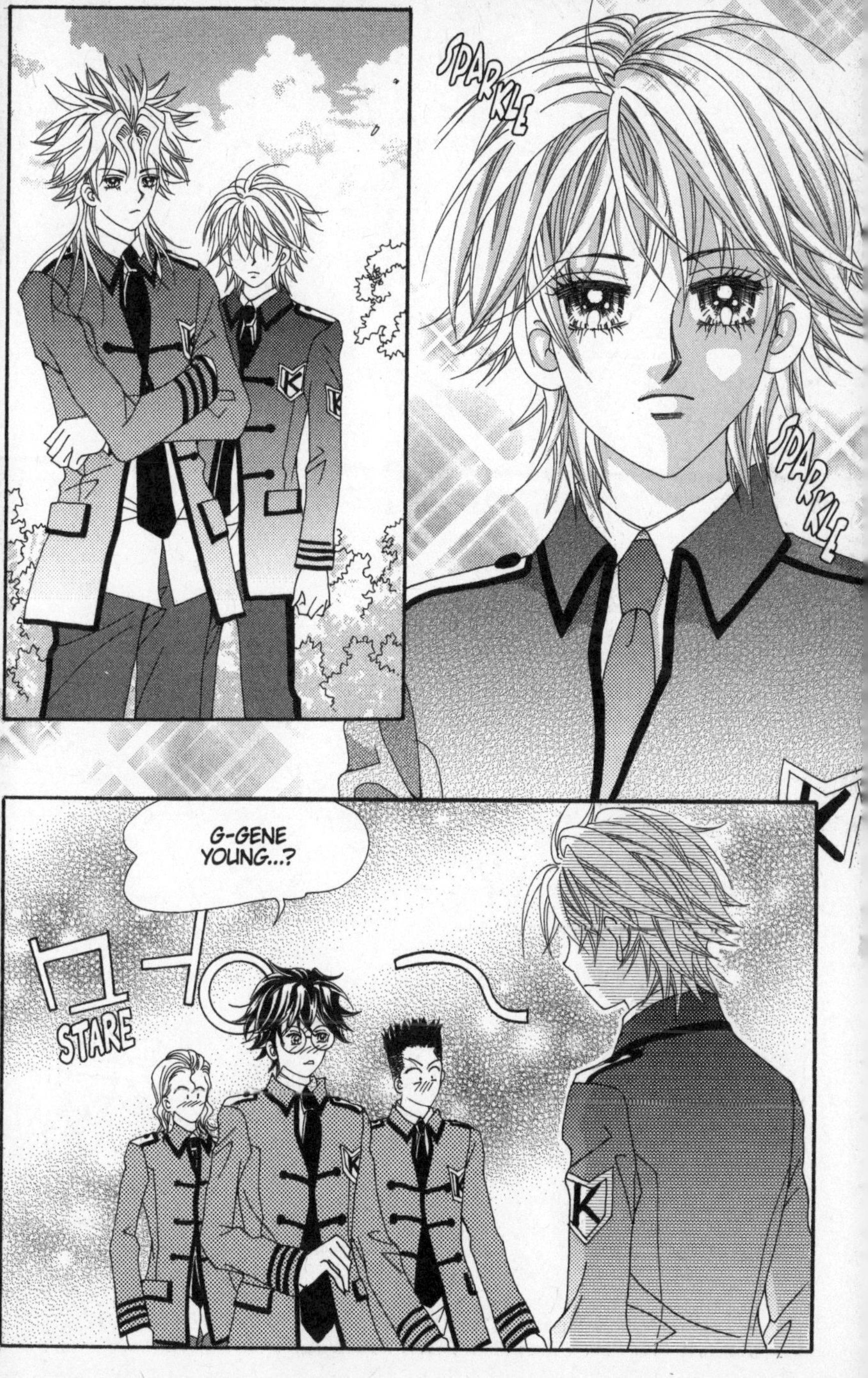
SPARKLE
SPARKLE
G-GENE YOUNG...?
STARE

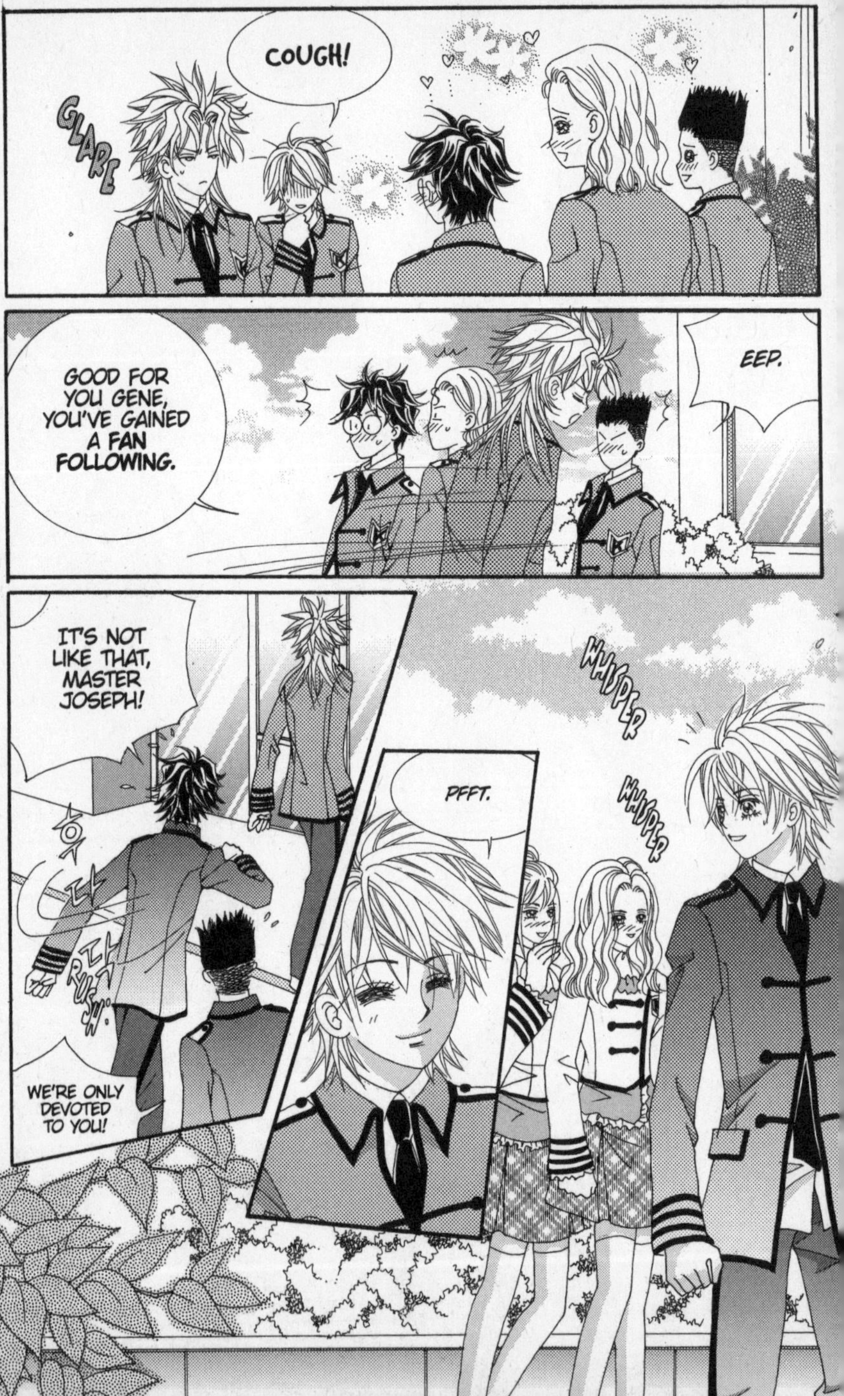
GLARE
COUGH!
GOOD FOR YOU GENE, YOU'VE GAINED A FAN FOLLOWING.
EEP.
IT'S NOT LIKE THAT, MASTER JOSEPH!
RUSH
WE'RE ONLY DEVOTED TO YOU!
PFFT.
WHISPER
WHISPER

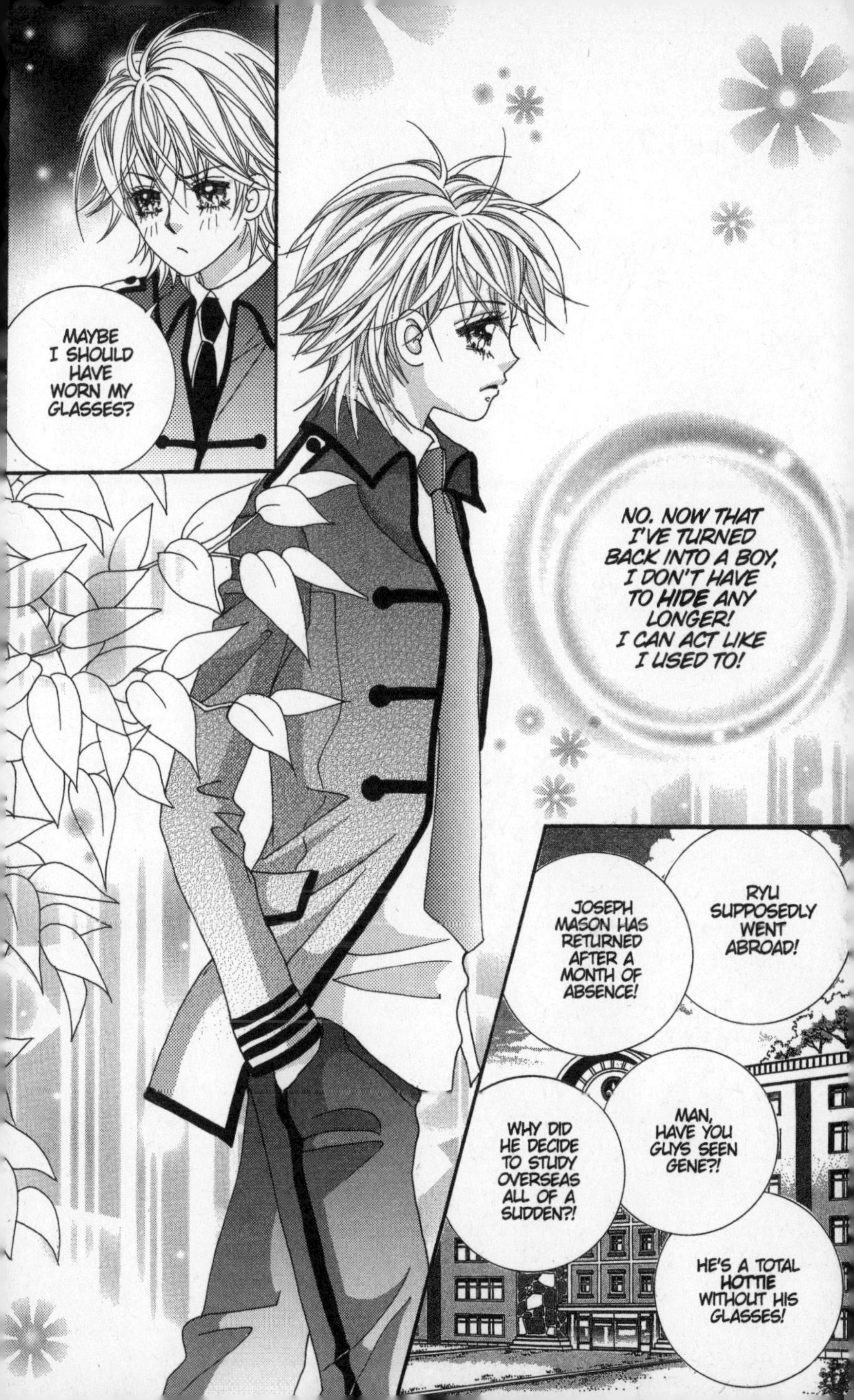
MAYBE I SHOULD HAVE WORN MY GLASSES?
NO. NOW THAT I'VE TURNED BACK INTO A BOY, I DON'T HAVE TO **HIDE** ANY LONGER! I CAN ACT LIKE I USED TO!
JOSEPH MASON HAS RETURNED AFTER A MONTH OF ABSENCE!
RYU SUPPOSEDLY WENT ABROAD!
WHY DID HE DECIDE TO STUDY OVERSEAS ALL OF A SUDDEN?!
MAN, HAVE YOU GUYS SEEN GENE?!
HE'S A TOTAL HOTTIE WITHOUT HIS GLASSES!

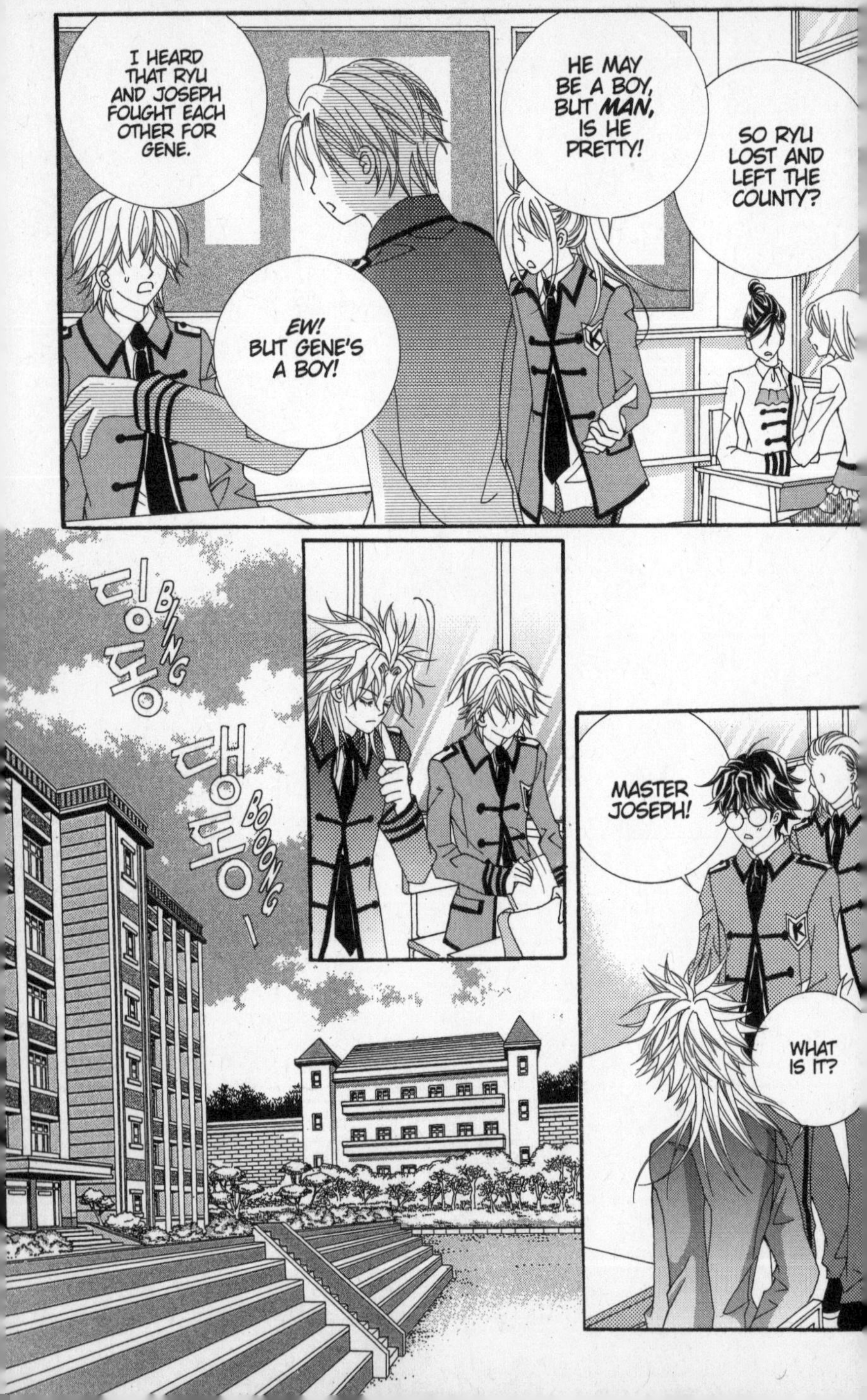
I HEARD THAT RYU AND JOSEPH FOUGHT EACH OTHER FOR GENE.
EW! BUT GENE'S A BOY!
HE MAY BE A BOY, BUT MAN, IS HE PRETTY!
SO RYU LOST AND LEFT THE COUNTY?
BING
BOOONG
MASTER JOSEPH!
WHAT IS IT?

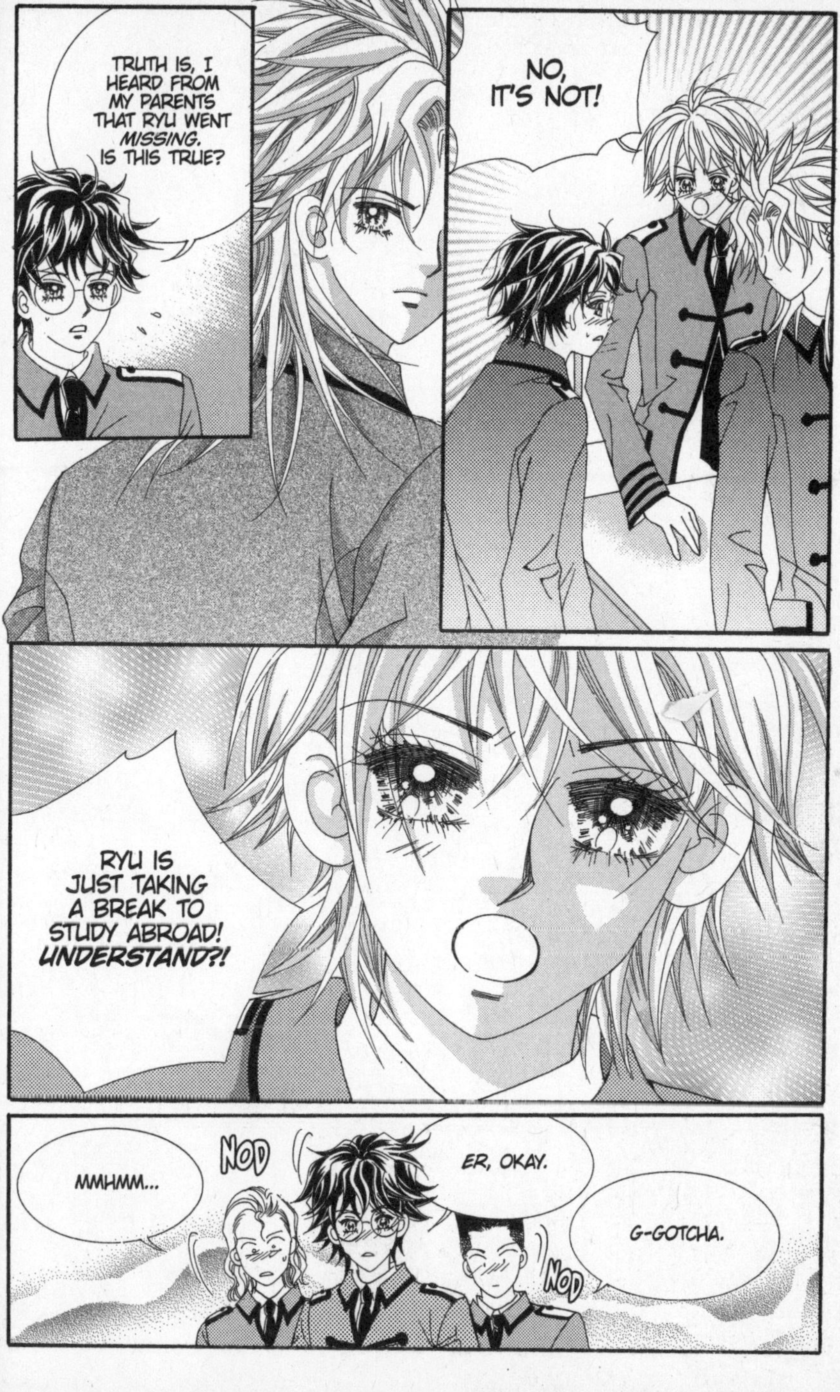
TRUTH IS, I HEARD FROM MY PARENTS THAT RYU WENT *MISSING*. IS THIS TRUE?
NO, IT'S NOT!
RYU IS JUST TAKING A BREAK TO STUDY ABROAD! **UNDERSTAND?!**
MMHMM...
NOD
ER, OKAY.
G-GOTCHA.
NOD

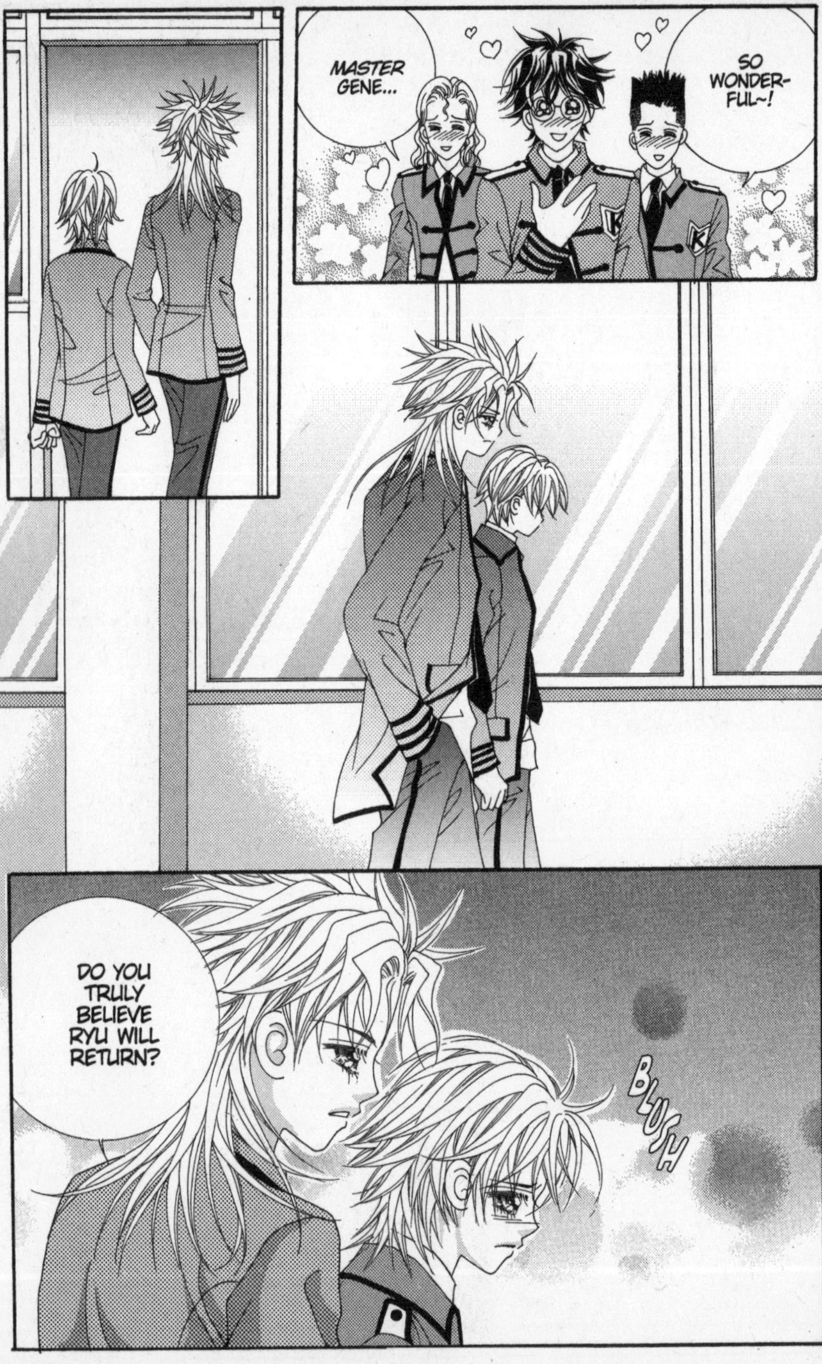
MASTER GENE...
SO WONDER-FUL~!
DO YOU TRULY BELIEVE RYU WILL RETURN?
BLUSH

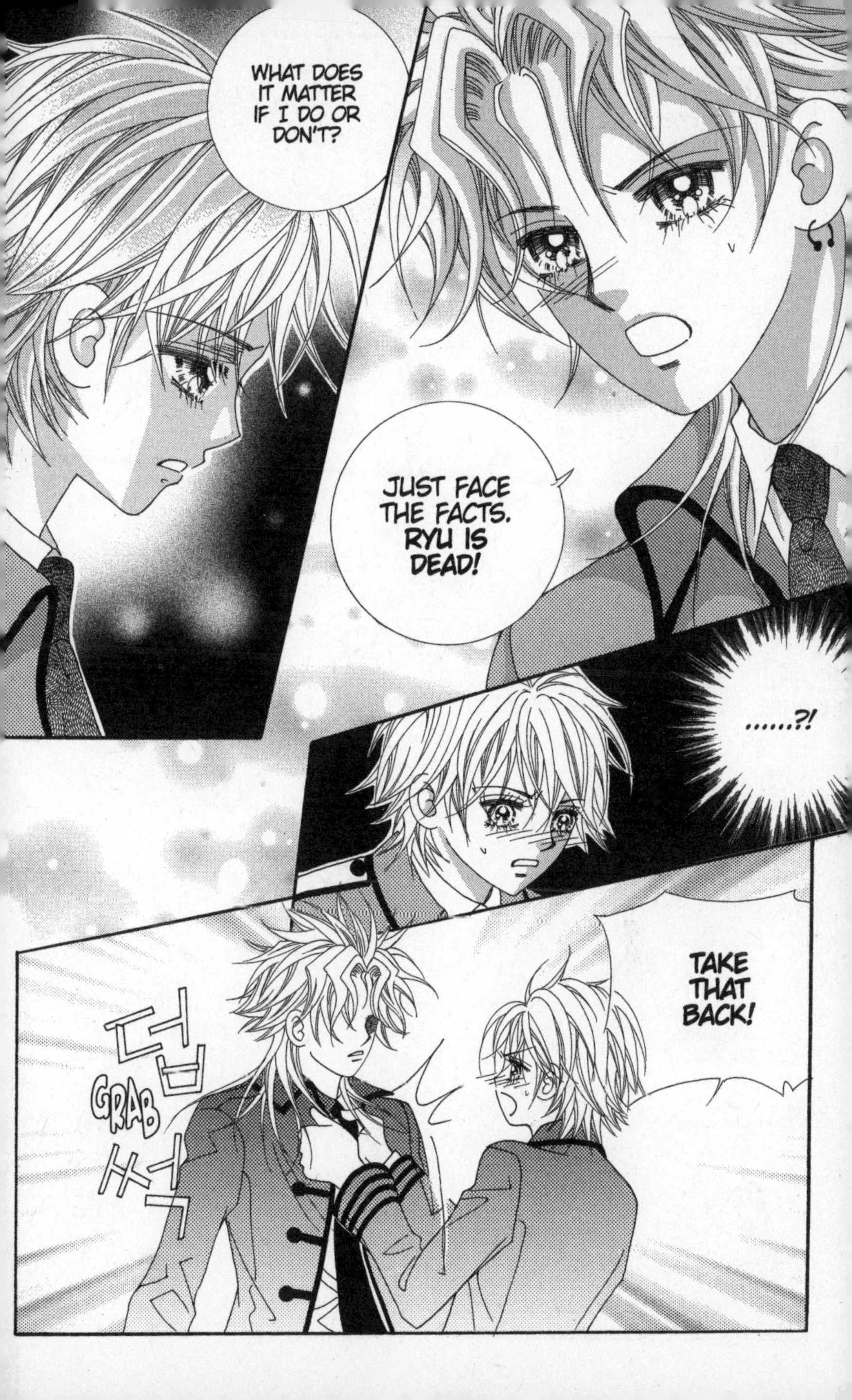
WHAT DOES IT MATTER IF I DO OR DON'T?
JUST FACE THE FACTS. RYU IS DEAD!
......?!
덥석
GRAB
TAKE THAT BACK!

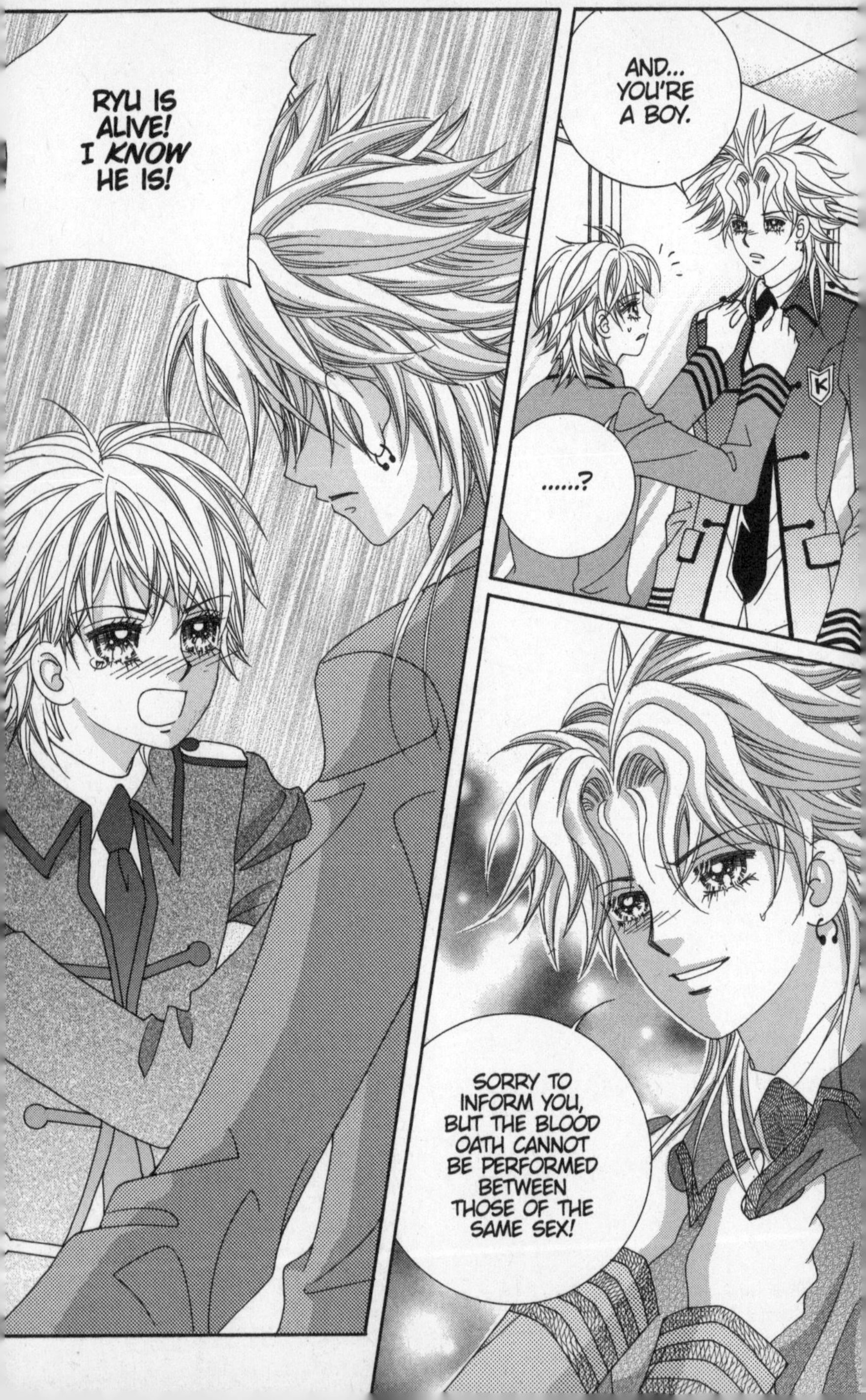
RYU IS ALIVE! I KNOW HE IS!
AND... YOU'RE A BOY.
......?
SORRY TO INFORM YOU, BUT THE BLOOD OATH CANNOT BE PERFORMED BETWEEN THOSE OF THE SAME SEX!

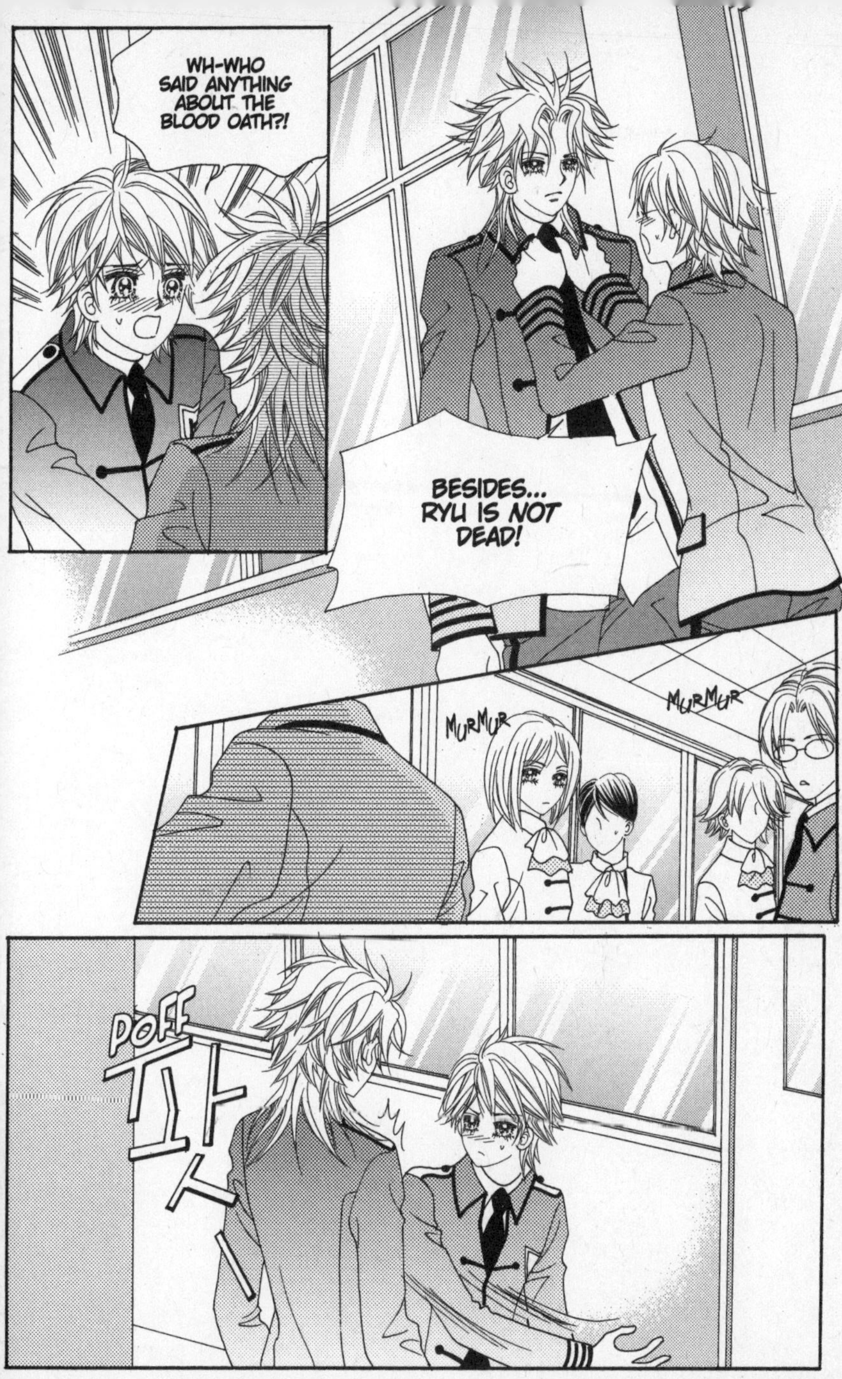
WH-WHO SAID ANYTHING ABOUT THE BLOOD OATH?!
BESIDES... RYU IS NOT DEAD!
MURMUR
MURMUR
POFF

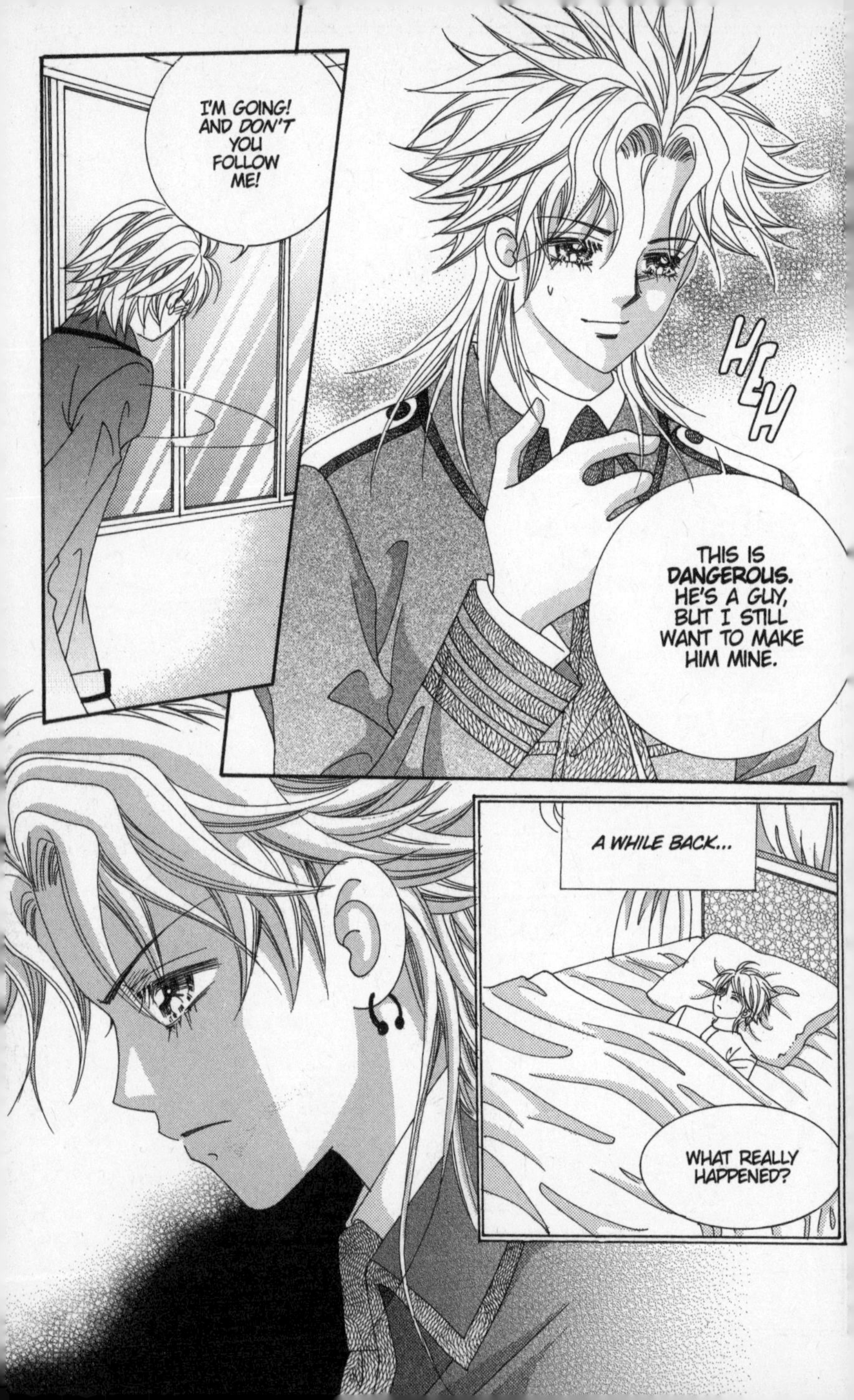
I'M GOING! AND DON'T YOU FOLLOW ME!
HEH
THIS IS DANGEROUS. HE'S A GUY, BUT I STILL WANT TO MAKE HIM MINE.
A WHILE BACK...
WHAT REALLY HAPPENED?

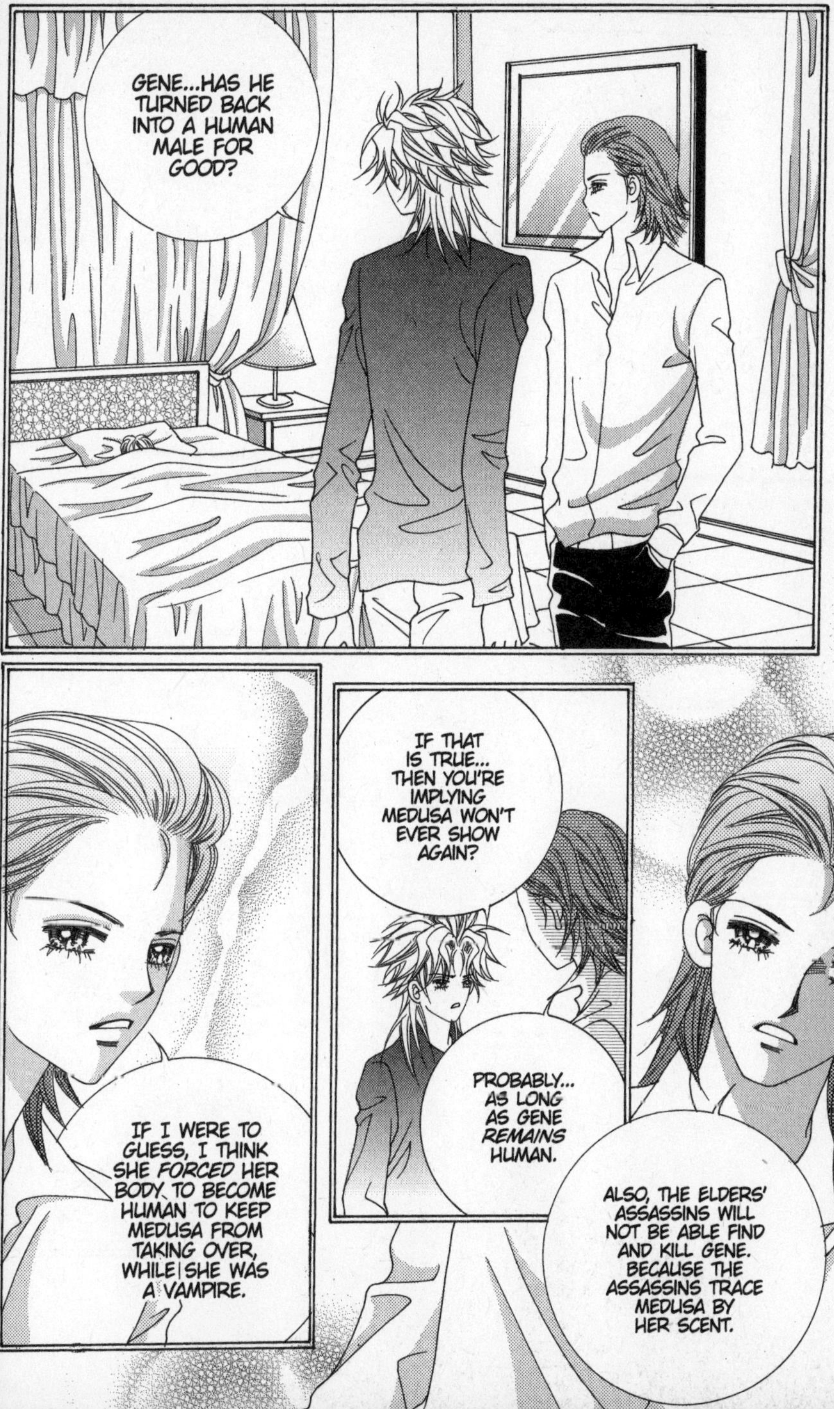
GENE...HAS HE TURNED BACK INTO A HUMAN MALE FOR GOOD?
IF I WERE TO GUESS, I THINK SHE *FORCED* HER BODY TO BECOME HUMAN TO KEEP MEDUSA FROM TAKING OVER, WHILE SHE WAS A VAMPIRE.
IF THAT IS TRUE... THEN YOU'RE IMPLYING MEDUSA WON'T EVER SHOW AGAIN?
PROBABLY... AS LONG AS GENE *REMAINS* HUMAN.
ALSO, THE ELDERS' ASSASSINS WILL NOT BE ABLE FIND AND KILL GENE. BECAUSE THE ASSASSINS TRACE MEDUSA BY HER SCENT.

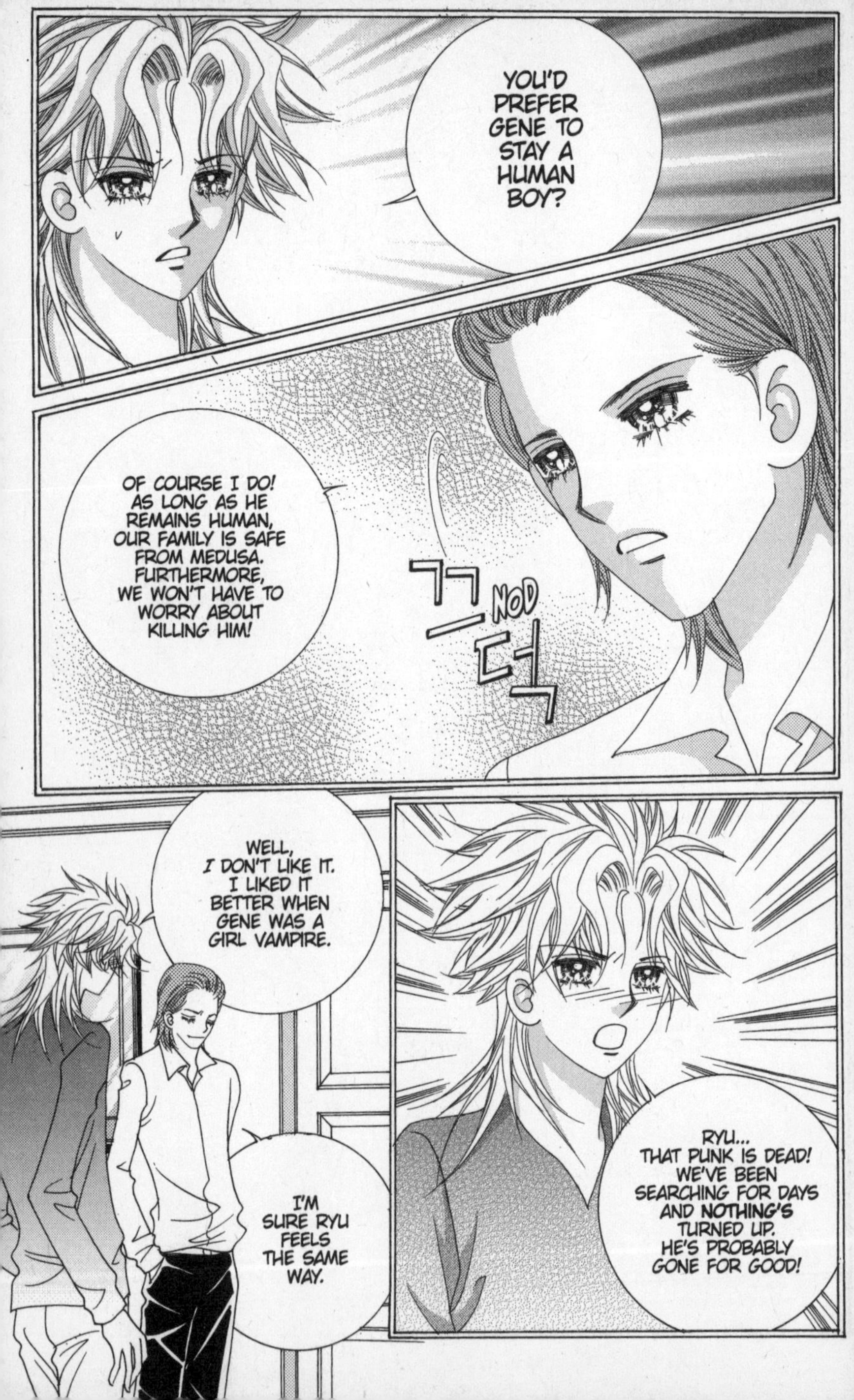
YOU'D PREFER GENE TO STAY A HUMAN BOY?
OF COURSE I DO! AS LONG AS HE REMAINS HUMAN, OUR FAMILY IS SAFE FROM MEDUSA. FURTHERMORE, WE WON'T HAVE TO WORRY ABOUT KILLING HIM!
끄덕
NOD
WELL, I DON'T LIKE IT. I LIKED IT BETTER WHEN GENE WAS A GIRL VAMPIRE.
I'M SURE RYU FEELS THE SAME WAY.
RYU... THAT PUNK IS DEAD! WE'VE BEEN SEARCHING FOR DAYS AND NOTHING'S TURNED UP. HE'S PROBABLY GONE FOR GOOD!

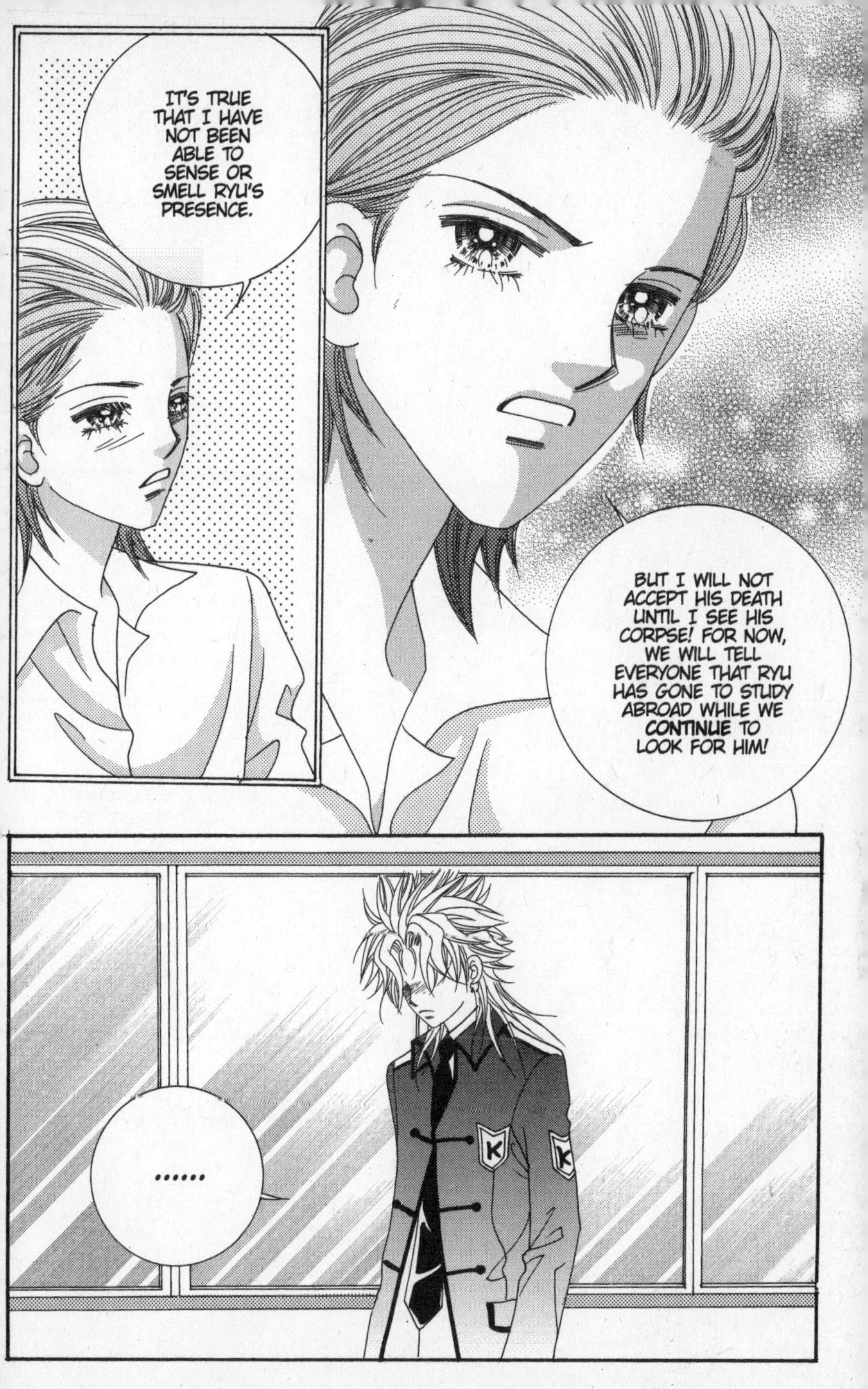
IT'S TRUE THAT I HAVE NOT BEEN ABLE TO SENSE OR SMELL RYU'S PRESENCE.
BUT I WILL NOT ACCEPT HIS DEATH UNTIL I SEE HIS CORPSE! FOR NOW, WE WILL TELL EVERYONE THAT RYU HAS GONE TO STUDY ABROAD WHILE WE CONTINUE TO LOOK FOR HIM!
......

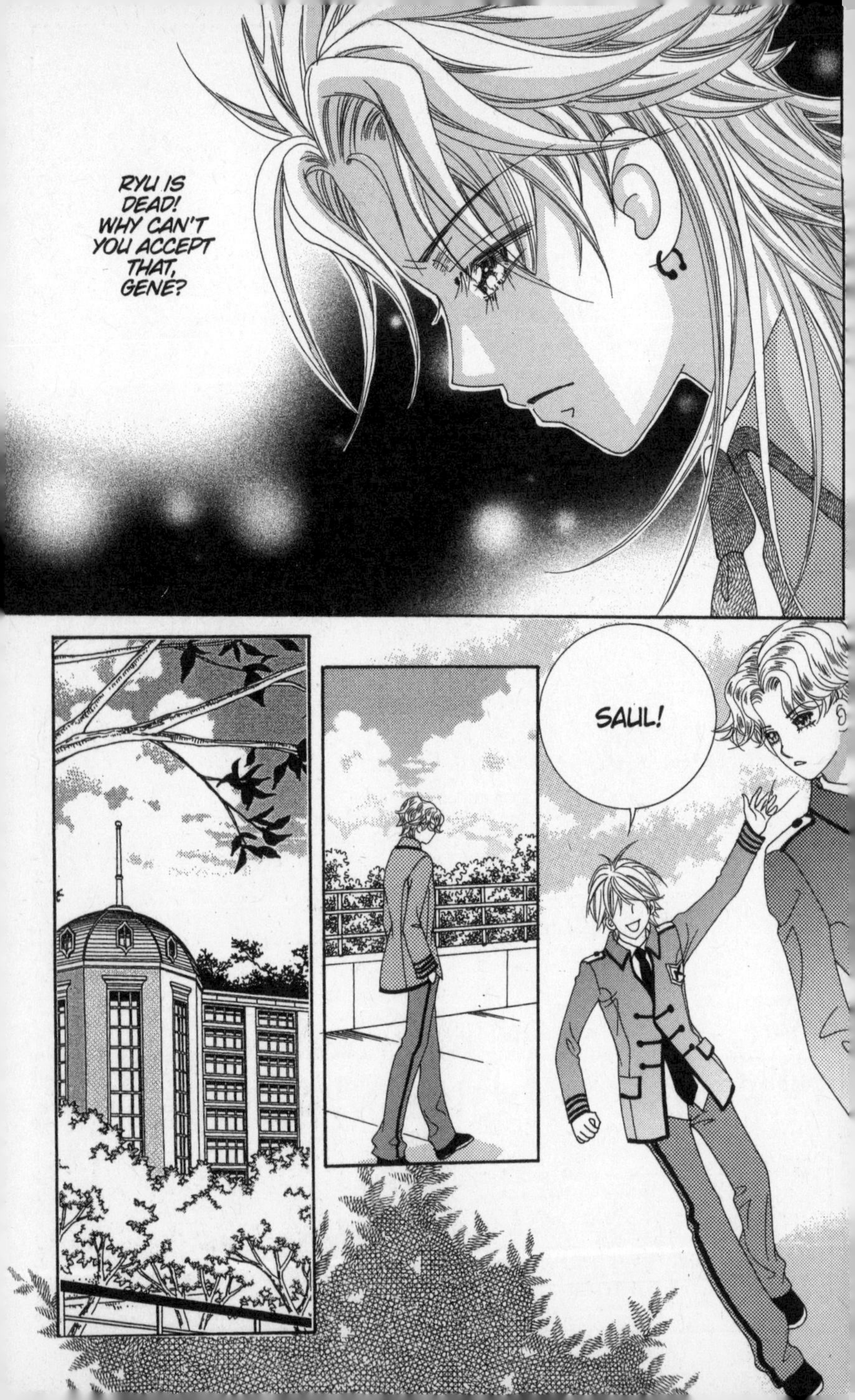
RYU IS DEAD! WHY CAN'T YOU ACCEPT THAT, GENE?
SAUL!

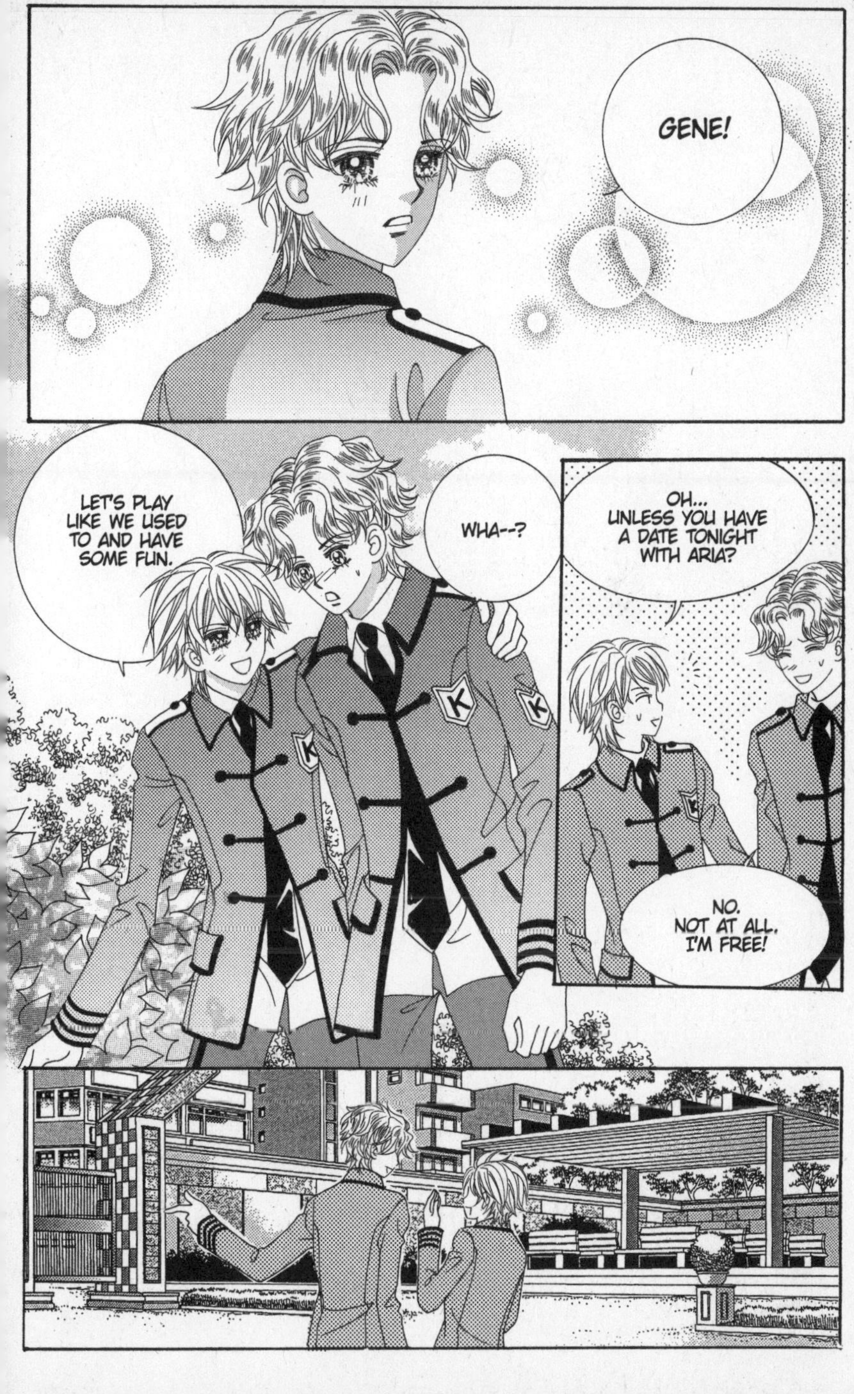
GENE!
LET'S PLAY LIKE WE USED TO AND HAVE SOME FUN.
WHA--?
OH... UNLESS YOU HAVE A DATE TONIGHT WITH ARIA?
NO. NOT AT ALL. I'M FREE!

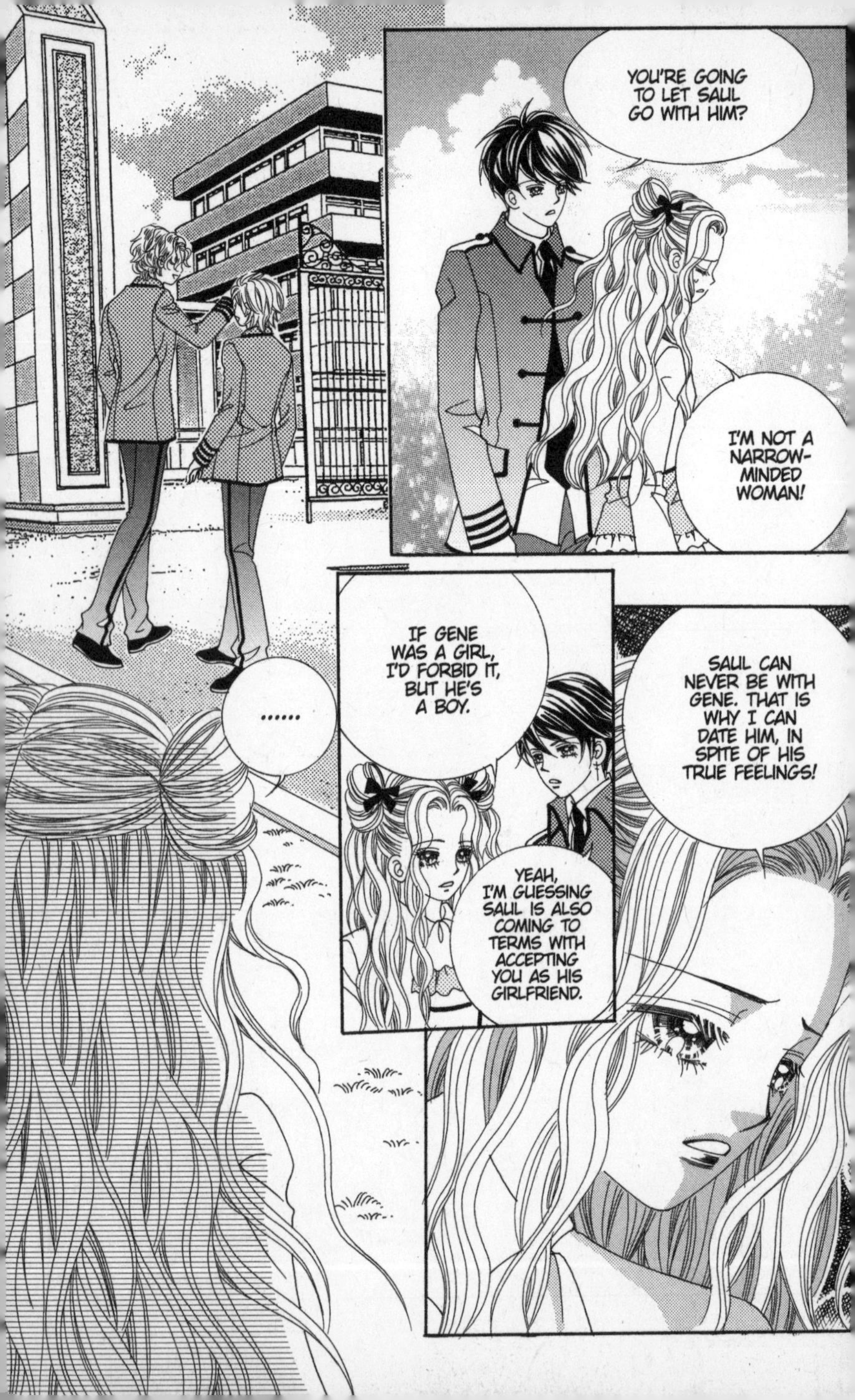
......
YOU'RE GOING TO LET SAUL GO WITH HIM?
I'M NOT A NARROW-MINDED WOMAN!
IF GENE WAS A GIRL, I'D FORBID IT, BUT HE'S A BOY.
YEAH, I'M GUESSING SAUL IS ALSO COMING TO TERMS WITH ACCEPTING YOU AS HIS GIRLFRIEND.
SAUL CAN NEVER BE WITH GENE. THAT IS WHY I CAN DATE HIM, IN SPITE OF HIS TRUE FEELINGS!

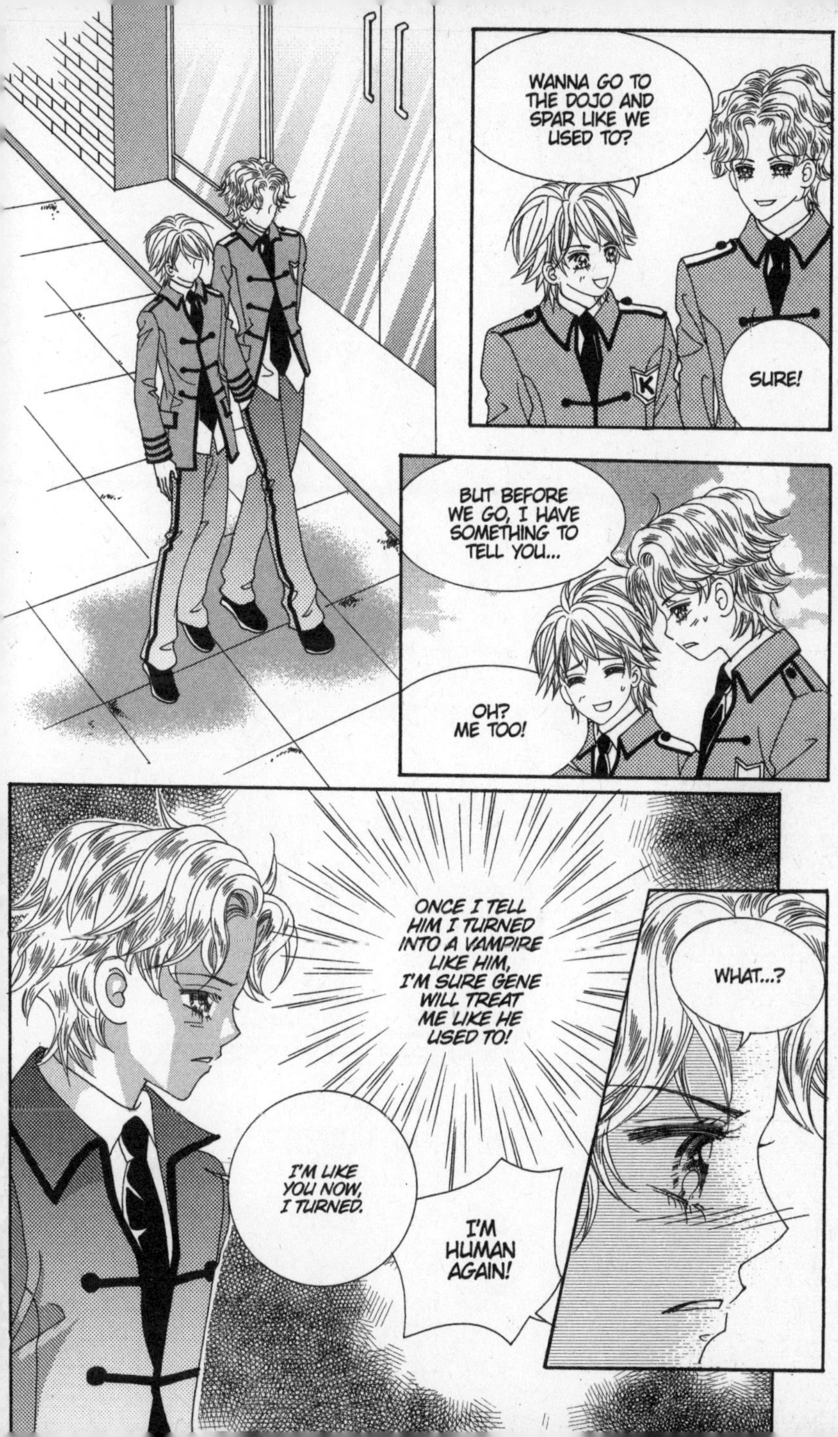
WANNA GO TO THE DOJO AND SPAR LIKE WE USED TO?
SURE!
BUT BEFORE WE GO, I HAVE SOMETHING TO TELL YOU...
OH? ME TOO!
ONCE I TELL HIM I TURNED INTO A VAMPIRE LIKE HIM, I'M SURE GENE WILL TREAT ME LIKE HE USED TO!
I'M LIKE YOU NOW, I TURNED.
I'M HUMAN AGAIN!
WHAT...?

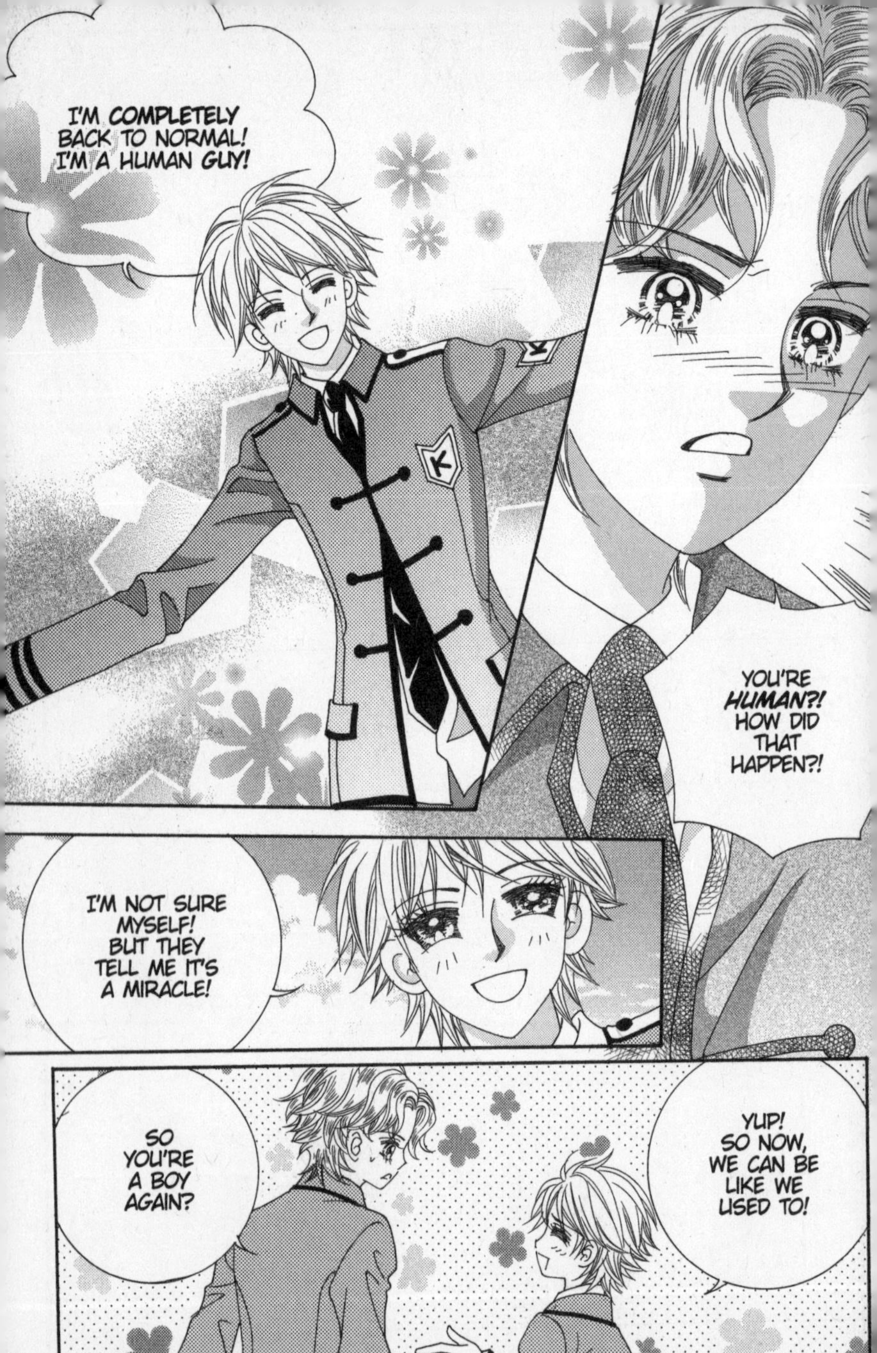
I'M COMPLETELY BACK TO NORMAL! I'M A HUMAN GUY!
YOU'RE *HUMAN?!* HOW DID THAT HAPPEN?!
I'M NOT SURE MYSELF! BUT THEY TELL ME IT'S A MIRACLE!
SO YOU'RE A BOY AGAIN?
YUP! SO NOW, WE CAN BE LIKE WE USED TO!

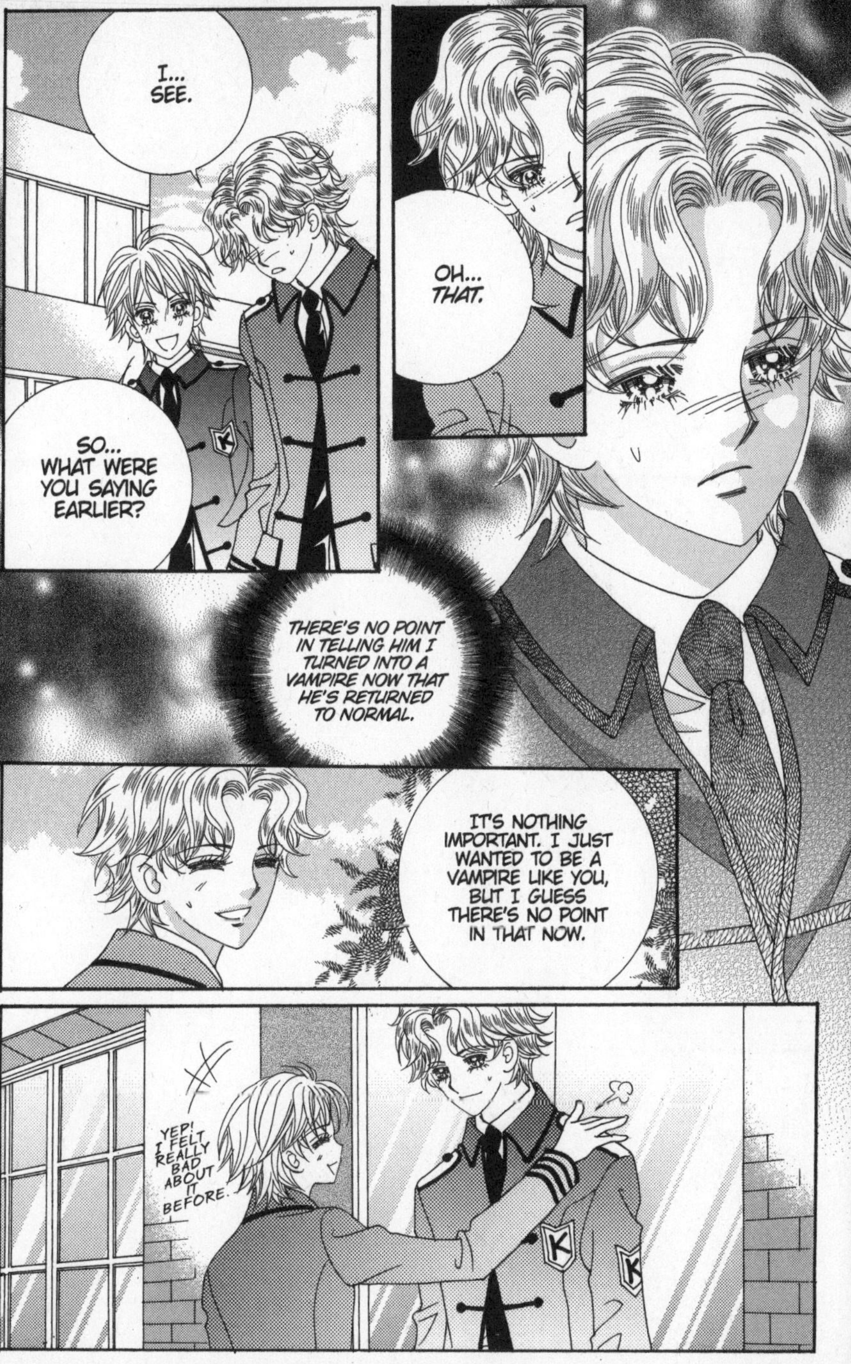
I... SEE.
SO... WHAT WERE YOU SAYING EARLIER?
OH... THAT.
THERE'S NO POINT IN TELLING HIM I TURNED INTO A VAMPIRE NOW THAT HE'S RETURNED TO NORMAL.
IT'S NOTHING IMPORTANT. I JUST WANTED TO BE A VAMPIRE LIKE YOU, BUT I GUESS THERE'S NO POINT IN THAT NOW.
YEP! I FELT REALLY BAD ABOUT IT BEFORE.

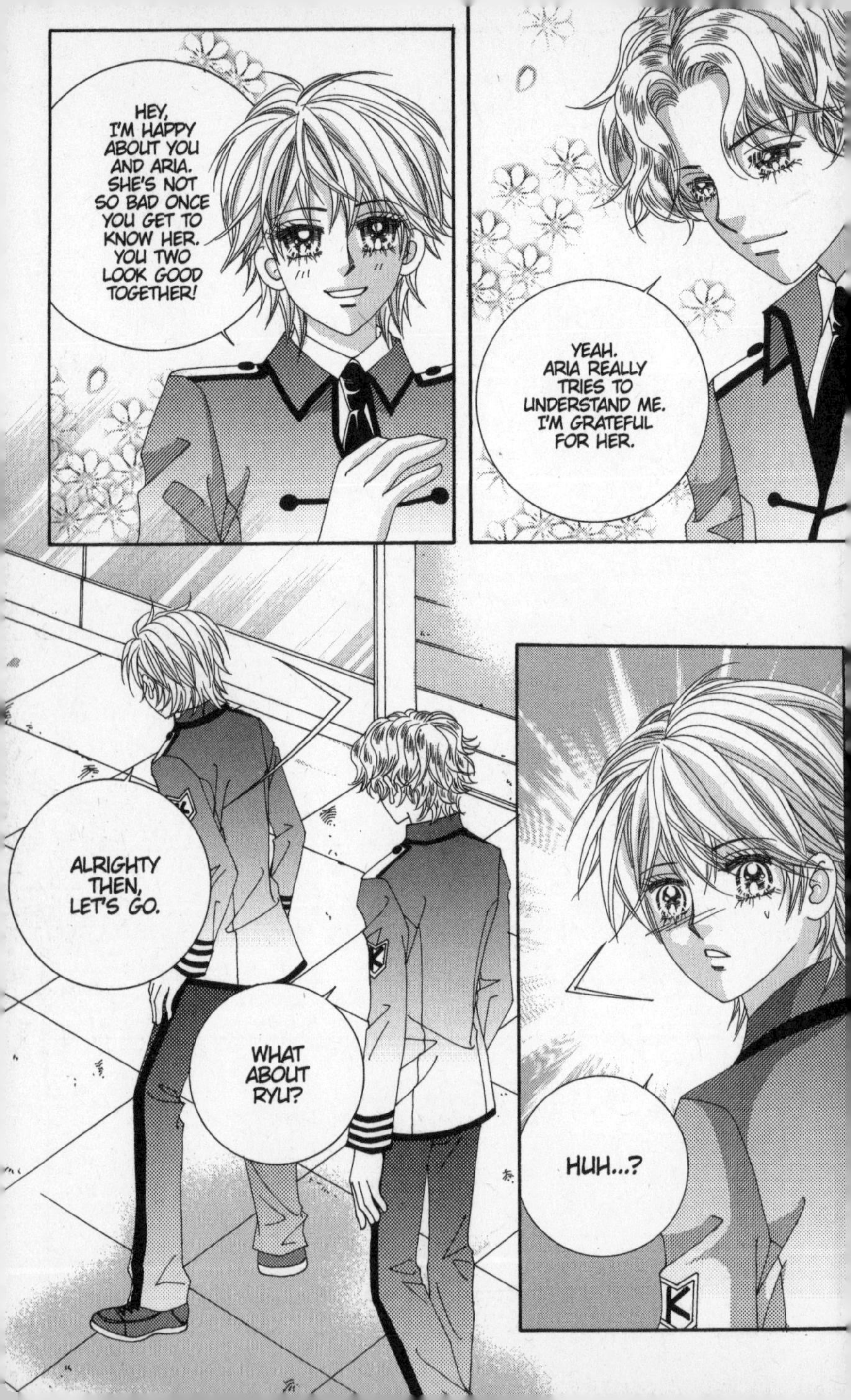
HEY, I'M HAPPY ABOUT YOU AND ARIA. SHE'S NOT SO BAD ONCE YOU GET TO KNOW HER. YOU TWO LOOK GOOD TOGETHER!
YEAH. ARIA REALLY TRIES TO UNDERSTAND ME. I'M GRATEFUL FOR HER.
ALRIGHTY THEN, LET'S GO.
WHAT ABOUT RYU?
HUH...?

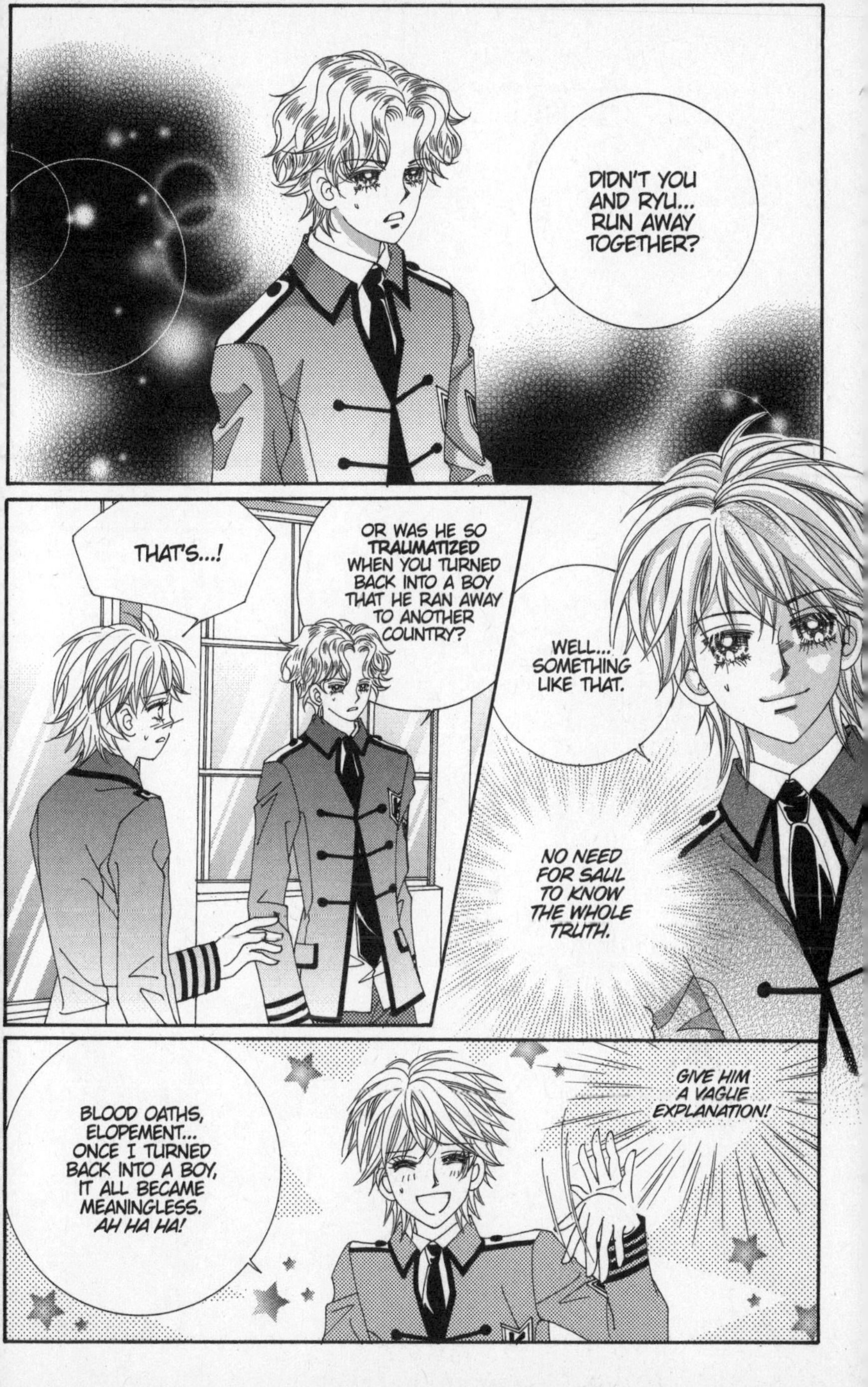
DIDN'T YOU AND RYU... RUN AWAY TOGETHER?
THAT'S...!
OR WAS HE SO TRAUMATIZED WHEN YOU TURNED BACK INTO A BOY THAT HE RAN AWAY TO ANOTHER COUNTRY?
WELL... SOMETHING LIKE THAT.
NO NEED FOR SAUL TO KNOW THE WHOLE TRUTH.
BLOOD OATHS, ELOPEMENT... ONCE I TURNED BACK INTO A BOY, IT ALL BECAME MEANINGLESS. AH HA HA!
GIVE HIM A VAGUE EXPLANATION!

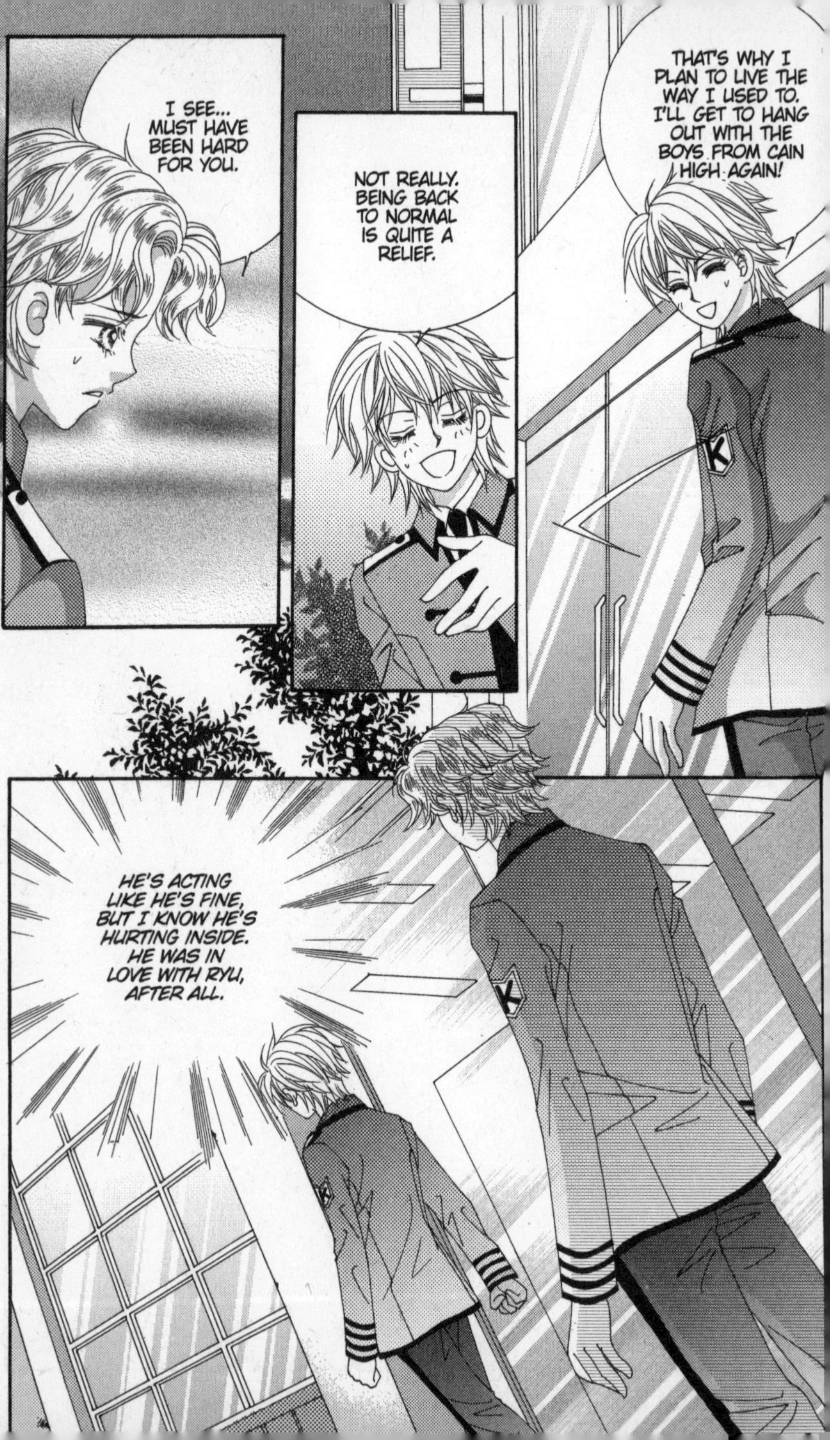
I SEE... MUST HAVE BEEN HARD FOR YOU.
NOT REALLY. BEING BACK TO NORMAL IS QUITE A RELIEF.
THAT'S WHY I PLAN TO LIVE THE WAY I USED TO. I'LL GET TO HANG OUT WITH THE BOYS FROM CAIN HIGH AGAIN!
HE'S ACTING LIKE HE'S FINE, BUT I KNOW HE'S HURTING INSIDE. HE WAS IN LOVE WITH RYU, AFTER ALL.

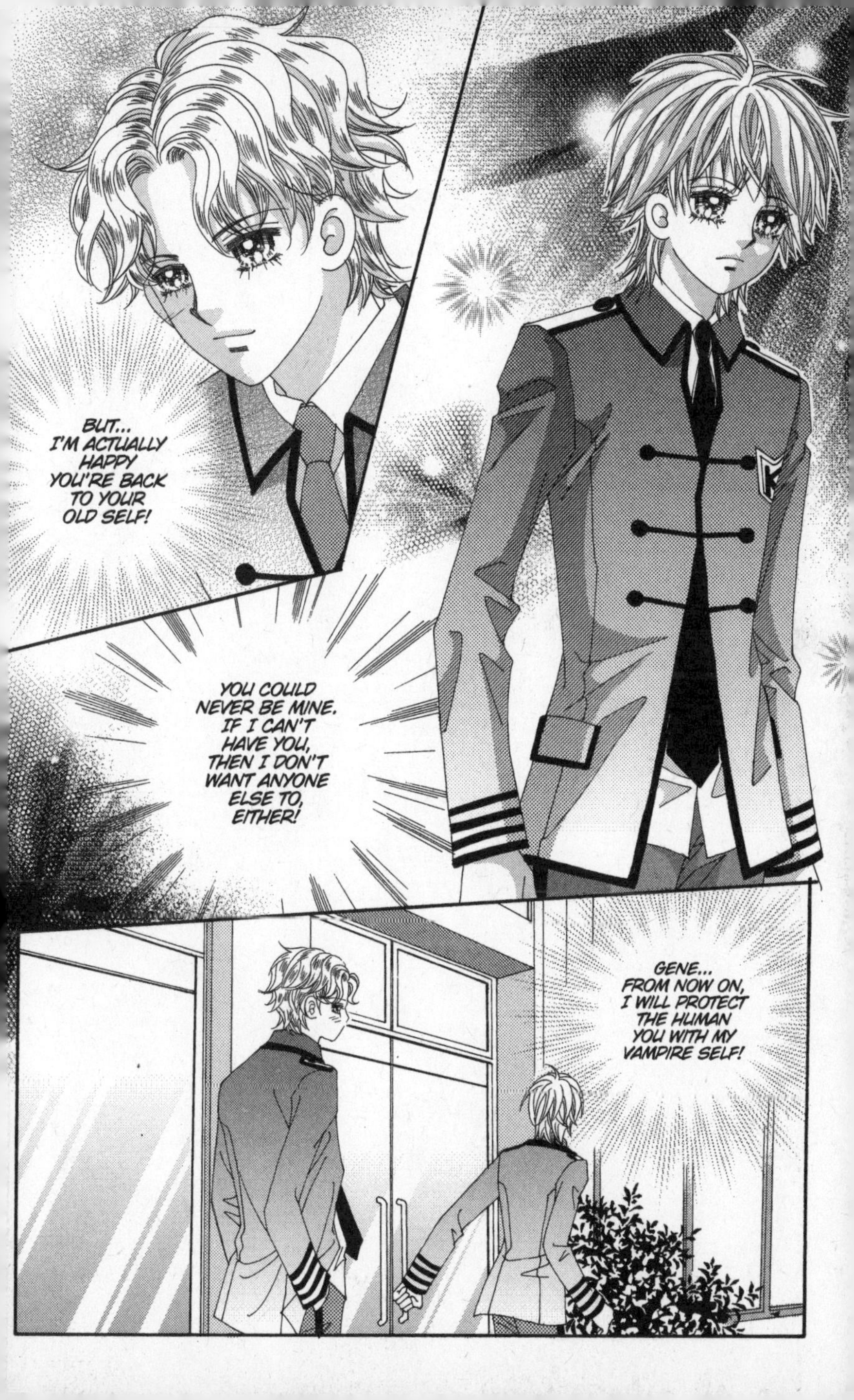
BUT... I'M ACTUALLY HAPPY YOU'RE BACK TO YOUR OLD SELF!
YOU COULD NEVER BE MINE. IF I CAN'T HAVE YOU, THEN I DON'T WANT ANYONE ELSE TO, EITHER!
GENE... FROM NOW ON, I WILL PROTECT THE HUMAN YOU WITH MY VAMPIRE SELF!

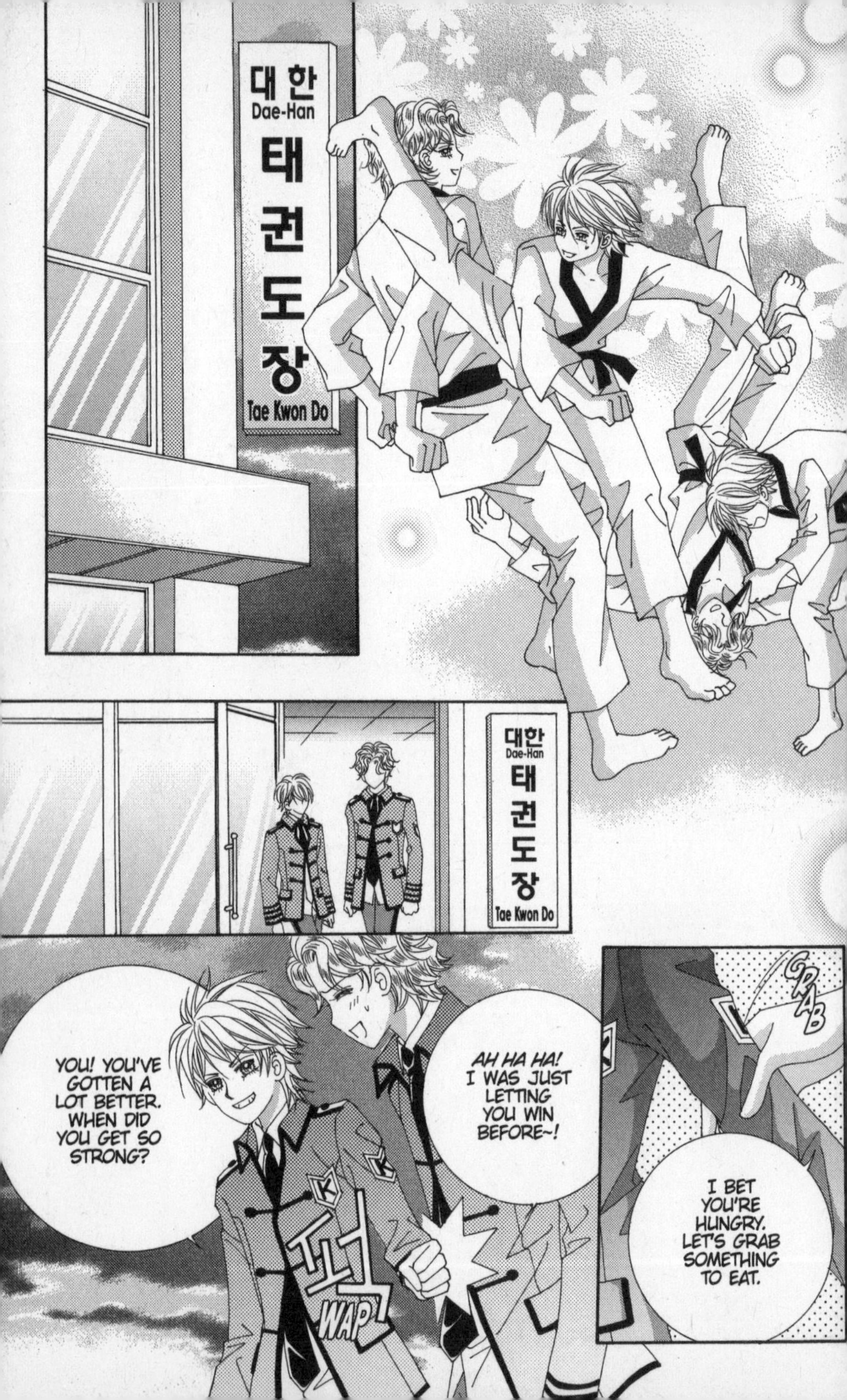
대한
Dae-Han
태권도장
Tae Kwon Do
대한
Dae-Han
태권도장
Tae Kwon Do
YOU! YOU'VE GOTTEN A LOT BETTER. WHEN DID YOU GET SO STRONG?
AH HA HA! I WAS JUST LETTING YOU WIN BEFORE~!
WAP
GRAB
I BET YOU'RE HUNGRY. LET'S GRAB SOMETHING TO EAT.

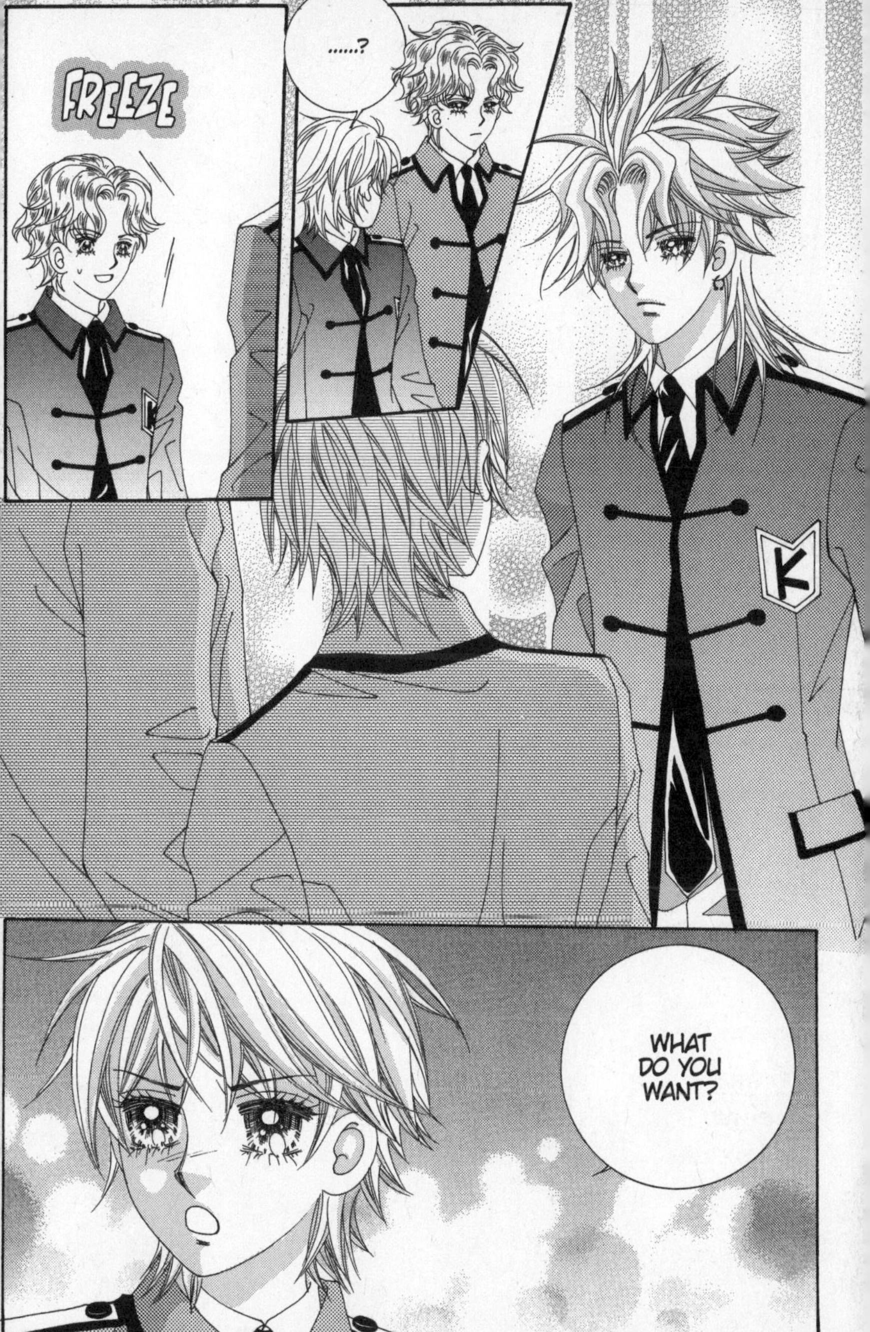
FREEZE
......?
WHAT DO YOU WANT?

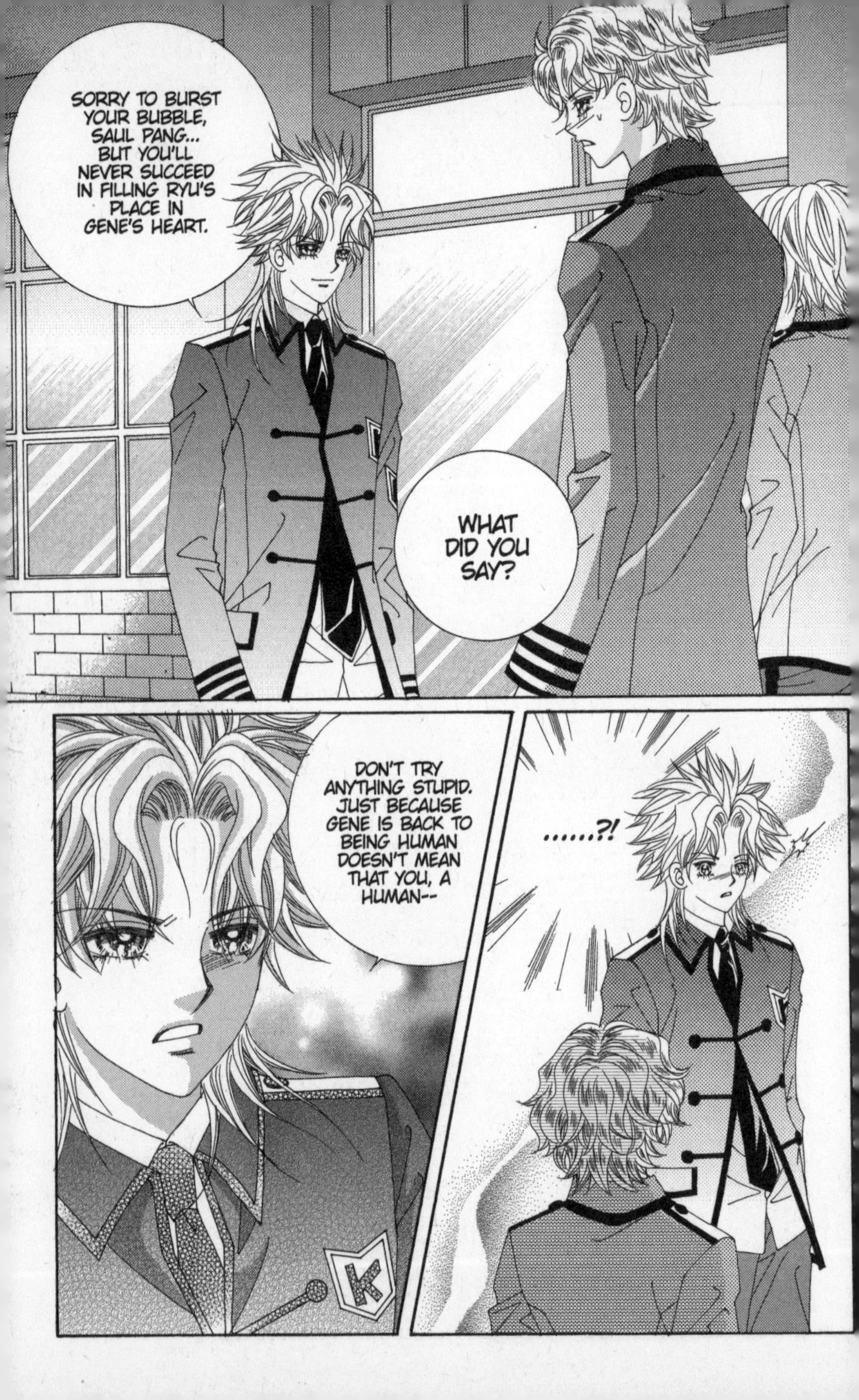
SORRY TO BURST YOUR BUBBLE, SAUL PANG... BUT YOU'LL NEVER SUCCEED IN FILLING RYU'S PLACE IN GENE'S HEART.
WHAT DID YOU SAY?
DON'T TRY ANYTHING STUPID. JUST BECAUSE GENE IS BACK TO BEING HUMAN DOESN'T MEAN THAT YOU, A HUMAN--
......?!

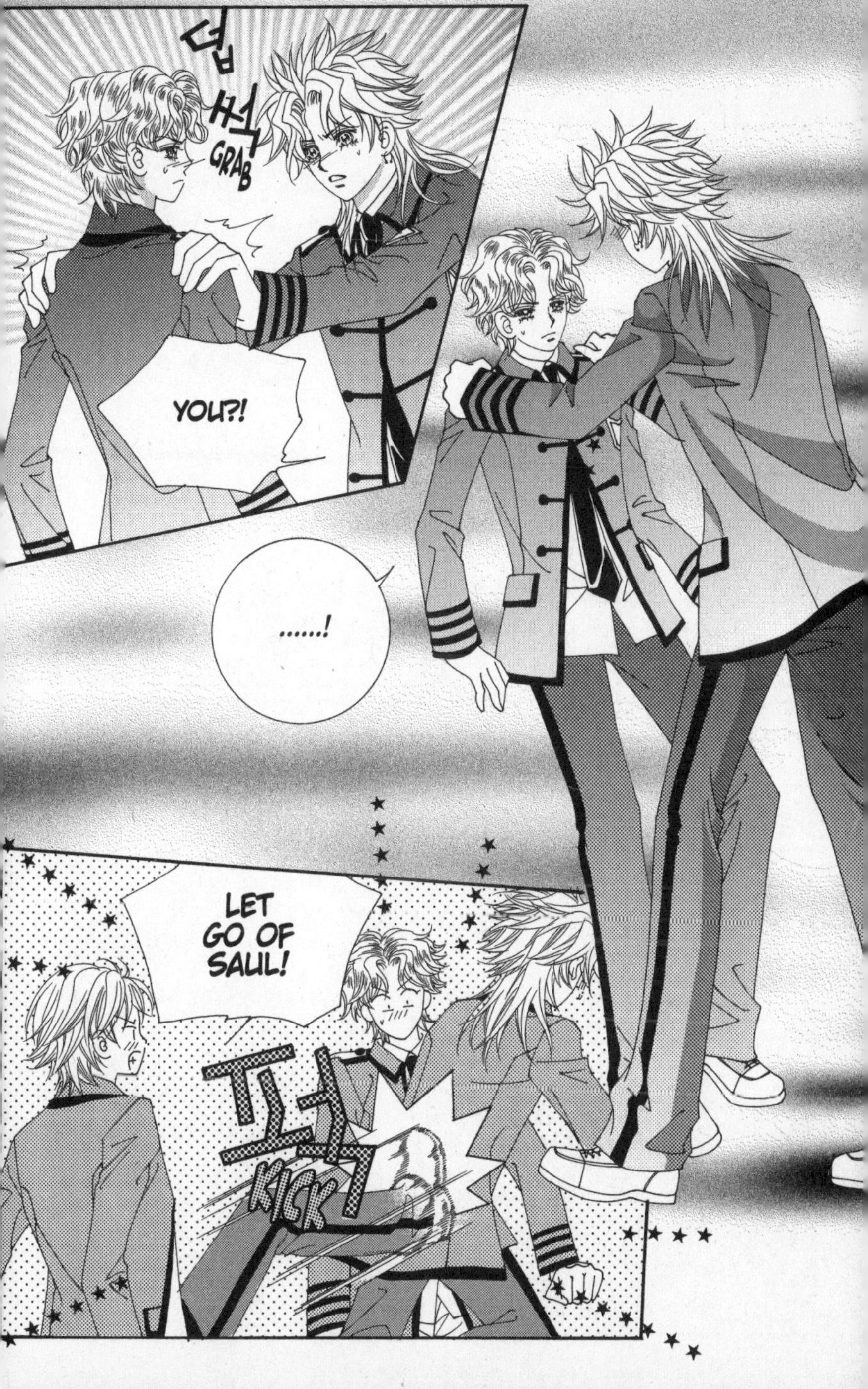
덥석
GRAB
YOU?!
......!
LET GO OF SAUL!
퍽
KICK

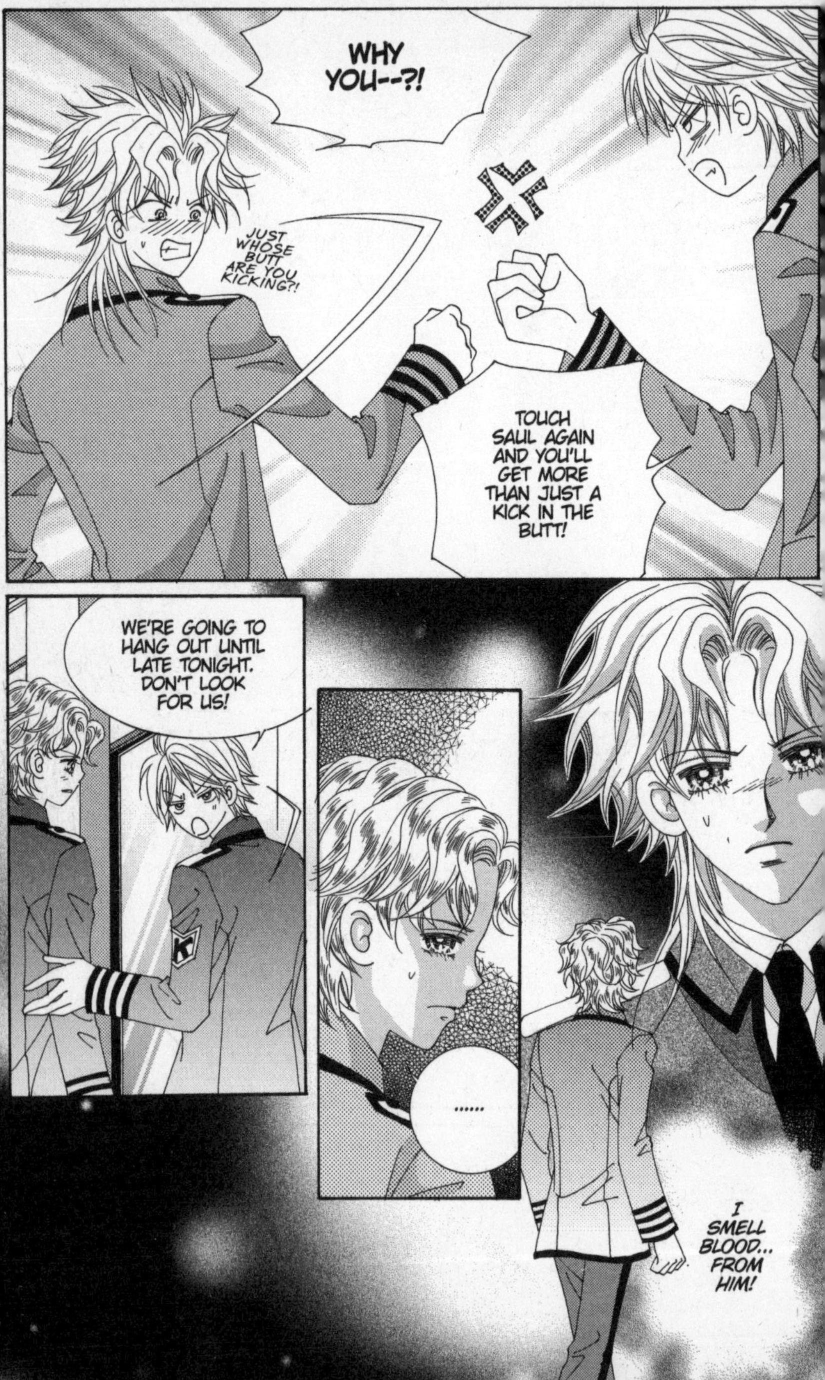
WHY YOU--?!
JUST WHOSE BUTT ARE YOU KICKING?!
TOUCH SAUL AGAIN AND YOU'LL GET MORE THAN JUST A KICK IN THE BUTT!
WE'RE GOING TO HANG OUT UNTIL LATE TONIGHT. DON'T LOOK FOR US!
......
I SMELL BLOOD... FROM HIM!

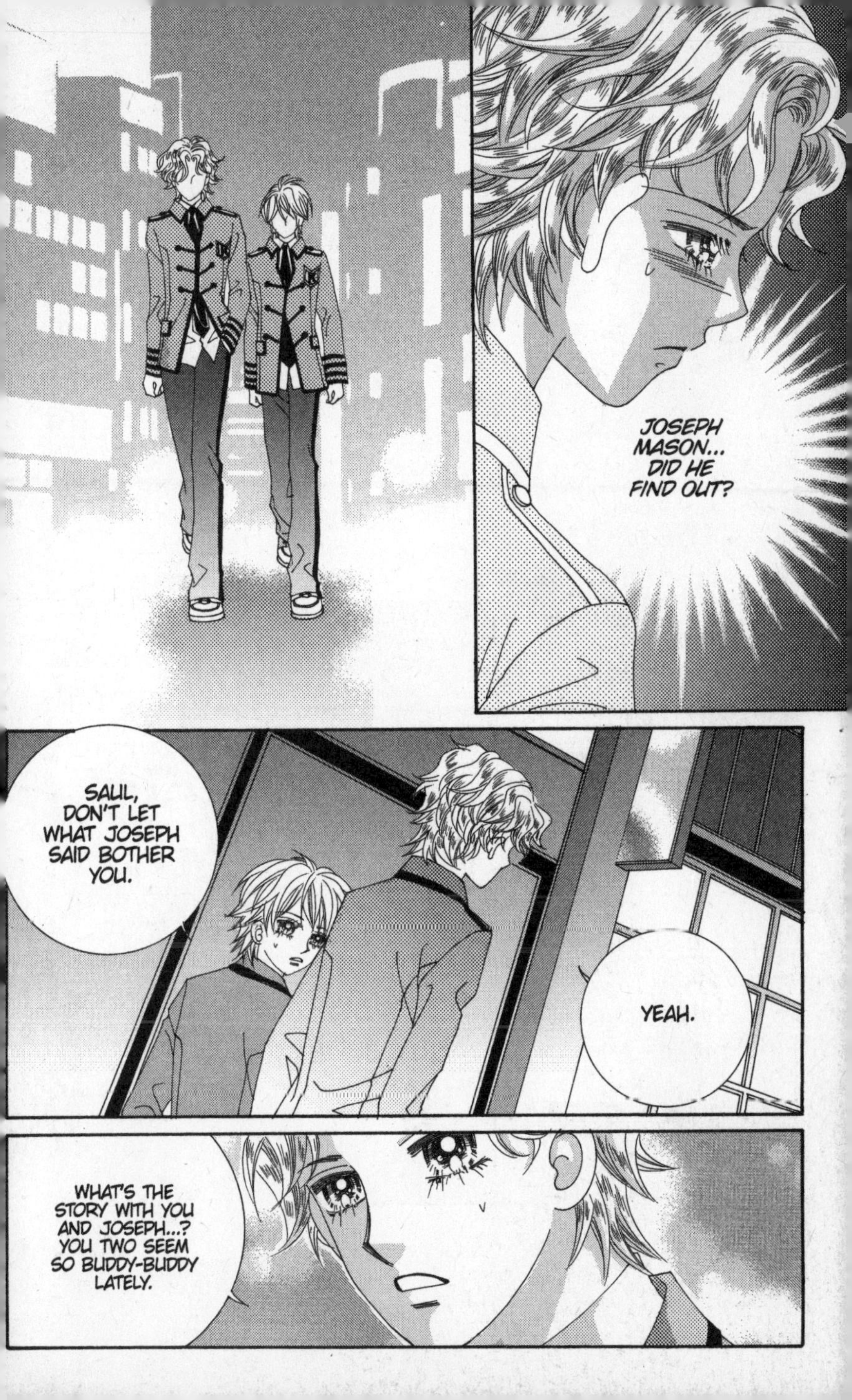
JOSEPH MASON... DID HE FIND OUT?
SAUL, DON'T LET WHAT JOSEPH SAID BOTHER YOU.
YEAH.
WHAT'S THE STORY WITH YOU AND JOSEPH...? YOU TWO SEEM SO BUDDY-BUDDY LATELY.

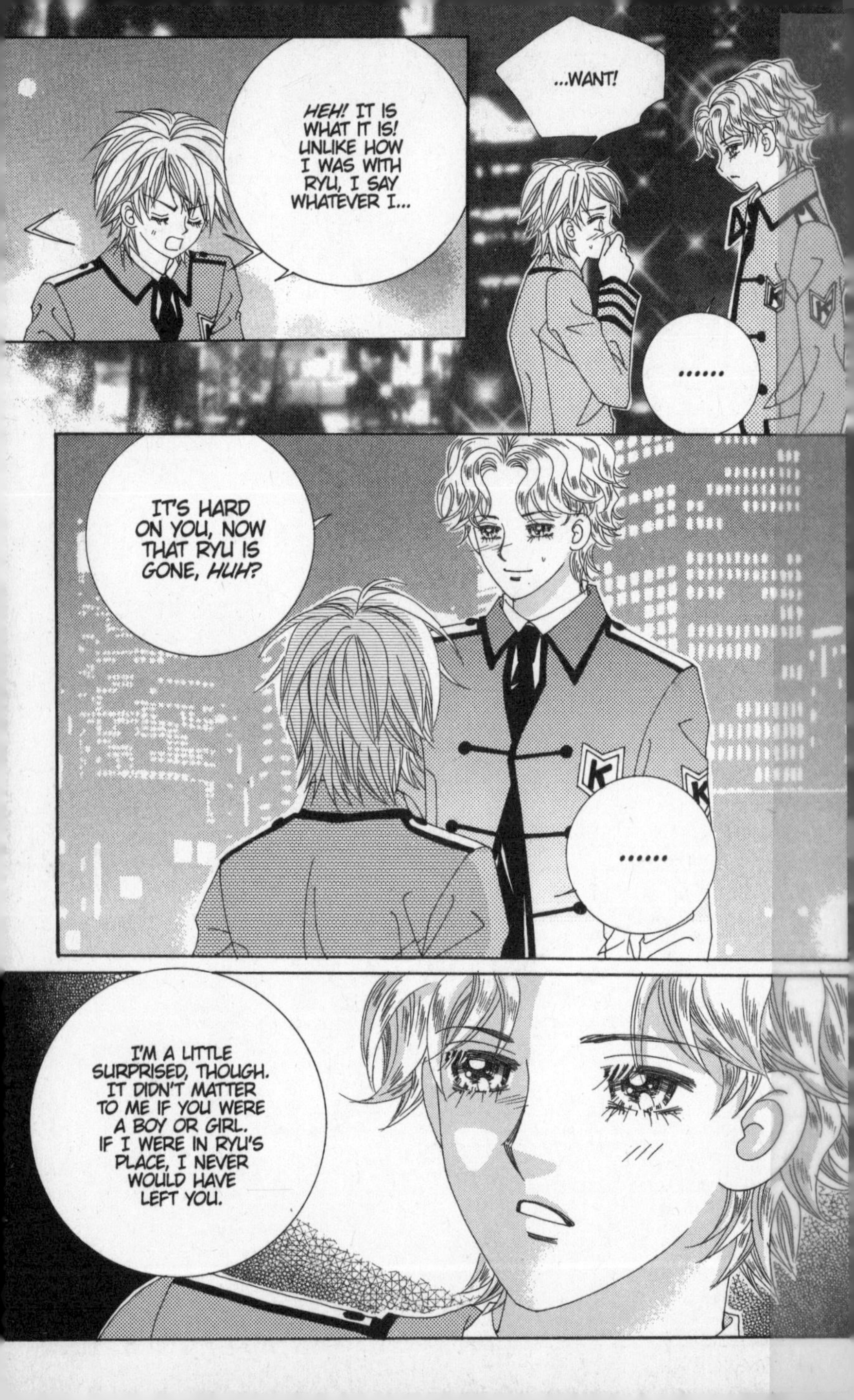
HEH! IT IS WHAT IT IS! UNLIKE HOW I WAS WITH RYU, I SAY WHATEVER I...
...WANT!
......
IT'S HARD ON YOU, NOW THAT RYU IS GONE, HUH?
......
I'M A LITTLE SURPRISED, THOUGH. IT DIDN'T MATTER TO ME IF YOU WERE A BOY OR GIRL. IF I WERE IN RYU'S PLACE, I NEVER WOULD HAVE LEFT YOU.

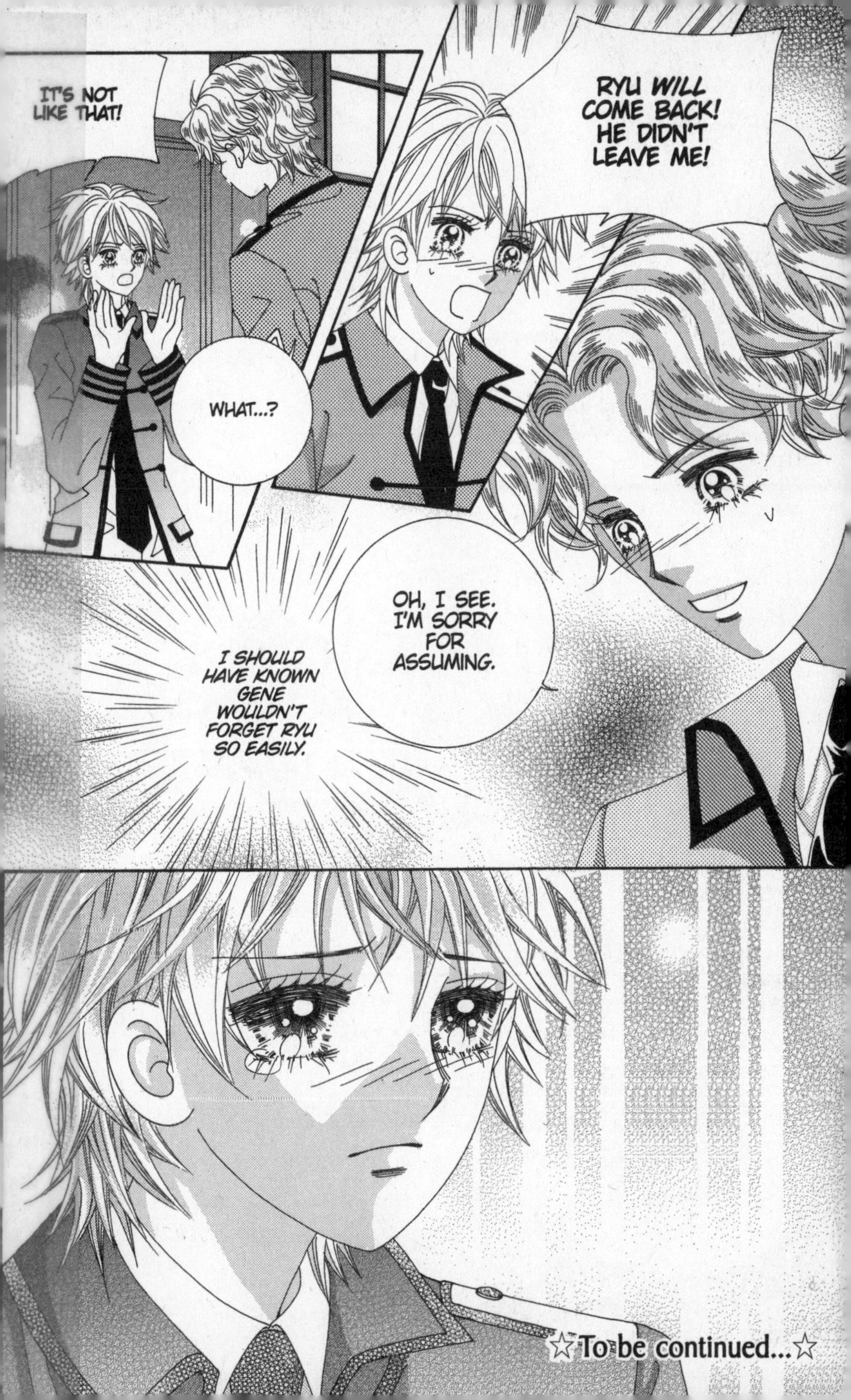
IT'S NOT LIKE THAT!
WHAT...?
RYU WILL COME BACK! HE DIDN'T LEAVE ME!
OH, I SEE. I'M SORRY FOR ASSUMING.
I SHOULD HAVE KNOWN GENE WOULDN'T FORGET RYU SO EASILY.
☆To be continued...☆